Management Science

A Survey of Quantitative Decision-Making Techniques

Madhukar V. Joshi

University of Massachusetts at Boston

DUXBURY PRESS

North Scituate, Massachusetts

Duxbury Press
A Division of Wadsworth, Inc.
© 1980 by Wadsworth, Inc., Belmont, California 94002.

*Management Science: A Survey of Quantitative
Decision-Making Techniques* was edited and
prepared for composition by Margaret Hill. Interior
design was provided by The Book Department. The
cover was designed by Elizabeth Anne Rotchford.

Library of Congress Cataloging in Publication Data
Joshi, Madhukar V   1938–
    Management science.

    Includes index.
    1. Management.   2. Management—Mathematical models.
3. Decision-making.   I. Title.
HD31.J64   658.4'03   78-10592
ISBN 0-87872-204-1

Printed in the United States of America
1 2 3 4 5 6 7 8 9 — 83 82 81 80 79

To

JYOTI, SWATI, CHITRA

and

**The Managers of Tomorrow
who keep asking:**

When will your weekends be free?

CONTENTS

PART TWO:

Decisions in Risky Situations   137

Preface

Quite frankly, I would like to make true believers out of my readers. For this reason, I have tried to provide as broad an overview of management science philosophy and techniques as is possible in an introductory text on this subject. This poses a dilemma to any textbook author. To fully appreciate the beauty and variety of management science applications in the real world situations, one must be conversant with the "language" of this discipline—mathematics. On the other hand, the typical management student is often not well versed in the intricacies of mathematics. Thus, several of the existing texts in Operations Research/Management Science are not "accessible" to such students. In fact, the mathematical notations in several of the otherwise excellent texts frighten the very students who will be the consumers of management science—the managers of tomorrow.

Accessibility. This text attempts to resolve the dilemma as follows. The major portion of each chapter is devoted to examining some of the simplest decision-making situations, the corresponding management science models, and the techniques for solving the problems so formulated. Each new concept is illustrated by an example. Furthermore, the concepts and techniques presented in each chapter are summed up at the end of that chapter. This much is, of course, standard pedagogy. This text goes two steps further. I end the discussion of each topic by outlining the extensions of that topic. It provides a glimpse at the more advanced techniques as well as more varied applications. I also provide a rather extensive set of selected readings, which include research articles on that topic as well as the advanced texts devoted to that topic alone. Thus, interested readers can familiarize themselves with what else has happened in that field. The "extensions" section and the readings together increase the readers' appreciation of the general applicability of management science in real world situations.

The primary readers of this text are those who are enrolled in a one-semester or two-quarter introductory course in management science, operations research, decision sciences, or quantitative techniques in management. This text is also appropriate for a survey course required during the first year of MBA programs. The presumed reader could also be a practicing manager who wishes to be updated on the new tools, concepts, and techniques of managerial decision making.

If they are to become the consumers of management science, the readers must understand what management science is and where it can be (and has been) helpful. Thus, they must grasp the conceptual foundations of the discipline, as well as the commonly used decision-making techniques. And, they must also be presented with proven suggestions on enhancing the chances of implementing the technically derived solutions. Finally, the discussion must be kept at an introductory level so as to not lose sight of the "forest" due to the numerous "trees."

Organization of the Text. This is what has been attempted in this text. The text is divided into four parts: foundations, decisions in risky situations, deterministic decision making, and the frontiers of management science. Part I provides an overview of management science, reviews the techniques for quantifying uncertainties (i.e., probability), and ends with describing the philosophy and general techniques of making decisions.

Part II examines some decision-making techniques in three common risky situations: planning a project, determining order size, and coping with waiting lines. This part also outlines simulation—an approach for solving managerial problems when formal models become too complex or too restrictive.

Part III describes the efficient search techniques for choosing among actions when the consequences of each action are known. Since properly formulating a problem is a crucial ingredient of managerial success, an entire chapter is devoted to formulating a variety of decision situations. The remaining chapters present a number of linear optimization techniques.

Part IV reviews the documented suggestions for successfully implementing the solutions obtained by applying the management science techniques. It also outlines where this discipline is likely to be in the next decade or two.

The "applied orientation" is maintained within each chapter. Each chapter begins with a statement explaining the significance of the specific technique. There is at least one fully worked out illustration taken from either the public or the private sector of the economy. Each chapter, except the first, also provides a "recipe" for solving such problems.

Mathematical Prerequisites. Most of what the practicing management scientists do might be termed refined common sense. As such, extensive knowledge of mathematics and computers is not necessary to understand the basics of management science. A course in college algebra or finite mathematics and a course in introductory statistics should be sufficient to understand this text. This is especially true since the necessary mathematical tools are reviewed whenever necessary, and all of chapter 2 is devoted to reviewing the probability concepts used in the rest of the text. Thus, perhaps the most important prerequisite for this book is an eagerness to learn and manipulate symbolic and numerical relationships.

Selection of Topics. A large number of quantitative techniques have been developed by the management scientists in the last twenty-five years. On the other hand, most management students are required to take only a one-semester or two-quarter course in this discipline. For this reason, only those topics that have been widely used in real world applications have been presented in this text. In other words, the topics are selected for their relevance to the managerial situations—as documented by the results of nationwide usage surveys—rather than for their mathematical elegance.

Flexibility. Personal experience indicates that a typical manager prefers to proceed from the particular to the general. I have, therefore, arranged the chapters (especially those on linear programming) in that order as much as possible. However, each chapter is essentially self-contained so that every instructor can customize the sequence of presenting the topics.

Exercises. Each chapter, except the last one, contains a problem set so that both the students and the instructors can judge the extent to which the students have understood the materials presented. The exercises follow the sequence in which the material was presented—so that an instructor who covers only a portion of the chapter can easily locate the corresponding exercises. The exercises have also been arranged in the order of increasing difficulty. The first few are essentially review exercises. Those at the end require a firmer grasp on the techniques discussed in the chapter. Those marked with an asterisk (*) are for the more advanced student.

Teaching Plans. From the instructor's point of view, the adjoining figure shows the organization of this text. Discussion of part I, the foundations, should perhaps precede that of either part II or part III. One can

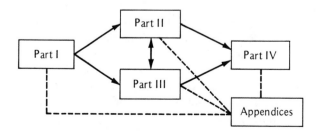

teach part II either before or after part III. Specific choice depends on the instructor. Part IV, the epilogue, should be covered so that students become aware of the "art" of managing. The appendices contain reference material to be used whenever necessary.

A school that follows the quarter system can cover the entire text in two quarters.

At the University of Massachusetts in Boston, chapters 1, 3, 4, 5, 7, 8, 10, 11, 12, 14, and 16 are covered in a one-semester, three-credit-hour course. Because of time limitations, the special purpose or more advanced topics in these chapters are generally not covered in a one-semester course. For example, we cover only the Poisson-Exponential models and the associated decision situations in chapter 7. Only the assignment technique is examined from chapter 11. The rest of the topics are then covered in the first half of the second semester.

The statistical concepts are reviewed when needed in the application chapters. Thus, expected values and variances are reviewed while discussing the decision theory of chapter 3. Normal distribution is reviewed when needed in chapter 5. The conditional probabilities are reviewed as a preparation for the Bayesian analysis of chapter 4. The Poisson and Exponential laws are discussed when needed in chapters 7 and 8. The Binomial Law is reviewed while covering the Monte Carlo techniques in chapter 8. The materials in chapter 2 and the appendices are used as reference materials, because a one-semester statistics course is a prerequisite to studying Operations Research where I teach.

Many other teaching plans can be devised by individual instructors since each chapter is essentially self-contained.

ACKNOWLEDGMENTS

This book draws heavily from management science and operations research literature. Specific materials have been cited when they have been used. The quality of this book has been improved by the comments and reviews of Edward Baldyga, Lowell University; D. James Croft, University of Utah; Jeffrey E. Jarrett, University of Rhode Island; Robert Jensen, University of Maine at Orono; David Murphy, Boston College; and James E. Reinmuth, University of Oregon. I must thank Margaret Hill for improving the readability of the final text by her careful editing. The Duxbury Press staff deserves special thanks; Robert West and Jerry Lyons who actively supported the project and Virginia Lakehomer who processed the manuscript into its textbook form.

I am deeply indebted to my wife, Jyoti, for successfully completing the unenviable task of typing the entire manuscript and the instructor's manual and for boosting my morale throughout the project.

Introduction

This text begins by describing two of its most important terms: management and management science. This is followed by a brief outline of the history and growth of this discipline: where it has been, where it is now, and what are some of the signs of its maturity. Finally, the introduction ends by explaining which of the many topics in management science have been included in this text: why they are included and in what order.

MANAGEMENT IS DECISION MAKING

To manage means to get things done—to achieve one's purpose. To this extent, each of us is a manager. A manager must decide what to do and why it must be done and then implement the decision. If decisions were to be made only once or very infrequently and then implemented forever, books on this topic would not be necessary. However, managers are constantly engaged in making and implementing decisions, examining the consequences of their actions, and then making newer and better decisions. Besides, even the best decisions should be reviewed periodically to verify their continued validity and utility.

Figure I-1 displays this function graphically. Consider the dean of a college who must decide whether to initiate a new curriculum. If the decision is affirmative, the dean must determine the number of additional faculty members to be hired. After implementing this decision, the dean must examine its consequences—the impact on budget, student satisfaction, faculty/student ratio, accreditation of the school and potential for acquiring research grants. If not fully satisfied with the results, the dean must then review the current decisions and make new ones. Even if the

1

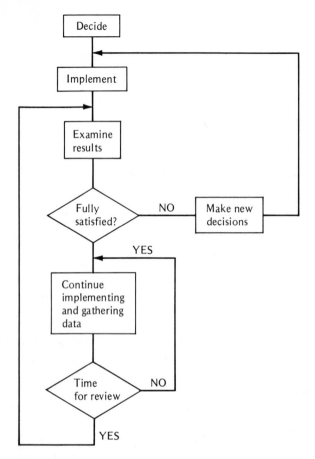

Figure I-1. *The Management Function*

dean is satisfied and continues to implement the decisions and acquire further data, such decisions must be reviewed at periodic intervals to ensure continued validity. Many other situations would follow this pattern.

Management can be described as a continuous cycle of decisions, implementations, and reviews. Or, as Herbert A. Simon (1960) states: *Management is decision making.**

At this stage, it is worth stressing the obvious. Even if the dean in the above illustration postpones action on the new curriculum, a decision has in fact been made and that decision has its own consequences. There is simply no way to avoid decisions.

For years, managers have considered decision making to be an art. It

*Italic wording denotes definition.

was to be mastered over many years through experience, i.e., through "trial and error." I recall working at a grain processing firm where one of the managers used to wonder openly what a freshly minted Ph.D. could possibly know about his grain business that he himself had not known in thirty years. What he did not realize was that through the application of management science techniques, especially when augmented by a computer, many of his experiences could be reproduced "on paper." Thus, the consequences of his past actions, as well as of the actions he had not yet tried, could be evaluated without risking actual capital. In other words, a management scientist could perform *experiments* that a practicing manager would not dare.

This is where the *science* of management enters the picture. Decision making based solely on experience and trial and error can be very costly in today's complicated world. Management science can help reduce such risks by conducting experiments and suggesting more proven solutions.

WHAT IS MANAGEMENT SCIENCE?

For many reasons this question does not have a unique answer. As formal disciplines go, management science is relatively new. Early practitioners in this field came from such diverse fields as: mathematics, engineering, accounting, and psychology. They each brought in their own viewpoint, and as a result, there are perhaps as many definitions as there are practitioners. Indeed, it is almost an annual ritual at the meetings of professional societies to coin new definitions.

A clue to what management science is can be derived by reviewing what management expects the management scientist to do, viz., solve managerial problems which involve operations of man/machine systems, gather and/or interpret relevant data, develop models of present operations, and experiment with models to make recommendations for the future. We may thus define:

Management science consists of applying the scientific method to solve the problems of man/machine systems using quantitative measures of system effectiveness. The solution consists of recommending specific courses of action.

Other Names

It is worth mentioning that this discipline goes by other names: operations research, operational research, and decision science. Corresponding to each name, there is a professional society, e.g., The Institute of Management Sciences (TIMS), the Operations Research Society of America (ORSA), the Operational Research Society of the United Kingdom (ORSoc), and the American Institute of Decision Sciences (AIDS).

In this text, we will use the terms *operations researcher* and *management scientist* interchangeably. Similarly, the terms *manager* and *decision maker* will be synonymous. For the sake of brevity, we may sometimes use OR/MS as a short form for operations research or management science.

Characteristics of Management Science

OR/MS Is Primarily Interested in Managerial Decision Making. Unlike physics, chemistry, or psychology, which focus on describing what is happening in some system, OR/MS focuses on finding what needs to be done. Its solutions constitute recommendations to management.

OR/MS Is Based on Scientific Methods of Inquiry. Such methods include: observing the symptoms of what is wrong with a system, identifying the causes of these symptoms, formulating hypotheses on the possible ways to alleviate or solve the problem, performing experiments in that system to determine which solution is more likely to succeed, and then implementing the now proven solution.

OR/MS Employs Quantitative Measures of Effectiveness. Effectiveness means the extent to which objectives are achieved. It should not be confused with *efficiency,* which is inversely proportional to the resources used for achieving an effect. If you wish your product to reach 20,000 customers and it reaches 18,000 customers, you have been 90 percent effective. If this could be accomplished by spending $4,500 on advertising and you have spent $6,000, then you are 75 percent efficient.

OR/MS Problems and Decisions Are Viewed from a Systems Perspective. A typical decision problem might read: "We can make products A, B, C, and D. The unit costs of making each product are known. The total capacity in person-hours, budget, or raw material is limited to so many hours, dollars, and tons, respectively. Market research has indicated what the demand for each product is. What is the most profitable combination of A, B, C, and D to make and sell?"

OR/MS Projects Require Knowledge from Many Different Subject Areas. Problem solving is, therefore, attempted by a heterogeneous team of experts rather than a homogeneous one. A typical team might include the subject area expert, statistician, psychologist, and computer professional, besides the management itself. Such combinations substantially increase the number and sources of analytical techniques which can be brought to bear on any problem. Professionals from different disciplines *cross-fertilize* ideas, so that custom-made solution techniques are often developed through such efforts. This is perhaps the chief advantage of the team approach.

OR/MS Problems Are Solved by First Constructing a Mathematical Model of the System and Then Experimenting on That Model. Most often, this is done by computers, since they are the most efficient manipulators of numbers. Computers, however, can only do what they are told. Thus, to use these devices for problem solving, the user must be familiar with typical decision problems and existing solution techniques. Breeding such familiarity is a purpose of this text.

A HISTORICAL PERSPECTIVE

Management science is a study of organizations—systems in which human beings are an important component. In this sense, it has been around since the dawn of history, even though as a formal discipline it came into being during the early 1940s.

Early Developments

Jericho, father-in-law of Moses, is said to have documented the organization principles in chapter 18 of the Book of Exodus. In India, Chanakya, a Brahman prime minister (advisor) to a sixth century king, Chandragupta, had written a treatise on the *science of governing people.* Venetian shipbuilders of the fifteenth century are known to have used an assembly line for outfitting ships.

The use of scientific method to solve managerial problems was uneven, however, until the Industrial Revolution. In the late nineteenth century, Frederick Taylor, an American engineer, formally began using the scientific approach for solving the problems of manufacturing. He wanted to find the "one best way" of doing a specified task. In other words, he was the first "industrial engineer" and "efficiency expert."

Henry L. Gantt, a contemporary of Taylor, brought into consideration the human aspect of management's attitude towards labor. In that sense, he is more of a "father" of management science/operations research than Taylor. Perhaps his greatest contribution was in the field of scheduling production.

In 1914, Frederick W. Lanchester, an Englishman, attempted to predict the outcome of military battles based on the number of soldiers and weapons. This is perhaps the first mathematical model of an organizational decision problem.

At about the same time (1915), Ford W. Harris published the economic lot size model for making inventory decisions. His economic order quantity (EOQ) model is still used today.

In 1917, A. K. Erlang, a Danish mathematician with Copenhagen's telephone company, founded the modern waiting line (queueing) theory.

In the 1930s, Horace C. Levinson studied the effects of advertising on sales, and those of income and residential location on purchases.

Though Sir Ronald A. Fisher (1890–1962) did not pursue the study of managerial problems per se, his work on the statistical methods must be mentioned. It is the basis for most of the applied statistics theory used in management science today.

1939 Onwards

The term operations research dates back to the 1939 study of military operations by the famous British group headed by P. M. S. Blackett. This group was composed of three physiologists, two mathematical physicists, an army officer, a surveyor, two mathematicians, an astrophysicist and a general physicist. This list is to emphasize that OR/MS projects are characteristically conducted by multidisciplinary groups.

The success of the British group influenced the U.S. military establishment immensely. In the U.S., such groups were called "operations analysis" groups. During this period, John Von Neumann developed the *Theory of Games and Economic Behavior,* and George Danzig worked out the Simplex technique for solving linear optimization problems.

In 1947, Danzig published his book, *Linear Programming.* It shows how to find the best allocation of scarce resources. At this point, operations research began to be regarded as relevant to solving business problems.

An important reason for the rapid acceptance of operations research in industry was the advent of electronic computers. These machines took the drudgery out of solving large numbers of equations and completing other computational tasks essential to successful OR/MS projects. Since then, this discipline has grown rapidly.

Some 20,000 persons now apply, research, or practice in the field of management science. Most large companies have management science departments, while smaller firms might employ operations researchers in consulting capacities. Many universities now offer undergraduate as well as graduate courses in operations research/management science/quantitative analysis—the actual title varies from place to place.

PROGRESS OF MANAGEMENT SCIENCE

Management science is a relatively new discipline, and it is still growing in importance as it matures. Perhaps it is this newness which is reflected in the much larger growth of management science theory as compared to actual practice. It does create an imbalance. Some of the researchers, especially those in the academic organizations, do tend to stress mathematical elegance rather than practical utility. However, these are perhaps the symptoms of nothing more serious than "growing pains."

John F. Magee, president of Arthur D. Little, Inc., has suggested taking this view to understand what has happened thus far, is happening now, and is likely to happen in the future. (See Magee's article, "Progress in Management Sciences," in *Interfaces*, February 1973.) He divides the development of management sciences into three broad and partially over-lapping phases.

The Primitive Phase

Toward the end of World War II and continuing through the 1950s, the main emphasis was on small and rather well defined *tactical* problems. The researchers in the field were busy developing quantitative techniques and seeking optimal solutions. The OR/MS professionals—far fewer than today—were drawn from related fields such as mathematics, physics, engineering, and psychology. Academic interest was quite limited—only three schools in the early 1950s had formal programs in OR/MS.

The Academic Phase

The early practitioners did a good job of "selling" the discipline. As business leaders began to see that OR/MS was at least somewhat relevant for solving their managerial problems, universities began to offer more programs in this discipline. Thus began the academic phase (most of 1960s and, to some extent, even today). During this period, the number of schools with OR/MS programs increased from 6 in 1962 to 37 in 1968. This growth was both good and bad. People with some exposure to OR/MS techniques in this period are now moving into executive positions. And familiarity can breed acceptability. In 1965, for example, I had to "sell" the management of a company on the utility of operations research. Nowadays, this is not necessary—at least not in industrial firms.

During the academic period, much work was done in developing solution techniques. To aid the practicing management scientists, a number of "canned" computer programs were developed. This helped increase the practical value of operations research. Since management scientists need an abundance of empirical data, many computer-based management information systems (MIS) were also developed during this period.

However, much of the research in the 1960s (and to a certain extent, in the 1970s) was "academic" in a bad sense. The same publish-or-perish syndrome which gave rise to excellent techniques also produced research on esoteric and arcane topics whose practical utility is questionable. Many management scientists are said to have roamed the world in search of problems whose solution they had found!

The Maturing Phase

In a sense, this phase has been around since the early 1950s. However, it is becoming more prominent now. For example, in contrast to the academic phase, more practitioners are now publishing their *experiences* in professional journals. Such journals are beginning to devote more space to the discussion of urban issues, management of health organizations, and water/air/noise pollution. In short, the focus is again on managerial problems rather than on techniques.

To quote from Magee's article in *Interfaces*,* the characteristics of this maturity are:

- More realistic understanding by both managers and management scientists of what the management sciences can and cannot accomplish
- More attention to getting the facts, describing what is going on and why, compared with development of abstract sophisticated techniques
- Less attention to finding "optimum" answers, more to developing processes for evolving successively better answers, adapted to evolving circumstances
- Better integration of behavioral, functional, and quantitative analysis, fuller appreciation of the importance of values as well as arithmetic, a clearer understanding of the importance of assumptions as well as of logic.

These characteristics constitute an excellent set of OR/MS objectives today.

ORGANIZATION OF THE TEXT

One purpose of this text is to acquaint you with the OR/MS techniques for solving managerial problems. Since a rather large number of techniques have been developed by OR/MS professionals, it is not possible to fully explain each one in such limited space. Instead, we will study only those techniques with wide applicability.

Table I-1 was prepared on the basis of a 1972 survey conducted by Efraim Turban. It shows the relative frequency with which those OR/MS professionals at the corporate level who responded to the survey have used these techniques. In this text, we will discuss the topics marked with an asterisk (*). Thus, the text covers most of the commonly used techniques.

*J. F. Magee, "Progress in Management Sciences," *Interfaces*, Vol. 3 (Feb. 1973), pp. 35–41. Reprinted with permission from The Institute of Management Sciences.

Table I-1 *Most Common OR/MS Techniques*

TECHNIQUES	FREQUENCY OF USE (percent)
*Statistical Inference	29
*Simulation	25
*Linear Programming	19
*Inventory Theory	6
*PERT/CPM	6
Dynamic Programming	4
Nonlinear Programming	3
*Queueing	1
Heuristic Programming	1
Other	6

*These techniques will be discussed in this text.
© Reprinted with permission from Efraim Turban.

The text is divided into *four parts*. The first part, chapters 1 through 4, outlines the basic *foundations* of this discipline. Specifically, we will discuss how to go about formulating and solving a decision problem, and quantifying the uncertainty. We will also examine some common ways to display problem situations. Finally, we will examine some decision-making criteria, their propriety in various circumstances, and the procedures for identifying the best course of action.

The second part, chapters 5 through 9, covers *decision making using statistics*. We will examine three prototype OR/MS problems, viz., how to plan and manage a project, how to manage inventories, and how to analyze the properties of waiting lines. Formal solutions of these problems are discussed in chapters 5, 6, and 7, respectively. However, the formal models of such situations often become too complex or too restrictive. These are then analyzed using the simulation approach—an extremely versatile problem solving tool. Chapters 8 and 9 sketch this tool.

In some situations, the future is known with reasonable certainty or can be so assumed—at least in the short run. Also, a fairly accurate representation of payoff as a linear function of a finite number of action variables may be possible. The resultant models, extremely popular in OR/MS literature, are called *linear optimization (allocation) models*. The third part, chapters 10 through 15, examines many such specific situations and the corresponding search techniques.

The fourth part, chapter 16, explores some of the documented suggestions for enhancing the chances of *implementing* the OR/MS generated *solutions*. We will also take some educated guesses at where this discipline might be in the near future.

Finally, there are the appendices, which include statistical tables, a table of natural logarithms, as well as two computer programs useful for solving the problems in part III.

The text is deliberately written at the exploratory level. Each topic is included only in its simplest form—enough to recognize the decision problems in each case, and to understand the solution presented by the experts in the field. On the other hand, each topic ends by outlining the possible extensions of the corresponding techniques. Each chapter lists readings where the interested reader can find additional materials. Each chapter also contains a variety of homework problems so that you can test your newly acquired skills.

SELECTED READINGS

MAGEE, J. F. "Progress in Management Sciences." *Interfaces* 3 (Feb. 1973), pp. 35–41.

SIMON, H. A. *The New Science of Management Decision.* New York: Harper & Row, Inc., 1960.

TREFETHEN, F. N. "A History of Operations Research." *Operations Research for Management* 1 (1954), pp. 3–35.

TURBAN, E. "A Sample Survey of Operations Research Activities at the Corporate Level." *Operations Research* 20 (1972), pp. 708–721.

PART ONE

Foundations

The technical discussion begins by describing the components of any decision-making situation: the object system, the environment in which the organization operates, the inputs, outputs, and the transformation that converts inputs into outputs. Then, the steps in a typical decision-making process are outlined.

The second chapter is intended only as a review of some of the basic concepts of probability: events, sample spaces, ways to assign probability to events, random variables, expected values, and variances. It also reviews the properties of binomial, Poisson, and normal variables.

The third chapter describes the construction of payoff matrices and decision trees—two ways to display decision-making situations. It also describes several criteria that are often used in choosing a suitable course of action.

The fourth chapter continues the discussion of decision-making criteria. It introduces the techniques of marginal analysis and Bayesian analysis, and then outlines the concepts of utility of money and adjusted expectations.

1

The Decision-Making Process

The *object system* of management science is an organization that currently faces a decision problem whose solution is desired by someone—the decision maker. Since an organization cannot exist in a vacuum, management science begins by identifying the environment in which an organization operates. The management scientist must also identify the input variables, the output variables, and how the inputs are transformed into outputs. This whole process is often known as the system analysis.

The chapter then continues to describe the steps in a typical decision-making process: formulating the problem, constructing and validating the model, solving the problem as modeled, performing sensitivity analysis, establishing controls, and implementing the solution. In other words, this chapter provides an overview of the entire decision-making process.

THE OBJECT SYSTEM AND ITS ENVIRONMENT

The introduction to this text mentioned that management science consists of applying the scientific method to solve the problem of man/machine systems using quantitative measures of system effectiveness. The solution consists of recommending specific courses of action. Several of these terms need further explanation.

The systems of interest to management science must include humans. Thus, collections consisting exclusively of hardware items cannot be considered. This means, for example, that management science does not study the properties of airplanes, plastics, or medicines, per se. That is the scope of "hard" sciences, such as physics, chemistry, or biology.

Rather, management science deals with the *operations* of plastic processing plants, since these include human beings as their essential components. Similarly, it studies air transportation systems with their planes, ticket clerks, passengers, food suppliers, reservation procedures, and ground transportation. Or, it could examine hospital systems, which are made up of patients, medical staff, emergency equipment, and billing procedures. In other words, by systems we really mean organizations.

A system of managerial interest, known as an *object system*, consists of human beings; machines; resources, such as, capital and technical know-how; concepts; and procedures. An object system, must be working towards achieving some objective. There must be some *measure of effectiveness*, i.e., an indication of the extent to which the objective has been reached. And, of course, there is a decision maker who is interested in improving some aspect of the object system. In fact, this person should be motivated enough to initiate management science projects for finding ways to improve these aspects.

But, an object system does not exist in a vacuum. Thus, an operations researcher likes to determine the object system's boundary and structure. This exercise reveals those aspects which (1) the decision maker cannot control, but which (2) nonetheless affect the achievement of the objective. According to C. West Churchman (1968), these aspects together constitute the system *environment*. The exercise also reveals the system inputs, controllable or otherwise, which give rise to system outputs. It furthermore reveals the *transformation* that converts inputs into outputs. Figure 1-1 displays this graphically.

Returning to the grain processing firm discussed earlier might further illustrate this. The company's objective is to maximize profits by selling finished products, such as, corn oil, soybean oil, or potato starch. The payoffs can be measured as total profit in dollars, tank-cars of oil sold, or tons of starch sold. The inputs consist of the soybean, corn, and potato crops; the person-hours at various skill levels; as well as technical know-how and business acumen. The company can make such decisions as, how

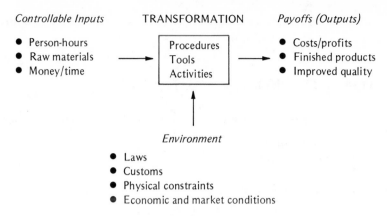

Figure 1-1. *A System and Its Environment*

many bushels of beans, corn, and potatoes to buy or what size labor force to employ. These are the controllable inputs. The environment for this firm includes weather conditions, the number of acres cultivated by the particular farmers, the strength of competing firms, state and local laws, and union contracts. The company converts *all* these inputs into the appropriate outputs by using specific tools and procedures, and by managing the necessary activities, such as, buying, marketing, and extracting oil.

How the environment is defined depends on the particular object system. For example, if the object system is the mathematics department of a college of a university, then *all* other departments in that college are likely to be part of the environment of that department. This environment would also include the admissions and financial assistance sections of that university. This follows because the quality of students entering the mathematics department depends on admissions policy (3.0 grade average or better) and whether or not brighter students receive scholarships or tuition exemptions. These are in the environment of the mathematics department because that department, by itself, probably does not control financial policies.

The environment of the college, on the other hand, consists of other colleges in that university and the administration of the university. The environment of the university may include other universities in the surrounding communities, the industries in those communities, as well as other socio-political influences. Thus, careful definitions of the object system and the environment are crucial to successfully completing an OR/MS project.

We briefly examined the meaning of the "scientific method" while discussing the characteristics of operations research. Now we will explore how a modification of that method helps a management scientist discover the most suitable course of action. The modification is necessary since a management scientist can seldom perform fully controlled experiments as required in the true scientific method.

BEFORE ATTEMPTING A SOLUTION

Typically, an OR/MS project goes through the following phases:

- Formulating a problem
- Constructing a model
- Validating the model
- Solving the problem as modeled
- Performing sensitivity analysis
- Establishing controls
- Implementing the solution

These phases are not necessarily executed in this exact order. Rather, the activities resemble a widening circle—often reverting back to problem formulation or model construction (reconstruction or upgrading) as additional "pieces of the puzzle" begin to complete the picture. For some semblance of order, the phases are discussed here sequentially.

Problem Formulation and Model Construction

These two phases are often called the system analysis. The decision maker observes the current system trying to identify its weaknesses/problems. Here, the operations researcher (team) operates like a diagnostician and identifies the root cause(s) of the observed system's problems.

For example, suppose that the director of a private outpatient clinic observes that the waiting room is often crowded, that the adjoining playroom (built for the convenience of patients and their children) is rather noisy, and that there is an unusually high turnover of cashiers. If so, he has observed the *symptoms* of some underlying malady. It is important to identify the problem in specific, operational terms now, to avoid spending time, money, and energy trying to solve the wrong problem. So, it is important to *keep* asking why something is or is not happening, in order to flush out the underlying problem. The director might initially attribute the cashier turnover to low pay, but further inquiries "around town" might indicate that this is not the case. He might also determine that, given the size of his clientele, both the waiting room and the adjoining playroom are adequate. Suppose he finally realizes that the typical patient experiences an excessive amount of waiting time. He has now located the problem, since this can explain *all* the symptoms.

To begin solving the problem, the OR/MS team constructs a model of the current situation. Since the patients do the waiting, it is logical to begin observing the process a typical patient goes through. Suppose, for simplicity, that this clinic employs two physicians, a cashier, and a recep-

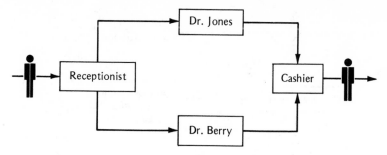

Figure 1-2. *A Patient's Journey Through the Clinic*

tionist. Figure 1-2 might show the encounters of a typical client with the "service providers" in this clinic.

This model provides a preliminary description of what happens to a patient. The patient arrives and meets the receptionist. Depending on his symptoms, the patient is guided towards the office of Dr. Jones or Dr. Berry. The patient waits to see the doctor, spends some time with that doctor, and then proceeds to the cashier. After waiting in the cashier's line, the patient spends some time with the cashier and then leaves the clinic.

Note a few things about this model. It contains no numbers. Nonetheless, its importance should not be underestimated. *It shows the direction of flow.* It does *not* discuss what a patient does with the receptionist, the assigned doctor, or the cashier. By such an omission, the model is stating that this information is irrelevant here. It is important to note just what is and is not relevant in a model. The decision maker must verify such preliminary models to avoid wasting money on solving "wrong" problems.

After verifying the model, the operations researcher quantifies it, i.e., introduces numerical data to describe the model in greater detail. First, all the relevant variables must be identified and classified, into input or output categories. For the clinic in figure 1-2, the input variables include: the rate at which the patients arrive, their arrival pattern, the time spent at the receptionist's desk, the doctor assigned to each, the time spent in that doctor's office, as well as the time spent with the cashier. The waiting times at each of these places and the money paid to the cashier are some of the output variables.

Having settled on a list of input/output variables of interest, the OR/MS team proceeds to gather data (either by searching through records, or more likely, by accumulating new data) and to analyze it. As diagrammed in figure 1-3, the team finds that the patients arrive in a Poisson manner, that the receptionist's service times follow a rectangular distribution, that 70 percent of the patients visit Dr. Jones, and that Dr. Jones's service times are normally distributed. These statements include several

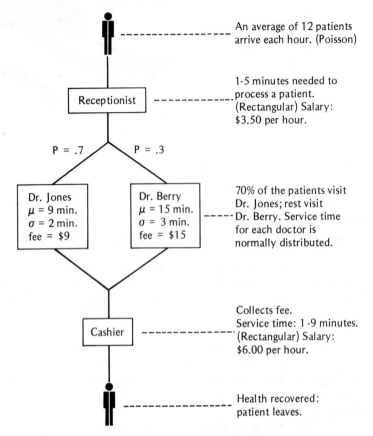

Figure 1-3. *A Quantitative Model of the Outpatient Clinic*

statistical terms which will be defined in chapter 2, and a more detailed, mathematical discussion of the model is provided in chapter 9.

The Model Types
The model in figure 1-3 represents the flow of many patients at the clinic. It can be used to determine the numerical values of all the relevant output variables. In this sense, the model *describes* the current state of affairs at the clinic. However, it does not show all the possible improvements or changes that might be made in the clinic. If the director decided to add another physician, the model could not represent it—we would have to create a different model for each such change. This model alone cannot lead us to the "best solution" to the clinic's problem, and for this reason, it is said to be a *descriptive model*.

A model that inherently contains *all* variations of a given situation, and thus includes the description of the best arrangement, is said to be a *normative model.* Table 1-1 shows one such model. A writer has completed drafting four chapters and can assign one chapter to each of four secretaries. To avoid confusion, he wants the typist who begins working on a chapter to stay with it until it is finished. Each typist can type any one chapter. The associated costs are shown in table 1-1. For instance, if Jyoti types chapter 1, 2, 3, or 4, the cost would be $96, $99, $105, and $108, respectively. The problem consists of deciding who should type which chapter. *All* possible solutions to this problem are contained in the model. Thus, "Jyoti typing chapter 1, Mary typing 2, Jackie typing 3, and Tammy typing 4" is a solution. It costs: $96 + 109 + 113 + 115 = $433. All the solutions and their associated costs can be found similarly. Therefore, it is a normative model.

Table 1-1 *An Assignment Model*

	CHAPTER			
TYPIST	1	2	3	4
Jyoti	$ 96	$ 99	$105	$108
Mary	116	109	107	96
Jackie	120	102	113	111
Tammy	114	105	118	115

Whether a model is descriptive or normative depends on the problem situation it is representing. These problem situations tend to cluster into a few well-known types. Because they occur frequently in managerial decision making, specific techniques exist for solving each type of problem. Though some of these techniques are beyond the scope of this text, note that the prototype problems include:

- Allocation of resources
- Inventory management
- Replacement of equipment
- Queueing (waiting lines)
- Sequencing and coordination
- Routing through networks
- Competition
- Search

Validating the Model

To *validate* a model means to verify that the model satisfactorily explains *all* the important and relevant aspects of reality. For example, by using the clinic model described in figure 1-3, it is possible to predict the values of relevant output variables, such as the waiting time at each "service station," the service time at each service station, and the number of patients visiting the clinic every hour it is open. The values of these output variables can also be obtained from direct observation of the clinic operations. (The observations already used to derive the model cannot be used to verify it—fresh data must be collected to verify the model.)

Validation consists of comparing the observed values with those predicted by the model. Statistical tests are used for this purpose. Two such tests, which belong to the class of "goodness of fit" tests, are the χ^2 test and the Kolmogorov-Smirnov test. Briefly, one poses two hypotheses: that the model represents reality and that it does not. Fresh data is collected and the hypothesis "the model represents reality" is accepted as being true, if it cannot be rejected with enough confidence. For a more technical discussion concerning the methods of testing hypotheses, refer to the statistical literature cited at the end of this chapter.

In any case, validating a model implies attempting to resolve the question: "What are the possible ways in which a model can fail to represent reality adequately and hence lose some of its potential usefulness?" Despite the objective procedures used in testing a model, any questions of adequacy or usefulness are inherently subjective. Three reasons why a model might fail are:

- Because an irrelevant variable was included or a relevant variable was omitted. The model postulates the dependent variable as a function of one or more independent variables.
- Because the relationship between dependent and independent variables is inaccurate.
- Because its parameters are not evaluated properly.

Once validated, the model can be used to search for the desired solution to the decision problem.

Principles of Choice

Before we continue our search for a *desirable* solution, we must examine the meaning of that adjective in the decision-making context. A discussion of common meanings of "desirable" follows.

Optimal A solution to the decision-making problem, i.e., a course of action, is optimal if it can be shown to be the *best of all* possible solutions to the system as a whole. Since the payoffs associated with any action are either desirable (e.g., profits or satisfaction) or undesirable (e.g., costs or losses or frustration), the optimal solution can also be described by the level of the associated payoff. An optimal solution has these characteristics:

1. The most desirable payoff for a given level of resources.
2. The least undesirable payoff that satisfies a required level of objectives.
3. The highest ratio of desirable to undesirable payoff.

Generally speaking, seeking optimal solutions is meaningful only if the problem has a normative model. See chapters 6, and 10 through 15 for additional details.

For example, the optimal (meaning, in this case, the least costly) solution to the typing assignment problem in table 1-1 is: "Jyoti types chapter 1; Mary, 4; Jackie, 3; and Tammy, 2." The cost of this arrangement is: $96 + 96 + 113 + 105 = $410. You can verify that this is the least costly arrangement.

Note one curiosity of an optimal solution. *Though it is best overall, it may not be the best for each component.* For example, the best assignment for Jackie would have been chapter 2, not 3. Similarly, the best typist of chapter 2 would have been Jyoti, not Tammy.

Suboptimal A solution that is optimal for some component of the system but not for the whole system is said to be suboptimal. For example, the cheapest way to produce an item, from a production department's point of view, would be to produce in large lots. However, such a plan would likely result in large inventories or undue shortages. Thus, it might not be optimal for the company as a whole.

This being the case, why should one think of obtaining a suboptimal solution? Because, it might be the only practical approach. Given that even today's computers are limited in their size and speed and that management science is still a growing discipline, some problems defy optimal solution. Occasionally, then, an OR/MS team deliberately ignores some aspects of a problem, finds a suboptimal solution, and then checks its potential impact on the initially ignored aspects. If the impact is not unacceptably negative, the current solution is accepted as desirable even though it is also suboptimal.

Satisfactory This is yet another pragmatic criterion. Essentially, the decision maker defines some *aspiration level* and any solution whose desirable payoff exceeds this level is considered *satisfactory*. This is because the decision maker may not have the time nor the money to find an optimal solution. This is what you do, for example, when you advertise to sell your car for $2,000. Instead of collecting and evaluating all possible offers (which could be a long, frustrating experience), you simply set an aspiration level of $2,000 and accept the first offer that exceeds $2,000. In fact, if no one calls within a week, you would probably consider selling it for $1,800. If so, you will be seeking a new solution at a reduced aspiration level.

If the decision problem only has a descriptive model, finding satisfactory solutions at some prescribed aspiration level is probably the only choice. See chapters 3, and 5 through 9 for additional details.

Other Meanings of Desirability So far we have assumed that *all* possible consequences of every action are known prior to making a decision.

When this is not the case, several other principles of choice are used. Among the most common of these are: best expected payoff, minimax cost or regret, risk aversion, and best expected utility. It is essential to review probability theory before these criteria can be meaningfully discussed. See chapters 3 and 4 for additional details.

THE SOLUTION TECHNIQUES

Once the model has been constructed and validated, and the decision criterion has been agreed upon, it is time to solve the model. The technique used to solve a model depends on the type of model and the amount of information available regarding the future. Some common techniques are outlined below.

Analytical Procedures
This technique employs deductive logic. When applicable, a solution is represented by a symbolic equation with all the known quantities on one side of the equation and the value of the dependent variable on the other side.

For example, suppose you own and operate a retail store. Your records indicate that the demand for a product is extremely steady—*exactly D* units per year at the rate of *D*/52 units per week. You order the product in batches. Past experience shows that *exactly L* workdays elapse between the placement of an order and its delivery. If you order a very large batch, it takes up too much space in the store and also too much of your capital is tied up. (It costs you *H* dollars to hold one unit in the store for a period of one year.) But, the cost of just placing the order is *K* dollars each time—regardless of how many units are ordered in the batch. So, ordering too few items at a time can also be costly. Obviously, you would like to know the most economical order quantity, *Q*. If *all* of the above assumptions are true, the best value of *Q* is shown to be:

$$Q = \sqrt{\frac{2KD}{H}}$$

For example, if $D = 62,400$, $H = \$0.60$, and $K = \$2.00$; then $Q = 645$. See chapter 6 for additional details on this model.

An analytical solution, such as this value of *Q*, is of course the most concise and definitive way to express a solution. A management scientist always dreams of obtaining an analytical solution. Since too many and often unrealistic assumptions are necessary for achieving this conciseness, most solution techniques are not analytical.

Complete Enumeration
If the total number of possible solutions to a decision problem is small, the management scientist can list each solution (i.e., the corre-

sponding course of action), compute the corresponding payoff, and then choose the solution with the best payoff. Table 1-2 shows this process for solving the typing assignment problem in table 1-1. The top line of the table lists the typists. Each entry shows an arrangement and the associated cost. For example, the first arrangement is: 1, 2, 3, 4. This means that Jyoti will type chapter 1; Mary, 2; Jackie, 3; and Tammy, 4. This will cost $433. All other entries are interpreted similarly. Obviously, the best arrangement is 1, 4, 3, 2 and it will cost $410.

Table 1-2 *Assignments of Typists to Chapters*

JYOTI	MARY	JACKIE	TAMMY	COST	JYOTI	MARY	JACKIE	TAMMY	COST
1	2	3	4	$433	3	1	2	4	$438
1	2	4	3	434	3	1	4	2	437
1	3	2	4	420	3	2	1	4	449
1	3	4	2	419	3	2	4	1	439
1	**4**	**3**	**2**	**410**	3	4	1	2	426
1	4	2	3	412	3	4	2	1	417
2	1	3	4	443	4	1	2	3	444
2	1	4	3	444	4	1	3	2	442
2	4	1	3	433	4	2	1	3	455
2	4	3	1	422	4	2	3	1	444
2	3	1	4	441	4	3	1	2	440
2	3	4	1	431	4	3	2	1	431

Iterative Procedures

Though theoretically simple, a complete enumeration technique is often impractical, because there is usually a very large number of possible solutions. Unless each solution is evaluated, the proposed solution *cannot be proven* optimal. Iterative procedures avoid this trap. With this technique, a proposed solution and the possibilities for improvement are obtained simultaneously. In other words, each solution explicitly indicates whether or not it is optimal; and if not, where to look next.

Consider, for example, a metropolitan area in which five general hospitals have formed a consortium. Let H_1, H_2, H_3, H_4, and H_5 denote the five hospitals. Suppose also that every day the hospitals need exactly 300, 400, 500, 600, and 300 pints (respectively) of a specific blood type. The consortium management knows three blood banks, B_1, B_2, and B_3, which can supply 900, 400, and 800 pints (respectively) of this blood type daily. Table 1-3 shows the per-pint cost of obtaining blood from each bank for each hospital. The cost of obtaining blood is independent of the amount purchased. Since each bank supplies exactly the same kind of blood, the blood obtained from different sources can be mixed together. The consortium wants to find the least expensive way of obtaining blood to meet the needs of each hospital without exceeding the capacity of any bank. (This

Table 1-3 *Unit Cost of Obtaining Blood ($ per Pint)*

			TO		
FROM	H_1	H_2	H_3	H_4	H_5
B_1	18	15	12	13	16
B_2	12	16	14	12	9
B_3	15	11	13	16	15

kind of problem is called a transportation problem, which will be discussed in more detail in chapter 12.)

The proposed solution and its improvement potential for this type of problem are usually displayed in a tabular form, commonly called the Transportation Tableau. Table 1-4 shows such a tableau. Each delivery route, such as from B_1 to H_1, is shown by a box. Each box shows the corresponding unit cost in the upper right-hand corner. A number preceded by an asterisk (*) is the number of pints of blood assigned to the corresponding route. Thus, table 1-4 proposes that blood bank B_1 should send 300 pints to hospital H_3 and 600 to H_4; B_2 should send 100 pints to H_1 and 300 pints to H_5; and B_3 should send 200 pints to H_1, 400 to H_2, and 300 to H_3. In short, the asterisked entries as a group represent a solution to the hospital's problem.

The nonasterisked entries, such as +4 in the B_1 H_1 box, are interpreted as follows. Each represents the *increase in cost* of assigning a pint of blood to that route. Since the consortium wishes to minimize cost, it follows that the route of B_1 to H_1 should remain unused. Since *all* nonasterisked entries are positive, *none* of those routes should be used for

Table 1-4 *The Optimal Solution of the Hospital Problem*

BLOOD BANKS	HOSPITALS					SUPPLY
	H_1	H_2	H_3	H_4	H_5	
B_1	$18	$15	$12	$13	$16	900
	+ 4	+ 5	*300	*600	+ 5	
B_2	$12	$16	$14	$12	$9	400
	*100	+ 8	+ 4	+ 1	*300	
B_3	$15	$11	$13	$16	$15	800
	*200	*400	*200	+ 2	+ 3	
Demand	300	400	500	600	300	2100

*Pints of blood assigned to the corresponding route.

delivering blood. In short, the solution shown in table 1-4 is in fact optimal.

Note that this conclusion—that table 1-4 represents an optimal solution—was derived without obtaining other solutions. The test of its superiority was contained in the tableau itself. All iterative models in management science share this property.

Simulation

The optimal solution of a normative model can be obtained by complete enumeration or iterative procedures. A strictly descriptive model may have either optimal or satisfactory solutions. However, it is often difficult to prove the optimality of any solution of a descriptive model. In fact, many descriptive decision problems cannot be solved at all, in the formal sense. (Turban's 1972 survey showed that nearly 25 percent of OR/MS situations are of this type.) In such situations, the OR/MS team engages in what is known as a *simulation exercise.*

To illustrate this approach, consider again the outpatient clinic in figure 1-3. Though it is an example of waiting line problems, it cannot be solved in the formal sense. Instead, one proceeds by generating on paper the arrival times of a large number of patients and the time each one spends with the receptionist, the doctor, and the cashier. This results in a *simulation run.* Based on that run, the system parameters (such as the average waiting time at each service station and the average throughput time) are derived. The alternative configurations of that system (such as, adding another doctor to the system, hiring paraprofessionals, or referring some clients to other clinics) are then modeled. Each such model is run for a large number of patients. When all conceivable alternative runs are complete, the model with the most desirable (or least undesirable) properties is chosen as the satisfactory solution.

A simulation approach is also the mainstay of many system development projects in which no reliable, well-tested pilot model exists. Simulation approaches are useful beyond the realm of operations research. Historians studying the manmade systems of the past or physicists studying galactic systems cannot readily manipulate their object systems. Although experiments are crucial for studying cause and effect relationships, some very desirable experiments may be impractical. Thus, the simulation technique is used as a last resort. Chapters 8 and 9 explore this technique in more detail.

POST-SOLUTION ACTIVITIES

Once the OR/MS team has established a desirable solution to the decision problem, it must also complete the three activities outlined below.

Performing Sensitivity Analysis

Recall that in order to construct a model of the situation at hand, one must know the values of many relevant parameters, such as:

- Average number of units arriving at a facility per hour
- Average time spent on servicing each unit
- Cost of performing a task
- Time necessary to complete a task
- Unit cost per day of storing an item in a warehouse
- Cost of transporting an item from place A to place B
- Unit profit associated with selling an item
- Probability that a client serviced by a service center will no longer experience problem days
- Probability that a client referred by agency A to agency B will be accepted for service by that agency

Whether or not a given solution of the model is optimal for that problem situation depends on the actual values of the parameters in that model. However, the exact parametric values are rarely known. Generally, the parametric values entering a model are, at best, the estimates available at the time. And, estimates are always subject to error. Therefore, it is important to know the extent to which parametric values can vary without changing the optimality of a solution.

This study of ranges of parametric values which do not affect the optimality of a solution is known as *sensitivity analysis*. The less sensitive the solution is with respect to a parameter, the more error one can tolerate while estimating that parameter. This translates into reduced costs of collecting data regarding that parameter. It follows that the sensitivity analysis is an important aspect of any OR/MS project. It delineates those parameters that require extremely accurate (and usually costly) data from those that can survive with moderate inaccuracies. It also helps to forecast the conditions under which the current optimal solution may become nonoptimal or even intolerable. Thus, it prepares management to cope with any such situations. It is very difficult to actually define sensitivity. But, its meaning should become clear as we observe it in the context of specific techniques that appear throughout the rest of the text.

Establishing Controls

Once the limitations of the model have been explored through sensitivity analysis, the decision maker is in a better position to decide which changes in the uncontrolled variables and among the functional relationships are *significant*. To paraphrase Churchman, et al. (1957), a change is significant if both of the following are true:

- Adjustment of the solution due to the change in variables results in an improvement in effectiveness
- The cost of implementing the adjustment does not offset the improvement in effectiveness.

Design of a control system consists of three steps:

- List the variables, parameters, assumptions, and relationships that either are included in the solution or should be if circumstances change.
- Develop a procedure to detect significant changes in each of the parameters and relationships listed.
- Specify the action to be taken or adjustments to be made in the solution in which a significant change occurs.

The first steps are in fact a by-product of activities carried out during the earlier phases—from problem formulation to sensitivity analysis.

The second requires the installation of a monitor (human or mechanical, depending on the system) who will *report* the current status of the system. The number of parameters and relationships whose status is to be monitored depends on the results of the sensitivity analysis and the cost of monitoring each such item.

The prescriptions derived in the third step are known as "feedback and correction." These depend on the nature of the model, the solution, and the OR/MS effort in general. They also depend on the decision maker's ability to persuade superiors, colleagues, and subordinates to abide by OR/MS derived solutions.

Implementing the Solution

Once the optimal solution has been derived and tested, and the mechanisms to control this optimality have been brought in place, the solution is ready to be implemented. Putting the solution into operation should be of concern to the operations researcher since an OR/MS project is judged not so much by the elegance of the solution as by its practical utility in the improved system. Two reasons (paraphrased from Churchman, et al.) why a management scientist should be interested in implementing the solution are stated below.

- No matter how carefully an optimal decision rule was derived and tested, shortcomings may still appear when it is put into operation or new ways to improve the solution may become apparent. If the adjustment of the decision rule (to take care of unforeseen operating problems) is left to those who do not understand how the solution was derived, the adjustment may seriously eat into its effectiveness.
- Carrying out a solution may not be as obvious in the context of complex operations as it initially appeared to the researchers.

Unfortunately, implementation continues to be an art rather than a science. Successful implementation of an OR/MS project depends upon psychological factors, such as, the decision maker's skills in the art of communication, motivation, and persuasion. These arts are usually discussed in textbooks on the management of human resources. Only recently have reference books provided guidelines for successful implementation of OR/MS projects. We will discuss some of the documented suggestions for enhancing the chances of implementing the OR/MS solutions in chapter 16.

Now that you have seen the whole decision-making process, we will discuss the specific problem formulation and solution techniques. The readings that follow will give you an appreciation of the breadth of OR/MS applications as well as additional details on the theory of decision making.

SELECTED READINGS

BAKER, N. R.; SOUDER, W. E.; SHUMWAY, C. R.; MAHER, P. M.; AND RUBENSTEIN, A. H. "A Budget Allocation Model for Large Hierarchical R & D Organizations." *Management Science* 23 (1976), pp. 59–70.

CHURCHMAN, C. W. *The Systems Approach.* New York: Delacort Press, 1968.

CHURCHMAN, C. W.; ACKOFF, R. L.; AND ARNOFF, E. *Introduction to Operations Research.* New York: John Wiley & Sons, Inc., 1957.

CLELAND, D. I. AND KING, W. R. *Management: A Systems Approach.* New York: McGraw-Hill Book Company, 1972.

COOK, T. M. AND ALPRIN, B. S. "Snow and Ice Removal in an Urban Environment." *Management Science* 23 (1976), pp. 227–234.

FRIES, B. E. "Bibliography of Operations Research in Health-Care Systems." *Operations Research* 24 (1976), pp. 801–814.

GITLOW, H. S. "A Methodology for Determining the Optimal Design of a Free Standing Abortion Clinic," *Management Science,* 22 (1976), pp. 1289–98.

GRAYSON, C. J., JR. "Management Science and Business Practice." *Harvard Business Review* 51 (1973), pp. 41–48.

HARRISON, E. F. *The Managerial Decision-Making Process.* Boston: Houghton-Mifflin Company, 1975.

JOSHI, M. V. AND EICKER, W. F. *DESIM: A Simulation Technique for Modeling and Evaluating Human Service Systems.* Waltham, Mass.: Florence Heller School, Brandeis University, 1973.

LINSTONE, A. AND TUROFF, M. The *Delphi Method: Techniques and Applications.* Reading, Mass.: Addison-Wesley Publishing Company, 1975.

MCGUIRE, J. W., ED. *Contemporary Management: Issues and Viewpoints.* Englewood Cliffs, NJ: Prentice-Hall, Inc., 1974.

MILLER, D. W. AND STARR, M. K. *Executive Decisions and Operations Research.* 2d ed. Englewood Cliffs, NJ: Prentice-Hall, Inc., 1969.

MONTGOMERY, D. B. AND URBAN, G. L., ED. *Management Science in Marketing.* Englewood Cliffs, NJ: Prentice-Hall, Inc., 1969.

RIVETT, P. *Principles of Model Building.* London: John Wiley & Sons, Ltd., 1972.

TURBAN, E. "A Sample Survey of Operations Research Activities at the Corporate Level." *Operations Research* 20 (1972), pp. 708–721.

WAGNER, H. M. *Principles of Operations Research.* 2d ed. Englewood Cliffs, N.J.; Prentice-Hall, Inc., 1975.

YOUNG, S. *Management: A Decision Making Approach.* Belmont, Calif.: Dickenson Publishing Co., 1968.

PROBLEM SET 1
MANAGEMENT SCIENCE PROJECTS

1. In any two of the following situations, *identify* the relevant input/output variables and the environment, *describe* the form a solution might take, and *choose* the appropriate measures of effectiveness and the appropriate principle of choice.

   a. As the dean of a college, decide whether and when to initiate a new academic program.

   b. Determine the most desirable schedules for maintaining equipment (servicing or replacing it).

   c. As the local public health official, decide whether to immunize a population against a disease.

   d. As the author of a textbook, choose among a number of publishers.

   e. As an active and influential citizen, decide whether to start an organization for maintaining the health of all persons in your community.

   f. As a bank's loan officer, determine whether customers who apply for a loan are worthy of credit.

   g. Determine if and where to open a new retail outlet of your company.

   h. Appoint a new marketing director for a consumer products company.

   i. Select the director of public relations for a new and expanding college.

   j. Select a mode of transportation for commuting to work.

   k. Decide whether to accept a new job in another town.

   l. Choose the right kind and amount of life insurance to buy.

   m. Pick the length, timing, and place of your next family vacation.

   n. Determine the number of dollars you should spend on Christmas and related festivities.

   o. Choose between two policies: one would increase the number of jobs in a community; another would increase probability of finding a cure for cancer.

2. Choose an organization to analyze.

   a. Identify: the whole system and its components, the environment, the inputs and outputs, and the objectives.

b. Identify a problem in that organization, a decision maker who is interested in solving it, the possible courses of action open to the decision maker, at least three factors over which the decision maker has no control, the recommended principle of choice, and the measure of effectiveness.

c. Identify the weak spots in your data and/or arguments used in the recommended solution to the problem identified in part b. Suggest sources of additional data required to strengthen your argument. Discuss how you will overcome any opposition to your proposed solution.

3. Identify at least five controllable and uncontrollable variables in three of the following systems: toy manufacturer, hospital, motel, bank, utility company, travel agency, public school, and state government.

4. Describe the scientific approach in the following situations:
   a. Introducing a new product

   b. Determining the utility of a drug

   c. Modifying the rates charged for flights between Boston and London

   d. Opening a new fast-food outlet

5. Provide at least two examples, other than those discussed in this chapter, to illustrate that effectiveness is not synonymous with efficiency.

6. Provide two other solutions (not necessarily optimal) to the problem of distributing blood from blood banks B_1, B_2, and B_3 to hospitals H_1, H_2, H_3, H_4, and H_5. Use table 1-4 to discuss the difference between an optimal and a suboptimal solution.

2

Review of Probability

Usually, not every parameter that influences a decision can be known with certainty. In such cases, the uncertainties inherent in any decision process must be handled somehow. This chapter briefly reviews the methods of quantifying uncertainties.

Sample spaces and events are the building blocks of probability theory. Working with events helps sharpen one's logical thinking abilities. Thus, the chapter begins with a review of these concepts. The remainder of the chapter examines the concepts and techniques that will be needed later in this text, including: computing the conditional probabilities, checking the independence of events, obtaining unconditional probabilities, and deriving the expected values and variances of random variables. The chapter then goes on to discuss the properties of binomial, Poisson, and normal variables—three of the often used probability distributions. Of the many excellent texts on this topic, a few are cited in the readings at the end.

31

SAMPLE SPACES AND EVENTS

The *probability* of a future is a number between 0 and 1 that quantifies your belief in the likelihood of that future. No matter how that number is derived, it will follow a specific set of rules. To understand these rules, we must first examine certain "building blocks" on which the theory of probability is based.

Definitions of Terms

An *experiment* refers to any process of observing or measuring. It might consist of counting the number of mistakes a typist makes on a page, observing the color of a randomly chosen flower from a garden, noting whether the light in a room has been switched on or off, or measuring the number of gallons of gasoline sold by a gas station on a specified day. A more complex experiment might consist of obtaining the per capita annual income of the households in a county, region, state, or country.

Each experiment results in certain *outcomes*. The typist may make 0, 1, 2, . . . mistakes on a page; the color of the chosen flower may be white, blue, red, or orange; the light in the room may be switched on or it may be off; and the number of gallons sold may lie between 800 and 1000. The number and kind of outcomes depend on the specific experiment. Some experiments, such as counting the mistakes on a page, have a finite number of outcomes. Others, such as measuring the gallons of gasoline sold, have an infinite number of outcomes. Some others, such as counting the number of persons with 15 fingers, have no outcomes. Also, the outcomes may be numbers, or they may describe attributes such as race, sex, or color.

The set of all possible distinct outcomes of an experiment, no matter how unlikely a specific outcome may be, is said to constitute its *sample space*. It is usually denoted by the letter S. If an experiment results in a finite number of distinct outcomes, its sample space is said to be *finite;* otherwise, it is said to be *infinite*. A finite sample space can be described either by making a *list* of all outcomes in that space or by defining a *membership rule* so as to easily determine whether a candidate outcome belongs to it. It is necessary to state the membership rule for describing an infinite sample space.

Consider, for example, the case of Sally Baker who attends a management school where the faculty assigns grades as 1, 2, 3, and 4 (rather than A, B, C, and F). Sally has enrolled in two courses: accounting and marketing. We will study the experiment of forecasting her grades. An outcome in this experiment can be represented by an ordered pair:

(grade in accounting, grade in marketing)

This means, for example, that if Sally gets a grade 1 in accounting and a 2 in marketing, this is shown by the pair (1, 2). If she gets a 2 in accounting and a 1 in marketing, this is shown by the pair (2, 1). With this convention, her sample space S can be described by the following list of outcomes:

$$S = \{ (1, 1), (1, 2), (1, 3), (1, 4), (2, 1), (2, 2),$$
$$(2, 3), (2, 4), (3, 1), (3, 2), (3, 3), (3, 4),$$
$$(4, 1), (4, 2), (4, 3), (4, 4) \}$$

More conveniently, this sample space can be described by using a membership rule, such as:

$$S = \{ (i, j) \text{ where } i \text{ and/or } j \text{ can be } 1, 2, 3, \text{ or } 4 \}$$

A sample space can also be described in a graph. Sally's grade in accounting can be shown along the i-axis and her grade in marketing along the j-axis. Each ordered pair (i, j) corresponds to a point on the graph (see figure 2-1). Her sample space would be a collection of 16 points, arranged in 4 rows of 4 points each.

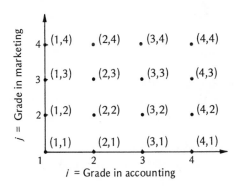

Figure 2-1. *Sally's Sample Space*

An *event* is a subset of a sample space. It may contain all, some, or none of the outcomes which comprise that sample space. If it contains none of the outcomes, it is said to be a *null event.* Three events in Sally's sample space are listed below for illustrative purposes.

> I = Sally gets a 1 in accounting. Note that this event happens if (1, 1), (1, 2), (1, 3), *or* (1, 4) happens. That is, event I consists of those four pairs.
>
> J = Sally receives a 2 in marketing. Event J's component outcomes are (1, 2), (2, 2), (3, 2), and (4, 2).
>
> K = Sally scores *better* in marketing than in accounting. Event K comprises the pairs (2, 1), (3, 1), (4, 1), (3, 2), (4, 2), and (4, 3).

Alternatively you can define the events I, J, and K by specifying their membership rules. Thus:

$$I = \{ (1, j), \text{ where } j = 1, 2, 3, \text{ or } 4 \}$$
$$J = \{ (i, 2), \text{ where } i = 1, 2, 3, \text{ or } 4 \}$$
$$K = \{ (i, j), \text{ where } j < i \}$$

Each of these events is depicted in figure 2-2. Note that events I and K have no points in common, i.e., these are *mutually exclusive events*. This means that these events cannot occur at the same time. Sally will *either* get a 1 in accounting *or* her marketing score will be better than her accounting score. She cannot have both.

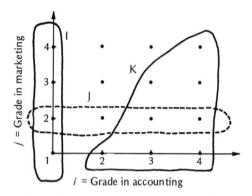

Figure 2-2. *Events in a Sample Space*

Unions, Intersections, and Complements

We are often interested in events which can be formed by combining two or more known events. There are three possibilities: unions, intersections, and complements.

Suppose we know the component outcomes of two events A and B. Then the union event $(A \cup B)$ and the intersection event $(A \cap B)$ are obtained as follows:

The event $A \cup B$ (also known as the event "A and/or B") is obtained by combining together all outcomes which are either in A, or in B, or in both.

The event $A \cap B$ (also known as the event "A and B") is obtained by using only the outcomes that are components of *both* A and B.

The events A and B are mutually exclusive if and only if $A \cap B$ is a null event, i.e., no outcomes common to both A and B can be found. The null event is often denoted by the symbol $\emptyset$.

If events A and B are mutually exclusive, i.e., if $A \cap B = \emptyset$, then the union event $A \cup B$ is often displayed by the symbol: $A + B$. To repeat:

If $A \cap B = 0$, then $A \cup B = A + B$

In Sally's case, for example, the event $I \cup J$ comprises $(1, 4)$, $(1, 3)$, $(1, 1)$, $(1, 2)$, $(2, 2)$, $(3, 2)$, and $(4, 2)$. Of these, the first four outcomes belong to event *I* and the last four belong to event *J*. You can also define *I* ∪ *J* by the membership rule:

$I \cup J = \{(i, j), \text{ such that } i = 1, \text{ or } j = 2, \text{ or both}\}$

In any case, the outcome (1, 2) belongs to both *I* and *J*:

$I \cap J = (1, 2)$

Similarly:

$J \cup K = \{(1, 2), (2, 2), (3, 2), (4, 2), (2, 1), (3, 1), (4, 1), (4, 3)\}$

Also:

$J \cap K = \{(3, 2), (4, 2)\}$

You can also define its membership rule:

$J \cap K = \{(i, 2), \text{ such that } i > 2\}$

We can now examine the third operation: taking a complement.

Given an event *A*, obtain its complement (known as the event "not *A*," event "*S* − *A*" or "the complement of *A*") by combining together *all* the outcomes that do not belong to *A*. Obviously, by construction:
$$A \cap A' = 0 \text{ and } A + A' = S$$

In Sally's case, for example, the complement of *K* consists of *all* points not in *K*. Thus, you can verify from figure 2-2 that:

$K' = \{(1, 4), (1, 3), (1, 2), (1, 1), (2, 2), (2, 3), (2, 4), (3, 4), (3, 3), (4, 4)\}$

The corresponding membership rule is:

$K' = \{(i, j), \text{ such that } j \geq i\}$

Practice obtaining complements by deriving events *I'* and *J'* yourself.

In Sally's case, it was possible to list all outcomes that constitute an event. Since this is usually not the case, you should practice defining the events by their membership rules.

Venn Diagrams

In Sally's case, the sample space *S* was finite and all the distinct outcomes that jointly constitute that space could be displayed graphically. There are several reasons why this cannot always be done:

1. Finite does not mean only a few members.
2. All decision situations do not possess a two-dimensional structure.
3. All sample spaces are not finite.

A different graphic tool, a Venn diagram, is used to display the relationships among events in general.

A Venn diagram uses a rectangle to represent a sample space. Circles or parts thereof represent the events of interest. (Actually, any closed figure with a definite "inside" and "outside" can be used.) For example, in Figure 2-3, the rectangle represents a sample space S. Event A is represented by the interior of a circle, and event A' is represented by that portion of the rectangle which is outside the circle. Describing the complement of A with the notation S − A becomes obvious from such a figure.

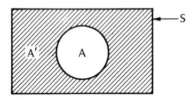

Figure 2-3. *Venn Diagram of Event A*

The Venn diagram in figure 2-4(a) displays two overlapping events: A and B. The *interior* of the appropriate circle represents event A or event B. These two events divide the sample space S into four sections, each representing a compound event. Thus, the section labeled 1 is common to both A and B; it represents A ∩ B. Any outcome in section 2 belongs to event A, but it does not belong to event B. Hence, section 2 represents event A ∩ B'. Similarly, section 3 represents A' ∩ B, and section 4 represents A' ∩ B'.

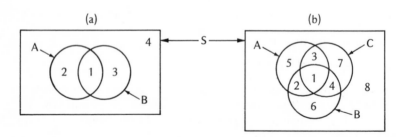

Figure 2-4. *Venn Diagrams for Multiple Events*

The Venn diagram in figure 2-4(b) represents three overlapping events A, B, and C. Each section can be interpreted as indicated in the preceding paragraph. Thus section 1 represents the event A ∩ B ∩ C, section 2 represents the event A ∩ B ∩ C', and so on.

Many other variations of Venn diagrams are possible. For example, if two events A and B are mutually exclusive, the corresponding circles would not intersect. Sally's situation (figure 2-2) shows yet another possibility.

It should be emphasized that a Venn diagram is a communication tool. A management scientist does not use it to actually solve a problem—unless, of course, lack of communication is the problem. A Venn diagram is used to clarify the existing relationships among various events. It is a tool for displaying logic. Since the formulation of a decision problem in the clearest possible terms is an important benefit of using management science, the utility of a Venn diagram should not be underestimated. This is equally true of other management science tools (decision trees, payoff matrices, Simplex tableaus, and flow diagrams), which will be discussed in greater detail in later chapters.

Algebra of Events

As an example of using Venn diagrams, consider the logical relationships between various compound events. Begin by using figure 2-3 to verify that, for any event A:

$$A + A' = S$$

The addition symbol in the above equation is equivalent to the union symbol because these two events, A and A', are mutually exclusive.

Using figure 2-4(a) you can verify that the events $A \cap B$, $A \cap B'$, $A' \cap B$, and $A' \cap B'$ are mutually exclusive and that:

$$A = A \cap B + A \cap B'$$
$$B = A \cap B + A' \cap B$$
$$A \cup B = A \cap B + A \cap B' + A' \cap B$$

In the first of these equations, event A can happen either with an event B or in the absence of B. Sally can get a 1 in accounting (event I) regardless of whether she gets a 2 in marketing (event $I \cap J$) or not (event $I \cap J'$).

The other two equations can be interpreted similarly. But, in the last equation, also note that the events $A \cup B$ and $A' \cap B'$ are mutually exclusive, and that together these two events cover the entire sample space:

$$(A \cup B) \cap (A' \cap B') = 0$$
$$(A \cup B) + (A' \cap B') = S$$

Hence, these two events are complements of each other.

$$(A \cup B)' = A' \cap B'$$

This means that if event "A and/or B" has not occurred, then event "neither A nor B" must have occurred. You can similarly interpret the following rule:

$$(A \cap B)' = A' \cup B'$$

Using figure 2-4(b), you can also verify the following rules regarding three events:

$$A \cap (B \cup C) = (A \cap B) \cup (A \cap C)$$
$$A \cup (B \cap C) = (A \cup B) \cap (A \cup C)$$

Now we are ready to review the techniques of probability and statistics.

BASIC CONCEPTS OF PROBABILITY

The probability of an event is a number between 0 and 1 which quantifies the decision maker's belief in the likelihood of that event. The more a decision maker believes an event will occur the closer its probability will be to 1. If the event is guaranteed to happen (e.g., the sun will rise tomorrow), its probability equals 1. This will be the case, for example, if the event coincides with the entire sample space S. Conversely, the less the decision maker believes an event will occur (e.g., Earth will explode tomorrow), the closer that event's probability will be to 0. The probability of a null event is always zero. Finally, if event A happens whenever B does, its probability must be at least as large as that of B.

The Probability Postulates

The previous remarks, of course, do not specify *how* one assesses the probability of an event. Presumably, this is done on the basis of some objective facts and/or the subjective feelings of a rational decision maker. Regardless of how the probabilities are assigned to various events in a sample space, they must obey certain rules. These rules are accepted without proof and are known as the probability postulates, three of which follow.

Postulate 1: The probability of an event is a positive real number or it is zero. Symbolically:

If $P(A)$ denotes the probability of an event A, then $P(A) \geqslant 0$.

Postulate 2: The probability of the entire sample space S equals one. Symbolically:

$$P(S) = 1$$

Postulate 3: If two events are mutually exclusive, the probability that either one or the other will happen equals the sum of their individual probabilities. Symbolically:

If $A \cap B = 0$, then $P(A + B) = P(A) + P(B)$.

In Sally Baker's case, for example, we have already identified three events: I, J, and K. The first postulate states that their probabilities will be nonnegative, i.e., $P(I) \geqslant 0$, $P(J) \geqslant 0$, and $P(K) \geqslant 0$. Her sample space S consists of 16 pairs (i, j), and one of these will definitely occur. The second postulate states that this is equivalent to saying that:

P(one of those 16 pairs will occur) = 1

In Sally's case, the events I and K are mutually exclusive. Sally can either score 1 in accounting or her marketing score will be better. She cannot have both. If she feels that $P(I) = .33$ and $P(K) = .37$, then according to Postulate 3, P(either I or K) must equal $.33 + .37 = .70$. Figure 2-5 illustrates this situation. If you think of probabilities as weights, Postulate 3 may become clearer. A decision maker whose probablity assessments follow Postulate 3 is said to be *consistent*. If these assessments do not satisfy Postulate 3, such a decision maker is said to be inconsistent. The probability assessments of an inconsistent person cannot be taken seriously.

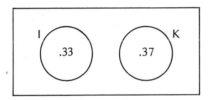

Figure 2-5. *Probability of an "Addition" Event*

It is now easy to verify the consequences of the three postulates. Recall from the algebra of events discussed earlier, that an event and its complement are mutually exclusive and together these cover the entire sample space. Symbolically:

$A \cap A' = \emptyset$ and $A + A' = S$

From Postulate 3:

$P(A + A') = P(A) + P(A')$

From Postulate 2:

$P(A + A') = 1$

It follows that:

$P(A) + P(A') = 1$
or equivalently:
$P(A') = 1 - P(A)$

This is known as *the law of probabilities of complementary events*. Since the probabilities must be nonnegative (Postulate 1), the above law also implies that for any event A:

$0 \leqslant P(A) \leqslant 1$

Also, since the events S and $\emptyset$ are complementary:

$P(0) = 0$

In other words, each of the remarks presented at the beginning of this section can be proven using the three postulates of probability and the algebra of events. However, since the purpose of this chapter is only to *review* the techniques of probability and statistics, the other results are stated here without proofs.

To begin, we can extend Postulate 3 to many mutually exclusive events.

Given k mutually exclusive events, $A_1, A_2, \ldots, A_k$, the probability that one of these will occur equals the sum of their individual probabilities. Symbolically:
$$P(A_1 + A_2 + \ldots + A_k) = P(A_1) + P(A_2) + \ldots + P(A_k)$$

This is the *addition rule* for mutually exclusive events. If a finite number of distinct outcomes together make up a sample space, then the above rule can also be used to obtain the probability of events from that of the constituent outcomes.

The probability of an event A equals the sum of the probabilities of the distinct outcomes which compose A.

This rule implies that probabilities need not be explicitly assigned to each possible event. The rule is quite handy since one can identify 2^n distinct events in a sample space made up of n distinct outcomes— especially since 2^n becomes unmanageably large for moderate values of n. Using this rule, you only need to define the probabilities of the individual outcomes. The probabilities of any events of interest to you are computed only as necessary.

Table 2-1 shows the probabilities of each outcome in Sally Baker's sample space. For example, Sally's chances of getting a 1 in accounting

Table 2-1 *Sally's Probability Assessments*

GRADE IN MARKETING	GRADE IN ACCOUNTING			
	1	2	3	4
4	.05	.05	.02	.01
3	.08	.07	.07	.02
2	.10	.08	.07	.05
1	.10	.10	.08	.05

and a 3 in marketing are: $P(1, 3) = .08$. Using the above rule, you can find the probability that Sally will get a 1 in accounting (event I) to be:

$$P(I) = P(1, 1) + P(1, 2) + P(1, 3) + P(1, 4)$$
$$= .10 + .10 + .08 + .05$$
$$= .33$$

Similarly, you can verify that:

$$P(J) = P(1, 2) + P(2, 2) + P(3, 2) + P(4, 2)$$
$$= .10 + .08 + .07 + .05$$
$$= .30$$

The addition rule can also be used to find the probability of a union when the component events overlap. This is known as the general addition rule:

Given any two events A and B:
$$P(A \cup B) = P(A) + P(B) - P(A \cap B)$$

In Sally Baker's case, events I and J overlap. In fact, $I \cap J = (1, 2)$. Hence, $P(I \cap J) = P(1, 2) = .10$. The general addition rule can, therefore, be used to find the probability of her getting a 1 in accounting or a 2 in marketing or both:

$$P(I \cup J) = P(I) + P(J) - P(I \cap J)$$
$$= .33 + .30 - .10$$
$$= .53$$

You can also verify the above result by enumerating the outcomes that make up the event $I \cup J$.

This rule can be extended to three or more events. For example, given three events A_1, A_2, and A_3, you can verify using a Venn diagram that:

$$P(A_1 \cup A_2 \cup A_3) = P(A_1) + P(A_2) + P(A_3)$$
$$- P(A_1 \cap A_2) - P(A_1 \cap A_3) - P(A_2 \cap A_3)$$
$$+ P(A_1 \cap A_2 \cap A_3)$$

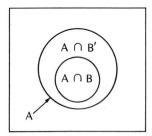

Figure 2-6. *A Venn Diagram Depicting a Subevent*

Finally, suppose that event *A* happens whenever event *B* happens. This implies that all outcomes that are part of *B* also belong to *A*, though some outcomes in *A* may not belong to *B*. The situation is depicted in the Venn diagram in figure 2-6. The inner circle represents event *B* and the outer circle shows event *A*. Clearly, $A \cap B = B$. For this reason, *B* is said to be a *subevent* of *A*. Since $A = A \cap B + A \cap B'$, then $P(A) = P(A \cap B) + P(A \cap B') = P(B) + P(A \cap B')$. Since $P(A \cap B')$ must be non-negative, we can state that:

If event *A* happens whenever event *B* happens, then $A \cap B = B$, and hence $P(A) \geqslant P(B)$.

In Sally's sample space, for example, define event *H* as happening whenever her marketing grade is one better than her accounting grade. In other words:

$$H = \{(2, 1), (3, 2), (4, 3)\}$$

Verify that:

1. Event *K* happens whenever event *H* happens.
2. $P(H) = .19 < .37 = P(K)$

Assessing Probabilities

Now that we have seen how probabilities must behave, we will describe three methods of assigning probabilities to an event.

Hypothetical In this method, probabilities are assigned on the basis of hypothetical reasons. For instance, if we assume that a perfectly balanced coin will turn up heads or tails equally often, then we can assign P (head on a single toss) = .5 and P (tail on a single toss) = .5. If each of the six faces of a perfectly balanced die show up equally often, we can assign P (1 dot) = P (2 dots) = . . . = P (6 dots) = 1/6. Many early assessments of probabilities were carried out in this manner. And, in later years, many formulas describing the statistical behavior of elementary particles were derived this way. Even Mendel's laws on genetics owe their existence to this technique.

Historical (Empirical) If an experiment has been performed many times in the past, one can count the number of occasions when event A occurred. Thus, if event A happened on k out of n occasions in the past, then one may assess:

$$P(A) = \frac{k}{n}, \text{ especially if } n \text{ is large}$$

From such past evidence (history), sociologists, psychologists, and economists often assign probabilities to the events in which they are interested. The basic assumption of this method is that the past is a guide for the future. To such decision makers, the world is essentially stationary or is in a dynamic equilibrium. If a certain disease has occurred in 8 of the past 100 years, according to this method one would assign a probability of .08 to its happening next year. This is how the risk of a policyholder being in an automobile accident within the next year would be derived.

Subjective This method is used when neither a formal theory nor empirical records of sufficient length exists to completely assess probabilities. Such might be the case when starting new ventures. The corresponding statements of probability are based on indirect information, educated guesses, and other subjective factors. In betting $5,000 against $2,000 that a certain enterprise will succeed, a person is in effect assessing:

$$P(\text{success}) = 5/(5 + 2) \approx .71$$

> If someone considers it equitable to bet x dollars against y dollars that event A will occur, this person's subjective assessment of its probability is:
>
> $$P(A) = \frac{x}{x + y}$$

Assigning probabilities to events of interest is an art as much as science. Technical knowledge of the specific situation must be used to generate hypotheses. Augment these with available empirical data, and then subjectively decide whether the past would continue to be a reasonable guide for the future.

Conditional Probabilities

Thus far, we had tacitly assumed that once we describe an experiment and define all of its outcomes, the *entire* sample space S would continue to be relevant while assessing probabilities. It often turns out that as new information becomes available, some portion of the original sample space becomes irrelevant. Occasionally a researcher wants to limit the investigations to within some subset of the original sample space. In either case, the relevant sample space "shrinks," and this affects the probability assessments.

Returning once again to the experiment of forecasting Sally Baker's final grades in marketing and accounting, suppose she reports that her grade in marketing is better than that in accounting. In other words, event K has occurred. How does this affect the probabilities of various events? For example, what is the new probability of event J that she will get a 2 in marketing?

The number that we now seek is the *conditional probability* of event J given that K has happened; symbolically: $P(J \mid K)$. In this notation, the vertical stroke, |, separates the event of interest from the *condition* that some "specified event has occurred." The condition is always shown on the right of the vertical stroke and the event of interest on the left. In fact, using this new notation, $P(K)$ is equivalent to $P(K \mid S)$, with the condition that the entire sample space S is relevant. Refer back to figure 2-2 and observe that the events J and K overlap. The corresponding Venn diagram (in fact, a reduced copy of figure 2-2) is shown here as figure 2-7. The original sample space S had 16 points. The report that event K has occurred makes all except five of these irrelevant. The event J can therefore happen only if the subevent $J \cap K$ occurs. Thus, $P(J \mid K)$ equals $P(J \cap K \mid K)$. Since K is now the only relevant sample space, $P(K \mid K)$ must

Figure 2-7. *Venn Diagram of Sally's Problem*

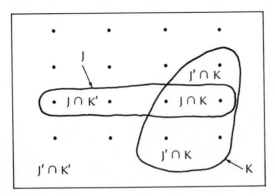

be one. It follows that the probability of each outcome within K must be inflated by the ratio: $1 \div P(K)$. Hence:

$$P(J \mid K) = \frac{P(J \cap K)}{P(K)} = \frac{.12}{.37} = .3243$$

Using the initial assessments of probability of each outcome, the conditional probabilities of any event can be derived similarly:

Given any two events A and B in a sample space S, the conditional probability of A given B, symbolically $P(A \mid B)$, is computed as the ratio:

$$P(A \mid B) = \frac{P(A \cap B)}{P(B)}$$

as long as $P(B)$ is not equal to zero.

Naturally, if events A and B are mutually exclusive, then $P(A \mid B)$ as well as $P(B \mid A)$ would both be zero.

The Multiplication Rule

If we multiply both sides of the above formula by $P(B)$, we get:

$$P(A \cap B) = P(A \mid B) \times P(B)$$

This is the multiplication rule used to obtain the *joint probability* that two events A and B would occur simultaneously. It can also be used to generalize the findings of an experiment from a smaller to a larger sample space.

Suppose, for instance, that you have found that 70 percent of the private physicians practicing in urban areas of the United States make over \$30,000 per year. You also know that 80 percent of all private physicians in the U.S. practice in urban areas. To generalize these findings to all private physicians in the U.S., you can use the multiplication rule.

Let S denote the set of all private physicians in the U.S. Let A denote the event that a randomly chosen private physician in the U.S. makes over \$30,000 per year. Let B denote the event that such a physician practices in an urban area. Your findings to this point can be expressed as:

$$P(A \mid B) = .7 \text{ and } P(B) = .8$$

Consequently, the chance that the above physician makes over \$30,000 annually *and* practices in an urban area, symbolically $P(A \cap B)$, can be determined by the multiplication rule:

$$P(A \cap B) = .7 \times .8 = .56$$

There is a $P(B') = 1 - P(B) = 1 - .8 = .2$ chance that the above physician does not practice in an urban area. Suppose that you have found through further research that $P(A \mid B') = .5$. (Provide a verbal equivalent of this last symbolic statement.) Another application of the multiplication rule would then yield:

$$P(A \cap B') = P(A \mid B') \times P(B')$$
$$= .5 \times .2 = .10$$

Since the events $A \cap B$ and $A \cap B'$ are mutually exclusive, you can use the additional rule (Postulate 3) to obtain:

$$P(A) = P(A \cap B) + P(A \cap B')$$
$$= .56 + .10 = .66$$

By skillful use of the multiplication rule (and by obtaining additional information), you can thus state that 66 percent of *all* private physicians in the U.S. make over $30,000 annually. In other words, the sample space can be expanded by using the multiplication rule.

Independence of Events

The multiplication rule can also be used to check the independence of events. If two events A and B are independent, then the knowledge that event B has or has not occurred should not affect the probability that A will occur. Symbolically, we must have:

$$P(A \mid B) = P(A \mid B')$$

In fact, since the knowledge of B is immaterial, each of these probabilities must also equal $P(A)$. But in that case, the multiplication rule becomes:

$$P(A \cap B) = P(A) \times P(B)$$

This is then the *test of independence* for two events.

As an illustration of its use, suppose that you meet a group of 20 adults at a party. Of these, 12 are men and 8 are women. Also, three of the men and two of the women are of Chinese origin. Table 2-2 shows the situation. The experiment consists of choosing a person at random and noting that person's sex and origin. Let C denote the event that the chosen person is of Chinese origin and let M denote the event that the chosen person is a male. You can verify that because the group contains 12 men:

$$P(M) = 12/20 = .6$$

Since three of the men are of Chinese origin:

$$P(C \cap M) = 3/20 = .15$$

Table 2-2 *The Sex and National Origin of Partygoers*

	CHINESE	OTHER	TOTAL
Men	3	9	12
Women	2	6	8
Total	5	15	20

Since there are five persons of Chinese origin:

$P(C) = 5/20 = .25$

Finally, since:

$P(C \cap M) = .15$ equals $P(C) \times P(M)$

it follows that in this group, the events M and C are independent events.

SUBSCRIPTS AND Σ NOTATION

We will pause in the discussion of probabilities to introduce a very useful notation which will be employed whenever convenient. Suppose that you know the take-home pay of each of the 100 employees of an organization. The act of computing the total of all these pays can be described as follows: Arrange the employee names in some order so that there will be a first, a second, . . . , and a hundredth employee. Add the take-home pay of the second employee to that of the first. Add to the resultant total, the take-home pay of the third employee. Add to this total, the take-home pay of the fourth employee. Continue this way until the take-home pay of the hundredth employee has been added. The result will be the sum of the take-home pays of all employees.

As you can see, the verbal description of even such a simple act is rather lengthy. Since we often need to make descriptions of this sort, we can use a shorthand notation. In that notation, the take-home pay total can be described as follows: Let $i = 1, 2, \ldots , 100$ denote the employee numbers and let x_i denote the take-home pay of the ith employee. This means that the take-home pay of the first employee ($i = 1$) is x_1, that of the second employee ($i = 2$) is $x_2, \ldots$, and that of the one hundredth employee ($i = 100$) is x_{100}. The sum of their pays equals:

$$\sum_{i=1}^{100} x_i$$

The variable i is said to be a *subscript* of the variable x. In effect, it is a device to keep track of which particular number, x_i, is of present concern. The i values are always *successive* integers. It is not necessary to begin with $i = 1$. Depending on the situation, you may begin counting with $i = m$, a *known* integer. You may also continue counting until $i = n$, also a *known* integer. Usually, m is less than or equal to n. (In the take-home pay situation, m equals 1 and n equals 100.) When $i = m$, the number of current interest is x_m. When $i = m + 1$, the number of interest is x_{m+1}, and so on.

With these conventions, the shorthand notation:

$$\sum_{i=m}^{n} x_i$$

stands for the following paragraph.

Set i to be m. Obtain x_m. Increase i by 1 (from m to $m + 1$). Obtain x_{m+1}. Increase i by 1 again. Obtain x_{m+2}. Continue until i equals n. Then add *all* of these numbers: $x_m + x_{m+1} + \ldots + x_n$. (The symbol Σ means "take the sum of.")

For example, suppose that a student's scores on successive tests are: $x_1 = 75, x_2 = 63, x_3 = 87$, and $x_4 = 91$. In this case, the initial subscript, m, equals 1. The final subscript n is 4. The sum of all the student's scores, in this notation, would be:

$$\sum_{i=1}^{4} x_i = x_1 + x_2 + x_3 + x_4$$

$$= 75 + 63 + 87 + 91 = 316$$

The sum of scores on only the last three tests would be:

$$\sum_{i=2}^{4} x_i = x_2 + x_3 + x_4$$

$$= 63 + 87 + 91 = 241$$

DISCRETE RANDOM VARIABLES

A situation described by a sample space has many aspects. Fortunately, a decision maker is generally interested in one or only a few of these aspects. Sally Baker, whose sample space was shown in figure 2-1, is probably only interested in her average grade. Though the world of private physicians can be interesting in many ways, the decision maker in the section on the multiplication rule was concerned only with their annual incomes. An investor is usually interested in the return on investment (ROI). A hospital administrator is interested in the cost of providing medical care. An urban planner is interested in improving the quality of life. A woman employee is concerned with job equality.

In each of these cases, the decision maker/researcher is interested in a *number* (or perhaps a set of numbers) that corresponds to the realization of a chance event. Such numbers are said to be values of the corresponding *random variables*. The adjectives random, stochastic, probabilistic, or chance, all imply the same thing—the values of such variables depend on the chance realization of specified events. In short, a random variable assigns numbers to events in a sample space.

Partitions of a Sample Space

Consider Sally Baker's sample space. Let X denote her average grade. If Sally scores a grade i in accounting and j in marketing, her average grade would be $(i + j)/2$. For example, if she scores a 2 in accounting *and* a 1 in marketing, X would be $(1 + 2)/2 = 1.5$. The first two columns of table 2-3 identify the outcomes that yield the corresponding

Table 2-3 *The Probability Function of X*

VALUES OF X	OUTCOMES NEEDED	PROBABILITY
1.0	(1, 1)	.10
1.5	(1, 2) or (2,1)	.20
2.0	(1, 3) or (2, 2) or (3, 1)	.24
2.5	(1, 4) or (2, 3) or (3, 2) or (4, 1)	.24
3.0	(2, 4) or (3, 3) or (4, 2)	.17
3.5	(3, 4) or (4, 3)	.04
4.0	(4, 4)	.01

values of X. Note that all outcomes that produce the same value for X are grouped together, e.g., $X = 1.5$ corresponds to the ordered pair (1, 2) or (2, 1). Since a group of outcomes defines an event, table 2-3 in fact displays seven events in Sally's sample space and the associated values of X. Note also that these seven events do not overlap—X is 1 *or* 1.5 *or* ... *or* 4.0. Also, taken together these span the entire sample space. This is always the case for any random variable in any sample space.

A random variable partitions a sample space into mutually exclusive and jointly exhaustive events, and assigns a unique number to each of these events. (By jointly exhaustive we mean that events span the entire sample space.)

The Probability Function

The last column of table 2-3 is obtained as follows. Since X will be 1 if and only if the grade outcome is (1, 1), the probability that X equals 1 is identical to the probability that the outcome (1, 1) will occur. From table 2-1, this latter probability is .10. Hence:

$$P(X = 1) = P(1, 1) = .1$$

Similarly, X will be 1.5 if and only if Sally's grade outcome is either (1, 2) or (2, 1). Hence, using table 2-1:

$$P(X = 1.5) = P(1, 2) + P(2, 1)$$
$$= .1 + .1 = .2$$

All other probabilities are obtained similarly.

Since the events $\{X = 1\}$, $\{X = 1.5\}$, . . . , and $\{X = 4\}$ are mutually exclusive and together cover the entire sample space S, it follows that $P(X = 1) + P(X = 1.5) + \ldots + P(X = 4)$ must be one. And it is. Because of this, the last column of table 2-3 is said to represent the *probability function* of X.

We need to introduce one other concept. If all possible values of a random variable, X, can be arranged in a *sequence* such as:

$$\{x_1, x_2, \ldots, \}$$

then it is said to be a *discrete random variable*. In other words, if it is meaningful to use a subscript notation to describe all possible values of X, then X is discrete. In Sally's case, you can easily identify a sequence: $x_1 = 1, x_2 = 1.5, x_3 = 2, \ldots, x_7 = 4$. In fact, all possible average grades in this sequence can be obtained by the rule:

$$X_k = \frac{(k + 1)}{2}, k = 1, 2, \ldots, 7$$

Thus, Sally's average grade is a discrete random variable.

If the random variable is discrete, we can also use a subscript notation to describe its probability function. Specifically, let x_k denote a typical member of the $x_1, x_2, \ldots$ sequence. Define a corresponding sequence of probabilities $p_1, p_2, \ldots$ by the rule:

$$p_k = P(X = x_k), k = 1, 2, \ldots$$

We can now state more precisely what we mean by a probability function.

The sequence of probabilities, $p_1, p_2, \ldots$, is said to be a probability function of a discrete random variable X, if and only if:

● Each p_k lies between 0 and 1.
and
● Their sum, $p_1 + p_2 + \ldots$, equals 1.

The third column of table 2-3 represents the probability function of Sally's average grade because each probability in that column is between 0 and 1, and because the sum of all entries in that column is 1.

The Expected Value

The probability function of a random variable tells us *all* there is to know about that variable. Frequently, it amounts to carrying too many individual items of information "in our head." Is it possible to find just a few numbers which would contain most of that information? In many cases, the answer is yes. The expected value of a random variable, its variance, its skewness, and its kurtosis are four such numbers. We will discuss the first two of these in some detail. Additional examples of their use are found throughout the remainder of this text. The last two will not be needed in the rest of this text. You can read more about any of these four parameters in a standard statistical text.

Consider Sally Baker's case again. The first and third columns of table 2-3 show the possible values of X and the corresponding probabilities. Based on this information, what can Sally *expect* to get this time? The symbolic answer is: $E(X)$, the expected value of X. This new number is computed as follows:

Multiply each value of X by the probability of realizing that value. Then add all such terms. The result is the expected value of X. Symbolically, let p_1, p_2, ... denote the probabilities of realizing $x_1, x_2, \ldots$. Then:

$$E(X) = \Sigma_k (p_k \times x_k)$$

Table 2-4 shows the process and the result of applying this rule. The first two columns are reproduced from their counterparts in table 2-3. The third column shows the cross-products $(x_k \cdot p_k)$ for line k. The sum of *all*

Table 2-4 *Sally's Expectation*

VALUES OF X (x_k)	PROBABILITIES (p_k)	CROSS-PRODUCTS $(x_k \cdot p_k)$
1	.1	.10
1.5	.2	.30
2	.24	.48
2.5	.24	.60
3	.17	.51
3.5	.04	.14
4	.01	.04
		2.17 = $E(X)$

entries in that column yield $E(X)$. Thus, Sally should expect to get 2.17. (In many U.S. universities, this would correspond to a letter grade of B−.)

The Law of Large Numbers

The importance of knowing the expected value of a random variable X, symbolically $E(X)$, can be summarized by the law of large numbers. The basic concept can be summed up as follows.

Suppose that you have observed the actual values of X on n successive occasions under essentially identical conditions, and that these were: $x_1, x_2, \ldots, x_n$. The *average* of these numbers, x, would be:

$$x = \frac{x_1 + x_2 + \ldots + x_n}{n}$$

The law of large numbers states that if n is sufficiently large, the difference between $\bar{x}$ and $E(X)$ can be negligible. Note that whereas the average is obtained empirically, the expected value is based on theory. Assume that the theory is correct. Then, this law also states that *in the long run, theory will coincide with experience.* Thus, if you are going to be in the same situation on numerous occasions, $E(X)$ can be your guide for the future. In the following chapters, we will have several opportunities to use this principle.

In particular, suppose that $X = 1$ if event A occurs and $X = 0$ if it does not. The sequence of observations $x_1, x_2, \ldots, x_n$ is a sequence of 1s and 0s. The average, $\bar{x}$, equals the relative frequency of event A. Since X will be 1 with probability $P(A)$ and it will be zero with probability $1 - P(A)$, it follows that in this case:

$E(X) = P(A)$

The law of large numbers, therefore, states that, *in the long run, the relative frequency of event A will equal its probability.* This is why relative frequencies are often used for assigning probabilities to various events.

Variance and Standard Deviation

The difficulty in using $E(X)$ as a guide for action is that it only indicates what would happen in the long run. If one is going to be in the same situation on numerous occasions, then $E(X)$ tells most of "the story." A grocer who must place an order for a product every day can effectively use $E(X)$ since the fluctuations in demand for that product would average out. But, if you are going to have only a few occasions on which to observe X, you need a measure of the variability inherent in that chance process. One such measure is known as the *variance* of X, symbolically Var(X). Another measure is known as the *standard deviation* of X, symbolically $\sigma(X)$. (σ is read "sigma.") These are defined by the formulas:

$$\text{Var}(X) = E[X - E(X)]^2$$

and

$$\sigma(X) = \sqrt{\text{Var}(X)}$$

Note that when a random variable X equals x_k, the difference between it and the expected value equals $x_k - E(X)$. To avoid canceling positive and negative differences, we will square this difference: $[x_k - E(X)]^2$. Since p_k is also the probability that this new variable, $[X - E(X)]^2$, would equal $[x_k - E(X)]^2$, variance can be computed by the summation formula:

$$\text{Var}(X) = \Sigma_k([x_k - E(X)]^2 \cdot p_k)$$

Note, however, that unless $E(X)$ is zero, computing the variance can become a chore. This can be avoided by noting that if X equals x_k with probability p_k, then X^2 equals x_k^2 with the *same* probability p_k. In short, X^2 is a random variable with:

$$E(X^2) = \Sigma_k (x_k^2 \cdot p_k)$$

After a few algebraic manipulations, the variance formula can be rewritten as:

$$\text{Var}(X) = E(X^2) - [E(X)]^2$$

This formula is usually much easier to work with.

As an illustration of its use, consider Sally Baker's average grade, X. We have already computed her $E(X)$ in table 2-4. The process of deriving $E(X^2)$ is similar and is displayed in table 2-5. Using the last line of that table, you can verify that in Sally's case:

$$\text{Var}(X) = 5.19 - (2.17)^2$$
$$= .4811$$

Table 2-5 *Obtaining $E(X^2)$ for Sally*

x_k	x_k^2	p_k	$x_k^2\, p_k$
1	1	.1	.10
1.5	2.25	.2	.45
2	4	.24	.96
2.5	6.25	.24	1.50
3	9	.17	1.53
3.5	12.25	.04	.49
4	16	.01	+ .16
			5.19 = $E(X^2)$

Consequently, the standard deviation of her grade is:

$$\sigma(X) = \sqrt{\text{Var}(X)} = \sqrt{.4811} \approx .6936$$

Linear Transformations

The significance of $\text{Var}(X)$ and $\sigma(X)$ in statistical literature will be discussed in the section on normal distribution. Now we should examine two important properties of $E(X)$ and $\sigma(X)$.

Choose any two numbers, $a(> 0)$ and b. Then define a new random variable Y to be $aX + b$. You now know enough to verify the following statements.

> If $Y = aX + b$
> then $E(Y) = aE(X) + b$
> and $\sigma(Y) = a\sigma(X)$

From these statements observe that:

1. $E(Y)$ has exactly the same relationship with $E(X)$ as Y has with X.
2. The standard deviation of a random variable is not affected by the addition or subtraction of a constant.
3. Multiplication by a constant changes the standard deviation of a random variable proportionately.

All of these results are obvious if you recall that:

1. $E(X)$ coincides with the average of X in the long run, so that *any* change in X will be reflected as a change in $E(X)$.
2. $\sigma(X)$ measures variability only and as such should not be affected by the addition or subtraction of a constant.

Recall from geometry that the equation $y = ax + b$ represents a straight line. For this reason, the transformation $Y = aX + b$ is known as a linear transformation. One special transformation of this type is:

$$Z = \frac{X - E(X)}{\sigma(X)}$$

You can easily verify that: $E(Z) = 0$ and $\sigma(Z) = 1$. These two numbers are independent of both $E(X)$ and $\sigma(X)$. For this reason, Z is known as a *standardized* variable. Its significance will become clearer in the section on normal distribution.

BINOMIAL DISTRIBUTION

In this and the next section, we will review the properties of three extremely useful, discrete random variables before proceeding with the discussion of continuous random variables. Their application in decision making appears throughout the next several chapters.

Binary Variables

The simplest of all the discrete random variables used by a management scientist is that which has only two possible values. Such a variable is encountered in numerous situations. A candidate will either get or not get a job; a randomly chosen person will or will not turn out to be a genius; a batch of a product will or will not be of acceptable quality; a proposal submitted to a funding organization will or will not be funded by that organization; a cure for cancer will or will not be found in the next five years. It is customary to denote one of the two possible outcomes in each such situation as a *success* and the other one as a *failure*.

The corresponding random variable is assigned a value 1 if the outcome is a success and 0 if it is not. (Since observing a success is an event, you have already encountered this variable in the discussion of the law of large numbers.) $P(X = 1)$ is usually denoted by the symbol p and $P(X = 0)$ is denoted by q. Since 1 and 0 are the only possible values of X, such a variable may be called a *binary* (meaning two-valued) variable. Note that the sum $(p + q)$ must equal 1, so that $q = 1 - p$. It is easy to verify that for a binary variable X:

$$E(X) = p, \text{ and } E(X^2) = p$$

so that:

$$\text{Var}(X) = p - p^2 = p(1 - p) = pq$$

Binomial Variables

Suppose now that the experiment consists of observing the values of a binary variable on n successive occasions or "trials." On each occasion, there is the *same* probability p of success. In other words, the knowledge that success has or has not occurred on an occasion does not influence the probability that it will or will not occur on following occasions. The random variable, X = *the number of successes* on n identical and independent occasions, is said to a *binomial* variable. Note again that both p and n must remain constant throughout the experiment.

If a student attempts a test consisting of 20 "true or false" questions, then each question represents a binary occasion. Hence, in this case $n = 20$. If the student just guesses at the answers, then the chance of success on any one question is $p = .5$. In that case, X = number of correct responses is a binomial variable.

If a manufacturing process is "in control," then there is only a small but fixed probability p of receiving a faulty unit. If, as a quality control inspector, you inspect a batch containing n such units, then you are performing a binomial experiment. The binomial variable in this case is X = number of faulty units in that batch.

Combinations and Permutations

At this stage, we need to introduce two new concepts. Given m distinct objects, how many different arrangements are possible? The symbolic answer is $m!$ (Read as "m factorial.") For example, with three objects: A, B, and C, you can make six different arrangements: ABC, ACB, BAC, BCA, CAB, and CBA. Hence, $3! = 6$. You can similarly find that $4! = 24$, $5! = 120$, etc.

If m is a positive integer, then:

$$m! = m(m - 1)(m - 2) \ldots \left[m - (m - 1)\right]$$

and

$$0! = 1$$

If a group must contain exactly k of the n distinct objects, then one can form nC_k such groups. For example, with $n = 4$ objects: A, B, C, and D, you can form 6 groups of $k = 2$ objects each: AB, AC, AD, BC, BD, and CD. Hence, $4C_2 = 6$. Similarly, working with $n = 5$ objects, you can verify that $5C_1 = 5C_4 = 5$, $5C_2 = 5C_3 = 10$, and $5C_0 = 5C_5 = 1$. In general, it can be shown that:

$$nC_k = \frac{n!}{k!(n - k)!} = nC_{n-k}$$

The symmetry in the above equation can be explained by noting that when you choose k objects to form a group, you automatically choose $n - k$ objects to *not* be in that group. These objects form a "leftover" group. Thus, there are just as many groups of k objects as there are of $n - k$ objects.

Binomial Properties

Using this notation, we can now state the following result without proof. Given a binomial experiment with parameters n and p, the probability of obtaining exactly k successes, p_k, is given by:

$$p_k = nC_k \, p^k (1 - p)^{n - k}$$

This formula defines the binomial probability function. In the past, the binomial function had been extensively tabulated. (Appendix C shows one such table.) But, since today's computers can use a software routine to compute the binomial function, the need for extensive tables of this function has been greatly reduced.

The expected value and the variance of a binomial variable are given by:

$$E(X) = np \text{ and } \text{Var}(X) = npq$$

These two formulas can also be obtained by noting that a binomial variable X is in fact the sum of n independent binary variables $(X_1, X_2, \ldots, X_n)$ each of which equals 1 with probability p and 0 with probability q. Hence:

$$E(X) = E(X_1) + \ldots + E(X_n) = np$$

and

$$\text{Var}(X) = \text{Var}(X_1) + \ldots + \text{Var}(X_n) = npq$$

Note one consequence: the variance of a binomial variable reaches its peak when $p = .5$, i.e., when success and failure on a single occasion are equally probable. This maximum value of variance is $.25n$.

POISSON DISTRIBUTION

If n is large and p is small, the binomial probabilities can be approximated using a formula first discovered by Simeon Poisson (1781–1840), a French mathematician. Specifically, let λ (read "lambda") equal the product $n \cdot p$. Then the probability of finding exactly k successes is given by:

$$p_k = \frac{\lambda^k e^{-\lambda}}{k!}, \text{ where } k = 0, 1, 2, \ldots$$

The symbol e in the above formula is known as the *base of the natural logarithms*. It equals 2.718282.... A random variable which follows the above law exactly is known as a Poisson variable. It can take on any nonnegative integral value. However, small values are far more likely than the larger ones. The proof that the above formula in fact represents a probability function is beyond the scope of this text.

The Poisson approximation to the binomial probability function becomes increasingly more accurate as p decreases and n increases without limit. For this reason, the above formula is also known as the *probability of rare events*. Thus, for instance, the chance that a randomly chosen person will be blind is very small indeed. However, in any large metropolis one can find several blind persons. The number of blind persons per 100,000 population, for example, is a Poisson variable. Similarly, the number of accidents on a given highway per week, or the number of policyholders (of an insurance company) who will report a fire in their house next week are additional examples of a Poisson variable.

The Poisson distribution is also important in the study of waiting lines which form behind almost any service facility. Empirical studies indicate that the number of people, for example, approaching a service facility in a specified amount of time is a Poisson variable. The annual number of failures of a piece of equipment, the number of cars approaching a toll booth on an expressway, and the number of telephone calls per hour are additional examples. More examples will be found in the chapter on waiting lines.

If X is a Poisson variable with a parameter λ, then it can be shown that:

$E(X) = \lambda$ and $\text{Var}(X) = \lambda$

In fact, $E(X) = \text{Var}(X)$ is one indication that X is a Poisson variable.

CONTINUOUS RANDOM VARIABLES

Many of the random variables in management science can be measured on a continuous scale. The speed at which a plane flies, the floor space of an office, the time necessary to complete a task, and the gallons of gasoline sold by a gas station per day are some examples of continuous random variables. In such cases, we are not really interested in probabilities of individual outcomes, such as the plane will travel at exactly 537.4 miles per hour or you will need exactly 35.3 hours to complete writing a chapter. Instead, the interest lies in questions such as: what is the chance that a plane will fly between 520 and 540 miles per hour or that you will need between 33 and 37 hours to complete a chapter.

Constructing a Probability Histogram

In general, given a continuous random variable X, we begin by dividing the range of its values into a number of nonoverlapping intervals and then record the probabilities that X will lie within each such interval. In a sense, these intervals take the place of the individual outcomes. Suppose, for example, that James Brown is a cattle farmer who owns a herd of 1000 cows. In weighing his cows every Monday he noticed that each of his cows gains between 70 and 105 pounds during their tenth week on the farm. Being curious, he has counted the number of cows that gain between 70 and 75 pounds, the number that gain between 75 and 80 pounds, etc. The results are shown in table 2-6. The first column shows the weight gained in pounds. The second column shows the number of cows who belong to each weight class. Since there are 1000 cows on Mr. Brown's farm, the last column is obtained by dividing each frequency by that total, i.e., 1000. Mr. Brown wishes to use these relative frequencies as probabilities of the corresponding weight class. In other words, let X = number of pounds gained by a randomly chosen cow on Mr. Brown's farm. Then, $P(70 \leq X < 75) = .006$, $P(75 \leq X < 80) = .061$, etc.

The same information can also be displayed in a *histogram of probabilities*, such as in figure 2-8. (Not all histograms are symmetrical as

Table 2-6 *Weight Gained by Farmer Brown's Cows*

WEIGHT GAIN* (POUNDS)		FREQUENCY (NUMBER OF COWS)	RELATIVE FREQUENCY
70⁻	75⁻	6	.006
75⁻	80⁻	61	.061
80⁻	85⁻	242	.242
85⁻	90⁻	382	.382
90⁻	95⁻	242	.242
95⁻	100⁻	61	.061
100⁻	105⁻	6	.006
Totals		1000	1.000

*The minus sign, such as in 75⁻, implies that only the cows gaining *less* than 75 pounds are in the 70–75⁻ class.

this one.) It is constructed as follows. The weights are shown along the horizontal axis. The width of each rectangle is that of the corresponding weight class. The *area* of each rectangle *equals the probability* of the corresponding class. Thus, the height of a rectangle for each weight class is given by:

$$\text{height} = \frac{\text{probability}}{\text{width}}$$

For example, consider the weight class 80–85⁻. It is 5 units wide and the probability of a cow gaining these many pounds is .242. Hence, that rectangle is .242/5 = .0484 units tall. Similarly, the rectangle with base 85–90⁻ is .382/5 = .0764 units tall.

If Mr. Brown needs more precise information, his rectangles must be narrower than the present ones. For instance, figure 2-9 shows a more precise histogram with weight classes 70–73.75, 73.75–76.25, . . . , up to

Figure 2-8. *Histogram of Mr. Brown's Cows*

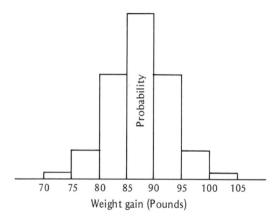

101.25–105. As long as his data can support it, there is no particular reason why Mr. Brown should not continue to subdivide his rectangles even more. If he does, he will eventually find that *the mid-points* of the top sides of his rectangles *follow a smooth curve*. That curve goes by the name of *probability density curve*. The height of that curve at any point *x* is denoted by the symbol $f(x)$. It represents the probability density function of Mr. Brown's random variable.

Probability Density Functions

It is worth noting that not all probability density functions (PDF, for short) have the shape (called a bell curve) shown in figure 2-9. We will review its properties in the following section. Figure 2-10 shows some of the commonly used probability density functions.

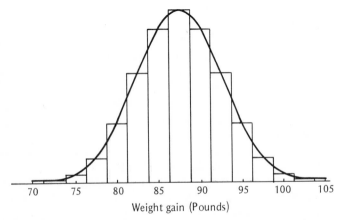

Weight gain (Pounds)

Figure 2-9. *A Refined Histogram and a Probability Curve*

Figure 2-10(a) shows simply a straight line parallel to the *X*-axis. The dotted lines are drawn only to "carry the eye." Since it looks like a rectangle, this function is called a rectangular distribution. It is written algebraically as: $f(x) = 1/(d - c)$ in some interval from *c* to *d*, and as $f(x) = 0$ outside that range.

Figure 2-10(b) shows an exponential density function. It is positive only on the positive side of the *X*-axis. The corresponding algebraic for-

Figure 2-10. *Some Commonly Used PDF's*

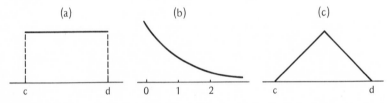

mula is: $f(x) = me^{-mx}$ for some constant number m. When $x = 0$, $f(x) = 1$. As x increases, $f(x)$ decreases. However, it never becomes zero.

The density curve in figure 2-10(c) looks like a triangle, and is hence called the triangular density function. It is positive only between two numbers, c and d. The corresponding $f(x)$ is 0, when $x = c$ or $x = d$. It reaches the peak value of $2/(d - c)$, when $x = (c + d)/2$.

There are many other probability density functions that are commonly used. Some are obtained empirically, others are derived using some theoretical reasoning. All such functions share three properties:

---

1. $f(x)$ is always nonnegative, $f(x) \geq 0$, for all x.
2. The area under a density function between any two constants, a and b, equals $P(a \leq X \leq b)$.
3. The total area under any density function always equals one.

A probability density function is thus very similar to a probability function discussed earlier. Given such a function, you can compute the probability of specified events. You can also obtain the $E(X)$, Var (X), and $\sigma(X)$ of the corresponding random variable X. However, since X is continuous, it is often necessary to use calculus to work with such variables. Instead, we will review one such variable in some detail in the following section.

GAUSSIAN (NORMAL) DISTRIBUTION

This probability law was extensively studied by the mathematician and astronomer Karl Friedrich Gauss (1777–1855) for describing the distribution of errors which can occur even in a carefully designed and controlled experiment. In such an experiment all the resultant errors are attributable to chance only. His reasoning might be summarized as follows.

1. Since the errors are presumed to be caused by chance rather than by deliberate design or experimenter's neglect, it is logical to assume that such errors are as likely to be positive as they are to be negative.
2. The size of the error caused by chance alone should not depend on whether that error is positive or negative. In other words, the density function of errors should be symmetrical around zero.
3. Since the experiment has been carefully designed and controlled, one should expect that small errors are far more likely than large ones.

4. There can be no conceivable limit to the size of individual
errors.

The variables, which behave very much as stated in this idealized description, have been found in many and diverse fields. Due to this empirical phenomenon, this probability law is also called the normal distribution.

The Standard Normal Variable
Let Z denote a random variable that follows all four of the above postulates. Then, $E(Z) = 0$. If, in addition, we assume that Var(Z) = 1, then Z is said to be a *standard normal variable*. The probability density function of Z is given by the formula:

$$f(z) = \frac{1}{\sqrt{2\pi}} \cdot e^{-z^2/2}$$

The corresponding density curve is bell shaped. It is displayed in figure 2-11. Unfortunately, calculus must be used to find the area under a standard normal curve. For this reason, appendix A of this text tabulates the areas in the "left-hand tail" of this curve. Specifically, for each z in that appendix, you can read off the value of:

$$F(z) = P(Z \leqslant z)$$

In other words, $F(z)$ corresponds to the shaded area of figure 2-11.

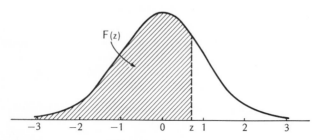

Figure 2-11. *A Standard Normal Density and Probabilities*

The random variable Z will almost always lie between −3 and +3. Also, because of the perfect symmetry of $f(z)$ around $z = 0$, it is unnecessary to tabulate $F(z)$ when z is negative. Appendix A, therefore, shows the $F(z)$ values only for positive z's less than 3. Since probabilities of normal variables are obtained by reading the appropriate $F(z)$ values from appendix A, it is beneficial to practice reading the tables. Some self-evident rules are listed below for ready reference.

1. $F(0) = .5$
2. If z is positive, read $F(z)$ directly from appendix A. If the desired z is not tabulated, you may either round off or interpolate.
3. $F(-z) = 1 - F(z)$
4. If $z_1 < z_2$, then $P(z_1 \leqslant Z \leqslant z_2) = F(z_2) - F(z_1)$

For example, if $z = .69$, you can read that $F(z) = .7550$. Also, $F(-1.44) = 1 - F(1.44) = 1 - .9251 = .0749$. Finally, $P(.51 \leqslant Z \leqslant 2.21) = F(2.21) - F(.51) = .9865 - .6952 = .2913$. With practice, you can figure probabilities very quickly.

The Inverse Function
We must frequently respond to the reverse type of situations. The probability in the left-hand tail of the standard normal curve is given or can be inferred, and we need to find the corresponding value of z. Symbolically, we are given $r = F(z)$, where $0 < r < 1$. We must derive the value of z that satisfies the above equation. The symbolic answer is:

$$z = F^{-1}(r)$$

The -1 in the above equation indicates that the question has been asked in reverse.

There are two possibilities: either $r \geqslant .5$ or $r < .5$.

If $r \geqslant .5$, the desired z will be positive (or zero). Hence, read down the column of $F(z)$ until either the desired $F(z)$ is found, or until you find two consecutive numbers z_1 and z_2 such that $F(z_1) < r < F(z_2)$. If some tabulated $F(z)$ equals r, then the corresponding z is $F^{-1}(r)$. If r lies between $F(z_1)$ and $F(z_2)$, you can either accept the "rounded" z or compute the necessary z by interpolation:

$$z = z_1 + \frac{r - F(z_1)}{F(z_2) - F(z_1)} \times (z_2 - z_1)$$

For example, suppose $r = .8924$. From appendix A, you can read that $F(1.24) = .8924$. Hence, $F^{-1}(.8924) = 1.24$. As another example, suppose $r = .8500$. You can check that: $F(1.03) = .8483$ and $F(1.04) = .8506$. Hence, $z_1 = 1.03$ and $z_2 = 1.04$. Consequently,

$$z = 1.03 + \frac{.8500 - .8483}{.8506 - .8483} \times (1.04 - 1.03)$$
$$= 1.037$$

If $r < .5$, the desired z will be negative. Using the symmetry of $f(z)$, you can verify that:

If $r < .5$, then $z = -F^{-1}(1-r)$

Suppose, for example, that $r = .3936$, so that $1 - r = .6064$. From appendix A, you can read that: $F(.27) = .6064$. Thus:

$F^{-1}(.6064) = .27$ and hence, $z = -.27$

In other words:

$F^{-1}(.3936) = -F^{-1}(.6064) = -.27$

The General Normal Variable

The normal probability law has wide applicability in managerial problems. Many such problems require repeated measurements of a process. If the process is under control, then each measurement follows the same probability law. And, the observations are independent of each other. Under these circumstances, the normal probability law is likely to be applicable. This can be stated more formally as follows.

Central Limit Theorem   Let $X_1, X_2, \ldots, X_n$ denote a set of n independent observations from a potentially continuous process. Let $E(X)$ and $\sigma(X)$ denote the mean and standard deviation of the observations produced by this process. Compute the average:

$$\overline{X} = (X_1 + X_2 + \ldots + X_n) \div n$$

If the histogram for this process is fairly symmetrical and contains only one prominent peak (i.e., it is unimodal), then:

$$Z = \frac{\sqrt{n} \cdot [\overline{X} - E(X)]}{\sigma(X)}$$

is approximately a standard normal variable. The approximation improves as n increases.

There will be several occasions in which we can use the normal law. PERT/CPM, inventory control, general decision theory, waiting lines, and quality control are some of the topics where the normal law is invoked. In general, however, a variable X can be normal even though $E(X) \neq 0$ and/or $\sigma(X) \neq 1$. The probabilities for such variables are derived by noting that:

$$Z = \frac{X - E(X)}{\sigma(X)}$$

is a standard normal variable. In other words, all questions about X are solved by formulating and solving the corresponding questions about Z.

WHAT A MANAGER SHOULD KNOW

Management is the art of the possible. As such, a manager should know not only what is possible but also the extent to which it is possible—and this is where probability theory can help. It helps quantify uncertainty.

Every manager should have a working knowledge of the theory of probability. This theory begins by defining an experiment and its outcomes. Then it identifies the events of interest to the decision maker and explores the logical relationships among them.

Having done this, we reviewed how probabilities of events can be derived given those of the constituent outcomes. We then reviewed an efficient technique to identify events, i.e., by defining suitable random variables. The random variables are either discrete or continuous. We reviewed the general properties of each. Two important parameters of any random variable are its expected value and its variance. The law of large numbers provides the rationale for using the expected value as a guide for action. The importance of variance is mostly due to the central limit theorem. To use it, a manager must know how to handle normal distribution. We have, therefore, reviewed the techniques of using a standard normal table.

There are too many important topics in the theory of probability and statistics to be covered in a single chapter such as this. I hope I have provided you with an incentive to study this science in greater detail. If so, you should read through some of the references cited next.

SELECTED READINGS

CAMPBELL, S. K. *Flaws and Fallacies in Statistical Thinking.* Englewood Cliffs, N.J.: Prentice-Hall, Inc., 1974.

FELLER, W. *An Introduction to Probability Theory and Its Applications,* vol. 1. 2d ed. New York: John Wiley & Sons, Inc., 1957.

FREUND, J. E. AND WILLIAMS, F. J. *Elementary Business Statistics: The Modern Approach.* 3d ed. Englewood Cliffs, N.J.: Prentice-Hall, Inc., 1977.

HAYS, W. L. *Statistics for the Social Sciences.* 2d ed. New York: Holt, Rinehart and Winston, 1973.

HUFF, D. *How to Lie with Statistics.* W. W. Norton & Company, Inc., 1954.

HOEL, P. *Introduction to Mathematical Statistics.* 4th ed. New York: John Wiley & Sons, Inc., 1971.

KENDALL, M. G. AND BUCKLAND, W. R. *A Dictionary of Statistical Terms.* New York: Hafner Press, 1971.

MENDENHALL, W. AND REINMUTH, J. E. *Statistics for Management and Economics.* 3d ed. North Scituate, Mass.: Duxbury Press, 1978.

MOORE, P. G. *Risk in Business Decisions.* New York: John Wiley & Sons, Inc., 1972.

PEARSON, E. S. AND HARTLEY, H. O. *Biometrika Tables for Statisticians.* 3d ed. Cambridge, England: Cambridge University Press, 1966.

PROBLEM SET 2
QUANTIFYING UNCERTAINTY

1. Suppose you flip four coins. Use the shortform H = head and T = tail on any one coin.

    a. Let A denote getting exactly two heads, B denote getting a head on the second coin, and C denote getting two or more tails. List the outcomes in A, B, and C.

    b. What are the outcomes in $A \cap B$? $A \cap C$?

    c. Verify the union law: $A \cup B = A \cap B + A \cap B' + A' \cap B$ by listing the outcomes in each event.

    d. Similarly verify that: $(A \cap B)' = A' \cup B'$

    e. Also verify the distribution law: $A \cap (B \cup C) = (A \cap B) \cup (A \cap C)$

2. Suppose that each of the four coins above is a fair coin so that $P(\text{head}) = P(\text{tail}) = .5$ for any one coin.

    a. Compute $P(A)$, $P(B)$, and $P(A \cap B)$. Are events A and B independent? Why or why not?

    b. Verify the addition law: $P(A \cup B) = P(A) + P(B) - P(A \cap B)$ by obtaining the corresponding probabilities.

3. In the sample space of problem 2 above,

    a. Compute $P(B \cap C)$ and $P(B \cap C')$.

    b. Compute $P(B \mid C)$ and $P(B \mid C')$. Are events B and C independent? Why or why not?

4. A stockbroker is willing to bet $2 against $1 that the price of Sure-Growth stock will be higher tomorrow. He will also wager $1 against $1.50 that the price will be lower.

    a. Obtain his subjective probabilities.

    b. Is he consistent? Why or why not?

5. The chance that a midwesterner will become the president of an insurance company is .3. Due to the advent of the feminist movement, a woman has .4 chance of reaching that same position. A midwestern woman has only .05 chance of being the president. What is the chance that the next president will be:

    a. Either a woman or a midwesterner?

    b. Neither a woman nor a midwesterner?

6. Jyoti Joshi is displaying a modern as well as a traditional oil painting in a suburban mall. She feels that the chances of selling the modern, the traditional, or both paintings are .27, .18 and .09, respectively. A modern painting is priced at $200, whereas the traditional is priced at $250.

   a. What is the probability of selling at least one painting?

   b. Of selling neither?

   c. Of selling the modern painting only?

   d. How much can she expect to earn from the display?

7. A country has entered two athletes in an Olympic event. The coach feels the odds to be 3 to 1 against player A winning the gold medal and 5 to 1 against player B winning it. To be consistent, what must the odds be that at least one of these two players will win the medal?

8. Abbott Associates, Inc., an urban planning firm, has responded to a request for proposals. Their chance of winning the contract is .9 provided that the competing firm of Plananalysis, Inc. does not submit a proposal. If they do, Abbott has only .6 chance of winning the contract. An informed guess is that there is .8 chance of Plananalysis submitting a bid. Given this information, what is Abbott's chance of winning?

9. There is .9 chance that Linda Smythe's plane will leave Boston on time. The chance that it will leave Boston on time and also reach Washington on time is .8.

   a. What is the chance that her plane will reach Washington on time if it leaves Boston on time?

   b. Past experience shows that this flight reaches Washington on time 85 percent of the time. Today, Linda has reached Washington on time. What are the chances that her flight did not leave Boston on time?

10. Five percent of all families in the world live in country A. If a family lives there, it has 90 percent chance of earning $10,000 or more annually. If it lives elsewhere, the chance of making that much income is only 20 percent. What proportion of families in the world have income of less than $10,000?

11. Boyce Slayman Associates, Inc., is bidding on four contracts: A, B, C, and D. Their chances of winning each contract are .7, .9, .6, and .8, respectively. Assume that each contract is judged independently of all the others. The results will be out a month from today. Let W = win and L = loss for each contract.

    a. Describe their contract sample space, and assign probabilities to each outcome. [For example, the outcome (W, W, L, L) would represent winning contracts A and B but losing C and D.]

    b. Let X = number of contracts won by this firm. Today, of course, X is unknown. Find the probability function of X.

12. Contract A above is worth $100,000. The worths of contracts B, C, and D are $70,000, $150,000, and $120,000, respectively.

    a. Using the probabilities of individual outcomes, derive the probability function of G = total monetary gain due to these contracts.

    b. What is their expected monetary gain?

13. On the basis of midterm results, Sally Baker now feels that she will avoid a grade of 4 in either of her two subjects. Believe her, and revise the probabilities of her outcomes. Then recompute the probability function of her average grade. What average grade should she expect now?

14. The management science course in an urban university is attended by 150 students. Their age distribution is shown in the adjoining table.

Age	21	22	24	27	30	32	35
Number of Students	5	10	20	50	30	25	10

    a. Derive the probability function of age.

    b. How old do you expect a student in this class would be?

    c. Compute the variance of their ages.

15. The number of times a machine will break down in one day is given by the adjoining probability function. Compute $E(X)$ and $\sigma(X)$.

Number of Breakdowns	0	1	2	3	4	5
Probability	.20	.30	.25	.18	.05	.02

16. The quality control department of a company claims that 95 percent of the units that are shipped out are perfect. You inspect eight of the units chosen randomly from a large batch. (This means that the probability of the unit being defective remains a constant.)

    a. What is the chance that one of those eight will be defective?

    b. If you find two that are defective, is it proper to reject the batch? Why or why not?

17. Chances are that 40 percent of the students graduating from a high school are weak in algebra. That high school graduates hundreds of students each year. You meet six of these students within a week of their graduation. What is the probability that at least two of these will be weak in algebra?

18. Five thousand cars pass each week through a mountain pass. Because of improper maintenance by the owners, there is a .0005 probability of a car developing carburetor trouble and hence stalling in the pass. What is the probability of fewer than three cars doing this in a specified week?

19. An average of five cars arrive at a toll booth each minute.

    a. Find the probability that fewer than three cars will arrive in a one-minute interval.

b. You watch the toll booth for two minutes. What is the chance of observing exactly eight cars in that time?

20. What is the probability that a standard normal variable, Z, will:

a. Be less than 2.1?

b. Exceed 1.43?

c. Lie between .5 and 2.3?

d. Be less than −.72?

e. Exceed −1.37?

f. Lie between −2.4 and −.6?

g. Lie between −.8 and .95?

21. Find z such that:

a. $F(z) = .7$

b. $P(Z > z) = .35$

c. $P(Z < z) = .4$

d. $P(0 < Z < z) = .28$

e. $P(z < Z < 2) = .65$

22. The weekly demand for a certain product is normally distributed with mean 700 and variance 3600. What are the chances that in a certain week, the actual demand will:

a. Exceed 800?

b. Be less than 550?

c. Lie between 620 and 750?

23. For the demand described in the preceding problem, how many units must be ordered each week so as to be sure of satisfying the demand 90 percent of the time?

3

Decision Theory: Basic Concepts and Techniques

Formulating Decision Problems
Decision-Making Situations
Decision Making Under Uncertainty
Decision Making Under Risk
Expected Value of Perfect Information
Summary
Selected Readings
Problem Set 3: Payoffs, Regrets, and Decisions

Management is synonymous with decision making. This chapter examines some of the basic concepts in the theory of making decisions. Through specific examples, we will study the process of formulating a decision problem and displaying its important ingredients. Then we will explore the commonly used decision criteria.

A basic assumption of this chapter is that the decision maker is aware of all the options, i.e., available courses of action, and that the effects of all possible futures can be determined—at least in the short run. Decision theory helps decision makers choose the best option, and this chapter will illustrate the mechanics of doing so. In the process, the meaning of payoffs, payoff matrices, and decision trees is illustrated, the difference between courses of action and states of nature is shown, and the impact of individual points of view (conservative, level, or optimistic) on a decision maker's choice of actions is estimated.

70

The extent of knowledge regarding the likelihood of a specific future plays an important role. This information, like any other commodity, can be purchased for a price. Therefore, this chapter discusses one measure of determining whether the ''price is right.'' (Another measure used for the same purpose will be discussed in the next chapter.)

The theory to be explored in this (and the following) chapter provides a quantitative, systematic, and normative approach to making decisions. It is a key to understanding the tools and techniques of management science.

FORMULATING DECISION PROBLEMS

Throughout this chapter, assume that:

1. There is only one decision maker.
2. The decision maker has only one objective.
3. The objective can be written in quantitative terms (e.g., maximize profit or minimize cost).
4. The potential states of nature and courses of action have been identified.
5. There are finite numbers of courses and states.
6. The decision problem consists of choosing the best courses of action. (The terms *future, state,* and *state of nature* are used interchangeably, as are the terms *course of action, option,* and *action.*)

A very simple inventory situation illustrates the basic concepts of decision theory.

Paul Pofcher's Retail Outlet

This gentleman owns and operates a small retail store. The items in his store belong to one of two categories: the items which are perishable and those which are not. The nonperishable items can be ordered in large lots and stored until it is time to order a new batch. However, the decisions regarding how much to order at any one time and when to place an order depend on such factors as the cost of carrying an item in the inventory, the cost of placing an order, as well as the cost of shortages. (The corresponding decision models will be discussed in a separate chapter devoted entirely to the study of inventories.)

We will limit this discussion to the problem of ordering the perishable items, such as, dairy products, vegetables, and newspapers. Assume that the item we wish to examine must be purchased and sold daily, and assume the following scenario.

Each evening, before going home, Paul must place an order with the local wholesaler. The wholesaler makes deliveries by 8 A.M. the next morning. Each time a unit is sold, Paul realizes a unit profit. Thus, as long as daily stock equals daily demand, there are no complications. The left-over units have no salvage value. On the other hand, if Paul places an order for fewer units than can be sold the next day, he not only misses a chance to make profit but often there is a loss of customer goodwill. Paul comes to you, his management consultant, for advice: *how much should he stock each day to make the most profit?*

The data needed to solve this problem include:

- Daily demand fluctuates between 11 and 14 units.
- The per unit purchase cost is $6.
  Each unit sells for $11.
- If there is a shortage, Paul loses his profit and some degree of customer goodwill. Paul estimates this loss to be worth $2 per unit short.
- Paul can always purchase the exact number of units needed each day.
- There are no quantity discounts, i.e., regardless of how much or how little he orders, the unit price is always the same, $6.
- The actual demand cannot be forecasted with assurance.

This situation is admittedly artificial. However, more realistic situations are that much more difficult to analyze; and these will be examined in more detail in the rest of this text.

Definition of Terms

Given a problem such as Paul's order quantity problem, you must first formulate it, i.e., present the information in a more systematic manner.

States of Nature In each decision-making situation, some factors can be controlled by the decision maker and others are beyond his control. For example, Paul cannot control demand, i.e., the number of items which will be sold the next day. The only assurance we have is that the actual demand will be for 11, 12, 13, or 14 units. In decision theory, a statement, such as "customers will buy 11 units tomorrow," is said to describe a *"state of nature."* In Paul's case, the possible futures, i.e., states of nature, are listed below:

S_1: There will be demand for 11 units.
S_2: There will be demand for 12 units.
S_3: There will be demand for 13 units.
S_4: There will be demand for 14 units.

The potential states of nature can be represented by the values of a suitably chosen random variable. In Paul's case, "the number of units demanded" is such a variable, and it assumes four possible values: 11, 12, 13, or 14. In general, such a random variable (sometimes referred to as the state variable) can assume a large number or even infinitely many values. In such cases, the set of possible values is identified by the membership rules, e.g., all integers between 100 and 400 or all numbers smaller than 500.

Courses of Action Paul cannot control demand. He can, however, decide on the number of units to be stocked in anticipation of the next day's demand. For example, he may decide to stock 10 units. That is a possible *course of action*. He may also decide to order 15 units. That is another course of action. Note that the sum of the courses of action does not have to equal the number of states of nature. In fact, when either of these two sets contain an infinite number of members, discussion of equality is irrelevant.

It is worth repeating that, whereas the states of nature are beyond the decision maker's control, the courses of action describe what he/she can do. They are options. Though you cannot control whether it will rain, snow, or be sunny tomorrow, you can choose to carry an umbrella, wear a topcoat, or bring your sunglasses. The choice is yours. Each is a possible course of action. The variations in tomorrow's weather are, on the other hand, the states of nature.

On the basis of his business acumen, Paul notes that ordering 10 units or fewer does not take full advantage of the market's potential. Ordering 15 units or more, on the other hand, is a waste of money. He has therefore decided to choose among the following options:

A_1: Order 11 units.
A_2: Order 12 units.
A_3: Order 13 units.
A_4: Order 14 units.

The Payoffs Having identified the states of nature and the courses of action, we must now determine the consequences of each action. In decision theory, the consequences are known as payoffs. The actual payoff depends on the joint occurrence of two events: following a specified course of action and realizing a specified state of nature. Payoffs can be measured in terms of money, satisfaction, hours saved, utility, or leisure. Obviously, a payoff can be either desirable (such as profit) or undesirable (such as cost). This chapter assumes that the payoffs are quantities, such as, profits, income, or cost.

For example, if Paul takes action A_1, i.e., he orders 11 units from the wholesaler, it will cost him \$6 per unit × 11 units = \$66. If S_1 happens, i.e., if there is a demand for 11 units tomorrow, he will receive $11 per unit × 11 units sold = $121. Thus, his payoff will be a net profit of $121 − $66 = $55. Or, you might compute his payoff as follows. Each unit sold yields a profit of $11 − $6 = $5. If S_1 happens, he will net a profit of $5 × 11 = $55.

You can similarly compute Paul's payoffs whenever *supply equals demand*. For example, his payoff corresponding to action A_2 and state S_2 will be: 12 units sold × $5 unit profit = $60. The profit with action A_3 and state S_3 will be $65, and that with action A_4 and state S_4 will be $70. (Verify.)

Of course, the actions might not always match the states of nature this perfectly. Consider for instance, that Paul takes action A_1 and the state of nature turns out to be S_2. As before, Paul has paid $66 to purchase 11 units. The demand is for 12 units. Hence, Paul gets $121 from selling the 11 units on hand. But, the twelfth customer will return emptyhanded, i.e., Paul experiences a goodwill loss of $2. His net payoff that day would be:

$121 from the sale of 11 units
− $ 66 purchase cost of 11 units
− $ 2 goodwill loss on 1 unit
_____
$ 53 net payoff

You can similarly compute the payoffs in all cases where the *demand exceeds supply*.

But, it is possible that *supply might exceed demand*. For instance, if Paul orders 12 units (action A_2) but only 11 units are sold (state of nature S_1), he would realize a profit of:

$121 from the sale of 11 units
−$ 72 purchase cost on 12 units
_____
$ 49 profit

Paul's payoffs in all cases where supply exceeds demand could be computed similarly.

Payoff Matrices and Decision Trees
The payoffs corresponding to each action and each state of nature can be jointly displayed by using one of the two devices: a payoff matrix or a decision tree. Each displays exactly the same information—but in a different form. The choice is a matter of personal taste. Payoff matrices are more compact, but decision trees have a visual advantage, e.g., a decision tree more clearly shows that a course of action precedes the knowledge of a specific state of nature. Let's look at each type in more detail.

The payoff matrix displays each course of action in the left-hand margin and each state of nature along the top of the table. (The table could be arranged the other way around with the same results.) The payoffs corresponding to a specific action are displayed in the corresponding row. Those associated with a state of nature are shown in the corresponding column. At the intersection of a row and a column is the payoff obtained by following the corresponding course of action and *then* realizing the specific state of nature.

For example, based on the available information, table 3-1 shows the payoff matrix for the retail outlet. There are four rows—one for each course of action, and four columns—one for each state of nature. The entry in the second row and the third column is 58. This means that if Paul orders 12 units (action A_2) but 13 units are demanded (state S_3), the payoff would be a net profit of $58. All other entries are to be interpreted similarly.

Table 3-1 *Paul's Payoff Matrix*

	DEMAND FOR			
PAUL'S CHOICES	11 UNITS (S_1)	12 UNITS (S_2)	13 UNITS (S_3)	14 UNITS (S_4)
Order 11 units (A_1)	55	53	51	49
Order 12 units (A_2)	49	60	58	56
Order 13 units (A_3)	43	54	65	63
Order 14 units (A_4)	37	48	59	70
Probabilities, $P(S_j)$	?	?	?	?

If the probabilities of the individual states of nature are known, these are displayed beneath each column. Since the states of nature are mutually exclusive and jointly exhaustive, their probabilities must always total one. In Paul's case, these probabilities are still unknown.

A decision tree is a collection of nodes and branches. The branches are straight lines emerging out of a node. There are two kinds of nodes: decision nodes and chance nodes. There are also two types of branches: action branches and state of nature branches.

To construct a decision tree, each course of action is drawn emerging from a decision node. A decision node is usually shown by a square. The branches usually emerge from the right of the decision node as in figure 3-1. Alternatively, the branches can be shown emerging from below the node. This is a more common practice when displaying the logic underlying the branch-and-bound technique which is used to solve some of the linear optimization models. (See chapter 11.)

Note that the decision to follow a specific course of action precedes the knowledge of which state of nature will in fact materialize. In a decision tree, this fact is made quite evident by the chance nodes shown at the end of each action branch.

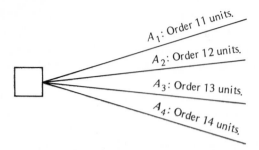

Figure 3-1. *The Retailer's Decision Node and Action Branches*

For example, after taking action A_2 (order 12 units), our retailer friend would learn whether there is a demand for 11 units (S_1) or for 12, 13, or 14. Figure 3-2 depicts this as the chance branches emerging out of the chance node at the end of an action branch (A_2). If the probability of realizing a state of nature is known, it is shown on the corresponding chance branch. The payoff received after realizing a state of nature is shown at the end of that branch. This is, in a sense, a "fruit" of that decision tree. The total number of payoffs equals the number of ultimate chance branches. In the retailer's problem, there are four options: A_1, A_2, A_3, and A_4, and each option has four chance branches. Thus, his decision tree would have $4 \times 4 = 16$ chance branches and hence 16 payoffs. You should now be able to display his decision tree.

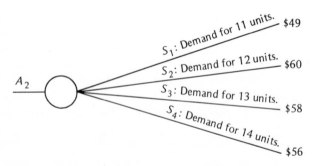

Figure 3-2. *The Payoffs of a Course of Action*

Note that the retailer's decision tree has only two stages: choosing a course of action and observing a state of nature. If the decision process itself had more stages, the corresponding decision tree would be more complex. Before introducing a new product on the market, for instance, a company might wish to conduct a market survey. In such situations, the decision process has the following stages: conduct or not conduct a survey (a decision), observe the results of survey (the chance value), decide to introduce or withhold the product (a decision), and observe the actual sales level (a chance value). The corresponding analysis, which we will examine in the next chapter, becomes more complex.

The Concept of Opportunity Loss (Regret)

There is yet another way of analyzing the payoff matrix. Corresponding to each state of nature, there is always a best course of action. It is found by comparing the payoffs associated with realizing that state. If in fact that particular option is chosen, the decision maker has done the best that can be done with the given facts. Consequently, the decision maker has not lost any opportunity to choose the best. On the other hand, if a different course of action is chosen (one that does not have the best payoff for this state of nature), the decision maker experiences a regret. The size of the regret equals the difference between the best payoff and that obtained by following the current option. Based on this reasoning, we can construct the *regret matrix* corresponding to any payoff matrix.

Consider again the retailer's payoff matrix shown in table 3-1. For the state of nature S_1, the possible payoffs are: \$55 for action A_1, \$49 for A_2, \$43 for A_3, and \$37 for A_4. Each payoff in this case equals the net profit. Hence, the best payoff is the largest of these four, i.e., \$55. Consequently, if the state is S_1, the best action would be A_1. There would be no regret if Paul had chosen A_1. On the other hand, if Paul had chosen A_2, his payoff would have been \$49, which is $55 - \$49 = \$6$ less than the best. This number represents Paul's opportunity loss for choosing action A_2. Similarly, the regret with action A_3 would be $55 - \$43 = \$12$, and with action A_4 it would be $55 - \$37 = \$18$.

Similarly, for the state of nature S_2, the best payoff would be \$60, a result of following action A_2. All other actions in this case have positive regrets. You can now obtain Paul's opportunity losses corresponding to each state of nature. The process and the results are summarized in table 3-2.

Table 3-2 *The Retailer's Regrets*

COURSES OF ACTION	STATES OF NATURE			
	S_1	S_2	S_3	S_4
A_1	55 − 55 = 0	60 − 53 = 7	65 − 51 = 14	70 − 49 = 21
A_2	55 − 49 = 6	60 − 60 = 0	65 − 58 = 7	70 − 56 = 14
A_3	55 − 43 = 12	60 − 54 = 6	65 − 65 = 0	70 − 63 = 7
A_4	55 − 37 = 18	60 − 48 = 12	65 − 59 = 6	70 − 70 = 0

Note several important features of opportunity loss:

1. One begins by locating the best payoff for each state of nature. If the payoffs are desirable, (e.g., profit, income, or satisfaction) the

best payoff is the largest payoff. If the payoffs are undesirable (e.g., costs or taxes), the best implies the smallest payoff.

2. The opportunity loss associated with a course of action always equals the *numerical difference* between its payoff and the best payoff. This means that an opportunity loss is never negative, and it is always measured in the same units as those used for measuring the payoffs. Opportunity loss equals the benefits not realized or the savings forgone.

3. An opportunity loss is not a loss in the usual sense—a decision maker can experience an opportunity loss even while making a million dollar profit (because an opportunity to make an additional 1,000,000 was lost). By marrying Jane, one may lose an opportunity to marry Judy. If you can vacation in Florida, you cannot at the same time enjoy being in Bermuda. The loss may be potential rather than real, while the associated regret is often quite real.

4. Paul's opportunity loss matrix had zeros along the main diagonal, but this might not always be the case. After all, the best opportunities do not necessarily follow a pattern; one must hunt for them wherever they might be.

DECISION-MAKING SITUATIONS

Now that you have seen how to formulate a decision problem, we will examine some techniques for choosing the best course of action. It turns out that there is no definitive answer to the question: "What should Paul, the retailer, do?" It depends on the criterion used to judge the alternative courses of action.

The best way to classify the criteria is to discuss the situation where each is suitable. Decision-making situations, in turn, can be grouped according to the amount of information a decision maker is presumed to have regarding the likely states of nature. Broadly speaking, there are three possibilities: certainty, risk, and uncertainty.

Certainty
If the future (e.g., demand for a product, needs of a population, or time needed to perform a task) can be forecasted with (nearly) complete assurance, the corresponding decision situation is one of *certainty*. This is not as farfetched as it sounds. For example, one may know from past experience the *average* demand and the *maximum likely variation* from that average. If this variation is a negligible fraction of the average, one may use average value of demand in place of certainty.

As another example, suppose the utility company of a town keeps extensive records on power usage. From such records it may know that tomorrow's demand for electricity is likely to be 300,000 kilowatt-hours (kWh) with a variation of no more than ± 10,000 kWh. The company may, therefore, assume that power demand to be 300,000 kWh with practical certainty. In a conservative company that wishes to "err on the safe side," the company engineer might assume tomorrow's power consumption to be 310,000 kWh.

If a specific state of nature has a 95 percent or better chance of being true, many decision makers will choose the course of action that is most suitable for *that* state of nature. In effect, such a decision maker is making decisions under certainty.

The decision criteria under certainty are easiest to define; choose that course of action which yields the largest desirable payoff (profit, income, or satisfaction), or the least undesirable payoff (cost, taxes, or pollution). Equivalently, one might compute the associated regrets and choose the action with zero regret.

The practical difficulty of applying these criteria is that the payoffs (or regrets) of each action must be compared. Since the number of alternative courses of action might be large or even infinite, an efficient search technique is necessary. The chapters on linear optimization models illustrate several such techniques.

Risk

Risk, the most common type of decision-making situation, occurs when the decision maker knows that many states of nature are possible and also knows the chance of realizing each different state. If Paul, the retailer, can estimate the probability of each demand, he would be operating under risk.

Looking at another example, some of the possible states of nature that you might encounter in your job are:

- Your boss will be very happy and will give you a substantial raise.
- Your boss will get a promotion and you will rise to his position.
- You will argue with your boss and be fired.
- You will become bored with your job and think of investigating the "greener pastures."

If these were the only possibilities and if you knew their probabilities, you would be operating under risk.

As an additional example, recall that most of us commute to work or school every workday. We can easily list various states of nature associated with commuting, and after some weeks of commuting, you can assign reasonably good probabilities to each of these. In other words, we often operate under conditions of risk; now we know what to call it.

Uncertainty

This is actually an extreme case of a risky situation. The decision maker can list the possible states of nature without being able to assign a specific probability to each. Insufficient information, the primary cause of uncertainty, can be a result of the novelty of the decision-making environment. The exploration of space is one example. Accepting your first job is another example. A drastic change in the operating conditions, such as that caused by the oil crisis of 1973, is yet another reason for uncertainty. Generally speaking, the dearth of reliable historical data leads to uncertainty.

Having classified the decision-making situations, the rest of this chapter will be devoted to examining the criteria used for making decisions under uncertainty and risk.

DECISION MAKING UNDER UNCERTAINTY

The less that is known about the future, the more criteria are needed to deal with the resulting situations. As can be expected, commonly used criteria are based on extreme caution, i.e., such criteria tend to be conservative. There are four such criteria:

- Laplace's criterion
- Best-of-the-worst payoff
- Savage's criterion
- Minimal range

Laplace's Criterion of Insufficient Reason

The user of this criterion, which was first developed by Pierre Simon Laplace, believes that since the knowledge regarding the states of nature is not forthcoming, one should assume that all states are equally likely. Thus, for n states of nature, each state has a probability of $1/n$. The user then proceeds to find the expected value of payoff for each course of action. The course with the best expected value (i.e., maximum expected profit or minimum expected cost) is chosen.

As an extension, consider the situation with infinitely many states of nature. For example, if the demand were continuous between 200 and 300 units, the Laplace criterion is equivalent to assuming a rectangular distribution of demand. Since, to compute the expected payoffs, a knowledge of integral calculus is required, we have not treated the continuous case here.

For example, Paul's payoff matrix presented in table 3-1 does not contain the probabilities of various demands. According to the Laplace criterion, since the demand has four possible values (11, 12, 13, or 14), each is arbitrarily assigned a probability 1/4 = .25. The resultant matrix is shown in table 3-3.

Table 3-3 *Laplace's Payoff Matrix*

COURSES OF ACTION	STATES OF NATURE			
	S_1	S_2	S_3	S_4
A_1	55	53	51	49
A_2	49	60	58	56
A_3	43	54	65	63
A_4	37	48	59	70
Assumed Probabilities $P(S_j)$	.25	.25	.25	.25

Now examine action A_1. There are four payoffs: $55, $53, $51, and $49. The payoff will be $55 if the state of nature is S_1 and this has a probability of .25. Hence, there is .25 chance of realizing $55. Similarly, there is .25 chance of realizing $53, .25 of realizing $51, and .25 chance of realizing $49. In short, the payoff of action A_1 is a random variable with these probabilities. Following the discussion in chapter 2, you can therefore find its expected value, $EP(A_1)$. The expected payoff of action A_1 is:

Σ (probability $\times$ payoff)
= .25 $\times$ $55 + .25 $\times$ $53 + .25 $\times$ $51 + .25 $\times$ $49
= $52

If Paul orders 12 units (action A_2), his payoffs will be $49, $60, $58, and $56. The corresponding probabilities are those of states $S_1, S_2, S_3,$ and S_4; i.e., .25 each. Hence, the expected profit of A_2, expressed as $EP(A_2)$, would be:

.25 $\times$ $49 + .25 $\times$ $60 + .25 $\times$ $58 + .25 $\times$ $56
= $55.75

You can similarly compute $EP(A_3)$ and $EP(A_4)$. The results are summarized in table 3-4. Since Paul is in the business to make money, the best payoff is the largest payoff. It follows that, according to Laplace's criterion, he should choose action A_3 (order 13 units) to expect a profit of $56.25.

Table 3-4 *Expected Payoffs a la Laplace*

ACTION	A_1	A_2	A_3	A_4
Expected Profit	$52	$55.75	$56.25	$53.50

The Best-of-the-Worst Payoff

This decision criterion is extremely conservative (you might even say pessimistic). The decision maker using this criterion assumes that the nature is "out to get him." When the decision maker chooses a course of action, this criterion assumes that the worst possible payoff (e.g., the least profit) will result. The decision maker therefore chooses that action which yields the "best among the worst" payoffs.

Maximin Profits Assume, for example, that the payoffs are profits. To use the maximin profits criterion, first find the least profit associated with each course of action, and then find the largest of these least profits. The action that corresponds to this "largest of the least" profit is the *maximin profit* action.

For example, if Paul chooses action A_1, his worst payoff is a profit of $49 (corresponding to the state S_4). Similarly, the worst payoff corresponding to action A_2 is $49 (state S_1), the worst payoff with A_3 is $43 (state S_1), and the worst payoff with A_4 is $37 (state S_1). In other words, the worst profits are: $49, $49, $43, and $37, respectively. Of these, $49 is the best profit. Hence the corresponding actions, e.g., A_1 and A_2, are maximin profit actions. Thus, this criterion indicates that Paul should order either 11 or 12 units each day. These computations and conclusions are summarized in table 3-5. Note one feature of this criterion. An application of maximin profit criterion assures Paul that he will not be stuck with the least desirable payoff (a profit of $37), but he must also forego any chance to make the most profit ($70).

Table 3-5 *Paul's Maximin Profit Choice*

COURSES OF ACTION	STATES OF NATURE			
	S_1	S_2	S_3	S_4
A_1	55	53	51	49
A_2	49*	60	58	56
A_3	43	54	65	63
A_4	37	48	59	70

*Boldface entries imply minimum profits.

Minimax Costs As another example of applying this criterion, suppose that the payoffs are costs. Then, to find the *minimax cost* solution, find the greatest cost corresponding to each course of action, and then find the smallest of these greatest costs. The action which has this "smallest of the greatest" cost is the *minimax cost* action.

Consider an electric company that must choose between installing a small, medium, or large transformer in an apartment complex. Since the

complex has not yet been built, its actual needs for electricity are unknown. A transformer that is too small is likely to break down more often,
so its operating costs are likely to be high. A larger than necessary transformer, on the other hand, is a more expensive investment. The company
would like to find the proper size transformer for this complex. Based on
the past data on similar complexes, the company's accounting department
has provided the total-cost information shown in table 3-6. What should
the company do?

Table 3-6 *The Transformer Costs (in $1,000)*

TRANSFORMER SIZE	NEED FOR ELECTRICITY		
	LITTLE	MEDIUM	HEAVY
Small	50	140	**190**
Medium	120	120	**180**
Large	**160***	160	160

*Boldface entries imply maximum costs.

A company that can prepare a cost matrix (such as shown in table 3-6)
very likely can also obtain the probabilities of the usage rates. But, let's
suppose this company cannot. It can then use the following minimax cost
criterion. If the company uses a small transformer, the largest cost would
be $190,000. The largest cost using a medium transformer is $180,000; and
that using a large transformer is $160,000. The smallest of these costs is
$160,000 and it corresponds to using a large transformer. Hence, minimax
cost criterion demands that the company install a large transformer.

Minimax Regret (Savage's Criterion)

If you were the retailer, would you implement the option of ordering
either 11 or 12 units daily as suggested by the maximin profit criterion?
Would you install a large transformer as indicated by the minimax cost
rule? The answers depend on your philosophical outlook. Some decision
makers would like to know what opportunity they might be losing by
following the above options. The minimax regret criterion provides them
with an answer.

Paul, the retailer, might argue that by choosing action A_2, he will lose
the chance to make $70 if S_4 were true. As you have already seen in table
3-2, this represents a regret of $14. (Paul would make $56 instead of $70.)
Had he chosen action A_1, also a maximin profit choice, his regret would be
$21. How can he minimize such regrets?

Professor Richard R. Savage (1925–) suggests using minimax regret
as a criterion for making decisions in the presence of uncertainty. Given a
payoff matrix, this implies first finding the corresponding regret matrix

and then performing the "best of the worst" computations on this regret matrix.

For example, using the retailer's regret matrix (table 3-2), you can argue as follows. The maximum regret in choosing A_1 is \$21; that for action A_2 is \$14; for action A_3, it is \$12; and for action A_4, it is \$18. The smallest of these regrets (\$21, 14, 12, and 18) is \$12 which corresponds to action A_3. Hence, according to the minimax regret criterion, Paul should choose A_3, i.e., order 13 units. The process is displayed in table 3-7.

Table 3-7 *Paul's Minimax Regret Option*

COURSES	STATES OF NATURE			
OF ACTION	S_1	S_2	S_3	S_4
A_1	0	7	14	**21**
A_2	6	0	7	**14**
A_3	**12** *	6	0	7
A_4	**18**	12	6	0

*Boldface entries imply maximum regrets.

Minimal Range

A decision maker who employs this rule is trying to create as certain a future as possible. To use the minimal range criterion, find the largest and the smallest payoffs for each course of action. Then, subtract the smallest payoff from the largest payoff to find the range. The course of action that corresponds to the smallest range of payoffs is the minimum range choice.

In Paul's case in table 3-4, you can see that the smallest payoff with action A_1 is \$49 and the largest is \$55, which yields a range of \$55 − \$49 = \$6. Similarly, action A_2 payoffs have a range of \$60 − \$49 = \$11; for A_3, the range is \$22; and for A_4, it is \$33. The smallest range (\$6) corresponds to action A_1. Hence, the minimal range option is A_1: order 11 units. The process and the findings are summarized in table 3-8.

As you can imagine, this type of decision maker is rather conservative, wanting to avoid risk at any cost. If he acted according to this rule,

Table 3-8 *Paul's Minimal Range Option*

PAUL'S	STATES OF NATURE				RANGE
CHOICE	S_1	S_2	S_3	S_4	
A_1	55	53	51	49	6
A_2	49	60	58	56	11
A_3	43	54	65	63	22
A_4	37	48	59	70	33

Paul would never earn more than $55 but he is assured of making at least $49.

Comparison of Rules

Were you surprised to find that even though all of these rules are conservative, Paul gets different answers to his "how much to order" question? You should not be if you consider the following differences.

The maximin profit criterion is very conservative—it assumes that regardless of the decision maker's action, the future will yield the smallest profit. Such decision makers are willing to forego the chance of making the maximum profit in order to be assured the minimum profit.

Minimax regret is based on the analysis of "after the fact" second thoughts. The decision maker is willing to take some risk (of making $43 by following action A_3 rather than making $49 by following A_2) in order to have a chance of making better profit ($65 rather than $60). In other words, a minimax regret is somewhat less conservative than maximin profit.

The minimax cost rule is based on exactly the same philosophy as that of the maximin profit. The Laplace criterion, on the other hand, assumes that all states are equally likely. The relative conservatism of this rule is not clear.

The minimal range criterion is perhaps the most conservative. Willing to forego the largest profit (smallest cost) in order to avoid the smallest profit (largest cost), this decision maker wants to introduce the most certainty to the decision-making process.

Which one of these rules is more correct? Since all of these decision makers are operating in an atmosphere of ignorance, it is not always easy to judge who is more right. A better judgment requires additional information, for example, the probability of realizing each state of nature.

DECISION MAKING UNDER RISK

Recall that in this case, there are a multitude of states of nature (and the consequent uncertainty about future), but the probability of realizing each state is known. (If the total number of states of nature were infinite, then we would say that the probability distribution of the state variable is known.) A natural extension of decisions under certainty is the use of expected value of payoff as a decision criterion.

Despite the knowledge of probabilities, however, the specific state of nature remains unknown until after a course of action is chosen. Even in this situation, there are many different decision rules. The commonly used criteria are:

- Most likely future
- Expected value of payoff
- Expected value of regret

We will examine each in some detail, but first we must update the retailer's story.

Suppose Paul's past records show that there is a 10 percent chance of a demand for 11 units, a 30 percent chance of a demand for 12 units, a 20 percent chance of a demand for 13 units, and a 40 percent chance of a demand for 14 units each day. In the notation from chapter 2:

$$P(S_1) = .1, P(S_2) = .3, P(S_3) = .2, P(S_4) = .4$$

These being the only possible states of nature, the probabilities total 1. Given this information, Paul's payoff matrix is as shown in table 3-9. The symbol S_j in that table denotes a possible state of nature, such that when $j = 1, 2, 3,$ or 4; S_j will be $S_1, S_2, S_3,$ or S_4. The corresponding probabilities are historical in the sense that they were obtained using his past records.

Table 3-9 *Paul's Payoff Matrix with Probabilities*

COURSES OF ACTION	STATES OF NATURE			
	S_1	S_2	S_3	S_4
A_1	55	53	51	49
A_2	49	60	58	56
A_3	43	54	65	63
A_4	37	48	59	70
Historical Probabilities $P(S_j)$	.1	.3	.2	.4

Most Likely Future

This criterion is based on transforming the probabilistic situation into a deterministic situation. It is most appropriate when one of the possible states of nature has extremely high probability. For example, despite the possibility of a crash or hijacking, most persons would choose to fly a commercial airline, because the probability of a safe journey is extremely high. In effect, the decision maker assumes a safe journey as the only state of nature.

To illustrate the computations, consider the retailer's payoff matrix in table 3-9. From the last line, note that the largest probability is .4, which causes the most probable future to be S_4 (a demand for 14 units). Assuming this to be the only future, the best payoff is a profit of $70. Hence the best course of action is A_4 (order 14 units).

Note that though S_4 is the most likely future, it will be realized only 40 percent of the time. This means that 60 percent of the time, the retailer will be making his choice on the basis of a wrong assumption. This warning is even more pertinent if the total number of futures is large and the "most likely future" occurs with a very small probability (.05 or less). As the highest probability approaches 1, this criterion becomes more appropriate.

The Expected Payoff

This is yet another natural extension of the decisions under certainty. A basic assumption here is that the decision maker will perform the corresponding activity on a large number of occasions. Each state of nature would thus occur roughly in the same proportion as its probability. In Paul's case, this is a reasonable assumption. He is in the business to buy and sell products. The customers arrive each working day and he must place an order each day. For instance, in a year of 260 workdays, there are approximately $.1 \times 260 = 26$ days in which demand will be for 11 units. Similarly, there are $.3 \times 260 = 78$ days with a demand for 12 units. Thus, the expected payoff would, *in the long run*, equal his average payoff. It is natural to seek a course of action which would optimize the expected payoff.

It is important to remember that the expected payoff would equal average payoff only in the long run. Specifically, suppose that Paul chooses action A_1 on each of the n consecutive occasions, and that his payoffs are $P_1, P_2, \ldots, P_n$, respectively. Let $\bar{P} = (P_1 + P_2 + \ldots + P_3) \div n$ denote his average payoff. Let $EP(A_1)$ denote his expected payoff from choosing action A_1. Then the difference $\bar{P} - EP(A_1)$ would approach zero as n becomes increasingly large, i.e., as Paul follows the same option for more and more days.

In the short run, however, there is no such warranty. For example, P_1 might be far less or far more than $EP(A_1)$. Thus, $EP(A_1)$ might not lead to a proper decision. To see this, suppose that Paul were a wildcatter, i.e., he were in the business of drilling for oil. The cost of drilling a hole is extremely large, and it will be lost unless Paul strikes oil. If Paul loses the first few times, he might no longer have enough cash on hand to drill additional holes. In short, *expected payoff might not be an appropriate criterion* for making decisions *in the short run*.

The situations where one does not have many chances to make errors will be considered in the following chapter. In the rest of this chapter, we will assume that the decision situation will be repeated often enough. In these circumstances, expected payoff is the most appropriate decision criterion.

Computing the expected payoff is fairly straightforward. In fact, you saw the process while applying the Laplace criterion. Suppose, for example, that Paul takes action A_1. His payoff is a net profit of $55 if the state of nature is S_1. In other words, as long as Paul chooses action $A_1, P(S_1) = .1$ is also the probability of gaining $55. (See table 3-10.) Similarly, $P(S_2) = .3$ is also the probability of gaining $53, $P(S_3) = .2$ is the probability of making

Table 3-10 *Expected Payoffs of Paul's Actions*

COURSES OF ACTION	STATES OF NATURE				$EP(A_i)$
	S_1	S_2	S_3	S_4	
A_1	55	53	51	49	51.20
A_2	49	60	58	56	56.90
A_3	43	54	65	63	58.70 ←
A_4	37	48	59	70	57.90
$P(S_j)$	.1	.3	.2	.4	

← Maximum expected payoff action

$51, and $P(S_4) = .4$ is the probability of making $49. The random variable, Paul's net profit, is thus fully defined. His expected profit associated with choosing action A_1, $EP(A_1)$, is computed as follows:

$$EP(A_1) = \Sigma \text{ (profit} \times \text{probability)}$$
$$= \$55 \times .1 + \$53 \times .3 + \$51 \times .2 + \$49 \times .4$$
$$= \$51.20$$

Similarly, the second row of table 3-10 shows profits due to action A_2 and, as before, the last row of that table contains corresponding probabilities. Hence, expected profit of action A_2 is:

$$EP(A_2) = \$49 \times .1 + 60 \times .3 + 58 \times .2 + 56 \times .4$$
$$= \$4.9 + 18.0 + 11.6 + 22.4$$
$$= \$56.90$$

You can similarly verify that:

$$EP(A_3) = \$58.70$$

and

$$EP(A_4) = \$57.90$$

Since profits are desirable, the best profit is the largest profit. In Paul's case, the largest of expected profits is $58.70 per day. So, according to this criterion, the best course of action is A_3: order 13 units each day. This process and the results are shown in table 3-10. Note that both the computations and the reasoning are identical to that employed by the Laplace criterion. The difference is one of information. Laplace assigns equal probability to each state of nature for lack of any specific information. The expected payoff criterion employs the probabilities derived from the past data.

Needless to say, if the payoff matrix shows the costs associated with following a course of action, the best action would be that which has the least expected cost. The computational process is identical to that used for finding the expected profit of each action.

Using a Decision Tree

In the preceding section, we used Paul's payoff matrix to obtain his best action. We could have used his decision tree for the same purpose. (Paul's decision tree was discussed earlier.) To be specific, his tree begins with a decision node from which four action branches (A_1, A_2, A_3, and A_4) emerge. There are four chance nodes, one at the end of each action branch. Four chance branches (S_1, S_2, S_3, and S_4) emerge from each chance node. The payoffs are profits, to be interpreted in the following manner. If Paul takes action A_1 and if S_1 results, Paul will realize a profit of $55. There is .1 probability of this happening. All other payoffs are to be interpreted similarly. See figure 3-3.

A decision tree is always solved, i.e., a proper action is found by proceeding from right to left—from the ultimate payoffs to the initial decision node. Begin, for example, by evaluating the chance node corresponding to action A_1. Since the profits $55, $53, $51, and $49 will be realized with probabilities .1, .3, .2, and .4, respectively, it follows that the expected profit at this node will be $51.20. (See the preceding section for the actual computations.) Similarly, the expected profit at the second node from the top is $56.90, that at the third node is $58.70, and that at the last node is $57.90.

These chance nodes are at the end of the action branches A_1, A_2, A_3, and A_4, respectively. Hence, the profits associated with actions A_1, A_2, A_3, and A_4 are $51.20, $56.90, $58.70, and 57.90, respectively. Since Paul always acts to maximize his profits, it follows that he will choose the branch with profit $58.70. *There is no randomness about this.* The remaining three branches (A_1, A_2, and A_4) are "cut off" from this node. The best profit, $58.70, is the profit at this decision node.

Since no more nodes remain to be examined, the search is ended. The decision tree has now been solved; its value is $58.70. Since the decision criterion is the same as that used while evaluating a payoff matrix, the conclusion is also the same. Whether you use a payoff matrix or a decision tree is up to you.

Least Expected Regret

If it is appropriate to use expected payoff as a decision criterion, it is equally appropriate to use expected regret as a decision criterion. The converse is also true: the inappropriateness of expected payoff implies that of expected regret.

The computations begin by obtaining the regret (opportunity loss) matrix and then determining the expected regret of each course of action. The course with the least expected regret is judged to be the best. In practice, it is unnecessary to compute both the expected payoff and the corresponding expected regret. It is sufficient to know just one to determine the best course of action. For example, given Paul's profit matrix and

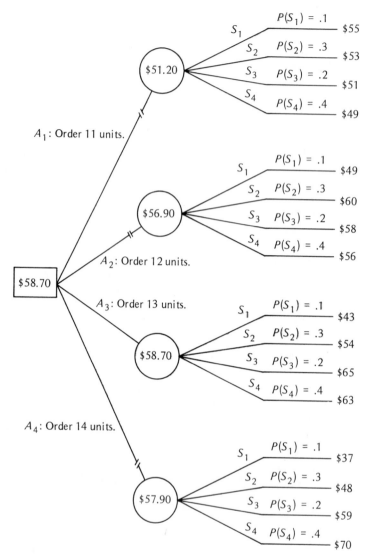

Figure 3-3. *Solving a Decision Tree*

a specific course of action, say A_1, you can check that for each possible state of nature the profit from action A_1 equals:

profit from the best action − opportunity loss due to choosing A_1

Multiply both sides of the above equation by the probability of realizing that state of nature, and then add all such terms. The result will be an equation in terms of the corresponding expected values. The expected profit of action A_1 equals:

expected profit of the best action − expected regret of action A_1

Similar arguments can be presented for each course of action. The point is that the largest expected profit action is *always* the smallest expected regret action. Thus, either criterion will lead to the choice of the very same option. The actual choice of a criterion depends on convenience.

EXPECTED VALUE OF PERFECT INFORMATION

We have just examined a number of decision criteria to deal with the uncertainty that results when there is insufficient information about the prevailing state of nature. Though it is better to deal with the situation when at least the probabilities are known than when even these are unknown, it would be preferable still if the actual state of nature were known prior to choosing a course of action. It is natural to wonder how much the perfect information would be worth. To answer this, consider the following.

How would Paul the retailer operate if he had an extremely knowledgeable friend who could *always* forecast the next day's demand perfectly? Obviously, Paul would always be operating under certainty. He would, therefore, always follow the most profitable action: A_1 if the future were S_1, A_2 if S_2, A_3 if S_3, and A_4 if S_4. His daily profit would be $55, $60, $65, or $70, respectively.

But Paul's friend, though knowledgeable, cannot order the future. It will be S_1 with probability .1, S_2 with probability .3, S_3 with probability .2, and S_4 with probability .4. Hence, with perfect information about the future, Paul's expected profit would be:

$$EP \text{ (perfect)} = \Sigma \text{ (profit due to the best action) (probability)}$$

$$= \$55 \times .1 + \$60 \times .3 + \$65 \times .2 + \$70 \times .4$$

$$= \$64.50$$

The process of computing the expected perfect profit is summarized in table 3-11. You can, of course, work through a similar process if the payoffs were costs.

To repeat, if Paul had an omniscient (but not omnipotent) friend, he would have an average net profit of $64.50 each day. From table 3-10, you also know that his average profit in the absence of such a friend would be $58.70 per day. The difference, $64.50 − $58.70 = $5.80, is known as the

Table 3-11 *Expected Payoff with Perfect Information*

FUTURE	BEST ACTION	PAYOFF a	PROBABILITY b	CONTRIBUTION a × b
S_1	A_1	$55	.1	$ 5.50
S_2	A_2	$60	.3	$18.00
S_3	A_3	$65	.2	$13.00
S_4	A_4	$70	.4	$28.00
			EXPECTED PAYOFF	$64.50

expected value of perfect information. In other words, knowing the future every day is worth $5.80 every day.

Since Paul's opportunity losses (regrets) are known, you can also compute his expected value of perfect information as follows. Given the regrets from table 3-2 and the probabilities of each state of nature, you can compute the *expected regret* of his actions as summarized in table 3-12. His minimum expected regret action is A_3. The least expected regret is $5.80.

Table 3-12 *Paul's Expected Regrets*

COURSES OF ACTION	STATES OF NATURE S_1	S_2	S_3	S_4	$ER(A_i)$
A_1	0	7	14	21	$13.30
A_2	6	0	7	14	$ 7.60
A_3	12	6	0	7	$ 5.80
A_4	18	12	6	0	$ 6.60
$P(S_j)$	.1	.3	.2	.4	

Notice that the least expected regret, $5.80, also equals the expected value of perfect information. Is this a coincidence? No. To see this, note that when you seek a minimum regret action, you are making the best use of available information. The regret in this case is caused only by the lack of knowledge about tomorrow, i.e., the lack of perfect information. Consequently, the *smallest expected regret also equals the expected value of perfect information.*

Perfect information about the future is, of course, only a dream. Then why bother computing its expected value? Providing information about the future is a business in itself. Many firms gather, process, and sell information. The amount that a manager pays to such firms in exchange for information depends on his negotiating skills. However, the expected value of perfect information indicates the maximum the manager should be willing to pay for obtaining *even* the perfect information.

It should be emphasized that management scientists are pragmatists. They realize that trying to obtain perfect information is likely to be an exercise in futility. They will, therefore, settle for the next best thing: obtaining information of known (though imperfect) reliability. This is a topic of the next chapter.

SUMMARY

The concepts introduced in this chapter are at the core of management science. All of the tools employed by a management scientist are ultimately justified only on the basis of their usefulness in making decisions. It is therefore crucial to examine the rational decision-making process. Any such process must enumerate the states of nature and the courses of action as well as their effects (or payoffs).

Throughout this chapter, we have examined a situation with only a few states, courses, and payoffs. Each such situation can be represented by using either a payoff matrix and/or a decision tree. In the following chapter, we will extend the discussion to situations with large or even an infinite number of states and/or courses.

Since six of the chapters in this text are devoted to studying decision-making techniques under certainty, the discussion in this chapter has been limited to the study of uncertainty and risk. Since the different decision makers have different philosophies, many different commonly used decision criteria have been presented here. The more conservative decision makers are, the more they try to avoid risk.

By no means have we exhausted the theoretical issues of decision making. However, since many new tools have been presented already, it is time to pause and check your understanding.

SELECTED READINGS

BAIRD, B. F. *Introduction to Decision Analysis.* North Scituate, Mass.: Duxbury Press, 1978.

BROWN, R. V.; KAHR, A. S. and PETERSON, C. *Decision Analysis for the Manager.* New York: Holt, Rinehart and Winston, Inc., 1974.

HARRISON, E. F. *The Managerial Decision-Making Process.* Boston: Houghton-Mifflin Co., 1975.

RAIFFA, H. *Decision Analysis,* Reading, Mass.: Addison-Wesley Publishing Co., Inc., 1968.

SCHLAIFFER, R. *Analysis of Decisions Under Uncertainty.* New York: McGraw-Hill Book Company, 1969.

TAHA, H. A. *Operations Research: An Introduction.* 2d ed. New York: MacMillan Publishing Company, Inc., 1976.

WHITE, D. J. *Decision Methodology.* London: John Wiley & Sons, Ltd., 1975.

PROBLEM SET 3
PAYOFFS, REGRETS, AND DECISIONS

1. Identify the courses of action and the states of nature in each of the following situations.

    a. You wish to invest your annual savings in bonds, common shares, savings account, term deposit certificates, or real estate.

    b. A developer has enough capital to build up to five single-family homes for speculation.

    c. You are going abroad and must decide whether to purchase foreign currencies before leaving home.

    d. On the way to work, your car develops a flat tire. You must reach your office soon.

2. In each of the following situations, assume that the appropriate probabilities are known. Then discuss whether expected payoff is a suitable criterion.

    a. A butcher must decide on the amount of beef to buy.

    b. A dietitian must determine the number of pounds of vegetables to purchase for a cafeteria.

    c. A building contractor must decide whether to submit a bid for constructing an industrial park. The cost of submitting the bid is $25,000. The net worth of the contract, if won, is $200,000. The contractor has a credit line worth $100,000.

    d. As a marketing manager, you must decide whether to introduce a new shampoo on the market. If successful, the company will increase its net worth by 5 million dollars. If unsuccessful, the million dollars spent on research and promotion would be lost.

    e. You must decide whether or not to insure a valuable diamond.

    f. As a drugstore owner, you must determine the number of aspirin bottles to order at a time.

3. Identify at least five different ways of commuting to work and/or school. Identify at least four different states of nature associated with such commuting. Suppose you measure the payoff as the "number of minutes of commute." Make sure to measure the time from the moment you leave your home till you arrive at your destination. Construct and display the corresponding payoff matrix.

4. For the situation of problem 3, you can also measure the payoff to be "the total cost of commuting." Note that this cost is the sum of two components: the travel cost and the lost-time cost. For example, if you drive your car, the travel cost includes the cost of gasoline, maintenance, insurance, highway tolls, as well as any parking fees. Also, if you are paid $5 per hour, then the lost-time cost of arriving 15 minutes late would be $1.25. Construct and display the corresponding payoff matrix.

5. Is decision making under certainty always simpler than that under risk? Explain your answer.

6. As a purchasing agent of a novelty store, Carol Johnson would like to know whether to stock 100, 120, 140, or 160 boxes of a specially gift wrapped holiday item in anticipation of the upcoming season. Each box costs $5 to purchase. During the holiday season it sells for $8. If a box cannot be sold during the holiday season, it must be sold (and customers will be found) during the post-season sale for the discount price of $4 each. On the other hand, the demand during the holiday season may exceed stock on hand. Carol has the option of buying 20, 40, or 60 additional boxes from the wholesaler as required. However, all such orders are shipped Special Air Freight to take advantage of the holiday mood. This costs $1 extra per box over normal shipping fees. Assume that all the specially ordered boxes will be sold during the holiday season. Assume also that either 100, 120, 140, or 160 boxes will be sold during the holiday season.

   a. Construct Carol Johnson's payoff matrix.

   b. Display her regret matrix.

7. Playperson, a manufacturer of sporting goods, wants to know whether to produce 100, 150, 200, 250, or 300 Spor-T-Shirts now for sale prior to Father's Day. Incremental cost of producing one shirt is $4, and it sells for $8 prior to Father's Day. Leftover shirts go "out of style" and thus have no salvage value. If, however, demand exceeds supply, Playperson can produce 50, 100, 150, or 200 additional Spor-T-Shirts as necessary at an incremental cost of $7 per shirt. Assume that a total of either 100, 150, 200, 250, or 300 Spor-T-Shirts will be sold prior to Father's Day.

   a. Construct the payoff matrix of Playperson.

   b. Obtain their minimax regret action.

8. Charlie Frown recently started selling his daily newspaper on a newsstand. Somedays as many as 80 copies are sold, on other days only 60 are sold. For some curious reason, the number of copies sold is always a multiple of 10. Charlie buys a copy for 50¢ and sells it for 75¢. A recycling plant has promised to buy Charlie's unsold copies for 15¢ each. Charlie is also in the process of convincing the newspaper publisher to buy back the unsold copies at cost. At present, Charlie does not know whether the publisher will do so. Construct his decision tree.

9. Construct and display the regret matrix corresponding to the payoff matrix of problem 3. Then identify your minimax regret action.

10. Because you are a newcomer in town, you do not know the probabilities of various states of nature identified in problem 4. Use the Laplace criterion and thus choose the best course of action.

11. After a few weeks on the job, Charlie Frown of problem 8 has estimated the probabilities of selling 60, 70, or 80 copies to be .3, .5, and .2, respectively. Also, Charlie has a 75 percent confidence that beginning tomorrow, the publisher will buy back all the leftover copies.

    a. Find the expected profit of each of Charlie's options.

    b. What is his best course of action?

12. After graduating from a management school, you are offered a choice between two jobs. Company A offers a straight salary of $13,500 per year. Company B guarantees a salary of $10,000 with possibilities of earning a commission through sales of high price merchandise (e.g., a computer). Being rather new in marketing, it is doubtful if you can sell more than three units next year. Your commission is $2,500 per unit sold.

    a. Construct your decision tree.

    b. What would be your best option using Laplace criterion?

13. Boyce Slayman Associates, Inc. is a growing firm. They are in the process of choosing a bigger location and then constructing permanent corporate head-quarters. In the meanwhile, however, the company must decide whether to sign a one-year or a two-year rental contract with the current landlord. The rent for the first year is $10,000 to be paid now. If the rent for the next two years is paid now, it will be $18,000. The interest rate is 10 percent per year. This means that $100 of today are worth $110 a year from now. Though the company plans to relocate sometime this year, there is a 50 percent chance that they will stay at their present location for an additional year. In that case, they will have to pay an additional rent of $10,000 a year from today. On the other hand, if the company rents for two years now but has to relocate next year, there is a 70 percent chance of subletting it for $9,000 at the beginning of next year. Use the expected cost of rental in today's dollars as the decision criterion. Should the company rent now for one or two years?

14. When a new apartment complex is built, the electric company must assign a transformer to that complex. Since this is done before the residents move in, one cannot forecast the electrical demand during peak load periods. A trans-former that is too small is likely to burn out, and one too large results in unnecessary expense (and capital tie-up). These and similar considerations lead to various effective cost figures (× $1,000) as shown in the adjoining table.

NEED FOR ELECTRICITY	TRANSFORMER SIZE		
(peak load)	SMALL	MEDIUM	LARGE
Little	50	120	160
Medium	140	120	160
Lots	190	180	160

    a. Obtain the corresponding opportunity loss matrix.

    b. What is this company's minimax regret action?

15. Suzie Wong owns a Chinese restaurant. Her daily costs for salaries of full time employees, general upkeep, and mortgage payments are 400 dollars. She also notes that 50 percent of the gross earnings are spent on groceries, direct cost of cleanup (tables, dishes, etc.), as well as taxes.

In addition, the demand is variable. On rainy days, 15 customers arrive each hour and spend an average of $8 per meal. On sunny days 30 customers enter the restaurant every hour. If Suzie hires two part-time cooks, all customers get satisfactory service. If she hires only one part-time cook, 20 percent of the sunny-day customers leave the restaurant in frustration. If she tries to operate the restaurant with only the help of full-time employees, half of the sunny-day customers go elsewhere. Sunny-day customers spend an average of $6 per meal.

In any case, Suzie must book the part-time cooks at least a day in advance. Each such cook charges $80 per 8-hour day that the restaurant is open.

a. What are Suzie Wong's options?

b. Construct Suzie Wong's decision tree showing her net profit each day.

c. If Suzie believes as Laplace does, what would her best option be?

16. Because you stayed up late Monday evening, you have overslept on Tuesday morning. There are three possible courses of action:
   - Take the bus (at a cost of $1.00 one way) and arrive 30 minutes late to work.
   - Drive your car (gas and parking cost is $7.00) and hope the traffic is light in which case you make it on time; if it is heavy, you will be 15 minutes late.
   - Call on the services of a friendly and daredevil taxi driver who guarantees to reach your office in time (cost $10); you can take the bus home.
   You must punch a time clock as you enter the office. Delay costs 25¢ per minute.

   a. Construct your regret matrix.

   b. What is the minimax regret course of action?

17. Given the adjoining cost matrix, identify the course of action that would minimize expected cost.

COURSES OF ACTION	STATES OF NATURE			
	S_1	S_2	S_3	S_4
A_1	300	340	380	420
A_2	280	360	400	440
A_3	260	340	420	460
A_4	240	320	400	480
$P(S_j)$	.3	.4	.2	.1

What is the expected value of perfect information in this case?

18. Given the following profit matrix (where negative entries indicate losses).

   a. Derive the associated regret matrix.

   b. Identify the option with the least expected regret.

   c. What is expected value of perfect information?

COURSES	STATES OF NATURE				
OF ACTION	S_1	S_2	S_3	S_4	S_5
A_1	400	450	500	550	600
A_2	200	600	650	700	750
A_3	0	400	800	850	900
A_4	-200	200	600	1,000	1,050
A_5	-400	0	400	800	1,200
$P(S_j)$	.1	.2	.3	.25	.15

19. Given this gross income matrix:

COURSES	STATES OF NATURE			
OF ACTION	S_1	S_2	S_3	S_4
A_1	13,500	13,500	13,500	13,500
A_2	10,000	12,500	15,000	17,500
$P(S_j)$	.2	.5	.2	.1

   a. Compute the expected gross income for each option.

   b. This is a one-shot deal. Which option would you choose?

20. Refer again to problem 16. History dictates that there is a 40 percent chance of finding light traffic. Construct your decision tree and identify the best course of action.

21. This payoff matrix shows the per-day profit in dollars of operating a small service organization.

COURSES	STATES OF NATURE	
OF ACTION	S_1	S_2
A_1	80	-40
A_2	0	96
A_3	-80	160
$P(S_j)$	.2	.8

   a. What is this organization's maximum expected profit option?

   b. What is their minimal range option?

   c. Which one of these two criteria is more appropriate in this case?

22. Given the following payoff matrix, determine the value of p when the decision maker is indifferent between options A_1 and A_2. Use expected payoff as the decision criterion.

COURSES OF ACTION	STATES OF NATURE	
	S_1	S_2
A_1	82,400	80,000
A_2	384,000	6,400
$P(S_j)$	P	$1 - P$

23. Christopher Woodward, a public health official in a rural county of 80,000 residents, is concerned about the possible outbreak of a flu epidemic. He must decide whether to implement a mass vaccination program. In order to compute the potential payoffs, he argues as follows. Each day a person experiences symptoms of flu is a "flu-day" for that person. The number of flu-days for the county as a whole equals the totality of flu-days experienced by each resident of the county. A vaccinated person experiences one flu-day on the day of vaccination. Each person who is not vaccinated will experience eight flu-days (if infected). The person who is vaccinated and still catches the flu will recover in three days. If the flu is epidemic as feared, 60% of the county residents will catch it unless everyone is vaccinated—in which case only 1% will catch the flu. Even if there is no flu epidemic, 1% will suffer from flu in the absence of a vaccination program—a vaccination program completely prevents such "stray" incidences of flu.

    a. Construct Mr. Woodward's payoff matrix.

    b. What is his minimax regret action?

    c. There is a 15 percent chance of flu epidemic. Should Mr. Woodward go ahead with mass vaccination?

    d. Is "expected flu-days" a proper criterion in question c? Why or why not?

24. James Doran owns a gasoline station which he can lease to a major oil company for a fee based on a percentage of profits. If the station is successful, the present value of his fee would be $1,000,000; otherwise it would be only $200,000. The oil company has offered to buy the property outright for $700,000 now. James believes in maximizing the "expected present value." What must the probability of successful operations be in order for "not selling" to be a better course of action?

25. A marketing manager must price a new product. She wants to know whether to set a high, average, or a penetration price. The desirability of a price depends on the demand for the product. The possible levels of demand are: light, medium, and heavy. The following table shows her estimates of likely profits in each situation ($1,000 dollar units).

PRICING OPTIONS	LEVELS OF DEMAND		
	LIGHT	MEDIUM	HEAVY
High	100	70	−50
Average	50	100	−20
Penetration	−80	0	90

a. Find her maximin-profit and minimax-regret option.

b. Which one would you prefer in this case? Why?

26. Suppose that the marketing manager in problem 25 believes the probabilities of demand to be .5 for light and .3 for medium. Derive her best option using the expected regret criteria. What would the expected value of perfect information be?

27. A supermarket chain must decide whether to build a standard, large, or a variety store in a particular location. The chain also has the option of not opening any store. The choice depends on the market potential of the candidate location. This potential might be very high, high, usual, or limited. The potential profits in each case are shown below ($1,000 units).

OPTIONS	MARKET POTENTIAL			
	VERY HIGH	HIGH	USUAL	LIMITED
Standard	$300	$200	$150	$ 50
Large	$450	$350	0	− $100
Variety	$700	$450	− $100	− $250
None	0	0	0	0

Determine what the company should do on the basis of maximin profit, minimax regret, and Laplace criterion, respectively.

4

Decision Theory: Extensions

This chapter assumes that decisions have to be made under conditions of risk. Building on the concepts discussed in the previous chapter, four extensions of those concepts will be described.

The first technique, *marginal analysis,* uses expected monetary value as the decision criterion, but it avoids actually computing the expected value of each action. It is useful when the total number of states of nature and/or courses of action is large or even infinite.

The second technique, *Bayesian analysis,* is based on revising the probabilities of futures as new information becomes available. There are, in fact, two decisions: whether to collect fresh data, and then, which course of action is best.

The third technique, which employs the *utility of money* to measure effectiveness, is useful when the decision maker has very few opportunities for making decisions. This technique allows the decision maker's views to be explicitly incorporated into the decision making process.

The fourth technique, which uses *adjusted expectations* to measure effectiveness, is based on using the standard deviation of an action's payoff to adjust the action's expected payoff. It is an alternative to using utilities.

MARGINAL ANALYSIS IN A DISCRETE CASE

To illustrate this technique, we will reexamine the retailer's problem posed in the preceding chapter. For the sake of ready reference, the situation is summarized below.

- Paul knows the daily demand for a perishable item to be either 11, 12, 13, or 14 units.
- Each unit costs $6 to purchase and it sells for $11. The unit profit of $11 − $6 = $5 is realized only if the daily supply equals daily demand.
- If supply exceeds demand, Paul loses $6 on each leftover unit. This is because, in Paul's case, such units have no salvage value.
- If demand exceeds supply, Paul experiences a loss of customer goodwill. This loss is valued at $2 per unit short.
- Because of random fluctuations, Paul does not know the precise value of next day's demand. He does know, however, that the probability of a demand for 11, 12, 13, or 14 units is .1, .3, .2, and .4, respectively.
- Paul has limited his options to ordering 11, 12, 13, or 14 units each day. He would like to know which of these options is the best.

Since the probabilities of various states are known, since the payoffs are quantifiable as net profits, and since Paul is going to follow the same course of action on numerous occasions, expected profit is an appropriate decision criterion in his case. Table 4-1 shows the results of applying this criterion to Paul's problem.

You can compute the expected profit associated with each course of action. By comparing the expected profits, you can also determine the best expected profit to be $58.70, and hence conclude that it is best to order 13 units each day. The above decision criterion is appropriate for Paul's problem and it has been properly applied. Notice, however, that to derive Paul's best course of action, we had to:

- Perform 4 × 4 = 16 multiplications of the payoff × probability type
- Perform 12 additions to obtain the four expected profits
- Perform 6 comparisons: order 11 v. 12 units, 11 v. 13 units, . . . , 13 v. 14 units

Table 4-1 *Expected Payoffs on Paul's Actions*

PAUL'S ACTIONS	NEXT DAY'S DEMAND, d				EXPECTED PROFIT $EP(i)$
	11	12	13	14	
Order					
11 units	$55	$53	$51	$49	$51.20
12 units	49	60	58	56	56.90
13 units	43	54	65	63	58.70
14 units	37	48	59	70	57.90
Probability of Demand, $P(d)$	.1	.3	.2	.4	

The Decision Rule

Is there a more efficient procedure for deriving the best course of action? In Paul's case, the answer is yes. This more efficient technique is called *marginal analysis.*

Marginal analysis is commonly used to solve inventory decision problems. In such problems, the states of nature correspond to the levels of demand, i.e., the number of units of a product that will be needed in the next time period. If we assume that the item in question is to be purchased from an outside source, the decision problem consists of finding the *best order size*, i.e., the number of units to be ordered at any one time. A course of action thus corresponds to choosing an order size.

In this context, *marginal means incremental*. Assuming that the order size is currently X, we examine the effect of increasing it by one unit to $X + 1$ (or decreasing it by one unit to $X - 1$). What does a decision maker expect to gain when the order size becomes $X + 1$ rather than X? The profit associated with selling one more unit might be realized. And, the cost of a unit shortage might be saved. The sum of these two quantities is called the *marginal gain*. Note, however, that the decision maker realizes this marginal gain only if that additional unit is sold. If it is not, that item will be left over. The corresponding purchase price might not be fully recovered. This implies a *marginal loss*, i.e., a loss incurred due to the unrealized demand.

These two events, the additional unit is sold or it is not sold, are *complementary*. Thus, if p_X denotes the probability of selling the additional unit, then the probability of not selling it is $1 - p_X$. It follows that the decision maker's *expected net gain* will be:

$$p_X \times \text{marginal gain} - (1 - p_X) \times \text{marginal loss}$$

Obviously, the decision maker should increase the order size by one if the expected net gain is positive. Equivalently, one more unit should be ordered if the chance of selling it, p_X, is sufficiently large. Specifically, by examining the inequality: expected net gain > 0, you can verify that the order size should be increased by one (from X to $X + 1$) as long as the probability of selling that unit, p_X, satisfies the inequality:

$$p_X > \frac{\text{marginal loss}}{\text{marginal gain} + \text{marginal loss}}$$

The ratio on the right-hand side of the above inequality might be viewed as a *probability threshold*. The chance of selling one more unit, p_X, must exceed this threshold before increasing the order size becomes profitable.

Solution to the Retailer's Problem

Returning to the retailer's problem, note that it satisfies all of the requirements for using this technique. Paul's states of nature correspond to the levels of demand between a low of 11 units and a high of 14. Each unit, if it is sold, yields a profit of $5. Paul would in that case not suffer a loss of goodwill valued at $2. In short, his *marginal gain* might be: $5 + $2 = $7. On the other hand, leftover units have no salvage value. Thus, his *marginal loss* due to not selling one unit is the same as that unit's purchase price, $6.

From the previous discussion, Paul's decision rule can be stated as follows: Let p_X denote the chance of selling one more unit. Paul should increase his order size from 11 to 12, from 12 to 13, or from 13 to 14, as long as:

$$p_X > \frac{\$6}{\$6 + \$7} = .4615$$

The only question is: how can Paul find the probability of selling one more unit? Suppose, for example, that now Paul orders 11 units each day. In other words, $X = 11$. The additional unit, i.e., *the twelfth unit will get sold if there is a demand the next day for 12 or more units.* From table 4-1, you can determine this probability as follows. There is .3 probability that the demand will be exactly 12, .2 that it will be exactly 13, and .4 that it will be exactly 14. The demand never exceeds 14. Hence, the twelfth unit will be sold as long as the next day's demand is either 12, 13, or 14. Using the law of addition of probabilities, you can obtain:

$$
\begin{aligned}
p_{11} &= P \text{ (demand} = 12, 13, \text{ or } 14) \\
&= P\,(12) + P\,(13) + P\,(14) \\
&= .3 + .2 + .4 \\
&= .9
\end{aligned}
$$

Since this probability, $p_{11} = .9$ exceeds .4615, Paul should increase his order size by one, i.e., he should order $11 + 1 = 12$ units each day rather than 11. If ordering 12 units is better, why not order 13? To answer this, we must again determine the chance of selling that additional unit, p_{12}. You should verify that in this case:

$$p_{12} = P \text{ (demand} = 13 \text{ or } 14)$$
$$= P\,(13) + P\,(14)$$
$$= .2 + .4$$
$$= .6$$

Since this probability, $p_{12} = .6$, exceeds .4615, we can conclude that Paul is better off ordering 13 units rather than 12 each day.

Why not increase the order size by one more unit? This additional unit, i.e., the fourteenth unit will be sold only if there is demand for 14 units. Hence, in this case,

$$p_{13} = P \text{ (demand} = 14)$$
$$= .4$$

Since this is smaller than the necessary .4615, Paul should not order 14 units each day.

The best order size is 13 units. Paul should always order 13 units each day. With this course of action, his gains will outweigh his losses. This conclusion is, of course, identical to that obtained from table 4-1, but the number of computations are fewer and simpler. This is the advantage of marginal analysis.

Obtaining the Probabilities of Sales

The process of computing the probabilities of selling one more unit, p_X can be made more systematic. Each time we examine the usefulness of ordering one more unit, the probability of selling that additional unit has to be computed. If the current order size is X, the probability of selling that additional unit equals:

$$p_X = P \text{ (demand exceeds } X)$$
$$= P\,(X+1) + P\,(X+2) + \ldots$$

You can, in theory, obtain p_X by adding all of the probabilities in the right-hand side of the above equation. In general, this could imply adding an infinitely long sequence of individual probabilities. (The corresponding decision situations are beyond the scope of this text.)

In Paul's decision situation, this difficulty does not arise because there are only a finite number of levels of demand. The process of obtaining p_X values is summarized in table 4-2. Begin with the highest level of demand, in this case, 14. Since no more than 14 units can be sold on any day, $p_{14} = P \text{ (demand} > 14) = 0$. This is shown in the last column of the table. To determine p_{13}, note that it equals the probability of selling 14 or more units. Hence,

$$p_{13} = p_{14} + P \text{ (demand = 14)}$$
$$= 0 + .4 = .4$$

Table 4-2 *The Cumulative Probabilities*

LEVEL OF DEMAND	PROBABILITY OF DEMAND	PROBABILITY OF SELLING MORE UNITS
11	.1	.6 + .3 = .9
12	.3	.4 + .2 = .6
13	.2	0 + .4 = .4
14	.4	0

This process is indicated in table 4-2 by the upward arrow, ∠+. In general, for each value of X:

$$p_X = p_{X+1} + P(\text{demand} = X + 1)$$

You can verify the rest of the entries in the last column of table 4-2.

Where are the promised savings? Note that we only need to perform three additions to find the cumulative probabilities, one addition to obtain the (marginal gain + marginal loss) value, one division to obtain the threshold value of probability, and, at most, three comparisons of the "$p_X >$ threshold?" type. With n levels of demand, one must perform $n - 1$ additions to obtain the cumulative probabilities, one addition followed by one division to obtain the threshold value, and at most $n - 1$ comparisons of the "$p_X >$ threshold?" type. These are far fewer and simpler computations than those needed to compute and compare the expected payoffs since that technique requires doing n^2 multiplications, $n(n - 1)$ additions, and $n(n - 1)/2$ comparisons.

MARGINAL ANALYSIS IN A CONTINUOUS CASE

We have assumed that the demand for a product can assume values from a discrete set only, but this need not always be the case. For example, the amount of gasoline sold by a gas station could assume *any* value between 0 and 1,000 gallons. There are infinitely many states of nature in such a decision problem. The number of potential courses of action can also be infinite. The method outlined in the previous chapter (i.e., computing the expected payoff of each course of action and then choosing the course with the best expected payoff) is obviously out of the question here. Marginal analysis is the only practical method.

The basic philosophy underlying marginal analysis remains the same. The differences are in detail only. Suppose the current order size is X units. The "marginal question" now becomes: when is it more profitable, in the expected value sense, to order $X + h$ units of a product rather than X? The h in the above question can be any number no matter how small. The answer is: as long as p_X = the probability of selling more than X units exceeds the probability threshold. The best order size is that value, X, for which:

$$p_X = \frac{\text{marginal loss}}{\text{marginal gain} + \text{marginal loss}}$$

To derive the best order size:

1. From the economic analysis of the decision situation, determine the marginal gain and marginal loss associated with a unit increase in order size.
2. Compute the value of the probability threshold:

$$\text{threshold} = \frac{\text{marginal loss}}{\text{marginal gain} + \text{marginal loss}}$$

3. Using the probability distribution of demand, obtain the probability, p_D, that actual demand will exceed D, for *all* possible values of D.
4. Using these probabilities, solve the equation:

$$p_X = \text{threshold}$$

and thus derive the best order size, X.

Two specific illustrations of applying these rules are examined in the rest of this section.

The Normally Distributed Demand

To illustrate how to derive the best order size, let us consider the following scenario. Susan Sanders finds that she sells an average of 120 units of a perishable product every day. The actual sales are normally distributed with a standard deviation of 20 units. Each unit costs her $9 and it sells for $14. A leftover unit can be sold to a discount outlet for $6. A shortage costs a loss in customer goodwill valued at $2 per unit. How many units should she stock every day?

Note that the demand for the above item is not really continuous since fractional values of demand might not be meaningful. However, the number of levels of demand is too large to be analyzed by the discrete variable procedures. A continuous distribution is therefore assumed as a convenient approximation. Also, Susan must have found that the actual probability distribution is single peaked and reasonably symmetrical about that peak. The normal distribution provides a reasonably good approximation under these circumstances. In the notation used in chapter 2, the mean of this distribution in Susan's case is μ = 120 units. The standard deviation is σ = 20 units. The distribution of demand is thus fully defined.

Notice that each unit, if sold, brings a profit of $14 − $9 = $5. Also, since it will help meet the customers' demand, goodwill worth $2 will *not* be lost. Thus, stocking an additional unit has a *marginal gain* value of $5 (profit) + $2 (goodwill not lost) = $7—but only if that unit is sold. If that unit is not sold, Susan can recover only $6 out of $9. In that case, she would lose $9 − $6 = $3 on each unit left over. In other words, her *marginal loss* equals $3.

In Susan's case, therefore, the probability of selling additional units must equal:

$$\text{threshold} = \frac{\$3}{\$7 + \$3} = .3$$

We must now determine the probability of selling more than D units (p_D) for each value of D.

Since the demand (D) is normally distributed with a mean of 120, and a standard deviation of 20, the random variable (Z), given by:

$$Z = \frac{D - \mu}{\sigma} = \frac{D - 120}{20}$$

is a standard normal variable, i.e., it is normally distributed with a mean of 0 and a standard deviation of 1. (Appendix A shows the probabilities that this variable Z will be less than z for various values of z.) Probabilistic questions about a normal variable are always answered by solving the corresponding questions about Z.

In Susan's case, the probability threshold is .3. Figure 4-1 depicts graphically what this means. The normal distribution is characterized by a bell-shaped curve with its peak at the mean value, in this case, 120. Most of the observed values of demand will fall ± 3 standard deviations from the mean. In Susan's case, this implies that nearly always the demand will fluctuate between 120 − (3 × 20) = 60 and 120 + (3 × 20) = 180 units.

Figure 4-1. *Depicting Susan's Best Order Size*

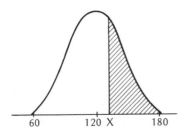

Our job is find a number X, such that P (demand $> X$) $= .3$. In terms of the normal curve, we must find an X so that the shaded area in figure 4-1 equals .3.

Most of the standard tables of the "area under normal curve" tabulate the probabilities of the type: $P(Z \leq z)$. Using tables such as shown in appendix A, you can argue as follows. Since the area to the right of X should be .3, the area on the left of X must be .7. Thus, to find X, solve:

$$.7 = P(\text{demand} \leq X)$$

$$= P \left(\frac{\text{demand} - 120}{20} \leq \frac{X - 120}{20} = z \right)$$

$$= P (Z \leq z).$$

$$= F(z) \text{ of appendix A}$$

Now, read from appendix A that:

$$F (.52) = .6987 \text{ and } F (.53) = .7022$$

The necessary z is approximately halfway between .52 and .53, i.e., $z \approx .525$.

The best order size, X, is now obtained by solving:

$$\frac{X - 120}{20} = z = .525$$

so that:

$$X = (20)(.525) + 120 = 130.5$$

Practically speaking, $X = 130.5$ might be accomplished by ordering 130 units or 131 units on alternate days. If Susan follows this policy, her supplies will equal or exceed demand 70 percent of the days, and she will run out of stock 30 percent of the days.

Other Distributions

The demand for a product can follow probability laws other than the normal distribution just examined. For example, the demand might be uniformly distributed or might be assumed to do so for lack of any other evidence. (This is an extension of the Laplace philosophy discussed in the preceding chapter.) Instead of following any specific distribution, however, we will illustrate a situation where the histogram of a demand is known.

Creature Comforts Inc. sells air conditioners at a special discount price each May. The probability distribution of next May's demand, based partly on the past data and partly on the owner's intuition is shown in table 4-3. The owner buys each unit for $100 and sells it for $155. Creature Comforts is not exclusively in the business of selling air conditioners.

Table 4-3 *The Distribution of Air-Conditioner Demand*

DEMAND FOR	ESTIMATED PROBABILITY	PROBABILITY OF SELLING MORE THAN THE RIGHT-HAND LIMIT
1 through 9	.25	.75
10 through 29	.35	.40
30 through 49	.20	.20
50 through 89	.15	.05
90 through 120	.05	0

The owner does this job once each year as a special favor to his regular customers, and also to earn a side income. Consequently, he sells all of the remaining stock in June to a discount outlet for $80 each. This year he plans to vacation in the Bahamas, so he wants you to determine the best order size.

You can verify that Comforts' *marginal gain* is $155 − $100 = $55 and that its *marginal loss* is $100 − $80 = $20. Thus, the best order size is X, such that:

$$p_X = \frac{\$20}{\$20 + \$55} \approx .27$$

To find X, we must first find the probability of selling more than D units (p_D) for each D between 0 and 120. To this end, you can argue as follows. From table 4-3, you notice that:

$$p_{120} = P\,(D > 120) = 0$$

Since there is a .05 probability of selling between 90 and 120 units, it follows that:

$$p_{89} = p_{120} + P\,(90 < D \leqslant 120)$$
$$= 0 + .05 = .05$$

Similarly,

$$p_{49} = p_{89} + P(50 < D \leqslant 89)$$
$$= .05 + .15$$
$$= .20$$

By working your way through table 4-3, you can similarly verify that:

$$p_{29} = .40,\ p_9 = .75,\ \text{and}\ p_0 = 1$$

This process is depicted by the upward arrows ⊿ in table 4-3.

The best order size corresponds to $p_X = .27$. Hence, X must exceed 0 since $p_0 = 1$. Similarly, X must exceed 9 since $p_9 = .75$, and it must also exceed 29 since $p_{29} = .40$. On the other hand, $p_{49} = .20$. It follows that the best order size must be between 29 and 49.

The actual order size is obtained by *linearly interpolating* between $D = 29$ and $D = 49$. The process is depicted in figure 4-2. Note that as the demand increases from 29 to 49, an increase of $49 - 29 = 20$ units, the probability of selling additional units decreases from .4 to .2, a decline of .2. The best order size lies between 29 and 49, and it corresponds to a probability decline of $.4 - .27 = .13$. The linear interpolation procedure is based on the concept of *equal decline in probability per unit increase in demand*. Thus, you can verify that:

$$X = 29 + \frac{49 - 29}{.4 - .2} \times (.4 - .27)$$

$$= 29 + \frac{20}{.2} \times .13$$

$$= 42$$

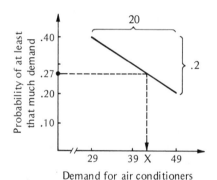

Figure 4-2. *Best Order Size Through Interpolation*

Conclusion: The owner of Creature Comforts Inc. should purchase 42 air conditioners for sale during May. This will help him realize the maximum profit without incurring excessive losses from having to sell the leftover units at a discount.

USING THE LATEST DATA (BAYESIAN ANALYSIS)

We have implicitly assumed that the future will resemble the past—at least in the probabilistic sense and in the short term. This is the rationale behind computing the historical probabilities of various states of nature, and then choosing that course of action which is best with respect to these past probabilities. In this section, we will examine two questions:

- How are the probabilities of states of nature revised based on the latest data?
- Is it worth gathering the latest information?

The latter question is important since it is usually costly to gather and analyze information. In effect, the decision process in this section has two stages. First, we must decide whether to collect data, and then we must find the best course of action on the basis of present and/or past data. We will illustrate the process by studying one specific situation.

PAI's Decision Problem

The Propose-Anything Incorporated (PAI) is a management consulting firm that survives and grows by bidding on government contracts. PAI is now developing a new proposal in response to a request by one of PAI's client agencies. PAI management wants to know whether they should bid high or bid low. It is not clear from the wording of the request for the proposal whether the client wants to spend more money to ensure quality.

If the client agency is looking for the highest quality work regardless of expense, then it is more profitable to bid high and propose that the highly paid executives will do the contract work. If the PAI management bids high when the agency is looking for an adequate job done inexpensively, PAI will likely lose that contract and this implies incurring actual as well as opportunity losses. (When you spend your resources chasing one contract, you can't at the same time effectively pursue another contract.)

Bidding low, i.e., proposing relatively inexperienced, lower paid professionals, also has its own problems. Even if PAI gets the contract, their gross income will be relatively less. Though the cost of developing such a proposal is relatively small, the time used to develop it could have been used to bid on other contracts.

Based on these and similar reasons (knowing which details are immaterial for the present purposes), PAI management has computed the payoffs of each course of action. They are displayed in table 4-4. On the basis of contract awards in the past, PAI has also assigned probabilities to client agency's intentions, which are also displayed in the table.

In short, PAI has two options: bid high (A_1) or bid low (A_2). There are two states of nature: the agency is looking for a quality job (S_1), or it is looking for an adequate job (S_2). The chances are .3 and .7, respectively. Since the situation is one of risk, you can proceed, as in the preceding chapter, to compute the expected profits:

$$EP\ (A_1) = \$400,000 \times .3 - \$50,000 \times .7 = \$85,000$$

Table 4-4 *Pai's Payoff Matrix (Profits)*

PAI BIDS	AGENCY IS LOOKING FOR	
	QUALITY JOB (S_1)	ADEQUATE JOB (S_2)
High (A_1)	$400,000	– $50,000
Low (A_2)	$ 80,000	$120,000
Probabilities $P(S_j)$	.3	.7

and

$$EP\ (A_2) = \$80,000 \times .3 + \$120,000 \times .7 = \$108,000$$

On the basis of past experience alone, PAI should bid low and expect a profit of $108,000.

However, several factors indicate that PAI should not accept this option without additional considerations. The payoffs vary widely. This is also confirmed by obtaining the expected value of perfect information. If PAI had perfect information, their expected payoff would be:

$400,000 × .3 (bid high if the agency wants quality)
+ $120,000 ×.7 (bid low if the agency wants adequacy) = $204,000

In this case, perfect information is worth:

$204,000 – $108,000 = $96,000

It is likely that the agency is shifting its emphasis from cost to quality. If so, PAI will acquire higher profits by bidding high. In short, PAI is looking for additional information if this can be done at a reasonable cost.

PAI's Decision Tree

PAI management is therefore thinking of hiring a market research firm, Omniscience Incarnate Limited (OIL) to inform them about agency's intentions. If hired, this firm will be responsible for generating a one-line report (i.e. the main conclusion of their research can be expressed in a one-line statement). The actual line being either:

I_1: Agency wants a high quality job

or

I_2: Agency wants an adequate job

OIL will charge $10,000 for producing this report. What should PAI do? As you see, PAI must now make two decisions: whether to hire OIL, and then how much to bid. Their situation is represented by the decision tree in figure 4-3.

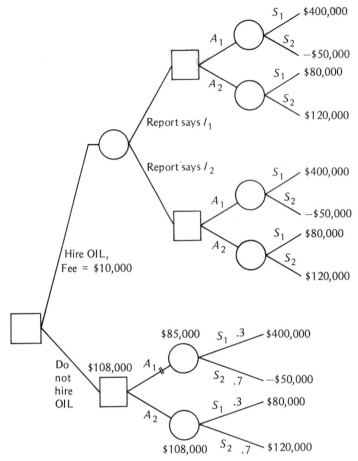

Figure 4-3. *PAI's Decision Tree*

A decision tree has two kinds of branches (action and chance) and two kinds of nodes (decision and chance). PAI's decision tree has a decision node with two branches: hire OIL and do not hire OIL.

If PAI does not hire OIL, they can either choose action A_1 or A_2. If PAI chooses A_1, the future will be either S_1 or S_2 with probabilities .3 and .7, respectively. The associated payoffs are $400,000 and $-$50,000, respectively. The corresponding chance node is "evaluated" by finding the expected payoff, in this case, $85,000. (This number is shown on top of the node.) Similarly, if PAI choose A_2, the evaluation of that branch is $108,000 (shown directly below the associated chance node). The worse of these two branches, A_1, is dropped from any further consideration. Hence, the payoff corresponding to decision branch, "do not hire OIL," equals that of the subbranch A_2, i.e., $108,000. We can conclude that if PAI does not hire OIL, their expected payoff is $108,000 which is obtained by bidding low.

The value of the branch labeled "hire OIL" is not yet known. We can only say that if PAI hires OIL, they will receive a report which says I_1 or I_2. After receiving the report, PAI can choose A_1 or A_2. Regardless of their choice, the future will be either S_1 or S_2 with the payoffs shown at the end of each branch.

Then why should PAI hire OIL? Because, depending on whether the report says I_1 (agency is looking for a quality job) or I_2 (it is looking for an adequate job), PAI can reassess the probabilities of futures S_1 or S_2. This in turn implies that their expected payoffs would be reassessed on the basis of what the report says. Before we can continue with this analysis, we must examine how to reassess the probabilities of futures.

Computing the Probabilities of Reports

To begin with, we must know the reliability of the reports presented by OIL. Specifically, we must know:

1. If the agency is looking forward to awarding a quality contract (state of nature S_1), what is the probability that the report will say I_1?
2. If the future is S_1, what is the probability that the report will say I_2?
3. If the future is S_2, what is the probability that the report will say I_1?
4. If the future is S_2, what is the probability that the report will say I_2?

In the notation given in chapter 2, each of these questions seeks the value of the corresponding *conditional probability*, $P(I_1 \mid S_1)$, $P(I_2 \mid S_1)$, $P(I_1|S_2)$, and $P(I_2|S_2)$, respectively. Suppose that because of past experiences with OIL, the management of PAI knows that:

$$P(I_1|S_1) = .85 \text{ and } P(I_1|S_2) = .2$$

Then you can argue that since I_1 and I_2 are the only possible reports and since only one of these will materialize, these two reports are *complementary*. Hence:

$$P(I_2|S_1) = 1 - P(I_1|S_1) = 1 - .85 = .15$$

Similarly, if the future is S_2:

$$P(I_2 \mid S_2) = 1 - P(I_1 \mid S_2) = 1 - .2 = .8$$

PAI can now use the *multiplication rule* to derive the *joint probability* of each of the following events.

- $I_1 \cap S_1$: report will say I_1 and the future will be S_1.
- $I_2 \cap S_1$: report will say I_2 and the future will be S_1.
- $I_1 \cap S_2$: report will say I_1 and the future will be S_2.
- $I_2 \cap S_2$: report will say I_2 and the future will be S_2.

The Venn diagram of figure 4-4 shows these events as the components of a sample space. In that figure, the rectangle represents the entire sample space. Event $I_1 \cap S_1$ is represented by the cross-hatched portion. Similarly, the events $I_1 \cap S_2, I_2 \cap S_1$, as well as $I_2 \cap S_2$ are shown by different shades.

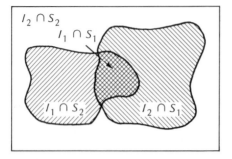

Figure 4-4. *Venn Diagram of PAI's Problem*

According to the multiplication rule discussed in chapter 2, you can now compute:

$$P(I_k \cap S_j) = P(I_k|S_j) \times P(S_j)$$

For example, the probability that the report will say I_1 and the future will be S_1, symbolically $P(I_1 \cap S_1)$, equals:

$$\begin{aligned} P(I_1 \text{ and } S_1) &= P(I_1 \mid S_1) \times P(S_1) \\ &= .85 \times .3 \\ &= .255 \end{aligned}$$

Similarly, you can verify that:

$$\begin{aligned} P(I_2 \text{ and } S_1) &= .15 \times .3 = .045 \\ P(I_1 \text{ and } S_2) &= .2 \times .7 = .14 \\ P(I_2 \text{ and } S_2) &= .8 \times .7 = .56 \end{aligned}$$

Why should we know these joint probabilities? Because, we can use them to derive the unconditional probabilities of reports. For example, PAI can now respond to a question such as: What is the chance that OIL will report I_1—regardless of what the future is? Referring again to figure 4-4, you should note that the event "Report says I_1" is composed of two mutually exclusive subevents: "Report says I_1 and future is S_1," and "Report says I_1 and future is S_2." Symbolically:

$$I_1 = I_1 \cap S_1 + I_1 \cap S_2$$

Similarly, you can verify that:

$$I_2 = I_2 \cap S_1 + I_2 \cap S_2$$

Hence, using the *addition law* (Postulate 3 of chapter 2), you can obtain:

$$P(I_1) = P(I_1 \text{ and } S_1) + P(I_1 \text{ and } S_2)$$
$$= .255 + .14$$
$$= .395$$

Similarly:

$$P(I_2) = P(I_2 \text{ and } S_1) + P(I_2 \text{ and } S_2)$$
$$= .045 + .56$$
$$= .605$$

You can check these computations by noting that the events I_1 and I_2 are *complementary.* One of these two must happen, or in other words $P(I_1) + P(I_2)$ must equal 1. In PAI's case, $.395 + .605 = 1$ which means that the computations have been properly executed.

Revision of Probabilities

Now that they know the unconditional probabilities of receiving the reports, $P(I_1)$ as well as $P(I_2)$, PAI can revise the probabilities of S_1 and S_2 depending on what the OIL report says.

Suppose for example, that the report says I_1: the agency is looking for a quality job. Referring to figure 4-4, you see that only a portion of that sample space is now relevant. Thus, the future S_1 can now happen only if the events I_1 and S_1 happen. Thus, the probability of S_1 is no longer $P(S_1)$, it must be revised for the condition that I_1 has *happened.* The proper symbol for this probability is: $P(S_1|I_1)$. Its numerical value can be computed by using the formulas discussed in chapter 2. Specifically:

$$P(S_1|I_1) = \frac{P(I_1 \text{ and } S_1)}{P(I_1)}$$

$$= \frac{.255}{.395} \approx .646$$

Note the drastic change in assessments. On the basis of past experience alone, the probability of S_1 was only $P(S_1) = .3$. If you know that the report says I_1, the probability of S_1 becomes considerably larger, $P(S_1 | I_1) = .646$. On the other hand, knowing that the report says I_1 will reduce the chance of future S_2. It will be $P(S_2|I_1)$. You can compute it by using a ratio formula as above. Since the future will be S_2 whenever it is not S_1, you can also use the complementary events formula:

$$P(S_2|I_1) = 1 - P(S_1|I_1) = 1 - .646 = .354$$

If, on the other hand, the OIL report says I_2, you can revise the probabilities of S_1 and S_2 as follows.

$$P(S_1|I_2) = \frac{P(I_2 \text{ and } S_1)}{P(I_2)} = \frac{.045}{.605} = .074$$

You can also revise the probability of S_2 by the complementary events formula:

$$P(S_2|I_2) = 1 - P(S_1|I_2) = 1 - .074 = .926$$

The point is that the knowledge of what the OIL report says affects PAI's assessment of the future. In standard statistical terminology, the probabilities $P(S_1)$ and $P(S_2)$ are known as *a priori* (before the fact) and the probabilities assigned after gathering data are called the *a posteriori* (after the fact) probabilities. The procedure for computing the a posteriori probabilities, first proposed by Rev. Thomas Bayes (1702–1761), is called the *Bayesian* procedure.

Analysis Based on Reports

Now that the revised probabilities are available, we can evaluate PAI's decision tree. The results are shown in figure 4-5, which we will examine step by step.

If PAI does not hire OIL, you have already seen that their best action will be A_2: bid low. It will yield the expected profit of $108,000. The course of action, A_1: bid high, is therefore discarded. The expected profit of not hiring OIL thus equals that of action A_2, i.e., $108,000

Now suppose that PAI chooses to hire OIL, that the OIL report says I_1: agency is looking for a quality job, and that PAI decide to bid high (action A_1). In other words, suppose we move to the uppermost chance node of figure 4-5. There are still two possible futures, S_1 and S_2, but their probabilities have been revised. Since the report says I_1, the appropriate probabilities are: $P(S_1|I_1) = .646$, and $P(S_2|I_1) = .354$. Using these, you can now determine the expected profit of action A_1, symbolically:

$$EP(A_1|I_1) = \$400,000 \times .646 - \$50,000 \times .354$$
$$= \$240,700$$

This value is shown on top of the corresponding chance node.

You can similarly compute $EP(A_2|I_1)$, i.e., expected profit of bidding low (action A_2) when the report says I_1.

$$EP(A_2|I_1) = \$80,000 \times .646 + \$120,000 \times .354$$
$$= \$94,160$$

Given these two numbers, it is obvious that PAI should bid high (action A_1) if the report says I_1. Hence, the action branch A_2 is closed off. If the report says I_1, PAI expects to make a profit of $249,700. This is shown next to the corresponding decision node.

If the report says I_2: agency is looking for an adequate job, the revised probabilities of the futures will be $P(S_1|I_2) = .074$ and $P(S_2|I_2) = .926$. In that case, the expected profit from action A_1 will be:

$$EP(A_1|I_2) = \$400,000 \times .074 - \$50,000 \times .926$$
$$= -\$16,700$$

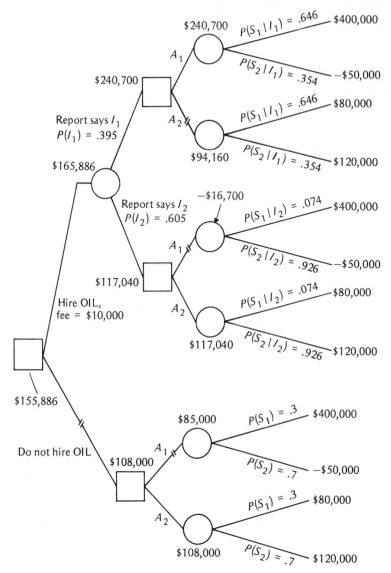

$240,700

A_1

$P(S_1 \mid I_1) = .646$ $400,000

$P(S_2 \mid I_1) = .354$ -$50,000

$240,700

Report says I_1
$P(I_1) = .395$

A_2

$P(S_1 \mid I_1) = .646$ $80,000

$94,160

$P(S_2 \mid I_1) = .354$ $120,000

$165,886

-$16,700

Report says I_2
$P(I_2) = .605$

A_1

$P(S_1 \mid I_2) = .074$ $400,000

$P(S_2 \mid I_2) = .926$ -$50,000

$117,040

A_2

$P(S_1 \mid I_2) = .074$ $80,000

$117,040

$P(S_2 \mid I_2) = .926$ $120,000

Hire OIL,
fee = $10,000

$155,886

Do not hire OIL

$85,000

A_1

$P(S_1) = .3$ $400,000

$P(S_2) = .7$ -$50,000

$108,000

A_2

$P(S_1) = .3$ $80,000

$108,000

$P(S_2) = .7$ $120,000

Figure 4-5. *Evaluation of PAI's Decision Tree*

Similarly, the expected profit of A_2 will be:

$$EP(A_2|I_2) = \$80,000 \times .074 + \$120,000 \times .926$$
$$= \$117,040$$

Each of these two profits are shown on top of the corresponding chance nodes. The action branch A_1 is closed off since, obviously, A_2 has better expected profit. Thus, if the OIL report says I_2, PAI's expected profit would be $117,040.

Expected Value of New Information

If PAI decides to hire OIL, the rest of their decision strategy is clear. Wait till OIL produces the report. If it says I_1, do A_1. The expected profit would be $240,700. If it says I_2, do A_2. The expected profit would be $117,040. We must now respond to the question: *should PAI hire OIL?* The answer depends on the expected value of the information contained in the OIL report.

Note again that this report will say I_1 with a probability of $P(I_1) = .395$. If it does, PAI's expected payoff would be $240,700. The report will say I_2 with a probability of $P(I_2) = .605$. In that case, PAI's expected payoff would be $117,040. Thus, the expected profit of hiring OIL can be computed in the usual manner:

$$EP(\text{hire OIL}) = EP(A_1|I_1) \times P(I_1) + EP(A_2|I_2) \times P(I_2)$$
$$= \$240,700 \times .395 + \$117,040 \times .605$$
$$= \$165,886 \text{ (to the nearest dollar)}$$

Thus, if PAI hires OIL, a profit of $165,886 is expected. If they don't, their profit expectation is $108,000. The difference between these two amounts ($165,886 − $108,000 = $57,886) is attributable to the information supplied by the newly gathered data. This number, $57,886, is the *expected value of new information.*

Should PAI hire OIL? Note that OIL will charge a fee of $10,000 to produce their report. The report itself is worth $57,886 in expected profits. Thus, even after paying the fee, PAI can expect to make a profit of $57,886 − $10,000 = $47,886 more than the expected profit without such a report. Conclusion: The OIL report more than pays for itself. Hence, PAI should hire OIL for a fee of $10,000.

The same conclusion can also be reached as follows. If PAI hires OIL, they would expect a profit of $165,886. After paying the fee, the net expected profit is $155,886. This is more than the expected profit from not hiring OIL, i.e., $108,000. Consequently, PAI should hire OIL.

PAI's decision tree, first shown in figure 4-3, has now been completely solved. It is worth repeating that a typical decision tree is always created from the first decision node to the ultimate payoffs. It is always "solved" in exactly the reverse direction: from the payoffs through the chance and decision nodes to the initial decision point. PAI's solution is shown in figure 4-5.

UTILITY OF MONEY

We have assumed till now that our decision maker will follow the same course of action on numerous occasions. Paul, the retailer, typifies such a decision maker. So do a vast majority of the decision makers in this text. When this assumption of repeated applicability of the same course of action is justified, the average payoff of such a course will always equal its expected payoff. This is why we have allotted so much space to exploring the techniques based on using the expected payoff criterion.

Analysis of Two Situations

However, the validity of expected payoff (whether profit, revenues, or cost in time and/or monies) is questionable if the decision maker has only one opportunity for making the decision. Consider two diametrically opposite situations of this type.

1. Sally Canterbury visits a popular new car show in which there is a "drawing" for a dream car valued at $7,000. The drawing can be entered for a nonrefundable fee of $2. Sally, aware that her chance of winning the car is only 1 in 10,000, wonders if she should enter the drawing.

2. Elizabeth Feller owns a diamond valued at $500,000. She is well aware that despite all the precautions, there is 1 in 1,000 chance of losing it during a one-year period. An insurance company is willing to insure it for an annual premium of $1,000. Should Elizabeth insure the diamond?

Instinctively, most of you are likely to answer yes to both of these questions. Yet, the corresponding courses of action do not have the best expected monetary values. For example, the expected profit from not entering the drawing is $0, whereas that from entering is:

$$[(\$7,000 - \$2) \times .0001] - [\$2 \times .9999] = -\$1.30$$

Similarly, the expected cost of insuring the diamond is $1,000, whereas that of not insuring it is:

$$(\$500,000 \times .001) + (0 \times .999) = \$500$$

Does it mean that you made a wrong choice? Not really. But how can you justify such a decision? To solve this puzzle, keep in mind that monetary value is but one of the many measures of success. Without getting overly philosophical about it, you can list several other measures of success such as: the amount of satisfaction, excitement or security achieved by following a course of action.

Von Neumann and Morgenstern (1944) quantified such subjective measures by introducing the concept of *utility*. They suggested that each individual has a measurable preference among various choices available in risky situations. Such preferences can be measured in arbitrary units called "utiles." If the utility of an outcome is negative, it is said to have disutility. In other words, the relationship between utility and disutility is similar to that between profit and loss. They also suggested a method for obtaining the numerical values of an individual's utility of winning (or losing) various amounts of money.

Suppose, for example, that Sally's utility scale in this situation is as follows. $0 is worth 0 utiles, $2 is worth 2 utiles, and $7,000 is worth

30,000 utiles. (Many other "points" on her utility scale must be known to properly "calibrate" it, but we will assume that this has been done.) Then, she can argue as follows. The expected utility of not gambling is 0 utiles, whereas that of gambling on the car is:

$$(30,000 - 2) \times .0001 - 2 \times .9999 \times 1 \text{ utile}$$

Thus, she will enter the drawing for the car so as to maximize her expected utility.

Elizabeth might similarly argue that the grief associated with losing her diamond is worth 2,000,000 utiles, whereas that associated with losing $1,000 in insurance is worth only 1,200 utiles. Furthermore, the utility of $0 is only 0. Given these utility values, the act of not insuring has an expected utility of:

$$(-2,000,000 \times .001) + (0 \times .999) = -2,000$$

The expected utility of insuring the diamond is $-1,200$. Hence, she will insure the diamond so as to minimize the expected disutility.

In short, both Sally and Elizabeth can justify their actions using *expected utility* as their decision-making criterion. The basic assumption underlying the utility theory is that:

> Given a risky situation, a decision maker acts so as to maximize the expected utility, or equivalently, so as to minimize the expected disutility.

Utility values reflect individual decision maker's preferences in a specific situation. As such, the repetition of the decision situation is not that crucial.

The Mechanics of Constructing a Utility Function

The mechanics of obtaining expected utility of a course of action are similar to those for obtaining its expected monetary payoff. All of the techniques we have discussed are applicable when payoffs are measured in terms of utility. The difficulty lies in assigning the utilities to various monetary outcomes, and hence in constructing the decision maker's utility scale—also known as a utility curve or function. This is done by measuring the decision maker's attitude toward risk. It should be emphasized that the act of constructing a decision maker's utility function is akin to psychoanalysis. The scientist performing this act must be a skilled interviewer.

Let's assume that you are a skilled interviewer, and that you must construct the utility curve of a decision maker. You have found that in a situation presently occupying his attention, the best outcome is a profit of $14,000, and the worst outcome is a loss of $5,000. In algebraic terms, you might say that the decision maker's profit varies from −$5,000 (meaning a loss) to $14,000.

To construct this decision maker's utility function, you should assign some utility value to $14,000 and a smaller value to −$5,000. Actual numbers might be chosen arbitrarily. For example, let the utility of $14,000 be +1, and let the utility of −$5,000 be −1. Symbolically, let:

$U(\$14{,}000) = 1$, and $U(-\$5{,}000) = -1$

These assignments of utility are represented by the points A(14, 1) and B(−5, −1) in figure 4-6.

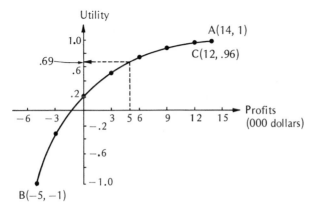

Figure 4-6. *The Utility Curve of a Decision Maker*

To obtain the utility of an intermediate profit value, say $12,000, you should ask your decision maker to compare the following two options.

Option 1: A project which guarantees a profit of $12,000.
Option 2: A gamble which will yield $14,000 with a probability of p, and −$5,000 with a probability of $1 - p$.

Obviously, if p equals 0, i.e., if there is *no chance* of winning $14,000, your decision maker would prefer option 1. On the other hand, if p were 1, he would be *certain* to choose option 2 (that is, unless he is morally opposed to gambling). By successively changing the values of p, you should obtain that value of p for which he is *indifferent* between option 1 and option 2.

Suppose, for example, that when $p = .98$, your decision maker says that option 1 (a certainty) is as good as option 2 (a gamble). Then the utility of $12,000 is computed by the formula:

utility of a certainty = expected utility of the equivalent gamble

In this case:

$$U(\$12,000) = .98 \times U(\$14,000) + (1 - .98) \times U(-\$5,000)$$
$$= .98 \times 1 + (1 - .98) \times (-1)$$
$$= .98 - .02$$
$$= .96$$

Point C (12, .96) in figure 4-6 represents this assignment of utility for $12,000.

Repeat the above experiment with various guaranteed profit values in option 1, obtain the corresponding values of p when the decision maker would be indifferent, and compute the appropriate values of that decision maker's utility. The process is summarized in table 4-5 for some intermediate profit values. The corresponding utility points are shown in figure 4-6. The utility function is obtained by joining the successive points by a smooth curve.

Table 4-5 *Utilities of a Decision Maker*

PROFITS ($)	PROBABILITY FOR INDIFFERENCE (p)	UTILITY $U\text{-}2p - 1$
14,000	—	1
- 5,000	—	-1
12,000	.98	.96
9,000	.95	.9
6,000	.88	.76
3,000	.75	.5
0	.6	.2
-3,000	.3	-.4

The utility of any intermediate point can be read off such a utility curve. Move vertically from the profit axis until you reach the utility curve. Then move horizontally toward the utility axis. Thus, for example, the utility of $5,000 to the above decision maker is .69.

Given a payoff matrix in monetary terms, you can now solve this decision maker's one-time decision problem by *first* converting the payoffs from money to utility, and *then* choosing that course of action which maximizes his expected utility.

On Utility Functions

The decision maker whose utility curve was plotted in figure 4-6 is said to be a *risk averse* decision maker. He tries to avoid risks. Such a decision maker might also be called cautious, conservative, or even pessimistic, depending on the extent of his risk aversion. This decision maker's utility curve is always *concave* with respect to the profit axis. Such a curve is relatively flat in the vicinity of the best payoff and steep in the vicinity of the worst payoff. In fact, at any specific profit, the marginal utility of unit profit is smaller than the marginal disutility of a unit loss. In other words, this person is much more afraid of losing his capital than he is anxious to add to it. Elizabeth Feller's utility curve would be of this type.

The utility curve of an optimist, as shown in figure 4-7, is of exactly the opposite type. Such a curve rises more sharply to the right of any monetary value than it drops to the left. Such a person is willing to gamble current assets for the sake of winning much higher payoffs. Sally Canterbury's utility curve would be of this type.

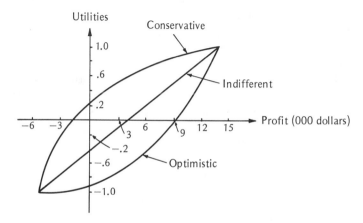

Figure 4-7. *Utility as a Reflection of Attitude*

The utility function of a decision maker who is not affected by the risks involved is always a straight line. For such a person, both the expected monetary and expected utility criteria lead to the same course of action. This can happen if the risk involved is small compared to this person's assets. Winning or losing $1,000, for instance, would not materially affect a millionaire either way—the utility curve for such a decision would be level.

Finally, note that the same decision maker might be conservative in some situations (e.g., while insuring assets), optimistic in others (e.g., while initiating a business venture), and level headed in still others— where the monetary gains or losses are relatively small. This implies that separate and individual curves must be established for each decision-making situation.

ADJUSTED EXPECTATIONS

Another technique for dealing with one-shot decision-making situations is to explicitly account for variations from the mean while choosing a course of action. A decision criterion that does this to some extent is:

$$E(X) - K \cdot \sigma(X)$$

where, $E(X)$ denotes the expected payoff, and $\sigma(X)$ is the standard deviation of that payoff. The constant K is called the *risk aversion factor*. Suppose that the decision maker is risk averse. Then, K is positive if X denotes a profit, and it is negative otherwise. The size of K depends on the importance a decision maker attaches to being safe. For example, if the profits are normally distributed, the actual profit on any one occasion will be less than $E(X) - \sigma(X)$ with a probability of .16 or less. A decision maker who is willing to take 1 chance out of 6 might, therefore, set $K = 1$. This person might set $K = 1.28$ if only 1 chance in 10 is desired. A 1 chance in 20 would correspond to a $K = 1.65$.

Reconsider the retailer's problem to illustrate computations. Paul's payoff matrix was shown in table 4-1. Suppose he wants to be 84 percent safe; he should set $K = 1$. If he is considering option A_1 (order 11 units), his profits would be $X = \$55, \$53, \$51$, and $\$49$, respectively with probabilities of .1, .3, .2, and .4, respectively. In that case, $E(X) = \$51.20$ as was noted earlier. Recall from chapter 2 that:

$$\text{Var}(X) = E(X^2) - [E(X)]^2$$

and that:

$$\sigma(X) = \sqrt{\text{Var}(X)}$$

When Paul chooses action A_1, you can compute:

$$
\begin{aligned}
E(X^2) &= \Sigma(X^2 \cdot \text{probability}) \\
&= (55)^2\,(.1) + (53)^2\,(.3) + (51)^2\,(.2) + (49)^2\,(.4) \\
&= 302.5 + 842.7 + 520.2 + 960.4 \\
&= 2625.8
\end{aligned}
$$

Hence, for profits associated with action A_1:

$$
\begin{aligned}
\text{Var}(X) &= E(X^2) - [E(X)]^2 \\
&= 2625.8 - (51.2)^2 \\
&= 2625.8 - 2621.44 \\
&= 4.36
\end{aligned}
$$

This, in turn, implies that for action A_1:

$$\sigma(X) = \sqrt{4.36} = 2.088$$

Table 4-6 summarizes the computations for each action.

Table 4-6 *Variation Corrected Expectations*

PAUL'S ACTIONS	$E(X)$	$E(X^2)$	$\sigma(X)$	$E(X) - \sigma(X)$
A_1	51.2	2525.8	2.088	49.112
A_2	56.9	3247.3	3.113	**53.787**
A_3	58.7	3492.3	6.827	51.873
A_4	57.9	3484.3	11.484	46.416

Since Paul is using $K = 1$, his adjusted expected profit equals: $E(X) - \sigma(X)$. From the last column of table 4-6, you can conclude that Paul's best action using this criterion would be A_2.

WHAT A MANAGER SHOULD KNOW

In these two chapters we have explored some aspects of making decisions. To begin with, managers should know what they can and cannot control. Whatever can be done by a manager becomes a course of action. Since managers operate within some environment, there are some aspects over which they have no control. Each of these becomes a state of nature. A state of nature can be described by the values of a suitably chosen random variable—also known as a state variable. Since the specific values of such a variable become known only after the decision maker has chosen a course of action, a state of nature is synonymous with a potential future.

The effect of bringing together a course of action and a state of nature is represented by a payoff. If the state variable is discrete, such payoffs can be displayed using a payoff matrix or a decision tree—the choice is a matter of personal taste. If the state variable is continuous, payoffs must be described by a rule rather than by a complete listing.

Most decision situations fall into the category of risky situations. The decision maker recognizes various states of nature and can either assign probabilities to each state or provide a probability distribution function. If the decision maker has repeated occasions on which to apply the same rule and if the payoffs can be expressed using a monetary scale, the decision maker acts to maximize expected profits or minimize expected costs. The *marginal analysis* technique is an efficient method for choosing the best course of action under these circumstances.

If fresh data regarding the states of nature can be obtained, the decisions are made by performing a *Bayesian analysis*. This technique uses the theory of conditional probabilities to revise the probabilities of various futures. Since gathering the necessary information can be costly, whether or not to engage in data collection activities must also be decided in such situations. The expected value of new information is used as a criterion to determine the worth of data collection efforts. The main advantage of Bayesian analysis is that it tends to minimize the risks associated with wrong decisions.

If the decision maker has only one opportunity to choose a course of action and/or if the payoffs are disruptive, the expected monetary value is not necessarily the best criterion. Two alternative techniques, each based on the decision maker's attitude towards risk, have been presented. In the first case, the decision maker's utility function is constructed. The decision maker is assumed to act so as to maximize expected utility. Alternatively, the expected payoff is adjusted by using the standard deviation—a measure of variability in payoffs. The difference, $E(X) - K \cdot \sigma(X)$, is then used to choose the best course of action.

In these two chapters we have presented some aspects of rational decision making. It should be clear by now that rationality is not a straightjacket. Everyone does not have to use an identical decision making rule. It does, however, imply "putting all of your cards on the table." The available options, anticipated futures and their likelihoods, the possible payoffs, as well as the decision-making criterion must be explicitly spelled out to qualify as a rational decision maker. Many specific situations using these guidelines will be explored in upcoming chapters.

SELECTED READINGS

BAIRD, B. F. *Introduction to Decision Analysis.* North Scituate, Mass.: Duxbury Press, 1978.

BEER, S. *Management Sciences: The Business Use of Operations Research.* Garden City, N.Y.: Doubleday & Co., Inc., 1968.

BIERMAN, H.; BONINI, C. P., JR.; and HAUSERMAN, W. H. *Quantitative Analysis for Business Decisions.* 4th ed. Homewood, Ill.: Richard D. Irwin, Inc., 1973.

BROWN, R. V. *Decision Analysis: An Overview.* New York: Holt, Rinehart and Winston, 1974.

CHURCHMAN, C. W.; AUERBACH, L.; and SADAN, S. *Thinking for Decisions: Deductive Quantitative Methods.* Chicago: Science Research Associates, Inc., 1975.

FISHBURN, P. C. *Utility Theory for Decision Making.* New York: John Wiley & Sons, Inc., 1970.

HARRISON, E. F. *The Managerial Decision-Making Process.* Boston: Houghton-Mifflin Company, 1975.

HOWELL, J. E. and TEICHROEW, D. *Mathematical Analysis for Business Decisions.* 2d ed. Homewood, Ill.: Richard D. Irwin, Inc., 1971.

MAGEE, J. F. "How to Use Decision Trees in Capital Investment." *Harvard Business Review* 42 (1964).

RAIFFA, H. *Decision Analysis.* Reading, Mass.: Addison-Wesley Company, 1970.

TURBAN, E. and METERSKY, M. "Utility Theory Applied to Multi-variable System Effectiveness Evaluation." *Management Science* 19 (1973), pp. 817–828.

VON NEUMANN, J. and MORGENSTERN, O. *Theory of Games and Economic Behavior.* Princeton, N.J.: Princeton University Press, 1944.

PROBLEM SET 4
DECISIONS IN RISKY SITUATIONS

1. The demand for a product varies from 41 through 80 units on any one day. For lack of sufficient data, the decision maker has assumed that all levels of demand are equally likely. A unit costs $10 to buy and it sells for $15. A unit left over at the end of the day can be sold for a markdown price of $7. If customer goodwill is worth $1 per unit, what is the optimal order quantity?

2. The weekly demand for a product varies between 101 and 110 units with probabilities .018, .073, .147, .195, .196, .155, .104, .059, .029, and .024, respectively. A unit costs $12 and it sells for $18. However, a unit left over at the end of the week must be sold at half its cost price. What is the best order quantity?

3. A large fashion store sells women's party dresses for $59.95 each during the holiday season. Each dress costs $35. When the season is over, it must be sold at the mark-down price of $25. Customer goodwill is valued at $4 per dress. Past data indicates that the demand is normally distributed with a mean of 500 and variance of 10,000. The store manager must purchase the entire stock prior to the beginning of the season. What is the best order quantity?

4. Casey, Morebuck, and Company must determine the number of junior slacks to be purchased from a wholesaler at $8 per slack. The slacks are to be sold in the month of September at the back-to-school sale price of $11.50 per slack. Any slack not sold in September will be auctioned off during October. The average price of such slacks is known to be $5.75. If the demand during September is known to be normally distributed with a mean of 2,000 and a standard deviation of 300, what would you recommend they do?

5. St. Nicholai tire company wants to be ready for the upcoming winter season in Buffalo, New York. It snows heavily in that part of the United States and hence there is a large but seasonal demand for snowtires. St. Nicholai estimates the following probabilities of demand during the November-December season.

Number of Tires	1 to 100	101 to 250	251 to 500	501 to 800	801 to 1,200	1,201 to 1,800
Probability	.10	.17	.27	.25	.13	.08

It costs $23 to produce, advertise and store a tire in the local warehouse. Each tire sells for $39.95 in the year it is manufactured. If a customer cannot get a St. Nicholai snowtire, he/she will buy a competing brand. St. Nicholai estimates the associated goodwill loss to be worth $4 per customer. A tire not sold by the end of December has to be sold at a lower price and/or stored for sale during the following season. This means, effectively, that they will lose an average of $13 on each such tire. How many tires should they produce for sale during the upcoming season?

6. Charlie Frown operates a newsstand in downtown Boston. Though he sells many copies of a particular newspaper each Sunday, he does not have a fixed clientele. The demand varies a lot as shown in the adjoining table. Each copy costs 50¢ to Charlie and he sells it for 75¢. Because Charlie has negotiated a deal with a local recycling plant, the Monday morning value of the Sunday paper is 15¢. How many copies should he purchase each Sunday?

Number of Copies Sold	101 – 120	121 – 140	141 – 160	161 – 180	181 – 200
Probability	.06	.21	.3	.24	.09

*7. Due to the near symmetry of demand in problem 6 above, solve that problem using the normal approximation for demand.

8. Peerless Hunt is the inventory controller for ABC Manufacturing Company. He can sell the entire line of ABC-15 AM/FM stereo receivers now or the following year. If he sells now, a wholesaler is willing to pay $1,000,000 for the entire line. If he waits till the next year, his company will get $1,200,000 provided there is no recession. If there is a recession, his company will receive $700,000 only. It costs $25,000 to store the receivers for one year. All prices and costs are quoted in today's dollars.

    a. Construct Mr. Hunt's payoff matrix.

    b. Since a recession has occurred ten times in the last 100 years, Mr. Hunt assumes that the probability of recession next year is 10 percent. Compute the expected payoff of each course of action.

    c. What should Mr. Hunt do?

9. Rising bad debts is a leading indicator of recession next year. In fact, Mr. Hunt of problem 8 believes that if the recession is going to occur next year; there is 90% chance that bad debts will rise this year. Otherwise, there is only 20% chance of bad debts rising this year.

    a. Compute the unconditional probability of rising bad debts.

    b. Mr. Hunt has noticed that bad debts have been rising recently. What is the probability of recession next year under these circumstances?

    c. Compute the expected payoff of selling next year.

    d. What should Mr. Hunt do?

10. Ezikiel Hardy, a manufacturer of cosmetics, is wondering whether or not to introduce a "revolutionary" shampoo on the market. He knows that his production and advertising costs can be recovered only if the sales volume turns out to be high. Otherwise, he may be better off continuing with the current line of products and get his current level of returns. The adjoining table shows his net profit (millions of dollars) matrix derived from this kind of reasoning. The "boom or bust" nature of the decision to introduce the new shampoo

*For the advanced student.

| | LEVEL OF SALES | |
HARDY'S ACTIONS	HIGH	LOW
Introduce Shampoo	6	− 2
Do Not Introduce Shampoo	2	2
$P(S_j)$	.3	.7

bothers Mr. Hardy; "sitting back" if the market is "ripe" bothers him even more. He can, of course, commission a market survey for a fee of $50,000. If the true level of sales is going to be high, market survey will indicate this with probability .8. There is a 30% chance that the survey will indicate high sales even if true sales turn out to be low. Note that whether or not to conduct the market survey is also a decision.

    a. What is the expected payoff if the survey forecasts high volume of sales?

    b. What if it forecasts low sales?

    c. Should Mr. Hardy commission the survey?

11. Florence Palmer has recently bought a motel in the New England area. She estimates that she will need to purchase 100,000 gallons of #2 oil for heat this winter. Both Albert Rousseau and David Nolan can supply the oil. Mr. Rousseau supplies it at the prevailing prices whereas Mr. Nolan is willing to negotiate a fixed price of 45¢ per gallon.

    Ms. Palmer feels with probability .7 that the OPEC nations would continue to operate as a cartel. In that case, the oil price would rise to 50¢ per gallon. If they don't, the price will drop to 35¢ per gallon. Thus, her payoff matrix is that shown in the adjoining table.

| | FORECAST | |
PURCHASE OIL FROM	OPEC CONTINUES	OPEC CEASES
Albert Rousseau	$50,000	$35,000
David Nolan	$45,000	$45,000
$P(S_j)$	.7	.3

Fahrud Motiiafshar, a Persian, claims to know which way the "wind is blowing." His forecasting services can be purchased for a fee of $200. His forecasts are judged to be 80 percent reliable. Thus, for example, if OPEC continues as a cartel, Fahrud will say so with probability of .8.

    a. What is the expected cost of heating if Fahrud's services are used?

    b. What is the expected value of using Fahrud's Forecasts?

12. Jyoti Jones is a professional housewife. This means that she likes to be a housewife and that she plans her home activities in a rational manner. She

knows that Mr. Jones is usually easy-going, sometimes even jolly; but there are days when he can be rather grouchy. Jyoti can prepare gourmet dishes, though doing so every day can be rather time consuming as well as expensive. She reserves such preparations for those days when Mr. Jones is likely to be grouchy. When the professor is in a jolly mood, he even helps Mrs. Jones prepare steaks. In his easy-going mood, of course, even a hamburger is a satisfactory fare. The adjoining table shows her utility-of-a-meal matrix.

| | PROFESSOR'S MOOD | | |
JYOTI'S MENU	JOLLY (S_1)	EASY-GOING (S_2)	GROUCHY (S_3)
Gourmet	30	65	100
Steak	80	50	70
Hamburger	60	90	0
$P(S_j)$	.25	.6	.15

Though the above matrix helps in general, it is of no use to plan the menu on a specific day. Today, therefore, she has decided to perform the following experiment. She would call her husband at 4 PM and tell a story beginning with: "Guess what happened when I stopped at the traffic light?" She anticipates the possible responses to be:

I_1: Did you call the police and the insurance agent?
I_2: I told you so.
I_3: Did you remember to smile? (You might be on candid TV.)

She anticipates the conditional probabilities of responses, $P(I_k \mid S_j)$, to be those summarized in the adjoining table. She calls and her husband responds I_2.

a. What should her menu be?

b. How much has she increased the expected utility today?

RESPONSES	JOLLY(S_1)	EASY-GOING(S_2)	GROUCHY(S_3)
I_1	.3	.5	.3
I_2	.2	.2	.6

13. Recall that Suzie Wong, the Chinese restaurateur of the previous chapter, must determine the number of part-time cooks to be hired on each day. This determination matrix must be made at least 48 hours in advance. Her payoff matrix is shown in the adjoining table. The entries are per day profits (losses) in dollars.

    Suzie Wong has learned that the local weatherman, John Dent, can forecast weather conditions up to 48 hours in advance, but that he charges special consulting fees for this service. Knowledgeable friends have told

SUZIE HIRES	WEATHER	
	SUNNY	RAINY
no cooks	−40	80
1 cook	96	0
2 cooks	160	−80
$P(S_j)$	.8	.2

Suzie that if the day is going to be sunny, John can forecast it 70 percent of the time. Also, if it is going to rain, John will say so 80 percent of the time.

   a. What is Suzie's expected profit if John forecasts rain?

   b. What is her expected profit if John forecasts sunshine?

   c. Are Mr. Dent's forecasts worth $25 per day?

14. A job candidate was given a choice between two positions. Position A carries a fixed salary of $12,000. Position B carries a fixed salary of $10,000 with 75 percent of making $5,000 in commissions (and 25 percent chance of getting no commission). The candidate felt indifferent between these two positions. The utility of $10,000 is 1 and that of $15,000 is 5.

   a. What is the utility of $12,000 to this candidate?

   b. Is this person an optimist or a pessimist about earning commissions?

15. The extreme payoffs in a new business venture were a profit of $50,000 and a loss of 15,000. This was a one-time decision situation. Hence, it was decided to plot a utility function prior to choosing one of the several available courses of action. The utility of $50,000 was fixed at +1 and that of −15,000 at −1. Then, the chief executive of the project was given a preference test. It turned out that this executive was indifferent between a certain profit of $40,000, and a gamble with .99 chance of winning $50,000 (a .01 chance of losing $15,000).

     The test was successively applied at certainty levels of $30,000, $20,000, $10,000, 0, and −$10,000. The executive was indifferent between each level of certainty and the above type of gamble whenever the probabilities of winning $50,000 were .95, .90, .8, .6, and .3, respectively.

   a. Determine this executive's utility for $40,000, $30,000, . . . , and −$10,000.

   b. Plot the corresponding utility curve.

   c. Obtain the dollar value corresponding to the utility of .4.

   d. At what dollar value will the utility be zero?

16. The executive of problem 15 is asked to examine the following options. Options A will have the sure profit of $15,000. In option B, there is probability p of making $30,000 and probability $1 - p$ of making 0 dollars. For which value of p will the executive be indifferent between these two options?

17. Suppose that the executive of problem 15 is faced with a one-time risky venture summarized by the adjoining profit matrix. The decision rule is to maximize the expected utility.
    What would be the best option?

	STATES OF NATURE		
OPTIONS	S_1	S_2	S_3
A_1	10,000	7,000	−5,000
A_2	5,000	10,000	−2,000
A_3	−8,000	0	9,000
$P(S_j)$	.5	.3	.2

18. A plant manager has a utility of 1 for $100,000, .6 for $50,000, 0 for $0, and −1 for a loss of $20,000.

    a. This manager is indifferent between receiving $50,000 for sure, and a gamble with .6 chance of winning $25,000 and .4 chance of winning $100,000. In that case, what is her utility for $25,000?

    b. Construct her utility curve.

    c. Using this curve, find her *certainty equivalent income* for the following gamble, i.e., the cash amount which would make her indifferent to the gamble:

    • Lose $10,000 with a probability of .2
    • Break even with probability .3
    • Win $15,000 with a probability of .3
    • Make $50,000 with a probability of .2

19. Stop-n-Buy, a supermarket chain, must decide whether to build a standard, large, or a variety store in a particular spot. The chain also has the option of not building a store. The adjoining payoff matrix shows the potential profits in thousands of dollars as well as the probabilities of experiencing very high, high, usual, or limited demand.

	MARKET POTENTIAL			
OPTIONS	VERY HIGH	HIGH	USUAL	LIMITED
Standard	$300	$200	$150	$ 50
Large	450	350	0	−100
Variety	700	450	−100	−250
None	0	0	0	0
$P(S_j)$	.2	.3	.4	.1

Since developing a supermarket is a capital intensive activity, the board of directors of Stop-n-Buy has decided to use expected utility as their measure of effect. Some points on their utility scale are shown in the adjoining table.

DOLLAR PROFIT ($\times$ 1,000)	700	450	250	100	0	-100	-200	-250
Utility	100	90	70	50	30	0	-55	-100

a. Determine the utility of each profit potential in the above payoff matrix by drawing a utility curve.

b. Identify the Stop-n-Buy option which maximizes their expected utility.

20. Reconsider the profit matrix shown in problem 17. Use the decision rule: maximize $E(X) - \sigma(X)$ to determine the best course of action.

21. Apply the decision rule: maximize $E(X) + \sigma(X)$ to derive the best course of action for the one-time decision situation shown in the following cost matrix.

COURSES OF ACTION	STATES OF NATURE			
	S_1	S_2	S_3	S_4
A_1	30	34	38	42
A_2	28	36	40	44
A_3	26	34	42	46
A_4	24	32	40	48
$P(S_j)$	.3	.4	.2	.1

PART TWO

Decisions in Risky Situations

This part will examine three common decision situations: planning and managing a project, managing the inventory of a product, and analyzing the service system to eliminate or reduce waiting lines. In each case, the necessary parameters are seldom known with certainty, but the probabilities of various futures are usually known. In short, each is a risky situation.

One chapter each is devoted to describing the formal models of PERT/CPM, inventories, and waiting lines. The discussion is deliberately kept at the exploratory level.

137

Each one of these three chapters ends with a section entitled ''What a Manager Should Know,'' which outlines the extensions and/or additional applications of the technique just discussed.

Most often, the formal models become either too complex, or too restrictive, or both. In such cases, the associated decision problem is ''solved'' by using the simulation approach. This approach is outlined in chapters 8 and 9 where we explore the techniques for generating the numerical values of the necessary chance variables and some ways of developing and testing the simulation models. Chapter 9 ends with a section entitled ''What a Manager Should Know,'' which outlines the extensions and additional applications of simulation.

5

Project Definition and Scheduling Techniques

The Process of Defining the Project
Deterministic PERT
Gantt Charts
The Critical Path Method
Stochastic PERT
What a Manager Should Know
Selected Readings
Problem Set 5: Projects and Completion Times

The purpose of this chapter is to explore some of the tools used in the planning and management of a project or a one-of-a-kind undertaking. Specifically, we will examine the following tools in some detail: task diagrams, PERT networks, Gantt charts, CPM, and Stochastic PERT. Each tool is prescriptive, i.e., each depicts what must happen if the work progresses as planned.

The technical discussion in this chapter begins by describing two methods to represent a project as a sequence of events: task diagrams and PERT networks. The process is illustrated by developing a task diagram and PERT network to perform market research. This is followed by a description of the procedures for estimating the duration of the entire project—first by assuming that the durations of individual tasks are fairly well known, and then by relaxing this assumption. In either case, the progress of the project can be supervised by developing the corresponding Gantt chart.

139

The critical path method (CPM) for performing time-cost tradeoffs is also described. Given that certain tasks can be rushed—for a price—this technique helps determine cost-effective ways to expedite the entire project.

These methods have been advantageously used while planning and managing large scale and complex projects. The Program Evaluation and Review Technique (PERT) was first used in the 1950s to manage the Polaris missile program. Since then the scheduling techniques to be described in this chapter have been successfully used by private industry in such areas as:

- Construction of new homes, shopping centers, and subways
- Major maintenance efforts
- Pilot production runs
- Introduction of new products

These tools should be used when starting new educational programs, designing experiments, publishing books, or planning vacations. In short, whenever faced with complex or novel problem situations, a manager should use these techniques. Generally speaking, their cost is less than the benefits.

THE PROCESS OF DEFINING THE PROJECT

A project is well defined when it can be represented as a sequence of events; i.e., observable stages in the progress of that project. It is vitally important to define each project in this manner. Identification of significant "landmarks" makes orderly development that much easier to plan. Managing the project becomes relatively easy due to the significant reduction in the number of "surprises." Furthermore, sequencing events helps clarify the logical precedence among events and thus improves communication among different professionals working on the same project. The communication is enhanced even more if the logical precedences among events can be displayed on a chart. Both the task diagrams and the PERT networks are valuable in this regard. This section is, therefore, devoted to describing how to construct such charts.

Defining the End State

The first step in the development of a project description is to define the end state of the corresponding project. This does not imply that a management scientist decides what the project must accomplish—that is the responsibility of the corresponding decision maker. However, a management scientist should ensure that the end products associated with a project have been defined in operational terms. Phrases such as: providing quality education, reducing poverty, and improving quality of life are philosophical statements of goals. Such descriptions are seldom useful in deciding whether or not a project has been successfully completed. The end products consist of observable states, such as:

- The house constructed by contractor X contains so many square feet of living space, is draft-free, conserves energy, and meets all the local building codes.
- The graduates of school Y can do A, B, and C.
- Your application to the school of your choice has been approved by the dean.

It is possible to provide several additional examples of the end states corresponding to a variety of projects. To limit the philosophical discussion and provide a "concrete" illustration of the project definition procedures we shall now examine one project in detail.

Note that a community is defined by some unambiguous rule of membership. Some possible rules are listed here. A community consists of all those who:

- Attend a specific college or university
- Own shares of a particular company
- Live within specified geographic boundaries
- Came to U.S. from one certain nation
- Buy products manufactured/distributed by a specific organization

Each community has persons who are responsible for planning the future of that community. We will say that these persons collectively constitute the *governance* for that community. To realistically plan the future, the governance must know the level of needs as currently experienced by the community members. Borrowing from accounting terminology, we shall say that a project undertaken to determine the current level of needs in the community is to be designated a *community needs audit* (CNA). Such an audit is equivalent to conducting market research.

The Black Box, the Arcs, and the Nodes

Suppose that the governance decides to conduct a community needs audit (CNA). This decision marks the beginning of the CNA project. When will the audit be complete? When the governance has enough information to plan the future. We can therefore define the end state of the CNA: the document containing the future guidelines is on hand. This information can be displayed as shown in figure 5-1. This figure provides a "black box" representation of the CNA project. The name, black box, a term borrowed from electrical engineering, indicates that even though the end points have been defined, the process of converting the inputs into outputs is unspecified. A stereo is a black box—you push a button (input) and

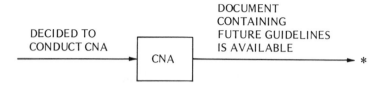

Figure 5-1. *The Black Box Representation of a Project*

out comes beautiful music (output). What happens inside is of no concern here. In fact, any diagram where the transformation is unspecified is called a black box. The end state is shown in figure 5-1 by placing an asterisk (*) in the front.

Note that operations research is end-products oriented rather than means oriented. The black box concept provides a very striking example of this orientation. To be sure, management scientists realize that means must be found to achieve the goals—that at least one transformation must be found to convert inputs into outputs. However, their first priority is to unambiguously define the end points of a transformation without getting bogged down in a discussion of how to get from here to there.

This philosophy of downplaying the process details until the broader picture has been brought into focus is also shared by PERT, a Project Evaluation and Review Technique. However, while task diagrams are based on the symbols borrowed from electrical engineering, PERT developers have chosen to "map out" their projects. Consequently, the PERT representation of CNA is shown in figure 5-2. The arrowhead sponding black box representation. PERT uses a *node* (circle) to represent an event. Two successive events are joined by an *arc* (a straight line). The PERT representation of CNA is shown in Figure 5-2. The arrowhead indicates the direction of progress. The event which initiates a task is at the base and the event which indicates the completion of that task is at the tip of the arrow.

It is important to review the two concepts introduced thus far. An *event* is any specific and observable state of the project. Contrary to common English usage, the word "event" does not specify something un-

Figure 5-2. *PERT Representation of a Project*

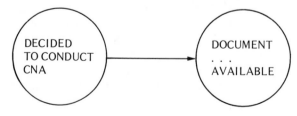

usual. That a man bit a dog is an event, but so is that a dog bit a man. If the project consists of building a nursing home, some of the events might be:

- A planning committee has been selected.
- Building funds have been secured.
- Shell of the building is complete.
- Opening ceremony is performed.

A *task* defines the work that must be done in order to proceed from one event to the next. In figure 5-1 a task is represented by a black box; in figure 5-2, it is represented by an arc. In either case, it is important to concentrate on the events rather than on the name of the task. For this reason, task names are often omitted in the definition of a project as the sequences of events.

Intermediate Milestones

Figures 5-1 and 5-2 both provide a specification of the CNA project. However, neither is detailed enough to identify even one well documented transformation that can convert DECIDED TO CONDUCT CNA into DOCUMENT CONTAINING FUTURE GUIDELINES. On the other hand, in keeping with the end-products orientation, a management scientist should not spell out the process. How can you specify what you want in sufficient detail without specifying the means to accomplish the end product? This dilemma might be resolved as follows.

Identify an event that should happen after the project has started but before it's completed (if the project is proceeding as planned). Such an event is called an intermediate milestone. Identifying an intermediate milestone is helpful because the manager should be able to think of at least one transformation that takes the project either between this milestone and the end of the project or between the initiation of the project and this milestone. Even if this is not the case, identifying an intermediate milestone has been a help. For one can continue to further define the project by identifying additional milestones between the initiation of the project and the currently known milestone or between the currently known milestone and the end state of the project—whichever is easier.

The Penultimate Event and Backward Development Having decided to conduct CNA (and thus initiated the project), it is logical to base future guidelines (the end product) on the findings of the audit report.

The event REPORT OF AUDIT FINDINGS IS AVAILABLE must lie between the events DECIDED TO CONDUCT CNA and DOCUMENT CONTAINING FUTURE GUIDELINES IS AVAILABLE. In effect we have begun to define the CNA project in more detail than shown in figure 5-1. The result is depicted as in figure 5-3. The labels JOHN and MARY serve to emphasize that a task is uniquely defined by the events that precede and follow it, and not by whatever name may be assigned to

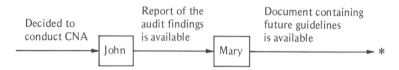

Figure 5-3. *An Intermediate Milestone for the CNA Project*

the task. The corresponding PERT diagram (not shown here) is comprised of three nodes joined by two arcs.

Since the task called MARY is fairly straightforward, it is not necessary to identify additional events between REPORT . . . AVAILABLE and DOCUMENT . . . AVAILABLE. In this sense, REPORT . . . AVAILABLE is the second-from-the-last event in the description of the CNA project. On the other hand, the transformation corresponding to the black box JOHN is not so obvious. The project definition procedure, therefore, continues to identify additional events between DECIDED . . . CNA and REPORT . . . AVAILABLE. Observe that in this case the procedure moves backward from the end state through the intermediate milestones to the initiation of the project.

The Second Event and the Forward Development The transformation necessary to move the project from its initiation to the newly identified event may also be fairly clear. In that case, such an event is the second event in the description of that project. For example, the event NEED AREAS (PRODUCT LINES) DEFINED must lie between the events DECIDED . . . CNA and REPORT . . . AVAILABLE; and the corresponding transformation is fairly straightforward. However, additional events must be identified between the events NEED . . . DEFINED and RE-PORT . . . AVAILABLE. The project definition procedure continues from the left to right.

Immediate Predecessor and Follower In PERT notation the event NEED AREAS DEFINED is said to be an immediate follower of the event DECIDED TO CONDUCT CNA. Conversely, the event DE-CIDED . . . CNA is an immediate predecessor of the event NEED AREAS DEFINED. The adjective, *immediate,* implies that the task connecting these two events is fairly straightforward. Thus, for example, the events REPORT . . . AVAILABLE and DOCUMENT . . . AVAILABLE are the immediate predecessor and follower, respectively. On the other hand, the transformation connecting the events NEED AREAS DE-FINED and REPORT . . . AVAILABLE is not immediately obvious, so at least one intermediate event must be identified. To this extent, these two events are not "neighbors" of each other.

Branch Formations Depending on the nature of the project, some events may have more than one immediate follower. For example, once the need areas have been defined, the CNA manager can recruit the data collector, establish the sample design (e.g., which of the community members should be contacted for soliciting the necessary information), design the audit instrument (e.g., a questionnaire asking for community members' current needs), inform the appropriate authorities (that a data collection effort is about to begin), and choose a satisfactory data processor. In other words, five events can be the immediate followers of the CNA event NEED AREAS DEFINED. Presumably, one could perform the corresponding tasks one after the other. It is, however, much more efficient to initiate all of these tasks simultaneously. This situation is represented by showing five *branches* emerging from the common event. See figure 5-4. Conversely, some events may have more than one im-

Figure 5-4. *An Event with Multiple Immediate Followers*

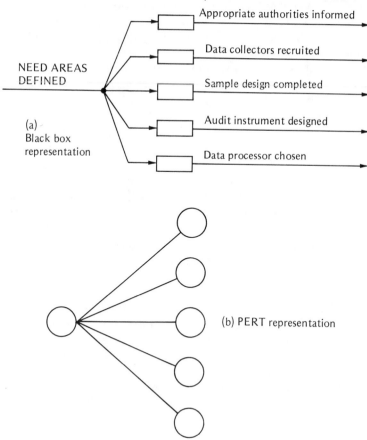

mediate predecessor. The corresponding black box and PERT representations are mirror images of those shown in figure 5-4.

Review of the Project-Definition Procedures

When a project has been fully defined in terms of significant events and the order of their occurrence, the corresponding black box representation is called a task diagram of the project, and the corresponding arcs and nodes representation is called a PERT network of that project. One such representation of the CNA project is shown in figure 5-5. Although the phrase, "the transformation is fairly clear" is obviously subjective, past experience in applying these techniques shows that the very exercise of developing either a task diagram or a PERT network is extremely informative and valuable. One of the greatest benefits of these techniques is that it forces the decision maker to plan the entire project in explicit detail—thus minimizing the number and intensity of unpleasant suprises. Another benefit is that it facilitates communication between the management scientist (who must "solve" such models for estimating quantitative parameters as the project completion time, the probability of meeting externally imposed schedules, and the monetary effects of speeding up the project operations) and the decision maker (who must agree to the inherent logic of the model, provide initial estimates of time and resources needed to complete the various tasks, and ultimately manage the project according to the management scientist's schedule).

One other point: note that hardly any work needs to be done to move the CNA project from event F: APPROPRIATE AUTHORITIES INFORMED along the branch to event L: DATA COLLECTION BEGUN. (The actual work is done in other parts of that project.) The black box between events F and L exists simply to show the logical precedence of F over L, i.e., that the collection of data cannot begin without informing appropriate authorities. For this reason, the task F→L is known to be a *dummy task*. In any project, a dummy task can be recognized by observing that no resources, time, or money need to be spent in performing such a task.

Of the two ways to graphically represent a project, drawing a task diagram has the advantage that it allows "free form" drawings. This implies that the graphics can be more easily modified in consultation with the decision maker. When the final definition of the project emerges, it is perhaps more aesthetically pleasing to show the project by a PERT network.

The rest of this chapter examines the methods of deriving schedules, estimating the probability of project completion on schedule, and evaluating the worth of speeding up project operations.

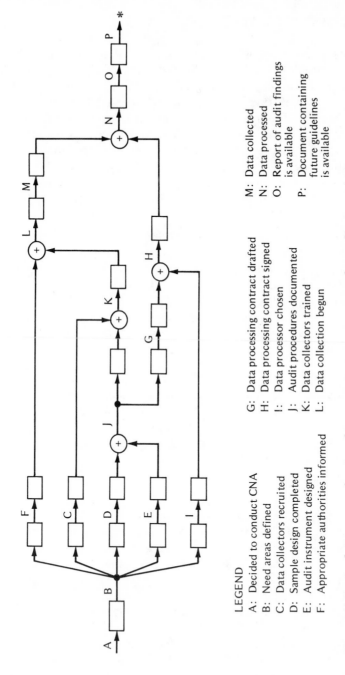

LEGEND

A: Decided to conduct CNA
B: Need areas defined
C: Data collectors recruited
D: Sample design completed
E: Audit instrument designed
F: Appropriate authorities informed

G: Data processing contract drafted
H: Data processing contract signed
I: Data processor chosen
J: Audit procedures documented
K: Data collectors trained
L: Data collection begun

M: Data collected
N: Data processed
O: Report of audit findings
   is available
P: Document containing
   future guidelines
   is available

Figure 5-5. *Task Diagram for Conducting a Community Needs Audit (CNA)*

DETERMINISTIC PERT

In this section we will assume that all the tasks that make up a project are sufficiently routine in the sense that the time needed to complete each task is known with reasonable certainty. Construction industry projects, such as, building single family homes, fall in this category. The tasks associated with normal repair and maintenance also belong to this category. Typing a nontechnical page, commuting to work in non-rush-hour traffic, and mowing 15,000 square feet of lawn are additional examples of routine tasks. Even though the individual tasks are fairly routine, the project as a whole may comprise a large number of such tasks. This section examines the methods to estimate project completion time.

Propose Anything Inc. Project #320

To illustrate the computations associated with PERT, we will pose a problem currently faced by the management of Propose Anything Inc. (PAI). This management consulting firm is in the midst of bidding on a small contract designated as Project #320. (To guard against intrusion by competitors, PAI prefers to use symbols and code names.) The project's management has already defined the ultimate objective (i.e., end product) and intermediate milestones (i.e., events) for this project. The project will begin with event A: the award of the contract to PAI and end with event G: delivery of the client-specified product. PAI proposes that the tasks leading to events B and C can be started simultaneously, and that the work leading to event E can be started after reaching event C, but that it cannot be finished until accomplishment of event D. They also propose that the events B, C, and E are essential for realizing F, and that E and F are both essential for accomplishing G. These interrelationships are displayed in figure 5-6 using three display techniques.

Earliest Possible Times

Developing a PERT network is a significant accomplishment, but by itself it does not contain enough information to derive a schedule of events. Along with the PERT network of events, we need to know or estimate the time necessary for completing each task. Taken together, this information is sufficient for deriving the schedule.

Suppose that, after consulting the various task leaders, PAI management has estimated the task completion times to be those shown in table 5-1. The task completion times are often exhibited graphically on the PERT network itself. See figure 5-7 in which the events are shown by letters A through G and the task completion times (measured numbers of weeks) are shown on the arcs connecting successive events.

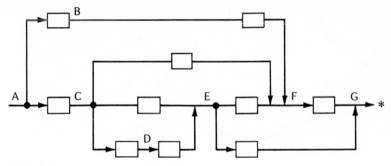

(a) Task diagram

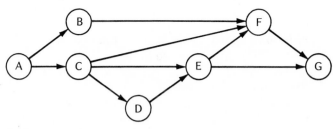

(b) PERT network

Event	Immediate predecessors	Immediate followers
A	—	B,C
B	A	F
C	A	D,E,F
D	C	E
E	C,D	F,G
F	B,C,E	G
G	E,F	—

(c) Logical interrelationships

Figure 5-6. *Three Displays of PAI's Project #320*

Table 5-1 *Task Completion Times (Number of Weeks)*

TASK	TIME	TASK	TIME	TASK	TIME
ab	9	ac	7	bf	12
cd	5	ce	10	cf	15
de	4	ef	6		
eg	10	fg	5		

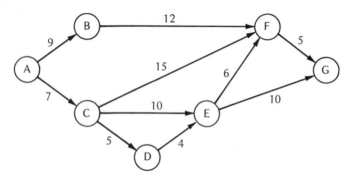

Figure 5-7. *PERT Network with Task Completion Times*

On Task Completion Times PAI management has chosen weeks to be the units of time. Depending on the nature of the project, any appropriate time unit, such as, days, weeks, or months may be chosen. If a task is a dummy task, corresponding task completion time would be set to zero. In all other cases, i.e., nondummy, one should be able to assign reasonably good time estimates. If this cannot be done, the implication is that the task is poorly defined or very complex. Additional review and perhaps splitting into more manageable subtasks is called for after which reasonable time estimates should be assigned. In PAI's Project #320, we assume that the time estimates are reasonably firm.

A Recipe to Compute Earliest Possible Times (EPT) for Realizing Each Event We will describe these procedures and apply them to PAI's Project #320 for illustrative purposes. To compute each event's EPT, follow these steps:

1. Identify the initial event (source) and set its EPT to zero. In a PERT network, this is the node without an arc entering it. In a task diagram, it is a milestone which is not a result (output) of any task. In a table of logical precedences, it is the event with no predecessors. For PAI's Project #320, it is event A. Symbolically:

$$EPT(A) = 0$$

2. Consider each event that has not been assigned an EPT, but *all* of whose immediate predecessors have been assigned their EPT. For PAI's project, events B and C are of this type.

3. For each immediate predecessor of the event under scrutiny, *add* the corresponding task completion time (TCT) to the EPT of that predecessor. The resulting number is a candidate value for the EPT of the event under scrutiny. For example, A is an immediate predecessor of B, and EPT(A) = 0. Since the task ab requires 9 weeks, TCT(ab) = 9. Hence $0 + 9 = 9$ is a candidate value for EPT(B). Two possibilities arise:

- *The event under scrutiny has only one immediate predecessor.* The candidate value computed above is the designated EPT. For example, if EPT(B) = 9 weeks and EPT(C) = 7, it follows that EPT(D) = EPT(C) + TCT(cd) = 7 + 5 = 12.
- *The event under scrutiny has two or more immediate predecessors.* In PAI's Project #320, event E has two immediate predecessors, C and D. We know that EPT(C) = 7 and that task ce requires 10 weeks. Consequently, 7 + 10 = 17 is a candidate value of EPT(E). Similarly, EPT(D) = 12 and TCT(de) = 4. Hence, 12 + 4 = 16 is yet another candidate value of EPT(E). The conflict is resolved by choosing the *largest* of all the candidate values. Therefore, EPT(E) = 17. To rationalize this rule consider that an event cannot happen unless *all* the tasks necessary for it to occur have been completed. Thus, one must wait until the *last* of such tasks has been completed.

4. Repeat steps 2 and 3 until each event in the PERT network has been assigned its EPT, the earliest possible time for its occurrence.

The computations performed on the PERT network of PAI's Project #320 are summarized in table 5-2. Note that this table is constructed from the top down, i.e., the results obtained in each line are used to derive the outputs for the lines below it. The EPT of the final event (i.e., the sink, or the event without followers) is also the earliest possible time for completing the project. This number, in PAI's case, EPT(G) is known as the "length" of the corresponding PERT network.

Latest Allowable Times

The computations in this subsection are designed to respond to the query: if the completion of the project is not to be delayed beyond a

Table 5-2 *Earliest Possible Times for Project #320*

EVENT	IMMEDIATE PREDECESSOR	EPT OF PREDECESSOR	TASK	TCT	EPT OF EVENT UNDER SCRUTINY
A	—	—	—	—	0
B	A	0	ab	9	0 + 9 = 9
C	A	0	ac	7	0 + 7 = 7
D	C	7	cd	5	7 + 5 = 12
E	C	7	ce	10	7 + 10 = 17
	D	12	de	4	12 + 4 = 16
F	B	9	bf	12	9 + 12 = 21
	C	7	cf	15	7 + 15 = 22
	E	17	ef	6	17 + 6 = 23
G	E	17	eg	10	17 + 10 = 27
	F	23	fg	5	23 + 5 = 28

specified date, when must each event happen? In this section, it is assumed that the entire project is to be completed as soon as possible. Under this assumption, the latest allowable time (LAT) of the very last event is set equal to the earliest possible time it can occur. The computations are summarized by the following sequence of steps:

1. Set the latest allowable time (LAT) for the final event to be equal to its own EPT. For PAI's Project #320, this implies that:

$$LAT(G) = EPT(G) = 28$$

2. Consider each event whose LAT has not been derived, but *all* of whose immediate followers have been assigned LAT values. F is such an event.

3. For each immediate follower of the event under scrutiny, *subtract* the corresponding task completion time, TCT, from LAT of that follower. The resulting number is a candidate value of LAT for the event under scrutiny. For example, LAT(G) = 28 and TCT(fg) = 5. Hence, $28 - 5 = 23$ is a candidate value of LAT(F). Two possibilities arise.

- *The event under scrutiny has only one immediate follower.* The candidate value is the designated LAT, e.g., LAT(F) = 23.
- *The event under scrutiny has two or more immediate followers.* The candidate LAT values are computed with respect to each follower. The smallest of all such numbers is the designated LAT value. For example, event E has two followers, F and G, with LAT(G) = 28 and LAT(F) = 23. Since TCT(eg) = 10 and TCT(ef) = 6, it follows that LAT(E) is the smaller of two numbers: $28 - 10 = 18$ and $23 - 6 = 17$. Hence LAT(E) = 17.

4. Repeat steps 2 and 3 until the LAT for each event in the PERT network has been designated.

The computations for PAI's project are summarized in table 5-3. Note that this table is computed from the bottom up, i.e., the results derived in each line are used in the lines above it.

Slacks, Critical Events, and Critical Paths

The manager of a project needs to recognize the critical events (i.e., the events which must happen at specific times) and the critical tasks (i.e., the tasks which must be started and finished on time). The "path" obtained by joining the critical tasks in the order of their occurrence is called a *critical path*. These parameters are obtained as follows:

1. Compute the difference:

$$TS = LAT(\text{final event}) - EPT(\text{final event})$$

This difference represents the maximum allowable slack, usually zero, in the completion of the project.

Table 5-3 *Latest Possible Times for Project #320*

EVENT	IMMEDIATE FOLLOWER	LAT OF FOLLOWER	TASK	TCT	LAT OF EVENT UNDER SCRUTINY
A	B	11	ab	9	11 − 9 = ~~2~~
	C	7	ac	7	7 − 7 = 0
B	F	23	bf	12	23 − 12 = 11
C	D	13	cd	5	13 − 5 = 8
	E	17	ce	10	17 − 10 = 7
	F	23	cf	15	23 − 15 = ~~8~~
D	E	17	de	4	17 − 4 = 13
E	F	23	ef	6	23 − 6 = 17
	G	28	eg	10	28 − 10 = ~~18~~
F	G	28	fg	5	28 − 5 = 23
G	—	—	—	—	28

2. Compute the slack associated with each event:

$$\text{Slack(event)} = \text{LAT(event)} - \text{EPT(event)}$$

3. Each event whose slack equals TS is a critical event.
4. Connect the critical events in the order of their occurrence. The resultant path is a critical path and all of the tasks on that path are critical tasks.

The results for PAI's Project #320 are summarized in table 5-4. (The asterisks (*) indicate the critical events.) Since LAT(G) = EPT(G) = 28, it follows that TS = 28 − 28 = 0. Hence, the critical events are those with slack 0. Thus, events A, C, E, F, and G are critical. (That events A and G are critical should not be a surprise.) Consequently, tasks ac, ce, ef, and fg are critical. The critical path (in this case there is only one) is A→C→E→F→G. Project completion time is 28 weeks. This can be

Table 5-4 *Slacks and Critical Events in Project #320*

EVENT	EARLIEST POSSIBLE TIMES	LATEST ALLOWABLE TIMES	SLACK TIME
A	0	0	0*
B	9	11	2
C	7	7	0*
D	12	13	1
E	17	17	0*
F	23	23	0*
G	28	28	0*

*Critical events

achieved only if the critical tasks are begun and completed on time. On the other hand, task ab can be delayed up to 2 weeks without affecting the project duration, i.e., it is not critical. If necessary, resources may be switched from these noncritical tasks—as long as such a shift does not make these tasks critical—to ensure the on-time completion of critical tasks and hence the entire project.

The next section examines a technique for displaying the results of the PERT analysis. After that is a reexamination of critical tasks in order to evaluate the costs of speeding up the project. Then, a statistical analysis of project completion time is presented. In each case, attention is focussed on the critical path—the longest path through the PERT network.

GANTT CHARTS

This graphic technique visually displays the beginning and ending times of each task in the project. The task names or other identifiers are shown along the vertical axis and the times are plotted along the horizontal axis. The display itself consists of a series of horizontal bars—one for each task. During the proposal stage of a project, time may be measured from the initiation of the project. Once funding has been secured, the time axis usually shows the "calendar." Assuming, for example, that PAI's Project #320 begins on June 6, figure 5-8 shows the corresponding Gantt chart. To prepare a Gantt chart, two items must be known: the time necessary to complete each task and the beginning and ending dates of each task. For PAI's Project #320, these information items are obtained from tables 5-1 and 5-4, respectively.

Figure 5-8. *Gantt Chart for PAI's Project #320*

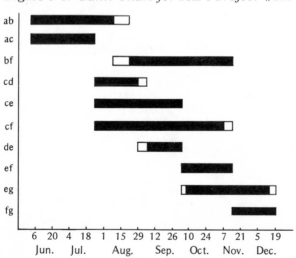

The critical tasks are indicated by solid bars. If a task is not critical, at least one end of the corresponding bar is not solid. The solid portion of such tasks indicates the amount of time required to complete that task; the hollow portion is proportional to the amount of slack. Gantt charts are most useful for monitoring the progress of the project.

THE CRITICAL PATH METHOD

The computations presented thus far assume that the work proceeds at normal pace—no one works overtime, additional help is not used, nor is more costly but faster working equipment used. The discussion in this section indicates some economical ways to speed up the project by speeding up the completion of chosen tasks. Note that we will use the phrase "to rush a task" to indicate its speedy completion.

Note also that a *critical path is always the longest path* through a PERT network. Consequently, it is pointless to rush noncritical tasks in order to rush the project. Thus, the methods of rushing the project are based on examining the possibilities of rushing the tasks on the critical path only. For this reason, the method used to evaluate time-cost tradeoffs is often called the Critical Path Method (CPM). It should be emphasized that CPM is most useful for evaluating projects that comprise relatively routine tasks and in which past experience in similar work can be used to effectively predict task durations and corresponding costs with reasonable certainty. The usefulness of CPM in developmental or one-of-a-kind projects is rather dubious. One other point—any good technique for estimating cost should account for two kinds of costs: the cost of producing an item as well as the cost of goodwill lost should rushing affect the quality of the output. The discussion in this section assumes that carefully prepared cost estimates are available. The computations are illustrated by reexamining PAI's Project #320.

CPM Nomenclature

The time needed to complete a task when the work is proceeding at a normal pace is called its *normal duration*. The corresponding cost is called the *normal cost*. CPM begins by investigating the possibilities of rushing a task and the cost of so doing. Generally speaking, tasks performed within an organization are more likely to be under the project manager's control and as such are more amenable to earlier than normal completion, though of course at a premium. The absolute minimum time necessary to accomplish a task is called its *crash time* and the corresponding cost is called its *crash cost*. Classic CPM assumes that the increase in cost is proportional to the reduction in task duration. The project manager should verify this assumption prior to applying the procedures illustrated in this section. Based on this assumption, CPM proceeds to compute the cost slope of each task which can be rushed. The cost slope of each such task is derived by the formula:

$$\text{cost slope} = \frac{\text{crash cost} - \text{normal cost}}{\text{normal duration} - \text{crash duration}}$$

The results for PAI's Project #320 are summarized in table 5-5. As an illustration of the procedure for computing the cost slope, note that the task ac can be completed normally in 7 weeks at a cost of $8,000. If one is willing to spend $11,000, it could be accomplished in 5.5 weeks. (A week has 5 working days.) Thus, the per week cost of rushing task ac is:

$$\frac{\$11,000 - \$8,000}{7 - 5.5} = \$2,000$$

All of the cost slopes are to be interpreted in this fashion.

Table 5-5 *Project #320 Task Completion Times and Costs*

| TASKS | NORMAL | | CRASH | | COST SLOPE ($/WEEK) |
	TIME (NO. OF WEEKS)	COST ($)	TIME (NO. OF WEEKS)	COST ($)	
ab	9	5,000	SAME	—	—
ac	7	8,000	5.5	11,000	2,000
bf	12	10,700	9.4	13,300	1,000
cd	5	6,000	4	7,600	1,600
ce	10	6,500	8	11,300	2,400
cf	15	11,900	SAME	—	—
de	4	3,700	SAME	—	—
ef	6	9,200	5	11,000	1,800
eg	10	8,400	9	11,600	3,200
fg	5	4,300	4	6,500	2,200

Rushing the Project by One Week

There are two questions of interest regarding any task in the project. Can it be rushed? And, should it be rushed? The former question deals with feasibility, the latter is of managerial interest.

Table 5-5 responds to the first question for PAI's Project #320. It indicates that tasks ab, cf, and de cannot be rushed. All others can be rushed provided the price is paid.

To illustrate the response to the second question, suppose we wish to rush Project #320 by one week, i.e., complete it in 27 rather than 28 weeks. Figure 5-9 shows the PERT network of this project, the normal duration of each task, and the corresponding critical (i.e., the longest) path: A→C→E→F→G. The project will normally continue for 28 weeks and will cost $73,700. That the tasks ab, cf, and de cannot be rushed at all

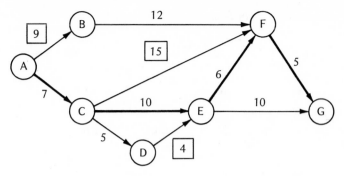

Figure 5-9. *Normal Times of PAI's Project #320*

is indicated in figure 5-9 by boxing in the corresponding tasked durations, e.g., the duration of task ab is shown as $\boxed{9}$.

Since the duration of the project equals the length of its critical path, the possibilities of shortening the path A→C→E→F→G without making it noncritical must be examined. Table 5-5 indicates that each of the critical tasks, ac, ce, ef, and fg can be rushed by one week. Also, the currently noncritical tasks have enough slack in them so that rushing ac, ce, ef, or fg would not make any task noncritical. So, the only question is one of cost. Since ef is the critical task with the smallest cost slope, $1,800, it follows that we should choose to rush ef by 1 week, i.e., from 6 to 5.

The consequences of this decision (as summarized in step 2 of table 5-6 and in figure 5-10) are:

1. Task ef will now last for 5 weeks only.
2. In addition to the currently critical tasks (ac, ce, ef, and fg) two new tasks (eg and cf) have also become critical.
3. The total cost of the project has increased by $1,800 to a new total of $75,500.

All of the critical tasks in figure 5-10 are shown with double lines. The currently critical paths are: A → C → E → G, A → C → E → F → G, and A → C → F → G. Also, since task ef has been rushed to its limit, the corresponding task duration (5) has been boxed in.

Further Reductions

To reduce the project duration by another week, one must examine the costs associated with rushing the currently critical tasks ac, ce, ef, fg, eg, and cf. Of these, task ef has been rushed to its limit. Also, task cf cannot be rushed at all. Can you see why there is no point in rushing task ce either? On the other hand, since task bf continues to have a slack of 1 week, task ac can be rushed by 1 week. This would cost an extra $2,000.

Table 5-6 *Consequences of Rushing the Critical Tasks*

STEP NUMBER	PROJECT DURATION	CRASH TASK AND DURATION	CRITICAL TASK AND DURATION	PROJECT COST
1	28	None	ac: 7 ce: 10 ef: 6 fg: 5	$73,700
2	27	ef: 5	ac: 7 ce: 10 ef: 5 fg: 5 eg: 10 cf: 15	$75,500
3	26	ef: 5 ac: 6	ac: 6 ce: 10 ef: 5 fg: 5 eg: 10 cf: 15 ab: 9 bf: 12	$77,500
4	25	ef: 5 ac: 6 fg: 4 ef: 9	ac: 6 ce: 10 ef: 5 fg: 4 eg: 9 cf: 15 ab: 9 bf: 12	$82,900
5	24.5	ef: 5 ac: 5.5 fg: 4 eg: 9 bf: 11.5	ac: 5.5 ce: 10 ef: 5 fg: 4 eg: 9 cf: 15 ab: 9 bf: 11.5	$84,400

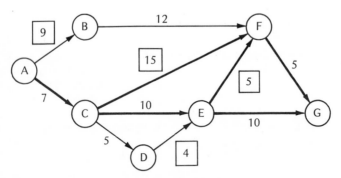

Figure 5-10. *Effects of Rushing Task ef*

Note that task eg can be rushed by 1 week provided that task fg is simultaneously rushed by 1 week. (Otherwise, task eg would no longer be critical.) And this would cost a total of $3,200 + 2,200 = $5,400 extra.

Obviously, the least expensive way of completing Project #320 in 26 weeks is to rush task ac by an additional week (from 7 to 6) at a cost of $2,000. If this is done, the project would now cost a total of $75,500 +

$2,000 = $77,500 and two more tasks, ab and bf, would become critical. The results are summed up in step 3 of table 5-6.

Were we to continue, you could read from table 5-6 that the project can be completed in 25 weeks for a total cost of $82,900. It can also be completed in 24.5 weeks by spending a total of $84,400. At this stage, however, one comes across a technological boundary. Since task fg needs a minimum of 4 weeks (see table 5-5) and task ac needs 5.5 weeks, it is impossible to complete Project #320 in less than 24.5 weeks.

One last point. The critical path method helps us create a time-cost tradeoff table such as that shown in table 5-6. It does not help us choose a specific option—that is left to the decision maker.

STOCHASTIC PERT

PERT is often used to plan either research or one-of-a-kind development projects because of the valuable insights gained by the very act of identifying intermediate milestones and establishing logical precedences among them. Due to the inherent novelty of the component tasks of such projects, however, it is usually not possible to estimate task durations precisely. Nevertheless, it is often possible to obtain a range of estimates of duration of each task. But, in the more difficult cases, advice must come from a panel of experts. The Delphi method and the Nominal Group method are the most frequently used techniques for obtaining and assimilating the experts' advice. Given these estimates, standard statistical theory is used to derive project completion times as well as to assess the chances of completing the project on time. Examination of such methods is the purpose of this section.

Three Estimates of Task Duration

First, the PERT network is constructed, and then the duration of each task is estimated. More specifically, the project planner in such cases would ask the task leaders to provide three estimates of the time necessary to complete each task: a, m, and b. These symbols are interpreted as follows.

a = *optimistic estimate*—the minimum reasonable period of time in which the task can be completed. The project planner may specify that the probability of completing a task in less than the optimistic time should not exceed 1 percent. If you drive to work each day, think of this as the time necessary to reach the office if there were no traffic jams, snow emergencies, or red lights.This is the optimistic estimate of the task: commute to work during rush hour.

m = *most likely estimate*—the best guess of the time necessary to complete the task. Having commuted to your present office for several months, you can anticipate the time necessary to reach the office on a "typical" day. This provides the most likely time estimate for performing that task.

$b = $ *pessimistic time*—the maximum reasonable period of time necessary for completing the task. The project planner may, for example, specify that he wants to be 99 percent certain of completing the task within this amount of time. This is the case in which, during your commute to work, there are two (instead of the usual one) traffic jams, the car develops a flat tire, and it is raining.

It is relatively easy to interpret the most likely estimate of task duration. Even when the task is new, m can be obtained by considering the most prevalent opinion among a variety of experts. The terms optimistic and pessimistic need much more careful scrutiny. No extraordinary phenomenon need happen to present us with either an optimistic or a pessimistic estimate. We only need to postulate "reasonable" extremes— for example, something which has 1 to 100 odds.

Consolidating the Estimates

PERT, as a technique for deriving the critical path and consequently the project completion time, is based on the use of a single estimate of the duration of each task. The three estimates of task duration that we just discussed are obtained out of necessity—a single and precise estimate is difficult to achieve. The resultant conflict is resolved as follows.

Expected Time For Task Completion, ET. This is computed for each task with the formula:

$$ET = \frac{a + 4m + b}{6}$$

The scientific rationale for choosing this formula is based on the properties of what is called Beta distribution. This distribution was chosen by the PERT developers as a probability law for task durations, because it is not necessarily symmetrical and because it has finite end points. During PERT applications, a and b designate these end points and m is used as the mode of the required Beta distribution. Since m is the most likely estimate, the above formula weights it much more than either of the two extreme estimates. As a manager you feel intuitively that it is correct.

One of the most compelling reasons for using any theory or formula, at least from the managerial point of view, is that it works. On this basis, use of the formulas above and below seems to be more than justified.

Variance of the Task Completion Times, VART This is derived by the formula:

$$\text{VART} = \left(\frac{b-a}{6}\right)^2$$

Since a and b are optimistic and pessimistic time estimates, respectively, the difference $(b-a)$ is the range of the possible time estimates. Recall from chapter 2 that if X is a normally distributed random variable, then almost certainly the observed values of X will lie within ± 3 standard deviations of its mean. Thus, we may approximate $b-a$ with 6 standard deviations. Hence:

$$\text{standard deviation} \approx (b-a)/6$$

The above formula is intuitively justified since variance is the square of the standard deviation.

PERT Procedures The earliest possible times, latest allowable times, slacks, critical events, critical tasks, and the critical paths are derived using the expected time (ET) in place of the task completion time (TCT). The "length" of the PERT network is interpreted as the expected project completion time (EPCT). It follows from normal theory that the chances of completing the project in less than EPCT are exactly 50 percent. Policy questions, such as, the probability of completing the project on some externally specified schedule, are answered by using the VART of the critical tasks and the table of probabilities "under a standard normal curve." More specifically let PCT denote the desired project completion time, let EPCT denote the sum of ET values of the critical tasks, and let $\sigma^2(\text{PCT})$ denote the total of VART values of the critical tasks. Then, the PERT developers assume that:

$$Z = \frac{\text{PCT} - \text{EPCT}}{\sigma(\text{PCT})}$$

is approximately normally distributed with mean 0 and variance 1.

PAI's Project #424

To illustrate the analytical procedures when the task durations are statistical, let us consider a new problem faced by the management of Propose Anything Incorporated (PAI). Having successfully completed Project #320 on schedule, PAI has been invited to bid on a similar project in another part of the country. This is designated as Project #424. Since the project is similar, the task diagram and/or PERT network need not be redesigned; the one used in Project #320 is applicable. However, PAI management has never been outside of New England, and they are not so sure about task completion times. After reading all available information about the proposed project site, the task leaders are more divided than before. Some task leaders feel that having performed the task once, a similar task can be completed faster than before. Others feel that change of site slows their work. After hearing both sides, PAI management feels that these two factors will balance each other, and therefore each task will be completed at the same speed as before. The resultant optimistic, most likely, and pessimistic task completion times are shown in table 5-7. For each of the 10 tasks, the table also shows the expected time for completing the task. For example, consider the task cf for which $a = 11$, $m = 15$, and $b = 20$. Hence:

$$ ET = \frac{11 + (4)(15) + 20}{6} = \frac{91}{6} $$

Table 5-7 *Task Completion Times for Project #424*

TASK	OPTIMISTIC (a)	MOST LIKELY (m)	PESSIMISTIC (b)	EXPECTED (ET)
ab	8	9	10	9
ac	6	7	9	43/6
bf	9	12	15	12
cd	5	5	5	5
ce	8	10	11	59/6
cf	11	15	20	91/6
de	3	4	6	25/6
ef	5	6	8	37/6
eg	8	10	12	10
fg	4	5	10	34/6

Using the ET column of table 5-7, we can compute the earliest possible and latest allowable time of each event. Having computed the resultant slacks, we can identify the critical events, critical tasks, and hence the critical path. We can also determine the earliest project completion time. The computations are similar to those shown for deterministic PERT and they are summarized in table 5-8. The critical path is A→C→E→F→G, the same as that for Project #320. But, the project completion time is expected to be 173/6 = 28 5/6 weeks. Note that unlike Project #320, the project completion time is no longer exactly 28 weeks (a firm statement) but rather it is expected to be 28 5/6 weeks (a statistical statement). Furthermore, there is only a 50 percent chance of completing Project #424 in the expected 28 5/6 weeks. It is a rather stiff price to pay for uncertainty.

Statistical Queries

An effective manager prefers to deal with uncertainties explicitly. It is easier to deal with a "known evil" than to ignore its existence. PERT is useful in this respect. It enables a project planner to:

Table 5-8 *Slacks and Critical Events for Project #424*

EVENT	IMMEDIATE PREDECESSOR AND ITS EPT	EARLIEST POSSIBLE TIME	IMMEDIATE FOLLOWER AND ITS LAT	LATEST ALLOWABLE TIME	SLACK
A	—	0	B: 67/6 C: 43/6	~~13/6~~ 0	0
B	A: 0	9	F: 139/6	67/6	13/6
C	A: 0	43/6	D: 77/6 E: 102/6 F: 139/6	~~47/6~~ 43/6 ~~48/6~~	0
D	C: 43/6	73/6	E: 102/6	77/6	4/6
E	C: 43/6 D: 73/6	102/6 ~~98/6~~	F: 139/6 G: 173/6	102/6 ~~113/6~~	0
F	B: 9 C: 43/6 E: 102/6	~~21~~ ~~134/6~~ 139/6	G: 173/6	139/6	0
G	E: 102/6 F: 139/6	~~162/6~~ 173/6	—	173/6	0

- Determine the length of a safe schedule (e.g., the one can be met with 99 percent confidence)
- Estimate the chances of meeting an externally determined schedule
- Judge the chances of time/cost overrun

These and related queries are resolved by assuming that the project duration is normally distributed with a mean of EPCT and a variance of σ^2 (PCT). Project #424 opens up new territory for Propose Anything Inc. and they would like to obtain answers to such questions as:

- What are the chances of completing the project in 30 weeks?
- If PAI wants to be 98 percent sure of on-time completion, what should the forecasted project completion date be?
- What are the chances that the project will be prolonged beyond 32 weeks?

The critical path for Project #424 comprises tasks ac, ce, ef, and fg. Table 5-9 shows the expected value and variance of these tasks obtained by using these formulas:

$$\text{ET} = \frac{a + 4m + b}{6} \quad \text{and} \quad \text{VART} = \left(\frac{b - a}{6}\right)$$

Table 5-9 *Statistics of the Critical Path*

TASK	COMPLETION TIMES				
	a	m	b	ET	VART
ac	6	7	9	43/6	1/4
ce	8	10	11	59/6	1/4
ef	5	6	8	37/6	1/4
fg	4	5	10	34/6	1
Critical Path				173/6	7/4

It follows that for Project #424:

$$\text{EPCT} = 173/6, \quad \sigma^2(\text{PCT}) = 7/4, \quad \text{and} \quad \sigma(\text{PCT}) = \sqrt{1.75}$$
$$= 28.83 \qquad\qquad = 1.75 \qquad\qquad = 1.32$$

so that:

$$Z = \frac{\text{PCT} - 28.83}{1.32} \quad \text{or} \quad \text{PCT} = 1.32Z + 28.83$$

This variable Z is used for responding to PAI's questions.

Planning Information

PAI's first question: "What are the chances of completing Project #424 in 30 weeks?" is equivalent to the symbolic question: "What is Prob (PCT ≤ 30)?" The response process is summarized as:

$$\text{Prob (PCT} \le 30) = \text{Prob} \left(Z \le \frac{30 - 28.83}{1.32} \right)$$

$$= \text{Prob (Z} \le .88)$$

$$= F(.88)$$

$$= .8104 \text{ (from appendix A)}$$

In other words, there is an 81.04 percent chance of completing Project #424 in 30 weeks or less.

PAI also wants to know the likely duration of the project with 98 percent or better confidence. Appendix A indicates that $F(2.05) = .98$. To find the project duration with 98 percent confidence, we must have Z = 2.05. Hence:

$$\text{PCT} = (1.32)(2.05) + 28.83 = 31.54$$

Suppose the contract specifies that the contractor will be fined $1,000 if the project continues beyond 32 weeks. While making the bid, therefore, PAI wants to know the chances of such penalty. This can be computed as follows:

$$\text{Prob (PCT} > 32 \text{ weeks}) = \text{Prob} \left(Z > \frac{32 - 28.83}{1.32} \right)$$

$$= \text{Prob } (Z > 2.4)$$

$$= 1 - \text{Prob } (Z \leq 2.4)$$

$$= 1 - F(2.4)$$

$$= 1 - .9917 \text{ (from appendix A)}$$

$$= .0083$$

In short, there is only an .83 percent probablity of running beyond scheduled completion date.

WHAT A MANAGER SHOULD KNOW

We have presented a number of techniques for defining and scheduling a project. Many experts believe that the very act of defining the intermediate milestones and their interrelationships yields many of the benefits associated with PERT/CPM. Therefore, we began this chapter by outlining a method to depict a project as an orderly progression of tasks and events. Graphically, this order can be displayed by presenting either a task diagram or a PERT network.

Having defined each task, it is usually possible to obtain reasonably good estimates of its duration. The latter parts of this chapter illustrated the methods of using this information. Estimates of task durations can be used for one or more of the following purposes:

- To derive a schedule of tasks by identifying the critical tasks
- To assess the costs of speeding up the project operations by identifying the tasks that should be rushed
- To estimate the probabilities of meeting the specified deadlines
- To obtain a schedule that can be met with stated confidence

This chapter presented some techniques to achieve these goals. Further improvements on these techniques can be found in the selected readings. For example, Burt and Garmon (1971), and Van Slyke (1963) discuss using the Monte Carlo approach to derive critical paths. (We will examine the Monte Carlo approach in chapter 8.) Doersch and Patterson (1977) use zero-one programming to schedule a project.

Nonetheless, it should be emphasized that PERT/CPM is not a technician's panacea. Task durations, for instance, are rarely known with certainty. Thus, the question of how to estimate task durations continues to be important. See Britney (1976), King and Wilson (1967), and Lindsey (1971) for some tips on this.

In any case, estimating task durations and developing milestone schedules will not, by themselves, ensure the successful and timely completion of the project. The responsibility for completing each task successfully and on time must be assigned to individual task leaders. One method to motivate task leaders is to involve each of them in the planning process, i.e., in determining how to accomplish each task and estimating the time requirements.

Since task durations can be estimated only reasonably well, one should be on guard if time/cost tradeoffs appear too unreasonably precise, or if the probabilities are computed to several decimal places. It is wiser to examine each of the underlying assumptions rather than be carried away by the apparent accuracy of analyses.

We have seen how PERT/CPM can be used at the initiation of a project. In complex projects, both of these should be on-going activities. The planned schedules should be compared with the actual progress at the termination of each task. Time estimates should also be updated as the "track record" of the accuracy of previous estimates becomes known.

SELECTED READINGS

BATTERSBY, A. *Network Analysis for Planning and Scheduling.* 3d ed. New York: John Wiley & Sons, Inc., 1970.

BRITNEY, R. R. "Bayesian Point Estimation and the PERT Scheduling of Stochastic Activities." *Management Science* 22 (1976), pp. 938–948.

BURT, J. M. and GARMON, M. B. "Monte Carlo Techniques for Stochastic PERT Network Analysis." *INFOR* 9 (1971), pp. 248–262.

DOERSCH, R. H. and PATTERSON, J. H. "Scheduling Project to Maximize Its Present Value: A Zero-One Programming Approach." *Management Science* 23 (1977), pp. 882–889.

ELMAGHRABY, S. E. "On the Expected Duration of PERT Type Networks." *Management Science* 13 (1967), pp. 229–306.

GISSER, P. "Taking Chances Out of Product Introduction." *Industrial Marketing* (1965).

HANSON, R. S. "Moving the Hospital to a New Location." *Industrial Engineering* 4 (1972).

HOARE, H. R. *Project Management Using Network Analysis.* Maidenhead, England: McGraw-Hill Book Company, 1973.

JOSHI, M. V. *Methods for Conducting an Audit of Community Member Needs.* Wellesley, Mass.: The Human Ecology Institute, 1976.

KING, W. R. and WILSON, T. A. "Subjective Time Estimates in Critical Path Planning—A Preliminary Analysis." *Management Science* 13 (1967), pp. 307–320.

LINDSEY, J. H., II. "An Estimate of Expected Critical-Path Length in PERT Networks." *Operations Research* 19 (1971), pp. 1586–1601.

RUSSELL, A. H. "Cash Flows in Networks." *Management Science* 16 (1970), pp. 357–372.

VAN SLYKE, R. M. "Monte Carlo Methods and the PERT Problem." *Operations Research* 11 (1963), pp. 839–860.

WEIST, J. D. and LEVY, F. K. *A Management Guide to PERT/CPM*. Englewood Cliffs, NJ: Prentice-Hall, Inc., 1969.

WONG, Y. "Critical Path Analysis for New Product Planning." *Journal of Marketing Research* 28 (1964).

PROBLEM SET 5
PROJECTS AND COMPLETION TIMES

1. Given the PERT network below:

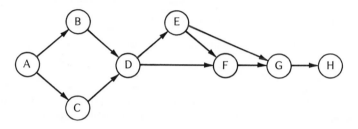

   a. Exhibit the corresponding task diagram, and

   b. Show the immediate predecessor(s) and follower(s) of each event in a table of logical interrelationships, such as that shown below.

EVENT	IMMEDIATE PREDECESSOR	IMMEDIATE FOLLOWER

2. A small project is comprised of 10 tasks. Their precedence relationships are shown in the task diagram below.

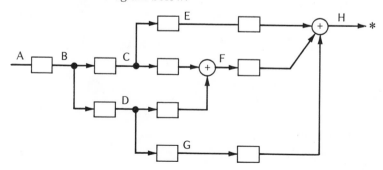

   a. Exhibit the corresponding PERT network.

   b. Display the interrelationships among events A through H in the tabular form such as that indicated in problem 1(b).

3. A table of precedences among events A through K is shown below.

EVENT	IMMEDIATE PREDECESSOR	EVENT	IMMEDIATE PREDECESSOR
A	—	B	A
C	A	D	A
E	B	F	B, C
G	C, D	H	E, F, G
I	G	J	H, I
K	J		

a. Display the corresponding PERT network.

b. Identify the immediate followers of each event.

4. Construct and display the PERT network corresponding to the task diagram in figure 5-5.

5. Some of the events in the production of a play are listed below. Arrange these in their logical order and display the corresponding PERT network.

A Play has been selected

B Actors/actresses chosen

C Set is designed

D Dress rehearsal completed

E Tickets printed

F Publicity campaign launched

G Costumes chosen

H Theater chosen

I Rehearsals completed

J Set construction begun

K Tickets sold

L Set is in place

6. A number of events must happen from the moment you decide to write a textbook until you receive your first royalty payment. Construct an appropriate PERT diagram.

A First royalty payment received

B Publisher chosen

C Book outline sent to prospective publishers

D Manuscript developed

E Lawyer consulted for contract review

F First edition printed

G Manuscript revised

H Reviewers' comments on hand

I Sales tallied

J First draft reviewed

K Reviewers chosen

L Problem sets constructed

M Book outline prepared

N Contract signed

O Publisher's representatives contact prospective adopters

P Book's potential market established

7. When you take your car to Quality Service Inc., they claim to perform the following activities. Arrange these in logical sequence(s) and hence construct a PERT network.

* Lift the car on a hoist

* Replace drain plug

* Grease the fittings

* Drain oil

* Lower car

* Check radiator

* Return your car

* Check the differential fluid

* Check the clutch fluid

* Remove drain plug

* Refill crank case

* Check battery

8. Some of the events encountered while building a house are listed below. Display the corresponding PERT network.

A Architect is chosen	O Building permit secured
B Decided to build a house	P Inside walls plastered
C Inside walls painted	Q Opening ceremony performed
D An empty lot chosen	R Building funds secured
E Plumber chosen	S Roof laid
F Foundation laid	T Electrician chosen
G Chosen lot cleared	U Exterior walls completed
H Sewage connections made	V Building contractor chosen
I Electrical connections completed	W Outside walls painted
J Landscaping completed	X Plumbing installed
K Windows in place	Y Doors in place
L Heating system installed	Z Ceiling finished
M Moldings and trim in place	α Heating system chosen
N Landscape artist chosen	β Driveway completed

9. Assume that you have decided to take a 7-day vacation in London at the end of this semester. Further assume that you are healthy and have money. Prepare a diagram showing all the tasks which *you* must perform in order to lawfully arrive in London, and to enjoy your vacation.

10. What is your current most important objective behind entering the management school? List the significant events, i.e. milestones, which would indicate that you are making progress. Arrange these milestones in their logical sequence and thus prepare a task diagram.

11. One of your friends is thinking of joining the management school of which you are a member. Prepare a task diagram to help him plan his steps until he begins attending classes in the first semester. (Had you followed these steps? If not, give reasons why these steps are valid.)

12. Prepare a task diagram showing the important milestones from the moment you become a "senior" in the management school till the time you are satisfactorily employed in a career of your choice.

13. Suppose that you are the chairperson of the "fun and games" committee. Prepare a task diagram for arranging a successful one-day picnic.

14. In the PERT network below, the number of weeks necessary to complete each task are shown on the corresponding arc.

   a. Compute the earliest possible and latest allowable time for the realization of each event.

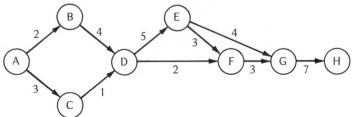

b. Identify the critical path(s).

c. Estimate the project completion date.

Show your computations in a tabular form such as that shown below.

EVENT	IMMEDIATE PREDE- CESSOR(S)	EARLIEST POSSIBLE TIME	IMMEDIATE FOLLOWER(S)	LATEST ALLOWABLE TIME	SLACK

15. The numbers on top of the black boxes in the task diagram below represent the days necessary to complete the corresponding task.

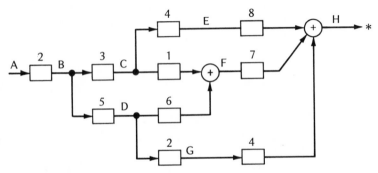

a. Compute the earliest possible and latest allowable times for each event.

b. Identify critical activities and hence the critical path.

c. Determine the project completion time.

Show your computations in a tabular form similar to that in problem 14.

16. The PERT network below shows a developmental project. The numbers on top of each task show the optimistic, most likely, and pessimistic times for task completion (number of weeks).

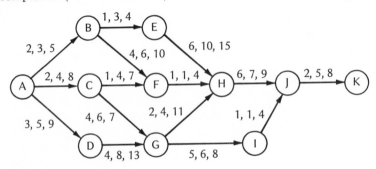

a. Compute the expected duration of each task.

b. Derive the critical path(s), i.e., the longest path(s).

17. For the PERT network in problem 16:

a. Compute the variance of task completion times for those tasks which are critical.

b. What is the probability of completing the project in 33 weeks or less?

18. The PERT network below shows the expected number of weeks to complete each task, and corresponding variance (in that order.) For example, task be is expected to need 13 weeks with a variance of 16.

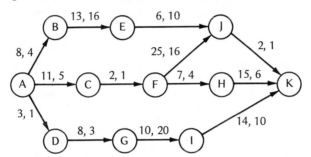

a. Derive the critical path and the expected time for project completion.

b. If you want to be 95 percent confident of completing the project on schedule, what should be the projected due date?

19. The PERT network below shows the expected number of weeks to complete each activity and corresponding standard deviation (in that order).
For example, task ab is expected to last 10 weeks with a standard deviation of $\sqrt{2}$ weeks.

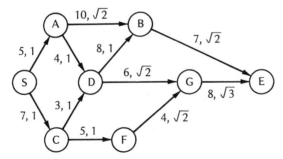

a. What is the expected time for project completion?

b. What are the chances that the project will continue beyond 28 weeks?

20. For the PERT network following, determine the expected duration of each task and hence the critical path. Compute the variance of task durations for the critical tasks only. If the management wishes to be 98 percent sure, what should be their predicted project completion date?

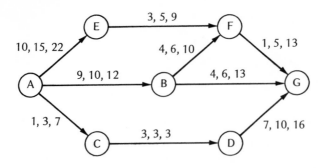

21–26. Display the Gantt chart for each of the projects described in problems 14 through 16 and 18 through 20.

27. Because of a new technological breakthrough, PAI may be able to complete their Project #320 much earlier than expected. Specifically, task cf can be completed in 12 weeks, provided PAI is willing to spend $17,000 instead of $11,900. Also task de can be rushed by 1 week for an added cost of $1,300. Find the earliest possible time for completing Project #320 and the corresponding total cost. Summarize your computations as in table 5-6.

28. The PERT network of a small project is shown below. Each arc, except D→E, shows two sets of numbers. The first set shows the normal duration in days and the corresponding cost in dollars. The second set shows the crash duration and crash cost. Determine the critical path(s) and the project completion time if each task proceeds at normal pace. What is the normal cost of the project?

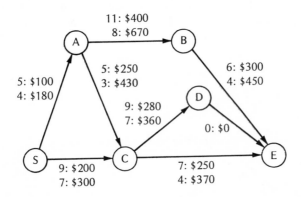

29. The project managment of problem 28 wishes to rush the project completion by 3 days. Find the least costly ways of accomplishing this. Summarize your process as in table 5-6.

30. The PERT network following shows the normal duration of each task (days) and the corresponding cost. Derive the normal time for completing the project and the corresponding total cost.

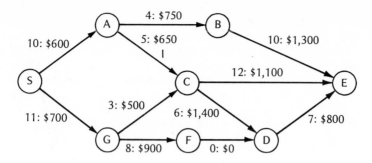

31. Investigation reveals that the task durations listed in problem 30 can be reduced at additional cost. The crash times and crash costs are summarized
below. Display the most economical ways of reducing the project completion
time by 1, 2, 3, or 4 days. In each case, derive the total project cost. Summarize
your reasoning as in table 5-6.

TASK	DURATION	COST	TASK	DURATION	COST
sa	8	$1,200	sg	7	$1,500
ab	same	$ 750	gc	same	$ 500
be	7	$2,500	ac	4	$ 900
ce	9	$2,000	cd	5	$1,900
gf	6	$1,500	de	5	$1,400

32. A small project comprises events A, B, C, D, E, and F. Their interrelationships and the time elapsing between successive events are summarized below. Derive the critical path, project duration, and the corresponding cost.

EVENT	IMMEDIATE PREDECESSOR	TIME TO COMPLETE THAT TASK (DAYS)	NORMAL COST ($)
A	—	—	—
B	A	7	800
C	A	6	600
D	A	13	1,300
	B	6	750
	C	9	1,000
	E	0	0
E	C	8	900
F	D	10	1,200
	E	7	500

33. It is possible to rush some of the tasks for the project described in problem 32. Specifically, task ab can be rushed up to 2 days at a cost of $200 per day rushed. Tasks ac and ad can each be rushed up to 2 days at an incremental cost of $250/day and $350/day, respectively. Task df can be completed in 9 days at a cost of $1,600 instead of $1,200; to rush it any further, outside help must be hired and this costs $600/day rushed. With the outside help, task df can be completed in 6 days. None of the other tasks can be rushed. Determine the *shortest* duration of the project and the corresponding minimum project cost.

6

Inventory Models

An inventory is a necessary evil—it is costly to store items in a warehouse. On the other hand, it can help smooth out production and meet unforeseeable demands. The issue is not whether to carry an inventory, but how large it should be. Related questions are: how much to order at one time, when to place the order, and what is the total annual cost. This chapter answers these questions in some simple situations.

RATIONALE FOR CARRYING AN INVENTORY

Inventory means having a quantity of goods or resources on hand, i.e., in stock. Since the items in the inventory are not being used for any productive purposes, carrying an inventory is costly. Why then, should an organization engage in this activity? For several good reasons:

175

1. To meet erratic or unforeseeable demand.
2. To smooth out production. The demand for a product is often seasonal (e.g., lawn equipment or snow tires). Carrying an item in inventory helps maintain a fairly steady production schedule and thus reduces the cost of hiring, firing, overtime, and idle time.
3. To guard against inflation or labor shortages (due to strikes, for instance).
4. To protect against irregularity of supply—especially in the farm and dairy related activities.
5. To obtain price discounts by buying/producing in large volume.
6. To minimize ordering cost. Since the amount of paperwork and searching expenses are usually independent of the amount ordered/produced, larger orders are often economical.

In short, inventories are important to modern managers. In this chapter, we will study some elementary models to answer three inventory-related questions:

1. How much to order at one time?
2. When to place an order?
3. What is the reasonable level of safety stock?

The answers to these questions depend on the values of several parameters, such as: the level of demand for a product, the cost of storing a unit of that product, purchase price per unit, and the cost of placing an order. To begin with, we will assume that these parameters are known precisely. The resultant models are known as the *deterministic* models. Towards the end of this chapter, we will discuss a *stochastic* model which assumes that the demand for a product is erratic. Questions 2 and 3 then become important. The marginal analysis technique discussed in chapter 4 will be employed to answer such questions.
Some other questions also examined by the inventory models are:

• where to stock (i.e., making the choice of warehouse location)
• how to staff the inventory (i.e., choosing the right mix of professionals) and
• whether to computerize the inventory records.

These questions will not be examined in this text. Instead, the interested reader is encouraged to consult the references in the Selected Readings at the end of this chapter.
Not all products are equally important to an organization. Thus, not each product need go through such a formal review. Therefore, we will end the chapter by discussing the A-B-C scheme of classifying the products.

PARAMETERS OF AN INVENTORY MODEL

In order to determine the proper model for representing an inventory situation, it is important to study its defining characteristics. This section lists the data items necessary to define a specific situation:

The Number of Products
Since this chapter intends to acquaint you with elementary models, we will assume that only one product is to be stocked.

Inventory Level
This is the number of units presently on hand, i.e., in stock. This number is also known as the size of the inventory.

Depletion Rate
This is the number of units leaving the inventory (i.e., being sold, used, or consumed) per unit amount of time. The depletion rate depends on the demand properties. There are three possibilities:

1. The depletion rate is constant over time (or nearly so). For example, the number of gallons of milk or the number of pounds of cereal sold by a supermarket per week is fairly constant. The actual level of inventory of such products is represented in figure 6-1(a). The inventory level in that figure decreases at a uniform rate of 50 per week.

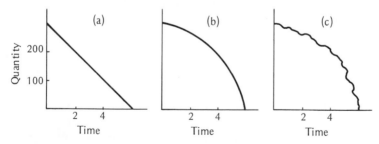

Figure 6-1. *Effects of Demand on the Inventory Level*

2. The depletion rate, though not constant, follows an easily recognizable pattern. [See figure 6-1(b).] Such a pattern would result if most of the items are drawn toward the end of the observation period. The inventory level is said to be a *convex* function of time. The inventory level would be a *concave* function if most of the items were drawn in the early part of the observation period.
3. The depletion rate is erratic. Figure 6-1(c) shows one such situation. Statistical procedures are essential to handle such cases.

The first two situations are examples of deterministic demand and the last is one of stochastic demand.

The Reorder Point
When inventory reaches a specified level, it is time to order a new batch to replenish the stock. That specified level is called a reorder point.

The Lead Time
This equals the time elapsed from the moment an order to replenish the inventory is placed to the moment when the items are in inventory. If the depletion rate is constant, the relationships among reorder point, lead time, shortage, and supply can be depicted as in figure 6-2. When reading this figure, assume that the demand is 50 units per week; that each time an order is placed, 300 units are ordered; and that the lead time is 2 weeks.

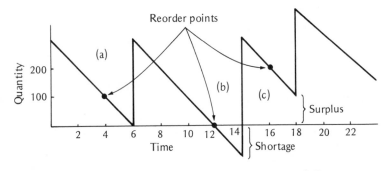

Figure 6-2. *Fluctuations in the Inventory Level Due to Depletion and Replenishment*

Since $50 \times 2 = 100$ units will be used up before the new delivery arrives, it follows that one should place a new order when the inventory level becomes 100. If this is done, the new order will arrive exactly when the current inventory is zero. If the new order is placed when one runs out of stock, i.e., if the reorder point equals zero, the decision maker will experience a *shortage* until the stock is replenished. If, on the other hand, the reorder point exceeds 100, the new delivery will be made before the current inventory is exhausted, i.e., there will be a *surplus*. Most inventory models determine the reorder point to be such that the new delivery will arrive precisely when the current stock is zero.

Order Quantity and Lot Size
Order quantity equals the amount to be ordered or produced at the moment the inventory level equals the reorder point. Lot size equals the quantity received.

Replenishment Rate and Replenishment Period

The replenishment period is the time during which units of a particular order are added to the inventory. In a purchasing situation, this might be insignificant. If the units are produced in-house, however, the situation is different—the units are added to inventory over a period of time, i.e., as they are produced. Consequently, in the production environment, one must also consider the replenishment rate, i.e., the number of units brought into the inventory per unit time. To be meaningful, the replenishment rate must exceed the depletion rate. In a purchasing situation, this rate is usually assumed to be infinite, i.e., the entire order is filled instantly.

The Average Inventory

This parameter is useful for decision making as well as for insurance and taxation. If the demand is constant, the replenishment is instantaneous, and there is neither shortage nor surplus. Thus, the average inventory equals exactly half of the initial inventory.

Ordering or Set Up Cost

Traditionally, inventory models seek to minimize costs rather than increase profits. There are several components of the inventory related costs. The first is the ordering cost, i.e., the cost of placing one order. This is obtained as the sum total of the following (and similar) costs: purchasing, inspection, receiving, bookkeeping, and data processing as well as the expenses of delivery, postage, and telephone. Usually the ordering cost is independent of the size of the order. If the units are produced in house, the ordering cost is equivalent to set up cost. In either case, the fewer the occasions for ordering, the smaller is the total ordering cost per year. This is a motivation for carrying an inventory.

Carrying or Holding Cost

This includes:

1. The cost of capital (i.e., interest paid (or forgone) on the capital invested in the inventory)
2. The cost of storage (e.g., rental, heat, light, and security)
3. Bookkeeping and taking of physical inventory
4. Taxes and insurance
5. Obsolescence and deterioration of the items stored

Often, the carrying cost is expressed as a percentage of the capital value of the inventory.

Shortage Cost

This occurs if the inventory is depleted prior to receiving the new order. This cost can be obtained by considering the cost of idle time, cost of placing an "express" order, as well as the cost of goodwill lost. This last component of the shortage cost is, of course, very difficult to compute. The following questions might serve as a guideline: Will you lose a customer? What are the chances? What is the dollar value of the anticipated sale?

Per Unit Cost

This is simply the price per unit produced/purchased. The per unit price could be independent of order quantity or lot size and if so, this cost should not be discussed while deriving optimal inventory policies. Often, however, there are price breaks, i.e., quantity discounts. In such cases, the per unit price must enter any discussion of optimal policies.

System Constraints

Though listed last, it is not the least important component of any inventory decision. Specifically, before recommending a policy, you must examine the environment in which the inventory problem occurs. Thus, if a parking lot cannot accommodate more than 100 cars, the potentially optimal order quantity of 300 is meaningless. Similarly, if the organization does not have large cash reserves, it cannot be asked to take advantage of price breaks. The constraints imposed by space, operating capital, scheduling period, or shortage should be examined prior to choosing an appropriate model and/or making specific recommendations. The rest of this chapter assumes that this has been done.

ECONOMIC ORDER QUANTITY (EOQ) MODEL

This is one of the most basic and the oldest of all the formal inventory models. We will begin by listing the underlying assumptions so that you can determine the extent to which each is valid in specific situations. We will continue with the formulas for EOQ and the related parameters of decision maker's interest. Finally, we will present an example in which this model is likely to be valid. Later sections examine variations of the basic EOQ model.

The EOQ Assumptions

It is usually preferable to use the simplest possible analytical model that adequately represents the real world situation. First, the simplicity of the model implies fewer computations and hence less cost. Second, being analytical, such a model yields optimal values of the relevant parameters of decision maker's interest. Third, the simpler the model, the easier it is to interpret both the model and the solution. This has important benefits when attempting to implement the solution. Unfortunately, there is a price to be paid in numerous and occasionally stringent assumptions. It is crucial to know the assumptions underlying any model. Those of the EOQ model are listed here for ready reference.

1. *The depletion rate is known and constant.* This means that the graph of inventory levels during a depletion cycle should resemble that shown in figure 6-1(a). If the demand is nearly constant, using the average demand in place of the desired constant would not materially affect the optimality.

2. *The per unit purchase or production cost, the per unit holding cost, and the ordering cost are independent of the quantity ordered.* This means that there are no quantity discounts — the purchasing agent cannot obtain price breaks or the production set up cost is insignificant. It also means that the storage capacity is more than that needed by the optimal solution. If a dealer's parking lot can accommodate only 100 cars, the carrying cost of the 101st car is likely to be much greater than the unit carrying cost of the first 100 cars. The EOQ model would not be valid in that case. The assumption that the ordering cost is constant is most likely to be valid.

3. *The replenishment is scheduled so that the new deliveries arrive precisely when the current inventory level becomes zero.* Since the demand is constant, this is equivalent to proposing that the lead time is either zero or else it is precisely known. Consequently, the reorder point equals:

lead time × depletion rate

In other words, the reorder point resembles that shown in figure 6-2(a). There is neither shortage nor surplus inventory.

4. *The replenishment rate is infinite,* i.e., it takes zero time to stock the inventory. This assumption is most likely to be true in a purchasing situation but not so likely if the units are being produced in-house.

5. *Only one product is being considered.* If the orders for two or more products have to be decided, each is examined on its own. This is a major drawback of the EOQ model. However, models in which the orders are to be placed simultaneously become much more complex.

6. *There is only one decision variable,* i.e., the amount to be ordered at any one time so as to minimize the associated total cost. This order quantity is commonly denoted by the symbol Q and its optimal value is denoted by EOQ or Q^*.

EOQ Formulas
Figure 6-3 shows an inventory system that satisfies all of the assumptions of an EOQ model. The inventory level goes through cycles—each of

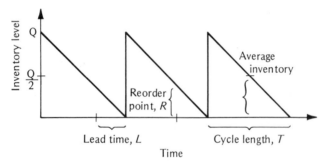

Figure 6-3. *The Parameters of an EOQ Model*

exactly the same length, say T. Each cycle begins with an inventory of size Q that is depleted at the rate Q/T per unit time. If the lead time is L, a new order is placed when the inventory level is $L \times Q/T$. In other words, the reorder point is $R = LQ/T$. Because the depletion rate is constant and because there are neither shortages or surpluses, the average inventory level is $Q/2$.

The Time Unit and Notations Traditionally, inventory operations are based on one year as a unit of time; though one month, one week, or one day might be more appropriate in specific situations. We will use the following notation:

Q = order quantity = number of units ordered in each cycle
T = length of each cycle
N = number of cycles per year
L = lead time
D = number of units demanded each year
R = reorder point
H = holding cost per unit per year
K = ordering cost per order
TC = total annual cost of inventory
C_h = annual holding cost
C_o = annual ordering cost

Annual Costs Since Q units are ordered each time and since the annual demand is D, there will be $N = D/Q$ orders each year. Since the per order cost is K, the annual ordering cost, C_o, equals:

$$C_o = \frac{KD}{Q}$$

Also, since the average inventory level is $Q/2$ units and since the per unit holding cost is H, the annual holding cost is:

$$C_h = \frac{HQ}{2}$$

The total annual cost of inventory, TC, is the sum of these two component costs since neither shortages nor surpluses are allowed in the basic EOQ model. Symbolically:

$$TC = C_o + C_h = \frac{KD}{Q} + \frac{HQ}{2}$$

The Economic Order Quantity, Q* Figure 6-4 shows the shapes of the TC, C_o, and C_h graphs as functions of Q. Note that as Q increases, C_o decreases and C_h increases. The total annual cost, TC, strikes a balance between these two. It first decreases rather sharply, reaches a low point,

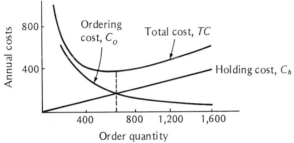

Figure 6-4. *The Components of EOQ Costs*

and then slowly rises as Q continues to increase. The value of the order quantity, say Q^*, as the lowest point on the TC curve is the required economic order quantity. There are two ways to obtain Q^*. From figure 6-4, you can note that TC is lowest when $C_o = C_h$. Thus, when order quantity is Q^*,

$$\frac{KD}{Q^*} = \frac{HQ^*}{2}$$

Alternatively, you can differentiate TC with respect to Q (an elementary exercise for those familiar with calculus), and then equate the derivative to zero. In either case, it is easy to verify that:

$$Q^* = \sqrt{\frac{2KD}{H}}$$

Other Parameters The model provides many other items of information besides the economic order quantity and the associated cost. For example, we have already seen that, the number of inventory cycles per year, N, equals:

$$N = \frac{D}{Q}$$

The length of a cycle, T, depends on the operational definition of one year. If every day is a workday, the year would consist of 365 or 366 days. If, a week contains only 5 workdays (say, Monday through Friday), a year would comprise $5 \times 52 = 260$ workdays. If you work for the U.S. Postal Service, each week has 6 workdays. Thus, a year would have $6 \times 52 = 312$ workdays. The specific figure depends on the nature of your decision maker's organization. If, for example, there are 365 workdays in a year, then the length of each cycle would be:

$$T = \frac{365}{N} = \frac{365 \times Q}{D}$$

Given the order size, Q, and the cost of purchasing (or producing) one unit, say U, you can compute the *dollar value of each order* to be: $U \times Q$. Similarly, the dollar value of average inventory equals: $U \times Q/2$.

When the order quantity is Q^*, each of these parameters would have its optimal value.

Example 1: The Milkland Dairy

The manager of this small, family-owned dairy products store has noticed that the demand for milk is independent of seasons. In fact, exactly 1,200 gallons of it is sold every week throughout the entire year. Because the demand is so steady, the manager buys just enough milk from a local farmer to meet each day's demand. The store is open six days a week. The farmer's milk truck arrives at the store early each workday.

Thus, customers can be served fresh milk without fail and everyone seems to be happy—that is, everyone except the manager's daughter who has been a student in the nearby school of management. Though she has yet to study inventory models, she knows by now that any manager who does not examine costs might not be operating at the optimal level.

After much discussion with her father and careful scrutiny of past records, she has found that:

1. It costs $2 to place each order for milk.
2. Half of a workday elapses between the placement of the order and the arrival of the milk truck.
3. Milk costs $1 per gallon.
4. Because milk must be stored at a carefully maintained temperature, the holding cost is rather high, in fact, 60¢ a gallon.

She has also noticed that the refrigerator in the store can hold up to 1,600

gallons of milk, if necessary. She feels that money can be saved by ordering a larger quantity of milk each time. Her father points out that when
more milk is ordered, the cost of carrying the inventory would rise also.
What would you recommend?

Having studied the EOQ model, you can recognize that both the
manager and his daughter have a point. Since the assumptions of the EOQ
model are valid in this case, a compromise is possible. In EOQ notation:

D = demand per year = $1,200 \times 52$ = 62,400 gallons
K = \$2 per order
L = lead time = 1/2 workday
H = 60¢ = \$0.6 per year per gallon

Hence, the economic order quantity, Q^*, equals:

$$Q^* = \sqrt{\frac{2KD}{H}} = \sqrt{\frac{2 \times 2 \times 62,400}{.6}} = 645 \text{ gallons}$$

If 645 gallons of milk is ordered each time, there will be D/Q^* =
62,400/645 = 96.75 orders each year, i.e., the milk inventory will go
through N = 96.75 cycles each year. The annual cost of ordering would
be:

$$C_o = KD/Q^* = \$2 \times 96.75 = \$193.50$$

The annual holding cost would be:

$$C_h = HQ/2 = \$0.6 \times 645/2 = \$193.50$$

The total annual cost would be:

$$TC = C_o + C_h = 2 \times \$193.50 = \$387.00$$

Compare this with the current policy of ordering Q = 200 gallons each
day. There are 6×52 = 312 cycles each year. This represents an annual ordering cost of $\$2 \times 312$ = \$624 plus annual holding cost of
$\$0.6 \times 100$ = \$60 for a total of $\$624 + 60$ = \$684. By following his daughter's advice, the manager will save $\$684 - \$387$ = \$297 each year.

On the other hand, since 200 gallons of milk are consumed each day
and since the lead time is a half day, the manager must place a new order
when the current supply is $200 \times 1/2$ = 100 gallons. In other words, the
reorder point, R, equals 100 gallons. This implies that he must now keep
track of his inventory instead of routinely accepting his daily milk delivery. That is an implicit requirement of the EOQ model.

Furthermore, the manager would need to have more cash on hand
than with the current policy. Since a gallon of milk costs him one dollar, in
the current policy he needs only $200 \times \$1$ = \$200 cash to accept the delivery of milk. The EOQ would require him to have \$645 on hand. The
standard EOQ model assumes that he can always do so.

We have not used the information that the dairy's refrigerator can store up to 1,600 gallons of milk, if necessary. Why, was this fact mentioned? When designing an inventory policy, it is crucial to know the system constraints. That the refrigerator cannot stock over 1,600 gallons is an important constraint. Since in this case, $Q^* = 645$ is less than the storage capacity, nothing more need be done about it. If, however, Q^* were to exceed 1,600, such a policy could not be implemented. Instead, we would have settled for $Q^* = 1,600$. We will return to this type of constraint in the following section. (See the discussion on price breaks.)

Sensitivity Analysis

Though the manager of Milkland Dairy is willing to put up with some of these inconveniences to minimize his total cost, he would like to know if a more convenient policy can be derived without an excessive increase in cost. He points out, for instance, that their store operates 6 days a week so that the inventory depletion rate is $1200 \div 6 = 200$ gallons each workday. Consequently, an order quantity of 645 gallons would last $645 \div 200 = 3.225$ workdays—a rather awkward fraction. Could he perhaps order either 600 or 800 gallons, so that the milk truck can always arrive in the mornings?

The answer in this case is yes since the total cost is relatively insensitive to moderate deviations from the optimal order quantity, Q^*. See figure 6-4 again which shows the graphs of TC, C_o, and C_h against order quantity, Q. That figure was constructed using the cost values in table 6-1. Both the figure 6-4 and table 6-1 convey the same message, i.e., moderate departures from Q^* produce only small changes in TC.

For example, consider $Q = 600$, a deviation of 45 gallons, i.e., $45/645 \approx 7$ percent from the optimal $Q^* = 645$. This rather moderate change is only \$1 (or equivalently only $1/387 \approx .25$ percent) more expensive than the optimal TC of \$387. Though the graph of TC might not be this "flat" in all situations, the point is that it is moderately so in all cases.

Table 6-1 *Annual Costs of Milkland Inventory*

ORDER QUANTITY (Q)	HOLDING COST (C_o)	ORDERING COST (C_h)	TOTAL COST (TC)
100	30	1,248	1,278
200	60	624	684
400	120	312	432
500	150	249.6	399.6
600	180	208	388
645	193.5	193.5	387
800	240	156	396
1,200	360	104	464
1,600	480	78	558

Furthermore, *positive deviations from Q* have less impact on the total cost than those of equally strong negative deviations.* Consider, for example $Q = 690$. You can check that $C_o = \$180.87$ and $C_h = 207$ so that $TC = 387.87$—an increase of 87¢ rather than \$1.

Refer again to the EOQ formula:

$$Q^* = \sqrt{\frac{2KD}{H}}$$

Note that the optimal order quantity does not increase or decrease as fast as the demand. For example, if the demand quadruples, the optimal order quantity only doubles. Similarly, if the demand is a quarter of what it used to be, the optimal order quantity would be half of its preceding value.

Both of these properties (the relative insensitivity of total cost to small deviations from the optimal order quantity and the relative insensitivity of the optimal order quantity to fluctuations in demand) are useful when deriving an optimal policy in the case of stochastic rather than constant demand. We will return to this point later.

VARIATIONS OF THE BASIC EOQ MODEL

The EOQ model is important for several reasons.

1. It is the simplest known model for cyclical inventory situations, i.e., those in which purchasing/production decisions have to be made repeatedly. As such, decision makers use it to avoid unnecessary clutter—as long as its assumptions are reasonably valid in specific situations.
2. Professors like it because it helps them explain several important concepts in a straightforward fashion.
3. Its insensitivity to moderate changes in input parameters allows the use of less than perfect data.
4. Its simplicity keeps the cost of obtaining optimal policies down—anyone with a pocket calculator can find Q^* in a few seconds.

In many real world situations, however, the basic model's assumptions cannot be met. Some of these include:

1. The basic model assumes that the *purchase/production price is independent of quantity ordered.* This assumption is perhaps the most untenable one in the face of frequent price breaks, also known as quantity discounts.
2. The basic model assumes *instantaneous replenishment* of stock. Though perhaps true in purchasing situations, it is often not the case when the product is manufactured in-house.

3. Even though the EOQ model is simple, when an organization must stock hundreds of products (e.g., in a supermarket or a department store) it cannot afford to collect the necessary data and compute Q^* for each item. Instead, they often use what is called an *A-B-C classification system.*

4. The basic model assumes that the *demand is known in advance and that it is steady.* This is seldom the case in real world inventory situations. There are two possibilities. If the demand is known with reasonable certainty but is seasonal, such as that for swimsuits or textbooks, the corresponding problems might be solved by the skillful use of transportation models (chapter 12), general linear models (chapters 10 and 15), or by dynamic programming methods. If, however, the demand is erratic but is reasonably normally distributed, the expected value of depletion rate can be used to obtain the optimal order quantity, Q^*. However, there is always a risk of shortages or surpluses which can be avoided (or at least minimized) by building what is known as *safety stocks.*

EOQ IN THE PRESENCE OF PRICE BREAKS

If you have done any purchasing, you know that sellers frequently offer discounts for buying larger quantities. But when you buy larger than necessary quantities of any product, annual holding costs rise. To derive an economic order quantity, there must be a trade off between price breaks and increases in holding cost. We will assume that all other assumptions of the basic EOQ model hold except that the unit purchase price is a function of the amount purchased.

Before proceeding with the technical discussion, let's review why quantity discounts exist. From the buyer's point of view, there is a lower unit price, less paperwork, cheaper transportation, and fewer stockouts (or at least fewer chances of a stockout). Also, since the units belong to the same batch, the products are more uniform. Furthermore, the buyer is secured against strikes in the seller's organization or delays due to bad weather. The seller is also happy because of the reduced paperwork, fewer trips, and the cost reduction realized with larger production runs. In short, both the buyer and seller get a better deal.

There are, of course, disadvantages associated with buying large quantities. As already mentioned, annual holding costs will be higher due to the larger inventories. Also, such products as medicine, film, vegetables, meat, and dairy products are more likely to spoil when purchased in larger quantities and hence stored longer. Such products as stereo equipment, pocket calculators, automobiles, and fashion items are more likely to become obsolete when stored for too long. Buying in larger quantities also requires more capital and more storage space. In short, obtaining quantity discounts is not necessarily the best policy. We will now consider the trade-off analysis in a simple situation.

Example 2: City General Hospital

The administrator of this hospital notes that 250 X-ray packages are used each month. When the cost of paperwork and transportation is included, it costs $10 to place a purchase order. Because X-ray plates must be stored in a dark, temperature controlled room, the storage costs are rather high. These costs and the quantity discounts available from the wholesaler of X-ray equipment are shown in table 6-2. The administrator would like to determine the most economical quantity after considering ordering, holding, and purchase costs.

Table 6-2 *Unit Costs of X-Ray Packages*

RANGE NUMBER	ORDER QUANTITY	UNIT COST ($) PURCHASE	HOLDING
1	0 – 199	14.00	10.00
2	200 – 999	13.00	9.50
3	1000 and up	12.00	9.00

Except for the price breaks, this model is similar to the basic EOQ model discussed in the preceding section. You can observe that:

$$D = \text{demand for X-ray plates per year}$$
$$= 250 \times 12 = 3,000$$

and:

$$K = \text{cost per order} = \$10$$

Hence, *if we were to ignore price breaks,* the optimal order quantity would be given by the formula:

$$Q^* = \sqrt{\frac{2KD}{H}} = \sqrt{\frac{60,000}{H}}$$

Since the smallest purchase price, $12.00, is obtained when the order quantity exceeds 1,000, let us begin by computing Q^* for that purchase price. The corresponding holding price is:

$$H = \$9$$

Hence, you can obtain the potentially optimal order quantity:

$$Q^* = \sqrt{\frac{60,000}{9}} \approx 82$$

The problem is that even though the unit price of $12.00 was used to derive Q^*, if we were to order 82 packages at a time, the supplier would not sell them for $12.00 a piece. As a matter of fact, to get the unit price of $12.00, *at least* 1,000 packages must be purchased at a time. However, since the optimal value (82) obtained by using the EOQ formula is *less* than the smallest order quantity in Range 3, it follows that ordering *more* than 1,000 plates at a time will not be most economical. In short, of all the order quantities in Range 3, the most economical order quantity is:

$$Q^*_3 = 1,200$$

The subscript, 3, identifies the applicable range.

The Procedure for Finding EOQ

As you can see from the previous example, if we ignore price breaks, we can obtain a most economical order quantity at each price level. If there were n price levels, there would be n potentially optimal order quantities: $Q^*_1, Q^*_2, \ldots, Q^*_n$. We must then decide among these optimal possibilities. This is the motivation underlying the following procedure. In following these steps let $P_1, P_2, \ldots, P_n$ denote the unit purchase prices and let $H_1, H_2, \ldots, H_n$ denote the unit holding prices in the order quantity ranges $R_1, R_2, \ldots, R_n$, respectively.

Step 1. Compute the EOQ for the smallest unit price, P_n, by using the formula:

$$Q^* = \sqrt{\frac{2KD}{H_n}}$$

If this EOQ belongs to the corresponding range, R_n, it must be optimal. STOP.

Otherwise, Set Q^*_n = smallest order quantity in range R_n. Compute the total cost at this price, TC_n, using the formula:

TC_n = ordering cost + holding cost + purchasing cost

$$= \frac{KD}{Q^*_n} + \frac{H\,Q^*_n}{2} + P_nD$$

Then proceed to Step 2.

In the case of City General Hospital, the smallest purchase price is: $P_3 = \$12.00$, the corresponding holding price is: $H_3 = \$9.00$ and in the range R_3, order quantity must be 1,000 or more. We have already seen that $Q^* = 82$ does not belong to this range, and hence that: $Q^*_3 = 1,000$. The total inventory cost, TC_3, in this case equals:

$$TC_3 = \frac{(\$10)(3,000)}{1,000} = \frac{(\$9)(1,000)}{2} + (\$12)(3,000)$$

$$= \$30 + 4,500 + 36,000 = \$40,530$$

Having done this, we can proceed to the next step.

Step 2. Compute EOQ for the next smallest price, P_{n-1}, and check if it belongs to the range R_{n-1}. If it does, compute the corresponding total cost, TC_{n-1} by using:

$$Q*_{n-1} = \text{computed EOQ}$$

Compare TC_{n-1} with TC_n and choose that order quantity which leads to the smaller total cost. STOP.

If the computed EOQ does not belong to R_{n-1}, set $Q*_{n-1} = $ smallest order size in range R_{n-1} and compute TC_{n-1}. Then continue the search at price level P_{n-2}.

For City General Hospital, the next smallest price is $P_2 = \$13.00$, the corresponding holding price is $H_2 = \$9.50$, and the order quantity must be between 200 and 999. Hence:

$$Q* = \sqrt{\frac{60,000}{H_2}} = \sqrt{\frac{60,000}{9.50}} \approx 79$$

Since it does not belong to the range R_2, we must set

$$Q*_2 = \text{smallest quantity in range } R_2$$
$$= 200$$

With this order quantity, the total cost will be:

$$TC_2 = \frac{(\$10)(30,000)}{200} + \frac{(\$9.50)(200)}{2} + (\$13)(3,000)$$
$$= \$150 + 950 + 39,000$$
$$= \$40,100$$

The search must continue since $Q*_2 = 200$ was not obtained using EOQ formula.

Step 3. At some price level, P_j, the computed EOQ will be in its appropriate range, R_j. At that stage, set $Q*_j = $ computed EOQ, derive TC_j, and choose the smallest of the total costs: $TC_j, TC_{j+1}, \ldots, TC_n$. The corresponding order quantity will be optimal.

At the next level, the purchase price is $P_1 = \$14.00$ per package and the unit holding price is $H_1 = \$10$. Hence, using the EOQ formula, you can obtain:

$$Q* = \sqrt{\frac{60,000}{H_1}} = \sqrt{\frac{60,000}{10}} \approx 77$$

Since this order quantity is in its proper range, we can set:

$$Q^*_1 = 77$$

The corresponding total cost will be:

$$TC_1 = \frac{(\$10)(3,000)}{77} + \frac{(\$10)(77)}{2} + (\$14)(3,000)$$
$$\approx \$390 + \$385 + \$42,000$$
$$= \$42,775$$

Since this order quantity was in its proper range, further search is unnecessary. Of the three potential total costs, the smallest is $TC_2 = \$40,100$. Hence, the optimal order quantity is EOQ = $Q^*_2 = 200$, and this means that 200 packages should be ordered at a time. With this quantity, you can achieve the best balance between ordering, holding, and purchase costs. The total cost with this policy would be $40,100 which is the smallest possible cost.

Note that this solution is not intuitively obvious. Many administrators would have chosen to order 1,000 packages at a time since it appears to provide "economies of scale." However, as we have seen, it is necessary to consider the increased holding costs associated with larger quantities before deciding an inventory policy. One must also consider the cash on hand necessary to take advantage of the quantity discounts. If, for example, only $2,000 could be spared for purchasing at any one time, then the policy of ordering 200 packages at a time becomes inoperative. In short, there is more to obtaining an inventory policy than just the knowledge of mathematical formulas.

ECONOMIC LOT SIZE (ELS) MODEL

The preceding two models, though applicable in some production situations, are more suitable when the necessary units are purchased from an outside source. In such cases, one can assume that the product arrives on a specific date and that it can be immediately stored, i.e., the replenishment is instantaneous and in effect occurs at an infinite rate. The model to be examined now is more suitable when the necessary quantities are produced in-house, say by another department of the company.

Some of the units will be used as soon as they are manufactured. Others will be stored to meet future demand. Naturally, the production rate must equal or exceed the depletion rate in order to have a meaningful inventory. The set up cost plays the role of the ordering cost.

All other assumptions of the basic EOQ model apply. For example, demand is known and it occurs at a uniform rate through the year. Lead time is known so that a new request for starting the production can be made as soon as the current inventory reaches the reorder point. In addition, the production rate is known. The only decision variable is the amount to be produced at any one time, i.e., the economic lot size (ELS). As in the basic EOQ model, this quantity is obtained by balancing the annual set-up cost and the annual holding cost—the only relevant components of the total cost.

ELS Concepts and Formulas

Let Q denote the lot size, i.e., the number of units to be produced during one production run. Since annual demand, D, is presumed to be known, you can see that the number of production runs per year, N, is given by the formula:

$$N = \frac{D}{Q}$$

Each production run starts a new inventory cycle of replenishment and depletion. Thus, the N of the above formula also denotes the number of inventory cycles each year. Since each production run implies a set-up cost of K dollars, the annual set up cost, C_o, equals:

$$C_o = K \times N = \frac{KD}{Q}$$

The length of each cycle, T, can be obtained as follows. Suppose that there are W workdays each year, then each cycle will last W/N workdays. Symbolically:

$$T = \frac{W}{N} = \frac{W}{D/Q} = \frac{WQ}{D}$$

Up to this point, the basic ELS model resembles the corresponding EOQ model. The lot size plays the role of the order quantity and the set-up cost is equivalent to the ordering cost.

Within each cycle, however, these two models differ considerably. In the production situation, each cycle is divided into two phases. In the first phase lasting T_1 workdays (see figure 6-5), the units are being pro-

Figure 6-5. *A Production-Depletion Cycle*

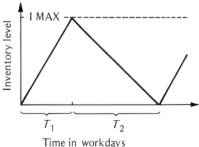

Time in workdays

duced as well as consumed. Since the production rate is larger than the depletion rate, the inventory continues to rise until it reaches a peak value, $IMAX$. At that moment, the production stops and the inventory goes through a depletion phase. This phase lasts for T_2 workdays—until there are no more units in the inventory. The next cycle begins at that moment. The complete cycle lasts for $T = T_1 + T_2$ workdays. We will now proceed to compute T_1, T_2, $IMAX$, and the other relevant items of information.

Let P denote the *annual production capacity* so that during the production phase lasting T_1 workdays, P/W units will be coming out of the assembly line each workday. Since production continues until a batch of Q units has been produced, it follows that:

$$T_1 = \text{number of production days in a cycle}$$
$$= \text{lot size} \div \text{production rate}$$
$$= Q \div \frac{P}{W} = \frac{WQ}{P}$$

Note that during the production phase, P/W units are produced and D/W units are consumed each workday. Hence, the inventory increases at the rate of $P/W - D/W = (P - D)/W$ units each workday. There being T_1 workdays in this phase, the maximum inventory, $IMAX$, is given by:

$$IMAX = (\text{accumulation rate}) \times (\text{production days})$$
$$= \frac{P - D}{W} \times \frac{WQ}{P} = \frac{(P - D)Q}{P}$$

During the depletion phase lasting T_2 workdays, the inventory is exhausted at the rate of D/W units each workday. Hence, the duration of the depletion phase is:

$$T_2 = \text{maximum inventory} \div \text{depletion rate}$$
$$= \frac{(P - D)Q}{P} \div \frac{D}{W} = \frac{W(P - D)Q}{DP}$$

The average inventory in any one cycle equals $IMAX/2$, so that the annual holding cost is:

$$C_h = \text{average inventory} \times \text{cost per unit per year}$$
$$= \frac{(P - D)QH}{2P}$$

Combining the annual set-up cost and the annual holding cost yields the total cost of inventory:

$$TC = C_o + C_h = \frac{KD}{Q} + \frac{(P - D)HQ}{2P}$$

The only unknowns in the above equation are TC and Q. The most economic lot size (ELS or Q^*) is obtained either by equating C_o and C_h or by differentiating TC with respect to Q and then setting the derivative to zero. Either way, the most economic lot size, Q^*, equals:

$$Q^* = \sqrt{\frac{2PKD}{H(P - D)}}$$

As in the case of EOQ, you can plot TC, C_o, and C_h as functions of Q. You will find that these graphs resemble those shown in figure 6-4. The graph of TC in the neighborhood of Q^* is relatively flat, so that small deviations from Q^* do not seriously increase TC. Practically speaking, any convenient lot size in the vicinity of Q^* can be used as the desired lot size.

Example 3: Production of Headlights

Suppose that an automobile manufacturer produces 50,000 cars in a year of 250 workdays and that the production continues at a steady rate of 50,000/250 = 200 cars per workday. The company uses 4 headlights per car. The headlight section of the company can manufacture 600,000 units each year. The set-up cost is $100 and then each unit costs an additional $1.00 to assemble. The storage cost is 20 percent of the incremental production cost. Given this data, what is the optimal lot size and what is the least annual inventory cost? If it takes 7 workdays to schedule a production run, what must the reorder point be?

Solution. You can easily check that:

P = 600,000 headlights per year
D = 50,000 cars per year × 4 headlights per car
   = 200,000 headlights per year
K = $100 per set up
H = 20 percent of incremental cost
   = 20¢ = $.2 per head lamp per year and
W = 250 workdays per year

Hence, the optimal lot size, Q^*, equals:

$$Q^* = \sqrt{\frac{2PKD}{H(P - D)}} = \sqrt{\frac{(2)(600,000)(100)(200,000)}{(.2)(600,000 - 200,000)}}$$

   = 17,321 headlights per batch

The annual set-up cost, C_o, equals:

$$C_o = \frac{KD}{Q} = \frac{(\$100)(200,000)}{17,321} = \$1,154.67$$

The annual carrying cost, C_h, equals:

$$C_h = \frac{(P-D)QH}{2P} = \frac{(600,000-200,000)(17,321)(.2)}{(2)(600,000)}$$

$$= \$1,154.73$$

Note that $C_o \approx C_h$, the difference of 6¢ being attributable to rounding off. As in the basic EOQ model, the optimal lot size balances the set-up and holding costs so that $C_o = C_h$ provides a check on computational accuracy.

$$TC = C_o + C_h = \$2,309.40$$

Finally, since 200 cars × 4 = 800 headlights are used daily, 800 × 7 = 5,600 of these will be used in the time it takes to reschedule a new run. Thus, the reorder point is 5,600 head lamps.

Additional Information Since the economical lot size is 17,321 headlights, it follows that there will be:

$N = 200,000/17,321 = 11.55$ inventory cycles each year

Each cycle will last:

$T = 250/11.55 = 21.65$ workdays

Each cycle will contain a production phase of T_1 workdays, where:

$T_1 = (250)(17,321)/600,000 = 7.22$ workdays

During this phase, the peak inventory will be:

$IMAX = (600,000 - 200,000)(17,321)/(600,000) \approx 11,547$ units

The inventory will be depleted in T_2 workdays, where:

$T_2 = T - T_1 = 21.65 - 7.22 = 14.43$

The new production phase will begin at this stage. Figure 6-6 summarizes the workings of one inventory cycle.

PROBABILISTIC DEMAND AND SAFETY STOCKS

To consider another variation of the basic EOQ model, we will continue to assume that the cost per order and the holding cost per unit stored in inventory are known and constant. It is often safe to make these two assumptions. However, the demand for a product rarely occurs at a steady rate—either because it changes from season to season or because it is erratic. Some simple situations of the former type will be considered in the chapter on general linear optimization models, as well as in the chapter on transportation models. (See chapters 10 and 12.)

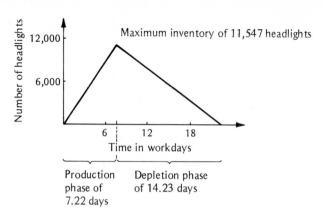

Figure 6-6. *The Headlights Inventory Cycle*

In this section, we will assume that the demand is erratic (random), i.e., the number of units consumed each workday is a random variable. We will also assume that the standard deviation of this variable is small compared to its mean. Under these circumstances, it is fairly safe to substitute the *average depletion rate*, $\bar{D}$, in place of the constant depletion rate, D, while deriving the economic order quantity. Specifically, let:

H = holding cost per unit per year
K = cost of placing one order
$\bar{D}$ = average annual demand

Then, arguing as in the basic EOQ model, you can verify the optimal order quantity to be:

$$Q^* = \sqrt{\frac{2K\bar{D}}{H}}$$

As we had already seen while examining that model, the total of the annual ordering and holding costs is rather insensitive to moderate deviations from Q^*. Furthermore, Q^* itself does not change as rapidly as the demand. For example, if the demand increases by 20 percent, Q^* increases only by 9.5 percent. Conversely, if the demand decreases by 20 percent, Q^* decreases only by 10.6 percent. In other words, using the average demand yields a satisfactory answer to the how-much-to-order question. The when-to-order question is much more difficult to answer.

The Buffer Stock and Service Level

Throughout this section, we will assume that lead time is known and is constant. That is, the time elapsed between the placing of an order to replenish and actual delivery of the product is known to us, and that it does not change from one ordering occasion to the next. Suppose, for example, that the lead time for a product is one week and that during that week, an average of 1,000 units would be needed.

According to the basic EOQ model, the reorder point would be $R = 1,000$ units, i.e., the order to replenish the inventory would be issued when the current inventory is 1,000 units. However, since the actual demand during lead time is random, this reorder policy can run into difficulty. Depending on whether the actual demand is more or less than anticipated, there would be either a surplus inventory or a shortage (stockout). See figure 6-7(a). A moderate surplus might not pose a serious problem except that both the maximum inventory level and the annual holding cost will be higher. A shortage, on the other hand, poses a more serious problem. There might be an associated loss of goodwill (customers seldom like to wait and they might turn to a competitor). If the product is an essential raw material, such as sheet metal used in automobiles, the stockout could shut down the automobile assembly line. This could cost as much as $20,000 per minute! A shortage of the appropriate type of blood during surgery might cost a patient's life. In general, a shortage tends to disrupt the smooth flow of activity (recall the long waiting lines during the oil crisis of the winter of 1973), and hence most organizations opt for an inventory policy which would either eliminate shortages or minimize the probability of their occurrence.

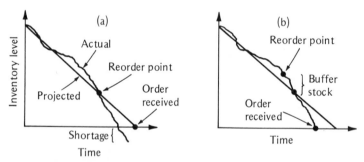

Figure 6-7. *Shortages and Buffer Stocks*

One obvious solution is to maintain what is known as a safety or buffer stock. See figure 6-7(b). To illustrate the concept, suppose we order a new batch of the product whenever the current inventory is $R = 1,300$ units. Then the difference: $1,300 - 1,000 = 300$ units represents the *buffer stock*. In general:

buffer stock = reorder point − average lead time demand

The buffer stock cushions the impact of unforeseen excess demand. Naturally, the larger the buffer stock, the smaller the chances of a stockout or shortage during lead time.

Note, however, that maintaining a safety stock in effect increases the inventory level and hence the inventory carrying cost. Thus, if the cost of a shortage is not prohibitive, management would probably plan to experience occasional shortages rather than carry an excessively large buffer stock. Thus, the question: When to reorder? is equivalent to the question: What is the desirable level of buffer stock?

To answer the latter question, it is necessary to introduce the concept of the *service level* of an inventory policy, which is the probability of not experiencing a shortage during lead time. Naturally, if the service level is higher, the buffer stock will be too. If the service level is lower, one is more likely to experience a shortage. How does one determine the service level? There are two possibilities:

1. If the cost of a unit shortage can be estimated with reasonable accuracy, the marginal analysis techniques discussed in chapter 4 can be used to derive the service level.
2. In many organizations, the operating room of a hospital for example, it is difficult if not impossible to estimate the cost of a unit shortage. In such cases, the service level is set by administrative decree.

In any event, having decided the service level, the value of the buffer stock is obtained by using the probability distribution (or probability density function, as the case may be) of the lead time demand. We will illustrate the procedures in the next two subsections.

The Economic Reorder Point

In this subsection we will assume that the cost of a unit shortage during lead time can be estimated with reasonable accuracy. In fact, let:

$$s = \text{cost of being one unit short}$$

Obviously, if we increase the reorder point from R to $R + 1$, i.e., if we place the new order when the current inventory is $R + 1$, rather than waiting till it becomes R, we can reduce the shortage by 1 unit. This translates into a saving of s dollars, as long as that additional unit is needed. In the terms used in chapter 4, the marginal gain due to a unit increase in reorder point is s dollars on each ordering occasion.

If the average annual demand is for $\overline{D}$ units of a product, and if we order Q^* units each time, it follows that there will be:

$$N = \frac{D}{Q^*} \text{ orders each year}$$

Putting together these two observations, we conclude that the gain due to a unit increase in reorder point is given by:

marginal gain $= s \times \overline{D}/Q$ each year

$\qquad\qquad = $ cost of a unit shortage $\times$ number of orders each year

On the other hand, if this additional unit is not used prior to receiving the new shipment, we would have incurred excessive holding cost.

Thus, the *marginal loss* due to a unit increase in reorder point *equals this carrying cost, H* dollars per year.

By using the arguments presented in chapter 4, you can now verify the following decision rules:

1. The desired service level equals the ratio:

$$\frac{\text{marginal gain}}{\text{marginal gain} + \text{marginal loss}} = \frac{S\bar{D}}{S\bar{D} + HQ}$$

2. If the demand during lead time is a continuous random variable, then the most economical reorder point, R, is obtained by solving:

$$F(R) = \text{service level}$$

where $F(R)$ is the probability of using, at most, R units of the product during lead time.

3. If the product must be ordered in an integral number of units, then increase the reorder point from R to $R + 1$ as long as:

$$F(R) < \text{service level}$$

We will now illustrate the process by solving a simple problem where the cost of unit shortage is known.

Example 4: Safety Stock of Washing Machines

A department store buys Brand X washing machines for $300 and sells them for $375 each. The selling cost (including the salesperson's time, displays, and advertising) is $30, so that the actual profit per machine is $45. This profit will be lost if the store does not have a machine on hand when the customer wants it. But, a large stockpile of washing machines can be expensive, the annual carrying cost being 20 percent of the inventory value.

The ordering cost, including paperwork, transportation and inspection, is $50 per order. The demand is probabilistic but without any pattern (as to season or trend). Table 6-3 shows the frequency distribution of weekly demand for the past two years, i.e., 100 weeks. Lead time is one week. The store manager would like to know: how often to place an order, how much to order each time, and when to place a new order.

Computing the Economic Order Quantity Note that this example satisfies all of the assumptions of the basic EOQ model except that the demand is stochastic rather than steady. You should have no difficulty in deriving the necessary parameters. Thus, the cost per order is: $K = \$50$ per order. The holding cost per machine per year is 20 percent of purchase price, i.e., $H = .2 \times \$300 = \$60$. Using the relative frequencies as estimated probabilities, you can determine the average demand to be 3

Table 6-3 *History of Washing Machine Demand*

WEEKLY DEMAND	FREQUENCY	RELATIVE FREQUENCY	CUMULATIVE PROBABILITY
0	1	.01	.01
1	8	.08	.09
2	23	.23	.32
3	34	.34	.66
4	26	.26	.92
5	8	.08	1.00
	100	1.00	

washers per week. Since this store operates for 50 weeks per year, the annual demand averages to: $\bar{D} = 50 \times 3 = 150$ washers per year. Hence, the economical order quantity is:

$$Q^* = \frac{\sqrt{2K\bar{D}}}{H} = \sqrt{\frac{(2)\,(\$50)\,(150)}{\$60}} \approx 15.81$$

As a practical matter, they should purchase $Q^* = 16$ washers each time. Thus, there will be:

$$N = \bar{D}/Q^* = 150/16 = 9.375 \text{ orders each year}$$

Given this data, we are now ready to derive the economical reorder point.

Deriving the Service Level and the Reorder Point Since a profit of $45 will be lost if the shop is out of a washing machine, $s = \$45$ so that:

$$\text{marginal gain} = \$45 \times 9.375$$
$$= \$421.875 \text{ each year}$$

Marginal loss equals the annual holding cost of $H = \$60$. Hence:

$$\text{service level} = \frac{\$421.875}{\$421.875 + \$60} \approx .875$$

The probability of selling at most x washing machines in one week, $F(x)$, is already shown in the last column of table 6-3. Since $F(3) = .66$ is less than the service level of .875, but $F(4) = .92$ exceeds .875, it follows that the most economical reorder point is: $R = 4$.

Reorder Point as a Function of the Service Level

As another example of deriving the reorder point given the desirable service level, consider a hospital that would like to maintain a service level of .95. This hospital uses an average of 60 gallons of a product each week. The actual usage each week has a standard deviation of 7 gallons.

Past data indicates that the usage is normally distributed. If the lead time is one week, when should the hospital order a new batch of this product?

In the notation used in chapter 2, the service level equals the "area under the standard normal curve." The numerical values of this area can be obtained from appendix A. In general, if you wish the service level to be α, then obtain the standard normal abscissa Z_α to be such that $F(Z_\alpha) = \alpha$. If the standard deviation of the lead time demand is σ units, then the buffer stock would equal: $Z_\alpha \cdot \sigma$. If the average demand during lead time is μ units, then the reorder point would be:

$$R = \mu + Z_\alpha \cdot \sigma$$

For the hospital problem, service level is $\alpha = .95$. From appendix A, you can obtain that $F(1.64) = .95$. Hence, $Z_\alpha = 1.64$. The standard deviation of the weekly usage is $\sigma = 7$ gallons. Hence, management should maintain a buffer stock of: $Z_\alpha \cdot \sigma = 1.64 \times 7 = 11.48$ gallons. Since the average weekly demand is $\mu = 60$ gallons, management should order a new batch when the present supply becomes $R = 60 + 11.48 = 71.48$ gallons. As a practical matter, the management should place a new order whenever the current inventory becomes 72 gallons. This would ensure a service level of at least 95 percent.

The A-B-C Classification

If you are considering only one product at a time, the computations necessary to use the basic EOQ model are fairly simple and straightforward. Many organizations carry such a large number of products in their inventories, however, that applying even this simple model to each product becomes impractical. L. M. Austin (1977) reports, for example, that Air Force Logistics Command carries an active inventory of 250,000 items. Thus, to properly apply the EOQ model, such organizations would have to keep track of demand, ordering cost, and carrying costs for literally thousands of items—a Herculean task indeed. Large department stores, grocery stores, and airlines are other examples of organizations that carry thousands of items in their inventories.

Such organizations, therefore, must decide which products deserve a thorough analysis using EOQ and/or more sophisticated models and others for which a "rule of thumb" policy might be satisfactory. One common scheme is the so called A-B-C classification system. Pareto analysis is another name for this scheme. It is based on an observation by Pareto (1848–1923), that a very small proportion of items usually accounts for the majority of value: profit or cost. The A-B-C scheme divides the total number of items in stock into three classes: A, B, and C and then recommends different analytical strategies in each case.

A items. This group contains 10 to 15 percent of all items which jointly account for 70 to 80 percent of the total annual inventory costs. As you can imagine, the actual percentages (and hence the demarcation boundaries) vary depending on the nature of the business. No absolute rule is proposed here. The EOQ or other more appropriate model is used to determine the best inventory policy (how much to order or when to order) for each product in this group. The relevant parameters (such as, demand, purchase price, and ordering cost) are updated frequently. Special-purpose forecasting techniques (such as, exponential smoothing; decomposition technique which isolates trend, seasonal, and cyclical effects; and linear regression) might be used as appropriate.

B items. Roughly 10 to 15 percent of the items are in this group and together they account for 15 to 20 percent of inventory costs. Applying an EOQ model might still be worthwhile, but input data is updated less frequently—once a month or once every quarter, depending on the speed and size of changes.

C items. The remaining 70 to 80 percent of the items account for only about 10 to 15 percent of inventory costs. Thus, keeping close watch on the changes in their input data or applying specialized inventory policies is more costly than potential savings accrued through such effort. The items are ordered on the basis of experience or whenever the stock is depleted. Management by exception is the guiding principle in this case.

WHAT A MANAGER SHOULD KNOW

The inventory models are important to modern managers because properly maintained inventories provide cost-effective ways of smoothing out the production process, meeting erratic or seasonal demand, guarding against inflation and irregularities in supply, obtaining quantity discounts, and minimizing the ordering or set-up costs. They are also important because, apart from accomplishing all of the above, inventory models also impart "a systems point of view." A properly derived inventory policy must consider all aspects of an organization: finance, marketing, production, and human relations.

A fully developed inventory policy responds to such questions as:

1. How much to order (on any one occasion)?
2. When to order?
3. What is the appropriate service level, and hence what is the reasonable buffer stock?
4. Where to stock the items, i.e., where to locate a warehouse?
5. What is the right mix of professionals for staffing an inventory?
6. How to keep track of inventory levels?
7. Should inventory records be computerized?

In this chapter, we have examined a few of the formal models for responding to questions 1 through 3. We will outline ways to respond to questions 4 and 5 in chapters 10 through 12. Questions 6 and 7 belong to the province of management information systems.

Most of the models in the present chapter study the issue of inventories from the viewpoint of a retailer, i.e., without regard to the production process. The models, wherein the effects of hiring, firing, overtime, idle time as well as inventory costs are explicitly examined over a planning horizon of several months, go by the name of aggregate planning. A simple situation of this type will be examined in chapter 10.

The models discussed in this chapter describe perhaps the simplest inventory situations. Yet, because the total inventory cost is rather insensitive to small deviations from the optimal solutions, the use of these models allows the management a great deal of flexibility. For this reason, such models give satisfactory results even when reality does not precisely match the formal models.

The models discussed in this chapter are known as the fixed reorder quantity models since the amount ordered (or produced) on each occasion is constant, though the time between orders might vary depending on demand. Alternatively, one can place a new order at fixed time intervals, e.g., once every month. Such policies are known as the fixed cycle policies. The amount ordered each time varies according to the perceived need till the next ordering occasion. The combination of these two policies is known as the optional replenishment policies. The interested reader should consult the references at the end of this chapter.

The models in this chapter implicitly assume that the product under scrutiny is nonperishable, so that only the ordering or set-up cost, storage cost, and purchase price or incremental production cost are the relevant costs. Many items, such as, vegetables, dairy products, and blood, do not belong to this category. Several references at the end of this chapter should be consulted if you need to make decisions about perishable items.

The references should also be consulted if you need to simultaneously decide the production schedules of multiple items, or in situations where storage capacity is limited or where backordering is allowed. The corresponding models are too complex to be explored at the level of an introductory text—knowledge of calculus and simulation is needed to derive the corresponding strategies.

In a sense, the inventories and waiting lines are two sides of the same problem. If an organization employs too many people, it would not only incur a large "holding cost" but the employees themselves would experience excessive idle time. On the other hand, employing too few people results in shortages as well as excessive delays. We have presented one view of the situation in this chapter. It will be re-examined from a different angle in the following chapter.

SELECTED READINGS

AUSTIN, L. M. "Project EOQ: A Success Story in Implementing Academic Research." *Interfaces* vol. 7, no. 4 (1977), pp. 1–14.

COHEN, M. A. "Analysis of Single Critical Number Ordering Policies for Perishable Inventories." *Operations Research*, 24 (1976), pp. 726–741.

DAELLENBACH, H. G. "A Model of a Multi-Product Two-Stage Inventory System with Limited Intermediate Bulk Storage Capacity." *Management Science* 23 (1977), pp. 1314–1320.

DUMAS, M. B. and RABINOWITZ, M. "Policies for Reducing Blood Wastage in Hospital Blood Banks." *Management Science* 23 (1977), pp. 1124–1132.

ELSTON, R. C. "BLOOD BANK INVENTORIES." *CRC Critical Reviews in Clinical Laboratory Sciences*, July 1976.

FRIES, B. E. "Optimal Ordering Policy for a Perishable Commodity with Fixed Lifetime." *Operations Research* 23 (1975), pp. 46–61.

GREEN, J. H. *Production and Inventory Control Handbook*. New York: McGraw-Hill Book Co., 1970.

JENNINGS, J. B. "Blood Bank Inventory Control." *Management Science* 19 (1973), pp. 637–645.

NAHMIAS, N. "On Ordering Perishable Inventory When Both Demand and Lifetime Are Random." *Management Science* 24 (1977), pp. 82–90.

NAHMIAS, S. AND PIERSKALLA, W. P. "Optimal Ordering Policies for Perishable Inventory–I." *Proceedings of the Twentieth International Meeting, TIMS* 2 (1973), pp. 485–493.

NAHMIAS, S. "Optimal Ordering Policies for Perishable Inventory–II." *Operations Research* 23 (1975), pp. 735–749.

NILAND, P., *Production Planning, Scheduling and Inventory Control: A Text and Cases*. New York: MacMillan Publishing Co., 1972.

ORAL, M.; SALVADOR, M. S.; REISMAN, A.; AND DEAN, B. V. "On the Evaluation of Shortage Costs for Inventory Control of Finished Goods." *Management Science* 18 (1972), pp. B344–351.

RESH, M.; FRIEDMAN, M.; AND BARBOSA, L. C. "On a General Solution of the Deterministic Lot Size Problem with Time-Proportional Demand." *Operations Research* 24 (1976), pp. 718–726.

ROSENSHINE, M. AND OBEE, D. "Analysis of a Standing Order Inventory with Emergency Orders." *Operations Research* 24 (1976), pp. 1143–1155.

SILVER, E. A. "A Simple Method of Determining Order Quantities in Joint Replenishment under Deterministic Demand." *Management Science* 22 (1976), pp. 1351–1361.

TERSINE, R. J. *Material Management and Inventory Control*. New York: Elsevier-North Holland, 1976.

THOMAS, A. B. *Inventory Control in Production and Management*. Boston: Cahners Publishing Co., 1970.

PROBLEM SET 6
OPTIMAL INVENTORY POLICIES

1. The Whirlwind Company buys the motors for its lawn mowers from Crag and Tatum Inc. for $25 each. The Whirlwind assembles 20 lawn mowers on each of the 250 workdays per year. When shipping, paperwork and inspection costs are added, the ordering costs are $100 per order. The carrying cost per motor is estimated to be 20 percent of the purchase price. Past experience shows that one must place the order 7 workdays in advance.

   a. How many Crag and Tatum motors should be in each batch?

b. What should be the reorder point?

c. What is sum of inventory related costs?

2. The manager of the Whirlwind Company would always like to receive the new batch of motors at the start of a workday. In that case,

   a. What is the most economical order quantity?

   b. What is the cash value of their average inventory?

3. Alpha Electronics purchases the transistors for its ABC-1500 stereo receivers at 40¢ a piece. The company assembles 60 receivers every day and each receiver uses 25 transistors. The holding cost is 25 percent of the purchase price and the ordering cost is $15 each time. The employees of Alpha Electronics enjoy liberal vacation benefits and so each year contains 240 workdays only. The transistors are shipped in boxes containing exactly 200 transistors per box. Only a whole number of boxes can be ordered.

   a. Determine the most economical number of boxes to be ordered each time.

   b. How long will each batch of transistors last?

   c. What is the average number of orders per year?

4. A manufacturer uses $60,000 worth of valves each year of 300 workdays. The cost per order is $40 and the carrying cost is 30 percent of the cash value. Under these circumstances, how many dollars worth of valves should be purchased each time?

5. The ABC manufacturing company buys a certain ingredient in containers which occupy 8 square feet of floor space each. The company's warehouse space for storing these boxes is limited to 2,000 square feet of floor space. Each year, the company needs 10,000 containers worth of raw material at a constant rate throughout the year. The ordering cost is $15 per order and carrying cost is $2.00 per container. Fractional number of boxes are not delivered.

   a. What is the most economical order quantity in this case?

   b. What is the total inventory cost per year?

   c. How much could the company save if the space were unlimited?

6. Baker Motor Inns operates an Innkeeper Training School for its prospective employees. Each session lasts a month. The Baker Inns must engage instructors on a variety of topics, provide living quarters for each instructor, as well as provide for laboratory sessions, etc. Hence, as long as the number of trainees per session does not exceed 20, the cost per session is practically independent of class size; past records show this cost to be $10,000 per session. The company pays each graduate $850 per month stipend until he/she can be employed as a full-time innkeeper. All positions are filled on a first come first served basis. Because the company is growing, 6 positions become available each month.

   a. How many graduates must the training school create in each session?

b. What is the optimal number of sessions per year?

c. What is the total annual cost of this program?

d. If only 4 out of 5 trainees successfully complete the course, how many trainees must be admitted each time?

7. Jason Morebuck and Company sells rug shampooers through its local outlet. Each machine costs $60. When the cost of storage, insurance and finance is considered, the carrying cost is 16 percent of purchase price. Ordering cost is $40. The store sells 5,000 shampooers each year.

   a. What is the economical order quantity?

   b. Each shampooer comes in a box. This box occupies 4 square feet of floor space. How much floor space must the store have for storing each complete shipment?

   c. If the store has only 600 square feet of floor space, is it worth renting additional space for $2 a square foot per year?

8. The automobile manufacturer of example 3 is inclined to close the headlights division of the company in favor of buying the lights from an outside source. The ordering cost would be $15 and each light could be purchased for $1.05. The demand for lamps would remain unchanged at 200,000 per year and the carrying cost would be 20 percent of the incremental cost.

   a. What would the economic order quantity be and how many orders would need to be placed each year?

   b. What is the total annual cost of this alternative (holding, ordering, and purchase)?

   c. Should the company buy or make headlights?

9. The Cheaper Motors Corporation is willing to sell its lawn mower motors to the Whirlwind Company of problem 1. If Whirlwind orders 1,000 or more motors at a time, Cheaper Motors is offering to sell them for $23.75 each.

   a. What is the most economic order quantity if the motors are purchased from the Cheaper Motors?

   b. What is the total annual cost of this alternative?

   c. Who should be Whirlwind's supplier: Crag and Tatum or Cheaper Motors?

10. A wealthy investor has expendable income of $1,000 per week. He deposits his money in a savings bank until he has Q dollars in the account at which time he buys tax-free bonds which yield an 8 percent return on investment. His broker's commission is 1.5 percent of the bond purchase price, plus $40 for paper work. Because of his tax bracket, the interest on the savings account is worth only 3 percent per year. Assume that a year has exactly 52 weeks, and that bonds can be purchased in multiples of $1,000.

    a. What is the optimal value of Q?

    b. What is the total annual cost (ordering, holding, and purchase) of his investment program? (Hint: The difference between the returns on investment is his "holding cost" per year. Broker's commission is similar to the purchase price, and paperwork cost is equivalent to ordering cost.)

11. A company has a petty cash fund which is used at the steady rate of $2,000 per month. The fund is replenished from a savings account which pays 5 percent interest. The company sends a "Go For" boy and a security guard to the bank whenever money is to be withdrawn from the savings account. This operation costs $8 in salary and transportation costs. What is the optimal withdrawal schedule?

12. Since the Alpha Electronics of problem 3 needs large number of transistors each year, the company is negotiating a price breaks policy with its supplier. The supplier is willing to offer a 35¢-per-transistor price if Alpha will order at least 12,000 units each time.

    a. What would be the most economic order quantity corresponding to the 35¢ purchase price?

    b. What would be the total annual cost at 35¢ purchase price?

    c. Which purchase price, 35¢ or 40¢, yields the smallest total cost each year?

13. Infant Village, a large day care center, needs 80 boxes of disposable diapers each of the 5 days per week the center is open. To ensure the sanity of its employees, the Village has a liberal vacation policy—two weeks off during August to relax on the beach, two weeks during January to enjoy ski season, and two more weeks to celebrate holidays. The ordering costs are $60 for orders of 2,000 or less boxes and $75 for larger orders. The carrying cost turns out to be 20 percent of purchase cost. A local wholesaler is willing to offer variable unit prices depending on the order quantity. These are shown in the adjoining table.

NUMBER OF BOXES	UNIT PRICE
0 – 1,999	2.50
2,000 – 5,999	2.40
6,000 and up	2.30

    a. Derive the economic order quantity at each unit price.

    b. Obtain the total annual costs for each candidate inventory policy.

    c. Identify the best policy.

14. An organization needs 3000 units of a product every year. The estimated ordering cost is $50 for a batch of 499 units or less, $75 for a batch of between 500 and 1999 units, and $100 each for larger batches. On the other hand, the unit purchase price is $12 each for up to 499 units; $11 each for between 500 and 1999 units, and $10 each for an order of 2000 units or more. It costs $6 to store one unit for one year.

    a. Find the most economic order quantity for each ordering cost-purchase price combination.

    b. Identify the best ordering policy.

15. Consider again the problem of Alpha Electronics. The management wants to know whether to produce the transistors in-house. A committee composed of engineers and accountants has determined that the cost of setting up a production run is $100, but once it is set up, manufacturing a transistor would cost 30¢ each. The holding cost is 7.5¢ per transistor per year. It is estimated that 4500 transistors can be manufactured each day. The factory is open 240 days each year.

    a. Determine the most economical number of transistors to produce in each batch.

    b. What is the total annual cost (set up, production, and holding) of this policy?

    c. Should Alpha Electronics make or buy their transistors?

16. An organization assembles a special component for later use in the production of a final product. For 250 workdays in the year, there is a demand for 10,000 components. The cost of storing a component is $15 per year.

    The production capacity using a small machine is 40,000 components per year. The set-up cost is $100. The daily cost of production is $300.

    a. Determine the most economical production run.

    b. What is the maximum number of components in the inventory?

    c. What is the total annual cost of production using the above production policy?

17. The organization in problem 16 can use a larger machine with a production capacity of 80,000 components per year. The set-up cost for this machine is $300 and daily cost of production is $500.

    a. Determine the most economical production run using the larger machine.

    b. What is the total annual cost using the larger machine?

    c. Which of these two machines should be used for assembling the components?

18. An electronics firm needs 120,000 feet of wire each day. The holding cost is $3 per thousand per day. The fixed cost (set-up or ordering) is $50 if purchased from an outside source and $300 if manufactured in-house. Incremental cost is $40 per thousand feet if purchased, but $35 per thousand if produced in-house. Also, the in-house production capacity is 600,000 feet per day whereas the replenishment is instantaneous if purchased.

    a. What is the least cost if the wire is made in-house?

    b. What is the least cost if the wire is purchased?

    c. What would you recommend?

19. The cost of a safety or buffer stock equals the cost of carrying the buffer stock units in inventory. The cost of safety stock rises much more rapidly than the increase in the service level. To see this, suppose that the lead time for a product is 1 week, and that the standard deviation of lead-time demand is $\sigma = 100$ units. Suppose the holding cost is $1 per unit per year. Assume the

lead-time demand to be normally distributed. Compute the costs of maintaining the buffer stocks corresponding to the service level of .5, .6, .7, .8, .85, .9, .95, .96, .97, .98, and .99. Then, plot these costs against service levels.

20. Noisy Mufflers Inc. has noticed that, on the average, 36 mufflers are used every week. The demand is erratic but without any pattern. The manager's statistician friend has noted that it would be safe to assume that the demand is normal with a standard deviation of 6 mufflers per week. Since the muffler manufacturer does not have a warehouse nearby, the mufflers must be purchased by mail. Consequently, there is a lead time of one week. The muffler shop would like to maintain a service level of 98 percent. What should their safety stock be? What is the reorder point? (Only integer values of these two parameters are meaningful.)

21. The Forever Needy Surgical Center has noted that it needs 20 pints of a particular type of blood per day. This is, of course, an average usage. The actual usage appears to follow the Normal Probability Law with $\sigma = 4$ pints. For various reasons, it takes 5 days to procure a new batch of blood. Running out of blood in the midst of a surgical procedure can be fatal. Thus, the center does not want this to happen more than once out of 500 times. What is the appropriate safety stock? What is the reorder point? If storage costs 50¢ per pint per day, what is the cost of safety?

22. A company has noticed that a shortage costs $50 per unit. Their EOQ analysis indicates that it is most economical to order 8 times each year. It costs $30 to store one unit for one year. The adjoining table shows $F(x)$, the probability of needing at most x units during lead time.

x	100	120	150	180	200	250
$F(x)$	.7	.8	.9	.93	.98	1

What should be their reorder point?

23. Compute the buffer stock given the following information: $\bar{D} = 1,200$ per year, EOQ = 150, lead time = 11 workdays, cost to store 1 unit for one year = $20, and the cost of a unit shortage = $30. The probability of using at most x units during lead time, $F(x)$, is shown in the adjoining table.

x	56	64	72	80
$F(x)$	.80	.90	.95	.98

24. The manager of Herman Thomas Sports Store has noticed that, in contrast to that for tennis rackets and skis, the demand for ping pong tables does not follow any special pattern, nor is the demand steady. His past record of sales is summarized in the adjoining table.

Number of Tables Sold	0	1	2	3	4	5
Number of Weeks	10	25	30	24	8	3

The store is open 50 weeks each year. The manager buys each table for $40 and sells it for $80. He spends $10 per table on sales related activities. It is his past experience that if a ping pong table is not available immediately, only 1 customer out of 10 will return to buy the table when a new shipment arrives. (The rest will go someplace else.) The ping pong tables are heavy and delicate. Thus, the cost of storing them is high, in fact, 30 percent of the value of inventory. The ordering cost is $80 per shipment. It takes one week to receive a shipment.

a. What is the most economical order quantity?

b. Calculate the optimal reorder point.

25. Davis Rent-A-Car wants to know how many cars to have in stock at their Santa Monica airport office for customers without reservations. There is no order cost and the storage cost is $5 per day. Average profit per car is $12 per day, and hence Davis uses this number as the unit cost of shortage. Past data regarding car usage is shown in the adjoining table. How many cars should the company store each day at this location?

Demand Per Day	10	11	12	13	14	15
Frequency	10	20	50	60	40	20

26. A committee of market researchers and accountants has provided the following values of the inventory parameters for a product:
Annual demand = 1,500 units
Unit carrying cost per year = $20
Ordering cost = $30
Unit cost of shortage = $60
Number of workdays per year = 300
Lead time = 7 workdays
The past records reveal that the most likely value of lead-time demand is 35, but that the actual demand might vary from 33 to 38. The adjoining table shows the probabilities.

Lead Time Demand	33	34	35	36	37	38
Probability	.08	.26	.34	.23	.08	.01

a. How often should the company purchase a new batch?

b. What is the optimal reorder point?

*27. The probability distribution of demand per week is shown in the adjoining table.

Demand	5	6	7	8
Probability	.1	.4	.3	.2

If the lead time is 2 weeks, derive the reorder point corresponding to the service level of .95.

Hint: The demand during a 2-week period varies from 10 to 16 units. Assume the statistical independence from week to week. Then the probability distribution of lead-time demand can be developed by considering all possible ways of getting the particular level of demand. For example, the probability of lead-time demand for 12 units, $P(12)$, can be obtained as follows.

DEMAND		
FIRST WEEK	SECOND WEEK	PROBABILITY
5	7	(.1)(.3) = .03
6	6	(.4)(.4) = .16
7	5	(.3)(.1) = .03
		.22

Hence, $P(12) = .22$. Similarly obtain $P(10)$ through $P(16)$. Then proceed as usual.

7

Formal Models of Waiting Lines

This chapter examines some of the formal models of a common phenomenon: the formation of waiting lines behind the service facilities. The models are formal in the sense that equations are solved to find the values of the parameters used to decide whether the existing situation should be improved. To accomplish this, model developers must posit some simplifying assumptions. These assumptions are explicitly spelled out when each new model is introduced.

A management scientist must carefully study the situation at hand, choose a model which closely approximates reality, satisfy the ultimate decision maker that the simplifying assumptions do not severely distort reality, and then recommend the best course of action to improve upon the existing state of affairs, if necessary. The models to be studied in this chapter help in this exercise.

The queueing models, by themselves, do not lead to the optimal course of action. Rather, such models provide the values of the parameters to be used to choose among the competing service systems. This chapter first lists some of the common means of judging system performance. This is followed by a review of the models that, when appropriate, provide the values of these performance measures in terms of the queueing system parameters.

INFORMATION PROVIDED BY QUEUEING MODELS

Waiting lines are an inherent feature of any service system. One reason is that the *calling units*, i.e., those who need services, seldom approach a service facility at a constant rate. A well-balanced assembly line is one of the few examples of a system with uniformly arriving calling units. Presumably in such situations the service rate can be adjusted to eliminate waiting lines. Presumably also, waiting lines could be eliminated by providing more or faster operating service facilities than those needed to satisfy even the "peak" demand. This, however, is likely to increase the cost of service beyond acceptable limits. In most reasonable circumstances, therefore, waiting lines occur when the unevenness present at the initiation of the system levels off.

The models to be explored in this chapter are formal in that their operating characteristics are obtained by inserting the values of certain exogenous (i.e., input) variables in the appropriate formulas. Examples of exogenous variables include the mean arrival rate, the mean service rate, and the number of service facilities. Before proceeding with the formulas, however, one must explore the organization of the queueing system.

THE STRUCTURE OF QUEUEING SYSTEMS

Figure 7-1 shows the components of a queueing system. Since the proper choice of a mathematical model depends on understanding the way queueing systems are organized, each of these factors will be examined in some detail.

The Calling Units

Calling units approach a service system, or are brought to it, for the sake of changing their current status. These units, which need not be alive

Figure 7-1. *Components of a Queueing System*

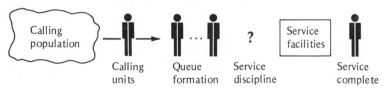

| Calling units | Queue formation | Service discipline | | Service complete |

or animate, might include: ships entering a port, withdrawal orders in an inventory, patients entering a hospital, welfare clients visiting a social worker, parts in an assembly line, or broken machines needing repair. Four things that should be known about these units are:

- How many such units might actually or potentially approach the service system?
- What is their pattern of arrival?
- What is their attitude regarding the length of queue?
- Do these units arrive singly or in groups?

Each aspect is examined below.

Population Size The set of all the possible units that may approach a service system is known as the *calling population* or the *input source*. The number of members in this population may be finite or infinite.

Examples of finite calling populations include: the faculty members of a department requesting secretarial services, the machines in a small factory serviced by one repairman, and students in a technical course looking for tutorial help. Typical infinite populations are: the cars approaching a toll booth, computer programs submitted to a large computing center, and customers entering discount stores during rush hours.

What distinguishes a finite population from an infinite one is the behavior of the probability of one more unit approaching the service system. If this probability is a constant (or nearly so), then the population is said to be infinite. If the probability depends on the number of calling units that have already approached the system, then the population is finite. As a rule of thumb, one may assume the population to be infinite if it contains 200 or more calling units.

The Poisson Process of Arrivals The units processed in an assembly line or those arriving according to some predetermined schedule might approach the service system at a relatively constant rate. Most often, however, the arrival pattern is random and must be studied over a period of time in order to describe its statistical properties. All of the models in this chapter assume that the calling units approach the service system according to a Poisson process. This means that:

- Regardless of how long the service system has been operating, the probability that one more unit will approach it for service in a *short interval* of time is proportional to the width of that time interval.
- The probability of two or more units approaching the service system in this short time interval is almost zero.

For example, if one expects 18 cars to arrive at a gas station every hour, then the probability that one car will arrive there within the next second is approximately:

$$\frac{(18)(1)}{3600} = .005$$

The chance of seeing 2 or more cars arriving in that second is negligible. In the Poisson process the above statements remain true irrespective of how long that gas station has been open.

That the above two assumptions are reasonable while modeling the arrival process has been validated in a number of empirical studies. See, for example, Churchman et al. (1957), Larson (1972), Morse (1967), Prabhu (1965).

In the general Poisson process, let λ (lambda) denote the mean number of arrivals per unit time. The probability of witnessing n arrivals in one unit of time, P_n, can be derived by solving the mathematical equations implicit in the above two assumptions. Generally called the Poisson distribution, this probability is given by the formula:

$$P_n = \frac{e^{-\lambda} \lambda^n}{n!} \quad n = 0, 1, 2, \ldots$$

See chapter 2 for additional properties of a Poisson random variable.

Attitude with Respect to Queue Length. Some of the models presented in this chapter assume that each calling unit will join the waiting line (if necessary) regardless of the line's length, i.e., irrespective of the number of units already in the queue. Consider, for example, that cars arriving at a toll booth have hardly any choice but to wait in line. In a number of situations, however, the calling units would refuse to join an excessively long queue. For example, would you join a gas station line which already contains more than 20 cars?

Group Size Formal queueing models assume that the calling units approach the service system individually rather than in groups. Such group situations (such as going to a restaurant or a theater) are not considered in this chapter, but rather in the next chapter on simulation.

The Service Systems

Proper selection of a queueing model also depends on knowing the relevant aspects of the service systems:

- Number of channels
- Number of phases
- Statistical properties of service times
- Queueing discipline

The Number of Channels Banks usually have only one drive-in window. A car approaches that window for service and waits in line, if necessary. Such a system is said to be a single-channel system. On the other hand, the cars approaching the toll booths or the persons approaching one of the tellers inside the bank are examples of multi-channel systems. Figure 7-2 shows some illustrative arrangements. Note, however, that an outpatient medical center operated by a group of physicians is *not* a multi-channel system of the kind examined in this chapter, because the patients of one doctor usually do not visit another doctor.

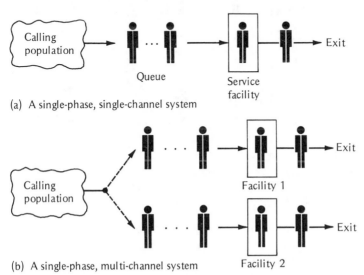

(a) A single-phase, single-channel system

(b) A single-phase, multi-channel system

Figure 7-2. *Configurations in a Single-Phase System*

The Number of Phases All of the examples in the preceding paragraph (as well as those illustrated in figure 7-2) assume a single-phased service system, i.e., any one calling unit enters only one service facility. In many service systems, however, each calling unit must enter several service facilities, one after another. Such a service system is said to be a multi-phase service system. Interstate 95 from Boston to New York City is an example of a multi-phase system for collecting tolls. Figure 7-3 illustrates two multi-phase systems. Figure 7-3(a) shows a three-phase system such as that of Interstate 95. A public welfare office where the clients visit one of the two receptionists and then meet one of the two social workers is illustrated in figure 7-3(b). The point is that the service facilities in a multi-phase system have a hierarchical structure.

The Exponential Distribution of Service Times The time necessary to serve one calling unit at one facility is known as the service time at that

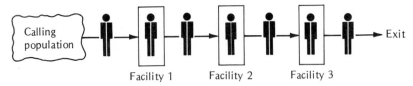

(a) A single-channel, three-phase system

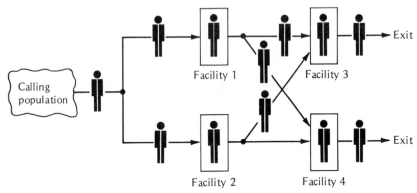

(b) A two-channel, two-phase system

Figure 7-3. *Multi-Phase Systems*
(a) A Single-Channel, Three-Phase System
(b) A Two-Channel, Two-Phase System

facility. The service times of a facility are seldom constant. Consequently, the statistical properties of the service times must be established before choosing an appropriate model.

A number of formal queueing models assume that the service times are *exponentially distributed*. This choice makes the derivation of the operating characteristics of the queueing systems that much easier, since the exponential distribution of service times is another aspect of the Poisson process discussed earlier. Let T denote the time between two occurrences of a Poisson event. If one expects to observe μ (mu) occurrences of a Poisson event per unit time, then the probability that t time units or more will elapse between successive occurrences, $F(t)$, equals:

$$F(t) = \text{Prob } (T \geq t) = e^{-\mu \cdot t}, t > 0$$

This formula is known as the *exponential law* and the corresponding random variable is said to be exponentially distributed. Figure 7-4 shows a graph of this law: the time units are shown along the X-axis and the corresponding probabilities are shown along the Y-axis.

The Queueing Discipline "Who will be served next when there are more than one calling units in the queue?" There are three possibilities:

- FIFO (first in, first out)

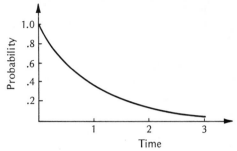

Figure 7-4. *The Exponential Law*

- FILO (first in, last out)
- Priority

Generally speaking, people prefer the queueing systems where FIFO is observed. Most formal models (all but one in this chapter) assume the queueing discipline to be FIFO. However, many queueing systems do employ other rules. In a number of parking lots or in elevators, for instance, the queueing discipline is FILO.

Priority rule implies that the calling units are divided into two or more classes and that within each class the queueing discipline is FIFO. Airline passengers are grouped in two classes: first and tourist. Hospital patients are divided into at least three classes: emergency, inpatient, and outpatient. Many computer centers divide incoming computer programs into a number of classes depending on the hourly rate charged and the core requirements.

QUEUEING STRUCTURES OF THE MODELS IN THIS CHAPTER

It must be clear by now that there is a large variety of queueing systems and that selecting an appropriate model requires a lot of care. Specifically, these factors must be examined:

- Arrival process
- Size of the calling population
- Statistical properties of service times
- Number of channels
- Number of phases
- Queueing discipline
- Queue length limitations

This chapter examines only those formal models that assume that the arrival process is Poisson and that the service systems are single-phased. Also, except where specifically noted, the queueing discipline will be

FIFO. Since all other factors vary from model to model, they will be specified in each model's description prior to the operating characteristics. The following notation will be used in each model.

λ = mean arrival rate = number calling per unit time
μ = mean service rate = number served per unit time
(In a multi-channel service system, μ denotes the mean service rate of *each* channel.)
k = number of channels

TWO MODELS BASED ON THE POISSON PROCESS

This section examines two models (single-channel and multiple-channel systems), each of which is based on the assumptions that the number of arrivals in a given amount of time can be represented by a Poisson distribution and that the service time at each facility is exponentially distributed. This implies that both the arrival and the service processes are Poisson. Each model further assumes that:

1. The calling population is infinite.
2. The queueing discipline is FIFO (first in, first out).
3. The service system is single-phased.
4. The calling units are extremely patient, i.e., they will join the queue regardless of its current length. The only difference between these two models is that the first model assumes a single-channel system and the second does not. In this sense, the first model is a particular case of the second one.

Single-Channel Systems
The drive-in window of a typical bank, the trucks arriving at the loading dock of a wholesaler, small airports with only one runway, and the checkout counter of your neighborhood pharmacist are some of the examples of single-channel systems of the type described by this model. For example, the validity of this model for the drive-in window might be justified as follows. A typical bank has at least several hundred depositors; the cars arriving at the drive-in window form a line that indicates the order in which they will be processed; and most customers, having completed a single transaction, leave the drive-in window (and the bank premises). Also, as long as drive-in operations are reasonably efficient, customers usually join the line regardless of the queue length.

Validity of the Poisson arrival process has been empirically checked by a number of researchers. That the service times are exponentially distributed must be verified in specific situations. We will assume it to be so in order to present the formulas.

Steady-State Statistics It can be shown that when a queueing system of this type has been operating for a while, i.e., after it has stabilized, it has the following characteristics:

1. The service utilization factor ρ (rho) equals:
$$\rho = \lambda/\mu$$
This means that the service facility is busy 100ρ percent of time.
2. The probability that the service facility is idle, i.e., that there is no calling unit in the system, equals:
$$P(0) = 1 - \rho$$
3. The probability of finding n units in the system equals:
$$P(n) = \rho^n \cdot (1 - \rho) = \rho^n \cdot P(0)$$
4. The average length of the queue, i.e., the number of calling units in the waiting line equals:
$$L_q = \rho^2/(1 - \rho)$$
5. The average number of calling units in the system (either waiting or being served) equals:
$$L_s = \rho/(1 - \rho) = L_q + \rho$$
6. The average time spent waiting for service equals:
$$W_q = L_q/\lambda = \lambda/[\mu(\mu - \lambda)] = \rho/[\mu(1 - \rho)]$$
7. The average time spent in the system (both waiting and being served) equals:
$$W_s = 1/(\mu - \lambda) = W_q + 1/\mu = L_s/\lambda$$

Note that, since $\rho = \lambda/\mu$ is the probability that the service facility is busy, ρ cannot exceed 1. Also, since:
$$L_s = \frac{\rho}{1 - \rho}$$
it follows that ρ must be strictly less than 1. This means that no service facility will be busy all the time. Most of the formal models in this chapter are based on this assumption.

Example 1: A Drive-in Window Suppose that an average of 20 customers arrive at the drive-in window of a bank every hour and that the bank teller can service an average of 25 customers every hour. In that case, $\lambda = 20$ per hour and $\mu = 25$ per hour. In the steady state, this drive-in window will have the following characteristics:

$$\rho = \frac{20}{25} = .8 \qquad\qquad P(0) = 1 - .8 = .2$$

$$L_q = \frac{(.8)(.8)}{1 - .8} = 3.2 \qquad\qquad L_s = \frac{.8}{1 - .8} = 4$$

$$W_q = \frac{3.2}{20} = .16 \qquad\qquad W_s = \frac{1}{25 - 20} = .2$$

On the average, the bank teller will be busy 80 percent of the time ($\rho = .8$), i.e., 48 minutes each hour. She will be idle 12 minutes each hour. However, do not confuse this idle time with free time—the teller can't leave her station for 12 consecutive minutes. Presumably, these 12 minutes might be spent performing some lower priority work whenever possible. Despite this idle time, an outside observer can expect to see $L_s = 4$ cars in the drive-in section of the bank, an average of $L_q = 3.2$ of these waiting to be served. Each driver expects to spend $W_s = .2$ hours $= 12$ minutes on this operation and $W_q = .16$ hours $= 9.6$ minutes of those 12 will be spent waiting to be served.

Multiple-Channel Systems

All of the assumptions of the preceding model continue to hold in this model except that, instead of just one channel (i.e., one service facility), the service system in this model consists of k parallel facilities. Figure 7-5 shows an example of such a system. It is assumed that an incoming unit may *freely choose* between Facility 1, Facility 2, . . . , Facility k; that the mean service rate of *each* facility is μ; and that the service times of each facility are alike in all respects. An expressway exit with k toll booths is an example of such a system.

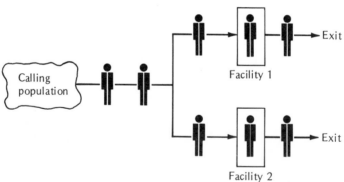

Figure 7-5. *A Two-Channel System*

Steady-State Properties Under these conditions, it can be shown that in the steady state, the k-channel system will exhibit the following characteristics:

$$\rho = \frac{\lambda}{k \cdot \mu}$$

$$\frac{1}{P(0)} = \sum_{n=0}^{k-2} \frac{(\rho k)^n}{n!} + \frac{(\rho k)^{k-1}}{(k-1)!\,(1-p)}$$

$$P(n) = \begin{cases} \dfrac{(\rho k)^n}{n!} \cdot P(0), \text{ when } n \leq k \\[3mm] \dfrac{\rho^n k^k}{k!} \cdot P(0), \text{ when } n \geq k \end{cases}$$

$$L_q = \frac{\rho^{k+1} \ k^{k-1}}{(k-1)! \ (1-\rho)^2} \cdot P(0)$$

$$L_s = L_q + \rho k$$

$$W_q = \frac{L_q}{\lambda}$$

$$W_s = W_q + \frac{1}{\mu} = \frac{L_s}{\lambda}$$

That the service utilization factor equals $\lambda/k\mu$ should be intuitively obvious. Also, as in the case of the single-channel system, no service facility can be busy all the time. In other words, ρ *must be less than 1*. The rest of the formulas are somewhat more complex than their counterparts in a single-channel system, the computation of $P(0)$ being the most tedious. However, once $P(0)$ has been derived, other parameters are obtained fairly easily. For this reason, the $P(0)$ values for up to eight channels have been graphed in figure 7-6. To use those graphs:

- Compute $\rho = \dfrac{\lambda}{k\mu}$
- Measure ρ units along the ρ-axis of figure 7-6.
- Move parallel to $P(0)$ axis until you reach the graph corresponding to the designated number of channel, k.
- Then the height of this point is $P(0)$.

For example, when $k = 3$ and $\rho = .78$, you can read that $P(0) = .06$ (up to 2 decimal places). This process is illustrated in figure 7-6.

Example 2: An Expressway Exit with Three Toll Booths To illustrate the computations, consider a busy exit on an expressway. An average of 420 cars per hour leave the expressway at this point and head toward one of the 3 toll booths. Each toll collector can service an average of 3 cars every minute. In other words: $k = 3$ channels, $\lambda = 420$ cars per hour = 7 cars per minute and $\mu = 3$ cars per minute. Consequently this toll booth will have the following properties in its steady state:

$$\rho = \frac{7}{(3)(3)} = .78$$

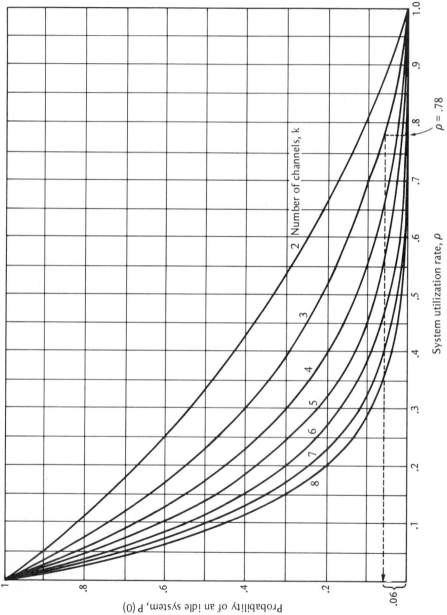

Figure 7-6 *P(0) as a Function of ρ and k*

Hence, from figure 7-6:

$$P(0) = .06$$

Consequently:

$$L_q = \frac{(.78)^{3+1} (3^{3-1})}{(3-1)! (1-.78)^2} \times (.06) = 2.06$$

$$L_s = 2.06 + (.78)(3) = 4.40$$

$$W_q = 2.06/7 = .29$$

$$W_s = .29 + 1/3 = .63$$

Thus, each toll collector will be busy 78 percent of the time. There is 6 percent chance that no cars are at the exit. On the average, there are 4.40 cars in the system, of which 2.06 are waiting for service. Each car needs an average of .63 minutes to get through the tolls, of which .29 minutes are spent just waiting. (These parameters are reliable up to at least one decimal place.) All in all, this appears to be a very tolerable situation from the driver's point of view.

DECISIONS BASED ON THE CHARACTERISTICS OF QUEUES

The queueing models help describe the important features of a queueing system so that the decision maker can design better service systems. In the notation of chapter 1, such models are descriptive. Queueing models alone do not yield optimal solutions. However, the information provided by the model can be used to design better service systems.

Generally speaking the decision maker cannot control the number or type of calling units which approach the service system. But, the service rate could be changed—by increasing the service capacity of each channel, by increasing the number of parallel channels, or by making the service more uniform to decrease the variance of service times (e.g., fast food chains). Or, the operating characteristics of the waiting lines might be influenced by changing the service discipline (e.g., to a priority scheme rather than FIFO).

When the calling units belong to the service organization itself, the decision maker can estimate the cost of "downtime" per hour, day, or week. The total cost to the system is then computed by adding the per hour costs of service and downtime. In such situations, the optimal service system is that which minimizes the total cost. For example, suppose a calling unit is normally worth $d per hour. If it spends W_s hours in the service facility, the cost to the organization equals $d \cdot W_s$.

If λ units call for services each hour, the per hour cost of downtime is: $\$\lambda \cdot d \cdot W_s$. Let OC denote the per hour cost of operating the service facilities. Then, the per hour total cost, TC, equals:

$$TC = OC + \lambda \cdot d \cdot W_s = OC + d \cdot L_s$$

The service system is chosen so as to minimize TC.

Calling units often do not belong to the service organization. The depositors of a bank, the customers of a grocery store, the airline passengers, or vehicles on an expressway are examples of this type. In such cases, it is usually difficult to accurately estimate the per hour cost of downtime. Instead, the least costly service system is selected as long as the resultant waiting lines are judged to be at least tolerably good. Some of the decision criteria are listed below:

- Average length of the queue (L_q) is less than m.
- Average downtime (W_s) is less than X.
- Probability of excessively many calling units in the system, say $P(n)$, is less than r.

In this section, we will illustrate some decision situations where the Poisson-Exponential models of the preceding section are applicable. This discussion of the optimal decision rules is continued in later sections as each new model is introduced.

Example 3: Operations of a Loading Dock A major retailer uses a central warehouse to load and unload goods brought in from wholesalers for delivery to local outlets. The trucks arrive at the dock randomly and may be assumed to follow the Poisson process with a mean rate of $\lambda = 4$ trucks per hour. A two-man crew can service, i.e., load or unload $\mu = 5$ trucks per hour. The time each truck spends at the loading dock is worth $\$25$ per hour and a crew member is paid $\$5$ per hour. The service time is exponentially distributed. Management believes that the service rate is proportional to the crew size. How many crew members should be hired to minimize the total cost?

In this case, $\lambda = 4$ per hour, $d = \$25$ per hour, and $k = 1$ channel. If the loading crew consists of n members, their pay will cost $\$5n$ per hour, and they will be able to service $\mu = 5n/2 = 2.5n$ trucks each hour. The corresponding downtime of a truck (W_s) would equal:

$$W_s = \frac{1}{\mu - \lambda} = \frac{1}{2.5n - 4}$$

Thus, the total system will cost the salary of n crew members at $\$5$ per hour and the truck downtime at $\$25$ per hour per truck. Symbolically:

$$TC = \$5n + (\$25)\,(4)/(2.5n - 4)$$
$$= \$5n + \$100/(2.5n - 4) \text{ every hour}$$

The *TC* values corresponding to the different crew sizes are:

$$n = 2 \quad TC = \$10 + \$100/(5 - 4) = \$110$$
$$n = 3 \quad TC = \$15 + \$100/(7.5 - 4) = \$43.57$$
$$\mathbf{n = 4 \quad TC = \$20 + \$100/(10 - 4) = \$36.67}$$
$$n = 5 \quad TC = \$25 + \$100/(12.5 - 4) = \$36.76$$

The lowest total cost occurs when the loading crew contains 4 members. In that case, each arriving truck will spend an average of $1/(10 - 4) = .1667$ hours = 10 minutes at the dock. Thus, the optimal service team consists of 4 crew members.

Example 4: The Number of Runways When the airport in a small but prosperous town was built, it was judged that one runway with a capacity of landing 20 planes per hour would adequately serve the flying public. Recently, however, traffic controllers have noticed an increase in the number of landings. The resultant increase in the number of planes waiting to land and the consequent air and noise pollution has bothered a number of prominent citizens, including those on the board of airport authority. A survey commissioned by the board forecasts that in the next three years the air traffic is likely to increase to 30 landings per hour. Since the airport will have to be redesigned, the board wishes to determine the number of runways essential to ensure that, on the average, no more than 1 plane will have to wait to land (after the airport construction is complete).

In this case $\lambda = 30$ landings per hour. Each runway can handle $\mu = 20$ landings per hour. We need to determine k = number of runways such that L_q = average number of planes waiting to land is 1 or less. Using figure 7-6 and the formula for L_q, you can verify that, when $k = 2$:

$$\rho = .75, \quad P(0) = .14, \quad L_q = \frac{(.75)^3(2)}{(1)(.25)^2} \times .14 = 1.89$$

and, when $k = 3$:

$$\rho = .50, \quad P(0) = .21, \quad L_q = \frac{(.5)^3(3)^2}{(2)(.5)^2} \times .21 = .47$$

It follows that the new airport should contain 3 runways to meet the forecasted demand.

TWO SINGLE-CHANNEL MODELS WITH ARBITRARY SERVICE DISCIPLINES

We will continue to assume that the calling units approach the service system in a Poisson fashion and that they are patient, i.e., that they will join the queue regardless of its length. However, in this section, we will no longer assume that the service times are exponentially distributed. The first of the two models in this section continues to assume that the service rule is FIFO (first in, first out). The second model investigates the affects of priority queueing. For both these models, it is assumed that:

1. The arrival process is Poisson, with an average of λ callers per hour.
2. There is potentially an infinite number of calling units.
3. The queues can be infinitely long (generally they are not).
4. There is only one service facility.
5. The service rate is μ calling units per hour, so the average service time is $1/\mu$ hours.
6. The variance of service times is known to be σ^2.

Queues with First-In, First-Out Rule

As in the case of a single-channel, Poisson-Exponential system, the service utilization rate ρ, equals λ/μ; and the probability of finding no calling unit in the system, $P(0)$, equals $1 - \rho$. Other results are generalizations of the corresponding formulas in the Poisson-Exponential model. Specifically:

$$\rho = \frac{\lambda}{\mu} \qquad\qquad P(0) = 1 - \rho$$

$$L_q = \frac{\rho^2(1 + \mu^2\sigma^2)}{2(1 - \rho)} \qquad\qquad W_q = \frac{L_q}{\lambda}$$

$$L_s = L_q + \rho \qquad\qquad W_s = W_q + \frac{1}{\mu} = \frac{L_s}{\lambda}$$

Effects of Variability in Service Times Consider two systems, each with the same arrival rate, λ, and the same service rate, μ. These systems appear to be alike. But, the value of σ^2 has a significant impact on the system's operating characteristics. In general, the larger the variance in service times, the longer the waiting lines. This, in turn, implies a more crowded service system and longer downtimes. In fact, it is possible to conceive of situations where the service facility with the smaller service rate, μ, might be more efficient than another system with better service rate but larger variability.

Two Extreme Possibilities If the service times are constant, σ^2 is zero. In that case, you can verify that:

$$L_q = \rho^2/[2(1 - \rho)]$$

Coin operated washing machines and automatic car washes are excellent approximations of this model. Generally speaking, it has been recognized that the highest variability occurs when the service times are exponential

$(\sigma^2 = 1/\mu^2)$. As we have already seen, L_q in that case is found to be:

$$L_q = \rho^2/(1 - \rho)$$

In general, the L_q values lie between these two extremes.

Example 5: Another Drive-In Window Reconsider the drive-in window of the bank discussed in example 1. We noted that an average of $\lambda = 20$ customers arrive each hour and that an average of $\mu = 25$ customers can be serviced each hour. In other words, the average service takes $1/25$ hours $= 2.4$ minutes. Suppose that the drive-in window has been limited to check cashing or deposit services to make it more efficient, and that because of this limitation, the standard deviation of the service times, σ, has been reduced to 1 minute $= 1/60$ hour. In short, $\sigma^2 = (1/60)^2 = .0003$. The corresponding waiting line properties are:

$$\rho = \frac{20}{25} = .8 \qquad\qquad P(0) = 1 - .8 = .2$$

$$L_q = \frac{(.8)^2\,[1 + (25/60)^2]}{2(1 - .8)} = 1.88 \qquad\qquad L_s = 1.8778 + .8 = 2.68$$

$$W_q = \frac{1.88}{20} = .094 \qquad\qquad W_s = \frac{2.68}{20} = .134$$

Compare these figures with their counterparts in example 1.

On the average, there are only 2.68 cars instead of 4 in the drive-in section of the bank, a 33 percent improvement. The average number of cars waiting to be served, L_q, has been reduced from 3.2 to 1.88, a 41 percent improvement. The expected downtime has been reduced from 12 minutes to $.134 \times 60 = 8.04$ minutes, a 33 percent improvement. These improvements have been achieved without hiring faster (and more expensive) bank tellers.

Queues with Priorities

The assumptions underlying this model are similar to those of the preceding model except that *all calling units are not treated alike.* Specifically, the calling units are divided into m classes according to a priority rule—each calling unit with a higher priority class is processed prior to any in the lower priority class. The units within each class are processed in the order of their arrival (i.e., FIFO). Usually, there is a cost associated with being in a higher priority class—a calling unit with higher priority pays a premium to move through the system faster. It is easier to understand the formulas that describe the operating characteristics of such a system if you note that, in effect, operating a multi-priority system is similar to serving a variety of calling populations simultaneously. Figure 7-7 depicts the operations of a two-class system.

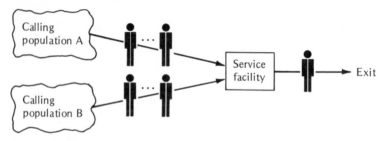

Figure 7-7. *A Two-Priority Queueing System*

Examples of multi-priority systems are: computer programs processed by large data processing facilities, passengers holding first or second class airline tickets, and the post office's classification of mail.

Mathematical Formulas Let m denote the number of priority classes. Let λ_i, μ_i, σ_i^2, ρ_i, $L_q(i)$, $W_q(i)$, $L_s(i)$, and $W_s(i)$ denote the queueing characteristics (with which you should be familiar) for class $i(= 1, 2, \ldots, m)$. Also, let:

λ = total number of calling units per hour, day, or week

W_q = expected waiting time of a "typical" client

$$S_j = \sum_{i=1}^{j} \rho_i \text{ (with } S_0 = 0)$$

W_s = expected time spent by a "typical" client in the system

Then, in the steady state, priority class i will have the following properties:

$$\rho_i = \lambda_i/\mu_i$$

$$W_q(i) = \frac{\sum\limits_{j=1}^{m} \rho_j^2(1 + \mu_j^2\sigma_j^2)/\lambda_j}{2(1 - S_{i-1})(1 - S_i)}$$

$$W_s(i) = W_q(i) + 1/\mu_i$$

$$L_q(i) = \lambda_i W_q(i)$$

$$L_s(i) = \lambda_i W_s(i)$$

System-wide characteristics are obtained from those of the individual classes:

$$\lambda = \sum_{i=1}^{m} \lambda_i$$

$$L_q = \sum_{i=1}^{m} L_q(i) \qquad\qquad W_q = L_q/\lambda$$

$$L_s = \sum_{i=1}^{m} L_s(i) \qquad\qquad W_s = L_s/\lambda$$

Example 6: To Board a Train in India Contrary to the situation in the United States, a large number of commuter trains operate in India to and from a number of large cities. It is, therefore, reasonable to investigate the situation at the ticket office of a suburban railway station using the steady-state formulas. At one such station, it has been observed that an average of $\lambda_1 = 20$ first class passengers and $\lambda_2 = 60$ second class passengers approach the only ticket office every hour. Though they both use the same counter, two different ticket agents service the passengers in round-robin fashion. This explains the high service rate. First class passengers often present bills in large denominations; second class passengers as a rule use exact or nearly exact change. This is one of the reasons that the service rates vary. In fact, the ticket office can process $\mu_1 = 60$ first class and $\mu_2 = 120$ second class passengers each hour. In other words, the average service time is $1/60$ hours, i.e., 1 minute to process a first class passenger and only $1/2$ minute for the second class passenger. The corresponding standard deviations are: $\sigma_1 = .85$ minutes $= .0141$ hour and $\sigma_2 = .38$ minutes $= .0063$ hours.

With this information, you can determine the operating characteristics of this ticket office as follows:

$$\rho_1 = 20/60 = .3333 \qquad\qquad \rho_2 = 60/120 = .5$$

$$S_1 = \rho_1 = .3333 \qquad\qquad S_2 = \rho_1 + \rho_2 = .8333$$

$$\frac{\rho_1^2(1 + \mu_1^2\sigma_1^2)}{\lambda_1} = .00956 \qquad\qquad \frac{\rho_2^2(1 + \mu_2^2\sigma_2^2)}{\lambda_2} = .00657$$

$$W_q(1) = \frac{.00956 + .00657}{2(1 - .3333)} \qquad\qquad W_q(2) = \frac{.00956 = .00657}{2(.6667)\,(.1667)}$$

$$= .0121 \text{ hours} \qquad\qquad = .0725 \text{ hours}$$

$$= .73 \text{ minutes} \qquad\qquad = 4.35 \text{ minutes}$$

$$W_s(1) = .0121 + 1/60 \qquad\qquad W_s(2) = .0725 + 1/120$$

$$= .0288 \text{ hours} \qquad\qquad = .0808 \text{ hours}$$

$$= 1.73 \text{ minutes} \qquad\qquad = 4.85 \text{ minutes}$$

$$L_q(1) = (.0121)\,(20) \qquad\qquad L_q(2) = (.0725)\,(60)$$

$$= .24 \text{ passengers} \qquad\qquad = 4.35 \text{ passengers}$$

$$L_s(1) = (.0288)\,(20) \qquad\qquad L_s(2) = (.0808)\,(60)$$

$$= .58 \text{ passengers} \qquad\qquad = 4.85 \text{ passengers}$$

On the whole, there will be an average of $L_q = .24 + 4.35 = 4.59$ passengers waiting in line; and $L_s = .58 + 4.85 = 5.43$ passengers in the system. A total of $\lambda = 20 + 60 = 80$ passengers arrive at the ticket office each hour. A typical passenger expects to wait $W_q = L_q/\lambda = 4.59/80 = .0574$ hours $=$ 3.44 minutes before reaching the counter and thus should reserve $W_s = L_s/\lambda = 5.43/80 = .0679$ hours $= 4.07$ minutes to get through the line. A rather tolerable system.

QUEUES WITH RESTRICTIONS

Each of the two models in this section represents a variation of the basic Poisson-Exponential model examined at the beginning of this chapter. Specifically, each model assumes that:

1. The arrival process is Poisson.
2. Service times are exponential.
3. The queueing discipline is FIFO. The first of the two models assumes that the population is finite; the second assumes that the queue length cannot exceed a specified limit.

Poisson-Exponential Systems with Few Callers

In a number of situations, the calling populations are rather small and thus the basic Poisson-Exponential model is not suitable. Specifically, the probability that one more calling unit will need service is no longer constant—it now depends on the number of units already in the system. The following are some real world situations where it is more proper to assume finite calling populations:

1. A small machine shop serviced by one repairman. Since any machine that is now operative might need repairs, all machines belong to the calling population. (Each repairperson in this case constitutes a channel.)
2. Patients in a hospital ward who are in the care of on-duty nurses.
3. The set of keypunch machines in a computing center.

In the first of these real world situations, there is $k = 1$ channel; in the second and third situations there are as many channels as service persons.

Steady-State Properties Let M denote the number of calling units in the calling population, let λ denote the mean arrival rate of *each* individual unit, and let k equal the number of channels. Compute $R = \lambda/\mu$. (In this case, R is *not* the service utilization rate). It can be shown that:

$$\frac{1}{P(0)} = \sum_{n=0}^{k-1} \binom{M}{n} R^n + \frac{M!}{k!} \sum_{n=k}^{M} \frac{R^n}{(M-n)!\, k^{n-k}}$$

where $\binom{M}{n}$ equals the number of ways of choosing n items out of M.

Once $P(0)$ is known, the remaining formulas are fairly straightforward:

$$P(n) = \begin{cases} \binom{M}{n} R^n P(0), & \text{when } 0 \le n \le k \\ \dfrac{M!\, R^n\, P(0)}{(M-n)!k!\,k^{n-k}}, & \text{when } k \le n \le M \end{cases}$$

$$L_s = \sum_{n=1}^{M} nP(n)$$

The calling units which are presently in the system, L_s, are *not* in the calling population at this moment. Hence, the *effective* arrival rate, λ_e, equals $\lambda(M - L_s)$. For this reason, this effective arrival rate, λ_e, is used to determine the average downtime, W_s; waiting time before being served W_q; and the number of units waiting, L_q. Specifically:

$W_s = L_s/\lambda_e$

$W_q = W_s - 1/\mu$

$L_q = \lambda_e \cdot W_q$

Properties of a Single Channel System When $k = 1$, the above formulas become much simpler. Specifically:

$$\frac{1}{P(0)} = M! \sum_{n=0}^{M} \frac{R^n}{(M-n)!}$$

$$P(n) = \frac{M!}{(M-n)!} \cdot R^n \cdot P(0)$$

$$L_q = M - \frac{\lambda + \mu}{\lambda} \cdot [1 - P(0)]$$

$L_s = L_q + 1 - P(0)$

$\lambda_e = \lambda(M - L_s) = \mu[1 - P(0)]$

$W_q = L_q / \lambda_e$

$W_s = L_s / \lambda_e$

Example 7: Peter McDonald's Antique Machinery Peter owns a manufacturing plant which utilizes five rather antiquated machines. When the machines operate correctly, the results are unique and beautiful indeed. However, Peter notices that, on the average, each machine needs to be readjusted once for every hour of its operation, and that the adjustment process requires an average of 20 minutes. Perhaps, Peter needs an additional repairman besides himself. What would the operating characteristics be with the resultant two-person crew?

In this case, $M = 5$ machines, $k = 2$ repairmen, $\lambda = 1$ breakdown per machine per hour of operation, and $\mu = 3$ repairs each hour; so that $R = 1/3$. Hence:

$$1/P(0) = 1 + \binom{5}{1}\frac{1}{3} + \frac{5!}{2!}\left\{\frac{(1/3)^2}{3!\,2^0} + \frac{(1/3)^3}{2!\,2^1} + \frac{(1/3)^4}{1!\,2^2} + \frac{(1/3)^5}{0!\,2^3}\right\}$$

$$= 1 + \frac{5}{3} + 60\left(\frac{1}{54} + \frac{1}{108} + \frac{1}{324} + \frac{1}{1976}\right)$$

$$= 4.5489$$

$$P(0) = .2198$$

$$P(1) = \binom{5}{1}\left(\frac{1}{3}\right)(.2198) = .3664$$

$$P(2) = \binom{5}{2}\left(\frac{1}{3}\right)^2(.2198) = .2443$$

$$P(3) = \frac{5!\,(1/3)^3\,(.2198)}{2!\,2!\,2^2} = .1212$$

$$P(4) = \frac{5!(1/3)^4\,(.2198)}{1!\,2!\,2^2} = .0407$$

$$P(5) = \frac{5!(1/3)^5\,(.2198)}{0!\,2!\,2^3} = .0068$$

$$L_s = (1)\,(.3664) + (2)\,(.2443) + (3)\,(.1221) + (4)\,(.0407)$$

$$+ (5)\,(.0068) = 1.4181 \approx 1.42$$

$$\lambda_e = (1)\,(5 - 1.4181) \approx 3.58$$

$$W_s = 1.42/3.58 \approx .40$$

$$W_q \approx .40 - 1/3 \approx .06$$

$$L_q \approx (.06)\,(3.58) \approx .21$$

There is 21.98 percent probability that Peter and an associate would be without repair work. In a typical hour, 1.42 machines are in the repair shop, and each such machine spends an average of .40 hours = 24 minutes there. Also, when a machine needs an adjustment, it must spend .06 hours = 3.6 minutes just waiting. The waiting line contains an average of .21 machines. (Fractional values are, of course, to be interpreted in the usual manner of reading statistical reports.) Whether Peter should hire an assistant depends on the value of Peter's free time and the cost of machine downtime.

Effective Arrival Rate The calling units *do not* arrive for service at the rate of $\lambda \cdot M$ per hour, day or week. A machine that is being serviced will not, by definition, call on the system at the moment. If L_s machines are in the repair shop, only $M - L_s$ are likely to need service at that moment. Since each calling unit might need service λ times per hour, the effective arrival rate is only $\lambda_e = \lambda(M - L_s)$.

In Mr. McDonald's case, $\lambda_e =$ (1) (5 − 1.42) = 3.58. This explains why Peter and his potential assistant could be idle a rather large percent of time. It also explains why Peter can service all the machines by himself without building an infinite queue—even though the waiting time, W_q, in that case would be substantial.

Ready-Made Tables Obviously, the computations necessary to derive the operating characteristics of such models can be rather laborious. For this reason, Peck and Hazelwood (1958) have published the finite population queueing tables for $m = 4$ through $m = 250$. The reader should refer to these tables when solving a real-life problem of finite population waiting lines. Alternatively, a computer can be programmed to yield the steady-state properties.

A Single-Channel Poisson-Exponential System with Truncated Queue

There are at least two reasons why a queue might not exceed a specified limit:

1. The calling units, particularly if they are human beings, might refuse to join an excessively long queue. Would you enter a barber shop if 10 other customers are already there and you can spot only two operators?
2. The service system is physically limited. For example, the waiting room of a typical physician cannot accommodate more than 15 patients.

Steady-State Properties We will consider one of the simplest models of this type—a variation of the basic single-channel, Poisson-Exponential model. Let M denote the maximum number of calling units in the system so that the maximum queue length is $M - 1$. Then, the operating characteristics are summarized by the following formulas, where $R = \lambda/\mu$ is no longer the service utilization factor:

$$P(0) = (1 - R)/(1 - R^{M+1})$$
$$P(n) = R^n P(0)$$

$$L_s = \frac{R}{1 - R} - \frac{(M + 1) R^{M + 1})}{1 - R^{M + 1}}$$

$$L_q = L_s + P(0) - 1$$

$$W_q = \frac{L_q}{\lambda_e}, \text{ where } \lambda_e = \lambda\left[1 - P(M)\right]$$

$$W_s = W_q + 1/\mu$$

Observations The quantity, $\lambda_e = \lambda\left[1 - P(M)\right]$ is also known as the *effective arrival rate*. The reasoning might be summarized as follows. Since no more than M calling units can be in the system, $P(M)$ equals the probability that the system is full, i.e., a calling unit arriving at this stage cannot (or will not) enter the system. Hence, $1 - P(M)$ equals the probability that a calling unit can or will enter the system. Thus, the Poisson arrival rate λ must be modified to the effective arrival rate, $\lambda_e = \lambda\left[1 - P(M)\right]$.

Since n, the number of calling units in the system, varies from 0 through M, it follows that:

$$\sum_{n=0}^{M} P(n) = 1$$

This implies that:

$$1 = \sum_{n=0}^{M} R^n \cdot P(0) = P(0) \cdot \sum_{n=0}^{M} R^n = \frac{1 - R^{M+1}}{1 - R} \cdot P(0)$$

It follows that:

$$P(0) = \frac{(1 - R)}{(1 - R^{M+1})}$$

This model allows the arrival rate to equal or exceed service rate. If the arrival rate equals the service rate (i.e., $\lambda = \mu$), then all states are equally likely. In fact, in that case:

$$P(0) = 1/(M + 1)$$

Hence, in that case, you can verify that the expected number of calling units in the system equals:

$$L_s = M/2$$

If λ exceeds μ substantially, the system will become saturated with $L_s \approx M$ and $P(M) \approx 1$.

Example 8: A Barber Shop Don Aubrey owns and operates a small shop in downtown Saxonville. Don has never bothered to hire an assistant, since he does not approve a hairdo given by anyone else. He can cut the hair of six customers (on the average) every hour. His shop contains four chairs besides the barber's chair. We shall investigate the evolution of Don's business over the past several years.

1. *The initial phase.* Since the shop is downtown, let us suppose that initially $\lambda = 3$ customers entered Don's shop every hour. In other words, in the beginning:

$\lambda = 3$, $\mu = 6$, $M = 5$ so that $R = 3/6 = .5$

His operating characteristics are summarized below.

$P(0) = (1 - .5)/(1 - .5^{5 + 1}) = .5079$

In other words, Don would have been idle more than half the time (but not free to go anywhere). Other probabilities would have been:

$P(1) = .5\,P(0) = .2540$
$P(2) = .5\,P(1) = .1270$
$P(3) = .5\,P(2) = .0635$
$P(4) = .5\,P(3) = .0317$
$P(5) = .5\,P(4) = .0159$

On the average, he would have:

$$L_s = \frac{.5}{1 - .5} - \frac{(5 + 1)\,(.5)^{5 + 1}}{1 - (.5)^{5 + 1}} = .9048$$

customers in the shop. Of these:

$L_q = .9048 + .5079 - 1 = .4127$

would be occupying one of the waiting chairs. A typical customer would have to wait:

$$W_q = \frac{.4127}{3(1 - .0159)} = .1398 \text{ hours} = 8.39 \text{ minutes}$$

before entering the barber's chair. Finally, a customer coming into Don's shop would expect to spend:

$W_s = .1392 + 1/6 = .3064$ hours $= 18.39$ minutes

before going out with freshly cut hair.

2. *The second phase.* Because of Don's good work, several more customers each hour started to frequent his shop. Suppose that within six months after opening the shop, $\lambda = 6$ customers begin to approach his shop every hour. In that case:

$R = 6/6 = 1$

$P(0) = 1/6 = .1667 = P(1) = \cdots = P(5)$

$L_s = (1 + 2 + 3 + 4 + 5)/6 = 2.5$

$L_q = 2.5 + .1667 - 1 = 1.6667$

$\lambda_e = \lambda\big[1 - P(M)\big] = 6(1 - .1667) = 5$

$$W_q = L_q/\lambda_e = 1.6667/5 = .3333 \text{ hours} = 20 \text{ minutes}$$

$$W_s = .3333 + 1/6 = .5 \text{ hour} = 30 \text{ minutes}$$

In other words, Don is busy most of the time but his customers expect to wait longer for getting a good quality haircut.

3. *Current state of affairs.* Nowadays $\lambda = 10$ customers per hour pass by Don's barber shop deciding whether to get their hair cut from Don or from one of his competitors. Thus,

$$R = \lambda/\mu = 10/6 = 1.6667$$

$$P(0) = (1 - R)/(1 - R^6) = .0326$$

$$P(1) = R \cdot P(0) = .0544$$

$$P(2) = R \cdot P(1) = .0906$$

$$P(3) = R \cdot P(2) = .1511$$

$$P(4) = R \cdot P(3) = .2518$$

$$P(5) = R \cdot P(4) = .4196$$

Don's idle time has become $.0326 \times 60 = 1.96$ minutes each hour. His shop is rather crowded most of the time. In fact, typically there are:

$$L_s = \sum_{n=1}^{5} nP(n) = 3.7941$$

customers in his shop. Of these:

$$L_q = 3.7941 + .0544 - 1 = 2.8485$$

are simply passing time. Each such customer will spend:

$$W_q = 2.8485/5 = .5697 \text{ hours} = 34.18 \text{ minutes}$$

just waiting to be served. Each customer expects to spend:

$$W_s = .5697 + .1667 = .7364 \text{ hours} = 44.18 \text{ minutes}$$

in Don's shop. Is Don's haircut worth this wait? The model cannot answer this question; it is a matter of personal choice.

WHAT A MANAGER SHOULD KNOW

We have examined six elementary models in this chapter. Queueing literature examines many other important situations. There are models of the multi-channel systems with truncated queues. Models have also been constructed for service times that follow the Erlang distribution. Models also exist for non-Poisson arrivals. Unfortunately, the formulas for describing the corresponding operating characteristics become increasingly more complex. Instead, we will briefly summarize the findings of some research reports to indicate the breadth of waiting line models.

A basic assumption of waiting line models is that the statistical properties of service times remain unchanged. Mine et al. (1976) examine the effects of modifying this assumption. This type of situation can arise because the server becomes increasingly more tired as time goes on or because the server becomes increasingly more efficient due to added experience.

Most multi-channel models assume that the calling unit chooses whichever server happens to be free, an assumption that is not true in some situations. Consider, for example, the problem of driving to the airport and finding a parking spot. Each parking spot is a "server," but the driver (the calling unit) does not choose an empty spot *randomly*. Rather, the driver wants a spot that is nearest the terminal. Bein (1976) discusses the corresponding waiting line model which might be applicable to other systems with customer preferences.

Driscoll (1975) applies the waiting line theory to model reservation systems. Iglehart and Whitt (1970) model the properties of waiting lines in heavy traffic (i.e., $\rho = \lambda/k\mu$ is close to 1). Koleskar et al. (1975) use queueing models to schedule patrol cars. Lemoine (1975) uses the model of a service system with multiple but nonidentical channels to describe a traffic control system.

Notice also the similarity between inventory and waiting line models. The servers of the waiting lines correspond to the inventoried units of the inventory model. (Consider again the example of parking spots discussed above.) Just as the customers of inventories need the stored products, the calling units of the waiting lines need the services provided by the server. Shortages correspond with delays; holding cost with the cost of idle servers. The point is that a thorough understanding of one system model can help understand the other.

This brings us to making decisions about a service system. If both the calling units and the servers belong to the same organization (corresponding statement in inventories: if inputs to a process are the finished products of another but internally controlled operation), then one can better estimate the cost of a unit downtime, e.g., that of delaying one calling unit by one hour. In that case, the total system related cost equals:

cost of a unit downtime
× average number of calling units in the system
+ cost of operating the service system

We have seen how to use this cost to design better service systems.

In a number of situations, however, the calling units do not belong to the service organization with the consequence that pricing downtime is difficult or impossible. (Compare this with the problem of estimating shortage costs.) Instead, one chooses the least costly service system that would keep the waiting line situation tolerable.

Many real-life systems are not amenable to modeling in the formal sense. This is true regardless of whether one is studying the PERT networks, inventories, or queues. One must then resort to solutions based on simulating the important aspects of the system of interest. This approach will be examined in the next two chapters.

SELECTED READINGS

BEIN, L. P. "An N-Server Stochastic Service System with Customer Preferences." *Operations Research* 24 (1976), pp. 104–117.

CHURCHMAN, C. W.; ACKOFF, R. L.; and ARNOFF, E. L. *Introduction to Operations Research.* New York: John Wiley and Sons, Inc., 1957.

COHEN, J. W. *The Single Server Queue.* London, North Holland Publishers, 1969.

COHEN, J. W. "On the Busy Periods for the M/G/1 Queue with Finite Waiting Room." *Journal of Applied Probability* 8 (1971), pp. 821–827.

COOPER, R. B. *Introduction to Queueing Theory.* New York: MacMillan, Inc., 1972.

DRISCOLL, M. F. and WEISS, N. A. "An Application of Queueing Theory to Reservation Networks." *Management Science* 22 (1975), pp. 540–546.

FISHMAN, G. "Statistical Analysis for Queueing Simulations." *Management Science* 20 (1973), pp. 363–369.

IGLEHART, D. L. and WHITT, W. "Multiple Channel Queues in Heavy Traffic, I." *Advanced Applied Probability* 2 (1970), pp. 150–177.

KOLESKAR, P. J.; RIDER, K. L.; CRABILL, T. B.; and WALKER, W. E. "A Queueing-Linear Programming Approach to Scheduling Police Patrol Cars." *Operations Research* 23 (1975), pp. 1045–1062.

LARSON, R. C. "Approximating the Performance of Urban Emergency Service Systems." *Operations Research* 23 (1975), pp. 845–868.

LARSON, R. C. *Urban Police Patrol Analysis.* Cambridge, Mass.: MIT Press, 1972.

LEMOINE, A. J. "A Queueing System with Heterogeneous Servers and Autonomous Traffic Control." *Operations Research* 23 (1975), pp. 681–686.

MINE, H.; OHNO, K.; and KOIZUMI, T. "A Single-Server Queue with Service Times Depending on the Order of Services." *Operations Research* 24 (1976), pp. 188–190.

MORSE, P. M. *Queues, Inventories and Maintenance.* New York: Wiley, 1967.

PALM, C. "Variation in Intensity in Telephone Conversation." *Ericsson Techniques.* (German), 1943, pp. 1–189.

PECK, L. G. and HAZELWOOD, R. N. *Finite Queueing Tables.* New York: Wiley, 1958.

PRABHU, N. V. *Queues and Inventories.* New York: Wiley, 1965.

SAATY, T. L. *Elements of Queueing Theory with Applications.* New York: McGraw-Hill, 1961.

SCHWARTZ, B. L. "Queueing Models With Lane Selection: A New Class of Problems." *Operations Research* 22 (1974), pp. 331–339.

TAKÁCS, L. *Introduction to the Theory of Queues.* New York: Oxford University Press, 1962.

WHITE, J. A. et al. *Analysis of Queueing Systems.* New York: Academic Press, 1975.

PROBLEM SET 7
QUEUES AND DECISIONS

1. Identify the calling units and the service facilities in each of the following systems. Discuss the likely structure of each system: the number of phases, channels, service discipline, size of the calling population, and its willingness to join and/or stay in the line. If necessary, visit the local systems of each type and diagram the calling unit flows.

 a. Airline ticket counters

 b. United States Post Office

 c. Airport runways

 d. Cafeterias

 e. Fast food outlet

 f. Telephone booth

 g. Secretarial pool

 h. Hospital

 i. Restaurants

 j. Soft drink assembly line

 k. Vending machines

 l. Computer center

 m. United States Congress

Assume in the rest of this problem set that the arrivals are Poisson and that the service systems are single-phased. Unless specifically noted, assume also that the queueing discipline is FIFO, and that the service times are exponentially distributed.

2. Consider a single-channel Poisson-Exponential queueing system with $\lambda = 7$ per hour and $\mu = 10$ per hour.

 a. Calculate and interpret the system parameters $\rho, P(0), W_s, L_s, W_q,$ and L_q.

 b. What is the probability of finding 4 calling units waiting to be served?

 c. What is the probability of finding at most 2 calling units in the system?

 d. What is the chance of finding the service facility busy even though no one has been waiting to be served?

 e. What is the probability of finding at least 2 calling units waiting to be served?

3. Compute the average number of calling units in the system, L_s, when ρ equals .95, .90, .85, . . , .5. Also compute L_s when $\rho = .96, .97, .98$ and .99. Comment on the resultant graph of L_s against ρ.

4. Parishioners arrive for confession at an average rate of 5 per hour. Father Xavier estimates that he spends an average of 10 minutes on each confession.

   a. What is the chance that Father Xavier will be idle when a parishioner arrives to confess?

   b. On the average, how many confessioners will one find in church?

   c. If you plan to confess in this church, how much time in all should you expect to spend?

5. On the average 9 planes arrive at an airport every hour. The airport has only one runway for landing which can process an average of 10 planes each hour.

   a. What is the runway utilization rate?

   b. What is the probability that 3 planes will be waiting to land?

   c. What is the average waiting time?

6. Linda Flair has just bought herself a grocery store. She believes that, on the average, a customer should not *wait* more than 2 minutes to pay for purchases. The store has only one checkout counter. An average of 15 customers approach that counter every hour. One cashier alone can service a typical customer in 4 minutes. Linda is thinking of adding 1, 2, or 3 baggers on her staff to assist the cashier. She notes that each additional bagger can save an average of 1 minute per customer.

   a. What is the average waiting time per customer if the cashier is alone? If she has 1, 2, or 3 assistants? (In each case, begin by deriving the service rate per hour.)

   b. What is the least number of baggers necessary to satisfy Linda's beliefs? (That is, ensure that W_q is 2 minutes or less.)

   c. In the proposed system of checkout, how many minutes per hour will the cashier be idle?

7. An average of 20 orders per week arrive at a small mail order store. These are filled by a single shipping clerk from the store's inventory at an average rate of 25 per week. A week consists of 5 workdays.

   a. How many days will a typical order spend in the system?

   b. What is the probability of finding 2 or more orders in the system?

   c. How many orders, on the average, will be waiting to be filled?

8. The duplicating center of a company is open 8 hours each workday (5 each week). An average of 15 employees per hour bring 3 pages each for duplication. The center is run on a self-service basis. An employee is paid $6 per hour (on the average). The duplicating center now has one copying machine which can duplicate an average of 60 pages per hour, and it costs $150 per week. A competing machine can duplicate 120 pages in a typical hour and costs $280 per week.

   a. What is the total cost per week of using the current duplicating machine?

   b. What will the corresponding cost of using the new machine?

c. Should the company replace the current machine? Why or why not?

9. Sorority Services Inc. is a group formed by the liberated coeds. Working as a team, they can wash a car in an average of 3 minutes. Because of the rather friendly atmosphere, 18 cars on the average arrive for wash every hour, but the service times are exponentially distributed.

   a. On the average, how many cars are just waiting?

   b. How many minutes is a typical wait?

10. Boyce Slayman owns a large number of slot machines in a town famous for its gambling houses. He finds that each machine yields a profit of $20 per hour. However, an average of 3 machines break down each hour. The company currently servicing these machines for Slayman charges $30 per hour and its crew needs an average of 15 minutes to fix a Slayman machine. A salesman of Quick-Fix Inc., a competing machine-repair firm, claims that their service is more than worth the service fee of $50 per hour. How fast, on the average, must Quick-Fix Inc. repair a slot machine to sustain their claim?

11. Suppose that in problem 4, another priest has been appointed to help Father Xavier hear confessions and that this new priest also spends an average of 10 minutes on each confession. Assume also that the parishioners do not show any preference between Father Xavier and his assistant.

    a. What will the λ, μ, and ρ be for the two-priest system?

    b. What is the probability that both priests will be idle?

    c. What is the probability that a parishioner will not have to wait to confess?

    d. How many confessioners do you expect to find in this church at any moment?

12. Suppose that the cashier in the problem 6 is paid $5 per hour and that each bagger is paid $3.50 per hour.

    a. What is the cost per hour of the checkout system proposed in problem 6?

    b. If Linda installs 2 checkout counters operated by 1 cashier each (no baggers), what would the average waiting time be per customer?

    c. Which of these two candidate systems is cheaper to operate?

13. Two parallel and identical runways have been built at the airport of problem 5. Answer parts a, b, and c of problem 5 again.

14. Each of the two managers has a personal secretary each of whom can type an average of 5 memos an hour. Each manager writes an average of 4 memos per hour.

    a. What is the average time a memo stays with a secretary?

    b. How many memos, on the average, are likely to be in that secretary's in-box?

    c. Suppose the managers agree to pool the secretarial services. Analyze parts a and b again.

    d. Which of these two situations (pooled and not pooled) is more efficient?

15. Forty-five customers per hour arrive at a facility randomly. Is it better to have 1 superfast operator who can process an average of 50 customers per hour or 2 slow operators each of whom can process an average of 25 customers per hour? (Average waiting time is the only criterion.)

16. The Instant-Go Company is opening a new gas station at the intersection of two expressways. The marketing research unit of the company forecasted that an average of 24 cars per hour will need regular gas. Instant-Go wants to know the number of regular-gas pumps to open in response to this need. Their criterion is that the probability that a new arrival must wait to gas up must be .20 or less. If an average car can be serviced in 3 minutes, what is the minimum necessary number of regular-gas pumps at this location? (Hint: Suppose that there are k regular-gas pumps. So long as at most $k - 1$ of these are in use, the new arrival will not have to wait. Beginning at $k = 2$, increase k until P(waiting) becomes .25 or less.)

17. Because of their rapid service, the Instant-Go Company of problem 16 has attracted additional business. In fact, their marketing research unit now forecasts that in less than 6 months the regular-gas seeking arrivals will increase to an average of 36 per hour. Should the company build more pumps? If so, how many?

18. Despite the rather friendly atmosphere at the Sorority Services car wash in problem 9, car owners are beginning to complain about the long waiting lines. Sorority's chairperson has recently located an automatic facility which can wash each car in *exactly* 3 minutes. Before installing it, they would like to know the associated waiting time and queue length statistics.

   a. Analyze the car wash situation again.

   b. Would you visit an efficient car wash facility or the one with friendly operators?

19. Suppose that the duplicating machines in problem 8 run at constant rates of 60 and 120 pages per hour, respectively. Analyze the copy machine choices again.

20. The Silverfox Bus Company notes that their reservation office receives 20 calls for tickets in a typical hour. Processing a call (i.e., checking vacant seats or finding alternative arrangement, if necessary) takes an average of 2 minutes. This being a routine operation, the service times are normally distributed with a standard deviation of 1/2 minute.

   a. On the average, how many calls have to be placed on hold?

   b. How long, on the average, will each call remain on hold?

21. Baker Hospital and the surrounding community is served by 1 ambulance. It receives 2 calls per hour. Bringing the patient to the hospital requires an average of 20 minutes with a standard deviation of 4 minutes.

   a. How many patients, on the average, must wait for the ambulance?

   b. How much time, on the average, elapses from the moment the ambulance is called till the patient reaches the hospital?

22. A computer facility divides incoming computer programs into 3 priority

classes: express, regular, and whenever. On the average, a computer needs 1/2 minute to process an express program, 3/2 minutes to process a regular program, and 5 minutes to process a whenever program. Corresponding standard deviations are 1/4, 1, and 3 minutes, respectively. An average of 50 express, 12 regular, and 2 whenever class programs arrive at the facility each hour.

    a. How many minutes, on the average, must an express program wait to be processed? A regular program? A whenever program?

    b. When you enter your program in the computer, how many other computer programs (do you expect) will be in the computer's memory?

23. It has been brought to the above computer manager's attention that service times can be reduced. Specifically, the average express processing time can be reduced to 1/4 minute (with a standard deviation of 1/8 minute) or the mean regular processing time can be reduced to 1/2 minute (with a standard deviation of 1/4 minute). If the average waiting time of the whenever programs is the decision criterion, which of these two is a better alternative?

24. Joan Little, a repairperson in charge of servicing 6 machines, notes that, on the average, each machine breaks down once each hour and that the repair time averages to 10 minutes per machine.

    a. Compute the probability that $n = 0, 1, \ldots, 6$ machines are in the repair-shop.

    b. Compute the average number of inoperative machines.

    c. What is the effective breakdown rate (λ_e)?

25. Suppose there are three repairpersons (one for each 8-hour shift) in problem 24 and each is paid $12 per hour. (Each is a skilled worker and belongs to a powerful union.) The machines, when productive, are worth $15 per hour. The factory operates around the clock.

    a. What is the average downtime per breakdown? What is the cost of each breakdown?

    b. What is the total per-hour cost to the system (repair person's pay + total downtime cost per hour)?

26. For the situation in problem 25, will it be cheaper to hire an additional repair-person on each shift? Justify your response.

27. Suppose that Peter McDonald's antique machines (in example 7 in the text) are worth $6 per productive hour and that Peter's assistant charges $4 per hour (he is the teenage son of Peter's neighbor).

    a. What is the per-hour cost of the system analyzed in example 7?

    b. Suppose that Peter decides not to hire the assistant. How many machines, on the average, will be nonproductive? At what cost per hour?

    c. Is it cheaper to hire an assistant?

28. An exclusive nursing home assigns one nurse to every seven residents. On the average, each resident needs the assigned nurse once every three hours for an average of 20 minutes (perhaps for some medical reasons, or perhaps because

the caller is bored). When not in the nursing room, the residents carry on the normal activities expected of such residents.

   a. What is the effective rate of calls per hour?

   b. How much is the expected waiting time?

   c. On the average, how many residents are engaged in the normal activities?

29. Joe Yablonski is an expert mechanic in a large city who specializes in tune ups. He can tune up a car in an average of 45 minutes and he charges $12 for his services (parts extra). His shop is open 8 hours a day, 5 days each week. An arrival is serviced immediately unless Joe is busy—in which case the waiting cars are parked in the adjoining lot which can store 2 customer cars. An average of 9 customers per day seek Joe's services but if the parking lot is full, a new arrival goes someplace else.

   a. How many hours, on the average, will Joe be idle every day?

   b. How many cars, on the average, does Joe service each week?

   c. What is Joe's average income each week?

30. A vacant lot next to Joe's repair shop is on the market. It can accommodate 4 cars and the mortgage payments will come to $86.67 per month (= 4.3 weeks).

   a. Answer parts a, b, and c of problem 29 assuming that Joe increases his customer parking area by purchasing the vacant lot.

   b. How much will be the net increase in Joe's income?

   c. Should he buy the next door lot?

31. A marketing research course includes a lab session where the students design questionnaires, develop sampling frames, and conduct surveys. An aide is available to help the students in case of difficulty. She responds to questions as these arise. A student with a question will "come back later" if 3 others are already waiting in line. An average of 4 students per hour approach the aide who can answer the question in an average of 12 minutes. Assume that there are a large number of students.

   a. How many students, on the average, will be waiting in line?

   b. What is the effective arrival rate?

   c. How long does a typical student remain in doubt?

32. A professor can assist an average of 6 students per hour. His office contains 4 chairs for the benefit of students. Students are discouraged from standing. Due to the professor's popularity, 10 students seek his help in a typical hour.

   a. Describe the steady-state values of $P(0)$, W_s, L_s, L_q, and W_q.

   b. What is the probability of finding 3 students in his office?

   c. Comment on the applicability of steady-state formulas.

8

Monte Carlo Simulation Techniques

Basic Process and Rationale
Obtaining Simulated Values in the Discrete Case
Simulating the Values of a Continuous Variable
Special Transformations
Summary
Selected Readings
Problem Set 8: Simulation of Chance Events

Since to simulate is to make believe, you might wonder why management scientists engage in this activity while trying to solve real world systems problems. You might also wonder how to go about creating a simulated history and how it can lead to policy decisions. Responding to such queries is the purpose of this and the following chapter. Of necessity, management scientists turn to computers for performing the actual computations. But, to understand the technique a few of these computations should be done manually. This chapter shows you how.

BASIC PROCESS AND RATIONALE

The question: "Why resort to simulation?" can be answered in a number of different ways. Generally, responses to this question belong to one of two categories.

The real system may be too complex to permit a compact mathematical model or to obtain an analytical solution. In studying waiting line models, for instance, you must have noticed that the more the real system deviates from the single-channel, single-phase, Poisson-Exponential model, the more complex its representation becomes and the harder it is to obtain an analytical solution. As another example, recall that, to ensure the relative simplicity of inventory models, we had to assume that all parameters (except possibly demand) were known and constant. Similarly, while solving a stochastic PERT model, only the variances along the critical path were examined. The tasks with shorter average durations (though possibly large variances) were excluded from any further discussion of project completion times—though such tasks could conceivably become critical.

It might be more practical or more possible to try out a new instrument or a new operating procedure in a realistic setting before deciding to use it in an actual system. A manager cannot buy and sell actual commodities on the Chicago Exchange just to try out a new investment policy. On the other hand, experience in performing such activities is necessary to becoming a successful trader of commodities. The dilemma is resolved by trading "on paper," i.e., by simulating the actual acts of trading and thus anticipating the potential impact of the proposed trading policies. It is possible to visualize many other situations where simulation can be a useful technique. For example, it is much cheaper to simulate on paper the effects of opening a new hospital, constructing a new highway, installing a new welfare program or instituting a new tax package.

In short, *simulation is a technique of last resort.* It should not be used when an appropriate formal model of the situation at hand can be constructed. Formal models are preferred since they yield analytical solutions, the corresponding solution techniques are usually more efficient, and the resultant policies are more likely to be optimal. When the models become complex or when gaining "hands on" experience in a real setting is impossible, expensive, or simply disastrous; one must resort to simulating the effects of the proposed policies, procedures, or instruments.

A majority of simulation models used by management scientists must deal with chance events, i.e., ones in which a course of action has more than one outcome. Ordering a new batch of widgets when only 100 are in stock is, for example, a course of action for an inventory controller. It can lead to one of three outcomes: shortage, surplus, or replenishment of inventory at just the right moment. In the chapter on inventory models, you saw how to deal with this decision problem using a formal model. In many real situations, however, both the lead time and the demand during lead time are stochastic. Yet, there must be a way to solve these and more complex inventory models, e.g., to determine how much and when to order or where to store the purchased/produced units.

The Monte Carlo technique of simulation (named after Monaco's famous gambling casino) comes in handy in situations of this sort. Suppose we institute a policy of reordering when exactly 100 widgets are in stock.

The possible consequences of this policy can be examined as follows. Using a random sequence of numbers (such as that shown in table 8-1), a known distribution of demand (such as that obtained from the study of demands for widgets in the past), one can obtain a possible numerical value of demand. Given this value for demand, you can easily determine the shortage or surplus likely to occur on this simulated occasion and hence the potential cost. By repeating the process many times, you can accumulate a *simulated history* of the consequences of using this policy of reordering when 100 widgets are in stock; and hence determine the average cost of using this policy. Alternative policies such as reordering when 80 or 120 widgets are in stock can be evaluated similarly. Having examined a number of candidate policies, the one that seems to yield the least cost (or some other decision criterion) is chosen to be the best policy on the basis of this simulated experiment.

The Monte Carlo technique consists of using random sequences of numbers and known probability distributions to obtain simulated values of chance variables. Using these values as chance inputs, the corresponding outputs on a *simulated occasion* can be derived. Repeating the process a large number of times yields a *simulated history* of the consequences of using a specific policy. Given a number of candidate policies, the one with the best simulated history is chosen as a "solution" to the decision-making situation.

The words "simulated occasion" and "simulated history" can take on different meanings depending on the decision-making situation. For instance, to obtain the possible completion time of a complex project, you can generate the simulated duration of each component task. Having done this, a critical path of the resultant PERT network on this occasion can be determined. The simulated history is derived by using different sets of task durations. Given this history, it is easy to assess the chances of completing the project in a specified amount of time.

To simulate the waiting lines, generate the moments in time when a new calling unit approaches the service system, generate the service times in minutes (hours, days, or weeks) at each service facility on its visit schedule, and thus compute the resulting waiting times and idle times on each occasion. The history is generated when a large number of such simulated calling units have progressed through the system. Each different configuration of the service system (e.g., the addition of new facilities and institution of new service rules) constitutes a different policy. When these simulated histories become available, the best possible service system under the circumstances can be determined.

Table 8-1 *A Uniform Random Sequence of Numbers*

86229	95389	19446	16176	07845	35176	61286
61784	27290	36298	20766	00401	85825	53112
09902	93274	95553	75427	24219	50461	68860
75719	78840	11241	20516	19634	60972	06576
79929	27262	36306	91086	51059	72701	46815
32064	57487	09399	37468	43024	10137	08774
49342	49274	35159	99620	16645	73024	99463
95794	05143	25526	71119	99680	29493	93742
54198	68940	86987	09048	29285	34042	45194
85463	47638	54067	21015	14915	06004	98308
88642	07035	45900	41138	53923	60983	12737
57663	32633	56808	12612	07665	70152	53832
04243	95309	40049	83573	63598	92149	59074
24697	58596	10903	56050	47498	71570	17514
32131	15411	06313	68993	50256	31062	20808
64542	90270	14338	12602	97458	08940	99999
11854	95319	40634	42814	02017	35947	77209
14233	16197	26663	64246	88584	43153	34310
51200	88812	80961	53568	32950	96737	75833
01043	20261	04851	83592	22640	76645	00646
91299	01720	59139	70467	36545	55532	00475
10405	61893	07433	70171	31715	41974	22383
52015	48266	20749	93229	75468	33527	96416
65259	38460	34576	91482	86548	59105	30650
45482	71583	93811	23716	67869	65662	59306
48584	88541	97581	96062	90038	43543	08106
10634	94516	33411	41713	34393	63802	91679
89123	36177	18263	01043	68112	26347	17112
94677	30099	89737	23203	80210	80024	85028
99857	23856	96999	48014	27220	32198	43245
36283	25648	69137	48806	52798	73633	45487
59554	85890	07750	18734	35958	03153	92141
40444	90155	36747	45028	88336	48785	97607
09758	24006	29116	56058	57878	03302	15948
26338	11747	94370	26800	92522	74167	23342
52875	13361	52562	95684	63300	43519	65170
27207	60199	08719	16784	22726	71916	72297
31509	39878	72196	30664	30059	75599	12510
75164	39087	12751	55222	57851	20035	64414
95024	98668	05030	53326	56150	71524	27298
63982	52879	06791	33620	04893	00810	47699
66311	18495	66422	98135	02237	76221	42421
99357	36354	96220	36358	73106	97292	21246
60036	68629	82456	94184	07194	51106	00169
68756	06973	68985	06338	92860	40669	37719
23158	02082	09256	77417	27345	60856	39200
41896	95396	88781	14051	76635	93388	09601
19314	43147	98802	60329	88105	47245	41882
98037	35087	08724	54019	41802	66183	09943
10677	87301	51579	60813	56343	31569	49502

*The Monte Carlo technique assumes a decimal point in front of each number so that the resultant numbers lie between 0 and 1. For example, the first three numbers in the first column are .86229, .61784, and .09902.

The Monte Carlo technique can also be used as an indirect aid to decision making. For example, it is used to select the respondents for market research, to numerically solve complicated integrals, and to obtain joint probability distributions. The trick lies in properly identifying the occasions and hence the history.

You can now see why one might use Monte Carlo simulation techniques for making real world decisions. You have also seen a broad sketch of how to use such techniques in practice. In the rest of this chapter, we shall examine the details—how to obtain the simulated values of chance variables and how to combine the variety of such variables called for by a model.

Actually, obtaining the simulated values of a chance (random) variable is a fairly straightforward task, as long as its probability distribution is known or can be presumed to be known. Given this information, the possible numerical values are obtained by constructing the corresponding cumulative probability distribution and then using a random sequence of numbers. There are two possibilities: the random variable of interest might assume any value from a continuous range, or it might be restricted to assuming its values from a disjoint set. The actual procedure for obtaining the numerical values differs somewhat, depending on the nature of the random variable. We will examine each possibility separately.

OBTAINING SIMULATED VALUES IN THE DISCRETE CASE

The number of units of a specific product sold during a week, the number of customers approaching a service counter in an hour, and the number of students registering for a course at the beginning of a semester are a few examples of discontinuous (also called discrete) random variables. The adjective "discrete" refers to the fact that the actual values of such variables can be arranged in a sequence. The adjective "random" implies that one cannot predict with certainty the actual value a variable might assume on any one occasion. See also chapter 2 for more formal definitions.

If you wish to generate a simulated value of a discrete random variable on a specific occasion, say that of the demand for a product next week, you should follow these steps:

Step 1. Determine the probability distribution for the variable of interest.

If the theoretical shape of this distribution is known, the above step is tantamount to obtaining the numerical values of specific parameters. For example, in the preceding chapter, we noticed that the number of customers approaching a service counter follows the Poisson distribution. Thus, knowing the average number of arrivals per hour, λ, is sufficient to completely define its probability distribution.

When the theoretical distribution is unknown, one must obtain the probability distribution on an empirical basis—either on the basis of past experience or by conducting a special experiment. Suppose, for example, that the demand for a product is known for each of the past 150 weeks and that the results can be summarized as in table 8-2. In that case, the *relative frequencies* can be used to approximate the probability distribution.

Table 8-2 *Weekly Demand for a Product*

x = NUMBER OF UNITS SOLD	$f(x)$ = NUMBER OF SUCH WEEKS
10	40
11	45
12	35
13	20
14	10
Total	150

Specifically, divide each observed frequency $f(x)$ by the total frequency (150 in this case) to obtain the corresponding relative frequency $p(x)$. Then $p(x)$ approximates the probability that the discrete random variable (X = demand during one week) equals x, where x = 10, 11, 12, 13, or 14. The results of these computations are:

x	10	11	12	13	14
$p(x)$	.27	.30	.23	.13	.07

Step 2. Arrange the x values in the increasing order and compute the cumulative probability distribution, $F(x)$.

For the random variable, X = weekly demand, the possible values, x = 10, 11, ... and 14, are already in the increasing order. The $F(x)$ values are obtained by noting that $F(10) = p(10) = .27$ and then successively using the formula:

$$F(x) = F(x - 1) + p(x)$$

Thus, you can verify that:

$$F(10) = p(10) = .27$$
$$F(11) = F(10) + p(11) = .27 + .30 = .57$$

and similarly:

$$F(12) = .80, F(13) = .93, \text{ and } F(14) = 1$$

For all other values of X, $F(x)$ is obtained by using the following argument. From the construction alone, you can see that $F(x)$ equals the probability that the random variable X is less than or equal to the number x. Since fewer than 10 units have never been demanded in the past, using that past as a guide for the future:

$$F(x) = 0, \text{ whenever } x < 10$$

Similarly, since more than 14 units have never been used in any of the previous 150 weeks:

$$p(x) = 0, \text{ whenever } x > 14$$

Hence:

$$F(x) = 1, \text{ whenever } x \geqslant 14$$

Also, since the demand is *never* fractional:

$$p(x) = 0, \text{ for any fraction } x$$

To summarize, the cumulative distribution of x is given by:

$$F(x) = \begin{cases} 0, & \text{when } x < 10 \\ .27, & \text{when } 10 \leqslant x < 11 \\ .57, & \text{when } 11 \leqslant x < 12 \\ .80, & \text{when } 12 \leqslant x < 13 \\ .93, & \text{when } 13 \leqslant x < 14 \\ 1.00, & \text{when } x \geqslant 14 \end{cases}$$

Figure 8-1 shows the graph of $F(x)$ against x, which is also known as the *ogive* of the random variable X. When X can assume integer values only, as is the case with weekly demand, its ogive is always a *step function*. This simply means that $F(x)$ remains steady over a range of values, jumps to assume its next higher value, and then remains steady until the moment of its next jump.

In general, suppose that $F(x)$ jumps when $x = c_1$ or c_2 or . . . or c_k, but at no other value. Suppose also that $c_1 < c_2 < \ldots < c_k$. The simulated

Figure 8-1. *The Ogive of Weekly Demand*

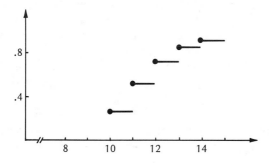

values of the corresponding random variable X can be obtained as in the next step.

Step 3. Choose any one member, say r, of a random sequence. Use r as if it were a probability. If r is smaller than the "height" of the first step of $F(x)$, i.e., if $r < F(c_1)$, set $x = c_1$. Otherwise, if $r < F(c_2)$, set $x = c_2$. If $F(c_{j-1}) \leq r < F(c_j)$, for some integer j (obviously, $2 \leq j \leq k$), then set $x = c_j$. This yields a simulated value of X. By choosing the consecutive members of the random sequence in succession, you can obtain as many simulated values of X as desired.

Obtaining a random sequence is fairly easy. Most textbooks on operations research, including this one, publish a table of such numbers (table 8-1). RAND Corporation (Santa Monica, CA) has published an entire book of random digits. Also, many computers have a program to generate a random sequence.

As an illustration of its use, refer to table 8-1. Suppose we choose $r = .86229$. To simulate the demand for a product on one occasion, notice that $r = .86229$ lies between $F(12) = .80$ and $F(13) = .93$. Hence, as per Step 3, x takes a simulated value of 13. Other simulated values of demand can be obtained by, for example, reading down the first column of table 8-1. Thus, the next number is $r = .61784$ and hence, the corresponding simulated demand would be for $x = 12$ units. The next simulated demand, corresponding to $r = .09902$ would be $x = 10$ units. You can now continue the process to obtain as large a sample of simulated demand as desired.

SIMULATING THE VALUES
OF A CONTINUOUS VARIABLE

Such variables as the number of minutes spent at the receptionist's desk, dollar volume of sales in a week, the amount of blood used during a surgery, and the height of a randomly chosen person are *continuous*. Fractional values of such variables have operational meanings. These are *random* in the sense that it is not possible to predict their values with certainty. In this section, we shall examine the general process of obtaining the simulated values of such variables. This process is similar to that described in the preceding section, the main difference being that the cumulative probability distribution $F(x)$ is no longer a step function.

If the shape of the theoretical distribution is assumed to be known, obtaining $F(x)$ is equivalent to finding the numerical values of the necessary parameters. For example, if a large number of students are each given an identical test, the distribution of their test scores can be approximated by the "normal" curve. To derive $F(x)$ in such cases, only the expected value $E(X)$ and the corresponding standard deviation $\sigma(X)$ need to be determined. The $F(x)$ value for any number x is obtained by referring to a table of "areas under a normal curve," such as that shown in appendix A.

Similarly, the time elapsed between two Poisson events is known to be exponentially distributed. (See the chapter on waiting lines.) Hence, knowing the average time between two consecutive Poisson events is sufficient to obtain the corresponding $F(x)$. Additional details will be given under "Special Transformations" in this chapter.

Empirical Derivation of $F(x)$

In case a theoretical justification for using some specific probability law cannot be given, empirical data must be used to derive $F(x)$. Suppose, for example, that table 8-3 summarizes the weekly expenditures of several four-person households and that no theoretical distribution fits this data.

To derive $F(x)$, begin by computing the relative frequencies to approximate the corresponding probabilities. As in the preceding section, this is accomplished by dividing individual class frequencies by the total, 125 in this case.

Table 8-3 *Summary of Weekly Expenditures*

DOLLAR AMOUNT	NUMBER OF HOUSEHOLDS
$50 – $79.99	20
$80 – $119.99	40
$120 – $179.99	50
$180 – $250	15
Total	125

The results are as follows:

Class	50 – 79.99	$80 – 119.99	$120 – 179.99	$180 – 250
Probability	.16	.32	.40	.12

First compute $F(x)$ values at each of the class boundaries, i.e., at 50, 80, 120, 180, and 250. Since no household has spent less than $50 per week, you should set:

$$F(50) = 0$$

The values of F at successive boundaries are now obtained by successively adding the relative frequency of the preceding class. Thus:

$$
\begin{aligned}
F(80) &= F(50) + .16 = .16 \\
F(120) &= F(80) + .32 = .48 \\
F(180) &= F(120) + .40 = .88 \\
F(250) &= F(180) + .12 = 1.00
\end{aligned}
$$

Since fractional values of expenditure are meaningful, the F values within each class are obtained by *linear* interpolation between the class boundaries. The effect of so doing is represented by the ogive of figure 8-2. To construct that figure, the points corresponding to $x = 50, 80, 120, 180,$ and 250 are plotted first, and then they are joined by straight lines.

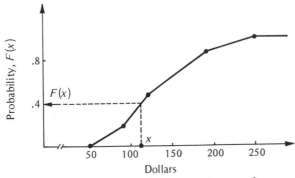

Figure 8-2. *The Ogive of Weekly Expenditures*

Algebraically, let a and b denote the boundaries of a class with $a \leq b$. Then, for each number x in this class:

$$F(x) = F(a) + (x - a) \cdot \frac{F(b) - F(a)}{b - a}$$

For example, in the lowest expenditure class, $a = \$50$ and $b = \$80$; $F(a) = 0$ and $F(b) = .16$. Whenever $\$50 \leq x \leq \$80$,

$$F(x) = 0 + (x - 50) \cdot \frac{.16 - 0}{80 - 50} = .0053x - .27$$

By repeating this process for each expenditure class, you will find that:

$$F(x) = \begin{cases} 0 & \text{if } x \leq 50 \\ .0053x - .2667 & \text{if } 50 \leq x \leq 80 \\ .0080x - .64 & \text{if } 80 \leq x \leq 120 \\ .0067x - .8 & \text{if } 120 \leq x \leq 180 \\ .0017x - .3086 & \text{if } 180 \leq x \leq 250 \\ 1 & \text{if } 250 \leq x \end{cases}$$

The Inverse Transformation

Given the cumulative probability function, whether theoretical or empirical, the numerical values of the corresponding continuous random variable can be simulated by using a random sequence of numbers. Specifically, let r denote a member of the random sequence. Then, the corresponding simulated value, x, is obtained by solving the equation:

$$r = F(x)$$

The resultant number x is often denoted by the formula:

$$x = F^{-1}(r)$$

where the exponent, -1, indicates that one is proceeding in the reverse direction—computing x given r, rather than finding $F(x)$ corresponding to x.

The process of finding x given r and the ogive of a continuous random variable can be depicted as in figure 8-3. Measure r units along the $F(x)$ axis. From that point (A in figure 8-3) draw a line parallel to the X-axis until it meets the ogive (at point B). From that point, draw a line parallel to the $F(x)$ axis until it meets the X-axis (at point C in the figure). Measure the distance, x, of this point from the origin. This x is the simulated value of the random variable of interest.

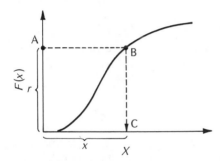

Figure 8-3. *Using an Ogive to Simulate the Values of a Continuous Variable*

As a specific example, consider again the four-person households. The cumulative probability function of their expenditures was computed and displayed earlier. To simulate the expenditure of a household, we must solve $r = F(x)$ either graphically or by algebraic formulas. Since the procedure has been indicated graphically in figure 8-3, we will illustrate the algebraic process. Either way, it is easy to verify that:

$$
\begin{aligned}
x &= \quad\$50, \text{ if } r = 0\\
x &= \quad\$80, \text{ if } r = .16\\
x &= \$120, \text{ if } r = .48\\
x &= \$180, \text{ if } r = .88\\
x &= \$250, \text{ if } r = 1
\end{aligned}
$$

If the random number r falls between $F(a)$ and $F(b)$, where a and b are the ends of a line segment with $a \leqslant b$, the corresponding $x = F^{-1}(r)$ is obtained by the interpolation formula:

$$x = a + [r - F(a)] \cdot \frac{b - a}{F(b) - F(a)}$$

For example, suppose r lies between .16 and .48 so that

$$a = F^{-1}(.16) = \$80 \text{ and } b = F^{-1}(.48) = \$120$$

Then:

$$x = \$80 + (r - .16) \cdot \frac{\$120 - \$80}{.48 - .16}$$

$$= \$60 + 125r$$

The results of similar computations can be summed up as follows.

$$x = \begin{cases} 50 + 187.5r & \text{if} & r \leqslant .16 \\ 60 + 125r & \text{if } .16 \leqslant r \leqslant .48 \\ 48 + 150r & \text{if } .48 \leqslant r \leqslant .88 \\ -333 + 583.33r & \text{if } .88 \leqslant r \end{cases}$$

Given these formulas and a random sequence of sufficient length, you can easily obtain a simulated sample of any desired size.

SPECIAL TRANSFORMATIONS

In the preceding two sections, we have seen the general approach for simulating the numerical values of a chance variable. Though the techniques examined in those two sections can be used in all cases, many of the random variables commonly used to simulate the operations of a system are of a few well-known types. This section examines these common variable types and some short cuts for obtaining their simulated values. To make the technical discussion both relevant and interesting, we will pause to describe a miniature system whose operations will be simulated to illustrate the techniques.

The Southboro Health Induction Project (SHIP)

This outpatient clinic is operated by two physicians, Dr. Jones and Dr. Berry, each of whom specializes in a different branch of medicine. Thus, there is no competition between them and each physician has his own set of patients. To this effect, we can think of SHIP as consisting of two parallel channels. The physicians do, however, share the services of a receptionist and a cashier. The SHIP contains a common waiting room stocked with the usual literature in the medical waiting rooms. It also contains a playroom for the convenience of patients who must bring their children with them. The physical setup of SHIP is shown in figure 8-4. SHIP is open for business from 1 PM to 5 PM, Monday through Saturday. This means that on any such day, SHIP admits its first patient as early as 1 PM and that anyone who enters SHIP prior to 5 PM is served that very day—no matter how long it takes.

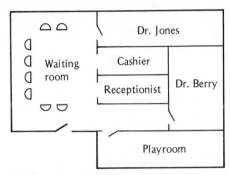

Figure 8-4. *Physical Layout of SHIP*

The Symptoms Recently, the management of SHIP has noticed that despite the good pay rate ($6 per hour), there is a high turnover of cashiers. Also, at times, the waiting room seems crowded (and the playroom is noisy). SHIP has therefore appointed a management consulting firm to identify the cause of their difficulties. This firm has decided to simulate the client-related activities of SHIP for performing that task. As a part of that job, the consultants have created a chart showing the flow of patients through SHIP. They have also collected some statistical data. These are summarized in figure 8-5.

The Arrival Process An average of 12 patients arrive each hour—the first one arriving at 1 PM or slightly thereafter. The Poisson distribution provides a good approximation of the process. After checking in with the receptionist each new arrival joins the end of the waiting line, the service discipline being first come, first served. (This is true of all the activities at SHIP.) The receptionist obtains each patient's prior records (if any) and notifies Dr. Jones or Dr. Berry, as appropriate. She needs between 1 and 5 minutes to perform these actions and any duration within these limits is equally likely. SHIP pays her $3.50 per hour.

Processing by the Doctors Depending on the type of complaint, a patient goes to see Dr. Jones or Dr. Berry. Past experience shows that 70% of all patients wish to see Dr. Jones; the rest go to see Dr. Berry. The patient is asked to enter the doctor's office if the appropriate doctor is free. Otherwise, the patient stays in the waiting room. The service times of each doctor, i.e., the time each doctor spends with his patient, follow the normal distribution. On the average, Dr. Jones spends 9 minutes with a

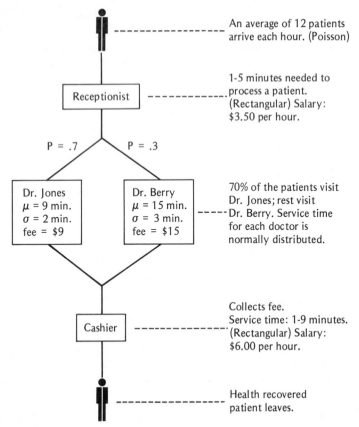

Figure 8-5. *The Client Flow at SHIP*

patient, and his service times have a standard deviation of 2 minutes. Dr. Jones charges $9 per patient. The corresponding figures for Dr. Berry are 15 minutes, 3 minutes, and $15, respectively.

Fee Collection The doctors, themselves, do not collect the fee. This work is done for them by the cashier who is paid $6 per hour. Since there are many different methods of paying for the doctor's services (cash, check, insurance, medicaid, or credit card), the time spent with each patient varies considerably. In fact, the cashier needs between 1 and 9 minutes to process each patient, and these times follow a rectangular distribution. At the end of this process, the patient leaves SHIP.

A thorough investigation of SHIP's difficulties may encompass such factors as the pay rates, the fee structures, the mortgage rates, and the possibilities of expansion. In this section, however, we will use the information regarding SHIP's client flows to illustrate some of the common transformations in a Monte Carlo simulation.

The Rectangular Distribution

A random variable, X, that follows this probability law is continuous and bounded. This means that we can always find two constants, a and b, with $a \leq b$, such that $F(a) = 0$ and $F(b) = 1$. In particular, one can determine the left-hand boundary, a, by finding the smallest possible value of X, and the right-hand boundary, b, by finding the largest possible value of X. Within these two limits, any number x is a possible value of X. Rectangular distribution is further characterized by the property that, given any two numbers, c and d, with $a \leq c < d \leq b$, the probability that X lies between c and d is proportional to the difference $d - c$. Specifically:

$$P(c \leq X \leq d) = \frac{d - c}{b - a}$$

It is easy to verify that under these circumstances, the cumulative probability function $F(x)$ is given by:

$$F(x) = \begin{cases} 0, & \text{if } x \leq a \\ (x - a)/(b - a), & \text{if } a \leq x \leq b \\ 1, & \text{if } x \geq b \end{cases}$$

The adjective "rectangular" is used because the corresponding probability density function $p(x)$ remains constant in the interval from a to b. In fact;

$$p(x) = \frac{1}{b - a}, \text{ whenever } a < x < b$$

The graph of $p(x)$ against x resembles a rectangle, as shown in figure 8-6. In short, a rectangular probability density is obtained by extending the concept of "equally likely outcomes" for all points in a finite interval.

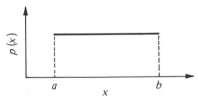

Figure 8-6. *A Rectangular Probability Density*

To simulate the numerical value of such a variable, find a random number r, and then solve: $r = F(x)$. Since $F(x)$ equals $(x - a) / (b - a)$ as long as $a \leq x \leq b$, the equation $r = F(x)$ becomes:

$$r = \frac{(x - a)}{(b - a)}$$

so that:

$$x = a + (b - a) \cdot r$$

The simulated sample of size n is obtained by choosing n consecutive members of a random sequence and then using the above equation repeatedly.

To illustrate the process, recall that the receptionist at SHIP needs between 1 and 5 minutes to process one patient and that the actual durations follow the rectangular distribution. See figure 8-5. Hence, in this case, $a = 1, b = 5$, and:

$$F(x) = \frac{x - 1}{5 - 1} = \frac{x - 1}{4}, \text{ whenever } 1 \leqslant x \leqslant 5$$

Hence:

$$r = \frac{x - 1}{4}$$

$$x = 4r + 1$$

Suppose we wish to simulate the receptionist's service times for each of the first 48 patients on a typical day at SHIP. The choice of a random sequence is arbitrary. Suppose we choose the first 48 numbers in the first column of table 8-1. The numbers as shown in that column are five digits each. Assume a decimal point to the left of each number. Thus, for example, read the first number to be .86229 rather than 86229. Since we are doing this activity for illustrative purposes only, we shall simplify our work by "rounding off" each number to two decimal places only. Thus, for instance, round off .86229 to .86; round off .61784 to .62; round off .09902 to .10.

This process yields $r_1 = .86$, $r_2 = .62$, $r_3 = .10$, ..., $r_{48} = .19$. Repeatedly using the equation:

$$x = 4r + 1$$

we get the required sample of 48 observations. For example:

$$x_1 = 4r_1 + 1 = (4)(.86) + 1 = 4.44$$

Similarly:

$$x_2 = (4)(.62) + 1 = 3.48$$

You can now determine $x_3, x_4, \ldots, x_{48}$ in this manner. These computations are summarized in table 8-4, where the receptionist's service times (i.e., the x values computed above) are denoted by SR. The service times (SR) are read in order from left to right across the table.

Also recall that the cashier's service times, i.e., the number of minutes necessary to settle the accounts, follow a rectangular distribution.

Table 8-4 *Receptionist's Service Times, SR*

r	SR	r	SR	r	SR	r	SR	r	SR
.86	4.44	.62	3.48	.10	1.40	.76	4.04	.80	4.20
.32	2.28	.49	2.96	.96	4.84	.54	3.16	.85	4.40
.89	4.56	.58	3.32	.04	1.16	.25	2.00	.32	2.28
.65	3.60	.12	1.48	.14	1.56	.51	3.04	.01	1.04
.91	4.64	.10	1.40	.52	3.08	.65	3.60	.45	2.80
.49	2.96	.11	1.44	.89	2.56	.95	4.80	1.00	5.00
.36	2.44	.60	3.40	.40	2.60	.10	1.40	.26	2.04
.53	3.12	.27	2.08	.32	2.28	.75	4.00	.95	4.80
.64	3.56	.66	3.64	.99	4.96	.60	3.40	.69	3.76
.23	1.92	.42	2.68	.19	1.56				

Figure 8-5 displays that she needs 5 ± 4 minutes per patient. Hence, $a = 5 - 4 = 1$ minute and $b = 5 + 4 = 9$ minutes. Thus, given a random number r, you can determine her service time to be: $x = 1 + 8r$. At this stage, it is necessary to remember the following rule.

> When simulating the values of two or more random variables, distinct sequences of numbers must be used to avoid introducing artificial correlations where none exist.

To simulate the cashier's service times, for example, we can no longer use the first column of numbers in table 8-1. But, you could use the second column. As before, round off the numbers to two decimal places. Also, let SC denote the service times of the cashier, i.e., let:

$$SC = 1 + 8r$$

You can now obtain the simulated service times of the cashier for each of the first 48 patients at SHIP on a typical day. The results are summarized in table 8-5. As in the previous table, the observations are read left to right, line by line across the table.

The Binary Variable

A random variable that follows this probability law arises in so many situations (and in so many disguises) that it is impossible to enumerate all the possibilities here. Such a variable has only two values, e.g., success or failure, true or false, and defective or good. In other words, such a variable represents a *dichotomy* of some kind. Traditionally, the corresponding variable is assigned a value $x = 1$ if the observation is of one type and $x = 0$ if it is not. Usually, $P(x = 1)$ is denoted by the symbol p, and $P(x = 0)$ is denoted by $q = 1 - p$.

Table 8-5 *Service Times of the Cashier, SC*

r	SC	r	SC	r	SC	r	SC	r	SC
.95	8.60	.27	3.16	.93	8.44	.79	7.32	.27	3.16
.57	5.56	.49	4.92	.05	1.40	.69	6.52	.48	4.84
.07	1.56	.33	3.64	.95	8.60	.59	5.72	.15	2.20
.90	8.20	.95	8.60	.16	2.28	.89	8.12	.20	2.60
.02	1.16	.62	5.96	.48	4.84	.38	3.04	.72	6.76
.89	8.12	.95	8.60	.36	3.88	.30	3.40	.24	2.92
.26	3.08	.86	7.88	.90	8.20	.24	2.92	.12	1.96
.13	2.04	.60	5.80	.40	4.20	.39	4.12	.99	8.92
.53	5.24	.18	2.44	.36	3.88	.69	6.52	.07	1.56
.02	1.16	.95	8.60	.43	4.44				

To simulate the value of a binary variable, assign $x = 1$, if the random number r is less than p; $x = 0$, if it is not. Symbolically:

$$x = \begin{cases} 1, \text{ if } r < p \\ 0, \text{ otherwise} \end{cases}$$

As usual, to simulate a random sample of size n, find a random sequence of n numbers and then assign $x = 1$ or 0, as appropriate for each r.

For example, a patient at SHIP is assigned to Dr. Jones with probability .7 and to Dr. Berry with probability .3. We may, therefore, equate p with .7 and describe the sampling process as follows. Using the fourth column of table 8-1 (rounded off to two decimals) as the random sequence, assign a simulated patient to Dr. Jones, if the corresponding number is less than .7; otherwise, to Dr. Berry. Consequent choices are shown in table 8-6.

Table 8-6 *Assignment of the First 48 Patients to the Doctors*

r	CHOICE	r	CHOICE	r	CHOICE	r	CHOICE	r	CHOICE
.16	Jones	.21	Jones	.75	Berry	.21	Jones	.91	Berry
.37	Jones	1.00	Berry	.71	Berry	.09	Jones	.21	Jones
.41	Jones	.13	Jones	.84	Berry	.56	Jones	.69	Jones
.13	Jones	.42	Jones	.64	Jones	.54	Jones	.84	Berry
.70	Berry	.70	Berry	.93	Berry	.91	Berry	.24	Jones
.96	Berry	.42	Jones	.01	Jones	.23	Jones	.48	Jones
.49	Jones	.19	Jones	.45	Jones	.56	Jones	.27	Jones
.96	Berry	.17	Jones	.31	Jones	.55	Jones	.53	Jones
.34	Jones	.98	Berry	.36	Jones	.94	Berry	.06	Jones
.77	Berry	.14	Jones	.60	Jones				

Multiple Splits

Sometimes, you might wish to split the population into three or more groups. For example, SHIP may get an additional doctor, you may want to assign work to one of your five colleagues, or cars arriving at a gas station may go to one of the eight pumps.

In general terms, suppose that the population is to be divided into k groups with membership probabilities $p_1, p_2, \ldots, p_k$. Arbitrarily, define $x = 1$ if the observation belongs to the first group, $x = 2$ if it belongs to the second group, $\ldots$, and $x = k$ if it belongs to the kth group. Since only the values $1, 2, \ldots, k$ are meaningful, the variable x is a discrete variable and as such, the corresponding cumulative probability function $F(x)$ is a step function. From the discussion in the previous section, you should recognize that:

$$F(0) = 0$$
$$F(1) = p_1$$
$$F(2) = p_1 + p_2$$
$$\cdots\cdots\cdots$$
$$\cdots\cdots\cdots\cdots$$
$$F(k - 1) = p_1 + p_2 + \cdots + p_{k-1}$$
$$F(k) = 1$$

Hence, following the logic of step functions, you should set:

$$x = j, \text{ if } F(j - 1) \leqslant r < F(j),$$

$$\text{where } j = 1, 2, \ldots, k$$

The simulated sample of size n can now be obtained by choosing a random sequence of size n and then obtaining the x values using the above formula.

Exponential Distribution

One of the best ways to identify a negative *exponential variable* is to look for *the time elapsed between two consecutive occurrences of a Poisson event*. The number of hours an electric light will last, the number of minutes elapsed between the arrival of two customers, and the length of a telephone conversation in a relaxed atmosphere are a few of the examples of such variables. An exponential variable is continuous, and takes only nonnegative values. On the other hand, there is no upper limit on the possible value of an exponential variable. In theory, at least, a conversation conducted in friendly and cozy atmosphere can last forever.

The cumulative probability function $F(x)$ of an exponential variable is given by:

$$F(x) = \begin{cases} 0 & \text{if } x \leqslant 0 \\ 1 - e^{\frac{-x}{M}} & \text{if } x > 0 \end{cases}$$

The constant M in the above formula *equals the average time* elapsed between two consecutive occurrences of a Poisson event, i.e., it is the expected value of x, and e denotes the base of a "natural logarithm." ($e \approx 2.71828$).

The Procedure for Obtaining x To simulate the numerical value x corresponding to a random number r, it is convenient to recognize that if r is random, so is $1 - r$. Hence, in this case, x is obtained by solving the equation:

$$1 - r = F(x)$$

This leads to the formula:

$$X = -M \cdot ln(r)$$

where $ln(r)$ is the natural logarithm of r. Obtaining $ln(r)$ is relatively easy. Many business and scientific calculators come equipped with an "lnx" key. Many operation research textbooks provide a table of natural logarithms—appendix B of this text gives $-ln(r)$ values for r = .001, .002, ..., .999. Since r lies between 0 and 1, you can recall from the theory of logarithms that $ln(r)$ is always negative. This is the reason for printing the values of $-ln(r)$ rather than $ln(r)$.

As an illustration of finding a natural logarithm using appendix B, suppose that r = .563 and that we wish to find $-ln(.563)$. Read the first two digits in the left-hand margin and the third digit in the top line of appendix B. The necessary logarithm is at the intersection of the corresponding row and column. Thus, to obtain $-ln(.563)$

- Read down the left-hand margin to .56
- Read across that row (i.e., horizontally) until you are in the column headed .003.

The number in that position is .574. Hence, $-ln(.563)$ = .574. You should similarly verify that when r = .418, $-ln(r)$ = .872.

Obtaining the Interarrival Times Referring again to figure 8-5, note that an average of 12 patients arrive at SHIP every hour. This is equivalent to an average of 5 minutes between consecutive arrivals. Thus:

$$M = 5$$

The random sequence can be chosen arbitrarily. We will, for example, use the fifth column of table 8-1. To illustrate that these numbers might be used in any direction, let us read the random sequence from bottom up. The resultant number will be rounded off to three decimals. Thus, for example, the first number from the bottom of the fifth column is .56343. After rounding it becomes:

$$r = .563$$

It follows that the first patient on the simulated day will arrive at SHIP x minutes after 1 PM, where:

$$x = M \cdot [-ln(r)]$$
$$= (5)(.574)$$
$$= 2.87$$

Recall that the exponential variable represents the time *between* consecutive occurrences of a Poisson event—in this case the time between successive arrivals. Thus, we must use the above procedure again to derive the number of minutes elapsed between the arrival of the first and second patient. The second (from the bottom) number in the fifth column is .418 (after rounding). We have already seen that $-ln(.418) = .872$. Hence, the second patient will arrive at SHIP x minutes *after* the first, where:

$$x = M \cdot [-ln(r)]$$
$$= (5)(.872)$$
$$= 4.36$$

For each of the 48 patients at SHIP, you can thus obtain the interarrival times—IAT, for short. The results are summarized in table 8-7.

Table 8-7. *Patient Arrival Times (Number of Minutes Since 1 PM) at SHIP*

r	IAT	TA	r	IAT	TA	r	IAT	TA
.563	2.87	2.87	.418	4.36	7.23	.881	.63	7.86
.766	1.33	9.19	.273	6.49	15.68	.929	.37	16.05
.072	13.16	29.21	.731	1.57	30.78	.022	19.08	49.86
.049	15.08	64.94	.562	2.88	67.82	.579	2.73	70.55
.301	6.00	76.55	.227	7.41	83.96	.633	2.29	86.25
.925	.39	86.64	.579	2.73	89.37	.883	.62	89.99
.360	5.11	95.10	.528	3.19	98.29	.272	6.51	104.80
.802	1.10	105.90	.681	1.92	107.82	.344	5.33	113.15
.900	.53	113.68	.679	1.94	115.62	.865	.73	116.35
.755	1.41	117.76	.317	5.74	123.50	.365	5.04	128.54
.226	7.44	135.98	.330	5.54	141.52	.885	.61	142.13
.020	19.56	161.59	.975	.13	161.82	.503	3.44	165.26
.475	3.72	168.98	.636	2.26	171.24	.077	12.82	184.06
.539	3.09	187.15	.149	9.50	196.65	.293	6.14	202.79
.997	.02	202.81	.166	8.98	211.79	.430	4.22	216.01
.511	3.36	219.37	.196	8.15	227.52	.242	7.10	234.62
.004	27.60	262.22						

The Moments of Arrival Now that you know when the first patient arrives at SHIP and also the interarrival times for each subsequent patient, you can compute the moment in time (number of minutes after 1 PM) when each patient arrives. Let *TA* denote the time of a patient's arrival.

Then, you can derive the formula:

TA of current patient = TA of the preceding patient
                       + IAT between these two

e.g. $TA_2 = TA_1 + IAT_{1 \to 2}$

For example, the second patient arrives at 2.87 + 4.36 = 7.23 minutes after 1 PM. Table 8-7 also displays these times.

Poisson Distribution

A random variable that follows this probability law is discrete and assumes nonnegative values only. Probability that it equals x is given by:

$$p(x) = \frac{e^{-\lambda}\lambda^x}{x!}, x = 0, 1, 2, \ldots$$

where λ is the average values of X. This being a discrete variable, you can simulate its numerical value by following the procedure described in a previous section. This illustrates an alternative method that makes use of the exponential formula.

Consider again the patients arriving at SHIP. Note that SHIP opens for business at 1 PM and that any patient who arrives prior to 5 PM will be admitted for service. From 1 PM to 5 PM is a span of 4 hours = 240 minutes. Hence, a patient whose TA is 240 or less will be admitted. Any patient whose TA exceeds 240 will find the door closed. From table 8-7 notice that the TA for each of the first 48 patients is less than 240, but that the 49th patient arrived at TA = 262.22 minutes after 1 PM—too late to enter SHIP. Thus, on this simulated day, x (the number of patients at SHIP) equals 48.

To describe the process in general terms, first, determine the average number of arrivals (λ) in some specified time span. For example λ = 12 (per hour) × 4 hours = 48 (on the average). Determine also, the average interarrival time, M (= 5 minutes in this case). Then:

1. Compute the TA of the first arrival. If the TA exceeds the allotted time span (240 minutes for SHIP), stop. In that case, $x = 0$.
2. Otherwise, obtain the next IAT and hence the next TA. If the new TA exceeds the allotted time, stop. In that case, $x = 1$.
3. Otherwise, continue this process of obtaining the next IAT and hence the next TA (and increasing x by 1 each time). Stop when TA exceeds the allotted time.

This procedure is more suitable for obtaining x by computer.

Normal Distribution

The probability function of a normal variable is defined completely when you know its expected value μ and its standard deviation σ. You have already become familiar with it in many of the preceding chapters.

Specifically, it was first introduced in chapter 2. It was used in chapter 5 to obtain the chances of completing the project in a given amount of time. In chapter 6, it was used to determine the service level of an inventory policy and again in chapter 7 as a possible distribution of service times.

You should also recall the standard procedure for using this distribution. Given a normally distributed random variable X, all inquiries regarding its value or probability are resolved by always obtaining the standardized variable:

$$Z = \frac{X - \mu}{\sigma}$$

and then using the cumulative probability function $F(z)$ of the standard normal variable. Appendix A provides the values of $F(z)$ for $z = 0$ in increments of .01 until $z = 3$. The $F(z)$ values when z is negative are found by noting the symmetry of the standard normal distribution. Specifically, use the formula:

$$F(-z) = 1 - F(z)$$

For example:

$$F(-1.49) = 1 - F(1.49)$$
$$= 1 - .932$$
$$= .068$$

The Normal Procedure To obtain the simulated value of X given a random number r, we must reverse the entire process. Specific steps are as follows.

1. First solve the equation $r = F(z)$ to obtain z. There are two possibilities.
   a. If $r \geq .5$, search through appendix A until, for some z, $r = F(z)$.* Then, z is the necessary number.
   b. If $r < .5$, compute $1 - r$. Then, search through appendix A until, for some w, $1 - r = F(w)$. the necessary standard value will be $z = -w$.
2. To obtain x, multiply the standard value z by the standard deviation σ. Then, add the expected value μ to obtain $x = z \cdot \sigma + \mu$.

---

*Occasionally, r will lie between two consecutively tabulated F values. If so, there are two options:
1. Round off both r and F values to three decimals and use the resultant z.
2. If z_1 and z_2 are consecutively tabulated z values with $F(z_1) < r < F(z_2)$, you may obtain the required z from the interpolation formula:

$$z = z_1 + [r - F(z_1)] \cdot \frac{z_2 - z_1}{F(z_2) - F(z_1)}$$

The specific choice of technique depends on the desired level of accuracy.

Suppose, for example, that $r = .862$, $\mu = 9$, and $\sigma = 2$. Since r exceeds .5, you can search through appendix A to find that:

$$F(1.09) = .862, \text{ so that } z = 1.09$$

In that case:

$$x = (1.09)(2) + 9$$
$$= 11.18$$

As another example, suppose $r = .195$, $\mu = 9$, and $\sigma = 2$. In this case, $1 - r = .805$. Searching through appendix A, you can find that:

$$F(.86) = .805, \text{ so that } z = -.86$$

In that case:

$$x = (-.86)(2) + 9$$
$$= 7.28$$

Service Times of Dr. Jones at SHIP Recall that for Dr. Jones, the service times, i.e., the number of minutes he spends with a patient, are normally distributed with $\mu = 9$ minutes and $\sigma = 2$ minutes. In other words, his service times are given by:

$$x = (2)(z) + 9 \text{ minutes}$$

From table 8-7, we have found that 48 patients will be admitted into SHIP on the simulated day. Table 8-6 indicates that 33 of those 48 patients will visit Dr. Jones. We will illustrate the drawing of a normal sample by generating the number of minutes each of these 33 patients spends with Dr. Jones.

We need 33 members of a random sequence, which we can take from the first 33 numbers in table 8-1 as follows: seven each from lines 1, 2, 3, and 4, and the remaining five from line 5. Each will be rounded off to three decimal points. The resultant sequence is shown in the column labeled "r" of table 8-8. The first line of that table contains the first three r numbers, the next line contains the next three r numbers and so on.

The corresponding z values, obtained using the normal procedure described earlier, are shown next to each r in table 8-8. The x values are obtained by evaluating: $x = 2z + 9$. In table 8-8, these are shown under the *SJ* heading.

Service Times of Dr. Berry at SHIP To complete the story of the Southboro Health Induction Project, one must also obtain the service times of Dr. Berry on this simulated day. A glance at table 8-6 reveals that 15 patients visited Dr. Berry on that day. Hence, we need 15 numbers from a random sequence, which we can read from the last column of table 8-1. The numbers, rounded to three places are shown in the "r" column of

Table 8-8 *Service Times of Dr. Jones at SHIP, SJ*

r	z	SJ	r	z	SJ	r	z	SJ
.862	1.09	11.18	.954	1.68	12.36	.195	−0.86	7.28
.162	−0.99	7.02	.079	−1.41	6.17	.352	−0.38	8.24
.613	.29	9.01	.618	.30	9.60	.273	−0.60	7.79
.363	−0.35	8.30	.208	−0.81	7.37	.004	−2.67	3.66
.858	1.12	11.30	.531	.08	9.16	.099	−1.29	6.42
.933	1.51	12.01	.956	1.70	12.40	.754	.69	10.38
.242	−0.70	7.60	.505	.01	9.02	.689	.49	9.98
.757	.70	10.39	.788	.80	10.60	.112	−1.21	6.57
.205	−0.82	7.35	.196	−0.85	7.29	.610	.28	9.56
.066	−1.51	5.98	.799	.84	10.68	.273	−0.60	7.79
.363	−0.35	8.30	.911	1.35	11.70	.511	.03	9.05

table 8-9. The z values, as before, are obtained by using the normal procedure with respect to each r.

Finally, recall from figure 8-5 that Dr. Berry spends an average of 15 minutes with each patient (i.e., $\mu = 15$) and that for him, $\sigma = 3$. Hence, Dr. Berry's service time, SB, is obtained by:

$$SB = (3)(z) + 15$$

The results are displayed in table 8-9. As usual, the statistics of the first three patients are shown in the first line, those of patients 4 through 6 are shown in the second line, and so on.

Table 8-9 *Service Times of Dr. Berry at SHIP, SB*

r	z	SB	r	z	SB	r	z	SB
.613	0.29	15.86	.531	0.08	15.24	.689	0.49	16.47
.066	−1.51	10.48	.468	−0.08	14.76	.088	−1.36	10.93
.995	2.56	22.68	.937	1.53	19.60	.452	−0.12	14.63
.983	2.12	21.36	.127	−1.14	11.58	.538	0.10	15.29
.591	0.23	15.69	.175	−0.94	12.20	.208	−0.81	12.56

SUMMARY

We began this chapter by discussing the reasons why management scientists use simulations to solve the real world problems in a variety of decision situations. The real systems are often too complex to permit a compact mathematical model or obtain an analytical solution. The application of a simulation model might be more practical and perhaps more possible. The simulation models are attractive because they allow the decision maker to represent the reality rather closely—without making an excessive number of restrictive assumptions.

In many simulation models, the input variables are motivated by chance. Thus, to operate a simulation model, the numerical values of such variables must be generated. In this chapter, we have studied a number of commonly used techniques for doing just that.

Of course, that is not the entire story. Having generated the numerical values of input variables we must bring these together in a model, i.e., "run the model" and predict the values of the appropriate output variables. These predicted values are helpful for validating the model. A validated model must then be "run" to respond to a variety of "what if" questions. These are some of the topics to be discussed in the following chapter.

SELECTED READINGS

CHASE, R. B. and AQUILANO, N. J. *Production and Operations Management.* Homewood, Ill.: Richard D. Irwin, Inc., 1973.

ECK, R. D. *Operations Research for Business.* Belmont, Calif.: Wadsworth Publishing Co., 1976.

MEIER, R. C.; NEWALL, W. P.; and POGER, H. L. *Simulation in Business and Economics.* Englewood Cliffs, N.J.: Prentice-Hall, Inc., 1969.

NAYLOR, T. H.; BALINTFY, J. L.; BURDICK, D. S.; and CHU, K. *Computer Simulation Techniques.* New York: John Wiley and Sons, 1968.

SHANNON, R. E. *System Simulation: The Art and Science.* Englewood Cliffs, N.J.: Prentice-Hall, Inc., 1975.

THE RAND CORPORATION. *A Million Random Digits with 100,000 Normal Deviates.* Glencoe, Ill.: Free Press, 1955.

PROBLEM SET 8
SIMULATION OF CHANCE EVENTS

In each of the following problems, you may use table 8-1 as a source of random numbers. Your primary job is to create random sequences of observations from the specified probability distributions. The questions marked by an asterisk (*) require you to put together the simulated observations so as to form a coherent whole. Since this is, however, a topic of the following chapter, answering such questions is presently an optional activity. If you have access to a computer, program each process.

1. Nancy Parr is a wholesaler of cheeses. She has found that the weekly demand for a certain variety of cheese varies from week to week. The data on the number of boxes of this cheese sold during each of the preceding 150 weeks is summarized in the adjoining table. Nancy orders a new batch of 70 boxes of cheese when the current stock is 24 boxes or less. It costs $15 to place an order. The new shipment always arrives a week later, i.e., the lead time is

x = Number Sold in a Week	20	22	24	26	28
f(x) = Number of Such Weeks	40	45	35	20	10

exactly one week. Because cheese spoils rather easily, she estimates the storage cost to be $10 per box per week. On the other hand, shortage costs her $50 per box.

a. Simulate the demand for cheese during the next 30 weeks.

b. Assume that her initial inventory is 50 boxes. Determine the inventory level at the end of each week, and hence the weeks when she orders a new batch.

c. Using the extent of demand during lead time, i.e., after she placed the order, determine whether she will experience a shortage or excess supply in the following week. Derive the associated cost on each ordering occasion.

*d. Determine the average cost per week of this operation. (*Hint*: While solving questions b, c, and d, imagine that you are balancing your checkbook. The demand is similar to making a withdrawal from your account, and receiving a new shipment is like making a deposit. Adjust the inventory levels each week. Her total cost for the 30 week period includes the cost of placing an order, storage as well as shortage.)

2. Professor Jones lives at point A and goes to work at point D in the adjoining diagram. He leaves his house at 7:45 in the morning and drives to the commuter bus stop at B. This journey takes 4 ± 2 minutes. Assume a rectangular distribution. The commuter buses leave point B at 7:50, 8:00, and 8:10. If the traffic is light (30 percent chance), this journey requires 25 minutes; if the traffic is heavy (10 percent chance), it takes 40 minutes; with intermediate traffic it is a 30 minute journey. From point C, the professor takes a university bus to reach the school at point D. These buses leave point C at 8:32 and 9:02. The journey from C to D takes between 15 and 25 minutes; assume a rectangular distribution.

a. Simulate the travel time for each of the 3 legs (A→B, B→C, and C→D) on each of the next 25 mornings.

*b. Compute the total time for the entire trip on each of these occasions, and hence derive the average time for the trip.

*c. What is the average waiting time at point B as well as at point C?
(*Hint:* To answer parts b and c, begin by finding the moment each morning when the professor arrives at points B, C, and D in his journey. Decide when he will leave points B and C, and thus obtain waiting time on each occasion.)

3. Suppose you were taking a survey of 25 randomly chosen households in a community. (See table 8-3.)

   a. List the simulated weekly expenditure of each household.

   *b. Determine the average expenditure of the sampled households.

   *c. What is the smallest expenditure of a household in the upper 20 percent of the sample?

4. The daily demand for a product follows the probability distribution shown in the adjoining table.

Number of Units	1	2	3	4	5
Probability	.17	.35	.30	.10	.08

The lead time is 2, 3, or 4 days with the following probabilities.

Number of Days	2	3	4
Probability	.2	.5	.3

Assume that the storekeeper orders a batch of 25 units whenever the current supply is exactly 6, that the inventory at the beginning is 15 units and that backordering is not allowed. (That is, if the product is not found in the store when a customer arrives, the customer will not return.) Simulate 30 days of demand and inventory levels. (*Hint:* Use the check balancing concept introduced in problem 1.)

5. Cars approach Quik-Fill gas station in a Poisson manner with an average interarrival time of 4.5 minutes. The gas station has only one pump. The time necessary to service each car is normally distributed with $\mu = 4$ minutes and $\sigma = 1$ minute. If two cars are already waiting to be serviced, the new arrival will not join the line—it will go someplace else. The gas station opens for business at 8 AM.

   a. Find the time of arrival of each car from 8 AM until 10 AM. Then, determine the number of cars which approach Quik-Fill during this period.

   b. Find the service time for each of the first 30 cars which might be served by Quik-Fill.

   *c. The service rule is first come, first served. Find the moments when each car begins and ends being served. Hence compute the waiting time, if any, for each car that joins the line. What is the average of waiting times?

*d. How many cars will go someplace else?

6. Quik-Fill of problem 5 has installed an additional gas pump to attract more business, and sure enough, the interarrival time now averages to 2.5 minutes. An arriving car will go to whichever pump is less busy. Because of the courteous service, no car goes someplace else.

  a. Simulate the arrival times of the first 30 cars.

  b. Simulate the corresponding service times.

  *c. Once a car joins the line behind one of the two pumps, it stays in that line. Find the moments when each car will begin and end being served.

  *d. Based on this information, compute the waiting time of each car. Derive the average of waiting times.

  *e. What is the maximum queue length in either line?

7. Mary Tchekowsky owns a chain of drive-in theaters. She has just purchased the land to start a new theater. Based on past experience, she estimates that between 100 and 300 cars will enter the theater for any one show. The probabilities of various audience sizes are as shown in the adjoining table.

x = Number of Cars	100	150	200	250	300
$p(x)$ = Probability	.10	.15	.40	.25	.10

Average gross profit per car per show is $1.50. On the other hand, a heater and a speaker must be in place to accommodate each car, and this costs $300 to install. Assume 2 shows each day, 6 days each week. She would like to determine the theater size that would maximize her profit in the first year.

  a. Simulate theater attendance for 20 days.

  b. Compute the average gross profit per day.

  *c. How many cars should she provide for? (Use net annual profit as decision criterion.)

8. An electric generator is known to fail an average of 3 times each year. The interfailure times are known to be exponential. When the generator fails, repairs take an average of 8 hours with a standard deviation of 2 hours. Service times are normally distributed. Each hour of downtime is worth $1,000 in lost profit. Besides, the repair operations cost $500 in parts and $75 per hour in labor charges.

  a. Determine the moments of (simulated) failures over a 10-year period. Assume that each year has exactly 52 weeks. Record the number of failures. (*Hint*: Ignore the service times when computing the moment of failures.)

  b. Simulate the service time and the associated total cost on each occasion.

*9. Suppose that the generator in problem 8 costs $100,000 to purchase and install, and that it has a useful life of 10 years. A heavy duty generator with the same useful life but average failure rate of 1 per year is available for $200,000. Which is the better buy?

10. The adjoining figure shows a small project with only four events and five tasks. The first number next to each arrow equals the expected duration of that task and the second number in each case equals its standard deviation.

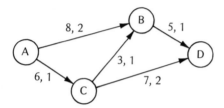

a. Obtain the simulated durations of each task on eight occasions.

b. Find the critical path and the project completion time on each occasion.

Albert Rousseau owns and operates a "system" consisting of: Ten Pin Bowling Alley, Clean Spoon Restaurant, and Happy Time Bar. The bowling alley has 5 lanes. The bar contains 20 stools. There are 30 tables in the restaurant: 20 of these are 2-person tables, the rest are 4-person tables. The system remains open for business from 5 PM to midnight. The system believes in "first come, first served" as modified by specific circumstances.

Patricia Feller, the hostess, has kept detailed records of the system operations for a number of months in the recent past. For example, she can tell you the arrival times of all the clients, the number of persons in each client group, and their initial destination (the bar, restaurant, or bowling alley). Problems 11 through 22 in this set are based on the information gathered by Ms. Feller and analyzed by the system's consultant, Professor Jones.

11. On the average, 15 customer groups per hour arrive at the system between 5 and 7 PM. After studying the records kept by Ms. Feller, Professor Jones has decided that the arrivals follow the Poisson process. Generate the arrival times (i.e. number of minutes after 5 PM) of those customer groups which arrive between 5 and 7 PM.

12. Ms. Feller's data also indicate that 15 percent of all the customer groups who arrive between 5 and 8 PM are 1-person groups, 40 percent are 2-person groups, 20 percent are 3-person groups and the rest are 4-person groups. Assign a size to each of the 35 customer groups who may arrive between 5 and 7 PM. Assume that the group size is independent of the moment of arrival.

13. Groups are homogeneous, i.e., all customers forming a group are either below 21 (minor), or above 21 (adults), or are treated as such. Also, a group stays together at all times (and performs the same set of activities). Minors comprise 50 percent of all groups, the rest are adult groups.

All minor groups who enter the system between 5 and 6 PM head towards the restaurant. Of those entering between 6 and 8 PM only 60 percent go to the restaurant, the rest go to bowl.

Of the adult groups entering between 5 and 6:30 PM, 20 percent go to the bar, 60 percent head towards the restaurant and the rest go to the bowling alley. Between 6:30 and 8 PM, these percentages changes to 30, 50, and 20, respectively.

Assign the age bracket to each of the 35 customer groups who may arrive between 5 and 7 PM and identify each group's initial destination.

14. A group which enters the Ten Pin Bowling Alley spends 45 ± 15 minutes in the act of bowling. Assuming the rectangular distribution of bowling times, derive the time (number of minutes) spent bowling by each of the 10 groups who may go bowling between 5 and 7 PM.

*15. Combine problems 11, 13, and 14 as follows. From problem 13, identify the groups (i.e. record their serial numbers) who go bowling. From problem 11, obtain the moment when each such group enters the bowling alley. As long as some lane is free, the newly arrived group will be assigned a lane; otherwise that group will wait until some lane becomes free. Record the moment when each group begins to bowl. From problem 14, determine the time each group will spend in the act of bowling.

Now derive these outcomes: the moment when each group begins to bowl, the moment when it exits from the bowling alley, and the time each group spends in there— both waiting and playing.

*16. Compute the expenses incurred by each of the groups who enter the bowling alley between 5 and 7 PM as follows. From problem 12, obtain the age bracket (minor or adult) and group size for each group that goes bowling. Problem 15 provides the number of minutes a group spends in the bowling alley.

Assume that the bowling alley costs $2.50 per hour and that the bowling charges are measured in 25¢ units. Each patron to the bowling alley consumes a drink every 20 minutes or part thereof. For example, someone who spends a total of 43 minutes there will consume 3 drinks. Minors have soft drinks only (30¢ a bottle); 50 percent of the adults have soft drinks; the rest consume beer (70¢ per glass).

17. When an adult group visits the Happy Time Bar, the apparently congenial atmosphere and the soothing qualities of alcohol affect the group members. Thus, the time necessary to consume a drink is exponentially distributed with an average of 15 minutes. Each group member consumes 1, 2, or 3 drinks with probabilities .3, .5, and .2, respectively.

Compute the number of drinks consumed by each member for each of the 10 groups who may enter the bar between 5 and 7 PM. Also, compute the total drinking time of each group.

*18. Compute the drinking expenses of each group and the moment when each will exit from the bar as follows.

From problem 13, derive the ordinal number (first, second, etc.) of the group which will go to the bar. From problem 12 obtain its group size. From problem 17, determine the number of drinks ordered by each group member. Assume that a drink costs $1.25, and hence compute the group's drinking expenses.

From problem 11, determine the moment when each group will enter the bar between 5 and 7 PM. If necessary, a group will wait to be seated until all of its members can find empty stools. Determine the moment when each customer group can be seated (and hence begin to drink). Then, add its drinking time to obtain the moment of its exit from the bar.

19. Up to 20 groups of minors may enter the Clean Spoon Restaurant between 5 and 7 PM. Since the minors have been raised in the "fast food" tradition, their eating time is normally distributed with a mean of 15 minutes and standard deviation of 3 minutes. Compute the eating time for each of these groups.

20. Up to 12 groups of adults may enter the Clean Spoon Restaurant between 5 and 7 PM. When the times necessary to consume a cocktail, dinner, and an after-dinner drink are added together, each group spends an average of 45 minutes at the dinner table with a standard deviation of 10 minutes. These times are normally distributed. Obtain the dinner times of these groups.

*21. Compute the food bill of each minor group as follows. From problem 13, obtain the serial number of each minor group that goes to the Clean Spoon Restaurant. From problem 12, obtain the size of each group. Assume that each member of any specific group spends exactly the same amount on his/her food, and that the actual amount is $1.50 ± .50 (rectangular distribution). Multiply the per member expense by the group size to obtain each group's food bill.

*22. Compute the food bill of each adult group as follows. The probability that a group will order a cocktail is .75, and it costs $1.25 per member. With a probability of .3, the group will also order an after dinner drink at a cost of $1.50 per member. The dinner costs $4–$7 per adult. Obtain the ordinal number of the adult group going to the restaurant from problem 13 and obtain its group size from problem 12. You now possess all of the information necessary to compute the food bill of each adult group which enters the restaurant between 5 and 7 PM.

9

Simulation of a System

The preceding chapter examined some techniques for generating the simulated values of the input variables. This chapter examines some methods of combining these input values using a model of the system. When the corresponding rules for combining the variables are developed and followed, you can obtain the values of output variables, i.e., the effects of the system. A thorough examination of these effects would tend to suggest modifications of the current system which can then be simulated and analyzed in turn. This process of simulating the changes and examining the consequences continues until a satisfactory solution is obtained.

Simulation of a system requires much more besides a knowledge of developing and running a computer program. To emphasize this point and also to provide a balanced view of this activity, this chapter begins by describing the major phases a simulation exercise goes through. This is followed by taking one case—that of the Southboro Health Induction Project (SHIP)—through these phases. The chapter ends with a brief discussion of other techniques of simulating a system.

279

OVERVIEW OF THE SIMULATION PROCESS

It should be clear by now that performing a simulation exercise is similar to conducting an experiment—except that the experiment is conducted on the mathematical model of a system rather than on the system itself. Any such exercise must abide by the principles governing a well designed experiment. The model must reflect all the relevant aspects of a reality and their interrelationships.

Simulating the values of an input variable is equivalent to drawing a random sample from the corresponding probability distribution. All other things being equal, the stability of simulation outputs increases with an increase in sample size. It follows that *one must simulate the drawing of a rather large sample* to ensure the desired level of output reliability. And, therein lies the difficulty of using simulations to choose among a number of candidate policies. Performing a simulation exercise manually is time consuming and tedious, and hence subject to human errors.

Simulations of managerial systems are, therefore, almost always carried out using a computer—a device known for its speed and consistency as well as for its ability to use simple rules of logic. On the other hand, a computer cannot actually think. When computers are used to simulate a system, the model must be defined to the last detail: the input variables, the output variables, and the process of obtaining the outputs given the values of input variables. A computer will not produce until all the i's have been dotted and t's crossed. Computers are also literal—they will do what you say rather than what you mean. Thus, you must think of all eventualities in order to create a valid and useful set of computer instructions. Thus, a decision maker's system must be thoroughly understood. In the opinion of many experts, this benefit alone is worth the long hours spent in developing a simulation model. Though we will spend a major portion of this chapter describing computer instructions written in the FORTRAN computer language, you need not be a computer programmer to become a simulation expert.

Figure 9-1 shows the typical phases in a simulation project. Such a project begins when the decision maker recognizes that something is wrong with the present system. The associated symptoms, if persistent and significant, will lead the decision maker to solicit the advice of a management scientist. A management scientist always works with a model of the system before recommending any changes in an operating system. Thus, when asked to solve a problem in an operating system or design a new system, a management scientist first constructs a preliminary (working or pilot) model of the decision maker's system. After verifying that this pilot model generally reflects reality, the management scientist collects and analyzes the data necessary to construct the detailed

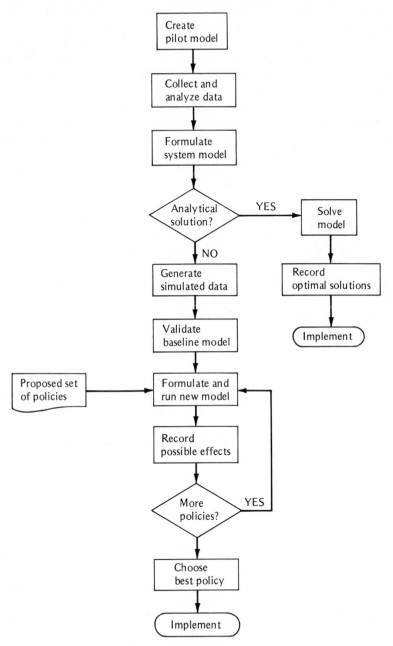

Figure 9-1. *Flow Chart of a Simulation Project*

model of the object system. A good understanding of sampling techniques and also the techniques of statistical inference is essential to properly perform this activity.

Having formulated a model, the management scientist determines if an analytical solution can be obtained. If so, the task of finding an optimal solution is relatively easy. You have already seen a variety of analytical techniques in the chapters on decision theory, PERT, inventories, and waiting lines. In the following six chapters, you will get to know many other techniques, generically known as linear optimization models. The applicability of these techniques depends on the validity of the associated assumptions in specific situations.

If the assumption(s) underlying the analytical techniques cannot be justified, simulation is the last resort. A simulation designer begins by constructing at least a block diagram of a simulation run and then proceeds to develop a complete set of computer language instructions. When these instructions are compiled, i.e., are found to be "grammatically" and "syntactically" correct, you can instruct the computer to generate the corresponding simulated history.

The resultant history should be sufficiently long to portray the current system characteristics as closely as possible. Checking the computer-generated data against available data or that gathered empirically is known as validating the baseline model. A good understanding of statistical hypotheses testing techniques is essential for performing this phase of a simulation project.

Now the model is ready for its real use—studying the effects of the alternate policies or procedures that might be implemented. By changing the current model as needed, we can construct and run a model corresponding to each proposed policy. When the effects of each policy have been documented and compared, the decision maker is in a position to choose the most desirable of all the proposed policies or procedures. Here is where simulation ends and implementation begins!

FORMULATING A MODEL

Every managerial system must deal with the effects of time. Some aspects of the system change with time, others remain the same—at least in the short run. In a production system, for example, the demand for a product and hence the size of inventory fluctuates with time; the size of the production staff on the other hand is relatively stable. In a research and development project, the planned events and tasks are likely to remain the same; the effort and time necessary to perform these tasks is likely to vary. In a waiting line model, the number of service facilities and their structural relationships do not change substantially; the number of customers using these facilities and the duration of service is likely to change from one customer to the next. Therefore, to simulate the operations of a system one must in some manner represent the passage of time. This is the first task in the construction of a simulation model.

A Preliminary Model

To illustrate the general concepts regarding the flow of time and materials in a system, we will pause to describe a specific system. Consider the situation at the Southboro Health Induction Project (SHIP). At this moment, assume that you have not read SHIP's case in the preceding chapter.

The outpatient clinic is operated by two physicians, Dr. Jones and Dr. Berry, each of whom specializes in a different branch of medicine. Thus, each physician has his own set of patients. The physicians do, however, share the services of a common receptionist and a cashier. SHIP also contains a common waiting room stocked with the usual literature found in the medical waiting rooms. There is a playroom at SHIP for the convenience of patients who must bring their children with them. SHIP is open for business from 1 PM to 5 PM Monday through Saturday. This means that on any of these days, SHIP will admit its first patient as early as 1 PM and that anyone who enters SHIP prior to 5 PM will be serviced that very day—no matter how long it takes. Recently, the management of SHIP has noticed that despite the rather good pay ($6 per hour), there is high turnover of cashiers. Also, the waiting room often seems crowded and the playroom is excessively noisy. SHIP has therefore asked you, a budding management scientist, to identify the cause of their difficulties and recommend any appropriate changes.

Where should you begin? Note that SHIP consists of a receptionist, two physicians, and a cashier. At least in the short range, they are the constants at SHIP. The patients, on the other hand, must "flow through" SHIP. As a first step, you should observe the patient processing at SHIP so that you could construct a model of their interactions with the service system.

Figure 9-2 displays such a flow model. In computer terminology, this is known as the *block diagram* of the flow process. From a typical patient's

Figure 9-2. *The Patient Flow at SHIP*

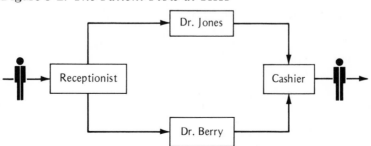

point of view, SHIP has four gates or barriers: the receptionist's desk, the offices of Dr. Jones or Dr. Berry, and the cashier's desk. Each patient must "navigate" through three of these gates. In the terminology of waiting line models, the patient's journey through SHIP has three processing phases: by the receptionist, by one of the two physicians, and by the cashier. In each phase, there is a possibility of experiencing a delay. Also, at each facility, some time will be spent receiving services. The visit with the cashier is always the patient's last encounter with SHIP. Since any patient entering SHIP prior to 5 PM is assured of "same day" service, the cashier cannot leave SHIP until the last patient has been processed. Thus, determining the moment when the last patient and hence the cashier can leave SHIP is likely to shed some light on the reason why the cashier turnover is high. If a patient has to spend many hours to get through SHIP, this might tend to explain both the crowded waiting room and excessive noise levels in the adjoining playroom. If this turns out to be the situation, any change that reduces the waiting time of patients would be a potential recommendation. In other words, consider using a waiting line model of SHIP.

The Exogenous and Endogenous Variables

To quantify the model of figure 9-2, you must now identify the variables of patient flow. There are two kinds of variables: input and output. The input variables (or factors) are also known as exogenous or causal variables. The object system acts on these exogenous variables to produce the outputs or endogenous variables. The model of the object system describes the transformation, i.e., how the outputs relate to inputs.

Given figure 9-2, you can easily identify the variables by following a typical patient's progress through SHIP. To begin with, you must know when the patient arrives at SHIP to be processed by the receptionist. At each gate in the model, you must know *when* the service begins and *how long* it continues. With these two items of information, you can easily determine the amount of waiting time experienced at each gate and also the moment of exit from that gate. The patient's path in figure 9-2 branches out after the patient leaves the receptionist. You can determine the probability of choosing each branch. Based on these and similar considerations, you can identify all of the relevant variables. The input variables and the corresponding shorthand notations are listed below.

- Arrival pattern of patients at SHIP, *AP*
- Service time of the receptionist, *SR*
- Probability that the patient wishes to visit Dr. Jones, *PJ*
- Probability that the patient wishes to visit Dr. Berry, *PB*
- Service time of Dr. Jones, *SJ*
- Service time of Dr. Berry, *SB*
- Service time of the cashier, *SC*

Some of the endogenous variables will be:

- Waiting time (delay) before seeing the receptionist, *WR*

- Waiting time prior to visiting Dr. Jones, *WJ*
- Waiting time prior to visiting Dr. Berry, *WB*
- Waiting time prior to meeting the cashier, *WC*
- Total time spent by a patient at SHIP, *TT*
- Time when the last patient (and hence the cashier) leaves SHIP, *TLAST*
- Number of patients in the waiting room, *NW*
- Idle times of cashier, *CIDLE*, of the receptionist, *RIDLE*, of Dr. Jones, *JIDLE*, and of Dr. Berry, *BIDLE*
- Take-home pay of the receptionist, *RPAY*, and of the cashier, *CPAY*
- Gross income of Dr. Jones, *JPAY*, and of Dr. Berry, *BPAY*

Separating the exogenous and endogenous variables is important. Whereas the value of an endogenous variable or its statistical properties become known after solving the model of a system, those of an exogenous variable must be known in order to fully define the model.

Quantification

If the detailed records have been kept, discerning the statistical properties of an exogenous variable is relatively straightforward. One begins by constructing the frequency charts, deriving the cumulative probability function, $F(x)$, and then comparing these with known, i.e., well documented, statistical distributions such as the rectangular, normal, Poisson, binomial, or exponential. The corresponding tests belong to the class of "goodness of fit" tests. The χ^2 statistic and Kolmogorov-Smirnov statistic are but two of the well-known statistics used for this purpose. A vast amount of standard statistical literature exists on the subject; some are cited at the end of this chapter.

More often, however, the detailed and reliable data necessary for constructing a mathematical model are not available. In such instances, you must specify the necessary data items whose values are to be obtained through direct observations over a sufficiently long period. This list may or may not be identical to that of the exogenous variables. In SHIP's case, for instance, you will need to obtain the values of the following items:

- Moment when each patient arrives, *TA*
- Moment when the receptionist begins to service that patient, *RBEG*
- Moment when that patient leaves the receptionist, *RDONE*
- Doctor assigned to that patient, *CHOICE*
- Moment when Dr. Jones (if applicable) begins to serve that patient, *JBEG*
- Moment when Dr. Jones has finished serving that patient, *JDONE*
- Moment when Dr. Berry (if applicable) begins to serve that patient, *BBEG*

- Moment when Dr. Berry has finished serving that patient, *BDONE*
- Moment when the cashier begins servicing each patient, *CBEG*
- Moment when that patient leaves cashier's office, *CDONE*

This list of data items becomes obvious if you think of these as the items necessary to keep track of where the patient is at any moment. A preliminary model, such as figure 9-2, should be used as a guide in this process.

How many patients should you observe? The answer depends on your budget as well as on the desired level of accuracy. Standard literature on sampling techniques provides specific answers in each case. Some of these are cited at the end of this chapter. However, you must observe the system operations long enough to average out the effects of chance fluctuations and thus identify the underlying pattern. In SHIP's case, for instance, you should observe their operations for at least one week to note any daily variations.

The relationships between the observed data items and the exogenous variables should be obvious. For example, the service time of the receptionist for a specific patient is given by:

$$SR = RDONE - RBEG$$

Similarly, for that patient:

$$SJ = JDONE - JBEG$$
$$SB = BDONE - BBEG$$
$$SC = CDONE - CBEG$$

If you have observed the choices of a sufficiently large number of patients at SHIP, you can estimate the probability that a patient will visit Dr. Jones as the ratio:

$$PJ = \frac{\text{number of patients visiting Dr. Jones}}{\text{total number of patients}}$$

Also, since a patient at SHIP must visit either Dr. Jones or Dr. Berry, it follows that:

$$PB = 1 - PJ$$

If the patients arrive at a constant rate (or very nearly so), their arrival rate equals the number arriving per hour or per minute. If, on the other hand, the interarrival times vary considerably, the statistical pattern of their arrivals must be determined. This is the next step.

Statistical Patterns

Since this is not a text on the techniques of making statistical inference, we will not dwell too long on the appropriate procedures for identifying statistical patterns. However, there are two major steps:

- Postulate a tentative pattern.
- Formally test the corresponding hypothesis.

For example, if the variable of interest assumes values from a discrete set only, if it is obtained by observing a relatively rare phenomenon (such as the number of blind persons in a city) or if it stands for the number of arrivals at a service facility, it is reasonable to expect that it would have a Poisson distribution. This suspicion is further reinforced if its expected value is (nearly) equal to its variance, i.e., if:

$$E(X) \approx \text{Var}(X)$$

Similarly, if the variable is continuous, if it represents the passage of times between two consecutive events, and if its expected value equals its standard deviation:

$$E(X) \approx \sigma(X)$$

it is reasonable to suspect that such a variable is exponentially distributed. The suspicion becomes stronger if the service occurs in a friendly and relaxed atmosphere.

If a variable is bounded both above and below, i.e., if you find two constants, a and b with $a < b$, such that $P(a \leq X \leq b) = 1$, and if there is no reason why a specific number within this range should occur more often than some other, you might suspect that it would follow the rectangular distribution. The suspicion grows stronger if you find that:

$$E(X) = \frac{a + b}{2} \quad \text{and Var} (X) = \frac{(b - a)^2}{12}$$

As one more example, if the histogram of a random variable appears to be symmetrical and unimodal, and if there is no logical reason why a variable should not assume large positive or negative values, you might wish to explore the possibility that it is normally distributed.

The above statements, of course, do not constitute proofs of the suitability of specific distributions. As a matter of fact, statistics never prove anything. A statistician is like a prosecutor whose job is to establish a strong case that reasonable persons would not refute. A good understanding of the techniques of making statistical inference is essential to building a strong case.

The Quantitative Model of SHIP

You should postulate and then verify the statistical distribution of each exogenous variable. To abbreviate the discussion, we will now suppose that having done this, you have evidence to support the following statements:

- The patients arrive at SHIP according to the Poisson process with an average of 12 per hour. The first patient arrives at 1 PM or shortly thereafter. Each arriving patient waits, if necessary, until the receptionist is free and then announces his/her arrival.

- The receptionist's service times, SR, are rectangular between 1 and 5 minutes. She obtains the patient's prior records, if any, and notifies Dr. Jones or Berry, as appropriate.
- 70 percent of the patients wish to see Dr. Jones, the rest visit Dr. Berry. In other words, $PJ = .7$ and $PB = .3$. If necessary, the patient waits until the chosen doctor is free.
- The service times of Dr. Jones, SJ, are normally distributed with $\mu = 9$ minutes and $\sigma = 2$ minutes.
- The service times of Dr. Berry, SB, are normally distributed with $\mu = 15$ minutes and $\sigma = 3$ minutes.
- Having visited the doctor, the patient waits, if necessary, until the cashier is free. The queueing discipline is first come first served.
- The cashier's service times, SC, are rectangular between 1 and 9 minutes. The cashier goes home when the last patient (in her office) has been served.

Figure 9-3 shows the detailed block diagram of the model of SHIP. Each patient goes through three phases: service at the receptionist's desk, service by one of the two doctors, and settling the account with the cashier. Thus, none of the models discussed in chapter 7 is directly applicable. The existence of multiple phases alone does not preclude the use of formal waiting line models. The literature on waiting line models states that the single-phase, Poisson-Exponential model can continue to be used if:

1. The arrivals at the initial phase are Poisson distributed with average arrival rate λ.
2. There are an infinite number of calling units.
3. The queues are not restricted to a finite length.
4. All service times are exponential.
5. All K equivalent channels *in any one phase* have identical service rate μ, with $\lambda < K\mu$.

Specifically, in that case, the output of each phase would also be Poisson distributed with a mean rate of λ so that, in effect, one can study each phase on its own. Such a neat statement cannot be made if the above five conditions are not met.

In SHIP's case, the assumptions are obviously invalid. The service rates are not exponential—in the second phase, Dr. Jones and Dr. Berry have unequal service rates. And, the patients do not choose their physician on the basis of whoever is available. Also, even if all of the conditions necessary to obtain a formal model were met by the current system, there is no assurance that this will keep on happening in the proposed variations on this model. Thus, we must resort to simulation technology for

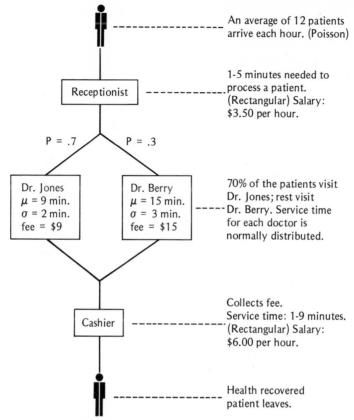

An average of 12 patients arrive each hour. (Poisson)

1-5 minutes needed to process a patient. (Rectangular) Salary: $3.50 per hour.

70% of the patients visit Dr. Jones; rest visit Dr. Berry. Service time for each doctor is normally distributed.

Collects fee. Service time: 1-9 minutes. (Rectangular) Salary: $6.00 per hour.

Health recovered patient leaves.

Figure 9-3. *The Client Flow at SHIP*

solving SHIP's problems. We will now examine the process of instructing computers to accomplish this end.

GENERATING A UNIFORMLY RANDOM SEQUENCE

It turns out that the modern computers are much faster at multiplying a pair of numbers than at referring to a standard table. Even though a large table of random numbers could be stored in a computer's memory, all simulation routines generate portions of their own random number sequence as needed. Computers do not use the table look-up procedure, since such tables tend to be extremely large and take up too much space in the computer's memory.

A Random Number Procedure

As an illustration of generating a random sequence, we will present one such procedure here. For a more technical discussion, see Payne, et al. (1969). Strictly speaking, since a computer generates such a sequence by following a specific set of rules, the resultant sequence is not random in the sense of being generated by a chance mechanism. Practically speaking, after a sequence is generated, it is subjected to a series of statistical tests of randomness. A sequence that passes all such tests is said to be statistically random. The Payne, et al. sequence is random in this sense.

This random number procedure is based on the *multiplicative congruence method.*

Begin by choosing three numbers: R_0, K, and M. The number R_0 is known as the "seed," K is the multiplier, and M is the "modulo." The successive members of the random sequence are found as follows:

1. Compute $B = K \cdot R_0$
2. Find the largest multiple of M which is smaller than B.
3. Subtract this multiple from B. The remainder becomes R_1. This is the first member of the desired sequence.
4. Replace R_0 by R_1 and return to Step 1.
   Successively repeat these steps to yield $R_1, R_2, R_3, \ldots$

For a more detailed discussion of the multiplicative congruence method and many other methods, as well as the statistical properties of the resultant sequences, see Naylor, et al. (1966).

For example, suppose $R_o = 1$, $K = 7$, and $M = 11$. Then, $B = 7$; and since it is less than 11, you can record that $R_1 = 7$. Using $R_1 = 7$ you can compute that $B = 7 \times 7 = 49$, which exceeds 44—a multiple of 11. According to step 3 above, $R_2 = 49 - 44 = 5$. Continuing this way, you can now determine that $R_3 = 5 \times 7 - 33 = 2, R_4 = 3, R_5 = 10, R_6 = 4, R_7 = 6, R_8 = 9$, $R_9 = 8$, and $R_{10} = 1$. Since $R_{10} = 1$ equals R_o, from now on, the entire sequence will repeat itself. Since this sequence has only 10 distinct members: 7, 5, 2, 3, 10, 4, 6, 9, 8, and 1, it is said to be of length (or period) 10.

The above sequence is, of course, too short to be of any value. To get a longer sequence a rather large M must be used. Computer programmers choose M to be the largest possible integer that can be stored in their computer. (An IBM 360 computer, for example, uses $M = 2,147,483,647$.) To find a random sequence of the maximum possible length, a proper value for K must be chosen. This is a problem in number theory. It is so important that the Association of Computing Machinery regularly publishes technical articles discussing the right choice of K. One such proven choice is $K = 630,360,016$ for the above M. Using this K, a 32-bit computer can generate a sequence of 2,147,483,646 members. Some idea of its vastness can be obtained as follows. A modern computer generating approximately 2,000,000 such numbers per minute will need nearly 1,074 minutes or 17.9 hours to generate the entire sequence!

Payne, et al. (1969) report that the above sequence has passed several tests of randomness: uniformity of distribution, serial tests of autocorrelation, and the run test. If R is a random integer generated by the above process, then $r = R/M$ is a random fraction between 0 and 1. This sequence of r values can be used as a uniform random sequence for the purposes of simulating a system.

A Computer Routine

A program in a computer language is a logical sequence of instructions in that language that jointly describe or solve a problem. Figure 9-4 shows a set of computer language instructions for generating this sequence as well as for generating the corresponding uniform random sequence, i.e., a random sequence of fractions between 0 and 1.

```
       SUBROUTINE RANDOM (I,J,RN)
C      I IS SUPPLIED BY THE USER.
C      COMPUTER RETURNS J, AN INTEGER BETWEEN 1
C      AND 2,147,483,646. IT ALSO RETURNS RN,
C      A FRACTION BETWEEN 0 AND 1.
       J = I * 630360016
C      AT THIS STAGE, J MIGHT BE NEGATIVE.
       IF(J) 3, 4, 4
     3 J = −J
     4 RN = J
       RN = RN * 0.4656613E − 9
       I = J
       RETURN
       END
```

Figure 9-4. *A FORTRAN Routine for Generating Random Numbers*

These instructions are shown here mainly to illustrate their correspondence with mathematical reasoning. To use these in a FORTRAN program of your choice, you only need to issue the command:

```
CALL RANDOM (I, J, RN)
```

from an appropriate place within your program. You are responsible for supplying the numerical value of I—an arbitrary integer. The computer will return J (an integer) and RN (a fraction). When this call is made repeatedly, the corresponding J values will be random integers and the RN values will be random fractions.

CREATING A SIMULATED HISTORY

Having created a quantitative model of the system, the next step is to generate the simulated data to test the basic model. Several substeps in this phase are:

- Decide on a procedure for representing the passage of time.

- Develop the mathematical formulas to generate the simulated values of each exogenous variable.
- Develop the rules for combining the simulated data.
- Run the resultant model, i.e., create a history.

Representing the Passage of Time

The systems whose properties are examined by a simulation exercise are dynamic. This means that in such systems, there are flows of some sort: of activities in a PERT network, of resources and materials in a production-inventory system, of messages in a communication network, of vehicles in a transportation system, or of calling units in a service system. It also implies that the corresponding simulation model must somehow represent the effects of time.

In each system, there are transactions which culminate in the occurrence of some events. In SHIP, for example, the patient arrives at SHIP, the patient meets the receptionist, the patient is assigned a physician, and the patient leaves the doctor's office. These are some of the events. When talking to the receptionist or while being serviced by a doctor, the patient is engaged in a transaction. In each transaction, there is a passage of time. There are two ways to represent the passage of time: the *event-based* and the *time-slice* approach.

In the event-based approach the simulation model updates the simulated clock only when an event takes place. The simulation continues until a specified sequence of events is completed. This approach will be illustrated in our simulation of the operations of SHIP.

In the time-slice approach, the system is seen as changing in all of its aspects over time, i.e., it is presumed to change continuously. Its status is updated, usually in fixed time increments, until a prescribed amount of time has elapsed. DYNAMO, a computer model described by Pugh (1963), takes this approach. The effects of time are represented by a set of differential equations. It has been used by Forrester to simulate industrial systems (1961) and urban systems (1969), and by Meadows, et al. (1972) to evaluate the effects of unplanned growth. Another example of the time-slice approach is DESIM, a computer model developed by Joshi, et al. (1973) to design and evaluate the human service systems. This model describes a client's progress through a network of public agencies as a Markov process. The passage of time is represented by a set of difference equations.

In either case, one must decide on the unit of time, i.e., whether to measure the passage of time in seconds, minutes, days, or weeks. Making this decision is more an art than a science. The smaller the unit of time, the more expensive it is to simulate a model. On the other hand, too large a unit of time might mean a loss of precision in measuring the system effects. The following is suggested as a compromise:

> *Rule. Choose the largest possible unit of time as long as two or more events do not happen "simultaneously" merely because the unit is too large.*

In SHIP's case, since the patients arrive every 5 *minutes*, receptionist's service time varies between 1 and 5 *minutes*, etc., minutes would seem to be the most natural unit of time. When simulating the commodity buy-sell actions on the Chicago Exchange, I had used days as the unit of time. When developing long-range plans, months might turn out to be a more adequate unit.

Developing the Formulas

From now on, we will concentrate on the simulation of SHIP and thus assume minutes to be the unit of time. Assume that we wish to simulate one day at SHIP, and that we begin measuring time (t) at 1 PM (e.g., $t = 0$ corresponds to 1 PM and $t = 60$ means 2 PM). Since SHIP remains open for business until 5 PM (i.e., until $t = 240$), any patient who arrives prior to $t = 240$ will be serviced that very day.

To perform the simulation, we need to generate:

- Moment of arrival of each patient, *TA*
- Service time of the receptionist, *SR*, and that of the cashier, *SC*
- Doctor assigned to each patient, *CHOICE*
- Service time of Dr. Jones, *SJ*, and that of Dr. Berry, *SB*

In the preceding chapter, we already saw how to manually generate these variables. This section illustrates how the corresponding formulas are written in FORTRAN.

There are no patients inside SHIP at the moment it opens, so we set the *TA* of the 0th patient to zero:

```
TA(0) = 0
```

Let *NR* denote the serial numbers of patients when they approach the receptionist. For the first patient:

```
NR = 1
```

Since the patients approach SHIP in a Poisson manner at an average of 12 per hour, the time between two arrivals is exponentially distributed. To simulate the actual arrival times, we can use the subroutine RANDOM and then use the resultant *RN* values to compute the interarrival times. Recall, however, that we need to supply the starting random integer. Arbitrarily, let us choose 935,784,206 to be this initial random integer. Figure 9-5 shows a possible set of FORTRAN instructions to generate the consecutive arrival times for each patient who might arrive before 5 PM.

```
            IPAT = 935784206
          5 CALL RANDOM (IPAT, JPAT, RPAT)
C           RPAT WILL BE THE RANDOM NUMBER USED FOR
C           OBTAINING INTER-ARRIVAL TIME, IAT
            IPAT = JPAT
            IAT(NR) = -5.0 * LN(RPAT)
C           TA STANDS FOR THE 'TIME OF ARRIVAL.'
            TA(NR) = TA(NR - 1) + IAT(NR)
            IF(TA(NR) - 240)10, 10, 300
         10 CONTINUE
```

Figure 9-5. *A FORTRAN Set of Instructions for Generating the Arrival Times*

Since this is not a text on FORTRAN language, figure 9-5 is intended merely to reinforce the notion that once you have a mathematical model, conversion to a computer program is relatively straightforward. Notice from the figure that a computer always processes these statements in the order of presentation. If you wish the computer to process the statements in any other order, use a GO TO statement or an IF statement.

A GO TO statement is of the form:

```
GO TO N
```

where n is the reference number of the statement to be processed next.

An IF statement is of the form:

```
IF (VARIABLE) M, N, K
```

The instruction processed next will be m if the variable is negative, n if it is zero, and k if it is positive.

Also, note that a "C" in the first column of a statement is for human convenience only. A computer will ignore it completely.

In figure 9-5, for instance, the very first statement provides the initial value of the starting random number, to be called *IPAT*. The statement numbered 5 yields a random integer *JPAT* and a random fraction *RPAT*. Since we need to use this particular statement each time we compute the next arrival time, it has been assigned a reference number—in this case, 5. The choice of a reference number is arbitrary, though it must not exceed 9999.

The next computer instruction ensures that we will keep on getting a new random number each time. The next time the computer returns to the statement numbered 5, *IPAT* will not be 935,784,206. Instead, it will be whatever *JPAT* was.

The interarrival time for this patient is computed using the formula: $IAT = -M \cdot ln(r)$, which was discussed in the preceding chapter. The FORTRAN language contains a "library" of commonly used functions. *LN* is one of these and it provides the natural logarithm of the corresponding number. Given the preceding patient's arrival time and the current value of the interarrival time, the next statement determines the arrival time of the current patient, *TA*.

At this stage, we must check to see if this patient has arrived too late, i.e., later than 240 minutes after 1 PM. This is the purpose of the next two statements. The patient who has arrived in time has a *TA* that is less than or equal to 240, so that $TA - 240 \leq 0$. In that case, we instruct the computer to CONTINUE processing. Otherwise, we ask it to process the statement numbered 300. (Physically, statement 300 appears at the end of a simulation run. From there, the computer engages in producing a statistical summary of data.)

You can similarly develop a FORTRAN set of instructions for obtaining *SR*, *SC*, and *CHOICE* values for each patient. (Be sure to use a *different* random integer in each case to avoid creating any correlations between the variables of SHIP.) Conceivably, you might also use the "table look up" approach outlined in the preceding chapter to find the values for *SJ* and *SB*.

However, as you have learned before, computers are much faster at generating and using random numbers on their own. Based on this fact, and the central limit theorem of chapter 2, computers sometimes generate the values of standard normal variable, *z*, using the formula:

$$z = \sum_{i=1}^{12} r_i - 6$$

The r_i values in the above formula can be obtained by repeatedly using the subroutine RANDOM. Given this *z*, you can find the *SJ* and *SB* values using the formulas:

$SJ = 2z + 9$ and $SB = 3z + 15$

In short, you can (with some effort) instruct a computer to generate the necessary exogenous values. To continue the discussion of SHIP's case, you may presume that tables 8-4 through 8-9 have been generated in this fashion. How should we combine these to obtain a simulated history for one day at SHIP?

Rules for Combining Data

The logic underlying the process of combining exogenous variables is based on tracking the flow: activities in a PERT network, resources and materials in a production-inventory system, or messages in a communication network.

In SHIP, the flow is that of the patients through the receptionist's, doctors', and cashier's offices. Thus, by tracking the patients, we can determine the logic of combining the exogenous variables.

The Tracking Aids To begin with, we must assign a serial number to each patient who meets the receptionist. This number, say *NR*, has the same function as taking a number in a crowded bakery—it helps determine who is to be processed next. If the entire system can be represented by a single channel, one serial number would suffice. In SHIP, however, there are two channels: one towards Dr. Jones's office and another towards Dr. Berry's office. Worse still, these two channels join again for processing by the cashier. Since the doctors do not have identical and constant service rates, the patients are likely to join the cashier's line in a sequence that does not match their incoming sequence. At each gate in the system, therefore, one must assign a new serial number, say *NJ* at Dr. Jones's office, *NB* at Dr. Berry's office, and *NC* at the cashier's office.

Next, we need to indicate the beginning and end of each transaction at each gate. We have already introduced the necessary variables while quantifying the SHIP model, viz., *RBEG, RDONE, JBEG, JDONE, BBEG, BDONE, CBEG,* and *CDONE*. Finally, whenever there is a branching, we need a variable to record which branch has been taken. In SHIP's case, there is only one branching and the corresponding variable is *CHOICE*.

Transaction Variables Each flow item comes across some gate in the system and is processed there. Thus, you must define a process variable, such as, the amount of lead time in an inventory system, the duration of each activity in a PERT network, or the service time in a waiting line. In SHIP's case, we have already defined these process variables to be *SR, SJ, SB,* and *SC*, corresponding to the four gates at SHIP.

Construct a Flow Chart Since you must keep track of many different variables for a large number of flow items, it is best to start this process by constructing a flow chart of the entire flow process. Figure 9-6 shows such a diagram for simulating the operations of SHIP for one day. When creating such a diagram, you must balance between showing too many or too few details. The more details you show, the easier it is to construct the corresponding set of computer instructions. If you show too many details, it is that much more difficult to grasp the entire process—your reader can't see the forest for the trees. Constructing a flow chart is thus an art to be mastered through practice.

Having defined all the necessary variables and drawn a flow chart, you can now proceed to follow each item of the flow as it enters the system. In SHIP's case, this implies following each patient from the moment of entry in the SHIP.

Initialization When SHIP opens there aren't any patients. Hence, to begin with, you should set *all* the serial numbers to zero. Symbolically:

$$NR = NJ = NB = NC = 0$$

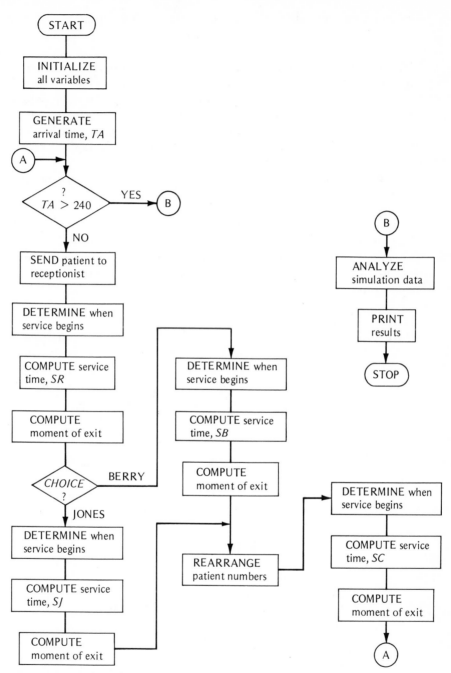

Figure 9-6. *The Flow Chart of a Simulation Run*

That there are no patients yet is also indicated by setting:

TA(0) = RDONE(0) = JDONE(0) = BDONE(0) = CDONE(0) = 0

You should also define distinct starting random integers necessary to use subroutine RANDOM for obtaining the random values of *TA, SR, SJ, SB, SC,* and *CHOICE*. If the waiting times at each gate are to be computed, you must also initialize all such variables to zero. Similarly, the idle times of each resource (the receptionist, the physicians, and the cashier) should be set to zero. The computer is now ready to process the first patient.

Patient Arrivals As each patient arrives at SHIP, you should increase *NR* by 1. Symbolically:

NR = NR + 1

The patient whose serial number is *NR* enters SHIP at *TA(NR)*, i.e., those many minutes after 1 PM. To instruct the computer, you should insert here all of the instructions from figure 9-5. The instruction numbered 5 in that figure corresponds to the point Ⓐ in figure 9-6.

Processing by the Receptionist If the receptionist is free, a patient entering SHIP will be processed immediately. In that case, *RBEG(NR)* = *TA(NR)*. If, on the other hand, the receptionist has been processing a previous arrival, patient *NR* cannot begin receiving service until patient *NR* − 1 leaves the receptionist's desk. Thus, *RBEG(NR)* is necessarily the larger of the two numbers: *RDONE(NR* − 1) and *TA(NR)*. This fact is reflected in the following equation:

RBEG(NR) = MAX(TA(NR), RDONE(NR-1))

where MAX $(a, b, \dots)$ equals the largest of all the numbers in the set: a, $b, \dots$.

The receptionist needs *SR(NR)* minutes to process patient *NR*. Recall from the preceding chapter that the receptionist's service times are given by the formula:

$$SR = 1 + 4r.$$

Insert the corresponding FORTRAN statements here.

When you add the receptionist's service time to the moment when service begins, you obtain the moment when that patient leaves the receptionist's desk. Symbolically:

RDONE(NR) = RBEG(NR) + SR(NR)

Branching The variable *CHOICE* is used to record which particular doctor the patient will visit. The actual value is obtained by using the binary rule of the preceding chapter. Specifically, *CHOICE* will be

Dr. Jones if $r < .7$. Insert the necessary FORTRAN instructions here. If the patient visits Dr. Jones, then:

```
20 NJ = NJ + 1
```

Similarly, if the patient visits Dr. Berry, this fact would be shown by recording:

```
50 NB = NB + 1
```

Processing by the Doctors If the patient visits Dr. Jones, the service can begin either when the patient leaves the receptionist, or when Dr. Jones has finished serving *his* preceding patient, whichever comes later. Hence, as in case of the receptionist, you will find that:

```
JBEG(NJ) = MAX(RDONE(NR), JDONE(NJ - 1))
```

Dr. Jones's service time, *SJ*, follows the normal distribution with $\mu = 9$ and $\sigma = 2$. You should provide the corresponding FORTRAN instructions here. Having done this, the moment when the current patient leaves Dr. Jones's office is obtained by the formula:

```
JDONE(NJ) = JBEG(NJ) + SJ(NJ)
```

The next stop for a patient who visits Dr. Jones is the cashier's office. To ensure that the computer will "send" the patient to the cashier's office, you will have to instruct it:

```
GO TO 100
```

This corresponds to the "by-pass" in figure 9-6. Just make sure that the very first statement in the cashier processing set of statements is numbered 100.

The transactions of a patient who visits Dr. Berry can be recorded similarly. Specific statements are:

```
50 NB = NB + 1
   BBEG(NB) = MAX(RDONE(NR), BDONE (NB - 1))
```

These are followed by the rules for computing *SB*: a normal variable with $\mu = 15$ and $\sigma = 3$. The moment of the patient's exit from Dr. Berry's office is given by:

```
BDONE (NB) = BBEG(NB) + SB(NB)
```

At the Cashier's Desk That the patient has reached the cashier's office is indicated by the numbered statement:

```
100 NC = NC + 1
```

Whether this patient has come from Dr. Jones or Dr. Berry would depend on when each patient left the doctor's office, i.e., on whether *BDONE (NB)* is smaller or larger than *JDONE* (*NJ*). Whoever comes to the cashier first is processed first. The moment of arrival of patient *NC*, say *TIME* (*NC*), is given by:

```
TIME(NC) = MIN(JDONE(NJ),BDONE(NB))
```

where MIN(*a*, *b*, . . .) equals the smallest of all the numbers in the set: *a*, *b*, ... The moment when the cashier begins to process this patient is given by:

```
CBEG(NC) = MAX(TIME(NC),CDONE(NC - 1))
```

The cashier's service times are rectangular between 1 and 9 minutes. Insert the appropriate formulas for obtaining *SC* here. Then determine the moment when the patient leaves the cashier:

```
CDONE(NC) = CBEG(NC) + SC(NC)
```

The End of a Run Is this the last patient to be processed today? The cashier cannot answer this on her own. She must find out if this was the last patient who entered SHIP prior to 5 PM. You must, therefore, ask the computer to send the next patient. In short, the next statement to be processed is the one numbered 5. It corresponds to point Ⓐ in figure 9-6. The appropriate instruction is:

```
GO TO 5
```

If this is the last patient of the day, the *TA* of the next patient would exceed 240. The computer would then process the statement numbered 300, which corresponds to point Ⓑ in figure 9-6. The appropriate statements for providing a summary of this simulation run (e.g., the average waiting time at Dr. Jones's office or the average throughput time for a patient) should be inserted here to complete this computer program.

Running the Model

The act of obtaining a simulated history is similar to processing the instructions in one giant loop. The computer goes around the loop once for each item of flow, i.e., each patient arriving at SHIP. When all arrivals have been processed, the computer exits from this loop and proceeds to do whatever else is required, which might include preparing statistical summaries or printing the recorded history. In order to actually run such a model on a computer, you will need to know much more about compiling and running a computer program than has been assumed here.

Instead, to complete the story here, we will assume that you have followed the instructions for generating the values of exogenous variables manually and have obtained the simulated values that were shown in tables 8-4 through 8-9 of the preceding chapter. Using the instructions in the preceding section, you can therefore create a simulated history of one day at SHIP. The results are shown in table 9-1.

Table 9-1 *Patient's Progress Through Ship*

NR	TA	RBEG	RDONE	CHOICE	JBEG	JDONE	BBEG	BDONE	NC	CBEG	CDONE
1	2.87	2.87	7.31	JONES	7.31	18.49	—	—	1	18.49	27.09
2	7.23	7.31	10.79	JONES	18.49	30.85	—	—	3	31.21	39.65
3	7.86	10.79	12.19	BERRY	—	—	12.19	28.05	2	28.05	31.21
4	9.19	12.19	16.23	JONES	30.85	38.13	—	—	4	39.65	46.97
5	15.68	16.23	20.43	BERRY	—	—	28.05	43.29	5	46.97	50.13
6	16.05	20.43	22.71	JONES	38.13	45.15	—	—	6	50.13	55.69
7	29.21	29.21	32.17	BERRY	—	—	43.29	59.76	8	64.11	65.51
8	30.78	32.17	37.01	BERRY	—	—	59.76	70.24	9	70.24	76.76
9	49.86	49.86	53.02	JONES	53.02	59.19	—	—	7	59.19	64.11
10	64.94	64.94	69.34	JONES	69.34	77.58	—	—	10	77.58	85.42
11	67.82	69.34	73.90	JONES	77.58	86.59	—	—	11	86.59	88.15
12	70.55	73.90	77.22	JONES	86.59	96.19	—	—	13	96.76	105.36
13	76.55	77.22	78.38	BERRY	—	—	78.38	93.14	12	93.14	96.76
14	83.96	83.96	85.96	JONES	96.19	103.98	—	—	14	105.36	111.08
15	86.25	86.25	88.53	JONES	103.98	112.28	—	—	16	113.28	121.48
16	86.64	88.53	92.13	JONES	112.28	119.65	—	—	17	121.48	130.08
17	89.37	92.13	93.61	JONES	119.65	123.31	—	—	18	130.08	132.36
18	89.99	93.61	95.17	JONES	123.32	134.55	—	—	20	140.86	143.46
19	95.10	95.17	98.21	JONES	134.55	143.71	—	—	21	143.71	144.87
20	98.29	98.29	99.33	BERRY	—	—	99.33	110.06	15	111.08	113.28
21	104.80	104.80	109.44	BERRY	—	—	110.06	132.74	19	132.74	140.86
22	105.90	109.44	110.84	BERRY	—	—	132.74	152.34	23	156.09	160.93
23	107.82	110.84	113.92	BERRY	—	—	152.34	166.97	25	166.97	173.73
24	113.15	113.92	117.52	BERRY	—	—	166.97	166.33	28	193.52	197.40
25	113.68	117.52	120.32	BERRY	143.71	150.13	—	—	22	150.13	156.09
26	115.62	120.32	123.28	BERRY	—	—	188.33	199.91	30	200.80	203.72
27	116.35	123.28	124.72	JONES	150.13	162.14	—	—	24	162.14	165.18
28	117.76	124.72	127.28	JONES	162.14	174.54	—	—	26	174.54	182.86
29	123.50	127.28	132.08	JONES	174.54	184.92	—	—	27	184.92	193.52
30	128.54	132.08	137.08	JONES	184.92	192.52	—	—	29	197.40	200.80
31	135.98	137.08	139.52	JONES	192.52	201.54	—	—	31	203.72	206.80
32	141.52	141.52	144.92	JONES	201.54	211.52	—	—	32	211.52	219.40
33	142.13	144.92	147.52	JONES	211.52	221.91	—	—	34	227.60	230.52
34	161.59	161.59	162.99	JONES	221.91	232.51	—	—	36	232.85	234.89
35	161.82	162.99	165.04	JONES	232.51	239.08	—	—	37	239.08	244.88
36	165.26	165.26	168.38	BERRY	—	—	199.91	215.20	33	219.40	227.60
37	168.98	168.98	171.06	JONES	239.08	244.46	—	—	39	249.08	253.20
38	171.24	171.24	173.52	JONES	246.46	253.75	—	—	40	253.75	262.67
39	184.06	184.06	188.06	JONES	253.75	263.31	—	—	42	267.91	270.35
40	187.15	188.06	192.86	JONES	263.31	269.29	—	—	43	270.35	274.23
41	196.65	196.65	200.21	JONES	269.29	279.97	—	—	44	279.97	286.49
42	202.79	202.79	206.43	BERRY	—	—	215.20	230.89	35	230.89	232.85
43	202.81	206.43	211.39	JONES	279.97	287.76	—	—	45	287.76	289.32
44	211.79	211.79	215.19	BERRY	—	—	230.89	243.09	38	244.88	249.08
45	216.01	216.01	219.77	JONES	287.76	296.06	—	—	46	296.06	297.22
46	219.37	219.77	221.69	BERRY	—	—	243.09	255.65	41	262.67	267.91
47	227.52	227.52	230.20	JONES	296.06	297.41	—	—	47	297.41	306.01
48	234.62	234.62	236.18	JONES	297.41	306.46	—	—	48	306.46	310.90

ANALYZING THE CURRENT SYSTEM

There are at least two reasons to analyze the data generated by running a model. First, no matter how good a model is, it is not synonymous with the real system. Some aspects of reality must be ignored in order to develop a manageable model, and, occasionally, relevant aspects of reality are ignored or incorrectly represented by a model. Thus, the model must be validated by comparing the model outputs with the corresponding values of a real system. The second reason is that an analysis of model outputs can reveal certain weaknesses in the current system, and might suggest ways of improving that system.

A complete discussion of various statistical techniques used to validate a model is beyond the scope of this text. (Consult the references cited at the end of this chapter for further detail.) Instead, we will prepare some simple summaries of data, and those of you who are statisticians can carry out the necessary analyses.

As we have discussed earlier, a much more elaborate model of SHIP would be necessary if SHIP were a real project asking us to help them design a better health delivery system. Such a model would be run much longer than one day to smooth out any irregularities in observations. But, the basic output data would be similar to that shown in table 9-1, which gives a log of patient-related activities for each simulated day. By performing simple arithmetic operations on several of the data items in that table, we can display a number of *operating characteristics* of SHIP. For example, the difference:

$$WJ(NJ) = JBEG(NJ) - RDONE(NR)$$

equals the time a patient spends waiting to see Dr. Jones. Conversely, the difference:

$$JIDLE(NJ) = JBEG(NJ) - JDONE(NJ - 1)$$

equals the time Dr. Jones spends between patients numbered $NJ - 1$ and NJ. Of course, in the case of any one patient, NJ, either WJ or $JIDLE$ must be zero.

Why is WJ important? Because it might tend to explain why the children's playroom at SHIP has been rather noisy; it might also explain why the cashiers keep quitting (two of the problems mentioned earlier).

You can similarly compute the values of other endogenous variables. In particular, the formulas for computing the waiting times are:

$$WR(NR) = RBEG(NR) - TA(NR)$$
$$WB(NB) = BBEG(NB) - RDONE(NR)$$
$$WC(NC) = CBEG(NC) - TIME(NC)$$

You can also verify the formula for computing the throughput time, i.e., the time from entry to exit, TT, of each patient.

$$TT(NR) = CDONE(NC) - TA(NR)$$

Analysis of Table 9-1 If you wish the computer to provide you with these endogenous values for each patient, you must insert the above instructions at proper places within your computer program. The simulation run will automatically compute WJ, WR, WB, WC, and TT for each patient. For the sake of illustration, these computations have been done for the simulated history of table 9-1. The results for some of the patients are shown in table 9-2. From the last line of that table you can read that *on the average:*

Table 9-2 *Analysis of Waiting*

NR	WR	WJ	WB	WC	TT	
1	0.	0.	—	0.	24.22	
2	.08	7.70	—	0.36	32.42	
3	2.93	—	0	0.	23.35	
26	4.70	—	65.05	0.89	88.10	
27	6.93	25.41	—	0.	48.83	
28	6.96	34.86	—	0.	65.10	
29	3.78	42.46	—	0.	70.02	
30	3.54	47.84	—	4.88	72.26	
36	0.	—	31.53	4.20	62.34	
37	0.	68.02	—	2.62	84.22	
38	0.	71.94	—	0.	91.43	
39	0.	55.69	—	4.68	86.29	
40	0.91	70.45	—	1.06	87.08	
46	0.40	—	21.40	7.02	48.54	
47	0.	65.86	—	0.	78.49	
48	0.	61.23	—	0.	76.28	
Mean	1.53	38.01	19.62	1.53	59.14	Jones
					43.67	Berry

- Patients wait 1.53 minutes to see either the receptionist or the cashier.
- Patients who visit Dr. Jones must wait an additonal 38.01 minutes (fortunately for Dr. Jones, SHIP is open for only four hours—otherwise, this number would be much bigger).
- Patients who visit Dr. Berry must wait 19.62 minutes to meet him.
- A patient visiting Dr. Berry can leave SHIP in 43.67 minutes, of which a total of 1.53 + 19.62 + 1.53 = 22.68 minutes are spent in the waiting room (i.e., 51.93% of the time inside SHIP).
- A patient visiting Dr. Jones can expect to spend 59.14 minutes inside SHIP, of which 1.53 + 38.01 + 1.53 = 41.07 minutes are spent in the waiting room (i.e., 69.45% of the time inside SHIP).

Proposed Policy Changes Suppose that you have simulated a large number of days at SHIP and that through a whole variety of statistical tests you have verified that the above results reflect the reality at SHIP. In other words, suppose that the deficiencies revealed above are more than a chance occurrence. That something must be done to improve SHIP seems clear. Two possibilities are:

- Reduce the caseload of Dr. Jones (perhaps by referring some of his patients elsewhere).

- Increase the number of physicians at SHIP (thus relieving the extra load carried by Dr. Jones and perhaps even expanding the total caseload in the process).

If you wish to examine the effects of implementing these policies, you must in each case construct the corresponding logic, i.e., tell the computer exactly what to do and then execute a simulation run. In the first case, you must decide on the new rate of arrivals of patients at SHIP and also modify the probability of going to Dr. Jones or Dr. Berry. In the second case, you need to introduce an additional physician at SHIP. This means adding one more "service facility" in the second phase of SHIP, recomputing the probability of each branch that emerges from the receptionist's station, assigning a service rate to the new physician and then running the model. The purpose of this chapter has been to illustrate the methods of constructing a model and setting up a simulation run. Solving SHIP's problem is secondary in this regard, so we will not study SHIP any further.

WHAT A MANAGER SHOULD KNOW

Simulation is a last resort technique. It should not be employed when an appropriate formal model of the situation at hand can be constructed. This is because formal models yield analytical solutions, the associated solution techniques are usually more efficient, and the optimality of the resultant solutions can be proven. Nonetheless, simulation is the most common activity of management scientists at the corporate level. A management scientist is engaged in this activity nearly 25 percent of the time. Based on a 1972 survey by Turban, this percentage will likely grow with the increased use and accessibility of computers and with the greater understanding of and confidence in management science techniques.

The reasons are not too difficult to understand. Many real world systems are too complex to permit a compact mathematical model or an analytical solution. Besides, a technical expert's notation might not correspond with the decision maker's, and translation would become necessary. A simulation model, on the other hand, can represent the system much more closely, and it uses the decision maker's terminology. And, the model outputs are easier to understand. Furthermore, once the model of the current system has been run and verified, the decision maker can easily try out a large number of candidate policies and "what if?" questions—especially with the advent of more versatile computers and easier computer languages.

There is, of course, a price to be paid. A simulation exercise is much more expensive than formal modeling. A simulation can evaluate a proposed solution, but it cannot by itself find an optimal solution, i.e., a solution whose optimality can be proven. The burden of proposing candidate solutions lies squarely on the shoulders of the decision maker and the simulation project team. As you must now realize, a simulation exercise is necessarily a team activity. A typical team must have expertise in computer programming and statistical inference as well as a knowledge of the system whose operations are to be simulated. The corresponding resources are scarce and hence expensive.

One other point. A manager whose problem is being solved through a simulation exercise must be an active member of the simulation team. Empirical evidence shows that, though this might make a simulation exercise even more expensive, the chance of ultimate success is greatly enhanced. Success, in this regard, is synonymous with the actual *implementation* of simulation-derived results.

Since a manager is not necessarily a technical expert, how far can he/she participate in a simulation activity? No firm answer to this question is likely to be satisfactory in all situations. However, a manager of tomorrow should understand and at least intuitively verify the quantitative model of the current system, i.e., verify the reasonableness of each proposed new policy or procedure. And, the outputs of each simulation run should be validated—the manager should insist on receiving such outputs in an easy-to-understand form, not in some obscure computer language.

We have used FORTRAN to illustrate the correspondence between mathematical formulas and computer instructions. The knowledge of these instructions alone would not make you a FORTRAN expert, but, if you are so inclined, you should pursue a course in FORTRAN programming. (A text that could help you is cited at the end of this chapter.) Though widely used for developing simulation models, FORTRAN is only one of the many such languages. Other languages, developed specifically for simulation purposes include DYNAMO, SIMSCRIPT, GASP IV, and GPSS. The corresponding reference materials are cited at the end of this chapter.

The references at the end of this chapter also indicate the wide range of situations in which simulation has been used as a decision-making tool, including making decisions about snow and ice removal, studying the operations of human service agencies, forecasting the effects of uncontrolled industrial and population growth, and studying the pollution control systems. So many ready-made models for corporate decision making alone are now on the market, that in 1974, Naylor, et al. published a rather extensive bibliography of such models.

In short, your imagination is the only limit on the applicability of simulation approach. To use any of these, however, you must first create a quantitative model of the situation at hand, and only *you* can do it best.

SELECTED READINGS

BURT, J. M. and GARMAN, M. B. "Monte Carlo Techniques for Stochastic PERT Network Analysis." *INFOR* (1971), pp. 248–262.

CONOVER, W. J. *Practical Non-Parametric Statistics.* New York: John Wiley & Sons, Inc., 1971.

COOK, T. M. and ALPRIN, B. S. "Snow and Ice Removal in an Urban Environment." *Management Science* 23 (1976), pp. 227–234.

COUGAR, J. D. and SHANNON, L. E. *FORTRAN IV: A P.I. Approach Including Structured Programming.* 3d ed. Homewood, Ill.: Richard D. Irwin, Inc., 1976.

DOWNING, P. B. and WATSON, W. D., JR. "A Simulation Study of Alternate Pollution Control Enforcement Systems." *Management Science* 22 (1976), pp. 558–569.

EMSHOFF, J. R. and SISSON, R. L., *Design and Use of Computer Simulation Models.* New York: MacMillan Publishing Co., Inc., 1970.

FISHMAN, G. "Statistical Analysis for Queueing Simulations." *Management Science* 20 (1973), pp. 363–369.

FORRESTER, J. W. *Industrial Dynamics.* Cambridge, Mass.: MIT Press, 1961.

FORRESTER, J. W. *Urban Dynamics.* 2d ed. Cambridge, Mass.: MIT Press, 1969.

GORDON, G. *System Simulation.* Englewood Cliffs, NJ: Prentice-Hall, Inc., 1969.

GORDON, G. *The Application of GPSS-V to Discrete System Simulation.* Englewood Cliffs, NJ: Prentice-Hall, Inc., 1975.

HAYS, W. L. *Statistics for the Social Sciences.* 2d ed. New York: Holt, Rinehart and Winston, 1973.

IBM *General Purpose Simulation System/360.* 4th ed. New York: IBM Corp. GH20-326-3, 1970.

JOSHI, M. V. and EICKER, W. F. *DESIM: A Simulation Tool for Modeling and Evaluating Human Service Systems.* Waltham, Mass.: The Florence Heller School, Brandeis University, 1973.

KIVIAT, P. J.; VILLENUEVA, R.; and MARKOWITZ, H. M. *The SIMSCRIPT II Programming Language.* Englewood Cliffs, NJ: Prentice-Hall, Inc., 1977.

KWAK, N. K.; KUZDRALL, P. J.; and SCHMITZ, H. H. "The GPSS Simulation of Scheduling Policies for Surgical Procedures." *Management Science* 22 (1976), pp. 982–989.

MAISEL, H. and GNUGNUOLI, G. *Simulation of Discrete Stochastic Systems.* Chicago: Science Research Associates, 1972.

MEADOWS, D. L.; MEADOWS, D. H.; RANDERS, J.; and BEHRENS, W. W., III. *The Limits to Growth.* New York: Universe Books, 1972.

MIZE, J. H. and COX, J. G. *Essentials of Simulation.* Englewood Cliffs, NJ: Prentice-Hall, Inc., 1969.

NAYLOR, T. H.; BALINTFY, J. L.; BURDICK, D. S.; and CHU, K. *Computer Simulation Techniques.* New York: John Wiley & Sons, Inc., 1966.

NAYLOR, T. H. and SCHAULAND, H. *Bibliography on Corporate Simulation Models.* Durham, NC: Social Systems, Inc., 1974.

PAYNE, W. H.; RABUNG, J. R.; and BOGYO, T. P. "Coding the Lehmer Pseudorandom Number Generator." *Communications of the ACM* vol. 12, no. 2 (1969).

PRITSKER, A. A. *The GASP IV Simulation Language.* New York: John Wiley & Sons, Inc., 1974.

PUGH, A. L. *DYNAMO User's Manual.* 2d ed. Cambridge, Mass.: MIT Press, 1963.

RAJ, D. *The Design of Sample Surveys.* New York: McGraw-Hill Book Co., 1972.

SCHMITZ, H. H. and KWAK, N. K. "Monte Carlo Simulation of Operating-Room and Recovery-Room Usage." *Operations Research* 20 (1972), pp. 1171–1180.

SHANNON, R. E. *Systems Simulation: The Art and Science.* Englewood Cliffs, NJ: Prentice-Hall, Inc., 1975.

SHYCON, H. M. "Perspectives on MS Applications." *Interfaces* vol. 7, no. 4, August 1977.

TURBAN, E. "A Sample Survey of Operations-Research Activities at the Corporate Level." *Operations Research* 20 (1972), pp. 708–721.

VAN SLYKE, R. M. "Monte Carlo Methods, and the PERT Problem." *Operations Research* 11 (1963), pp. 839–860.

PROBLEM SET 9
PUTTING IT TOGETHER

While creating FORTRAN-like instructions for a computer, assume the following symbols:

SYMBOL	INTERPRETATION
$a * b$	Product of a and b.
$a = b$	Assign the value b to the unknown a.
a/b	Divide a by b.
$a ** b$	Raise a to b^{th} power, i.e., a^b.
MAX $(a, b, \ldots)$	The largest of all numbers $a, b, \ldots$
MIN $(a, b, \ldots)$	The smallest of all numbers $a, b, \ldots$
LN (a)	Natural logarithm of a.
SQRT (a)	Square root of a.
GO TO n	Process statement numbered n.
IF $(v)\, i, j, k$	Process statement numbered i if v is negative, j if v equals zero, and k if v is positive.

1. Display the sequence of instructions necessary to:

   a. Deterime whether patient numbered NR visits Dr. Jones or Berry at SHIP, and

   b. Compute the number of minutes the receptionist at SHIP will spend serving patient NR.

2. Assume that you plan to obtain the values of a standard normal variable by using the formula:

$$z = \sum_{i=1}^{12} r_i - 6$$

Display the sequence of instructions necessary to compute the service time of Dr. Jones at SHIP.

In each of the following situations, create a quantitative model of that situation such as the one shown in figure 9-3. Identify the input/output variables in each case. Then, create a FORTRAN-like set of instructions for producing a simulation run. If you have access to a computer, run the model and analyze the outputs.

3. A machine shop has two identical machines A and B. The shop remains open for business 8 hours each workday. During that period, the jobs to be processed by either machine arrive at an average of 3.2 per day. Assume a Poisson process. Each job is processed on a FIFO basis, i.e., the first job to arrive is assigned to the first machine which becomes free.

   The time necessary to do a job depends on its complexity. The probability distribution in the adjoining table describes the time in hours to do a typical job. A job remaining unfinished one day will be processed the following workday.

   Management would like to run a simulation model to determine the average throughput time for a typical job, i.e., the number of working hours a typical job spends in the machine shop. A 200-day run would be satisfactory.

Time in Hours	1 – 2⁻	2 – 4⁻	4 – 8⁻	8 – 12
Probability	.40	.15	.20	.15

4. The management of the machine shop in problem 3 above would like to investigate the effects of implementing another policy. As per this policy, all the complex jobs, i.e., those needing more than 6 hours would always be run on machine A. All other jobs would be run on machine B unless machine A is free when a short job arrives. A simulation run of 200 workdays is called for. Prepare the computer instructions to test this policy.

5. Dr. Jones at SHIP has decided to reduce *his* patient load by 20 percent. Practically speaking, some of his patients would be referred elsewhere. They will not enter SHIP. Generate the computer instructions to study this policy so as to find the average throughput time in hours of those patients who visit Dr. Jones. A simulation run of 150 days would be satisfactory for this purpose.

6. Dr. Jones is also investigating the effects on throughput time of employing a paramedic to help him with routine cases. In this model, *all* patients of Dr. Jones will be assigned to the helper who can service each client in an average of $\mu = 5$ minutes with $\sigma = 1$ minute. Fifty percent of these clients are likely to need additional medical attention. They will be sent to Dr. Jones; the rest will join the cashier's line as soon as they exit from the helper's office. A simulation run of 150 days would be sufficient. Generate the appropriate instructions.

7. The adjoining network shows a small project, the least time to complete each

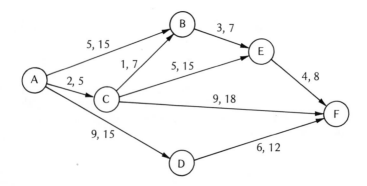

task and the corresponding pessimistic time. For example, task AB is expected to need at least 5 days but no more than 15 days. Suppose that the task completion times are rectangular.

Develop a sequence of computer instructions to simulate 100 occasions of completing the project and to obtain the corresponding project completion times.

8. A youth services director has found that when one of her young salesgirls goes door-to-door to sell cookies, the chance of making a sale and the size of sale depends on who opens the door. If the mother opens the door, the chance of making a sale is 40 percent; the probability of selling 1, 2, or 3 boxes of cookies to the mother is shown in the adjoining table.

Number of Boxes	1	2	3
Probability (Mother)	.5	.3	.2

If the father opens the door, there is 30 percent probability of making a sale; the size of the sale and the associated probabilities are shown in the adjoining table.

Number of Boxes	1	2	3	4
Probability (Father)	.4	.3	.2	.1

If one of the children comes to the door, the likelihood of a sale is 60 percent but in that case, only one box will be sold.

Experience shows that when a salesgirl approaches a household, 20 percent of the time, no one is home; 40 percent of the time, the mother opens the door; and 25 percent of the time, father opens the door. Travel from household to household needs 1 minute, a "no sale" transaction costs 3 minutes of the salesgirl's time, whereas, a sale needs 6 minutes. A salesgirl is on the road four hours each day.

The youth services director would like to find the average number of boxes sold each day. A simulation run of 200 days is desired.

9. Professor Jones lives at point A and goes to work at point D in the adjoining diagram. He drives from A to B in 4 ± 2 minutes. From point B, he takes a bus

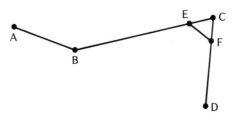

which stops at E and then at C. At point C, he gets on yet another bus which stops at point F before going to D. Read problem 2 from the preceding problem set for additional details. It turns out that the bus from B to C reaches point E four minutes earlier than at C. Also, the bus from C to D needs 3 minutes to travel from C to F. A brisk walk from E to F needs 2 minutes.

Develop a sequence of computer instructions to simulate 100 mornings of Professor Jones and to find average travel time from A to D.

10. Develop a computer program to answer question 9 of the preceding problem set, i.e., for choosing between two electricity generators.

*11. A restaurant has twelve 2-person tables and eighteen 4-person tables. The adjoining bar can accommodate up to 35 customers as they wait to be seated in the restaurant. Anyone unable to find accommodations in either the restaurant or the bar will go someplace else.

Customers arrive in a Poisson process but the arrival rate depends on the time of day. Specifically, an average of 15 customer groups arrive between 4:30 PM and 5:30 PM. This rate increases to 25 per hour between 5:30 and 7:30 PM but then drops to 10 per hour between 7:30 and 10 PM. The establishment does not accept anyone after 10 PM. Those inside are, however, always served—no matter how long it takes. Customers, once seated, do not go someplace else either.

Customers arrive in groups of 1, 2, or 4 persons. Fifty percent of the groups have two members and 30 percent are 4-member groups. Each group always stays together and behaves as one body, i.e., each member of a group eats and drinks alike.

Reservations are not accepted. Service rule is first come first served with the following modification. A 4-person table is generally used for 4-person groups only. But if more than ten 4-person tables are vacant, an incoming 2-person group is seated at a 4-person table, if necessary.

A customer group spends 60 ± 20 mintues eating food. Fifty percent of 4-person groups and 30 percent of 2-person groups also order an after dinner drink and this implies an additional 15 to 20 minutes at the dinner table. A customer spends $10 per hour at the dining table. The tip varies between 10 and 15 percent of the bill.

Those waiting in the bar order a drink every 20 minutes or part thereof. For example, a person who spends 43 minutes in the bar will have three drinks. Sixty percent of the 2-person groups order wine ($1.00 per glass), 20 percent order cocktails ($1.50 per drink), the rest drink beer ($0.85 per bottle). The corresponding proportions are 30, 50, and 20 for members of 4-person groups and 10, 60, and 30 for 1-person groups.

Develop a computer program to describe 100 days of this restaurant/bar system, to compute the average time a customer spends in each component of the system, as well as to determine each customer's expense and hence the gross income of the establishment.

*Should not be assigned unless students are FORTRAN experts or have access to special purpose language such as SIMSCRIPT II.s.

PART THREE

Deterministic Models

The models to be discussed in this part—linear optimization models—assume that the values of all the relevant parameters are known with certainty. Thus, the primary focus is on finding efficient search techniques.

To properly solve a decision problem, it must be formulated correctly—chapter 10 describes the necessary steps. Several particular cases of these models are discussed in chapters 11, 12, and 13. Each of these chapters also illustrates the corresponding solution techniques.

If the optimization problem consists of only two decision variables, the corresponding problem can be solved graphically, as illustrated in chapter 14. That chapter illustrates several of the concepts used by the Simplex technique—the most general method of solving such problems. Chapter 15 concludes this part by describing both the Simplex and the Dual Simplex techniques and by summarizing the Duality theory and the branch-and-bound technique for solving these problems when some of the decision variables must have integer values.

10

Formulation of Linear Optimization Models

The primary concern of the models to be explored in this and the next few chapters might be summarized by the question: "How does one allocate the available resources and/or meet the requirements imposed by the decision maker's environment in the best possible, i.e., optimal, manner?" Computers have made it unnecessary to "solve" such questions by scratch-pad computation, usually an inefficient procedure in most real life situations. In fact, many software packages, i.e., fully developed and tested computer programs, are available for problem solving on today's high-speed computers.

However, to take full advantage of these packages, one must know *how to formulate* the above question in a variety of decision-making situations. This is an art as well as a science. It is somewhat like doing a jigsaw puzzle—you become better at it only through extensive practice. Therefore, this chapter explores seven such decision-making situations and how to formulate them in algebraic form.

Traditionally, these models go by the name of linear programming models—LP for short. However, the name linear optimization more closely identifies their principal reason for being. The short form, LP, will be used to save space.

Though the basic models assume that the decision maker has only one objective, three different ways to handle multiple objectives are examined at the end of the chapter.

EXAMINATION OF TERMS

Several terms used in formulating optimization problems should be examined before we go on. These terms include: resources, activities and action (decision) variables, the objective of the decision maker and the objective function of the model, the constraints that must be satisfied by any feasible solution of the model, and optimality.

To allocate means to apportion for specific purposes. This is one of the problems most frequently faced by a decision maker, who must decide how the available resources are to be apportioned among a variety of activities so as to achieve the organizational goal (objective). For example, qualified persons, including the decision maker, are a resource of an organization. Their time must be apportioned between production, marketing, and planning activities so as to maximize their effectiveness. Similarly, an investor, to maximize the return on an investment, might purchase common stocks or municipal bonds, buy real estate, or leave cash in a savings account. In each case, the decision problem is one of allocating the available resources.

The Resources

As the above examples suggest, a *resource* is that which one possesses or employs to achieve an objective. A resource is necessary to conduct an activity, i.e., to follow a course of action. Thus, qualified persons, free time, investment capital, and food products are examples of resources. Linear optimization (LP) models make the following assumptions:

1. Resources are limited.
2. A resource can be used in more than one way, i.e., in performing two or more activities.
3. Payoffs are comparable, i.e., there is a common unit of measurement.
4. Each resource is made up of interchangeable components.

For example, the secretaries employed by an organization constitute one of its resources, and it is obviously limited. A secretary can perform a number of activities, such as, taking dictation, filing reports, and typing memos. The extent to which this resource has been used can be measured by units, such as, the number of hours spent or dollars paid. Similarly, the payoff can be measured in such terms as the amount of work done or the benefits gained. Finally, an organization usually employs more than one secretary. LP models assume that any one of them can do the assigned tasks—though perhaps with differing efficiencies.

Activities and Action Variables

Optimization models assume that the activities have been defined to be mutually exclusive. The extent to which an activity is performed is measured by the value of a suitably chosen *action* or *decision* variable. Such variables can be denoted by the symbols $X_1, X_2, \ldots, X_n$, where the subscripts, 1 through n, are used to distinguish the variables.

A marketing manager, wishing to know what number of TV spots, radio spots, pages in a periodical, and columns in the local newspaper to buy for advertising a product, could *arbitrarily* define:

$X_1 =$ number of TV spots
$X_2 =$ number of radio spots
$X_3 =$ number of pages in a periodical
$X_4 =$ number of columns in the local newspaper

The allocation problem consists of deriving the values of such variables, i.e., the level of each activity.

A Solution

In the general optimization problem, one must determine the numerical values of n action variables: $X_1, X_2, \ldots, X_n$. A statement that specifies the *numerical values* of these variables constitutes a *solution* to the allocation problem. For example, a solution to the above marketing manager's problem might be $X_1 = 15$, $X_2 = 27$, $X_3 = 2$, and $X_4 = 5$ (i.e., buy 15 spots on TV, 27 spots on radio, 2 pages in the periodical, and 5 columns in the local newspaper.) Note that each solution describes a course of action. Symbolically, a solution of the optimization problem is represented by an ordered n-tuple, $(X_1, X_2, \ldots, X_n)$. The above marketing manager's solution can be shown by the 4-tuple: (15, 27, 2, 5). Note also that the level of each activity in that problem is either positive or zero. This can be expressed by the condition:

$$X_1 \geq 0, X_2 \geq 0, X_3 \geq 0, X_4 \geq 0$$

In most optimization problems, this continues to be the case. This requirement on the solution of an n-variable problem is expressed by the *nonnegativity* condition:

$$X_1 \geq 0, X_2 \geq 0, \ldots, X_n \geq 0$$

The Objective Function

It is usually possible to obtain numerous solutions to a linear optimization (LP) problem. For example, if $(X_1, X_2, \ldots, X_n)$ and $(Y_1, Y_2, \ldots, Y_n)$

are any two solutions, and if p is a fraction between 0 and 1, then we find $(W_1, W_2, \ldots, W_n)$ is also a solution, where:

$$W_1 = pX_1 + (1 - p)Y_1, \ldots, W_n = pX_n + (1 - p)Y_n$$

To determine whether a specific solution is the best, one must know the decision maker's objective. Usually, this objective is expressed in one of the following two forms: *maximize* some desirable output (such as, profit, happiness, quality of products, quantity of products, security, or health) or *minimize* some undesirable consequences (such as, cost, time, pollution, or shortages).

Also, a unit of measurement must be defined to determine the extent to which the objective has been fulfilled by a proposed solution. Given this unit, the effectiveness of a proposed solution can be measured. The corresponding value is denoted by Z, and it depends on $(X_1, X_2, \ldots, X_n)$. For this reason, Z is said to be a function of $(X_1, X_2, \ldots, X_n)$, and is commonly denoted by the name of the *objective function*. In this notation, the decision maker's objective can be expressed in one of two forms:

maximize Z or minimize Z

The choice depends on whether the effect is desirable, e.g., profit, or undesirable, e.g., loss. When Z has the best possible value, the corresponding solution is said to be an *optimal solution*.

Though a decision maker can have more than one objective (e.g., maximize profit and minimize pollution), we will concentrate on formulating LP models in which there is only one objective. (We will outline some multiobjective situations at the end of this chapter.)

Constraints

As we have already noted, the resources available to the decision maker are limited in some sense. Such limitations are explicitly noted in LP methodology by constructing the corresponding constraints. Constraints also arise for accommodating secondary objectives. In any case, only those n-tuples, $(X_1, X_2, \ldots, X_n)$, which satisfy *all* constraints are said to be the feasible *solutions*. The set of all feasible solutions to a decision problem constitutes its *feasible solution space*. An optimal solution is the best of all such feasible solutions.

TYPICAL LP SITUATIONS

Typical situations where LP models can be used include: product mix, blending, physical distribution, assignment, production scheduling, and purchasing. Each is examined next.

Product Mix

In these problems, one determines the kinds and quantities of products to be manufactured so as to maximize total profit or some other desirable attribute. In a sense, this is a marketing manager's view of the production function. The product's demand levels are assumed to be known, or else it is assumed that whatever is manufactured will be sold. Constraints usually arise due to a shortage of resources. The objective function is constructed by deriving contributions toward the goal due to the production of a unit of each product.

Blending

These formulations generally express a production manager's problem of how much of which raw material should be used in manufacturing a product. The objective is to minimize the total cost or some other undesirable payoff without sacrificing quality. The dietitian's problem of deciding on the least expensive menu without sacrificing the minimum daily requirements of vitamins and minerals is a classic example of blending. Each ingredient contributes toward the required quality and also adds to the cost. The optimal solution equals or exceeds all requirements in the least expensive manner.

Distribution (Transportation)

In classic formulation, one wishes to decide how much of a homogeneous product to ship from each of the M sources (e.g., plants or warehouses) to each of the n destinations (e.g., retail outlets). The requirements of each destination must be met without exceeding the supply at any of the sources. The optimal solution identifies the amounts to be shipped along each delivery route so as to minimize the total cost of shipping. The decision maker is, in a sense, wearing the retailer's hat.

Assignment

The resources are generally persons who can do any of the many similar jobs—though with differing efficiencies. In the classic formulation, one person is assigned one job only and a job is performed by one person only. The objective is to minimize the total cost or to maximize the total productivity.

Production Scheduling

The demands for many a product fluctuate over time rather than remain constant. But, production levels cannot fluctuate too much from one time period to the next without affecting employee morale and productivity. The problem is therefore to derive a relatively steady production schedule, i.e., determine the amount to be produced in each time period so as to meet the anticipated demands while maintaining reasonable inventory levels. The optimal schedule minimizes total costs.

Purchasing

A number of vendors can supply a variety of products which are similar in some sense. However, they might differ with respect to quality and/or costs and/or supply capabilities. The purchasing agent must establish the right "vendor mix" so as to maximize total profit.

SAMPLE FORMULATIONS

As the preceding section indicates, optimization problems occur in a variety of situations. Formulating an appropriate model, i.e., constructing the objective function and identifying the constraints algebraically, is an art as well as a science.

The Formulation Process

Begin by identifying the decision maker's objective in operational terms. Then ask yourself: what contributes to that objective? Each distinct answer isolates one action variable. Determine how much one additional unit of that variable increases the effectiveness. This amount is known as the *objective coefficient* of that variable. The total contribution of that activity to the objective is the product:

unit contribution × value of the decision variable

The objective function is the sum of these individual contributions.

To identify the constraints, ask yourself: what prevents the decision maker from achieving the objective? Each distinct answer isolates one constraint. If some resource is limited, determine the amount needed to increase the value of a decision variable by one unit. This is the corresponding *technological coefficient*. Multiply the technological coefficient by the value of that decision variable to obtain the total consumption of that resource due to that activity. The sum of all such consumptions must be less than or equal to the resource available. This defines a resource-related constraint. Similarly obtain all of the resource-related and requirements-related constraints.

Complete the formulation by documenting whether an action variable can assume fractional values or whether it must be integer-valued. Also, determine whether negative values of a decision variable are meaningful. If they are not, impose the corresponding nonnegativity requirement.

In short, the formulation process has these steps:

- Identify the objective and hence the decision variables.
- Determine objective coefficients and hence the objective function.
- Determine the resource limitations and requirements.
- Determine technological coefficients.
- State all conditions in algebraic terms.

The following examples illustrate this process by formulating a variety of decision situations. Problem set 10 and the next several chapters provide additional opportunities for formulation.

Example 1: Product Mix

A television manufacturer is considering how to utilize its production facilities to maximize total profit. The company produces four types of TV sets: Regular, Super, Deluxe, and Fantastic. The company believes that it is enjoying a seller's market, i.e., that it can sell all it can produce. Each set goes through subassembly, final assembly, and testing. The number of person-hours of labor needed to produce a set and the number available each day are summarized in table 10-1. The company must produce at least 15 Regular and 20 Deluxe sets daily. The profit contribution of the Regular, Deluxe, Super, and Fantastic sets is $30, $40, $60, and $75, respectively. What should the manufacturer do?

Table 10-1 *Labor Requirements and Availability*

DEPART-MENT	REGULAR	DELUXE	SUPER	FANTASTIC	PERSON-HOURS AVAILABLE EACH DAY
		TV MODEL			
Subassembly	14.0	18.0	18.0	25.0	3,000
Final Assembly	10.0	12.0	13.0	17.0	2,400
Testing	.5	.7	1.0	1.5	200

The Objective and the Decision Variables It is best to start the formulation by identifying the decision maker's objective in words. The TV manufacturer wants to maximize profits. He can do so by producing and selling TV sets. Since the company can sell all it can produce, the decision maker's *objective* is to maximize profit by producing the proper number of TV sets of each type each day. This statement also identifies the decision variables, viz., the number of TV sets of each type to be produced each day. Arbitrarily, let us define:

$$X_1 = \text{number of Regular sets}$$
$$X_2 = \text{number of Deluxe sets}$$
$$X_3 = \text{number of Super sets}$$
$$X_4 = \text{number of Fantastic sets}$$

The problem consists of finding the numerical values of X_1, X_2, X_3, and X_4.

The Objective Function Note that each Regular set yields a profit of $30. Hence, the profit obtained by producing X_1 regular sets is $30X_1$. Similarly, the profit obtained by producing X_2 Deluxe sets, X_3 Super sets, or X_4 Fantastic sets is $\$40X_2$, $\$60X_3$, or $\$75X_4$, respectively. Since the company produces X_1 Regular, X_2 Deluxe, X_3 Super, and X_4 Fantastic sets, their total profit would equal:

$$Z = \$30X_1 + 40X_2 + 60X_3 + 75X_4$$

The TV manufacturer's objective is to maximize this profit.

Constraints From table 10-1 it is clear that the person-hours are limited to 3,000 in subassembly, 2,400 in final assembly, and 200 in the testing departments. Let us consider each constraint in turn.

Each Regular set needs 14 hours of subassembly; hence X_1 of these sets would need $14X_1$ hours of subassembly. Similarly, X_2 Deluxe sets need $18X_2$ hours; X_3 Super sets need $18X_3$ hours; and X_4 Fantastic sets need $25X_4$ hours of subassembly. Thus, the company needs a total of $14X_1 + 18X_2 + 18X_3 + 25X_4$ subassembly hours. But, only 3,000 hours are in fact available. We can represent this constraint by the inequality:

$$14X_1 + 18X_2 + 18X_3 + 25X_4 \le 3,000 \text{ (subassembly)}$$

Note that we do not have to use *all* of the available assembly hours. The above equation only states that no more than 3,000 hours can be used for this purpose.

The constraints due to the limitation on the final assembly and testing hours can be constructed similarly:

$$10X_1 + 12X_2 + 13X_3 + 17X_4 \le 2,400 \text{ (final assembly)}$$

$$.5X_1 + .7X_2 + 1X_3 + 1.5X_4 \le 200 \text{ (testing)}$$

Policy Constraints According to company policy, at least 15 Regular sets must be produced each day. This can be represented by the inequality:

$$X_1 \ge 15 \text{ (policy)}$$

Similarly, the company must produce at least 20 Deluxe sets each day. This implies:

$$X_2 \ge 20 \text{ (policy)}$$

Obviously, the company must produce *some* sets of each type. Making a negative number of sets is meaningless. Hence, we must impose the nonnegativity condition:

$$X \ge 0, X_2 \ge 0, X_3 \ge 0, X_4 \ge 0$$

This completes the formulation of the TV manufacturer's problem. The resultant model is summarized as follows:

Maximize:
$$Z = 30X_1 + 40X_2 + 60X_3 + 75X_4 \text{ (profit)}$$

Subject to:

$$14X_1 + 18X_2 + 18X_3 + 25X_4 \leq 3{,}000 \quad \text{(subassembly)}$$
$$10X_1 + 12X_2 + 13X_3 + 17X_4 \leq 2{,}400 \quad \text{(final assembly)}$$
$$.5X_1 + .7X_2 + X_3 + 1.5X_4 \leq \phantom{2{,}}200 \quad \text{(testing)}$$
$$X_1 \geq \phantom{2{,}0}15 \quad \text{(policy)}$$
$$X_2 \geq \phantom{2{,}0}20 \quad \text{(policy)}$$

Nonnegativity:
$$X_j \geq 0, \text{ for } j = 1, 2, 3, 4$$

The Meaning of Linearity

Now that you have seen how to formulate a linear optimization (or LP) problem, let us pause to discuss the meaning of linearity. An LP problem has three properties: proportionality, additivity, and divisibility.

Proportionality This implies that the amount of resource used up in performing an activity is proportional to the value of the corresponding action variable. It also implies that the payoff associated with that activity is proportional to the level of that activity. For example, consider the production of Regular sets. According to the model of example 1, *each* such set needs 14 subassembly hours—no more, no less. The model does not allow for possible fatigue at the end of the day, nor does it consider the increase in workers' speed due to familiarity.

One obvious situation where proportionality may not apply is shown in figure 10-1. Suppose that because of high volume discounts, a Regular set brings in a profit of $30 per set up to a limit of 30 sets, and that each additional set brings a profit of only $25. Figure 10-1 shows the graph of total profit as a function of the number of Regular sets produced. Suppose that the manufacturer does not anticipate making over 50 sets a day. Then one solution is to replace the curve OAB by the straight line OB. This is equivalent to assuming an average profit of $1{,}400 \div 50 = \$28$ per Regular set. Alternatively, one may assume a per unit profit of $30, solve the model, and then accept the results if the optimal value of X_1 is in fact less

Figure 10-1. *Approximating a Nonconstant Rate of Return*

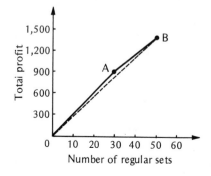

Number of regular sets

than 30. This is similar to the procedure used for obtaining EOQ in the presence of discounts. (See chapter 6 for additional details.)

The point is that proportionality is likely to be invalid in specific circumstances. The management scientist must examine each situation and provide suitable approximations to reality.

Additivity This means that the total profit (cost) can be obtained by adding the profit (cost) contribution of each activity. In example 1, for instance, we obtained the profit due to selling X_1 Regular sets and X_2 Deluxe sets as simply the total of the component profits, $30X_1$ and $40X_2$. This implies that the sales of Regular sets do not compete with those of Deluxe sets. If this is not true, then the assumption of additivity and hence that of linearity would be invalid.

Divisibility The implication is that the action variables are allowed to assume fractional values. When the action variables are naturally divisible (e.g., the number of tons of potato starch, number of gallons of paint, or the number of tank cars of corn oil), the divisibility requirement poses no problem. However, great care must be exercised when interpreting the fractional values of action variables, such as, the number of TV sets or the number of typists. Since the assembly continues day after day, the fractional number of TV sets might be interpreted to mean the average per day. Similarly, the fractional number of typists poses no problem if part-time help is available.

If the divisibility cannot be assured, the resultant model is said to be an *integer programming* model if every decision variable must be an integer, and *mixed integer programming* if some of these might assume fractional values. In any case, this requirement must be specified while formulating the decision problem.

We will now continue to explore additional situations that can be formulated by linear or integer linear optimization models.

Example 2: Personnel Allocation in a Community-Based Organization

A community-based, direct-service organization wishes to maximize its value to the community. The organization employs four types of professionals. Two professionals of Type 1 are as valuable as three of Type 2 or four of either Type 3 or Type 4. The salaries of the professionals are 20, 16, 10, and 8 thousand, respectively, and the organization's budget for professional salaries is 200 thousand. The organization must service at least 80 clients every day. A Type 1 professional can service ten clients each day; Type 2, eight; Type 3, six; and Type 4, five. In addition, the organization has a pool of five secretaries, each of whom works eight hours a day. Each professional needs two hours of a secretary's time every day. Assume that part-time professional help at each level of expertise can be obtained. How many professionals of each type must be employed by this organization?

The Objective and the Decision Variables To begin formulation process, note the objective of this organization: *to maximize its value to the community*. They plan to accomplish this by employing the necessary number of professionals of each type. Thus, the action variables are the number of professionals of each type. There are $n = 4$ worker types. Hence, for the sake of convenience, we can label the action variables to be:

$$X_j = \text{number of workers of Type } j, \text{ where } j = 1, 2, 3, \text{ or } 4$$

The Objective Function The corresponding objective coefficients are C_1, C_2, C_3, and C_4. The third sentence of the problem states the relative values of these coefficients:

$$2C_1 = 3C_2 = 4C_3 = 4C_4$$

Clearly, the values of C_1 through C_4 are measured on a relative scale only. Thus, by choosing a value for any one of these four coefficients, all others can be determined on that scale. Suppose that we choose C_1 to be 6. Then, using the above scale, you can verify that:

$$C_1 = 6, C_2 = 4, \text{ and } C_3 = C_4 = 3$$

The objective function is, therefore, given by the equation:

$$Z = 6X_1 + 4X_2 + 3X_3 + 3X_4$$

The organization wishes to maximize Z. Note that any solution which maximizes Z also maximizes $aZ + b$ for any arbitrary constants a and b. Thus, it is sufficient to define the objective coefficients on a relative scale as is done here.

Constraints You can check that there are three constraints.

1. The organization's budget for professional salaries is $200,000.
2. It must service 80 or more clients a day.
3. The secretarial help is limited to (5 secretaries) × (8 hours) = 40 typing hours a day.

Construct the inequalities as follows.

Each Type 1 professional is paid $20,000 per year so that X_1 of these will need $20,000$X_1$ each year. Similar arguments forecast the total salary cost to be: $20X_1 + 16X_2 + 10X_3 + 8X_4$ in *thousand dollar units,* and it cannot exceed 200 thousand dollars. Hence, the algebraic statement of the first constraint is:

$$20X_1 + 16X_2 + 10X_3 + 8X_4 \leq 200 \text{ thousand dollars}$$

or equivalently:

$$10X_1 + 8X_2 + 5X_3 + 4X_4 \leq 100 \text{ in units of 2000 dollars}$$

Since each Type 1 professional can service ten clients each day; Type 2, eight; Type 3, six; and Type 4, five; it follows that service constraint is:

$$10X_1 + 8X_2 + 6X_3 + 5X_4 \geq 80 \text{ clients each day}$$

Similarly, the typing constraint is expressed by:

$$X_1 + X_2 + X_3 + X_4 \leq 20 \text{ in units of two typing hours}$$

The community organization's optimization problem can be summarized as:

Maximize:

$$Z = 6X_1 + 4X_2 + 3X_3 + 3X_4$$

Subject to:

$$10X_1 + 8X_2 + 5X_3 + 4X_4 \leq 100$$
$$10X_1 + 8X_2 + 6X_3 + 5X_4 \geq 80$$
$$X_1 + X_2 + X_3 + X_4 \leq 20$$
$$X_1 \geq 0; X_2 \geq 0; X_3 \geq 0; X_4 \geq 0$$

Comments on Example 2 The problem statement specifies that part-time professional help at each level is available, e.g., the organization may be able to hire consultants. Because of this, it is meaningful to allow fractional values of X_1 through X_4. Otherwise, it would have been a problem in integer programming.

Note also that within each constraint, the unit can be chosen conveniently. For example, the first constraint measures salaries as well as budget in $2,000 units. The third constraint measures the typist availability in two-hour units. Though not a part of the formulation process per se, choosing the proper units becomes important since it could prevent or minimize rounding-off errors that often enter large-scale models. On the other hand, an analyst using "unnatural" units must be sure to document them so as to avoid misinterpreting the computer-generated results.

Example 3: The Cost-Effective Diet

The minimum daily requirements for a healthy adult are: 2,400 calories, 70 grams protein, 10 milligrams iron, 800 milligrams calcium, 5,000 international units of vitamin A, 1 milligram of vitamin B_1, 1.6 milligrams of vitamin B_2, and 70 milligrams of vitamin C. Furthermore, calorie intake should not exceed 2,800 and vitamin A intake should not exceed 40,000 international units. Note that these daily requirements are not universal. The requirements depend on the person's age, sex, state of health, height, weight, etc. Further information on this issue can be found in the texts on nutrition.

Susan, the dietitian, wants to determine the daily food program for a correctional facility. In the real situations, the food products come in a variety of forms. We have limited the discussion to only six of them. The nutritional content of these six foods is summarized in table 10-2. The per unit costs of foods 1 through 6 are $ .50, .13, .15, .30, .10, and .40, respectively. Even though food 5 is nutritionally almost worthless, Susan has found that at least one unit of it must be on the plate to help consume other foods. She wants to minimize her costs without sacrificing health of the inmates. What should be her menu?

Table 10-2 *Nutritional Content per Unit of Food*

FOOD	CALO-RIES	PRO-TEIN	FAT	IRON	CAL-CIUM	A	B_1	B_2	C
1	700	35	40	.5	1100	1500	.3	1.5	6
2	250	13	20	2.1	70	1200	0	.5	0
3	175	20	10	1.5	9	250	0	.1	0
4	200	30	7	1.5	20	0	0	0	0
5	150	1	8	.8	11	0	0	0	9
6	330	2	0	1.0	75	1500	.6	.2	350

Susan's Objective She wants to minimize the total cost per inmate per day. Six activities, viz., serving foods 1 through 6 contribute to this total cost. Hence the action variables are:

X_j = number of units of food j on an inmate's plate, where $j = 1, 2, \ldots, 6$

Before proceeding further, note that the actual unit used might vary from food to food. Thus, one might measure milk or orange juice consumption in quarts and chicken, fish, or beef in ounces. That this has been done is an implicit assumption in most of these types of models.

Using the unit costs described in the problem statement, you can check that Susan's objective is to minimize:

$$Z = .50X_1 + .13X_2 + .15X_3 + .30X_4 + .10X_5 + .40X_6 \text{ dollars}$$

The Constraints An adult must consume at least 2,400 but no more than 2,800 calories each day. The calories contained in a unit of each food are shown in the first column of table 10-2. Hence, the calorie constraints are:

$$700X_1 + 250X_2 + 175X_3 + 200X_4 + 150X_5 + 330X_6 \geq 2,400 \text{ calories}$$

and:

$$700X_1 + 250X_2 + 175X_3 + 200X_4 + 150X_5 + 330X_6 \leq 2,800 \text{ calories}$$

The constraint related to protein can be constructed similarly:

$$35X_1 + 13X_2 + 20X_3 + 30X_4 + X_5 + 2X_6 \geq 70 \text{ grams}$$

Other constraints are as follows:

Iron: $5X_1 + 21X_2 + 15X_3 + 15X_4 + 8X_5 + 10X_6 \geq 100$
Calcium: $1100X_1 + 70X_2 + 9X_3 + 20X_4 + 11X_5 + 75X_6 \geq 800$

Vitamin A requirements need two constraints:

Minimum: $30X_1 + 24X_2 + 5X_3 + 30X_6 \geq 100$
Maximum: $30X_1 + 24X_2 + 5X_3 + 30X_6 \leq 800$

Other vitamin requirements are:

B_1: $3X_1 + 6X_6 \geq 10$
B_2: $15X_1 + 5X_2 + X_3 + 2X_6 \geq 16$
C: $6X_1 + 9X_5 + 350X_6 \geq 70$

Furthermore, to help consume the nutritious diet, Susan must include at least 1 unit of food 5. In other words:

$$X_5 \geq 1$$

The formulation is complete when one adds the nonnegativity constraints:

$$X_j \geq 0 \text{ for } j = 1, 2, \ldots 6$$

Obviously, it is most efficient to solve such problems by computer, though "hand computations" are not impossible.

Example 4: Financing the Production

The Buildmore Company wants to expand its production of two very successful products over a given production period, say the next six months. The company is enjoying a seller's market, i.e., it can sell all that it can produce. The problem is that the company's cash on hand is only $50,000. However, because of the company's past record, a local bank is willing to lend it up to $100,000 for six months at 12 percent annual interest provided that the company's *acid test ratio* for this operation is at least 2.5. By this, the banker means that the following must be true:

$$\frac{\text{cash on hand} + \text{accounts receivable}}{\text{accounts payable}} > 2.5$$

Apart from banker-imposed conditions, the company must also meet various production restrictions which are summarized in table 10-3. How can it make the most of its seller's market?

Table 10-3 *Manufacturing Details*

PRODUCT	SELLING PRICE	PRODUCTION COST	PERSON-HOURS REQUIRED PER UNIT		
			ASSEMBLY	INSPECTION	PACKAGING
1	250	200	15	1/2	1
2	210	170	11	1/3	1
Person-Hour Limits			8,000	500	900

The Objective Obviously, the Buildmore Company wants to make the most of its seller's market. As in case of example 1, Buildmore can do this by controlling its production, i.e., by deciding on the amount of products 1 and 2 to be manufactured. It must also finance some of its operations. Hence, the decision variables are as follows:

X_1 = number of units of Product 1
X_2 = number of units of Product 2
X_3 = amount to be borrowed from the bank

Each unit of Product 1 contributes $250 - 200 = \$50$ toward profit; each unit of Product 2 contributes $210 - 170 = \$40$. The interest in six months will be, $\$12 \times 1/2 \div 100 = .06$ per dollar borrowed. Hence, total profit equals:

$$Z = 50X_1 + 40X_2 - .06X_3$$

Buildmore wants to maximize Z.

Production Constraints These are derived from the information in table 10-3. The company needs $15X_1 + 11X_2$ hours for assembly work and 8000 such hours are available. Hence:

$$15X_1 + 11X_2 \leq 8,000 \text{ (assembly hours)}$$

Similarly, the inspection and packaging constraints are:

$$3X_1 + 2X_2 \leq 3,000 \text{ (inspection)}$$
$$X_1 + X_2 \leq 900 \text{ (packaging)}$$

Capital If the company borrows X_3 dollars from the bank, its total operating capital will be $\$50,000 + X_3$. It can use this capital to support the production cost of $200X_1 + 170X_2$ dollars. Hence, the capital constraint is:

$$200X_1 + 170X_2 \leq 50,000 + X_3$$

or equivalently:

$$200X_1 + 170X_2 - X_3 \leq 50,000 \text{ (capital)}$$

The amount that the bank is willing to lend is limited:

$$X_3 \leq 100,000 \text{ (borrowing)}$$

The Acid Test Cash on hand after production is $50,000 + X_3 - 200X_1 - 170X_2$, whereas the accounts receivable (due to the sale of Products 1 and 2) would equal $250X_1 + 210X_2$. The accounts payable (to the bank) would equal $\$X_3$ borrowed from the bank $+ .06X_3$ interest on that loan (six months at 12 percent per year). Hence, the acid test ratio ≥ 2.5 is equivalent to:

$$\$50,000 + X_3 - 200X_1 - 170X_2 + 250X_1 + 200X_2 \geq 2.5(X_3 + .06X_3)$$

After some readjustment of terms, this is equivalent to:

$$-50X_1 - 40X_2 + 1.65X_3 \leq 50,000 \text{ (acid test)}$$

Finally, the nonnegativity constraints complete the formulation:

$$X_j \geq 0 \text{ for } j = 1, 2, \text{ and } 3$$

To recapitulate, the Buildmore Company's decision problem is as follows:

Maximize total profit:

$$Z = 50X_1 + 40X_2 - .06X_3 \text{ dollars}$$

Subject to:

$15X_1 +$	$11X_2$	$\leq$	8,000	assembly hours
$3X_1 +$	$2X_2$	$\leq$	3,000	inspection hours
$X_1 +$	X_2	$\leq$	900	packaging hours
$200X_1 + 170X_2$	$- X_3$	$\leq$	50,000	capital
	X_3	$\leq$	100,000	loan limit
$-50X_1 -$	$40X_2 +1.65X_3$	$\leq$	50,000	acid test

Nonnegativity:

$$X_j \geq 0, \quad j = 1, 2, 3.$$

Comments Notice that as the number of constraints increase, it becomes increasingly more important to label each one carefully. In the absence of such labeling, it is relatively easy to get lost. Labeling also helps the interpretation of computer outputs.

In real life situations, it cannot be assumed that the value of the dollar will remain unchanged over the entire planning period. In such formulations, the "present value" of the dollar must be used in constructing the objective function. If the interest rate is r per dollar per year, and if the planning period is t years long, then a return of A dollars at the end of that period is worth only $A \div (1 + r)t$ now. This is the present value of A dollars.

Example 5: Minimizing the Trim Loss

This classic problem occurs in a variety of situations. For example, the standard plywood sheets come 4 feet wide by 8 feet long. A furniture manufacturer might want to use plywood in 3-foot widths (to make dining tables or desks), in 16-inch widths (for sewing cabinets and typing tables), and in 10-inch widths (for making bookshelves). Naturally, there is some waste and a decision problem usually involves minimizing such wastage. Trimming masking tapes or adhesive tapes is another example—usually, there can be many trim patterns. Let's examine a simplified version.

The Problem A Paper Company buys 12-inch wide × 500-foot long rolls of paper and sells the more popular trimmed versions—rolls that are 1½, 2½, or 3½ inches wide. The company has orders for producing 700 rolls of 1½-inch wide paper, 1000 rolls of 2½-inch wide paper and 1200 rolls of 3½-inch wide paper. Excess rolls in any of these widths can be sold in the future, so producing extra rolls poses no problem (except that excessive overproduction in any one width might create an inventory problem). However, any roll narrower than 1½ inches has no market value and hence represents waste. How many rolls of which size should it produce to fulfill the order with minimum waste?

The Objective and the Decision Variables The company's objective is to minimize waste, i.e., the rolls that are narrower than 1½ inches. Identifying the action variables is more difficult. Given a 12-inch wide roll it could produce one 1½-inch, one 2½-inch, and two 3½-inch rolls. This is one alternative mode of trimming and the associated waste is an inch-wide roll. Similar considerations yield 13 possible alternative trim patterns as shown in table 10-4. That table is constructed as follows. Given

Table 10-4 *Paper Trimming Alternatives*

ALTERNATIVE	NUMBER OF ROLLS			WASTE
	1½	2½	3½	
1	1	0	3	0
2	0	2	2	0
3	1	1	2	1
4	3	0	2	½
5	0	3	1	1
6	2	2	1	½
7	4	1	1	0
8	5	0	1	1
9	1	4	0	½
10	3	3	0	0
11	4	2	0	1
12	6	1	0	½
13	8	0	0	0

a 12-inch roll, one can cut at most three 3½-inch rolls out of it; the leftover becomes one 1½-inch roll and there is no waste. This is the first alternative. The remaining alternatives are obtained by successively making fewer numbers of 3½-inch rolls. In each case, the leftover width is used to make the most rolls of 2½-inch width; the next lower level of 2½-inch rolls, etc. The remaining is to be used to make the 1½-inch rolls. This process ensures that all possible cutting alternatives with waste less than 1½ inches are listed. There are 13 possible patterns and the action variables are:

$$X_j = \text{number of 12-inch rolls cut as per alternative } j$$
$$\text{where } j = 1, 2, \ldots, 13$$

The objective is to minimize waste. From the last column of table 10-4, this is equivalent to minimizing:

$$Z = X_3 + .5X_4 + X_5 + .5X_6 + X_8 + .5X_9 + X_{11} + .5X_{12}$$

The alternatives 1, 2, 7, 10, and 13 produce no waste and hence are not shown in the objective function.

The Constraints These are obtained by translating the production requirements. Since the alternatives 1, 3, 4, and 6 through 13 result in 1½-inch rolls, and since 700 such rolls are required to fill the order, the following is true for 1½-inch rolls:

$$X_1 + X_3 + 3X_4 + 2X_6 + 4X_7 + 5X_8 + X_9 + 3X_{10} + 4X_{11} + 6X_{12} + 8X_{13} \geq 700$$

Similarly, the 2½-inch order can be filled if the following is true for 2½-inch rolls:

$$2X_2 + X_3 + 3X_5 + 2X_6 + X_7 + 4X_9 + 3X_{10} + 2X_{11} + X_{12} \geq 1000$$

Finally, of 3½-inch rolls, there must be:

$$3X_1 + 2X_2 + 2X_3 + 2X_4 + X_5 + X_6 + X_7 + X_8 \geq 1200$$

The formulation is complete with the specification of nonnegativity:

$$X_j \geq 0, \text{ for } j = 1, 2, \ldots, 13$$

Note, however, that fractional values of the action variables in this case are meaningful only if they can be interpreted as "average." Otherwise, it is an integer programming problem.

Example 6: Aggregate Planning

The ABC Corporation manufactures two kinds of stereo receivers: ABC-15 and ABC-18. Gordon Morebuck and Company has placed an order for 900 ABC-15 and 600 ABC-18 receivers for delivery on September 1. The work on this order can begin on July 1. In other words, ABC

Corporation has two months to assemble these receivers. Since the unit prices and quantities are fixed by contract, maximizing profit is equivalent to minimizing costs. The unit production costs (labor + material) and the availability of labor vary from month to month. The specific values are shown in table 10-5. The ABC employees need 12 hours to assemble an ABC-18. When storage space and interest on tied-up capital are taken into consideration, the monthly storage costs of ABC-15 and ABC-18 receivers are $8 and $10, respectively. Each of the two receivers is built using an identical FM tuner. And, 800 tuner units are received each month. An unused tuner costs $4 per month for storage and interest. How many receivers of each type should be produced each month?

Table 10-5 *Variable Supplies and Costs*

	JULY	AUGUST
Per Unit Cost ($)		
ABC-15	180	200
ABC-18	210	240
Labor Available (Person-Hours)	12,000	10,000

The Action Variables By now, you can spot that there are four action variables (two receiver types times two months). We will use the following notation:

X_j = number of ABC-15 receivers produced in month j

and:

Y_j = number of ABC-18 receivers produced in month j

where $j = 1$ for July and 2 for August

The Objective Function To determine Z we must identify and compute the three components of the total cost: production of receivers, storage of receivers, and storage of FM tuners.

Using the information in table 10-5, you can compute the *total production cost* to be:

$$\$180X_1 + 200X_2 + 210Y_1 + 240Y_2$$

Computing the receiver storage cost is somewhat more difficult. A receiver assembled on July 1 will have to be stored for two months (all of July and August), whereas the one assembled on July 31 must be stored for only one month. Assume the production rate to be constant throughout

July. Then, each receiver manufactured in July remains in storage for an average of 1.5 months, and the corresponding storage cost is:

$$\$1.5(8X_1 + 10Y_1) = \$12X_1 + 15Y_1 \text{ (July)}$$

With similar arguments, the storage cost of the units manufactured in August is:

$$\$.5(8X_2 + 10Y_2) = \$4X_2 + 5Y_2 \text{ (August)}$$

The *total receiver storage cost* for both months is the sum of these two amounts:

$$\$12X_1 + 4X_2 + 15Y_1 + 5Y_2$$

At the beginning of July, no tuners have been used. But, by the end of July, $X_1 + Y_1$ will have been used for an average usage level of $(X_1 + Y_1)/2$ in July. Consequently, $800 - (X_1 + Y_1)/2$ tuners remain unused in July. This translates into a July storage cost of:

$$\$4 \times [800 - (X_1 + Y_1)/2]$$

or, simplified:

$$\$3,200 - 2X_1 - 2Y_1$$

Similarly, the tuner usage level in August is $(X_2 + Y_2)/2$. In addition to the $800 - X_1 - Y_1$ tuners left over from July, 800 additional tuners arrive at ABC Corporation in August. Consequently, the tuner storage cost in August is:

$$\$4 \times \left[800 - X_1 - Y_1 + 800 - \frac{(X_2 + Y_2)}{2} \right]$$

or, simplified:

$$= \$6,400 - 4X_1 - 4Y_1 - 2X_2 - 2Y_2$$

Thus, the *total FM tuner storage cost* for both months is the sum of these two simplified amounts:

$$\$9,600 - 6X_1 - 2X_2 - 6Y_1 - 2Y_2$$

Adding the three components yields the total cost:

$$Z = \text{production cost} + \text{receiver storage cost} + \text{tuner storage cost}$$

or:

$$
\begin{aligned}
Z = \ \$180X_1 + \ & 200X_2 + 210Y_1 + 240Y_2 \ \text{(production)} \\
+ \ 12X_1 + \ & 4X_2 + \ 15Y_1 + \ \ 5Y_2 \ \text{(receiver storage)} \\
- \ 6X_1 - \ & 2X_2 - \ \ 6Y_1 - \ \ 2Y_2 + 9,600 \ \text{(tuner storage)}
\end{aligned}
$$

This simplifies to:

$$Z = 9,600 + 186X_1 + 202X_2 + 219Y_1 + 243Y_2$$

The constraints come in four groups.

The Labor Availability There are two constraints, one for each month. Each ABC-15 needs 12 hours and each ABC-18 needs 15 hours for assembly. Hence, the labor constraints are:

$$12X_1 + 15Y_1 \leq 12,000 \text{ (hours in July)}$$

and:

$$12X_2 + 15Y_2 \leq 10,000 \text{ (hours in August)}$$

FM Tuner Availability Since 800 tuners are received in both July and August, and since each receiver needs exactly one tuner, it follows that:

$$X_1 + Y_1 \leq 800 \text{ (tuners available in July)}$$

And, since the FM tuners not used in July can be used in August:

$$X_2 + Y_2 \leq 800 + (800 - X_1 - Y_1) = 1,600 - X_1 - Y_1$$

In other words:

$$-X_1 + X_2 - Y_1 + Y_2 \leq 1,600 \text{ (tuners in August)}$$

Supply Requirements As of September 1, ABC Corporation must deliver 900 ABC-15 and 600 ABC-18 receivers. Hence, by adding the corresponding production figures in each of the two months, one must have:

$$X_1 + X_2 \geq 900 \quad \text{ABC-15 receivers}$$
$$Y_1 + Y_2 \geq 600 \quad \text{ABC-18 receivers}$$

The Nonnegativity Requirements These complete this formulation:

$$X_j \geq 0 \text{ and } Y_j \geq 0, \text{ for } j = 1, 2$$

The entire problem can be summarized by:

Minimize:

$$Z = \$9,600 + 186X_1 + 202X_2 + 219Y_1 + 243Y_2$$

Subject to:

$$
\begin{array}{rrrrr}
12X_1 & & +\ 15Y_1 & & \leq 12,000 \\
& 12X_2 & & +\ 15Y_2 & \leq 10,000 \\
X_1 & & +\ Y_1 & & \leq\ \ \ 800 \\
-X_1 + & X_2 & -\ Y_1 + & Y_2 & \leq\ 1,600 \\
X_1 + & X_2 & & & \geq\ \ \ 900 \\
& & Y_1 + & Y_2 & \geq\ \ \ 600 \\
\end{array}
$$

Integer value:

$X_1, Y_1, X_2,$ and Y_2 must be integers.

Nonnegativity:

$$X_1, X_2, Y_1, Y_2 \geq 0$$

Comments on Aggregate Planning

The problem statement in example 6 does not clarify whether Gordon Morebuck and Company is the sole customer of the ABC corporation. However, if that were the case, the supply requirements would have to be fulfilled exactly (producing any extra units would be a waste). In that case, the supply constraints would be:

$$X_1 + X_2 = 900 \quad \text{(ABC-15 receivers)}$$

and:

$$X_1 + Y_2 = 600 \quad \text{(ABC-18 receivers)}$$

This implies, however, that in such a problem there would be only two decision variables, say X_1 and Y_1. Given these, the values of X_2 and Y_2 could be derived by solving:

$$X_2 = 900 - X_1 \text{ and } Y_2 = 600 - X_1$$

Though still somewhat complex, this problem can be solved graphically—without using a computer. (See chapter 14 for details of the graphical procedure.) The point is that careful scrutiny of data can occasionally simplify the problem.

The above problem represents a very much simplified version of the aggregate planning situation in general. The planning horizon is usually a year rather than two months. The demand for a product is likely to be seasonal. Rather than being known perfectly, it represents a forecast of the likely demand. Along with the cost of carrying an inventory, one must also consider the cost of increasing as well as decreasing production. This includes the cost of hiring, firing, overtime, and slacktime. For detailed discussion of the general problems in aggregate planning, the reader is encouraged to study some of the references cited at the end of this chapter.

Example 7: Assembly Line Balancing

The complete unit of a finished product is made up of four units of component A and three units of component B. Either component, A or B, can be produced in either of two production locations. Each component needs three raw materials, P, Q, and R. However, the amounts used depend on the location, since each location uses a different production technique. There are 400 units of P, 300 units of Q, and 500 units of R available now. The rest of the production data is shown in table 10-6. It is necessary to determine the number of production runs at each location that maximizes the production of complete units of the finished product.

Table 10-6 *Production Data*

Location	NUMBER OF UNITS NEEDED PER PRODUCTION RUN			NUMBER OF UNITS PRODUCED EACH RUN	
	P	Q	R	A	B
1	7	3	10	5	4
2	5	6	5	6	5

Since the objective is "to maximize the production of complete units," let us begin by identifying the action variables:

X_j = number of production runs at location j, where $j = 1, 2$

The Objective Function Each production run at location 1 produces 5 units of component A, the corresponding number at location 2 is 6. Hence, with X_1 and X_2 production runs at locations 1 and 2, respectively; there will be a total of $5X_1 + 6X_2$ units of component A. Similarly, there will be a total of $4X_1 + 5X_2$ units of components B.

The finished product needs 4 units of A *and* 3 units of B. Hence, the number of units of finished product would be the smaller of the two ratios:

$$\frac{(5X_1 + 6X_2)}{4} \text{ and } \frac{(4X_1 + 5X_2)}{3}$$

Consequently, the objective is to maximize:

$$Z = \min \left\{ \frac{5X_1 + 6X_2}{4}, \frac{4X_1 + 5X_2}{3} \right\}$$

Unfortunately, Z is not a linear function of X_1 and X_2. This difficulty is resolved by introducing a new variable, say X_3, which is the *smaller* of the two quantities on the right-hand side above. Specifically:

$$X_3 = \min \left\{ \frac{5X_1 + 6X_2}{4}, \frac{4X_1 + 5X_2}{3} \right\}$$

In this notation, the objective is to maximize:

$$Z = X_3$$

In order to use this objective function, however, one must impose two constraints on X_3. These are:

$$X_3 \leq \frac{5X_1 + 6X_2}{4}, \text{ i.e., } 5X_1 + 6X_2 - 4X_3 \geq 0$$

and

$$X_3 \le \frac{4X_1 + 5X_2}{3}, \text{i.e.,} \; 4X_1 + 5X_2 - 3X_3 \ge 0$$

Other Constraints There are three constraints due to resource limitations:

$$7X_1 + 5X_2 \le 400 \quad \text{(raw material P)}$$
$$3X_1 + 6X_2 \le 300 \quad \text{(raw material Q)}$$
$$10X_1 + 5X_2 \le 500 \quad \text{(raw material R)}$$

Also, the number of production runs at each location, X_1 and X_2, must be integers. Similarly, X_3 must be an integer.

Thus, the complete formulation is as follows:

Maximize:

$$Z = X_3$$

Subject to:

$$5X_1 + 6X_2 - 4X_3 \ge 0$$
$$4X_1 + 5X_2 - 3X_3 \ge 0$$
$$7X_1 + 5X_2 \le 400$$
$$3X_1 + 6X_2 \le 300$$
$$10X_1 + 5X_2 \le 500$$
$$X_1, X_2, X_3 \text{ integers}$$
$$X_1 \ge 0, X_2 \ge 0, X_3 \ge 0$$

THE GENERAL LINEAR MODEL

As the preceding examples illustrate, linear or integer linear optimization models can be constructed in a wide variety of situations. The preceding examples also illustrate that strict linearity is not always possible. Yet, linear approximations can often be used to represent the situation adequately. The approximation of a nonlinear function by a linear function is one of the necessary evils of using LP models. Why acquire linearity at the expense of accuracy? Because a model must be solved once it has been formulated. And at that stage, linearity is extremely useful. LP models are the simplest and most efficient from a computational standpoint. The point is that linearity should be assumed as long as the resultant model is not "too" inaccurate.

Mathematical Description

In general, an LP model has the following form. There are n decision variables, $X_1, X_2, \ldots, X_n$, and these contribute $C_1, C_2, \ldots, C_n$ per unit, respectively, towards the objective function. There are m constraints of the $\leq$, $=$, or $\geq$ type. Corresponding to the ith constraint ($i = 1, 2, .., m$) and jth variable ($j = 1, 2, .., n$), one can establish a technological coefficient, a_{ij}. Also, the ith constraint has a right-hand side constant, b_i, which represents either a resource limitation or a requirement. Given these constants, $\{c_j\}$, $\{a_{ij}\}$, and $\{b_i\}$, the following describes the *general LP model:*

Optimize (i.e., maximize or minimize):

$$Z = C_1 X_1 + C_2 X_2 + \ldots + C_n X_n$$

Subject to constraints:

$$a_{1,1} X_1 + a_{1,2} X_2 + \ldots + a_{1,n} X_n \leq (= \text{ or } \geq) b_1$$
$$a_{2,1} X_1 + a_{2,2} X_2 + \ldots + a_{2,n} X_n \leq (= \text{ or } \geq) b_2$$
$$a_{m,1} X_1 + a_{m,2} X_2 + \cdots + a_{m,n} X_n \leq (= \text{ or } \geq) b_m$$

Nonnegativity conditions:

$$X_1 \geq 0; X_2 \geq 0; \ldots X_n \geq 0$$

Using the Σ notation discussed in chapter 2, we can abbreviate this model to:

Optimize:

$$Z = \sum_{j=1}^{n} C_j X_j$$

Subject to:

$$\sum_{j=1}^{n} a_{ij} X_j \leq (= \text{ or } \geq) b_i, i = 1, 2, \ldots, m$$

$$X_j \geq 0, \; j = 1, 2, \ldots, n$$

Software Packages

When an LP model is expressed in this mathematical form, it can be solved by using a software package available on the user's computer. A large number of such packages are available on today's high-speed computers. A few are listed as examples.

The International Business Machines Corporation (IBM) has MPSX (mathematical programming system extended) for use on their System/360 and System/370 computers. Using this package, you can solve linear as well as integer linear optimization problems. Depending on the operating system, these problems can be solved in batch or interactive mode. IBM also has PL-Math, SL-Math, and APL "libraries" which can be used by PL/I, FORTRAN, or APL users so that they can develop their own software.

The Digital Equipment Corporation (DEC) has LINPRO on their PDP-1170 computers. LINPRO works under their RSTS-11 operating system in the time-sharing mode. LINPRO was developed by Project Delta working out of the University of Delaware. Written in Basic-Plus, LINPRO can be ordered through DECUS (Digital Equipment Corporation Users Society).

The Control Data Corporation (CDC) makes available APEX on their CYBER 170 series, 6000 series, 7600, CYBER 70 series, and CYBER 76 computers using NOS, NOS/BE, or SCOPE 2.1 operating systems. The APEX package can be used in batch mode (under SCOPE 2.1) or time-sharing mode.

Actually, all major computer companies (e.g., Honeywell, Univac, Burroughs) make linear programming software available to their users.

Dealing with Uncertainty

Note yet another feature of basic LP models. The implicit assumption is that the values of the necessary parameters, such as, the demand for a product, are known exactly. This is seldom the case in real life situations. Thus, having solved such problems using the best estimates, one must investigate the effects of variations from these presumed values. This study of ranges of parametric values over which an optimal solution remains optimal is called *sensitivity analysis*. The beauty of LP models is that when such models are applicable, performing sensitivity analysis is relatively straightforward. In fact, the Duality theory is a built-in part of the Simplex algorithm, and it answers a wide range of "sensitivity" questions. This is yet another reason why management scientists try to "linearize" a decision problem. We will return to discuss this issue in chapter 15.

In short, though precise knowledge of parametric values and exact linearity are seldom achieved, it is not necessary to despair. Empirical evidence (e.g., Turban's 1972 survey) shows that business leaders have been using it rather extensively. With further reductions in the cost of computer time and the increased acceptance of OR/MS in public sector organizations, the diversity and use of LP models is likely to increase even more. Some of this diversity is reflected in the references at the end of this chapter. The basic LP model can also be extended in a number of different ways, as we will see next.

MULTIPLE OBJECTIVES: AN EXTENSION OF LP

So far, we have tacitly assumed that a decision maker has only one objective (goal). In real life situations, this is not always the case. The decision maker often has multiple and conflicting goals. For example, a marketing manager may want to maximize profits *and* market share. A production planner may wish to minimize idle labor and overtime, as well as maximize profits. A school district supervisor may wish to provide equal educational opportunity, avoid underutilization of schools, achieve 70:30 racial balance, avoid overcrowding, minimize transportation costs, and limit busing time to 20 minutes or less—an actual case study prepared by Lee and Moore (1977).

In situations of this sort, it is not possible to optimize with respect to each objective. Instead, management science suggests three alternative techniques for "satisficing" the decision maker.

Dominant Objective

In the first alternative, one of the objectives (say maximize profit) is considered to be the only objective. The tolerable levels of other objectives are established by statements, such as, pollution shall not exceed 5 parts per million, or the market share must exceed 8 percent. In effect, each statement yields an additonal constraint. The corresponding situation can thus be formulated in the usual LP fashion.

Goal Programming

In this approach, the objectives are ranked with respect to their importance to the organization and the appropriate aspiration level is established with respect to each goal. Each such aspiration level yields one constraint. Then we find the set of solutions that minimizes the *relevant* deviation from the aspiration level of the highest ranked goal. Within this set, we find the solution that minimizes the *relevant* deviation from the *next* important goal and continue in this manner.

Formally, suppose that the decision maker has K goals, which have been arranged in order of their importance. Then the goal programming objective can be defined as:

$$\text{Minimize: } Z = \sum_{k=1}^{k} P_k(W_k^+ d_k^+ + W_k^- d_k^-)$$

Where P_k is the priority of the kth goal, d_k^+ and d_k^- are the deviations from the aspiration level of kth goal, and W_k^+ and W_k^- are the weight or importance of d_k^+ and d_k^-, respectively. The deviations d_k^+ and d_k^- are defined as follows:

$$d_k^+ = \text{amount of overachievement in goal } k$$

and:

$$d_k^- = \text{amount of underachievement in goal } k$$

The priorities P_k ($k = 1, 2, \ldots, K$) are such that:

$$P_k > m\, P_{k+1}$$

for *any* multiplier m, no matter how large m is.

For example, suppose that a manufacturer has three goals in manufacturing X_1 units of product 1 and X_2 units of product 2. In decreasing order of importance, the goals are:

1. Utilize all of the 3,000 hours of regular time labor.
2. Keep the necessary overtime hours below 400.
3. Exceed $50,000 in profit.

Then, you can verify that:

$$d_1^+ = \text{regular hours used} - 3,000$$
$$d_1^- = 3,000 - \text{regular hours used}$$

Note that only one of these two deviations, d_1^+ and d_1^-, will be positive; the other will be zero. You can also verify that:

$$d_2^+ = \text{overtime} - 400$$
$$d_2^- = 400 - \text{overtime}$$
$$d_3^+ = \text{profit} - 50,000$$
$$d_3^- = 50,000 - \text{profit}$$

Obviously, it does not matter if d_1^+, d_2^-, and d_3^+ are positive. Hence, we can set:

$$W_1^+ = W_2^- = W_3^+ = 0$$

Suppose that this manufacturer feels that the deviations d_1^-, d_2^+, and d_3^- are equally important. Then, we can set:

$$W_1^- = W_2^+ = W_3^- = 1$$

Thus, the goal programming objective for this manufacturer is:

Minimize: $Z = P_1 d_1^- + P_2 d_2^+ + P_3 d_3^-$

In general, suppose that the decision maker's aspiration levels are $G_1, G_2, \ldots, G_k$. (For example, to the above manufacturer, $G_1 = 3,000$, $G_2 = 400, G_3 = 50,000$.) Then the goal-related constraints are of the form:

$$\sum_{j=1}^{n} C_{kj} X_j + I_k^- d_k^- - I_k^+ d_k^+ = G_k$$

In the above equation, C_{kj} is the objective coefficient of X_j in the kth objective function, d_k^+ measures the amount of *overachievement* and d_k^- measures the amount of *underachievement* of goal k. If overachievement is permissible, the corresponding multiplier, I_k^+, is set to 0; otherwise, it is set to 1. Similarly, the underachievement multiplier, I_k^- is set to 0 or 1 as appropriate. In the manufacturer's case, suppose it takes 3 hours to make a unit of product 1, and 4 hours for product 2. The first goal-related constraint reads:

$$3X_1 + 4X_2 + d_1^- = 3,000$$

This follows because, to this manufacturer, positive values of d_1^+ are permissible so that $I_1^+ = 0$. On the other hand, positive values of d_1^- are not acceptable, hence I_1^- is set to 1. All other goal requirements can be defined similarly.

In short, given the priorities, the aspiration levels, and the deviation weights; it is fairly easy to formulate a goal program. The difficulty arises in establishing the aspiration levels and weights. Several of the references at the end of this chapter should be consulted for additional details on this technique.

Multiple Objective Linear Program

In this approach, each of the K objective functions is assigned a weight which depends on the importance of that objective. The aspiration level is not explicitly specified, thus avoiding one of the difficulties in the use of goal programming. Specific details are as follows. Suppose that the K objective functions are:

$$Z_k = \sum_{j=1}^{n} C_{kj} X_j \text{ for } k = 1, 2, \ldots, K$$

and that the decision maker wishes to maximize each one of these functions. The Multiple Objective Linear Program (MOLP) assigns nonnegative weights, $W_1, W_2, \ldots, W_k$, to each objective function, such that:

$$W_1 + W_2 + \ldots + W_k = 1$$

The MOLP can be summarized as follows:

Maximize:

$$Z = \sum_{k=1}^{K} W_k Z_k = \sum_{k=1}^{K} W_k \left(\sum_{j=1}^{n} C_{kj} X_j \right)$$

Subject to:

$$\sum_{j=1}^{n} a_{ij} X_j \leq (= \text{ or } \geq) b_i, i = 1, 2, \ldots, m$$

$$X_j \geq 0, j = 1, 2, \ldots, n$$
$$W_k \geq 0, k = 1, 2, \ldots, K$$

$$\sum_{k=1}^{K} W_k = 1$$

Note that, formally, it resembles the usual LP model. The user does not specify the objective weights—the computer finds these. The user may specify the lower and upper bounds on each weight, i.e., specify two numbers, L_k and U_k for each k, such that W_k must lie between these. Symbolically:

$$0 \leq L_k \leq W_k \leq U_k \leq 1, k = 1, 2, \ldots, K$$

See Steuer (1976) for further information on multiple objective linear programs.

SELECTED READINGS

BEALE, E. M. L. *Applications of Mathematical Programming Techniques*. New York: American Elsevier Publishing Co., Inc., 1970.

BUDNICK, F. S.; MOJENA, R.; and VOLLMAN, T. E. *Principles of Operations Research for Management*. Homewood, Ill.: Richard D. Irwin, Inc., 1977.

CARLTON, W. T.; KENDALL, G.; and TANDON, S. "Application of the Decomposition Principle to the Capital Budgeting Problem in a Decentralized Firm." *Journal of Finance* 29 (1974), pp. 815–827.

CARLTON, W. T.; DICK, C. L., JR.; and DOWNES, D. H. "Financial Policy Models: Theory and Practice." *Journal of Financial and Quantitative Analysis* 8 (1973), pp. 691–709.

COCHRANE, J. L. and ZELENY, M. eds. *Multiple Criteria Decision Making*. University of South Carolina Press, 1973.

COOPER, L. and STEINBERG, D. *Linear Programming*. Philadelphia: W. B. Saunders Company, 1974.

DAELLENBACH, H. G. and BELL, E. G. *User's Guide to Linear Programming*. Englewood Cliffs, N.J.: Prentice-Hall, Inc., 1970.

DANZIG, G. B. *Linear Programming and Extensions*. Princeton, N.J.: Princeton University Press, 1963.

DRIEBECK, N. J. *Applied Linear Programming*. Boston: Addison-Wesley Company, 1969.

GASS, S. I. *An Illustrated Guide to Linear Programming*. New York: McGraw-Hill Book Company, 1970.

GRAY, P. "The Shirt Allocation Problem." *Operations Research* 24 (1976), pp. 788–792.

KORNBLUTH, J. S. H. "Accounting in Multiple Objective Linear Programming." *Accounting Review* 49 (1974), pp. 284–295.

KORNBLUTH, J. S. H., "A Survey of Goal Programming." *Omega* (1973), pp. 193–206.

LEE, S. M., *Goal Programming For Decision Analysis*. (Philadelphia: Auerbach Publisher, Inc.), 1972.

LEE, S. M. and MOORE, L. J. "Multi-Criteria School Busing Models." *Management Science* 23 (1977), pp. 703–715.

LOOMBA, N. P. *Linear Programming: A Managerial Perspective*. (New York: Macmillan Publishing Co., Inc.), Second Edition, 1976.

MAIER, S. F. and VANDER WEIDE, J. H. "Capital Budgeting in the Decentralized Firm." *Management Science*, 23 (1976), pp. 433–443.

MARKOWITZ, H. *Portfolio Selection: Efficient Diversification of Investments*. New York: John Wiley & Sons, Inc., 1970.

PARASURAMAN, A. and DAY, R. L. "A Management-Oriented Model for Allocating Sales Effort." *Journal of Marketing Research* 14 (1977), pp. 22–33.

ROY, B. "Problems and Methods with Multiple Objective Functions." *Mathematical Programming* 1 (1971), pp. 239–266.

SALKIN, G. R. and KORNBLUTH, J. S. H. *Linear Programming in Financial Planning*. London: Haymarket Publishing Ltd., 1973.

SCHNEIDER, D. P. and KILPATRICK, K. E. "An Optimum Manpower Utilization Model for Health Maintenance Organizations." *Operations Research* 23 (1975), pp. 869–889.

STANCU-MINASIAN, I. M. and WETS, M. J. "A Research Bibliography in Stochastic Programming, 1955–1975." *Operations Research* 24 (1976), pp. 1078–1119.

STEUER, R. E. "Multiple Objective Linear Programming with Interval Criterion Weights." *Management Science* 23 (1976), pp. 305–316.

THOMAS, L. J. "Linear Programming Models for Production-Advertising Decisions." *Management Science* 17 (1971), pp. B474–B484.

TURBAN, E. "A Sample Survey of Operations-Research Activities at the Corporate Level." *Operations Research* 20 (1972), pp. 708–721.

WEINGARTNER, H. M. *Mathematical Programming and the Analysis of Capital Budgeting Problems*. Englewood Cliffs, NJ: Prentice-Hall Inc., 1963.

ZIONTS, S. and WALLENIUS, J. "An Interactive Programming Method for Solving the Multiple Criteria Problem." *Management Science* 22 (1976), pp. 654–663.

PROBLEM SET 10
FORMULATION EXERCISES

1. What are the basic assumptions of an LP model?

2. Illustrate, using some situation not discussed in the text, the following terms: action (decision) variables, objective coefficients, technological coefficients, and resource limitations.

3. An LP model assumes that the parametric values are known. How reasonable is this assumption? Discuss why LP models are useful even when the parametric values are only the best estimates.

4. If a linear optimization problem has two solutions, it has infinitely many solutions. Illustrate this by using the financial mix situation in example 4.

5. Basic LP models assume that the values of model's parameters are known exactly. In the terminology of chapter 3, there is only one state of nature. Could not such problems be solved through complete enumeration? Discuss using example 1: Product Mix.

6. Which of the following objective functions are linear?

   a. $Z = \max(X_1, X_2)$ b. $Z = 2X_1 - 3X_2 + X_3^2$

   c. $Z = 4X_1 X_2 + X_3 - 2X_4$ d. $Z = (3X_1 + X_2)/X_3$

   e. $Z = 5X_1 + \sqrt{X_2} + X_3$ f. $Z = 4X_1 - 3X_2 + X_5$

7. Express the following constraints in their standard form.

   a. $\dfrac{X_3 + X_4}{X_1 + 2X_2 + X_5} \le .7$

   b. $6X_1 + 10X_2 + 20X_3 \le 15 (X_1 + X_2 + X_3)$

In each of the following problems:

   a. Formulate the LP model.
   b. Solve it only if you have access to a computer with the appropriate software package. In that case, ignore the fact that some of the decision variables must be integer valued.

8. A poultry farmer can feed four types of grain to his birds. The nutritional content of grains, cost per unit of feed and the minimum daily requirements are summed up in the following table. (The daily requirements are for all the birds on his farm.) Find the least-cost grain mix.

	CONTENTS PER UNIT OF GRAIN				MINIMUM
NUTRIENT	1	2	3	4	REQUIREMENTS
A	4	3	8	—	1,600
B	1	1	—	2	300
C	6	4	—	3	900
D	1	.8	.3	—	100
Unit Cost (¢)	50	70	40	30	

9. The Supreme-Wheelers Company sells new cars in four sizes. The average characteristics of its cars can be summed up as follows.
   Sub-compact: Costs $4,000, sells for $4,250, and needs 110 square feet of space and 4 hours of a salesperson's time.
   Compact: Costs $4,800, sells for $5,100, and needs 150 square feet of space and 6 hours of a salesperson's time.
   Intermediate: Costs $5,500, sells for $6,000, and needs 170 square feet of space and 9 hours of a salesperson's time.
   Full-size: Costs $6,000, sells for $6,600, needs 190 square feet of space and 8 hours of a salesperson's time.
   The company has 24,000 square feet of display space exclusive of driveways and customer parking areas. At least 10 cars of each size must be on display to attract customers. The company has an operating capital of $700,000. The dealership is open 225 hours each month and 5 salespersons are on duty each working hour. How many cars of each size should be in the company's display area?

10. The coins used in India are: 1, 2, 3, 5, 10, 25, and 50 paise. (100 paise make 1 Rupee which is a note.) A cashier giving back change in these coins wishes to minimize the number of coins used. Formulate this as an LP problem.

11. Consider the following capital budgeting problem. A firm has $25 million to invest. Six projects are presently being considered. The adjoining table shows the investment details.

PROJECT	RATE OF RETURN (% per year)	BUDGET LIMITS (million $)
A	18	5
B	10	6
C	16	7
D	12	8
E	8	4
F	20	9

Projects A and F are speculative, (e.g., buying interest in an amusement park) projects B and E are financial (e.g., reducing the outstanding loan), whereas projects C and D are capital expenditure projects (e.g., buying new equipment or remodeling the plant). The management feels that the amount invested in financial projects should be no more than 50 percent of that invested in capital expenditure projects. Also, the speculative investments should be at least one-third of the sum of financial and capital expenditure investments. Formulate the LP model to derive the firm's optimal choices.

12. A newly established farming cooperative owns 20 acres of land. In the upcoming season, it intends to plant lettuce, tomatoes, corn, onions, watermelons, and potatoes on this land. The latest data regarding these crops are summarized in the accompanying table. (If the cost and person-hour values appear high, these include the allowance for soil preparation, fertilizers,

| | | PER-ACRE NEEDS | | | |
CROP	YIELD PER ACRE	WATER (GAL.)	COST ($)	PERSON-HOURS	SELLING PRICE PER UNIT
Lettuce	40,000 heads	1,100	16,000	4,000	49¢/head
Tomatoes	7,000 pounds	1,300	3,500	5,000	59¢/lb.
Corn	25,000 ears	1,500	2,000	5,000	10¢/ear
Onions	24,000 pounds	800	7,000	3,500	30¢/lb.
Watermelons	12,500 fruits	1,600	15,000	2,500	$1.25/fruit
Potatoes	20,000 pounds	1,200	1,300	3,000	8¢/lb.

insecticides, harvesting, as well as marketing expenses.) The cooperative cannot purchase more than 21,000 gallons of water. Its operating capital is limited to $120,000. The labor supply is limited to 50,000 person-hours, and no more than 30,000 watermelons can be sold this year. What is the optimal acreage for each crop?

13. The Twentieth-Century Kosmetics Company has manufactured a Revolutionary New Shampoo and would like the world to know about it. The management has allocated $160,000 to advertise this product. The possible choices and presumed consequences are summed up below.

Afternoon TV: A 30-second spot costs $6,000 and reaches 600,000 members of the target population; 1 percent will buy the shampoo.

The National Weekly: A full-page color advertisement costs $6,500 and reaches 400,000 members of the target population; 2 percent will buy the product.

Radio Spots: A one-minute spot at "drive time" costs $3,600 and reaches 200,000 members of the target population; 2.5 percent will buy the product.

The Fashion Leader (monthly): A full-page color advertisement costs $8,000 and reaches 400,000 members; 3 percent will buy the product.

Assume that each medium reaches a different segment of the population so that the total effect is cumulative. Management wishes to maximize the number of advertisement-induced buyers.

Management insists that the amount spent in buying the commercials in print should be at least 30 percent but not more than 70 percent of the expense of radio and TV commercials. No more than 20 TV spots or 30 radio spots can be purchased during this period. Also, there are only six Sundays (when the *National Weekly* reaches its readers) during this period. The *Fashion Leader* will be issued twice.

What is the most profitable mix of the media?

Note: The exercises in this problem set emphasize the problem formulations skills only. To solve these problems on a computer, you may use SIMPLEX, a fully interactive computer package available from the author.

14. A company makes three kinds of hats. Three hats of Type 1 bring as much profit as four of Type 2 or six of Type 3. A Type 1 hat needs 1 hour to make, 1 cubic foot of storage space, and $6 worth of material. For Type 2 hats, these figures are 3/4, 1, and 5, respectively. The corresponding figures for Type 3 hats are 2/3, 2/3, and 4, respectively. The company insists that at least 30 percent of all hats must be of Type 2. If they have 40 employees each of whom works 8 hours a day, if the storage space is limited to 1,600 cubic feet, and if the company can buy no more than $3,000 worth of material each day; what should their product mix be?

15. As you know, commercial wines are usually blended. John Runner manufactures and sells his wines under three labels: White Cow, Bullish, and Ladylove. Each is a blend of up to four components: A, B, C, and D. Currently 1,200 gallons of A, 1,600 gallons of B, 1,000 gallons of C, and 1,300 gallons of D are available for blending. John sells the resultant wines in quart bottles. There is a market for at least 6,000 bottles of White Cow, 7,000 bottles of Bullish, and 4,500 bottles of Ladylove. The alcohol contents of A, B, C, and D are 10, 12, 14, and 20 percent, respectively. White Cow contains at least 12 but no more than 16 percent alcohol. Bullish contains at least 16 percent alcohol. Ladylove contains no more than 14 percent alcohol. The accompanying profit table is to be interpreted as follows: the profit associated with using 1 quart of component A for producing White Cow is 50¢.

		WINE LABEL	
COMPONENT	WHITE COW	BULLISH	LADYLOVE
A	50¢	35¢	55¢
B	40¢	25¢	45¢
C	65¢	50¢	70¢
D	55¢	40¢	60¢

All other entries are to be interpreted similarly. How much of which component should be used in the blend of each wine? (Hint: Use double subscripts to define action variables. For example, let $X_{A,W}$ denote the number of quarts of component A allotted to produce White Cow.)

16. Elaine has $200,000 to invest. She is thinking of the following investment options:
Buy saving certificates. Return on investment (ROI) is 6 percent per year. This means that $100 invested now would become $106 next year. Being FDIC insured, there is no risk of losing money.
Buy municipal bonds. Income from such bonds is tax-sheltered. Her effective ROI would be 11 percent. However, there is a 4 percent risk.
Repay the home mortgage. She owes $25,000 to the bank and is paying 8

percent annual interest. She could pay some or all of that loan. There is a 2 percent risk of not being able to sell the house.

Buy real estate. ROI is 15 percent due to the likely increase in land prices. Risk of losing the capital is 7 percent.

Buy common shares. ROI, due to appreciation in the price, is 10 percent. Risk of losing capital is 6 percent.

Elaine wants to maximize the return on investment. If she invests $80,000 in real estate and $120,000 in common shares, her average risk would be:

$$\frac{\$80,000 \times 7 + 120,000 \times 6}{80,000 + 120,000} = 6.4 \text{ percent}$$

She does not like her average risk to exceed 5 percent. Derive her optimal investment plan.

17. A wholesaler buys 70-inch wide rolls of self-sticking paper and sells it to local retailers in the more popular 4-inch, 10-inch, 15-inch, and 36-inch widths used for the interior decorating purposes. One can, for example, use a 10-inch wide roll to cover pine shelves or a 36-inch wide roll to cover plywood table tops. Currently, the wholesaler has orders for producing 1,000 rolls, 4 inches wide; 1,500 rolls, 10 inches wide; 1,600 rolls, 15 inches wide; and 1,200 rolls, 36 inches wide. Any rolls narrower than 4 inches have no value. Though excess production in any usable size can be stored, the wholesaler's shelf space is limited to 1,500 linear feet. How many rolls of which size should be produced?

18. The Gordon Morebuck and Company has placed an order for 20,000 units of 13-channel citizen band (CB) radios and 12,000 units of 20-channel CB radios. The contractor, World-Wide-Voice-Senders Inc., is not prepared to fulfill the total order on its own. However, CB-Helpers Inc. is willing to supply World-Wide with enough radios of each kind at $85 per 13-channel unit and $109 per 20-channel unit. The management of World-Wide must determine the number of units of each kind to produce in its shop and those to be bought from CB-Helpers Inc. The manufacturing details are summarized in the accompanying table. World-Wide will receive $95 from Gordon Morebuck for each 13-channel unit and $120 for each 20-channel unit.

	PERSON-HOURS NEEDED PER UNIT		PERSON-HOURS AVAILABLE
DEPARTMENT	13-CHANNEL	20-CHANNEL	IN-HOUSE
Production	3	4	90,000
Inspection	1/2	3/4	17,000
Packaging	1/4	1/4	7,500
Unit Cost	$80	$100	

Obviously, World-Wide wants to fulfill its contract in the most profitable manner. What would you recommend?

19. The nurses in a hospital normally work in six-hour shifts. For example, a nurse who begins work at 4 PM will be on duty till 10 PM. A nurse is paid $10

per hour. the hospital administration has divided each day into eight periods of three hours each. The minimum necessary number of nurses required to be on duty during each period is shown in the accompanying table. (Note that Period 1 follows Period 8.)

PERIOD	FROM	TO	NUMBER REQUIRED	PERIOD	FROM	TO	NUMBER REQUIRED
1	7 AM	10 AM	30	5	7 PM	10 PM	35
2	10 AM	1 PM	50	6	10 PM	1 AM	35
3	1 PM	4 PM	60	7	1 AM	4 AM	30
4	4 PM	7 PM	50	8	4 AM	7 AM	25

The nurses may also work overtime for an additional three hours at $15 per hour. But, in that case, such nurses must work three full hours. How many nurses should begin working at 7 AM, 10 AM, etc.? How many should be assigned to overtime duty so as to minimize the total cost provided all the minimum requirements are met? (Hint: Let X_j equal the number who begin work at the start of period j for normal duty; and let Y_j equal the corresponding number who will work overtime.)

*20. The governing board of a Multi-Service Center wishes to judge the impact of its services on the surrounding community. It wants to gather this information by conducting a household survey.

The surveys are to be conducted in the afternoons, evenings as well as weekends. Not everyone is willing to be interviewed. The accompanying table shows the probabilities of successfully completing an interview. It also shows the minimum quota of completed interviews by respondent type.

RESPONDENT TYPE	PROBABILITY OF SUCCESS			MINIMUM INTERVIEWS
	AFTERNOON	EVENINGS	WEEKENDS	
Singles	.1	.5	.3	75
Families in				
Apartments	.3	.7	.4	125
Homes	.4	.7	.8	200
Elderly	.8	.8	.9	50

A call is an attempt to interview the designated respondent; if successful, it results in a completed interview. A weekend call costs twice as much as either an afternoon or evening call. However, to ensure representativeness of the sample, the governing board wants at least 20 percent of all the calls to be made on the weekend. Similarly, the ratio of afternoon to evening calls must exceed 30 percent.

Determine the number of calls by respondent type and time of the day so as to fulfill the expected quotas at a minimal cost.

*21. John Small is considering a 3-year investment program. The investments are to be made once every six months. He has $100,000 with him now (Jan. 1). His investment options are as follows.

Investment 1. Available on Jan. 1 and July 1 each year. Yields 18 percent every 18 months.

Investment 2. Available on July 1 each year. Yields 15 percent every year. John does not wish to invest more than $50,000 in this investment.

Investment 3. Available Jan. 1 beginning next year. Yields 28 percent in 2 years.

Investment 4. Six-month certificates. Available Jan. 1 and July 1 each year. Yields 6 percent in six months.

    Describe the investment program which will maximize his financial worth at the beginning of the fourth year. (Hint: Divide the planning horizon into six-month periods. For $i= 1, 2, 3, 4$, and $j= 1, 2, \ldots, 6$, define $X_{ij} =$ dollars invested in option i at the beginning of period j.)

*22. An electronics firm manufactures three types of television sets. For the next three months, its sales forecasts are as shown in the accompanying table.

TELEVISION TYPE	MONTH		
	1	2	3
1	2,000	1,500	1,500
2	1,200	1,500	1,000
3	900	800	500

(Assume the forecasts to be perfect.) Presently, there are 100 sets of each type on hand, i.e., the current inventory level is 100 sets of each type. The management wants to maintain or exceed this level at the end of each month. In each month there are 11,000 normal production days; each normal day costs $60. Also, the management can use up to 2,000 overtime production days each month at the rate of $100 per day. A Type 1 set requires 2.5 production days to assemble, a Type 2 needs 3 days, and a Type 3 needs 4 days. Because of the sagging demand, the company does not want to produce any Type 3 sets in the third month (so that it can dismantle the Type 3 machinery). Additionally, there is a storage cost: any set left in the storage at the end of a month costs $5.

    How many sets of each type should it produce each month so as to meet all these requirements at minimal cost?

*23. Three factories located on the same river discharge their industrial waste into their own treatment plants. From there, the treated waste flows into the river. For technological reasons, a treatment plant cannot remove more than 95 percent of the waste. The treatment cost is proportional to the plant's operating efficiency, i.e., the percent of waste it can remove from the factory discharge. Law requires that the quality of the river water must exceed a specified standard as measured by the biological oxygen demand (BOD), i.e., pounds of oxygen per gallon of water needed to neutralize the pollutants through natural biochemical activity. Obviously, a higher BOD implies poorer quality of water. Thus, the water quality requirement may be specified as BOD $\leq b$ pounds per gallon. If factory j discharges a_j pounds of BOD every day and if the efficiency of treatment plant j is X_j, then for $j = 1,$

2, 3, the total BOD discharge from plant j would be $a_j(1 - X_j)$ pounds each day. Assume that the river flow is Q gallons per day of pure water just before it reaches treatment plant 1, and that Q_j gallons flow out of plant j every day. Assume also that for $j = 1$ and 2, plant $j + 1$ is l_j miles downstream from plant j; that there are no other polluters along the way; and that the fraction of BOD removed by natural biochemical action between plant j and $j + 1$ equals $p \times l_j$. Formulate the LP model to determine the optimal values of X_j if the cost of removing one pound of BOD at plant j is $C_j, j = 1, 2, 3$.

*24. A small auditing firm is made up of three auditors. In this planning period, they need to determine X_{ij}, the number of hours ith auditor should spend on jth accounting project. If auditor i spends an hour on project j, the firm can collect d_{ij} dollars from the corresponding customer. Being a progressive firm, however, they have devised three other measures of hourly benefits to the firm. These are:

r_{ij} = value of past experience of working on a similar project
t_{ij} = value of training ith auditor on project j
U_{ij} = utility of assigning ith auditor to jth project

For example, if the customer prefers auditor i to work on project j, then U_{ij} is positive. If he/she cannot get along with auditor i, then U_{ij} is negative. Each of these measures is expressed in monetary equivalent terms, and the benefit to the firm is the sum of these individual components.

Accountants 1 and 2 are available for 160 hours each during this planning period, whereas accountant 3 is due a small vacation. He is available 120 hours only. The firm knows the efficiency with which auditor i can do project j. It equals a_{ij} which is to be interpreted as follows. If a "standard" auditor were to do project j, he would need a_{ij} hours to do what auditor i does in one hour. No less than 40 but no more than 70 standard hours are available to do project 1. Exactly 160 standard hours are to be devoted to project 2. At least 160 hours must be spent on project 3. At most 50 hours can be spent on project 4. Formulate an LP model to determine the optimal values of X_{ij}.

11

Assignment and Traveling Salesman Models

This chapter examines some techniques for solving special purpose linear optimization models. One of the specific problems involves assigning indivisible resources (such as qualified personnel) for performing indivisible jobs (such as typing a book containing several chapters) in the most productive manner.

The associated technique will then be used to solve another classic optimization problem—that of finding the least cost tour for a salesman who must visit a number of cities just once as a part of his job. Solving that problem will illustrate a general problem solving approach known as the branch-and-bound approach. Another topic to be studied in this chapter is the cost-effective methods of scheduling a variety of jobs on a single machine. And, the chapter ends with a brief discussion of assignment situations with nonmonetary payoffs as well as the formulation of generalization assignment programs (GAP).

ASSIGNMENT PROBLEMS

The prototype assignment problem can be stated as follows. There are m workers, each of whom can do any of m jobs at varying costs. A worker must be assigned only one job, and conversely a job must be performed by only one worker. An assignment problem of this type is said to be *balanced*. The technical discussion begins by presenting the balanced assignment problem of assigning four typing jobs to four secretaries.

Not all the assignment situations are necessarily balanced. At times there can be more workers than jobs as well as more jobs than workers, so we will examine how to restore balance without changing the decision problem. The prototype problem also assumes that any job can be assigned to any worker, but we will examine how to formulate the assignment problem when some workers cannot or will not do some jobs.

The decision maker of the prototype problem wishes to assign workers to jobs in the *least costly manner*. This cost might of course be expressed using a variety of measures, such as, dollars spent or lost, person-hours needed to do a job, number of complaints received due to assignment of workers to jobs, and the probability of failure associated with specific worker-job pairs. In fact, any interval-scale measure of undesirable payoffs can be used in place of cost. Opportunity loss is one such measure which is used while solving assignment problems. This last point is important to remember, for it means that a problem with a maximization objective can be formulated as a problem with the objective of minimizing opportunity loss.

We have talked of assigning workers to jobs. The crucial property is that each worker, as well as each job, is an *indivisible object* and that these belong to *two distinct groups*. The assignment problem consists of finding the one-to-one correspondence of the objects in one group with those in the other group in an optimal fashion. For example, an employment agency matches employees with employers; many computer-supported agencies match single men with single women; and a garage sale is designed to match buyers with sellers.

In short, assignment problems arise in a variety of situations. In the remainder of this section, a few of these situations will be illustrated.

Professor Jones's Book

Professor Jones has at last completed the remaining four chapters of his book and is now looking for typing help. Ordinarily, the professor would have asked his favorite typist, but the publisher's deadline approaches and, since time is of the essence, the work must be done simultaneously. To shorten the story, assume that he has determined that four typists: Jyoti, Mary, Jackie, and Tammy should each type one of the four chapters. To avoid confusion, he wants a typist who begins working on a chapter to stay with it until it is finished. Each typist can type any chapter. Even though the typists' hourly rates are about equal, the cost per finished page varies due to the difference in speed and accuracy. The cost also varies because the chapters are of different lengths and complexities. The historical data indicate that the final costs are likely to be those shown in table 11-1. For example, if Jyoti types chapter 13, the cost will be $96. Similarly, if Jackie types chapter 15, the cost will be $113. Since Jones's salary is not designed to make him excessively wealthy, he would like to minimize the typing costs. What should he do?

Table 11-1 *Typing Costs ($) of Various Assignments*

	CHAPTERS			
TYPIST	13	14	15	16
Jyoti	96	99	105	108
Mary	116	109	107	96
Jackie	120	102	113	111
Tammy	114	105	118	115

Professor Jones's problem is already in the standard form of assignment problems. This follows because the number of objects in one group (in this case, the typists) equals that in the matching group (the chapters), and his objective is to minimize the undesirable payoff (costs, in this case). An assignment problem is always converted into the corresponding standard form prior to initiating the search for optimality.

Table 11-1 shows one possible presentation of the assignment problem. It can also be presented as a linear optimization problem. To see this, define the action variables as follows:

$$X_{ij} = \begin{cases} 1, \text{ if the } ith \text{ row is matched with } jth \text{ column} \\ 0, \text{ otherwise} \end{cases}$$

For example, if Jyoti ($i = 1$) is assigned chapter 13 ($j = 1$), then $X_{1,1} = 1$; otherwise $X_{1,1}$ would be 0. Obviously, each $X_{i,j}$ can assume one of only two values: 1 and 0. It follows that if Jyoti is assigned chapter 13 ($X_{1,1} = 1$), she cannot be also assigned chapter 14, 15, or 16. Thus, in that case: $X_{1,2} = X_{1,3} = X_{1,4} = 0$. In other words, you can check that:

$$X_{1,1} + X_{1,2} + X_{1,3} + X_{1,4} = 1$$

This equation will be true regardless of whether Jyoti is assigned chapter 13, 14, 15, or 16; as long as she is assigned only one chapter—a requirement on any assignment problem.

You can similarly check that since chapter 13 is assigned to only one typist, we must also have:

$$X_{1,1} + X_{2,1} + X_{3,1} + X_{4,1} = 1$$

All of the row and column requirements can be represented by similar equations.

Since the assignment matrix of table 11-1 shows the per unit costs, it follows that Professor Jones's objective function is:

$$Z = \$96X_{1,1} + 99X_{1,2} + \ldots + 115X_{4,4}$$

The general formulation of any *standard assignment problem* follows.

Let n denote the number of objects in any one of the two matching groups. Define $X_{ij} = 1$, if the *ith* object in the first group is matched with the *jth* object in the second group; otherwise, define $X_{ij} = 0$. Let C_{ij} denote the cost (or some other undesirable payoff) associated with matching the *ith* object in the first group with the *jth* object in the second group. The assignment problem can be described by the following statements:

Minimize:

$$Z = \sum_{i=1}^{n} \sum_{j=1}^{n} C_{ij} X_{ij}$$

Subject to the constraints:

$$\sum_{j=1}^{n} X_{ij} = 1, \text{ for } i = 1, 2, \ldots, n$$

$$\sum_{i=1}^{n} X_{ij} = 1, \text{ for } j = 1, 2, \ldots, n$$

In the rest of this section, we shall illustrate how to convert *any* assignment problem into its standard form.

Unacceptable Assignments

A community organization has divided that community into five target areas. The organization has employed five social workers to service each area exclusively. For personal reasons, social worker A would rather not service any client from Area 3, and the clients from Area 4 would rather not choose social worker C for resolving their difficulties. Apart from this, any social worker can be assigned any one (and only one) area of the community. The director of the organization has kept a record of the number of complaints lodged against each worker by the clients in each area. The resultant "complaint matrix" is shown in table 11-2. An entry in that table represents the number of complaints per 100 clients served. The director is aware that not all of these complaints are legitimate. However,

Table 11-2 *Complaints Against Social Workers*

SOCIAL WORKER	TARGET AREA 1	2	3	4	5
A	8	5	X	3	4
B	11	4	3	7	5
C	6	8	2	X	3
D	10	3	5	4	6
E	5	3	4	3	7

for public relations purposes, she would like to find the least troublesome assignment of workers to target areas. In the table, X denotes the assignments which should not be attempted. What should she do?

This assignment problem is obviously a balanced one, but it violates one of the other assumptions: not all the assignments are feasible. You and I can live with this restriction, but a computer, the most common tool for solving such problems, cannot. It needs specific "cost" values. The difficulty is resolved by attaching exorbitantly high cost to each infeasible assignment, say 100,000 in this case. Since what is exorbitant depends on the values of the other cost figures in the corresponding assignment matrix, mathematicians use the symbol M to denote these exorbitant costs. A decision maker who is willing to pay this high price can make the corresponding assignment despite someone's protest. Since the computer is instructed to find the least costly solution, the high priced assignment will not be included in the optimal solution.

Rule 1. Formally attach cost M to each unacceptable assignment. Then proceed as usual.

Unbalanced Matrix

A company has orders to make deliveries at each of four locations before the end of the day. Due to some misunderstanding, only three trucks (and drivers) have arrived at the dispatch area this morning. Each delivery location is at least 300 miles away from the dispatch area as well as from each other. Thus, no truck can be assigned to more than one location. Table 11-3 shows the costs of deliveries. Which location will not be supplied today? Which truck and driver should be assigned to which location?

When the problem is this small, you can find the optimal assignments by "scratch-pad" computations. For much larger problems, how-

Table 11-3 *Costs ($) of Delivering Goods*

	LOCATIONS			
TRUCKS	1	2	3	4
A	110	140	150	130
B	120	130	150	120
C	130	160	180	160

ever, systematic solution techniques must be used. And, this implies that the truck problem must be stated in balanced form.

Add a "pretend" truck, known as the *dummy truck*, to those actually on hand. This dummy truck makes a "pretend" delivery at one of the four locations—whichever location is assigned to the dummy truck will not be served today.

We must also state the cost of sending the dummy truck to each possible location. Again, this is easy. Since the dummy truck will not in fact make deliveries, the cost of so doing (i.e., of transporting nothing nowhere) is zero. Note that the cost of any lost goodwill or of any penalties due to not making the fourth delivery are not considered in structuring an assignment matrix.

The balanced version of the truck problem is presented in table 11-4. Note that despite appearances, the managerial problem has not changed. Since the cost of using truck D is zero, it will be assigned to some location and that location will be unhappy. All we did was standardize the format.

The assignment problem will also be unbalanced if the number of rows, i.e., the associated number of objects, exceeds the number of columns. The imbalance is resolved by adding enough dummy columns at cost zero. We can therefore state the following rule.

Rule 2. Given an assignment matrix, check to see if the number of rows, m, equals the number of columns, n. If $m > n$, add $m - n$ columns to the assignment matrix. In each row, set the corresponding costs to zero. Symbolically:

$$C_{ij} = 0, \text{ for all } i \text{ whenever } j = n + 1 \text{ through } m$$

If $m < n$, add $n - m$ rows to the assignment matrix. In each column, set the associated costs to zero. Symbolically:

$$C_{ij} = 0, \text{ for all } j \text{ whenever } i = m + 1 \text{ through } n$$

If $m = n$, the assignment matrix is already balanced.

Table 11-4 *Truck Problem*

	LOCATIONS			
TRUCKS	1	2	3	4
A	110	140	150	130
B	120	130	150	120
C	130	160	180	160
D (dummy)	0	0	0	0

Maximization Objective

The marketing manager of a company has divided that company's sales territory into four regions. Each region will be managed by one of the four salespersons: A, B, C, or D. The associated profit potentials (in 1,000 dollar units) are shown in table 11-5. The marketing manager wants to make the most profitable assignments of salespersons to sales regions.

Table 11-5 *Profit Potentials of Salespersons*

	SALES REGION			
SALESPERSON	1	2	3	4
A	7	11	9	14
B	5	8	10	17
C	5	9	8	9
D	8	7	6	10

This problem can be transformed into the corresponding standard form by using the following rule.

Rule 3. Locate the most profitable entry in the current assignment matrix. Then subtract from it, every entry in the original assignment matrix. Use the resultant opportunity loss matrix to find the optimal assignments.

For example, the largest entry in this case is $C_{2,4} = 17$. The corresponding opportunity loss matrix is obtained as follows:

$$C_{1,1} = 7 \text{ is replaced by } 17 - 7 = 10$$
$$C_{2,1} = 5 \text{ is replaced by } 17 - 5 = 12$$
... ...
$$C_{4,4} = 10 \text{ is replaced by } 17 - 10 = 7$$

The resultant matrix is shown in table 11-6. That the two problems are managerially equivalent can be seen as follows. When salesperson B is assigned to region 4, the manager realizes the maximum potential, and the opportunity loss is zero. All other entries represent the corresponding opportunity losses. When the profit is maximized, by definition, the opportunity loss has been minimized. Thus, the two problems are equivalent and the latter one is in standard form.

Table 11-6 *Marketing Manager's Opportunity Losses*

	SALES REGION			
SALESPERSON	1	2	3	4
A	10	6	8	3
B	12	9	7	0
C	12	8	9	8
D	9	10	11	7

SOLVING A STANDARD ASSIGNMENT PROBLEM

From now on, we will assume that the assignment problem has been stated in standard form as we examine the methods of deriving optimal assignments. To illustrate the solution methods, we will completely solve Professor Jones's typist assignment problem. Table 11-1 is reproduced here as table 11-7 for reference purposes.

Table 11-7 *Typing Costs ($) of Various Assignments*

	CHAPTERS			
TYPIST	13	14	15	16
Jyoti	96	99	105	108
Mary	116	109	107	96
Jackie	120	102	113	111
Tammy	114	105	118	115

A Review of Solution Techniques
A variety of solution techniques and their merits for solving an assignment problem are summarized below.

Complete Enumeration Note that a solution to the assignment problem is described by a complete set of assignments, i.e., by identifying those X_{ij} that equal 1. One such solution is:

(Jyoti, 13), (Mary, 14), (Jackie, 15) and (Tammy, 16)

Symbolically:

$$X_{1,1} = X_{2,2} = X_{3,3} = X_{4,4} = 1$$

Conceivably, one could identify all such solutions and then choose that which has the lowest cost. However, there is a practical difficulty, e.g., if the assignment matrix has n rows and n columns, there will be $n! = n \times (n-1) \times \cdots \times 1$ possible solutions. For example, when $n = 8$, there will be 40,320 solutions, and evaluating each one of these is a rather formidable task.

The Simplex Technique Every assignment problem is a problem in (integer) linear programming and hence can be solved using the Simplex technique (which will be discussed in chapter 15). However, this technique in its general form does not make use of the special structure of the assignment problem. As such, it is rather inefficient.

The Transportation Technique The arguments against using this technique (to be illustrated in the following chapter) are similar to those against using the Simplex technique, though not that forceful.

The Hungarian Method This is the most efficient technique for finding the optimal assignment set since it takes full advantage of the structure of the assignment matrix. In what follows, we shall examine this method in detail.

The Hungarian (Konig) Method
Refer to table 11-7 and note that the best assignment for Jyoti is to type chapter 13. This statement remains true even if the cost values in the first row were reduced by an arbitrary constant, say $50, i.e., even if the first row were to read:

$$\$46 \quad \$49 \quad \$55 \quad \$58$$

This follows because the best assignment for Jyoti is based on *relative*, rather than actual, costs. So long as we add or subtract a constant number to every entry in the first row, the best assignment remains best. You can verify that similar statements apply for the other rows also. As a matter of fact, this same argument can be presented for each column also. The Hungarian method is based on this observation, which is rephrased as:

Rule 4. If a constant number is added to (or subtracted from) each entry in any row, and/or if a constant number is added to (or subtracted from) each entry in any column, the best assignment set remains the best.

The technique consists of finding suitable numbers to add or subtract from each row and/or column. It is presented below as a sequence of steps.

> *Step 1*. Subtract the smallest number in each row from every entry in that row.

For example, the smallest number in the first row is 96. Subtracting it from every entry in the first row transforms that row into: 0 3 9 12. The smallest number in the second row is again 96; subtracting it transforms that row into: 20 13 11 0. The consequences of performing similar subtractions in each row are shown in table 11-8. Note that Step 1 does more than just reduce the numbers, it identifies the best assignment in each row. Since the objective is to minimize costs, it follows that the best assignment for each row is indicated by the zero entries in that row.

Table 11-8 *Effects of Row Reductions*

	CHAPTERS			
TYPIST	13	14	15	16
Jyoti	0	3	9	12
Mary	20	13	11	0
Jackie	18	0	11	9
Tammy	9	0	13	10

The above entries can also be interpreted as opportunity losses in each row.

> *Step 2*. Subtract the smallest number in each column from every entry in that column.

The rationale and computations are similar to those in step 1. The resultant matrix is shown in table 11-9. The best assignment in each column is identified by the zero in that column.

> *Step 3*. Test for optimality.

Table 11-9 *Effects of Column Reductions*

	CHAPTERS			
TYPISTS	13	14	15	16
Jyoti	0	3	0	12
Mary	20	13	2	0
Jackie	18	0	2	9
Tammy	9	0	4	10

Note that any matrix such as that shown in table 11-9 can be interpreted as a row-and-column opportunity loss matrix. Searching for an optimal assignment set is equivalent to minimizing opportunity losses. It follows that in an optimal arrangement, all assignments are made using only zero entries. Note also that when one such assignment is made, all other zeros in that row and/or that column become useless. The procedure for checking the optimality of a matrix is based on these observations. It verifies that the zero entries have been well placed. First, cover the zeros with the *minimum* number of horizontal/vertical lines and then check to see that there are enough such lines. Specific details are listed as follows.

1. Cover each row that contains two or more uncovered zeros. Then, cover each column that contains two or more uncovered zeros.
2. If any row contains an uncovered zero, cover that row. Then, if any column contains an uncovered zero, cover that column.
3. Each covered row and/or column constitutes *one covering line*. If there are n such lines (n = number of rows or columns in the assignment matrix), the assignments can be made in an optimal fashion. If there are fewer than n covering lines, the zero entries must be rearranged.

For example, covering the first row, the second column, and then the second row covers all zeros in table 11-9. (Try it.) Only three covering lines, rather than four, are enough to cover all zeros; hence improvements must be found.

Step 4. Rearrange the zeros.

Zeros as shown in table 11-9 will not yield an optimal solution. This simply means that the initial set of constants used to obtain the above zeros was inadequate, and thus new constants must be found. However, there is no need to begin at the beginning. Use the information contained in the current matrix (table 11-9) to find the new one.

a. Find the *smallest* entry in the *uncovered* positions. *Subtract* it from all uncovered entries.
b. *Add* the above smallest entry to all entries where the covering lines intersect.

For example, covering the first row, the second column, and then the second row will cover all the zeros of table 11-9. These covering lines are shown in table 11-10. There are six uncovered entries: 18, 9, 2, 4, 7, and 10. The smallest uncovered entry, 2, occurs in the third row and the third column, i.e., Jackie typing chapter 15. Subtracting it from all uncovered entries yields $18 - 2 = 16$, $9 - 2 = 7$, and so on. This completes step 4a. Entries 3 and 13 lie at the intersection of the covering lines. Hence, according to step 4b, these entries are replaced by $3 + 2 = 5$ and

Table 11-10 *Rearranging the Zeros*

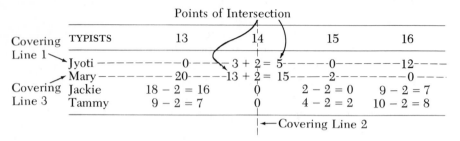

Points of Intersection

Covering	TYPISTS	13	14	15	16
Line 1	Jyoti	– – – – – – – – – 0 – –	3 + 2 = 5 – – – – –	0 – – – – – – –	12 – – – –
	Mary	– – – – – – – 20 – – – –	–13 + 2 = 15 – – – –	–2 – – – – – – –	–0 – – –.
Covering	Jackie	18 – 2 = 16	0	2 – 2 = 0	9 – 2 = 7
Line 3	Tammy	9 – 2 = 7	0	4 – 2 = 2	10 – 2 = 8

←— Covering Line 2

$13 + 2 = 15$. The new opportunity loss matrix, less all the procedural clutter, is shown in table 11-11.

Table 11-11 *The Improved Opportunity Loss Matrix*

	CHAPTERS			
TYPISTS	13	14	15	16
Jyoti	0	5	0	12
Mary	20	15	2	0
Jackie	16	0	0	7
Tammy	7	0	2	8

Repeat step 3. Then repeat step 4 (and consequently step 3 again, if necessary). For the matrix in table 11-11, you can check that covering the first row, and then the second, third, and fourth columns (in that order) covers all zeros. Since four covering lines are necessary, an optimal set of assignments can be found. We can, therefore, proceed to the next and final step.

Step 5. Make the optimal assignments.

a. Locate a row (or column) which contains only one zero.
b. Make an assignment in that row (or column).
c. Cross out any other zero(s) in that column (or row).
d. Repeat steps 5a through 5c until all assignments have been made.

Table 11-12 shows both the assignment process and the optimal assignments for Professor Jones's problem. Column 1 contains only one zero; hence make the first assignment there, i.e., at the intersection of row 1 and column 1. (Ask Jyoti to type chapter 13.) In table 11-12, an assignment is shown as the "boxed" zero. Row 1 contains one other zero. Cross it out. Table 11-12 shows this by placing an X on top of the zero at row 1, column 3. At this stage, column 3 contains only one zero. Hence,

Table 11-12 *The Optimal Assignments*

This zero becomes
useless after the
first assignment

First Assignment

TYPISTS	CHAPTERS			
	13	14	15	16
Jyoti	$\boxed{0}$	5	$\not{0}$	12	Fourth
Mary	20	15	2	$\boxed{0}$	Assignment
Jackie	16	$\not{0}$	$\boxed{0}$	7	
Tammy	7	$\boxed{0}$	2	8	

Third Assignment———

Second
Assignment

make an assignment there, i.e., at row 3, column 3. Then cross out the zero at row 3, column 2. Make an assignment at row 4, column 2. Finally, make an assignment in row 2, column 4.

In other words, Professor Jones should ask Jyoti to type chapter 13, Mary to type chapter 16, Jackie to type chapter 15, and Tammy to type chapter 14. Referring back to table 11-7, you can check that the total costs due to these assignments will be: $96 + 96 + 113 + 105 = \$410$. This is the least possible total cost. The symbolic solution to Jones's problem is:

$$X_{1,1} = X_{2,4} = X_{3,3} = X_{4,2} = 1$$

Summary of the Assignment Process

The entire technique can be summarized by the following sequence of steps:

1. Balance the assignment payoff matrix, if necessary.
2. If the problem has the maximization objective, compute the corresponding opportunity loss matrix.
3. If the assignments are forbidden at any positions in the matrix, allocate some exorbitantly high loss, M, at each such position.
4. Reduce each row by subtracting the smallest entry in that row from every entry in that row. Then, reduce each column.
5. Test for optimality. (Count the minimum necessary covering lines.) If the optimal assignments are possible, proceed to step 7; otherwise to step 6.
6. Find the smallest uncovered entry. Subtract it from all uncovered entries; and add it to each entry at the intersection of two covering lines. Then return to step 5.
7. Make the optimal assignments.

Now that you know how to formulate and solve the assignment problems, we shall examine an extension of the technique.

TRAVELING SALESMAN PROBLEMS

The classical formulation of such problems reads as follows. A traveling salesman plans to visit each of the n cities, starting and ending at his home city. Each city (except, of course, the home city) is to be visited once and only once, and he need not stay anywhere "forever." Any traveling plan which satisfies these rules is to be called a *tour*. The distance between City i and City j is known to be C_{ij}. The salesman wants to determine the shortest tour.

Problems of this type occur in a variety of managerial situations. For example, a publisher's representative or a campus recruiter must visit a number of colleges and universities. Though the symbol C_{ij} in classic formulation represents distance, the nature of the decision problem remains unchanged if C_{ij} represents cost or traveling time.

The model can also be used by a job scheduler who must sequence a variety of jobs on a versatile machine, such as a lathe. The "traveling salesman" in this case is the machine. The "cities" correspond to the different jobs (such as, cutting, stamping or sawing), the "home city" begin the situation where the machine is idle. C_{ij} is the cost of changeover from one operation to the next. The job scheduler would be interested in sequencing the jobs so as to minimize the changeover or set-up cost. As you can see, C_{ij} is any measure of undesirable payoff. It also means that, unlike the distance in the classic formulation, the cost matrix need not be symmetric, i.e., we need not insist on the condition: $C_{ij} = C_{ji}$. The solution methods to be presented here do not depend on such symmetry. See the references cited at the end of this chapter for additional formulations of "Traveling Salesman" situations.

Express Delivery Services Inc.

This truckers' cooperative specializes in making home deliveries of merchandise within the Boston metropolitan area. Presently one of its trucks must deliver furniture to the homes of four of its customers: Kent, Doran, Liddy, and Jones, and then return to the dispatch office for further orders. On the basis of past experience, the supervisor has prepared the cost matrix shown in table 11-13. For example, the cost of going from the office to the Kent residence to unload the furniture equals $22. Symbolically, $C_{1,2} = \$22$. Similarly, the cost of going from the Kent residence to Liddy's home (and unloading the furniture) equals $30. Symbolically, $C_{2,4} = \$30$.

The truck is forbidden to stay in any one location "forever." Equivalently, it cannot go from any place back to that same place. This restriction, which is present in any traveling salesman problem, is represented in table 11-13 by assigning the cost M (an exorbitantly large number) to each diagonal entry. Symbolically, for $i = 1$ through 5, $C_{ii} = M$. Finally,

Table 11-13 *The Trucking Costs ($)*

			TO		
FROM	1 OFFICE	2 KENT	3 DORAN	4 LIDDY	5 JONES
1 Office	M	22	30	45	60
2 Kent	18	M	20	30	40
3 Doran	25	24	M	27	50
4 Liddy	40	28	32	M	35
5 Jones	52	42	36	40	M

the lack of symmetry in table 11-13 (for instance, $C_{1,3} = \$30$ but $C_{3,1} = \$25$) is perhaps a result of the way the furniture has been loaded on the truck; perhaps due to the existence of one-way streets or detours in the Boston metropolitan area. It is unnecessary to establish the precise causes.

The Solution Techniques

Since a traveling salesman problem deals with a finite number of locations or jobs, one possibility is to list all possible tours, determine the corresponding costs, and then choose the tour with the smallest cost. For example, the cost of the tour from the office to the residences of Kent, Doran, Liddy, and then Jones and back to the office (symbolically: $1 \rightarrow 2 \rightarrow 3 \rightarrow 4 \rightarrow 5 \rightarrow 1$) equals:

$22 (from the office to the Kent residence)
$$+ \$20 + \$27 + \$35 + \$52 = \$156$$

That is:

$$\text{Cost}(1 \rightarrow 2 \rightarrow 3 \rightarrow 4 \rightarrow 5 \rightarrow 1) = \$156$$

The cost of any other tour can be computed similarly. In this problem, there are only 24 possible tours; hence enumerating can be practical. In general, however, the number of tours can quickly become unmanageably large. With n locations to visit (excluding the home location), you can check that there can be $n! = n(n-1) \ldots 1$ possible tours. For example, when $n = 10$, there will be $10! = 3,628,800$ tours. The enumeration method is, therefore, not always practical.

Since the cost matrix of a traveling salesman problem is in fact an assignment matrix with the "from location" forming one set of objects and the "to locations" forming another, one alternative is to solve this assignment problem and hope to obtain a tour. This is done for the trucker's problem as follows. To save space, all locations are denoted by their serial numbers. Begin by reducing the columns. The effect is shown in table 11-14(a). Then, reduce the rows (if any) and check for optimality. These operations are shown in table 11-14(b). Since only four lines cover all zeros, this arrangement is not optimal. The smallest uncovered entry, 3,

Table 11-14 *Solving the Assignment Problem*
(a) Column Reductions

			TO		
FROM	1	2	3	4	5
1	M	0	10	18	25
2	0	M	0	3	5
3	7	2	M	0	15
4	22	6	12	M	0
5	34	20	16	13	M

(b) Row Reductions (Row 5 only) and Covering Lines

			TO		
FROM	1	2	3	4	5
1	M	0	10	18	25
2	0	M	0	3	5
3	7	2	M	0	15
4	22	6	12	M	0
5	21	7	3	0	M

Smallest Uncovered Entry ⟶ (row 5, column 3: 3)

(c) The Optimal Set of Assignments

			TO		
FROM	1	2	3	4	5
1	M	[0]	7	18	22
2	[0]	M	0	6	5
3	4	2	M	[0]	12
4	22	9	12	M	[0]
5	18	7	[0]	0	M

occurs at row 5, column 3. The new arrangement of zeros, obtained by using the covering lines of table 11-14(b), is shown in table 11-14(c). As before, the optimal assignments are shown as the boxed zeros.

This set of assignments will cost: $22 + 18 + 27 + 35 + 36 = \$138$. There is only one difficulty: these assignments do not constitute a tour! In fact, there are two subtours: $1 \rightarrow 2 \rightarrow 1$ and $3 \rightarrow 4 \rightarrow 5 \rightarrow 3$. According to this plan, the delivery truck would go from the office to the Kent residence and back to the office. Presumably, someone else (without the furniture) would go from the Doran residence to those of Liddy and Jones and back to Doran's. But, why do that? In short, *this is not an acceptable solution*.

In general, any assignment set with subtours is not an acceptable solution of the traveling salesman problem.

Fortunately, there is an approach that enables us to use the efficiency of the assignment technique without sacrificing the requirement that the resulting plan must be a tour. This is discussed in the next section.

THE BRANCH-AND-BOUND APPROACH

This approach has been applied successfully to many different types of problems, though each type of problem might require a different variation of it. It is most widely used to solve *combinatorial optimization problems*, where the number of feasible solutions is finite but large. In such cases, neither the general Simplex technique nor the complete enumeration is practical.

For the sake of definiteness, assume that the decision maker seeks a least cost (in general, a least undesirable payoff) solution. To start, find an optimal solution ignoring one of the binding constraints. If this solution also satisfies the so far ignored constraint, *stop*—you have found a feasible optimal solution. Otherwise you can argue as follows. Insisting on feasibility reduces the number of available options. Thus, any feasible solution will cost at least as much as the value of the above optimal (but infeasible) solution. Consequently, that value is *a lower bound* on the cost of any feasible solution.

For the trucker's problem, the optimal but infeasible solution is that shown in table 11-14(c). The corresponding cost is $138. Thus, any feasible solution (i.e., a tour) will cost $138 or more.

Next, *a feasible solution* of the decision maker's problem *is found ignoring optimality*, and the corresponding objective function is computed. Remember that optimal means least costly. Hence, a feasible optimal solution must cost no more than the objection function value of the first feasible solution. That value provides *an upper bound* on the cost. In the trucker's problem, $1 \to 2 \to 3 \to 4 \to 5 \to 1$ is a tour and it costs $156. Hence, an optimal tour must cost $156 or less.

The word "branch" in the name of this technique refers to the fact that we partition the solution space into two subsets:

1. One that contains the optimal feasible solution(s).
2. One that need not be explored.

The first subset is successively "shrunk" and the new upper/lower bounds are established until, at some stage, the upper bound equals the lower bound. You can see that the corresponding solution must be both feasible and optimal.

The branch-and-bound approach appeals to pragmatists for yet another reason. Note that the upper bound corresponds to a feasible solution whereas the lower bound is, at each stage except the very last, only a dream. Also, the lower bound can only increase and the upper bound can only decrease. Thus, at each stage in the search process, you always know how far you are from a potentially optimal solution. The search process can therefore always be stopped (and the currently feasible solution accepted) when you are reasonably close to the optimum. For example, you might decide to "stop when the ratio of upper bound to lower bound is smaller than 1.1." A rule such as this can be derived by comparing the cost of searching against the potential savings to be realized by finding the true optimum.

This discussion has assumed that the payoffs are undesirable, but the branch-and-bound technique applies equally well when the payoffs are desirable—except, the roles of upper and lower bounds are reversed. A feasible solution yields a lower bound and an optimal solution provides an upper bound.

SOLUTION OF THE DELIVERY PROBLEM

The solution shown in table 11-14(c) is optimal but unacceptable since it is not a tour. The corresponding cost, $138, provides *a lower bound* on the cost of any tour. A branch-and-bound approach must be used to solve this delivery problem. To minimize the likely number of iterations, it is preferable to find an upper bound that is close to the lower bound.

Note that the zeros in table 11-14(b) represent the best assignment in each row. Use these to create a tour. In the first row, the zero occurs in column 2. So, the first leg of the tour is: $1 \rightarrow 2$. To find the next leg, search in the row (in this case, row 2) corresponding to the current point of departure. Note that since one has already reached Destination 2, the second column is no longer open for discussion. At each stage, the search continues in those columns that are still open. Of the two least costly open positions in row 2, choose the one in column 3. (Choosing column 1 at this stage would not yield a tour.) The first two legs of the tour are: $1 \rightarrow 2 \rightarrow 3$. *Complete the tour by always choosing the least costly open position from each successive departure point.* In this case, the resultant tour is: $1 \rightarrow 2 \rightarrow 3 \rightarrow 4 \rightarrow 5 \rightarrow 1$ with a cost of $156. This value, $156 is an upper bound for any subsequent tour.

With the lower bound of $138 and upper bound of $156, we will use what is called the Eastman-Shapiro algorithm to search for an optimal. The assignments shown in table 11-14(c) represent two subtours: $1 \rightarrow 2 \rightarrow 1$ and $3 \rightarrow 4 \rightarrow 5 \rightarrow 3$. To try to find a tour, we will *break up the smallest tour and create two new problems*, then solve each one in the hope of finding a better tour. This is the beginning of the branching process and is illustrated in figure 11-1. To break up the (smallest) subtour, $1 \rightarrow 2 \rightarrow 1$, in one

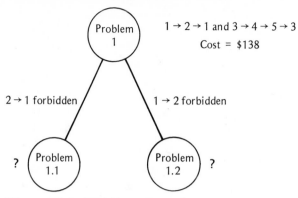

Upper bound = $156 (1 → 2 → 3 → 4 → 5 → 1)

1 → 2 → 1 and 3 → 4 → 5 → 3
Cost = $138

2 → 1 forbidden

1 → 2 forbidden

? Problem 1.1

Problem 1.2 ?

Figure 11-1. *The First Branching*

problem the assignment 1→2 (i.e., do not go from the office to Kent) is forbidden. In another problem, the assignment 2→1 (i.e., do not go from Kent to the office) is forbidden. The resultant branches are shown in figure 11-1. Since additional branching might become necessary, the terminology in figure 11-1 should be carefully examined. Problem 1 was described in table 11-13 and solved using table 11-14(c). The solution to problem 1 is spelled out just outside the initial *node*. Two new problems, 1.1 and 1.2 are identified on each branch. In each case, the last digit is arbitrary. The first digit, 1, indicates that each was derived by "splitting" a subtour in problem 1. In other words, each is a subproblem of problem 1. The fact that neither problem 1.1 nor 1.2 has been solved is indicated by placing a question mark outside the corresponding nodes.

Problems at the Second Level

We will begin the search process with the prior optimal matrix (i.e., the one that is to be split to create the branches). In this case table 11-14(c) contains the necessary matrix.

Problem 1.1 That the route 2→1 is forbidden is indicated by placing an M in row 2, column 1. See table 11-15(a). Since this M removes the only zero existing in the first column, that column must be reduced. Table 11-15(b) shows the resultant matrix and also the optimal assignments. Check that the cost of these assignments is $142 and that they do not form a tour. The subtours are: 1→2→3→1 and 4→5→4.

Problem 1.2 Begin again at the optimal matrix of problem 1, i.e., from table 11-14(c). Place an M in row 1, column 2 to indicate that the route 1→2 is forbidden. See table 11-16(a). This M eliminates the only zero in the first row as well as in the second column. Hence, that row and column must be reduced. The resultant matrix and the optimal assignments are

Table 11-15 *The Search When 2 → 1 Is Forbidden*

(a) Introduce M

	TO				
FROM	1	2	3	4	5
1	M	0	7	18	22
2	M	M	0	6	5
3	4	2	M	0	12
4	22	9	12	M	0
5	18	7	0	0	M

(b) Reduce Column 1 and Assign Zeros

	TO				
FROM	1	2	3	4	5
1	M	[0]	7	18	22
2	M	M	[0]	6	5
3	[0]	2	M	⊗	12
4	18	9	12	M	[0]
5	14	7	⊗	[0]	M

Table 11-16 *Finding the Assignments with 1 → 2 Forbidden*

(a) Introduce M

	TO				
FROM	1	2	3	4	5
1	M	M	7	18	22
2	0	M	0	6	5
3	4	2	M	0	12
4	22	9	12	M	0
5	18	7	0	0	M

(b) Reduce Row 1 and Column 2, Then Assign Zeros

	TO				
FROM	1	2	3	4	5
1	M	M	[0]	11	15
2	[0]	M	⊗	6	5
3	4	[0]	M	⊗	12
4	22	7	12	M	[0]
5	18	5	⊗	[0]	M

shown in table 11-16(b). Check that the total cost of these assignments is $147 and that these do not form a tour. There are two subtours: 1→3→2→1 and 4→5→4.

Evaluating the Branches The solution of problem 1.1 costs $142, which is less than the current upper bound of $156. The solution is not a tour. Hence, $142 is the new lower bound—at least on this branch. Similarly, the optimal assignments of problem 1.2 cost $147, which is less than the current upper bound of $156. The solution is not a tour.

Of these two solutions, that of problem 1.1 has the smaller cost. That cost, $142, is the new lower bound. Both nodes are open for further investigation. The upper bound, $156, has not changed. These findings are displayed in figure 11-2.

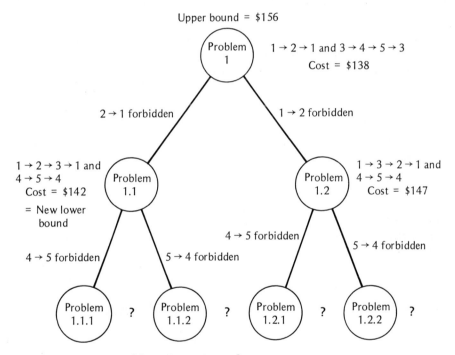

Figure 11-2. *Adding New Branches*

Problems at the Third Level

Of the four branches of figure 11-2, those emerging from problem 1.1 are investigated first in the hope of finding a tour that costs $147 or less. Problems, 1.1.1 and 1.1.2 are both created by starting with the optimal matrix of problem 1.1, i.e., with table 11-15(b). In problem 1.1.1, place an *M* in row 4, column 5 to indicate that the route 4→5 is forbidden. In problem 1.1.2, place an *M* in column 5, row 4 to indicate that route 5→4 is forbidden.

You should check the following results:

1. The optimal assignments for problem 1.1.1 cost $159, which is *more* than the current upper bound of $156. Hence, *reject* this solution and *close* that branch.
2. The optimal assignments for problem 1.1.2 cost $148, which is *less* then $156. Also, the solution is a tour: $1\rightarrow2\rightarrow4\rightarrow5\rightarrow3\rightarrow1$. Hence, $148 is *the new upper bound*, and further search along this branch is unnecessary.

Closing these two branches also implies that a tour costing less than $147 (the cost of the solution to problem 1.2) does not exist. Thus, $147 is *the new lower bound*. Will there be a tour costing exactly $147? To answer this, we must solve problems 1.2.1 and 1.2.2 each of which is created by starting with the optimal matrix shown in table 11-16(b).

You should check that:

1. The optimal assignments for problem 1.2.1 (obtained by placing an M in row 4, column 5) cost $163, which is *more* than $148. Hence, *reject* that solution and *close* that branch.
2. The optimal assignments for problem 1.2.2 cost $152, which is also *more* than $148. Hence, *reject* that solution and *close* that branch.

It follows that a tour costing less than $148 cannot be found. Thus, $148 is both an upper and lower bound. The corresponding tour, $1\rightarrow2\rightarrow4\rightarrow5\rightarrow3\rightarrow1$, is therefore the optimal tour. Figure 11-3 depicts the process. Part (a) in that figure logically precedes part (b).

We can conclude that the truck should make the first delivery at the Kent residence and then proceed to the residences of Liddy, Jones, and Doran (in that order) before returning to the office. This tour will cost $148, which is the smallest of all such costs.

SUMMARY OF THE BRANCHING TECHNIQUE

When reading this section, assume that the traveling salesman must visit each of the n cities before returning to City 1. Also, the intermediate cities are denoted by the letters i, j, and k, as necessary. The search process is summarized as follows:

1. Construct the assignment matrix by placing an M in each of the diagonal elements. To begin the solution process, *first reduce each column and then reduce each row*, if necessary. Create a tour as follows. Begin at City 1, i.e., examine row 1. Find the column, i, that has a zero in row 1. The first leg of the tour will be: $1 \rightarrow i$. Next, examine row i. Find the column, $j(j \neq i)$, that has

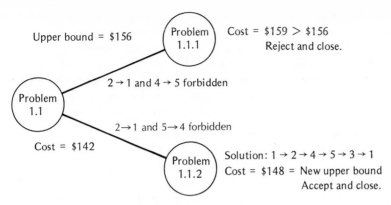

Figure 11-3 (a). *Branches from Problem 1.1*

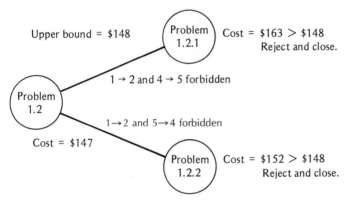

Figure 11-3 (b). *Branches from Problem 1.2*

a zero in row i (or that is the least costly in row i). The first two legs of the tour will be: $1 \to i \to j$. Complete the tour by examining the columns that remain open at each stage; and finally returning to City 1. If each leg was found using zero entries only, you have found an optimal tour. *Stop*. Otherwise, use the cost of this tour as *the initial upper bound*. (This tour is based on the specific costs. Hence, this upper bound will be usually much smaller than the cost of the tour: $1 \to 2 \to \ldots \to n \to 1$.)

2. Find the optimal solution of the assignment problem. If it is a tour, *stop*. This will be the least costly tour. Otherwise, use the cost of these assignments as *the initial lower bound*. This is the first node of the branch-and-bound tree; the corresponding optimal matrix describes problem 1.

3. Examine the problem whose solution provides the current lower bound. Split the smallest subtour in that solution. If two or more

subtours are the smallest, split each one in turn. This creates the branches coming out of that node. A subtour $i{\to}j{\to}i$ is split by forbidding the routes $i{\to}j$ and $j{\to}i$, in turn. A subtour $i{\to}j{\to}k{\to}i$ is split by forbidding the routes $i{\to}j$, $j{\to}k$, and $k{\to}i$, in turn. In general, create the new assignment problems— one along each branch—by beginning with the prior optimal matrix and placing an M along the forbidden route in that branch.

4. Evaluate the solution along each branch:
   a. If the cost exceeds the current upper bound, reject that solution and discontinue the search along this branch.
   b. If the solution is a tour, check that its cost equals the current lower bound. If so, you have found an optimal tour. *Stop*. Otherwise, *establish a new upper bound*. Discontinue the search along this branch.
   c. Otherwise, proceed to step 5.

5. All branches of Type 4(c) are "open" for investigation. Establish a new lower bound by finding the smallest of the corresponding solution costs.
   a. If the new lower bound equals the new upper bound, *stop* and accept the corresponding tour as being optimal.
   b. Otherwise, return to step 3, as long as there is at least one open branch.

As you can see, the deceptively simple condition of insisting on a tour makes the traveling salesman problem much harder to solve than the corresponding assignment problem. Though not an instant cure, the branch-and-bound algorithm will lead to an optimal tour in finitely many steps.

ADDITIONAL FORMULATIONS

A number of allocation problems naturally occur as assignment problems or can be transformed in that form. This section outlines three such possibilities. Many more can be found in OR/MS literature, some of which is cited at the end of this chapter.

Subjective Values of Costs

Suppose that there are m professional workers in an organization and that they are to be assigned to n projects. Suppose that the workers have been judged on the basis of their skills in each of K skill categories, and that the relative ability of the ith person in the kth skill category is r_{ik} ($i = 1, 2, \ldots, m$ and $k = 1, 2, \ldots, K$). Suppose further that the importance of possessing the kth skill while working on the jth project ($j = 1, 2, \ldots, n$) is determined to be W_{kj}. Finally, suppose that the priority of the jth project to this organization is P_j. Then, the effectiveness of the ith worker on the jth project can be defined by:

$$E_{ij} = P_j \sum_{k=1}^{K} r_{ik} W_{kj}$$

These E_{ij} values can be used to determine the optimal assignment of workers to projects during a planned period. The rest of the formulation can proceed as usual. For example, if:

$$V = \max\{E_{ij}\}$$

then the "cost" of not assigning ith worker to jth project would be:

$$C_{ij} = V - E_{ij}$$

Note that $\{P_j\}$, $\{r_{ik}\}$, and $\{W_{jk}\}$ are all subjective measures. Thus, the success of using the above formulation in real life situations depends on obtaining proper values of these parameters. For a discussion of the necessary methodology, see Child and Wolfe's paper (1972). That paper also describes the results of applying the resultant model in the Research Office of the Pittsburgh Board of Public Education.

Generalized Assignment Problem (GAP)

The basic assignment model assumes that there is a one-to-one correspondence between workers and jobs. In LP notation, this was expressed by the pair of conditions:

$$\sum_i X_{ij} = 1 \text{ and } \sum_j X_{ij} = 1$$

The first states that a job is assigned to only one worker. The second condition states that each worker is assigned only one job. If some workers can be assigned more than one job, the resultant model is known as the generalized assignment program (GAP). More specifically, GAP is defined as follows.

There are m workers and n jobs to be done in this planning period. The cost of assigning ith worker to the jth job is C_{ij}. Worker i needs r_{ij} hours (days or months) to do job j. Presently, worker i is free at least a_i but no more than b_i hours. The question, as usual, is to determine the least costly assignment of workers to jobs. More formally, GAP is summarized by the following model:

Minimize:

$$Z = \sum_{i=1}^{m} \sum_{j=1}^{n} C_{ij} X_{ij}$$

Subject to:

$$a_i \le \sum_{j=1}^{n} r_{ij} X_{ij} \le b_i, \text{ for } i = 1, 2, \ldots, m$$

$$\sum_{i=1}^{m} X_{ij} = 1, \text{ for } j = 1, \ldots, n$$

$$X_{ij} = 1, \text{ if worker } i \text{ is assigned job } j$$
$$= 0, \text{ otherwise}$$

Ross and Soland (1975) have developed a branch-and-bound algorithm for solving such problems.

Facility Location Problems

So far, we have assumed that the suppliers of service can be distinguished from the receivers of that service. But, this may not always be the case.

As a specific example, suppose that we are deciding on where to locate p facilities (hospitals, manufacturing plants, warehouses, or community clinics) within N communities. A community can have at most one facility within it. However, a facility may service more than one community. Obviously, each community will be assigned to the facility nearest it. The term "nearest" can signify distance, cost, or travel time depending on the circumstances.

Notice that even though each community receives the services, some communities will both supply and receive services. In this sense, the distinction between suppliers and receivers is somewhat fuzzy. The decision problem consists of identifying the communities that would both supply and receive service. It can be formulated as follows. For $i, j = 1, 2, \ldots, N$, let:

d_{ij} = distance from community i to community j
W_j = level of demand in community j
C_{ij} = cost of assigning community j to the facility located in community i
$X_{ij} = 1$, if community j is assigned to the facility located in community i
$\quad = 0$, otherwise

Then obviously, $C_{ij} = W_j d_{ij}$, for $i, j = 1, 2, \ldots, N$. We want to locate the facilities so as to minimize $\Sigma_i \Sigma_j C_{ij} X_{ij}$. It is necessary to determine whether each of the N communities will also be a supply center. This is done by adding N more "jobs" and one more "worker." The problem is then equivalent to GAP with $m = N + 1$ and $n = 2N$. Other details are as follows. (The notation is that of the preceding subsection.)

Minimize:

$$Z = \sum_{i=1}^{N+1} \sum_{j=1}^{2N} C_{ij} X_{ij}$$

Subject to:

$$a_i = 0, b_i = N \text{ for } i = 1, 2, \ldots, N$$
$$a_{N+1} = b_{N+1} = p,$$
$$C_{ij} = W_j d_{ij}, \text{ and } r_{ij} = 1 \text{ for } i, j = 1, 2, \ldots, N$$
$$C_{i,N+i} = 0, \text{ and } r_{i,N+i} = N \text{ for } i = 1, 2, \ldots, N$$
$$C_{N+1,N+i} = 0, \text{ and } r_{N+1,N+i} = 1 \text{ for } i = 1, 2, \ldots, N$$

For further information consult Ross and Soland (1977) in which many other types of facility location problems are also discussed.

SELECTED READINGS

BAKER, K. R. and MARTIN, J. B. "An Experimental Comparison of Solution Algorithms for the Single-Machine Tardiness Problem." *Naval Research Logistics Quarterly* 21 (1974), pp. 187–199.

BELLMORE, M. and NEMHAUSER, G. L. "The Traveling Salesman Problem: A Survey." *Operations Research* 16 (1968), pp. 538–558.

CHILDS, M. and WOLFE, H. "A Decision and Value Approach to Research Personnel Allocation." *Management Science* 18 (1972), pp. B269–278.

GASS, S. I. *Linear Programming: Methods and Applications*. 4th ed. New York: McGraw-Hill Book Co., 1975.

GAVETT, J. W. "Three Heuristic Rules for Sequencing Jobs to a Single Production Facility." *Management Science* 11 (1965), pp. B166–B176.

KAN, A. H. G. R.; LAGEWEG, B. J.; and LENSTRA, J. K. "Minimizing Total Costs in One-Machine Scheduling." *Operations Research* 23 (1975), pp. 908–927.

KHUMAWALA, B. M. "An Efficient Branch-Bound Algorithm for the Warehouse Location Problem." *Management Science* 18 (1972), pp. B718–B729.

KOLESKAR, P. J.; RIDER, K. L.; CRABILL, T. B.; and WALKER, W. E. "A Queueing-Linear Programming Approach to Scheduling Police Patrol Cars." *Operations Research* 23 (1975), pp. 1045–1062.

KWAK, N. K. *Mathematical Programming with Business Applications*. New York: McGraw-Hill Book Co., 1973.

LAWLER, E. L. and WOOD, D. E. "Branch-and-Bound Methods: A Survey." *Operations Research* 14 (1966), pp. 699–719.

LIN, S. and KERNIGHAN, B. W. "An Effective Heuristic Algorithm for the Traveling Salesman Problem." *Operations Research* 20 (1973), pp. 498–516.

LIPPMAN, S. and ROSS, S. "The Streetwalker's Dilemma: A Job-Shop Model." *SIAM Journal of Applied Mathematics* 20 (1971), pp. 336–342.

NORBACK, J. P. and LOVE, R. F. "Geometric Approaches to Solving the Traveling Salesman Problem." *Management Science* 23 (1977), pp. 1208–1233.

PICARD, J. C. and QUEYRANNE, M. "The Time-Dependent Traveling Salesman Problem and Its Application to the Tardiness Problem in One-Machine Scheduling." *Operations Research* 26 (1978), pp. 86–109.

REVELLE, C. and SWAIN, R. "Central Facilities Location." *Geographical Analysis* 2 (1970).

ROSS, G. T. and SOLAND, R. M. "Modeling Facility Location Problems as Generalized Assignment Problems." *Management Science* 24 (1977), pp. 345–357.

ROSS, G. T. and SOLAND, R. M. "A Branch and Bound Algorithm for the Generalized Assignment Problem." *Mathematical Programming* 8 (1975), pp. 91–105.

SHAPIRO, D. "Algorithms for the Solution of the Optimal Cost Traveling Salesman Problem." D. Sc. Thesis, Washington University, St. Louis, 1966.

SHRINIVASAN, V. and THOMPSON, G. L. "An Algorithm for Assigning Uses to Sources in a Special Class of Transportation Problems." *Operations Research* 21 (1973), pp. 284–295.

PROBLEM SET 11
SOME INTEGER OPTIMIZATIONS

1. Recall that in a standard assignment matrix, the payoffs are undesirable, the number of rows equals the number of columns, and any row can be matched with any column. Standardize each of the following matrices:

   a. The adjoining matrix shows profits associated with using machines A, B, and C to do jobs P, Q, R, and S.

MACHINE	JOB			
	P	Q	R	S
A	60	53	65	50
B	80	75	85	70
C	75	80	75	60

   b. The adjoining matrix shows the cost of assigning jobs A, B, or C to Joe, Mary, Terry, and Don.

JOB	WORKER			
	JOE	MARY	TERRY	DON
A	35	35	39	40
B	39	34	38	38
C	41	36	43	42

   c. Given below is a matrix showing the effectiveness per dollar of a doctor, nurse, and an aide with respect to bed making, patient care and routine examination. Of course, a doctor will not make a bed and an aide would not be asked to examine a patient.

	BED-MAKING	PATIENT CARE	PATIENT EXAMINATION
Doctor	✕	20	15
Nurse	12	10	22
Aide	15	10	✕

2. Four cost matrices are shown below. In each case, find the optimal assignments.

(a)

M	20	16	22	30
M	M	10	11	14
15	23	M	5	21
24	21	13	M	M
29	28	10	5	M

(b)

M	M	20	16	22
5	M	22	13	14
7	10	M	5	19
18	10	25	M	15
21	15	20	M	M

(c)

11	20	13	16	17
9	10	13	7	16
13	16	15	11	16
21	24	18	27	25

(d)

35	28	29
30	21	23
32	26	26
32	25	25

3. Using the standardized matrices in problem 1, find the optimal assignments of rows to columns.

4. Two profit matrices are shown below. In each case, find the optimal assignments.

(a)

35	22	27	44
51	39	42	47
32	28	40	46
27	31	35	31

(b)

44	58	49	42
52	47	55	64
60	53	45	39

5. Find the optimal assignments for the social workers using the complaint scores shown in table 11-2.

6. Using the delivery costs shown in table 11-4, determine the location which should not be supplied today. Also, which truck (and driver) should be assigned which location so as to minimize the delivery cost?

7. The dispatcher of problem 6 does not like to disappoint a customer. Instead, he has located a truck and driver who will make delivery to any location provided she is paid $5 more than the most expensive driver along the corresponding route. Find the optimal assignments and the total cost.

8. Solve the marketing manager's problem using the opportunity loss matrix of table 11-6. Then compute the total profit due to these assignments.

9. The Boston Foxes, an ice hockey team, has four more games to go before the end of this season. Unfortunately, the recent snowstorm has crowded the schedule—with games now being planned on four consecutive days. The team has five goalkeepers: McShane, O'Connor, White, Hudlow, and Corton. However due to the unusually long season this year as well as other hardships, none can be trusted to be his best for more than one game. The manager of the Boston Foxes knows that he should assign one goalkeeper to one game only. He has estimated the probability of winning each of the four games with each of five goalkeepers. These are shown in the adjoining table.

	GAME			
GOALKEEPER	1	2	3	4
McShane	.60	.80	.65	.70
O'Connor	.45	.50	.55	.60
White	.55	.55	.60	.65
Hudlow	.35	.60	.45	.50
Corton	.50	.45	.55	.55

a. Based on that information, determine who should be the goalkeeper in which game.

b. It turns out that McShane has come down with flu. How does this change the assignments?

10. McBride Associates Inc. believes that when an employee accepts a job, he/she should complete it, i.e., there must be "single point accountability." Currently, four research reports are ready to be typed and five secretaries are available to do the work. The estimated costs of typing ($) are shown in the adjoining table.

If McBride wishes to minimize costs:

a. Whose services must be declined?

b. Who should type which report?

	REPORTS			
TYPISTS	1	2	3	4
A	140	136	141	147
B	144	134	150	142
C	142	140	148	148
D	156	139	145	146
E	150	137	143	144

11. The Department of Energy Research wants to study four projects on energy conservation/generation alternatives. Four leading energy research firms have submitted bids to work on each project. Their bid amounts in thousands of dollars are shown in the adjoining table. For political reasons, each bidder

	PROJECT			
FIRM	1	2	3	4
A	120	86	98	77
B	124	84	107	72
C	122	90	105	78
D	136	89	102	76

must be assigned one project. If cost minimization is the objective, make optimal assignments of projects to firms.

12. Four applicants have applied for three job openings. Each has been administered an aptitude/skill test and the scores are shown in the adjoining table.

	APPLICANT			
JOB	A	B	C	D
1	95	103	115	99
2	120	118	130	109
3	107	119	108	123

The higher the score, the better is the applicant-job match.

a. Whose services must be declined?

b. Of those hired, who should be assigned which job?

13. A toy manufacturer employs four account executives each of whom would be responsible for dealing with one of the four major retailing firms. It is estimated that Firm 1 can place an order for toys worth $100,000. The corresponding "purchase potentials" of Firms 2, 3, and 4 are: $120,000, $90,000, and $140,000, respectively. Rapport with the corresponding purchasing agents is important for securing the order. The adjoining table shows the probabilities of sale for each executive-agent pair. For example, the probability is .8 that executive C will secure an order from the purchasing agent

employed by Firm 1. What are the optimal assignments? (Hint: expected payoff = purchase potential × probability of sale.)

AGENT	EXECUTIVE			
	A	B	C	D
1	.7	.6	.8	.6
2	.5	.8	.7	.6
3	.8	.8	.7	.6
4	.6	.5	.6	.6

Note: Problems 14 onward can be done by hand; however, a computer package would be more suitable. One such package, ASSIGN, can be obtained from the author.

14. Find the optimal tours given the following cost matrices:

(a)

M	20	30	30	50	40
20	M	50	50	35	45
35	50	M	15	30	20
15	50	15	M	50	30
45	40	30	45	M	25
45	40	20	35	25	M

(b)

M	59	35	23	43	63
50	M	25	40	42	70
30	28	M	27	30	48
25	35	30	M	40	30
45	45	25	40	M	37
70	60	40	30	40	M

15. Four different jobs must be done using the same machine. The adjoining table shows the set-up time between jobs in minutes. The "set-up times" in the first column represent the time to clean up, return the tools, etc. Currently, the machine is idle. Find the optimal sequence of jobs.

FROM JOB	TO JOB				
	IDLE	1	2	3	4
Idle	—	30	20	40	20
1	10	—	20	30	40
2	10	15	—	25	30
3	10	35	30	—	40
4	10	35	25	35	—

16. Circular Tours Inc. conducts guided tours of the Northeast and wants to start an eight-site tour of sites chosen for historical importance, natural beauty, or industrial significance. Each tour must return to the city of its origin. Since the intersite distance matrix is symmetrical, only half of it is shown in the adjoining table. Since Circular Tours must pay mileage for the bus and

2	320							
3	220	480						
4	500	700	390					
5	450	570	370	240				
6	280	280	400	580	400			
7	300	640	100	300	360	500		
8	600	650	480	320	100	380	540	
Sites	1	2	3	4	5	6	7	

driver, as well as the accommodations for each night's stay, they would prefer to find the shortest tour. However, they would be willing to accept a tour that is no more than 10 percent longer than the conceivably optimal tour—provided that you produce the necessary evidence. What would you recommend? (Hint: The above condition is equivalent to: upper bound ÷ lower bound ≤ 1.1.)

17. The Rainbow Company manufactures seven varieties of ice cream. The same machine is used to produce all varieties. The company has found that extra clean up is necessary when a mild flavored ice cream follows a strong flavored one. Similarly, an ice cream containing nuts requires additional clean up. For these kinds of reasons, the intervariety set-up times are asymmetric. These times are shown in the adjoining table. In that table, variety 1

	TO							
FROM	1	2	3	4	5	6	7	8
1	—	10	12	12	10	15	12	15
2	10	—	25	25	20	25	30	30
3	15	20	—	20	20	25	30	20
4	10	25	25	—	20	24	24	27
5	20	10	15	15	—	16	18	20
6	10	15	20	20	20	—	26	28
7	15	25	35	24	20	23	—	30
8	10	20	25	30	24	24	26	—

represents a clean machine; all others are actual varieties. A production run consists of making the designated amounts of each variety of ice cream beginning and ending with a clean machine. A run that will minimize total set-up time is desired. However, the management will accept a run whose total set-up time is at most 15 minutes more than the conceivable optimum—if the evidence to support this conclusion is presented. Make recommendations.

*18. The research section of a small company employs five professionals. The section manager has rated her employees on each of the four skill categories. The results are shown in the first of three adjoining tables.

		SKILL TYPE		
EMPLOYEE	1	2	3	4
John Symes	.30	.28	.20	.25
Mary Maloney	.45	.48	.32	.35
Linda Smythe	.25	.40	.45	.30
Jerry Clein	.28	.30	.40	.38
Sam Davis	.40	.41	.33	.35

The company must finish work on six small projects each of which needs one research employee for three months. Consequently, an employee who begins working on a project must stay with it throughout the next three months. Obviously, one of the six projects would have to be subcontracted and the president wishes to know which one. The president's priority ratings are shown in the following table.

Project	A	B	C	D	E	F
Priority Weights	.25	.30	.35	.25	.35	.40

The president could subcontract one of the two lowest priority projects, but he is not sure whether his employees could do the remaining projects competently. He consults with the chief of the research section who has prepared the following matrix of importance of various skills for each of the projects.

			PROJECTS			
SKILL	A	B	C	D	E	F
1	.33	.40	.39	.42	.45	.25
2	.15	.22	.25	.29	.39	.33
3	.41	.36	.34	.35	.42	.30
4	.37	.27	.20	.43	.30	.24

The company's methodologist and psychometrician has certified that each of the three tables have been constructed with utmost care.

a. Which project should be subcontracted out?

b. Who should be engaged on which of the remaining five projects?

*19. Four accountants must work on six customer accounts next month. The benefits to the firm because of assigning the accountants to the various accounts are summarized in the adjoining table.

ACCOUNTANTS	CUSTOMER ACCOUNTS					
	1	2	3	4	5	6
Bill Schwartz	95	80	75	85	90	80
Don Aubrey	85	90	60	65	70	75
Mary Jones	80	80	85	90	65	70
Pearson Murphy	90	95	70	80	85	60

Once assigned, an account stays with that accountant till its completion. The number of person-hours needed to complete the work on each account are shown in the following table.

ACCOUNTANTS	CUSTOMER ACCOUNTS					
	1	2	3	4	5	6
Bill Schwartz	90	80	60	70	100	75
Don Aubrey	95	85	65	60	95	70
Mary Jones	80	75	50	80	80	75
Pearson Murphy	70	70	80	75	90	65

Because of prior commitments, Pearson is available for 120 hours only. Mary needs at least 60 hours of work this month to cover the anticipated downtime. Bill and Don have no such difficulties; each can work full 180 hours this month. Each of the three men can also work on something else if none of the six accounts is assigned to them. What would be optimal assignments? (Formulate only.)

*20. An auto manufacturer has five dealers in the New England region. John Croke needs 50 cars each month. The corresponding needs of Bill Vronsky, Paula Karenina, Sammy Dunkin, and Eileen Karten are 60, 70, 55, and 65 cars, respectively. The auto manufacturer is planning to open two regional centers in New England for supplying the cars to dealers. The company has not chosen the sites as yet. Suitable sites are available in the vicinity of each dealer. The cost of transporting a car from the vicinity of each dealer to all other dealers in the region are shown in the adjoining table. Because of the differing pay rates in the surrounding communities, the cost matrix is not symmetric. Formulate the problem to determine the optimal locations of the proposed regional centers.

FROM	TO				
	JOHN	BILL	PAULA	SAMMY	EILEEN
John	$ 2	$36	$41	$43	$56
Bill	43	0	22	49	49
Paula	50	24	3	29	30
Sammy	44	45	24	4	25
Eileen	64	47	26	26	1

12

Transportation (Distribution) Models

Distribution Problems
Steps for Solving a Distribution Problem
Vogel's Approximation Method (VAM)
Evaluating the Proposed Solution
Better Solutions and Special Cases
Additional Formulations
Selected Readings
Problem Set 12: Optimal Source-Destination Pairs

The models in this chapter assume that, in effect, the decision maker is a distributor. There are a number of sources (factories, warehouses, or distribution centers) from where the products (goods and/or services) can be obtained, and there are a number of destinations (customer outlets or dealerships) which require these products.

There is a prototype distribution model which makes the following assumptions:

1. A central authority, the decision maker, is responsible for making the best possible match of sources and destinations.
2. The costs of obtaining a product from each source on behalf of every destination are known.
3. The products are homogeneous in the sense that the items obtained from different sources can be freely interchanged. Only the costs might vary from one route (i.e., the source-destination pair) to another.
4. There are no economies or diseconomies of scale (i.e., the total cost along any one route is proportional to the number of items allocated to that route).

5. Total supply equals total demand (i.e., the distribution problem is balanced).
6. All routes are acceptable.

Given these assumptions, the standard transportation model answers the question: *how much of the product should be allocated along each route so as to minimize the total cost of such allocations?*

The chapter begins by showing how to convert each decision problem into the standard form. Having done this, Vogel's method of finding a near-optimal solution to that problem is examined. Then ways to check the optimality of a proposed solution (and hence find better solutions) are illustrated.

The chapter ends by illustrating how the transportation technique can be applied to solve the problems of production planning as well as of transshipment.

DISTRIBUTION PROBLEMS

In this section, we will construct the transportation tableau of a prototype problem. We will then consider how to standardize any distribution problem. Also, we will present the prototype problem in its linear optimization form.

Blood Banks and Hospitals

Consider a metropolitan area in which five medical surgical hospitals have joined together to form a consortium.

Let H_1, H_2, H_3, H_4, and H_5 denote the five hospitals that are managed by this consortium. Every day the member hospitals need a fresh supply of one type of blood to use for transfusions during surgical procedures. Past experience reveals that the daily needs of the member hospitals can be summarized as shown in table 12-1. The total daily demand is for 2,100 pints. Assume further than the blood is always used on the day it is purchased—so the decision situation is not one of detemining the op-

Table 12-1 *Blood Needed by Member Hospitals*

HOSPITAL	DAILY NEEDS (NUMBER OF PINTS)
H_1	300
H_2	400
H_3	500
H_4	600
H_5	300
Total	2,100

timum inventory levels, nor of deriving the aggregate level of purchase for a number of months in the future.

The consortium management knows three reliable and quality-conscious suppliers of blood. Together, they can meet the daily needs of the hospital consortiums. The number of pints each blood bank can supply every day are shown in table 12-2. Even though the consortium management buys the blood on behalf of all its members, the purchased blood

Table 12-2 *Supply Capacities of Blood Banks*

BANK	DAILY SUPPLY (NUMBER OF PINTS)
B_1	900
B_2	400
B_3	800
Total	2,100

is delivered directly to the member hospitals. (The possible blood delivery routes are shown in figure 12-1.) Though each blood bank supplies the same type of blood, their unit prices vary considerably. Also, the cost of delivering the blood varies according to the delivery route chosen (i.e., from which bank to which hospital). The total cost per pint of blood has

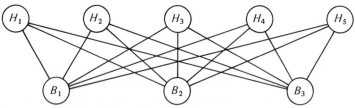

Figure 12-1. *Possible Blood Delivery Routes*

been computed for each delivery route by combining these two factors, viz., the cost at origin and the cost of delivery. These unit costs are shown in table 12-3.

The management wishes to know the answer to the following question: How much blood (number of pints) should be transported each day along each delivery route (i.e., from each bank to each hospital) so as to minimize the total cost? The transportation technique is an efficient method of responding to this query.

The Transportation Tableau

Presumably, this problem could be solved by enumerating all possible combinations of *source-destination pairs*, which are the routes and the amounts to be shipped along each route (i.e., the size of *allocations*). The

Table 12-3 *Unit Costs of Blood ($/pint)*

	TO				
FROM	H_1	H_2	H_3	H_4	H_5
B_1	18	15	12	13	16
B_2	12	16	14	12	9
B_3	15	11	13	16	15

rationale is that there is a finite number of such combinations. But since a finite number does not necessarily mean a few, it is preferable to follow some systematic procedure. Such a procedure, the transportation technique, begins by constructing the *transportation tableau*. For the blood banks and hospitals problem, BB/H for short, this tableau is shown in figure 12-2.

		Hospitals					
		H_1	H_2	H_3	H_4	H_5	Supply (S_i)
Blood banks	B_1	$18	$15	$12	$13	$16	900
	B_2	$12	$16	$14	$12	$ 9	400
	B_3	$15	$11	$13	$16	$15	800
Demand (D_j)		300	400	500	600	300	

Figure 12-2. *A Transportation Tableau for BB/H*

Such a tableau presents all of the known items of information in a concise form. Familiarize yourself with how to read transportation tableaus:

1. The sources, also known as origins, are shown in the left-hand margin. In general, there will be m of these.
2. The destinations are shown at the top of each column. In general, there will be n of these.
3. Each source-destination pair constitutes a *route*. There will be $m \times n$ such routes—n from each source. These routes are represented by the "cells" of the tableau. For example, B_1H_1 (from Bank 1 to Hospital 1) is a route. In the tableau, it is shown as the cell that lies at the intersection of row B_1 and column H_1, i.e., the northwest corner.

4. The per unit cost of using a route is shown in the top left corner
of the corresponding cell. The per-unit cost along a route from
source i to destination j is denoted by C_{ij}, e.g., $C_{1,1}$ = per unit
cost from B_1 to H_1 is \$18. Since there can be m sources and n
destinations, it follows that i varies from 1 to m, and that j varies
from 1 to n.
5. The amount of supplies at source i (also known as the capacity of
source i) is denoted by S_1, and it is shown in the extreme right-
hand column of the tableau.
6. The amount needed at destination j is denoted by D_j, and it is
shown in the very last row of the tableau.
7. In a standard tableau, the total supply equals total demand.
Symbolically:

$$S_1 + S_2 + \ldots + S_m = D_1 + D_2 + \ldots + D_n$$

In the mathematical shorthand discussed in chapter 2,

$$\sum_{i=1}^{m} S_i = \sum_{j=1}^{n} D_j$$

8. The amount to be shipped from source i to destination j is not
shown in the tableau in figure 12-2, because it is not yet known.
We can denote the amount by X_{ij}. The transportation problem,
when solved, will provide the numerical values of X_{ij} for all i
and j.

In the process of describing the tableau, we have also introduced the
necessary mathematical notation. Using that, the standard transportation
problem can be summarized as follows.
Minimize:

$$TC = \sum_i \sum_j C_{ij} X_{ij}$$

Subject to the constraints:

$$\sum_i X_{ij} = D_j, \text{ for } j = 1 \text{ through } n$$

$$\sum_j X_{ij} = S_i, \text{ for } i = 1 \text{ through } m$$

Nonnegativity requirements:

$X_{ij} \geq 0$, for all i and j

It is assumed that:

$$\sum_i S_i = \sum_j D_j$$

(i.e., supply equals demand)

The BB/H problem is standard because:

1. Total supply = 900 + 400 + 800 = 2,100 pints equals total demand = 300 + 400 + 500 + 600 + 300.
2. The objective is to minimize the total cost of allocations.
3. All routes are acceptable by default. (We never said that a specific route was unacceptable.)

Before proceeding to solve it, let us study the ways to standardize transportation tableaus.

When Supply Does Not Equal Demand

This turns out to be a very common situation in formulating the transportation problems. From a managerial point of view, at least, the condition that total supply must equal demand is both artificial and seldom realistic. The main rationale behind the insistence that supply should equal demand is the algebraic need to solve simultaneous equations. Since the condition itself is artificial, the methods of resolving the difficulty when supply does not equal demand are equally artificial—but effective.

If the total supply exceeds total demand, create a new destination, and set the demand at this artificially created destination (also known as a dummy destination) equal to the excess supply. Since nothing is in fact transported to this dummy destination, the unit cost of transportation from any origin to this destination is set equal to zero.

Algebraic requirements having been met, the solution procedures are applied to the resultant tableau. Any allocations in the dummy column are interpreted as the amount of the product left over at the origin. In other words, the dummy column helps the decision maker distribute the slack among the various origins.

Conversely, if the demand exceeds supply, create a dummy source and set its "supply potential" equal to the shortage. The per unit costs in the dummy row are set equal to zero. In effect, the shortage is distributed in a rational manner.

As an example of a situation when supply does not equal demand, consider the following scenario. Suppose that the economy of the metropolitan area has experienced a downturn, and that many more persons are now selling blood than used to when the BB/H problem was initially formulated. Specifically, suppose that blood bank B_1 can supply 900 pints, that B_2 can supply 600 pints, and that B_3 can supply 850 pints. The rest of the scenario is identical to that in the past.

A quick computation shows that the banks can supply a total of 2,350 pints of blood, i.e., there is an excess supply of 250 pints. The corresponding transportation tableau is shown in figure 12-3.

		Hospitals					
		H_1	H_2	H_3	H_4	H_5	H_6 (Dummy)	(S_j)
Blood banks	B_1	\$18	\$15	\$12	\$13	\$16	\$0	900
	B_2	\$12	\$16	\$14	\$12	\$ 9	\$0	600
	B_3	\$15	\$11	\$13	\$16	\$15	\$0	850
Demand (D_j)		300	400	500	600	300	250	

Figure 12-3. *A Tableau When Supply Exceeds Demand*

Unacceptable Routes

The classic transportation tableau is based on the notion that any of the origins can supply the products to any of the destinations. At times, however, some of the routes are not acceptable to one or both parties. Labor disputes, personality conflicts, or political incompatibility might be some reasons. If a route is not acceptable, it is customary to represent this by assigning an extremely high unit cost to that route. This very high unit cost is denoted by the symbol M. The resultant tableau is, then, in the standard form since, *officially*, all routes are acceptable.

This is, of course, a contrived scheme, employed mainly for computational convenience. Since M is a very high cost and since the transportation technique always seeks a least cost solution, the route with the assigned cost M can never be in the optimal solution.

Maximization Problems

A production manager is usually interested in reducing production and distribution costs. A marketing manager generally attempts to find the distribution channels that maximize profits. Thus, the discussion so far has assumed that our decision maker is in a sense, a production manager. However, the transportation technique can be modified to solve maximization problems as well.

Let P_{ij} denote the per unit profit of using the route from source i to destination j. Let $PMAX$ equal the largest of all the per unit profits. Then, compute the regret, C_{ij}, of not making all deliveries along the most profitable route:

$$C_{ij} = PMAX - P_{ij}, \text{ for all } i \text{ and } j$$

Use the resultant C_{ij} values in place of cost for all routes.

To illustrate this technique, consider the problem faced by the management of Make-More-Money, Inc. (MMM). The company has three production plants and four retail outlets. The production capacities of each plant, the forecasted level of sales at each outlet, and the net profits along each route are summarized in figure 12-4.

		Outlets				
		O_1	O_2	O_3	O_4	Production capacity (S_i)
Plants	P_1	\$50	\$80	\$100	\$70	500
	P_2	\$90	\$110	\$60	\$80	400
	P_3	\$120	\$90	\$50	\$80	300
Possible sales (D_j)		450	200	250	300	

Figure 12-4. *Transportation Tableau for MMM Inc. (Profits)*

Notice that the largest net profit of \$120 per unit sold occurs along route P_3O_1. In other words, $PMAX = \$120$. Hence, for example, the regret associated with delivery route P_1O_1 is $\$120 - \$50 = \$70$; that associated with P_2O_3 is $\$120 - \$60 = \$60$. The resultant matrix of regrets is shown in figure 12-5. It is now in the standard form.

Figure 12-5. *Transportation Tableau for MMM Inc. (Regrets)*

		Outlets				
		O_1	O_2	O_3	O_4	S_i
Plants	P_1	\$70	\$40	\$20	\$50	500
	P_2	\$30	\$10	\$60	\$40	400
	P_3	\$0	\$30	\$70	\$40	300
Demand (D_j)		450	200	250	300	

STEPS FOR SOLVING A DISTRIBUTION PROBLEM

The procedure for obtaining an optimal solution, i.e., an optimal set of allocations, can be summarized as the following sequence of steps.

1. Create a transportation tableau that displays the sources, destinations, the capacities of each source, the requirements at each destination, and the unit costs or benefits along each route.

2. Balance the tableau by creating a dummy source or destination, as necessary, if the supply does not equal demand. The per unit cost or benefit in the dummy row (or column) is set to zero.

3. If the distribution problem has a maximization objective, convert the corresponding tableau to its standard form by computing the associated opportunity losses and using these in place of costs.

4. If certain routes are unacceptable, assign a per unit penalty, M, at each such route. M must be large enough so that the corresponding routes will never be part of the optimal solution.

5. Find a feasible solution (i.e., a complete set of allocations) of the now standardized tableau so that both:
   a. The sum of allocations in each row equals the supply capacity of the corresponding source, and
   b. The sum of allocations in each column equals the demand at the corresponding destination.

6. Check for optimality. The current solution is optimal if no other feasible solution has a lesser cost. If better solutions can be found, return to Step 5. Otherwise, you must have reached the optimum; proceed to Step 7.

7. If the original objective was to minimize costs, compute the total cost as the sum of products:

$$\sum \sum C_{ij} \cdot X_{ij}$$

If the original objective was to maximize benefits, compute the total benefit as the sum of products:

$$\sum \sum P_{ij} \cdot X_{ij}$$

You have already seen the details of the first four of these seven steps. In the remainder of this chapter, we will assume that the transportation tableau either is or has been standardized. So, let us perform Steps 5 through 7.

VOGEL'S APPROXIMATION METHOD (VAM)

A method that guarantees to find the optimal solution on the very first try is yet to be devised. Consequently, as was mentioned in the preceding section, we end up using an iterative method—finding a feasible solution; checking its optimality; if necessary, finding a better feasible solution; and then repeating the cycle. The closer the first solution is to the true optimum, the fewer the number of iterations. So, Vogel's method tries to find the optimal (or near-optimal) solution on the very first try. To illustrate the step-by-step sequence, let's find a feasible solution of the BB/H problem. The concept of opportunity cost *(OC)*, also known as penalty or regret, plays the central role in the search process.

Step 1. In each row of the standard tableau, find the least costly and the next least costly routes. Compute the opportunity cost *(OC)* in each row as the difference: unit cost of the next best route *less* that of the best route. Similarly, compute the opportunity cost in each column.

Figure 12-2 shows the transportation tableau of the BB/H problem. In the first row, the smallest unit cost is $12 along route B_1H_3; the next smallest cost is $13 along route B_1H_4. Hence, the opportunity cost in the first row equals: $13 - $12 = $1. Similarly, the opportunity costs in the second and third row are: $12 - $9 = $3 and $13 - $11 = $2, respectively. The opportunity costs in the columns are: $15 - $12 = $3 in the first column, $15 - $11 = $4 in the second column, etc. Figure 12-6 shows the resultant tableau when these opportunity costs are appended to the tableau in figure 12-2.

Having found the opportunity costs *(OC)*, we certainly want to guard against the largest of such regrets. We also want to establish a rule that can be used at each stage in the search process.

Step 2. There are two possibilities:

a. The current tableau contains only one row or only one column. Make the allocations necessary to satisfy the remaining demands or to exhaust the remaining supplies. Then *stop*—you have the required solution.
b. The current tableau contains more than one row *and* more than one column. Find the row (or column) with the largest opportunity cost. In that row (or column) find the least costly cell and make the maximum possible allocation in that cell. (If there are two or more such cells, choose the one where the maximum amount can be allocated.) Reduce the supply in the corresponding row by the amount just allocated.

		H_1	H_2	H_3	H_4	H_5	Supply (S_i)	OC_i
				Hospitals				
Blood banks	B_1	$18	$15	$12	$13	$16	900	$1
	B_2	$12	$16	$14	$12	$9 \quad 300	100 ~~400~~	$3
	B_3	$15	$11	$13	$16	$15	800	$2
Demand (D_j)		300	400	500	600	~~300~~ 0		
OC_j		$3	$4	$1	$1	$6 ↑		

Figure 12-6. *The Opportunity Costs (OC) for the BB/H Problem and the First Allocation*

The First Allocation

For example, the largest OC in figure 12-6 is $6, and it occurs in Column H_5. Thus, the first nonzero allocation is made in that column. The least cost cell is B_2H_5 ($9 per pint). Since, at present, B_2 can supply 400 pints but H_5 only needs 300 pints, the most that can be allocated at B_2H_5 is 300 pints (the smaller of the two quantities: available supply and remaining demand). Hence, allocate 300 pints along B_2H_5. Having made this allocation, B_2 has an additional supply of only $400 - 300 = 100$ pints, and H_5 need not be considered any longer. In other words, we can ignore the contents of Column H_5 in all future allocations. These findings are displayed in figure 12-6. In effect, from now on the BB/H tableau contains only three rows and four columns.

Step 3. There are three possibilities:

a. The total supplies in the row are exhausted. If so, eliminate that row; recompute the opportunity costs in the currently active columns; and return to Step 2.
b. The column needs have been met. If so, eliminate that column; recompute the opportunity costs in the currently active rows; and return to Step 2.
c. The column needs have been met and the row supplies have been exhausted, *simultaneously*. Eliminate both that row and that column; recompute the opportunity costs in the rest of the tableau; and return to Step 2.

The Second Allocation

In the BB/H problem, since the H_5 needs have been met, eliminate Column H_5. You can show the elimination by shading that column in the transportation tableau. See figure 12-7. The first through the third rows are still active. Hence, recompute the penalties as in Step 1. The new penalties are: $13 − $12 = $1 in Row B_1, $12 − $12 = $0 in Row B_2, and $13 − $11 = $2 in Row B_3. These findings are shown in figure 12-7. Column H_5 has been shaded to indicate that it is no longer active. Return to Step 2(b). The largest penalty in the remaining 3 × 4 tableau now occurs in Column H_2. The smallest cost in that column, $11, is along the route B_3H_2. The blood bank B_3 can supply 800 pints, but the hospital H_2 needs only 400 pints. Thus, at most, 400 pints can be allocated along B_3H_2. Allocate 400 pints at B_3H_2. Column H_2 is no longer active. The supply at B_3 is now reduced to 800 − 400 = 400 pints. These findings are also shown in figure 12-7.

		Hospitals					Supply		
		H_1	H_2	H_3	H_4	H_5	(S_j)		
Blood banks	B_1	$18	$15	$12	$13	~~$16~~	900	~~$1~~	$1
	B_2	$12	$16	$14	$12	~~$9~~ 300	100 ~~400~~	~~$3~~	$0
	B_3	$15	$11 400	$13	$16	~~$15~~	400 ~~800~~	~~$2~~	$2
Demand (D_j)		300	~~400~~ 0	500	600	~~300~~ 0			
		$3	$4 ↑	$1	$1	~~$6~~			

Figure 12-7. *The Second Set of Penalties and the Second Allocation*

The Third and Subsequent Allocations

Since we have eliminated a column, the row penalties are recomputed to be: $13 − $12 = $1 in Row B_1, $12 − $12 = $0 in Row B_2, and $15 − $13 = $2 in Row B_3. The largest penalty now occurs in Column H_1. The smallest unit cost in that column is $12 at B_2H_1. Though H_1 needs 300 pints, B_2 can supply only 100 pints. Hence, allocate 100 pints at B_2H_1. Since B_2 supplies have been exhausted, eliminate Row B_2 and recompute the penalties in the still active Columns H_1, H_3, and H_4.

Now continue the process until all nonzero allocations have been found. The actual work is left as an exercise. The final set of nonzero allocations, i.e., a feasible solution is shown in figure 12-8. The sequence of making allocations and the size of allocations, i.e., number of pints allocated, is shown in table 12-4.

		H_1	H_2	H_3	H_4	H_5	Supply (S_i)
				Hospitals			
Blood banks	B_1	$18	$15	$12 *300	$13 *600	$16	900
	B_2	$12 *100	$16	$14	$12	$9 *300	400
	B_3	$15 *200	$11 *400	$13 *200	$16	$15	800
	Demand (D_j)	300	400	500	600	300	

Figure 12-8. *Vogel's Solution for the BB/H Problem*

Note that figure 12-8 shows a method of displaying a complete set of allocations. Since an allocation is either positive or zero, it is traditional to show only the nonzero allocations. A blank in any cell implies that the corresponding allocation is zero. To further focus attention on these positive allocations, an asterisk has been placed in front of each amount. Of the $3 \times 5 = 15$ possible routes, only 7 will be used for distributing the blood. This is a feasible solution because all row and column constraints have been met. For example, the amount allocated in Row B_1 equals the supply at B_1. Similarly, the allocations in Column H_1 equal the demands at H_1. The compliance of other constraints can be checked similarly.

Table 12-4 *Summary of the BB/H Search*

ALLOCATION NUMBER	ROUTE	NUMBER OF PINTS
1	$B_2 H_5$	300
2	$B_3 H_2$	400
3	$B_2 H_1$	100
4	$B_1 H_4$	600
5	$B_1 H_3$	300
6	$B_3 H_1$	200
7	$B_3 H_3$	200

Vogel's approximation method is a systematic procedure for obtaining a feasible solution, and it appears to use the cost information rather effectively. But, is the solution shown in figure 12-8 the best solution? If it is not, how can we obtain a better solution?

EVALUATING THE PROPOSED SOLUTION

Vogel's approximation method is an excellent heuristic for obtaining a feasible solution of the standard transportation tableau. But, it falls short of guaranteeing that the resultant set of allocations is the least costly. As we've said, a method that assures the optimal solution on the first try is yet to be devised. It follows that any proposed feasible solution must be proved optimal, i.e., that a better one cannot be found.

Two methods for checking the optimality of any feasible solution are discussed in this section. Both lead to the same conclusion—but neither will work unless the current solution is *a basic solution*. We will, therefore, examine the concept of a basic solution and then illustrate the evaluation procedures.

Basic Feasible Solutions
Recall that a feasible solution must satisfy two constraints:

- The total amount allocated in each row must equal the total supply at the corresponding origins.
- The total amount allocated in each column must equal the total needed at the corresponding destinations.

For example, both figures 12-8 and 12-9 display solutions to the same BB/H problem. Whereas the solution displayed in figure 12-8 contained only seven nonzero allocations, the one in figure 12-9 contains nine nonzero allocations. Which one of these two solutions is preferable? The Simplex technique (to be explored in chapter 15) assures us that if there is only one optimum, it will always be at an *extreme point*, i.e., *it will use the least number of positive valued action variables*. Thus, the solution in figure 12-8 has a much better chance of being optimal than the one in figure 12-9. From now on only the solutions with the least number of positive allocations will be checked for optimality.

How many positive allocations are enough? Note that the standard transportation tableau has m rows and n columns. Each row and each column represents one equation. However, since total supply equals total demand, *one* of these $m + n$ equations is unnecessary; $m + n - 1$ equations would be enough to describe a transportation tableau. Because of this, the general theory of simultaneous linear equations assures us that $m + n - 1$ positive allocations would be enough. A feasible solution that contains exactly $m + n - 1$ positive allocations is said to be a *basic feasi-*

400 Chapter 12

		Hospitals					Supply
		H_1	H_2	H_3	H_4	H_5	(S_i)
Blood banks	B_1	$18	$15 *100	$12 *400	$13 *400	$16	900
	B_2	$12 *100	$16	$14	$12	$ 9 *300	400
	B_3	$15 *200	$11 *300	$13 *100	$16 *200	$15	800
	Demand (D_j)	300	400	500	600	300	

Figure 12-9. *A Feasible Solution of the BB/H Problem*

ble solution. In the BB/H problem, there are $m = 3$ rows and $n = 5$ columns. Hence, a basic feasible solution contains exactly $3 + 5 - 1 = 7$ positive allocations. The solution in figure 12-8 is of this type; the one in figure 12-9 is not.

The Evaluation Process

Basic feasible solutions are important because their optimality can be judged in a straightforward manner. The current solution is optimal if none of the others is better. Thus, the test consists of:

1. Creating another feasible solution.
2. Computing the increase or decrease in the total cost.

This turns out to be a rather elementary process as long as the current solution is basic.

To create the next feasible solution, it is not necessary to start the solution process from scratch. Beginning with the current basic solution, a delivery route with current allocation of zero is identified. Then, it must be determined if making a positive allocation along that route, without disturbing its feasibility, will increase or decrease the total cost of the solution. If the cost decreases, then obviously a solution better than the current solution exists and hence the current solution is not optimal. Otherwise, the examination of *all* zero allocation delivery routes continues for possible improvement in costs. If the evaluation score of each currently empty cell indicates that a positive allocation along such routes would increase the total cost, then the current solution is in fact optimal and we have reached our goal.

We will now illustrate two methods of evaluating the cells of Vogel's solution to the BB/H problem.

The Circuit of Allocations

Referring to figure 12-8 notice that the delivery route B_2H_2 has an allocation of zero pints. Consider how the solution would change if we were to assign one pint along B_2H_2. Since the new set of allocations must be a feasible solution, we must not disturb the supply and demand constraints. In other words, the row totals and column totals must add up to 900, 400, etc.

Evaluation of B_2H_2 In order to allocate one pint along B_2H_2, we must take one pint away from some other delivery route in the second column and also in the second row. We must "rob Peter to pay Paul." B_2H_1 is such a delivery route in the second row; B_3H_2 is that delivery route in the second column. This, unfortunately, creates imbalances in the first column and third row. Allocating one extra pint along B_3H_1 resolves both of these difficulties. In other words, *we have found another feasible solution*. The changes in allocations and the corresponding cost implications are:

> 1 pint extra at B_2H_2—cost increase of \$16
> 1 pint less at B_2H_1—cost savings of \$12
> 1 pint less at B_3H_2—cost savings of \$11
> 1 pint extra at B_3H_1—cost increase of \$15

Thus, the total cost will increase by:

$$\$16 - \$12 - \$11 + \$15 = \$8$$

Both the computations and results are summarized in figure 12-10.

Figure 12-10. *Evaluating a Potential Allocation at B_2H_2*

		H_1	H_2	H_3	H_4	H_5	Supply (S_i)
				Hospitals			
	B_1	\$18	\$15	\$12 *300	\$13 *600	\$16	900
	B_2	\$12 (−) *100	\$16 (+) +8	\$14	\$12	\$ 9 *300	400
	B_3	\$15 (+) *200	\$11 (−) *400	\$13 *200	\$16	\$15	800
	Demand (D_j)	300	400	500	600	300	

Blood banks

Note that in reading figure 12-10 (and the figures that follow) the routes with currently positive allocations are indicated by an asterisk (*) to the left of the amount allocated. The arrowheads show the circuit of non-zero allocations. In that circuit, allocations are to be increased along each route which contains an enclosed plus sign (+). Similarly, (−) indicates that the corresponding allocation is to be decreased. The numbers with a plus or a minus sign attached denote the evaluation scores. A positive score equals cost increase per pint; a negative score equals cost savings per pint allocated along that route.

Evaluation of B_2H_4 Some circuits are a bit more complex. See, for instance, the circuit necessary to decide whether a positive allocation should be made along the delivery route B_2H_4. It is shown in figure 12-11. The circuit contains the routes B_2H_4, B_2H_1, B_3H_1, B_3H_3, B_1H_3, and B_1H_4. The cost of allocating one pint along B_2H_4 would be:

$12 (a pint extra at B_2H_4) − $12 (a pint saved at B_2H_1)
+ $15 (at B_3H_1) − $13 (at B_3H_3) + $12 (at B_1H_3) − $13 (at B_1H_4) = $1

This finding is displayed in figure 12-11.

As the number of rows and columns increases, the circuits can become rather complex making route evaluation a chore. But, there is another way to evaluate potential allocations which we will now examine.

The Dual Variables
You must wait till chapter 15 for a complete understanding of the theory underlying this method. Though the mathematical justification of

Figure 12-11. *Evaluating of the B_2H_4 Route*

	H_1	H_2	H_3	H_4	H_5	Supply (S_i)
			Hospitals			
B_1	$18	$15	$12 (+) *300	$13 (−) *600	$16	900
B_2	$12 (−) *100	$16	$14	$12 (+) +1	$9 *300	400
B_3	$15 (+) *200	$11 *400	$13 (−) *200	$16	$15	800
Demand (D_j)	300	400	500	600	300	

(Blood banks)

the method is rather complex, its application is straightforward. In fact, the process is completely mechanical and hence well suited for computer use.

It is enough to know now that corresponding to every linear optimization problem of interest to the decision maker, there is another optimization problem that shares the same data and is a mirror image of the original problem. If the decision maker wants to minimize some payoff, this other problem, known as the *dual problem*, has the objective of maximizing an associated payoff. *The Duality theory states that the optimum of the decision maker's problem is also the optimum of the dual problem*. In fact, both of these problems must be simultaneously feasible in order to be optimal.

The action variables of the dual problem are known as the *dual variables* of the decision maker's problem. There is one dual variable corresponding to each constraint. Since the transportation tableau has m rows and n columns (each yielding one constraint on any feasible solution), such a tableau also defines a set of $m + n$ dual variables (one for each row and column). On the other hand, only $m + n - 1$ such constraints are necessary. Hence, *one* of the $m + n$ dual variables can be arbitrarily set to equal zero. This fact helps us identify the dual variables of any tableau.

Denote the dual variable corresponding to Row i by the symbol U_i. Denote the dual variable for Column j by the symbol V_j. Set one of these dual variables to zero. The choice is arbitrary. Obtain all other dual variable values, in turn, using the following rule. If an allocation X_{ij} is positive, the corresponding unit cost C_{ij} equals the sum of U_i and V_j. Symbolically:

$$C_{ij} = U_i + V_j, \text{ whenever } X_{ij} > 0$$

In words: Obtain the complete set of dual variables by the formula:

Unit cost along a positive allocation route
= value of the dual variable in that row
+ value of the dual variable in that column.

Obtaining a Set of Dual Variables There are three rows in the BB/H tableau. The corresponding dual variables are U_1, U_2, and U_3. There are five columns and the corresponding dual variables are V_1, V_2, V_3, V_4, and V_5. Set one of these, say U_3, to zero:

$$U_3 = 0$$

That we began by setting U_3 to zero is indicated in figure 12-12 by placing a ① next to U_3. Note that we have recorded the value of U_3 in dollars. This is because the dual variables are always measured in the same units as the costs, C_{ij}.

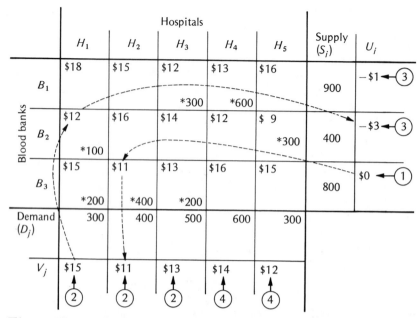

Figure 12-12. *The Dual Variables of Vogel's Solution*

U_3 is a dual variable in row 3 and it has a known value ($U_3 = 0$). Use this fact to obtain the values of the dual variables in those columns with positive allocations in row 3. In this case, columns 1, 2, and 3 have positive allocations in row 3. The corresponding unit costs are: $15 in column 1; $11 in column 2; and $13 in column 3. Hence, according to the above specified rule, the values of the column dual variables V_1, V_2, and V_3 can be obtained as follows:

$$C_{3,1} = U_3 + V_1, \quad \text{hence, } \$15 = 0 + V_1 = V_1$$
$$C_{3,2} = U_3 + V_2, \quad \text{hence, } \$11 = 0 + V_2 = V_2$$
$$C_{3,3} = U_3 + V_3, \quad \text{hence, } \$13 = 0 + V_3 = V_3$$

In other words, $V_1 = \$15$, $V_2 = \$11$, and $V_3 = \$13$. These three values became known at the second stage of computations. This fact is indicated by placing ② under V_1, V_2, and V_3.

These values of V_1, V_2, and V_3, in turn, are used to obtain the values of the dual variables in those rows with positive allocations in Columns V_1, V_2, or V_3. For instance, the B_2 and B_3 rows have positive allocations in the H_1 column. Ignore the allocation at B_3H_1, since it was already used to obtain the value of V_1. The other positive allocation, B_2H_1, has a per unit cost of $12. Hence:

$$C_{2,1} = \$12 = U_2 + V_1 = U_2 + \$15 \text{ yields: } U_2 = -\$3$$

Column H_2 contains only one positive allocation and it was already used to obtain the value of V_2. Finally, Column H_3 contains two positive allocations—at B_3H_3 and B_1H_3. The one at B_3H_3 was already used to obtain the value of V_3. The remaining allocation, B_1H_3, has a per unit cost of $12. Hence, it is used to obtain the value of U_1:

$$C_{1,3} = \$12 = U_1 + V_3 = U_1 + \$13 \text{ yields: } U_1 = -\$1$$

The U_1 and U_2 values were obtained at the third stage, as indicated by placing a 3 next to these.

Finally, the values of the column dual variables, V_4 and V_5, are obtained by using the allocations at B_1H_4 and B_2H_5. Thus, from B_1H_4:

$$\$13 = U_1 + V_4 = -\$1 + V_4 \text{ yields: } V_4 = \$14$$

The per unit cost of B_2H_5 yields:

$$\$9 = U_2 + V_5 = -\$3 + V_5, \text{ i.e., } V_5 = \$12$$

At this stage, all the dual variables have known values.

Evaluating the Zero-Allocation Routes What good is the knowledge of these dual variables? They help us find the additional cost of making positive allocations at the currently unused route, i.e., we can find an *evaluation score* for each zero-allocation route. The additional cost due to a unit allocation along a route equals the unit cost along that route *less* the value of the dual variable in that row *less* the value of the dual variable in that column. Symbolically, let E_{ij} denote the additional cost. Then:

$$E_{ij} = C_{ij} - U_i - V_j$$

For example, the route B_1H_1 has a zero allocation in the present tableau. See figure 12-12. The per unit cost along B_1H_1 is $18. The dual variable in that row, U_1, equals $-\$1$ and the dual variable in that column, V_1, equals $15. Hence, the evaluation score of B_1H_1 is:

$$E_{1,1} = C_{1,1} - U_1 - V_1$$
$$= \$18 - (-\$1) - \$15$$
$$= \$4$$

As another example, consider the zero-allocation route B_2H_3. The unit cost at B_2H_3 is $14. The dual variable in that row, U_2, equals $-\$3$ and the dual variable in that column, V_3, equals $13. Hence, the evaluation score of B_2H_3 is:

$$E_{2,3} = C_{2,3} - U_2 - V_3$$
$$= \$14 - (-\$3) - \$13$$
$$= \$4$$

You can similarly compute the evaluation scores of all zero-allocation routes for the Vogel solution of the BB/H problem. The results are shown in figure 12-13. The dollar signs ($) have been omitted in that figure to avoid the extra clutter.

		H_1	H_2	H_3	H_4	H_5	S_i	U_i
				Hospitals				
Blood banks	B_1	$18	$15	$12	$13	$16	900	−1
		+4	+5	*300	*600	+5		
	B_2	$12	$16	$14	$12	$ 9	400	−3
		*100	+8	+4	+1	*300		
	B_3	$15	$11	$13	$16	$15	800	0
		*200	*400	*200	+2	+3		
Demand (D_j)		300	400	500	600	300		
V_j		15	11	13	14	12		

Figure 12-13. *Evaluation of All Zero-Allocation Routes*

Test for Optimality

Recall that the evaluation score of a zero-allocation route equals the per unit increase in cost if a positive allocation were to be made along that route. This observation helps us check the optimality of the current solution by the following test:

> If a route with zero allocation has a positive evaluation score, that route should remain unused, i.e., its allocation should continue to be zero.
>
> If a route with zero allocation has a negative evaluation score, making positive allocation along that route would reduce the total cost of allocations. In other words, a better-than-the-current feasible solution can be obtained, i.e., the current solution is not optimal.
>
> If a route with zero allocation has an evaluation score of zero, introducing that route in the solution (i.e., making a positive allocation along that route) would neither increase nor decrease the total cost.

For example, from figure 12-13, you know that $E_{1,1} = \$4$. This means that each pint of blood sent from B_1 to H_1 increases the total cost of allocation by $4. You can also verify this statement by identifying the circuit of allocations: B_1H_1, B_1H_3, B_3H_3, and B_3H_1. In order to maintain feasibility, we would:

• Allocate 1 pint at B_1H_1

- Reduce the allocation at B_1H_3 by 1 pint
- Increase the allocation at B_3H_3 by 1 pint
- Reduce the allocation at B_3H_1 by 1 pint

Effective increase in the total cost can be computed as:

$$\$18 - \$12 + \$13 - \$15 = \$4$$

The point is that making deliveries using the route B_1H_1 would increase the total cost by \$4 and hence, the allocation at B_1H_1 should remain at zero.

Compute the evaluation score at each zero-allocation route.

   If every evaluation score is positive, the implication is that the current solution must be optimal.

   If at least one score is negative, a better solution can be found, i.e., the current one is not optimal.

   If an evaluation score is zero, another equally good solution can be found by making a positive allocation along that route.

Since every evaluation score in figure 12-13 is positive, it follows that the solution first displayed in figure 12-8 is, in fact, an optimal solution of the BB/H problem. All that remains to be done is to compute the total cost and make recommendations to the management. Since the asterisked entries in figure 12-13 represent the amounts allocated at each route, computing the total cost (TC) is straightforward:

$$
\begin{aligned}
TC = \quad & \$12 \times 100 \ (\text{at } B_2H_1) + \$15 \times 200 \ (\text{at } B_3H_1) \\
& + \$11 \times 400 \ (\text{at } B_3H_2) + \$12 \times 300 \ (\text{at } B_1H_3) \\
& + \$13 \times 200 \ (\text{at } B_3H_3) + \$13 \times 600 \ (\text{at } B_1H_4) \\
& + \$9 \times 300 \ (\text{at } B_2H_5) \\
= \quad & \$25,300
\end{aligned}
$$

This means that we should:

- Purchase from bank B_1: 300 pints for hospital H_3 and 600 for H_4
- Purchase from B_2: 100 pints for H_1 and 300 for H_5
- Purchase from B_3: 200 pints for H_1, 400 for H_2, and 200 for H_3.

This costs a total of \$25,300—the smallest cost.

BETTER SOLUTIONS AND SPECIAL CASES

That the very first feasible solution obtained by using the Vogel's approximation method turned out to be optimal is a lucky coincidence for the BB/H management. Vogel's method cannot guarantee that this would always be the case. Consequently, we should study how to obtain better solutions if the current solution turns out to be less than optimal. For this reason, we will now derive yet another solution of the BB/H problem.

The Northwest Corner Rule

Prior to the discovery of Vogel's method, this rule was generally used to obtain the first feasible solution. As the name suggests, one begins by making the maximum possible allocation in the northwest corner, i.e., in the top left-hand corner of the standard tableau. The procedure is summarized as:

> Begin at the northwest corner of the standard tableau. Allocate the smaller of the two quantities: available supply at that source and current demand at that destination. If it satisfies all of the demand, move across in the row, if it exhausts the supply, move down in the column. In the new position, allocate the smaller of the two quantities: remaining supply in that row and unsatisfied demand in that column. Repeat the process until all supplies are exhausted and all demands have been satisfied.

For example, in the BB/H tableau of figure 12-2, begin at the route B_1H_1. The supply in that row is 900 pints and the demand at H_1 is 300 pints. Hence, allocate 300 pints (the smaller of 300 and 900) at B_1H_1. The needs of the hospital H_1 having been met, move across row B_1 to the route B_1H_2. Presently, B_1 can supply $900 - 300 = 600$ pints and H_2 needs 400 pints. Hence, allocate 400 pints at B_1H_2. Adjust the supply at B_1 to $600 - 400 = 200$ pints. Since the demands of H_2 have been met, move to B_1H_3. The hospital H_3 needs 500 pints, but B_1 can only supply 200 pints. Hence, allocate 200 pints at B_1H_3 and move to B_2H_3. You can now complete the allocation process. The final allocations are shown in figure 12-14. The supply and demand entries in that figure also depict the allocation process.

Why use the northwest corner rule? Because its application is very simple. Also, if a basic feasible solution exists, the northwest corner rule will find it. Prior to the advent of more cost conscious methods, this rule also responded to the ever-present question of optimization techniques, i.e., where to begin. Obviously, since this rule makes the allocations disregarding the costs, the feasible solution is seldom optimal.

Dual Variables

That the solution in figure 12-14 is not optimal can be proved by first obtaining the values of the dual variables and then the evaluation scores. Following the rules in the preceding section, we can proceed as follows.

Arbitrarily, set $U_1 = 0$. In the first row, there are three positive allocations: at B_1H_1, B_1H_2, and B_1H_3. The corresponding unit costs are: \$18, \$15, and \$12. The values of V_1, V_2, and V_3 can be found as follows.

$$\$18 = U_1 + V_1 = \$0 + V_1 \text{ yields: } V_1 = \$18$$

Similarly, $V_2 = \$15$ and $V_3 = \$12$.

		Hospitals				Supply
	H_1	H_2	H_3	H_4	H_5	(S_i)
B_1	$18 *300	$15 *400	$12 *200	$13	$16	~~600~~ 0 ~~900~~ ~~200~~
B_2	$12	$16	$14 *300	$12 *100	$ 9	0 ~~100~~ ~~400~~
B_3	$15	$11	$13	$16 *500	$15 *300	0 ~~800~~
Demand (D_j)	~~300~~ 0	~~400~~ 0	~~500~~ ~~300~~ 0	~~600~~ ~~500~~ 0	~~300~~ 0	

(Blood banks)

Figure 12-14. *The Northwest Corner Solution of the BB/H Problem*

Now, using $V_3 = \$12$, and the unit cost, $14, of the positive allocation at B_2H_3, you can obtain U_2:

$$\$14 = U_2 + V_3 = U_2 + \$12, \text{ hence, } U_2 = \$2$$

In turn, using $U_2 = \$2$ and the unit cost, $12, of the positive allocation at B_2H_4, you can obtain V_4:

$$\$12 = U_2 + V_4 = \$2 + V_4, \text{ hence, } V_4 = \$10$$

Now, using the allocation at B_3H_4, obtain $U_3 = \$6$. Finally, using the allocation at B_3H_5, obtain $V_5 = \$9$. The results (and the discovery sequence) is shown in figure 12-15.

Evaluation Scores These are obtained using the $E_{ij} = C_{ij} - U_i - V_j$ formula discussed in the preceding section. For example, B_1H_4 has an allocation of zero pints, a unit cost of $13, and the dual variables $U_1 = \$0$ and $V_4 = \$10$. Hence, its evaluation score $E_{1,4}$ equals: $C_{1,1} - U_1 - V_4 = \$13 - \$0 - \$10 = \$3$. Similarly, B_2H_1 has a zero allocation, a unit cost of $12, and the dual variables $U_2 = \$2$ and $V_1 = \$18$. Hence, $E_{2,1} = \$12 - \$2 - \$18 = -\$8$. You can check all other evaluation scores in figure 12-15 in a similar fashion.

Deriving a Better Solution
Since a number of evaluation scores are negative, the solution in figure 12-14 is not optimal. A better-than-the-current solution can be found. But, this does not mean that we must begin at the beginning. The

Blood banks		H_1	H_2	H_3	H_4	H_5	Supply (S_i)	U_i
	B_1	$18	$15	$12	$13	$16	900	$0 ←①
		*300	*400	*200	+3	+7		
	B_2	$12	$16	$14	$12	$ 9	400	$2 ←③
		−8	−1	*300	*100	−2		
	B_3	$15	$11	$13	$16	$15	800	$6 ←⑤
		−9	−10	−5	*500	*300		
Demand (D_j)		300	400	500	600	300		
V_j		$18	$15	$12	$10	$9		
		②	②	②	④	⑥		

Hospitals (spanning H_1 through H_5)

Figure 12-15. *The Dual Variables and Evaluation Scores for the Northwest Corner Solution*

information contained in the evaluation scores of figure 12-15 can be used to find a better-than-the-current solution as follows:

Find the largest negative evaluation score and the corresponding circuit of positive allocations. Such a circuit is obtained by alternatively increasing and decreasing the size of allocations. The maximum amount that can be allocated at the currently empty route equals the most that can be taken away from any of the existing positive allocations without making any of the current allocations negative. Allocate this amount at the route with the largest negative evaluation score.

The Second Solution of the BB/H Problem The largest negative evaluation score is −10 and it occurs at $B_3 H_2$. Consequently, we will allocate some positive amount at this route. To determine the amount of allocation, first locate the circuit (figure 12-16). You can verify that the circuit of allocations is given by:

$$B_3 H_2 \rightarrow B_3 H_4 \rightarrow B_2 H_4 \rightarrow B_2 H_3 \rightarrow B_1 H_3 \rightarrow B_1 H_2$$

The allocation is to be increased at $B_3 H_2$, $B_2 H_4$, and $B_1 H_3$. It is to be decreased at $B_3 H_4$, $B_2 H_3$, and $B_1 H_2$. This is indicated by placing plus (+) and minus (−) signs in the appropriate cells. The *smallest* of the allocations with a minus sign attached is 300 pints at $B_2 H_3$. Hence, allocate 300 pints at $B_3 H_2$ and then adjust all the allocations in this circuit by adding/subtracting 300 pints where indicated. The resultant solution is shown in

Hospitals

Blood banks	H_1	H_2	H_3	H_4	H_5	Supply (S_i)
B_1	$18 *300	$15 (–) *400	$12 (+) *200	$13	$16	900
B_2	$12	$16	$14 (–) *300	$12 (+) *100	$ 9	400
B_3	$15	$11 (+)	$13	$16 (–) *500	$15 *300	800
Demand (D_j)	300	400	500	600	300	

Figure 12-16. *A Circuit of Allocations for B_3H_2*

figure 12-17. The route B_3H_2 is now an active route, whereas B_2H_3 is no longer active.

Further Improvements How much better is this solution? Since B_3H_2 had an evaluation score of -10 and since we have now allocated 300 pints along that route, it follows that this solution is cheaper by:

$$\$10 \text{ per pint} \times 300 \text{ pints} = \$3{,}000$$

than that shown in figure 12-14.

Figure 12-17. *The Second Solution of the BB/H Problem Using the Northwest Corner Rule*

Hospitals

Blood banks	H_1	H_2	H_3	H_4	H_5	Supply (S_i)
B_1	$18 *300	$15 *100	$12 *500	$13	$16	900
B_2	$12	$16	$14	$12 *400	$ 9	400
B_3	$15	$11 *300	$13	$16 *200	$15 *300	800
Demand (D_j)	300	400	500	600	300	

Is this best? You must again compute the values of the dual variables and then the evaluation scores to answer this question. If at least one evaluation score is negative, you must then find a better solution and check that it is optimal. Repeat this procedure until, at some stage, none of the evaluation scores are negative. When this happens, you have found an optimal solution. As you can see, this process yields successively better solutions always starting from the most current solution.

Degenerate Transportation Tableau

Recall that a basic feasible solution contains $m + n - 1$ positive allocations, i.e., these many delivery routes are active. A transportation tableau that yields a feasible solution with fewer than $m + n - 1$ positive allocations is said to be *degenerate*. This adjective reflects an algebraic—rather than a managerial—interpretation of the situation. Thus, the assignment problem (which is a perfectly legitimate decision problem) is said to be a degenerate case of the transportation problem. Most often, the degeneracy becomes known only when a feasible solution has been obtained. The degeneracy is removed by making "token" allocations along appropriately chosen routes. The solution is then evaluated in the usual manner.

As an illustration of degeneracy and its resolution, consider what would happen if hospital H_1 needs 200 pints of blood and if blood bank B_2 can supply a total of only 300 pints. Suppose that the rest of the circumstances remain unchanged. A feasible solution of the corresponding tableau is shown in figure 12-18. Note that it contains only six positive allocations and that solution is degenerate.

A consequence of this degeneracy becomes evident in determining the values of the dual variables. For example, starting with $U_3 = \$0$, you can obtain $V_1 = \$15$, $V_2 = \$11$, and $V_4 = \$16$. These, in turn, yield $U_1 = -\$3$ and from this you can compute that $V_3 = \$15$. However, there is no way of computing either U_2 or V_5. (Beginning with some other dual variable set to zero, you may conceivably obtain different sets of dual variable values. However, none of these will produce a complete set. The verification of this statement is left as an exercise for the reader.)

You can verify that if the second row had contained one more positive allocation, then the dual set would have been complete. This difficulty can be resolved by making a positive allocation along *any* route in the second row, e.g., at B_2H_3. However, such an allocation creates a problem in that either:

1. The solution does not remain feasible.
2. The solution does not remain the original solution—whose optimality was to be tested.

Both difficulties are resolved simultaneously by making a *token* allocation, say one drop of blood, along B_2H_3. The mathematical symbol for this kind of token allocation is ϵ (epsilon)—a very small number which is

Hospitals

Blood banks	H_1	H_2	H_3	H_4	H_5	S_i	U_i
B_1	\$18	\$15	\$12 *500	\$13 *400	\$16	900	−3 ← (3)
B_2	\$12	\$16	\$14	\$12	\$ 9 *300	300	?
B_3	\$15 *200	\$11 *400	\$13	\$16 *200	\$15	800	0 ← (1)
Demand (D_j)	200	400	500	600	300		
V_j	15 ↑ (2)	11 ↑ (2)	15 ↑ (4)	16 ↑ (2)	?		

Figure 12-18. *A Degenerate Tableau (Modified BB/H Problem)*

just barely positive. An ϵ is too small to affect the feasibility of the resultant solution; yet being positive, it enables us to determine the values of the remaining dual variables. (For instance, using a computer, we could set ϵ to be .00000001.) Figure 12-19 depicts the process of obtaining the values of the remaining dual variables as well as the corresponding evalu-

Figure 12-19. *Token Allocation for Resolution of Degeneracy*

Hospitals

Blood banks	H_1	H_2	H_3	H_4	H_5	S_i	U_i
B_1	\$18 +6	\$15 +7	\$12 *500	\$13 *400	\$16 +9	900	−3 ← (3)
B_2	\$12 −2	\$16 +6	\$14 6	\$12 −3	\$ 9 *300	300	−1 ← (5)
B_3	\$15 *200	\$11 *400	\$13 −2	\$16 *200	\$15 +5	800	0 ← (1)
Demand (D_j)	300	400	500	600	300		
V_j	15 ↑ (2)	11 ↑ (2)	15 ↑ (4)	16 ↑ (2)	10 ↑ (6)		

ation scores. You can now find an optimal solution in the usual manner. (The details are left as an exercise in the iterative process.)

Evaluation Score Zero

Thus far, we have concentrated on interpreting positive or negative evaluation scores only. This is mainly because the thrust of the discussion so far was on finding better solutions. We will now assume that an optimal solution has been found. The evaluation scores for this set of allocations contain no routes with negative scores, but they can contain routes with zero scores. The implication is obvious. Allocation along such routes would neither increase nor decrease the total cost. In other words, we have found two or more optimal solutions. In fact, if fractional allocations are meaningful in the corresponding decision problem, a zero score implies finding infinitely many solutions.

To illustrate the situation, reconsider the BB/H problem. Assume that the unit cost along B_2H_4 has become \$11 per pint. Under these conditions, figure 12-20 shows an optimal solution and the corresponding evaluation scores. Not surprisingly, route B_2H_4 has evaluation score 0. This means that B_2H_4 can be an active delivery route in an optimal solution. You can verify that:

1. The B_2H_4 evaluation circuit consists of B_2H_4, B_1H_4, B_1H_3, B_3H_3, B_3H_1, and B_2H_1.
2. Maximum allocation along B_2H_4 can be 100 pints.

Figure 12-20. *An Optimal Solution of a Modified BB/H Problem and Its Evaluation Scores*

		Hospitals						
		H_1	H_2	H_3	H_4	H_5	S_j	U_i
Blood banks	B_1	\$18 +4	\$15 +5	\$12 (+)←(−) *300	\$13 (−) *600	\$16 +5	900	−1
	B_2	\$12 (−) *100	\$16 +8	\$14 +4	\$11 (+) 0	\$9 *300	400	−3
	B_3	\$15 (+) *200	\$11 *400	\$13 (−) *200	\$16 +2	\$15 +3	800	0
Demand (D_j)		300	400	500	600	300		
V_j		15	11	13	14	12		

3. When 100 pints are allocated along $B_2 H_4$, route $B_2 H_1$ becomes inactive (i.e., has a zero allocation).

These two optimal solutions are displayed in table 12-5.

Given these two extreme solutions, many more optimal solutions can be derived. In fact, let p denote a fraction between 0 and 1 ($0 \le p \le 1$).

Table 12-5 *Two Basic Optimal Solutions*

	NUMBER OF PINTS ALLOCATED	
DELIVERY ROUTE	SOLUTION A	SOLUTION B
$B_2 H_1$	100	0
$B_3 H_1$	200	300
$B_3 H_2$	400	400
$B_3 H_3$	200	100
$B_1 H_3$	300	400
$B_1 H_4$	600	500
$B_2 H_4$	0	100
$B_2 H_5$	300	300

Then, every solution of type:

$$p \times \text{Solution A} + (1 - p) \times \text{Solution B}$$

is also an optimal solution. For example, if $p = .25$, then the allocation along $B_2 H_1$ equals $(.25)(100) + (.75)(0) = 25$ pints, that along $B_3 H_1$ equals $(.25) (200) + (.75) (300) = 275$ pints, etc.

Why bother computing a variety of optimal solutions? For at least two reasons. First, it allows management to exercise a great deal of flexibility in allocating resources. Also, if in the future, some of the routes become unacceptable, then the existence of multiple solutions may be useful in reducing the economic impact of such unacceptability.

ADDITIONAL FORMULATIONS

The transportation model can be used to formulate a variety of planning situations by correctly identifying the sources and destinations—it is not necessary to physically transport anything. We will outline a few such situations in this section.

Production Planning with Overtime

A manufacturer is planning the production of a single product over the next T months in response to a *known* demand of D_j units in the jth month ($j = 1, 2, \ldots, T$). (The assumption that D_j is known is reasonably valid only in the short term. Most such models, also known as "aggregate planning" models, work with small values of T, say $T \le 12$. When $T = 12$, one has an annual plan, with $T = 3$, one has a quarterly plan, etc.) In the ith month, the manufacturer can produce up to a_i units with regular labor and b_i units with overtime labor. It costs C_R dollars to manufacture 1 unit during regular time, and C_o dollars with overtime. It costs C_S dollars to store 1 unit in the company's warehouse for 1 month. *Backordering is not permitted*, i.e., if $i < j$, then the demand in month i cannot be satisfied with production in month j. For example, January's demand cannot be met with production in February or March of that year. The manufacturer wishes to know the optimal values of:

> X_{ij} = the number of units to be produced with regular time labor in month i for meeting the demand in month j

> Y_{ij} = the corresponding number produced with overtime labor (Both X_{ij} and Y_{ij} are meaningful only if $i \leq j$.)

Note that this problem can be formulated as a transportation problem if we identify the *source* to be the month of production and the *destination* to be the month of consumption. Furthermore, the condition that i should not exceed j is equivalent to the statement that route $i \rightarrow j$ is forbidden if $i > j$. Formally, this can be achieved by assigning an exorbitantly large cost, M, whenever $i > j$. Thus define:

$$C_R^* = \begin{cases} C_R, \text{ when } i \leq j \\ M, \text{ when } i > j \end{cases}$$

Similarly, define:

$$C_o^* = \begin{cases} C_o, \text{ when } i \leq j \\ M, \text{ when } i > j \end{cases}$$

Note also that the cost of storing a unit is 0, if $i > j$. Thus, define:

$$C_s^* = \begin{cases} C_s, \text{ when } i \leq j \\ 0, \text{ when } i > j \end{cases}$$

With these conventions, we can proceed as follows. The total cost is the sum of the costs of regular time production, overtime production, as well as storage. The objective is to minimize this total cost, Z. You can verify that

$$Z = \sum_{i=1}^{T} \sum_{j=1}^{T} [\underbrace{C_R^* X_{ij}}_{\substack{\text{Regular Time} \\ \text{Production}}} + \underbrace{C_o^* Y_{ij}}_{\substack{\text{Overtime} \\ \text{Production}}} + \underbrace{C_s^* (j - i) (X_{ij} + Y_{ij})}_{\substack{\text{Storage for } j - i \\ \text{Months}}}]$$

The formulation will be complete when we represent the constraints. These are:

1. Regular time production in month i cannot exceed a_i:

$$\sum_{j=1}^{T} X_{ij} \leq a_i$$

2. The overtime production month i cannot exceed b_i:

$$\sum_{j=1}^{T} Y_{ij} \leq b_i$$

3. The demand in each month must be met:

$$\sum_{i=1}^{T} (X_{ij} + Y_{ij}) \geq D_j$$

Furthermore, if the final inventory equals zero, then we would also have:

$$\sum_{i=1}^{T} (a_i + b_i) = \sum_{j=1}^{T} D_j$$

The resemblance to the standard transportation model is now complete.

Transshipment Problems

Thus far, we assumed that each source is *directly* connected to the ultimate destination. In many circumstances, however, this may not be the case. For example, factories often send the product to warehouses or regional centers, which in turn send it to retail outlets. In such cases, the warehouses or regional centers are neither the sources nor really the ultimate destinations. They are technically known as the *transshipment points*. This nomenclature describes their true function—to act as facilitators of product flows.

We will now illustrate how a transshipment problem can be represented by a transportation model. See figure 12-21. Assume in that figure that F_1 and F_2 are two factories with capacities to produce S_1 and S_2 units per month. Each is a net "exporter" of goods. The factories can send these units to warehouses W_1 and/or W_2. Warehouse W_1 also acts as a retail store with a monthly demand of D_4 units. That it is a net "importer" is shown by placing a negative sign in front of D_4. Warehouse W_2, however, is a true transshipment point—it neither produces nor demands units. This is shown by placing a "0" next to it. R_1, R_2, and R_3 are three retail outlets with demand levels D_1, D_2, and D_3, respectively. Their needs are satisfied by warehouses W_1 and W_2. The *direct costs* of transporting a unit are shown along each arc of the network.

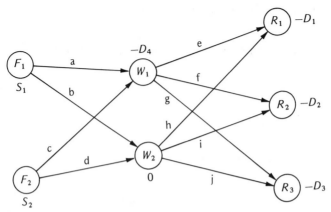

Figure 12-21. *A Transshipment Network*

The rationale behind this method is summed up as follows. A transshipment point acts as both a destination for the primary sources and as a source for the ultimate destinations. To prevent shipments between points that are not directly connected, exorbitantly high costs (M) must be assigned to such routes. Finally, there must be a buffer stock to ensure nonnegative flows along each route. Thus, we can construct the equivalent transportation model as follows.

1. Reserve a row for each source. Assign it the specified supply capacity. Thus, F_1 and F_2 are assigned capacities S_1 and S_2, respectively.
2. Reserve a column for each destination. Assign it the specified demand. Thus, R_1, R_2, and R_3 are assigned demands D_1, D_2, and D_3, respectively.
3. Reserve both a row *and* a column for each transshipment point. Let B be the sum of stocks available at all points. Also, let T_k be net stock position of the kth transshipment point. ($T_k = 0$, if pure transshipment point, positive if net exporter, and negative otherwise.) Thus, $T(W_1) = -D_4$ and $T(W_2) = 0$. Then assign the supply capacity of $B + T_k$ and the demand capacity of B to the kth transshipment point.
4. Assign the *direct cost* from a row to a column only if the corresponding direct link exists. Otherwise, assign cost M, an exorbitantly large number. Also, the cost of transporting from a transshipment point to itself should be set to zero.

The results of applying these rules to the network of figure 12-21 are shown in table 12-6. The quantity B in the above formulation is known as the *buffer stock* and it is introduced to ensure nonnegative flows along all arcs. Note also that there can be multistage *transshipments*. The above rules are completely general.

Table 12-6 *The Transportation Model of a Transshipment Network*

FROM	TO					SUPPLY CAPACITY
	W_1	W_2	R_1	R_2	R_3	
F_1	a	b	M	M	M	S_1
F_2	c	d	M	M	M	S_2
W_1	O	M	e	f	g	$B - D_4$
W_2	M	O	h	i	j	B
Demand	B	B	D_1	D_2	D_3	

Other Situations

A transportation or a "near transportation" model can be formulated in numerous other situations. By "near" we mean that either the decision variables must obey additional constraints, or the transportation costs are obtained as the sum of fixed and variable charges. The former situation was discussed at the end of chapter 10 in the context of accounting assignments. See, for example, problem 24 in chapter 10, as well as the articles by Balas, et al. (1964), Glover, et al. (1974), Klingman, et al. (1975), and Summers (1972). The latter results when, for example, a delivery route must be established prior to making shipments along that route.

Thus, in such cases, there are in fact two decisions: whether to open a delivery route; and, if so, how much to ship along it. The reader is encouraged to consult several of the references cited at the end of this chapter to gain additional insight into the formulation and solution technology of transportation models.

SELECTED READINGS

BALAS, E. and IVANESCU (HAMMER), P. L. "On the Generalized Transportation Problem." *Management Science* 11 (1964), pp. 188–202.

DAELLENBACH, H. G. "A Model of a Multi-Product Two-Stage Inventory System with Limited Intermediate Bulk Storage Capacity." *Management Science* 23 (1977), pp. 1314–1320.

GLOVER, F. and ROSS, G. T. "Finding Equivalent Transportation Formulations for Constrained Transportation Problems." *Naval Research Logistics Quarterly* 21 (1974), pp. 247–254.

HEFLEY, G. L. and BAIR, B. O. "Fixed Charge Transportation Problem: A Survey." Presented to the 43rd ORSA National Meeting in Milwaukee, Wisconsin (1973).

KENNINGTON, J. and UNGER, E. "A New Branch-and-Bound Algorithm for the Fixed-Charge Transportation Problem." *Management Science* 22 (1976), pp. 1116–1126.

KHUMAWALA, B. M. "An Efficient Branch-Bound Algorithm for the Warehouse Location Problem." *Management Science* 18 (1972), pp. B718–B729.

KLINGMAN, D, and RUSSELL, R. "Solving Constrained Transportation Problems." *Operations Research* 23 (1975), pp. 91–106.

ORGLER, Y. *Cash Management: Methods and Models*. Belmont, Calif.: Wadsworth Publishing Company, Inc., 1970.

SALKIN, G. R. and KORNBLUTH, J. S. H. *"Linear Programming in Financial Planning."* London: Haymarket Publishing Ltd., 1973.

SHRINIVASAN, V. "Benefit-Cost Analysis of Coding Techniques for the Primal Transportation Algorithm." *Journal of the Association of Computing Machinery* 20 (1973), pp. 194–213.

SUMMERS, E. L. "The Audit Staff Assignment Problem: A Linear Programming Analysis." *Accounting Review* 47 (1972), pp. 443–453.

WAGNER, H. M. *Principles of Management Science: With Applications to Executive Decisions*. Englewood Cliffs, NJ: Prentice-Hall, Inc., 1975.

WAGNER, H. M. "The Lower Bounded and Partial Upper Bounded Distribution Model." *Naval Research Logistics Quarterly* 20 (1973), pp. 140–151.

ZOLTNERS, A. A. "Integer Programming Models for Sales Territory Alignment to Maximize Profit." *Journal of Marketing Research* 13 (1976), pp. 426–430.

PROBLEM SET 12
OPTIMAL SOURCE-DESTINATION PAIRS

*1. You have seen the mathematical description of a general linear model in chapter 10. Compare it with the description of a transportation model. Then identify the additional constraints which convert a general LP model to a transportation model. Identify further constraints which make it an assignment model.

2. Explain the statement that an assignment model is necessarily a degenerate transportation model.

3. Formulate the BB/H problem as a linear optimization problem.

4. Standardize the following tableaus.

(a) The cell entries are opportunity costs.

	TO				
FROM	1	2	3	4	SUPPLY
A	63	60	37	48	600
B	49	55	35	43	400
C	55	60	49	50	200
Demands	350	400	300	250	

(b) The entries corresponding to each route are profits per unit delivered along the route.

			TO		
FROM	A	B	C	D	SUPPLY
1	49	53	61	63	5,000
2	53	49	55	70	7,000
3	57	51	52	67	9,000
Demand	3,000	4,000	7,000	5,000	

5. Find the optimal allocations for the distribution problem shown in table 12-3. Compute the total cost of the optimal assignments. Compare it with the cost of the solution in figure 12-13. Explain the difference in the two costs.

6. The new administrator of hospital H_1 cannot get along with the president of bank B_2. In other words, B_2H_1 is not an acceptable route. Solve the BB/H problem with this restriction. How much more costly is the new optimum as compared with that shown in figure 12-13?

7. Find the optimal production schedule for the MMM company's problem shown in figure 12-5. Then compute their optimal profit.

8. Beginning with the solution in figure 12-19 show all the intermediate tableaus necessary to derive the optimal solution for the BB/H problem.

9. What is the optimal set of allocations and the associated minimum cost of the BB/H problem if the blood banks can supply 900, 300, and 800 pints respectively and the hospitals need 200, 400, 500, 600, and 300 pints respectively?

10. The Rent-It-Here-Leave-It-There (RIHLIT) company has its truck rental shops in 7 cities. Presently, it finds that the shops in 4 of these cities, A, B, C, and D, experience a shortage of 10, 14, 20 and 12 trucks, respectively, whereas the shops in cities E, F, and G have an excess supply of 18, 24, and 14 trucks, respectively. (Presumably, more families move into E, F, or G than in the other direction.) The RIHLIT company must bring these excess trucks back so as to stay in business. It is known from past experience that the costs of bringing the empty trucks back are as those shown in the adjoining table. Determine the optimal allocation of surplus trucks.

			TO	
FROM	A	B	C	D
E	$50	$70	$75	$65
F	58	50	68	55
G	65	43	48	45

11. The Comfortable Homes Inc. must purchase fuel for heating each of the four apartment buildings owned by the company. The company has estimated that it needs 3, 4, 7, and 5 thousand gallons of fuel each month. Three suppliers: Johnson, Rousseau and Williams can each supply 5, 7, and 8

thousand gallons each month. Their per gallon delivered prices are shown in the adjoining table. Find how much fuel should be bought from which dealer.

| | APARTMENT | | | | SUPPLIES |
DEALER	1	2	3	4	(GALLONS)
Johnson	.49	.53	.61	.63	5,000
Rousseau	.53	.49	.55	.70	7,000
Williams	.57	.51	.52	.67	8,000
Demands (Gallons)	3,000	4,000	7,000	5,000	

12. An electronics firm has a production plant in each of the three cities: Chelsea, Prairie, and Saxony. It has a customer outlet in each of the three cities: Boston, Chicago, and New York. The cost in dollars of transporting a receiver from each plant to each outlet is shown below. That table also shows

| | OUTLETS | | | |
PLANTS	BOSTON	CHICAGO	NEW YORK	CAPACITY
Chelsea	4.50	7.00	5.50	500
Prairie	5.50	4.00	6.50	400
Saxony	7.00	5.00	8.00	600
Demand	500	400	500	

customer demands at each outlet and production capacities of each plant. The unit production costs are $100, $110, and $95 at the plants in Chelsea, Prairie, and Saxony, respectively. Obtain a minimum cost distribution plan.

13. Because of the local market conditions, the receivers in problem 12 above sell for $130, $140, and $120 at Boston, Chicago, and New York, respectively. Also, the demand at the Chicago outlet has increased to 500 receivers. Find the most profitable distribution plan.

14. The Kneehigh Company manufactures quality slacks. Each of the three production plants can produce any of four kinds of slacks. Plant 1 can produce 40,000 slacks; Plant 2, 50,000; and Plant 3, 60,000. The company has orders for 25,000 slacks of Style 1; 40,000 of Style 2; 50,000 of Style 3; and 35,000 of Style 4. Though workers in each plant can produce a slack of any style, their efficiencies differ. The adjoining table shows the per unit production costs in dollars. The selling prices of slacks of each style are also shown in that table. Find the most profitable production plan. How much is the net profit?

		SLACK TYPES		
PLANT	1	2	3	4
1	$6.	$10.	$14.	$11.
2	7.5	9.	12.	12.
3	8.	8.5	13.	10.
Selling Price	10	13	17	11

15. A plywood supplier has contracts to supply 4' × 8' sheets of 3/4″ plywood to each of the three construction projects. He has warehouses at three locations. The adjoining table shows the per sheet transportation costs from warehouses to projects, the stock at each warehouse and the needs of each project. What is the minimum cost of transportation?

	PROJECT			WAREHOUSE
WAREHOUSE	1	2	3	CAPACITY
1	$ .70	$ .60	$ .90	4,000
2	1.05	1.30	.75	3,000
3	.95	.90	1.15	2,000
Project Requirements	3,000	3,500	2,500	

16. *Continuation of problem 15.* Because of personnel conflicts, trucks carrying plywood from Warehouse 1 will not make deliveries at Project 2.

   a. Derive the minimum transportation cost.

   b. What is the "cost of conflicts"?

*17. Consider the following problem in financial planning. A small firm must raise the necessary capital through one or more of the following means.

   • Float corporate bonds worth up to $50,000 at 6 percent annual interest.
   • Issue preferred stocks worth $150,000 by paying a dividend of 7.5 percent annually.
   • Issue common stocks worth $200,000 where the dividend must be 9 percent per year.
   • Borrow $150,000 from a commercial bank at 8.5 percent annual interest.
   • Mortgage some of the equipment for $100,000 at 10 percent annual interest.

   Capital is needed for several projects:

   • Purchase new equipment and upgrade the working conditions. Estimated cost is $175,000. The benefit due to modernizing is expected to be

12 percent increase in productivity, i.e., return on investment (ROI) is 12 percent.

- Buy patents for up to $150,000. Expected ROI would be 15 percent
- Buy controlling interest in a noncompeting industry. This would cost $300,000 and would result in 18 percent more profit.
- Send selected employees to management training programs at a cost of $75,000 with anticipated increase in productivity of 16 percent.
- Invest in new product research with a budget of $100,000. The expected ROI is 10 percent.

The company has a one-year planning horizon. Recommend a financial plan, i.e., decide how the funds should flow to maximize total net profit.

*18. Reconsider any transportation model whose optimal solution you know. Verify that this solution would remain optimal (though, of course, the total cost would change), if for *any* constant, k, the unit costs were to change from C_{ij} to $C_{ij} + k$. Can you prove it mathematically? Explain why this is not true for the general linear models.

19. You are in charge of obtaining a most profitable production plan given the following data. The company has a production capacity to manufacture 30,000 units of a nonperishable product in the Spring and Fall of this year. Due to the days lost to sickness, bad weather, vacations, and holidays, however, the company's production capacity will be only 25,000 units in the Summer or Winter. The demand for this product is also seasonal. In fact, the marketing department has forecasted the sales to be 25,000 in Spring, 40,000 in Summer, 30,000 in Fall, and only 15,000 in Winter of this year. The per unit production costs have been rising due to inflation, though these are also influenced by the seasonal factors. Specifically, the production costs are estimated to be: $80, 85, 82, and 86 in Spring, Summer, Fall, and Winter of this year. Any excess production can be stored in the warehouse but at a cost of $10 per unit per season. Meeting one season's demand in following seasons, i.e., backlogging, is not allowed. A unit sells for $120, $140, $125, and $105 in Spring, Summer, Fall, and Winter, respectively. Initial inventory is 10,000, and final inventory must also be 10,000. What will the maximum profit be according to your plan?

20. A manufacturer must derive the "second quarter production plan" for a nonperishable item on the basis of the following information. The marketing department has forecast the demand to be 5,000, 8,000, and 7,000 in April, May, and June, respectively. There are 12,000, 13,000, and 11,000 regular production hours in April, May, and June, respectively at $6 per hour. It takes two person-hours of labor and $6 worth of materials to manufacture one unit of the product. Obviously, the forecasted demand cannot be met using regular labor only. The company has therefore decided to use up to 3,000 hours of work each month at overtime rates of $10 per hour. Excess production in any month can be stored at a cost of $3 per unit per month. Backordering is not permitted. Initial inventory is zero and final inventory must also be zero. Derive the minimal cost production plan.

*21. Reconsider problem 20. Suppose that backordering for up to two months is permitted. However, due to increased administrative costs as well as potential loss of goodwill, the cost of backordering is $2 per unit for one month and $7 per unit for two months. What would the least cost production plan be?

*22. A mine operator has two mines located at A and B from where he ships ores to the processing plants located at C and D. The final product is shipped to stores E, F, and G. The mines can extract 500 and 700 tons of ore daily at a cost of $4 and $5 per ton, respectively. The shipping cost per ton are $3 from A to C, $5 from A to D, $4 from B to C, and $7 from B to D. The processing at plants C and D costs $15 and $18 per ton of ore. The shipping costs per ton-equivalent of ore from the plants are $10: C → E, $12: C → F, $16: C → G, $13: D → E, $15: D → F, and $11: D → G. The daily demands at stores E, F, and G are for 450, 300, 350 ton-equivalents of ore, respectively. Derive the optimal production-and-shipment plan.

*Note: Though all of the problems in this set can be done manually, a fully interactive software package, TRANSPO, is available from the author for solving these problems on a computer.

13

Network Models

Network Terminology
The Minimal Spanning Tree Problem
The Shortest Route Problem
The Maximal Flow Problem
Network Formulations
Selected Readings
Problem Set 13: Optimization in Networks

Chapter 5 examined some network problems with its discussion of PERT networks. The assignment, traveling salesman, and transportation models of the preceding chapters can also be represented by networks. This chapter concludes the study of networks with three additonal network problems and their managerial applications.

NETWORK TERMINOLOGY

A network is a collection of *nodes* and the *arcs* connecting pairs of nodes. The networks to be studied in this chapter are said to be *connected* in the sense that we can always find at least one way of proceeding from one node to any other node in that network. The resulting set of connections constitutes a *path*. The distance from one node to its neighbor is the *length of the associated arc*. The *length of a path* is obtained by adding the lengths of the associated arcs. The arcs are also called branches, links, or edges. The path is also known as a route or a chain. Occasionally, it is possible to start from some node and return there through a sequence of intermediate nodes—this path constitutes a *cycle*. The traveling salesman problem, discussed earlier, finds the complete cycle of the shortest

426

length. In some problems, each branch has a *capacity*, i.e., an upper limit on the amount of flow that can be handled through that branch. These capacities need not be identical in each direction. For example, to accommodate the specific traffic flow, highway planners might open four lanes in one direction and only two in the opposite direction at certain times of the day. Finally, a node might be called a *source* or *origin* if the flows are always moving away from that node. Conversely, a node is a *sink* or *destination* if all flows are directed towards that node.

Using this notation and suitable interpretations of nodes, arcs, lengths and capacities, we will now examine three decision problems in networks.

THE MINIMAL SPANNING TREE PROBLEM

Even though this problem could be solved by complete enumeration, we will use it to illustrate the standard algorithm for solving such problems. If there are n nodes, this algorithm finds the optimum in exactly $n - 1$ steps.

The Ecology Associates Inc.

A progressive real estate firm has acquired a virgin forest for developing a planned community. They envision building each structure in this community—a hospital, an industrial complex, recreation facilities, supermarkets, schools, private homes, and apartments—with the least possible ecological damage. In keeping with that philosophy, the company wants to connect all the planned sites with the smallest possible road surface.

Figure 13-1 (not drawn to scale) shows the locations of seven important sites in the community, the proposed set of roads connecting these sites, and the estimated intersite distances in miles. Note that even though the potential roads are shown on the map, the company does not wish to in fact build all roads. It wants to connect all the sites using the least amount of road surface.

Figure 13-1. *A Proposed Network of Roads*

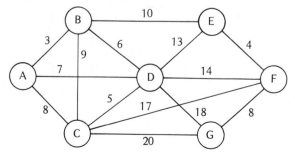

This is the typical problem where the minimal spanning tree algorithm is useful. In the standard terminology of network models, sites A through G constitute the *nodes*. The connecting roads such as A $\longleftrightarrow$ B are called the *arcs* or *branches*, and the entire diagram is said to form a *tree*. The minimal spanning tree problem consists of finding the set of arcs that connect all nodes with least possible total length.

The Algorithm

The minimal spanning tree algorithm is a sequence of three steps, each of which is illustrated by solving the Ecology Associates problem:

Step 1. Prepare a table of direct distances. Let d_{ij} denote the distance between node i and node j. If these two nodes are planned to be connected by an arc, read d_{ij} from the diagram showing the nodes. Otherwise, set d_{ij} to be M—a very large number.

Select any one node and mark the corresponding row by placing an asterisk (*) to the left of it. Cross out the corresponding column.

For example, nodes A and B of figure 13-1 are connected by the arc AB. Hence, from that figure, $d(AB) = 3$. Similarly, you can read that $d(CF) = 17$. On the other hand, nodes B and F are not connected by an arc—no road is planned to connect B and F *directly*. Hence, set $d(BF) = M$. Obviously, for each node i, $d_{ij} = 0$. Obviously also, for each pair of nodes i and j, $d_{ij} = d_{ji}$. In other words, the distance matrix is symmetric. We will *arbitrarily* choose node A to be the initial node, and mark it by an asterisk (*). The corresponding column has been crossed out.

Table 13-1 shows the results. In that table, the "from nodes" are shown in the left-hand column, and the "to nodes" are shown in the top row. The reason for crossing out the selected column should be obvious. Node A is obviously connected with itself and hence it is unnecessary to consider it any further. The next step indicates where to go from here.

Table 13-1 *Direct Distances among the Planned Sites*

	FROM NODE			TO NODE			
		A	B	C	D	E	F	G
*A		0	3	8	7	M	M	M
B		3	0	9	6	10	M	M
C		8	9	0	5	M	17	20
D		7	6	5	0	13	14	18
E		M	10	M	13	0	4	M
F		M	M	17	14	4	0	8
G		M	M	20	18	M	8	0

This column is no longer open.

*Initial Node

Step 2. Consider *all* the marked rows. Find the smallest distance and box it in. The corresponding node is now connected.

For example, now only row A has been marked. The smallest element in that row is 3 and it occurs in column B. Hence, connect node B to node A, i.e., plan to build the road from A to B. In figure 13-2, this is indicated by the boxed entry, $\boxed{3}$. We must now decide on any further connections from A and/or B.

Step 3. Mark the row containing the newly connected node. Cross out the corresponding column. As long as at least one column in the table of direct distances is open for examination, return to Step 2. Otherwise, you must have found all connections. Compute the total length of this tree and then stop.

From node	A	B	C	D	E	F	G
* A	0	3	8	7	M	M	M
* B	3	0	9	6	10	M	M
C	8	9	0	5	M	17	20
D	7	6	5	0	13	14	18
E	M	10	M	13	0	4	M
F	M	M	17	14	4	0	8
G	M	M	20	18	M	8	0

(Column header "To node" spans columns C, D, E, F, G)

Figure 13-2. *The First Connection (A↔B)*

For the Ecology Associates problem, node B has been connected (to node A). Mark row B, and cross out column B. Columns C through G continue to be open. Hence, return to Step 2. The progress thus far is depicted in figure 13-2.

The remaining connections are obtained by repeating Steps 2 and 3 as long as at least one column is open, i.e., as long as at least one node remains disconnected. For example, figure 13-2 shows that rows A and B are marked and that columns C through G are open. In other words, 2 rows × 5 columns = 10 distances are to be examined. The smallest of these distances, 6, occurs at the intersection of row B and column D. Hence, connect node D to node B.

D is the newly connected node. Cross out column D, and mark row D. Those entries in columns C, E, F, and G which lie in row A, B, or D are now examined. The smallest entry, 5, lies at the intersection of row D and column C. Hence, connect the node C to D.

You can now continue to find all of the remaining connections. The connections, the order in which these are found, and the length of each branch are shown in table 13-2. The resultant minimal spanning tree is shown in figure 13-3.

Table 13-2 *Locating the Branches*

CONNECTION NUMBER	NODE	BRANCH	DISTANCE
1	A	—	—
2	B	A ↔ B	3
3	D	B ↔ D	6
4	C	C ↔ D	5
5	E	B ↔ E	10
6	F	E ↔ F	4
7	G	F ↔ G	8

Total 36

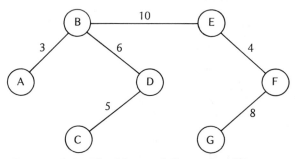

Figure 13-3. *The Minimal Spanning Tree*

Comments

Since at each stage of the search, we looked for the smallest distance from the connected to the unconnected nodes, it follows that the resultant tree is of the smallest total length. The complete tree can always be found using exactly $n - 1$ arcs. In the Ecology Associates problem, the distance was measured in miles. Alternatively, we could measure the distance in terms of costs or opportunity losses.

It is important that the cost used in this algorithm is the construction cost. Similarly, the distance is in terms of road surface. The resultant tree is not necessarily the best with respect to operating costs or traveling miles. For example, to travel from node C to node G, one would have to travel a distance of $5 + 6 + 10 + 4 + 8 = 33$ miles, rather than the direct distance of 20 miles! If reducing travel or operating costs (rather than construction or set-up costs) is your objective, it is better to use the shortest route model which we will now discuss.

THE SHORTEST ROUTE PROBLEM

We will illustrate the process of finding the shortest path through a network by finding such a path from node A to G of the Ecology Associates network shown in figure 13-1. As an example the general applicability of this technique, we will then find the optimal schedule for equipment replacement using this technique.

The Algorithm

Refer again to the network of nodes and arcs shown in figure 13-1. Assume that all the roads shown in that figure will be built. In that case, what is the shortest route from node A to all other nodes?

Begin by constructing the associated table of direct distances. Table 13-1 is the result. From this point on, the shortest route algorithm differs from the minimal spanning tree algorithm.

Step 1. Label the initial node with a permanent value of zero. Label all other nodes with a temporary value of M.

For the nodes in figure 13-1, it follows that node A has a permanent value of 0. Nodes B through G have the value M. Symbolically, denote the length of the path by 1. Then:

$$1_A = 0$$

All this means is that we have begun the journey at node A. Since we have not gone anywhere, the length 1_A is zero. M denotes the upper limit on distances to nodes B, C, . . . , G. Next, we will find the node closest to A.

Step 2. Consider each node that does not yet have a permanent label. Compute the sum of the label on the latest permanent node and the direct distance from there to the current node. Compare this number with the current tentative label of the node in question. The smaller of these two numbers is the new tentative label of that node. If the tentative label of a node has been changed, identify the preceding node which enabled this change.

Now, only the node A has a permanent label and it is known to be zero. Using the direct distances shown in table 13-1, we can therefore find new tentative labels for nodes B through G. The process is shown in table 13-3. It follows that the labels on nodes B, C, and D have changed and that in each case, the preceding node is A.

The smallest of the new labels is 3 for node B. In other words, we can reach from A to B by following the path which is 3 miles long. Can there

Table 13-3 *Shortest Route to B*

TENTATIVELY LABELED NODE	CURRENT LABEL	LENGTH COMPUTATIONS	NEW LABEL	PRECEDING NODE
B	M	$1_A + d_{AB} = 0 + 3 = 3$	3	A ←
C	M	$1_A + d_{AC} = 0 + 8 = 8$	8	A
D	M	$1_A + d_{AD} = 0 + 7 = 7$	7	A
E	M	$1_A + d_{AE} = 0 + M = M$	M	—
F	M	$1_A + d_{AF} = 0 + M = M$	M	—
G	M	$1_A + d_{AG} = 0 + M = M$	M	—

be a shorter route from A to B? The answer is no, since any other path from A to B would have to go via nodes C through G, each of which already has a higher label than that of B. Obviously, then, *the shortest route* from A to B is 3 miles long. We can now store this information by creating a new permanent label for B. Symbolically:

$$l_B = 3$$

This reasoning can be summed up as follows:

> *Step 3.* Declare the smallest of the new tentative labels to be the latest permanent label. The corresponding node is permanently labeled. If all nodes have been permanently labeled, go to Step 4. Otherwise, return to Step 2.

In other words, Steps 2 and 3 constitute a loop. By repeatedly following these steps, we will successively identify new permanently labeled nodes. Now, nodes C through G do not have permanent labels. Hence, we must return to Step 2. The latest permanent node is B and its label is 3. Using the direct distances of table 13-1, specifically those shown in row B of that table, you can obtain the new tentative labels for nodes C through G. Table 13-4 shows the process.

Table 13-4 *Finding the Permanent Preceding Node of D*

TENTATIVELY LABELED NODE	CURRENT LABEL	LENGTH COMPUTATIONS	NEW LABEL	PRECEDING NODE
C	8	$l_B + d_{BC} = 3 + 9 = 12$	8	A
D	7	$l_B + d_{BD} = 3 + 6 = 9$	7	A ←
E	M	$l_B + d_{BE} = 3 + 10 = 13$	13	B
F	M	$l_B + d_{BF} = 3 + M = M$	M	—
G	M	$l_B + d_{BG} = 3 + M = M$	M	—

The current label of C is 8. The sum of the legs A→B and B→C is $3 + 9 = 12$. Hence, the new tentative label of C continues to be 8. Similarly, the new label of D continues to be 7. The smallest of all the new labels is 7 and the associated node is D. Hence, according to Step 3, D is the newly permanent node with a permanent label of 7. Since the nodes C, E, F, and G are yet to be labeled, we must return to Step 2. Table 13-5 shows the rest of the process.

At this stage, each node has been permanently labeled and its permanent preceding node has been found. The next step shows how to identify the shortest route to each node from node A.

> *Step 4.* To find the shortest route to a given node, find the node's permanent predecessor. Then, find *its* permanent predecessor. Continue until you reach the initial node. The resultant route is the shortest.

Table 13-5 *Finding the Permanent Preceding Nodes for the Nodes C Through G*

ITERATION NUMBER	TENTATIVELY LABELED NODE	CURRENT LABEL	LENGTH COMPUTATIONS	NEW LABEL	PRECEDING NODE
3	C	8	$l_D + d_{DC} = 7 + 5 = 12$	8	A ←
	E	13	$l_D + d_{DE} = 7 + 13 = 20$	13	B
	F	M	$l_D + d_{DF} = 7 + 14 = 21$	21	D
	G	M	$l_D + d_{DG} = 7 + 18 = 25$	25	D
4	E	13	$l_C + d_{CE} = 8 + M = M$	13	B ←
	F	21	$l_C + d_{CF} = 8 + 17 = 25$	21	D
	G	25	$l_C + d_{CG} = 8 + 20 = 28$	25	D
5	F	21	$l_E + d_{EF} = 13 + 4 = 17$	17	E ←
	G	25	$l_E + d_{EG} = 13 + M = M$	25	D
6	G	25	$l_F + d_{FG} = 17 + 8 = 25$	25	D or F

For example, the permanent predecessor of G is either D or F. The permanent predecessor of F is E, that of E is B, and that of B is A. Hence, tracing forward, the shortest route to G is: A→B→E→F→G. Alternatively, the permanent predecessor of D is A. Hence, an equally short route to G is: A→D→G. Table 13-6 shows the shortest routes to all nodes.

Table 13-6 *The Shortest Routes from A*

NODE	ROUTE	DISTANCE
B	A → B	3
C	A → C	8
D	A → D	7
E	A → B → E	13
F	A → B → E → F	17
G	A → B → E → F → G OR A → D → G	25

In this problem, the distance was measured in terms of miles traveled. In general, the internode distance can also be measured in terms of operating cost or travel time. The next example shows how to make purchasing decisions by using the shortest route algorithm. The trick lies in suitably identifying the nodes, arcs, and direct distances.

When to Replace a Machine?

Suppose that a company has decided to manufacture and market a certain model of computers for the next five years. The company must purchase a special purpose machine which can only be used for manufacturing this model of computers. The machine can be purchased now for $5,000. However, it is estimated that after two years the purchase price will be $6,000. Because an older machine will need more repairs, the operating cost will increase with the age of a machine. At the same time, the resale price will decrease with age. Specifically, table 13-7 shows the effects of age. The resale price in that table is shown as a fraction of the corresponding purchase price, P_0. For example, at the beginning of year 1, the purchase price is $5,000. Hence, according to the ratios in table 13-7, it will resale for .70 × 5,000 = $3,500 at the beginning of year 2. Similarly, the resale price will be .64 × 5,000 = $3,200 at the beginning of year 3. You can similarly compute the resale prices at the beginning of years 4 through 6 to be: $2,800, $2,500, and $2,000, respectively.

Table 13-7 *Resale Price and Annual Operating Cost*

AGE OF THE MACHINE	RESALE PRICE AT END OF YEAR	ANNUAL OPERATING COSTS ($)
1	$.70P_0$	600
2	$.64P_0$	900
3	$.56P_0$	1,500
4	$.50P_0$	2,000
5	$.40P_0$	2,500

The decision problem can be stated as follows. Since the resale price decreases and annual cost increases with age, keeping a machine for all five years might not be financially desirable. On the other hand, trading in the machine each year might not be cost effective either. The company, therefore, wants to find an optimal replacement schedule, i.e., the number of years to keep the machine purchased at the beginning of year 1; and the number of years to keep the machine that will replace the initial machine.

Formulating the Shortest Route Problem

As you must have realized, we need to find a "travel plan" across time. Specifically, we must determine a strategy that will take us from the beginning of year 1 to the beginning of year 6 as cheaply as possible. The analogy with the shortest route problem can be summarized as follows:

1. The beginning of each year plays the role of a node. Thus, this equipment replacement problem contains six nodes: the beginning of year 1, beginning of year 2, etc.
2. The arc from node i to node j corresponds to purchasing the machine at the beginning of year i and selling it at the beginning of year j. This formulation is meaningful as long as: $1 \le i < j \le 6$.
3. The length of the arc: $i \rightarrow j$ is the *net cost* associated with the transaction described in part 2 above.

With this set of conventions, the machine replacement problem is equivalent to finding the shortest route through the network shown in figure 13-4.

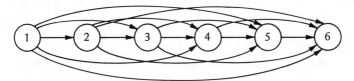

Figure 13-4. *The Network of a Replacement Problem*

Deriving the Arc Lengths To complete the formulation of the replacement problem, we need to obtain the net cost of purchasing a machine at the beginning of year i and selling it at the beginning of year j. The two components of the net cost are:

1. The difference between purchase and sales price
2. The totality of annual operating costs.

The net cost is the sum of these two component costs.

Table 13-8 summarizes the computations necessary to derive the lengths of arcs from node 1, i.e., the net cost of purchasing the machine at the beginning of year 1 and selling it at the beginning of year j for $j = 2$, $3, \ldots, 6$. In each instance, the first row lists the purchase price in year 1, i.e., \$5,000. Next, we list the operating cost of keeping the machine for 1 year, i.e., till the beginning of year 2. From table 13-7, this cost is \$600.

Table 13-8 *Net Cost (\$) Along the Arcs $1 \rightarrow j$*

	SELL AT THE BEGINNING OF YEAR j				
	2	3	4	5	6
Buying Price	\$5,000	\$5,000	\$5,000	\$5,000	\$5,000
Operating Costs for Year					
1	600	600	600	600	600
2	—	900	900	900	900
3	—	—	1,500	1,500	1,500
4	—	—	—	2,000	2,000
5	—	—	—	—	2,500
Cash Outlay	5,600	6,500	8,000	10,000	12,500
Selling Price	3,500	3,200	2,800	2,500	2,000
Net Cost	2,100	3,300	5,200	7,500	10,500

The cash outlay is the sum of purchase price and the operating cost, i.e., $5,000 + $600 = $5,600$. If the machine is sold at the beginning of year 2, i.e., when it is one year old, table 13-7 shows that it will sell for 70 percent of the purchase price, i.e., for $.70 \times \$5,000 = \$3,500$. Hence, the net cost is the difference: $\$5,600 - \$3,500 = \$2,100$.

If the machine is kept for two years, i.e., sold at the beginning of year 3, the operating cost is $600 in year 1 plus $900 in year 2 for a total of $1,500. Since the machine will then sell for $.64 \times \$5,000 = \$3,200$, the net cost of this alternative is $\$6,500 - \$3,200 = \$3,300$. You can now verify all other net costs shown in the last line of table 13-8.

You can similarly compute the net costs associated with purchasing the machine at the beginning of year 2 and selling at the beginning of year j for $j = 3$ through 6. However, since the purchase price continues to be $5,000, it is unnecessary to repeat the computations of table 13-8. The relevant net costs can be obtained by simply shifting the entries in the last line of table 13-8. For example, the net cost along the arc $2 \rightarrow 3$ is the same as that along the arc $1 \rightarrow 2$, i.e., $2,100; the net cost along the arc $2 \rightarrow 4$ is the same as that along $1 \rightarrow 3$, etc. All such costs are shown in table 13-9.

Table 13-9 *Net Cost ($) Along the Arcs $2 \rightarrow j$*

j	3	4	5	6	7
Net Cost	$2,100	3,300	5,200	7,500	10,500

Deriving the Net Costs Along the Arcs $3 \rightarrow j$ Since the purchase price changes to $6,000 at the beginning of year 3, the net costs along the arcs $3 \rightarrow j$ (for $j = 4$ through 6) must be recomputed. The computations are similar to those carried out in table 13-8. The results are shown in table 13-10.

Table 13-10 *Net Cost ($) Along the Arcs $3 \rightarrow j$*

	SELL OF THE BEGINNING OF YEAR j		
	4	5	6
Buying Price	$6,000	$6,000	$6,000
Operating Costs for Year			
3	600	600	600
4	—	900	900
5	—	—	1,500
Cash Outlay	6,600	7,500	9,000
Selling Price	4,200	3,840	3,360
Net Cost	2,400	3,660	5,640

Since there are no additional price changes, the net cost along the arc 4→5 is the same as that along 3→4; the net cost along 4→6 is the same as that along 3→5; and finally, the net cost along 5→6 is the same as that from 3→4. Table 13-11 displays the complete set of net costs as the corresponding direct distances. That a certain route is unacceptable is shown, as usual, by placing an M at the intersection of the corresponding row and column.

Table 13-11 *Direct Distances for the Replacement Problem*

PURCHASE AT THE START OF YEAR	SELL AT THE START OF YEAR				
	2	3	4	5	6
1	2,100	3,300	5,200	7,500	10,500
2	M	2,100	3,300	5,200	7,500
3	M	M	2,400	3,660	5,640
4	M	M	M	2,400	3,660
5	M	M	M	M	2,400

Recommendations to Management Now that the lengths of all arcs are known, the least costly equipment replacement schedule, i.e., the shortest path from ① to ⑥ can be found by the rules discussed in the preceding section. The shortest routes from node 1 to all other nodes are shown in figure 13-5. If the company wishes to manufacture the specific model of computers for the next five years, the least costly plan is keep the initially purchased machine for three years, get a new machine at the beginning of the fourth year, and use it for the next two years. The total cost of so doing is $8,860. Figure 13-5 also shows the shortest routes to nodes 2 through 5. Each can be interpreted similarly.

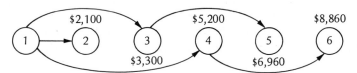

Figure 13-5. *The Shortest Routes*

THE MAXIMAL FLOW PROBLEM

Consider a network of flows (e.g., vehicles, aircrafts, messages, fluid, or jobs) with only one source node and only one sink. Assume that the flow capacities of each arc are known in both directions. Note that only the arcs (roads, air lanes, channels, pipes, or material handling routes) have capacities. At the corresponding nodes (intersections, traffic circles, airports, switching points, pumping stations, or work-stations), one assumes the conservation of flow (i.e., that the total flow into a node must equal the total flow out of that node). Under these circumstances, the maximal flow problem consists of finding the most flow that can proceed from the source to sink and identifying the actual flows on each path.

Consider the network shown in figure 13-6. Visualize the nodes in that figure to be switching centers, the flow to consist of messages, and the arcs to be the message carrying cables. Each message must begin at node A and reach node G. In other words, A is the source and G is the sink. Each branch is equipped to carry a certain number of messages per minute, i.e., it has a specified capacity. The capacity of a branch from i to j is shown along that branch by the number nearest node i. The capacity in

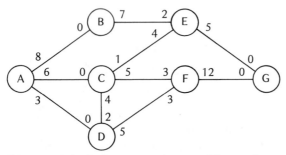

Figure 13-6. *A Communications Network*

the reverse direction is shown by the number nearest node j. Thus, for example, 8 messages per hour can be sent from A to B but none from B to A. Similarly, 7 messages per hour can move from B to E, but only 2 from E to B. This could mean, for instance, that the telephone company does not wish to allow more than 2 messages per minute from E to B at this time.

As an alternate scenario, you might visualize the above network to be one of highways and intersections, the flow to consist of cars leaving the downtown area at the end of the day, and the capacities to mean the number of cars (in 1,000-car units) passing every hour. Highway authorities often close several incoming lanes to speed up the outgoing traffic—thus creating an imbalance in capacities.

In any case, given this network with specified capacities, what is the maximum rate of flow from node A to G? The above problem can be formulated using linear optimization model. It could conceivably be solved by using the Simplex method to be discussed in chapter 15. It is, however, much more efficient to use your intuition! With some reflection, you should be able to develop an algorithm such as the one below:

1. Find a path with *some* flow from the source to sink.
2. Assign the *most* flow that is possible along this path.
3. Continue searching for the paths with some flow from the source to sink and assign the most that can be assigned along such path.

For example, consider the path A→B→E→G. It can carry 8 messages per minute from A→B, 7 from B→E, and 5 from E→G. If you do not wish to create bottlenecks at nodes B and E, you can assign no more than 5 messages per minute along this path. In other words, the most that can be assigned along a path equals the smallest capacity of any component branch. Hence, according to Step 2 above, assign a flow of 5 along A→B→E→G. When this is done, branch E→G can no longer handle any additional flow; branch B→E can carry 7 − 5 = 2 more messages per minute; and branch A→B can carry 8 − 5 = 3 more messages. It follows that the message carrying capacities of these three branches must be modified to: 3 along A→B, 2 along B→E, and 0 along E→G. This is depicted in figure 13-7.

Figure 13-7. *Revision of Flow Capacities*

You can similarly analyze the flows along the remaining paths from A to G. Will this process yield the optimal flow pattern? For the network shown in figure 13-9, the answer is yes. In general, however, it does not guarantee finding an optimal flow pattern in complex networks. The proof of this statement is beyond the scope of this book. We will instead present a slightly modified algorithm which assures finding the maximal flow for *any* kind of network.

The maximal flow algorithm is comprised of the following steps:

1. Find a path from the source to the sink with positive flow capacity. If none exists, the current pattern of flows is already optimal.
2. Along this path, search for the branch with the smallest capacity in the right direction, i.e., from source to sink. Assign a flow equal to this smallest capacity, say C, along the entire path.
3. Decrease by C the flow capacity in each branch of that path. Also, *increase* by C the flow capacity in the reverse direction along each branch in this path. Then return to Step 1.

Applying Step 3 as modified above to the path A→B→E→G of figure 13-6 yields the network of figure 13-8. Note that the flow capacities A→B, B→E, and E→G have been reduced by 5. On the other hand, the capacities in the reverse direction (i.e., B→A, E→B, G→E) have been increased by 5. It is not possible to assign any more flow along A→B→E→G. However, many other paths are still open.

For example, path A→C→F→G of figure 13-8 can carry a flow of 5 units (the smallest of the three numbers: 6 along A→C, 5 along C→F, and 12 along F→G). Reduce the capacity of these branches by 5 in the source-

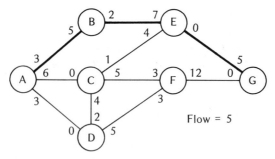

Figure 13-8. *Changes Due to a Flow of 5 along A→B→E→G*

to-sink direction and increase the capacity by 5 in the sink-to-source direction. See figure 13-9.

In the network of figure 13-9, you can assign a flow of 3 along A→D→F→G. The results are shown in figure 13-10. In that figure, the path A→B→E→C→D→F→G can carry a flow of 2. The results are shown

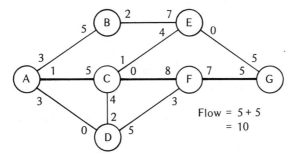

Figure 13-9. *Effects of Assigning a Flow of 5 along*
A→C→F→G

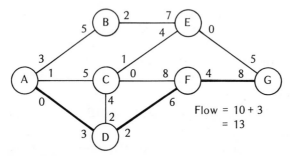

Figure 13-10. *Changes Due to a Flow of 3 along A→D→F→G*

in figure 13-11. At this stage, no path from A to G with positive flow capacity remains to be discovered. (Check this.) According to Step 1 of the algorithm, we must have found the optimal flow pattern. From figure 13-11, the maximal flow is 15 messages per minute.

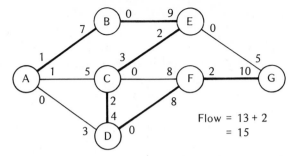

Figure 13-11. *Assigning a Flow of 2 along the Path*
$A \rightarrow B \rightarrow E \rightarrow C \rightarrow D \rightarrow F \rightarrow G$

Thus, the decision maker whose problem is represented in figure 13-6 can send up to 15 messages per minute without overworking the communications network. Figure 13-11 can also be used for identifying the "weakest links" in the network, e.g., A→D, B→E, C→F, D→F, and E→G. These branches are similar to the critical tasks of the PERT network. Unless at least one of these branches has a higher capacity, it would be meaningless to improve any of the remaining links. This knowledge can be useful when designing a network of higher capacity.

NETWORK FORMULATIONS

As we have seen, many decision problems can be advantageously formulated as a network formulation problem. Generally speaking, this is true for any problem with double-subscripted decision variables. Given a variable X_{ij}, one can identify the nodes i and j. In most such cases, $X_{ij} = 1$, if the arc $i \rightarrow j$ belongs on the optimal path and $X_{ij} = 0$, otherwise. In chapter 5, for example, $X_{ij} = 1$, if the activity $i \rightarrow j$ is on the critical path. In chapter 11, $X_{ij} = 1$, if the row i is matched with column j. In this chapter, you can identify $X_{ij} = 1$, if the arc is on the shortest path while solving the shortest path problems. In the minimal spanning trees, $X_{ij} = 1$, if the arc from $i \rightarrow j$ is to be retained in such a connected tree. Many a decision problem can then be formulated by suitably defining C_{ij}, the length of the arc from node i to node j.

In other words, each of the prototype problems examined in chapters 5, 11, 12, and 13 can be described by an appropriately constructed network model. However, the term *network model* is most often used to describe only those situations in which the decision variables assume only two values, 0 and 1. Even with this qualification, a large number of OR/MS models belong to this category. See Baker (1974), Elmaghraby (1970), Glover and Klingman (1975), and Whitehouse (1973) for many more managerial applications of network models.

Though the models themselves are relatively easy to understand due to their obvious visual appeal, the solution techniques are not always so obvious. In fact, a number of different algorithms have been devised to take advantage of the specialized structures of these models. The branch-and-bound approach, the cutting-plane algorithm, and the out-of-kilter algorithm are three of the famous algorithms used for solving network problems. The interested reader is encouraged to consult some of the references for additional information on these.

SELECTED READINGS

BAKER, K. R. *Introduction to Sequencing and Scheduling.* New York: John Wiley & Sons, Inc., 1974.

DOERSCH, R. H. and PATTERSON, J. H. "Scheduling a Project to Maximize Its Present Value: A Zero-One Programming Approach." *Management Science* 23 (1977), pp. 882–889.

ELMAGHRABY, S. E. *Network Models in Management Science.* Springer-Verlag Lecture Series on Operations Research, 1970.

GARFINKEL, R. S. and NEMHAUSER, G. S. *Integer Programming.* New York: John Wiley & Sons, Inc., 1972.

GLOVER, F. and KLINGMAN, D. "Recent Network Applications in Industry and Government." *Research Report #CCS247*, Center for Cybernetic Studies, The University of Texas at Austin (1975).

GLOVER, F.; KLINGMAN, D.; and NAPIER, A. "An Efficient Dual Approach to Network Problems." *OPSEARCH* 9 (1972), pp. 1–18.

GLOVER, F. and MULVEY, J. "Equivalence of the Zero-one Integer Program to Discrete Generalized and Pure Networks." *MSRS* 75–19 University of Colorado (1975), p. 75.

HELD, M. and KARP, R. M. "The Traveling-Salesman Problem and Minimum Spanning Trees." *Operations Research* 18 (1970), pp. 1138–1162.

HELD, M. and KARP, R. M. "The Traveling-Salesman Problem and Minimum-Spanning Trees, Part II." *Mathematical Programming* 1 (1971), pp. 6–25.

HOUCK, D. J. and VEMUGANTI, R. R. "The Traveling Salesman Problem and Shortest n-Paths." ORSA-TIMS Meeting, Philadelphia, May 1976.

HU, T. C. *Integer Programming and Network Flows.* Reading, Mass.: Addison-Wesley Publishing Co., 1971.

MINIEKA, E. *Optimization Algorithms for Networks and Graphs.* New York: Marcel Dekker, Inc., 1978.

TRUEMPER, K. "Maximal Flows in Networks with Positive Gains." Research Report. The University of Texas at Dallas, Texas, 1973.

WHITE, L. S. "Shortest Route Models for the Allocation of Inspection Effort on a Production Line." *Management Science* 15 (1969), pp. 249–259.

WHITEHOUSE, G. E. *Systems Analysis and Design Using Network Techniques.* Englewood Cliffs, NJ: Prentice-Hall Inc., 1973.

PROBLEM SET 13
OPTIMIZATION IN NETWORKS

1. The John B. Winters Memorial Committee is planning to construct an amusement park in honor of Mr. Winters. (It will also be a source of income for his
   descendants.) The committee has chosen the sites of the main entrance to the
   park, the hotel, the rides, and a fast-food stand. The park also contains a
   beautiful natural lake and the committee wants to establish a beach along the
   lake. The committee wants to construct a miniature railroad connecting all
   sites.

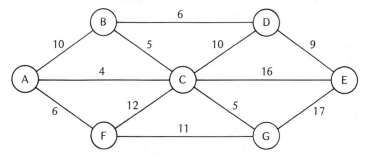

   The distances between sites are shown in the adjoining figure in thousands of
   feet. Since the construction costs are high, design a network which will connect all sites with the least amount of roadbed. What is the minimum total
   length?

2. The physical layout of a large manufacturing plant is shown in the adjoining
   figure. Each product must be processed in each of the seven work centers
   shown in that figure. Since the products are bulky, the company uses carts to
   move these from workcenter to workcenter. The potential set of "cart ways"
   and the corresponding distances in hundreds of feet are shown along the
   branches of that figure.

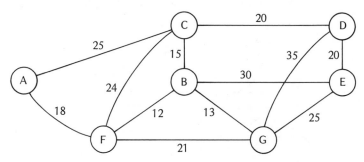

   Design a network of cart ways which would connect all centers with the least
   amount of concrete. What is the minimum total length?

3. Find the minimal spanning tree for the network shown in the adjoining figure.

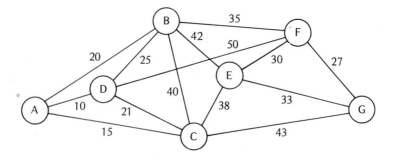

4. A large electrical firm has obtained a contract to provide several jet engines to a major manufacturer. The engines are to be assembled in city A and transported to city H. Since the jet engines are heavy, the transportation costs are rather large. Many potential routes and the corresponding cost ($) are shown in the adjoining figure.

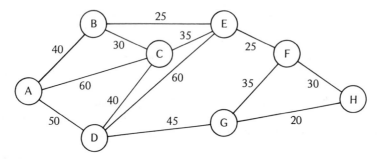

Find the cheapest route from A to H.

5. In response to a recent energy crisis, the Frontier Metropolitan Authority (FMA) has initiated a number of direct transportation routes connecting the major locations within this metropolis. Each route is serviced by an FMA vehicle. These routes and the average time in minutes to proceed from location to location are shown in the adjoining figure. Joseph P. Disa lives at A.

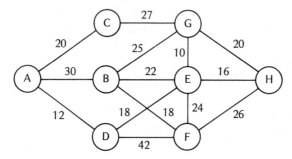

Being a firm advocate of public transportation systems, he always moves within the metropolis using the FMA vehicles only. Find the least amount of time he should set aside to go from his residence to any of the other locations within the Frontier Metropolitan Region.

6. Due to construction in the branch D→E of problem 5, that branch has been temporarily closed for traffic. Compute the least amount of time necessary to proceed from D to each of the other locations.

7. Let C_{ij} denote the net cost of purchasing a machine at the beginning of year i and replacing it at the beginning of year j. Given the C_{ij} values shown in the adjoining table, find the least costly replacement schedule over a five-year period.

	j				
i	2	3	4	5	6
1	2,000	2,400	4,000	M	M
2	—	2,000	3,000	4,500	M
3	—	—	3,000	3,600	4,000
4	—	—	—	3,200	3,800
5	—	—	—	—	3,600

8. A special purpose machine must be used for up to five years since the date of purchase. Currently it can be bought for $4,000. It is estimated that the purchase price will rise to $5,000 two years from now. The resale price will be 80, 70, 60, 45, and 35 percent after 1, 2, 3, 4, and 5 years of machine usage, respectively. The annual operating cost will be $600 in the first year of machine usage. Subsequently, it will rise to $1,000, $1,500, $2,400, and $3,000 in the second through the fifth year of its life. Given these circumstances, find a least costly replacement schedule.

9. The probabilities of failure through a communications network are shown in the adjoining figure. Assuming that the various links are statistically independent, find the most reliable, i.e., least-failure-prone route from A to G. (Hint: Let P_{ij} denote the probability of success from node i to node j. Then the probability of success along a path such as A→E→G is the *product* of component probabilities. $P(A→E→G) = P(A→E) \times P(E→G)$. Taking logarithms on both sides yields $\log P(A→E→G) = \log P(A→E) + \log P(E→G)$. Hence, use $d_{ij} = -\log P_{ij}$ as "distance" along arc $i→j$. Then find the shortest route.)

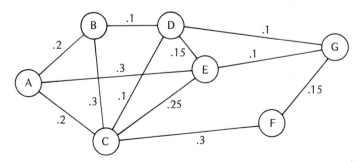

10. Find the optimal replacement policy over the next five years given the following information about prices, resale values and operating costs. The purchase

prices at the beginning of year i, P_i, are estimated to be: $P_1 = \$300$, $P_2 = \$330$, $P_3 = \$350$, $P_4 = \$375$, and $P_5 = \$400$. A one-year-old machine will resale for $200, a two-year-old machine will resale for $100 and a three-year-old machine will sell for $50. Beyond that, it has no salvage value. The operating cost in the ith year of machine usage will be $Y_1 = \$50$, $Y_2 = \$70$, $Y_3 = \$100$, $Y_4 = \$180$ and $Y_5 = \$300$.

11. The data kept by the manager of a small, privately owned delivery firm is shown in the adjoining figure. A substantial number of parcels originate at city

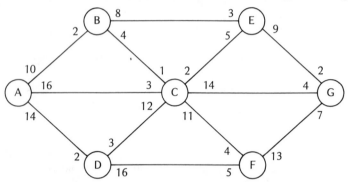

A with the eventual destination being city G. The number of deliveries which can be made along each arc in each direction are indicated on that arc. What is the maximum possible number of deliveries from A to G? Which links should be improved to increase the flow capacity from A to G?

12. Find the maximal flow from A to G of the following network. Which links need most improvement?

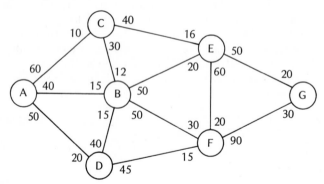

14

Graphical Method

The primary motivation behind this chapter is to discuss how to solve linear decision problems that contain only two decision variables and in the process, illustrate the meaning of linearity and several other concepts on which the Simplex technique is based. Solving these problems will also illustrate how to solve simultaneous equations. And, the Simplex technique, to be examined in the following chapter, requires this ability. In that sense, this entire chapter is designed to prepare you for the one that follows.

THE GEOMETRY OF SOLUTION SPACES

Let us assume a very much simplified version of a real world problem, as we examine the following situation.

Example 1: A Hospital Design

Suppose you are an advisor to a hospital planning committee and that the committee must decide on the number of beds to be assigned to the inpatient and outpatient sections. The outpatient beds are to be used for minor surgical cases in which the patient can be discharged the same day. The committee has determined that an inpatient bed is twice as

447

valuable as an outpatient bed. Two million dollars are available quarterly for operating this expansion. Each inpatient bed (and the associated facilities) costs $7,000; each outpatient bed costs $4,000. The inpatient section requires one resident physician per six beds; the corresponding physician in the outpatient section can supervise 15 patients. Only 40 residents can be hired. The committee also wants to diversify its service offerings. Therefore, it feels that the ratio of inpatient beds to outpatient beds should neither exceed 2 nor be less than .25. What would you recommend?

Let X_1 denote the proposed number of inpatient beds and let X_2 denote the proposed number of outpatient beds. Since the inpatient bed is twice as valuable as an outpatient bed, it follows that the committee's objective is to:

Maximize: $Z = 2X_1 + X_2$

There are four constraints. The budget is limited to $2,000,000. Since each inpatient bed needs $7,000 to operate, X_1 inpatient beds require $7,000X_1. Similarly, X_2 outpatient beds at $4,000 each require $4,000X_2. This total must be within the budget. Thus, the first constraint, in $1,000 units is:

$$7X_1 + 4X_2 \le 2,000$$

The number of residents is limited to 40. Since one resident can handle six inpatient beds, X_1 inpatient beds require $1/6\,X_1$ residents. Similarly, X_2 outpatient beds need $1/15\,X_2$ residents. Thus, the "number of residents available" constraint is:

$$1/6\ X_1 + 1/15\ X_2 \le 40$$

It is more convenient to multiply both sides of this constraint by 30 to eliminate fractions. In this form, the above constraint becomes:

$$5X_1 + 2X_2 \le 1,200$$

The ratio of inpatient beds to outpatient beds is X_1/X_2. According to the committee's stipulation, it must not exceed 2 nor must it be less than .25. This gives rise to *two* constraints:

$$X_1/X_2 \le 2 \text{ and } X_1/X_2 \ge .25$$

or equivalently:

$$X_1 - 2X_2 \le 0 \text{ and } 4X_1 - X_2 \ge 0$$

Thus, the hospital's problems can be summarized as follows:

Maximize:

$$Z = 2X_1 + X_2$$

Subject to:

$$7X_1 + 4X_2 \leq 2{,}000 \text{ (budget)}$$
$$5X_1 + 2X_2 \leq 1{,}200 \text{ (residents)}$$
$$4X_1 - X_2 \geq 0 \text{ (ratio} \geq .25)$$
$$X_1 - 2X_2 \leq 0 \text{ (ratio} \leq 2)$$

Nonnegativity:

$$X_1 \geq 0 \text{ and } X_2 \geq 0$$

The rest of this section prepares the geometrical description of this problem. We will begin by defining terms.

An ordered pair of numbers (X_1, X_2) is said to be a *feasible solution* of a decision problem if the X_1 and X_2 values satisfy *all* of the associated constraints. The set of all feasible solutions to an optimization problem constitutes its *solution space*. An optimal solution is to be sought in this space. Geometrically, one proceeds as follows.

The coordinate axes are identified corresponding to each action variable. Traditionally, the X_1 axis is shown by a horizontal line and the X_2 axis by a vertical line. The point where these axes meet is called the origin, which is represented by the ordered pair $(0, 0)$. Suitable scales are chosen along the X_1 and X_2 axes. The positive values of X_1 are shown to the right of the origin and the negative values to the left. The positive values of X_2 are shown above the origin and the negative values below it. Since the action variables in standard LP models are always nonnegative, the corresponding solutions are said to lie in the *first quadrant*, i.e., above and to the right of the origin. See figure 14-1. In that figure, a unit length along the X_1 axis represents 100 inpatient beds and a unit length along the X_2 axis represents 300 outpatient beds. A potential course of action is shown by a point in this space. For example, the point $(125, 225)$ represents planning for 125 inpatient beds and 225 outpatient beds $(X_1 = 125, X_2 = 225)$. Other courses of action can be represented by the corresponding points.

Figure 14-1. *Geometrical Representation of a Course of Action*

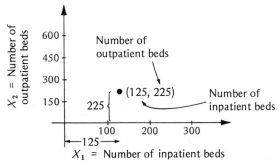

Not every point in the first quadrant represents a feasible solution to a given problem. We must construct the solution space by first finding the *feasible region* of each constraint and then finding the common points of all such feasible regions. As you can imagine, each additional constraint tends to shrink the solution space. There are two types of constraints: resource limitations and requirements. The corresponding feasible regions are obtained as follows.

Describing Resource Limitations

Only a fixed quantity of any one resource is available to the decision maker. Hence, a resource limitation takes the form: $AX_1 = BX_2 \leq C$, for suitable values of A, B, and C. (A, B, and C are all nonnegative.) The corresponding feasible region is always a triangle whose boundaries are the straight lines: $AX_1 + BX_2 = C$, the X_1 axis, and the X_2 axis.

Consider, for instance, the constraint imposed by the budget: $7X_1 + 4X_2 \leq 2,000$. To define the associated boundary, ignore the inequality portion of the constraint, i.e., consider the equation:

$$7X_1 + 4X_2 = 2,000$$

Such an equation represents a straight line and thus the knowledge of any *two points on that line uniquely defines it*. The points can be chosen in any convenient fashion. For example, when $X_1 = 0$, you can check that $X_2 = 2,000 \div 4 = 500$. Thus, (0, 500) lies on the "budget line." Similarly, when $X_2 = 0$, X_1 equals $2000 \div 7 = 285.7$. Hence, (285.7, 0) is yet another point on the budget line. The boundary of the budget constraint is obtained by joining these two points. See figure 14-2.

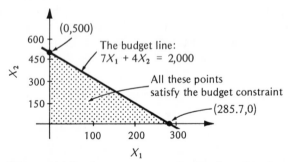

Figure 14-2. *Representing the Budget Limitation*

The budget constraint is an inequality rather than an equation. To represent it, proceed as follows. Note that for any point in the first quadrant that lies inside the triangle formed by the X_1 axis, the X_2 axis, and the budget boundary $7X_1 + 4X_2 = 2,000$, the value of $7X_1 + 4X_2$ is always *less* than 2,000. In other words, each point inside this triangle satisfies the budget constraint. Figure 14-2 shows the set of all points that satisfy the budget constraint, i.e., the corresponding feasible region. It includes both the inside of the triangle and its boundaries.

The triangle that represents the limitation on the number of residents is obtained in a similar fashion. It is shown in figure 14-3.

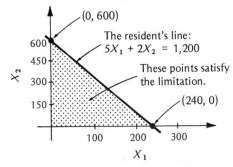

Figure 14-3. *Representing the Limitation on the Number of Residents*

Representing the Requirements

The process of representing a requirement also begins with the act of graphing its boundary. However, since requirements can assume a variety of forms, it is not possible to provide a general rule, such as that of deriving a limitation triangle. Having graphed a requirement boundary, the corresponding feasible region must be determined in an individualistic fashion.

The Hospital's Case The committee's diversification objective is stated as a pair of requirements:

$$4X_1 - X_2 \geq 0 \text{ (inpatient/outpatient ratio } \geq .25)$$

$$X_1 - 2X_2 \leq 0 \text{ (ratio } \leq 2)$$

In either case, the right-hand side of the constraint is zero. Hence, the corresponding boundary passes through the origin, i.e., $(0, 0)$ lies on each of the two boundaries. Each boundary is uniquely identified by finding one more point on it. For example, $4X_1 - X_2 = 0$ is equivalent to $X_2 = 4X_1$. It follows that any point whose X_2 coordinate is four times its X_1 coordinate lies on this boundary. $(150, 600)$ is such a point. Similarly, the other boundary, $X_1 - 2X_2 = 0$, passes through $(300, 150)$. The set of all points for which $.25 \leq$ ratio ≤ 2 constitutes the open-ended triangle bounded on two sides only by:

$$4X_1 - X_2 = 0 \text{ and } X_1 - 2X_2 = 0$$

It is shown in figure 14-4.

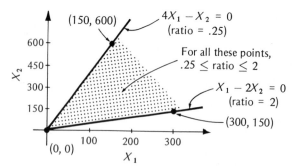

Figure 14.4. *Representing the Diversification of Beds Requirement*

Other Possibilities To illustrate the other possibilities of representing a requirement, let us propose three different requirements. The hospital planning committee could have specified these requirements:

1. There must be at least 150 inpatient beds, i.e., $X \geq 150$. Figure 14-5(a) shows the corresponding feasible region.
2. There must be at least 300 outpatient beds, i.e., $X_2 \geq 300$. Figure 14-5(b) shows the corresponding feasible region.
3. The totality of beds must be 400 or more, i.e., $X_1 + X_2 \geq 400$. Figure 14-5(c) shows the resultant feasible region.

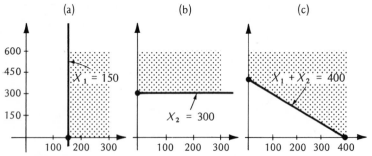

Figure 14-5. *Potential Requirements*

Note that all of these feasible regions are open-ended. This is usually the case with requirements.

Constructing the Solution Space

You must have already noticed that each constraint defines its own feasible region and that not every point in the first quadrant belongs to each feasible region. To be in the solution space, a point must satisfy *all* constraints. Geometrically, this implies that such a point must belong to all the feasible regions. The set of all points, each of which belongs to every feasible region, constitutes the solution space. In the two-variable decision problems, such points can be obtained by superimposing the feasible regions. Since the constraints are imposed for managerial rather than geometric reasons, two possibilities arise in the process of super-imposing the constraints. Each is discussed below.

Infeasibility This means that the constraints are such that no point in the first quadrant belongs to all feasible regions. In other words, the solution space is empty. If this happens, the constraints must be re-examined and the cause of such infeasibility must be eliminated before proceeding any further. Only managerial acumen, not mathematical skill, can save such situations.

Redundancy This means that, though managerially important, some constraints need not be stated at all since they do not in fact limit the solution space. All such constraints are eliminated from the problem statement before proceeding to find the optimal solutions. Figure 14-6 shows this situation graphically.

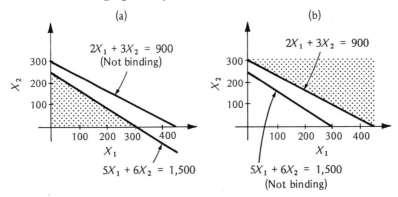

Figure 14-6. *Constraints That Are Not Binding*

The solution space of the decision problem in figure 14-6(a) is defined by two resource limitations:

$$5X_1 + 6X_2 \leq 1,500$$
$$2X_1 + 3X_2 \leq 900$$

The feasible region of the first constraint is shown by the dotted portion of figure 14-6(a). It follows that imposing the additional constraint, e.g., $2X_1 + 3X_2 \leq 900$, is unnecessary. It does not limit the solution space of the decision problem any more that that limited by the first constraint, e.g., $5X_1 + 6X_2 \leq 1,500$. For this reason, the second constraint is said to be a redundant or nonbinding constraint. On the other hand, the two constraints for the decision problem in figure 14-6(b) are:

$$5X_1 + 6X_2 \geq 1,500$$
$$2X_1 + 3X_2 \geq 900$$

You can check that in this case the first constraint is redundant or non-binding.

In general, a constraint that does not further restrict a solution space is said to be redundant. A constraint which helps define a boundary of the solution space is said to be an active or binding constraint. Only active constraints are examined while searching for an optimal solution.

The Solution Space of the Hospital Problem

The hospital problem is defined by four constraints and two non-negativity requirements. Each is represented in figures 14-1 through 14-4. Superimposing these results obtains figure 14-7. To avoid cluttering the

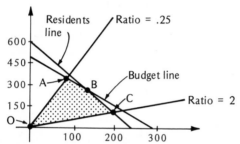

Figure 14-7. *The Solution Space of the Hospital Problem*

figure, only the important items of information from the component figures have been preserved. Thus, all the boundaries are shown, but only those points that belong to the hospital's solution space are shown by the dotted region. The solution space is bounded by four straight lines. OA, AB, BC, and OC. The corresponding equations are shown below.

OA: $4X_1 - X_2 = 0$ (ratio = .25)
AB: $7X_1 + 4X_2 = 2,000$ (budget)
BC: $5X_1 + 2X_2 = 1,2000$ (number of residents)
OC: $X_1 - 2X_2 =$ (ratio = 2)

Deriving the Coordinates of the Corners

The point O being the origin has coordinates $(0, 0)$, i.e., $X_1 = 0$ and $X_2 = 0$. The coordinates of the remaining corner are obtained by simultaneously solving the equations of the corresponding lines.

For example, OA and AB intersect at A. Hence, solve the corresponding equations: $4X_1 - X_2 = 0$, i.e., $X_2 = 4X_1$ and $7X_1 + 4X_2 = 2,000$, simultaneously. The idea is to eliminate one of two unknowns from one of the two equations to obtain the value of the remaining unknown. Having found this, the value of the second unknown is obtained. To find the coordinates of A, it is convenient to use the information that $X_2 = 4X_1$ in the equation of AB. This yields:

$$2{,}000 = 7X_1 + 4X_2 = 7X_1 + 4 \times 4X_1 = 23X_1$$

Hence, $X_1 = 2{,}000 \div 23 = 86.96$ and, from the equation of OA:

$$X_2 = 4X_1 = 4 \times 86.96 = 347.84$$

It follows that A has coordinates (86.96, 347.84). You can similarly find that C has coordinates (200, 100).

Deriving the coordinates of B is only slightly more difficult. One method is illustrated here. Multiply the entire equation of BC by 2 to obtain: $10X_1 + 4X_2 = 2{,}400$ as the new equation for BC. Now, subtract the entire equation of AB from that of BC term by term. This yields: $3X_1 = 400$ or $X_1 = 133.33$. Consequently, from the equation of AB, $4X_2 = 2{,}000 - 7X_1 = 2{,}000 - 933.33 = 1{,}066.67$. Hence, $X_2 = 266.67$. Thus, B has coordinates (133.33, 266.67).

A Cross-Multiplication Technique The above method of obtaining the coordinates of the corners is based on the inspection of coefficients and, as such, it is individualistic. A more systematic method follows:

1. Multiply each term in the first equation by the coefficient of X_1 in the second equation.
2. Multiply each term in the second equation by the coefficient of X_1 in the *original* first equation.
3. Subtract the new second equation, term by term, from the new first equation.
4. Now, compute X_2, since the second equation no longer contains X_1.
5. Finally, compute X_1 from the first equation.

For example, let AB, i.e., $7X_1 + 4X_2 = 2{,}000$, denote the first and BC, i.e., $5X_1 + 2X_2 = 1{,}200$, denote the second equation. An application of the above procedure yields the following results:

Step 1: $35X_1 + 20X_2 = 10{,}000$ (Coefficient of X_1 in BC is 5)
Step 2: $35X_1 + 14X_2 = 8{,}400$ (Coefficient of X_1 in AB is 7)
Step 3: $6X_2 = 1{,}600$ (Subtract line 2 from line 1)
Step 4: $X_2 = 2{,}600 \div 6 = 266.67$ (Solve for X_2)
Step 5: $7X_1 + 4 \times 266.67 = 2{,}000$ (Substitute $X_2 = 266.67$)

Hence,
$7X_1 = 2{,}000 - 4 \times 266.67 = 933.33$, so that $X_1 = 933.33 \div 7 = 133.33$
Thus B has coordinates (133.33, 266.67).

To summarize, the solution space is bounded by the quadrangle QABC where the corners have the following coordinates: O(0, 0); A(86.96, 347.84); B(133.33, 266.67); and C(200, 100). However, the quadrangle OABC contains infinitely many points, each representing a feasible solution. How do we find the best of these many solutions? That is the topic of the next section.

FINDING OPTIMAL SOLUTIONS

Actually, even though the solution space of the hospital design problem contains infinitely many points, finding an optimal solution is extremely easy. It is represented by one of the four corners: O, A, B, or C.

Convex Spaces and Vertices

Convexity This simplicity (one need compare only the corners) is a consequence of the shape of this solution space: it is convex. By this we mean the following: Given any two points in a convex solution space, all the points on the corresponding line segment also belong to that solution space. Graphically speaking, convex spaces do not "cave in." Thus, for example, the solution space OLN in figure 14-8(b) is convex; but OLMN in figure 14-8(a) is not. To see this, note that the points R and S belong to the solution space OLMN, but that none of the points between R and S belongs to it. However, don't worry—if the solution space is not convex, it can be enclosed within a suitable *convex hull*. Having done that, the solution process can investigate the corners of this convex hull to find an optimum.

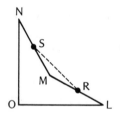   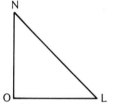

Figure 14-8. *(a) A Concave Space   (b) A Convex Space*

Such a hull is created by filling in the concave portions of the solution space. For example, since in figure 14-8(a) the points between S and R do not belong, simply include these in the corresponding convex hull. In effect, *pretend* that the triangle OLN [see figure 14-8(b)] is the solution space. When this is done, the new triangle OLN is known as the convex hull of the original space OLMN. The search for the optimum now proceeds as if OLN were always the true solution space.

When only the integer values of the action variables are acceptable, the solution space consists of unconnected points. Such spaces are obviously not convex. Also, the corners of the corresponding convex hull might not belong to the solution space. In such cases, a point that is nearest to the optimal corner represents an optimal solution. The mathematical technique of finding such points is known as *integer programming*.

In short, the graphical technique continues to evaluate only the corners of the feasible space. Vertex and extreme point are other names for a corner.

Why Vertices? To illustrate why vertices are important, reconsider the solution space of the hospital design problem. Figure 14-9 shows that space (less all the clutter in figure 14-7). Note that it is convex. Consider

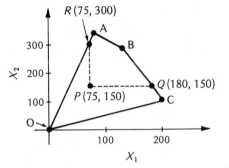

Figure 14-9. *Why P Is Not Optimal*

an inside point, say $P(75, 150)$, and compare it with $Q(180, 150)$ which is obtained from P by moving horizontally to the right edge of the solution space. Both P and Q represent the same number of outpatient beds, but Q represents more inpatient beds than at P. Thus, Q is better than P. You can check that R is also better than P. In fact, given any optimization problem and the corresponding convex hull, you will always find that the following is true.

> Corresponding to every inside point, there is at least one point somewhere on the boundary which is *better*. Therefore, an optimal solution must always lie on the boundary.

Because the objective function is linear, its value will either steadily increase or steadily decrease or remain constant as one moves along some boundary from corner to corner. Consequently, a specific corner is either the best or the worst point on that boundary. Since the optimum is always on some boundary, it follows that only the corners must be examined to find an optimum. (You should verify these conclusions for the problem in figure 14-9.)

The Enumeration Method

Since the number of corners is finite, presumably the best corner can be found by simply computing the objective function at each corner. For example, recall that the hospital planning committee's objective function is $Z = 2X_1 + X_2$. There are four corners in the solution space of that problem, i.e., O, A, B, and C. The search for the optimum is summarized in table 14-1, in which the coordinates of A and B have been rounded off to the nearest integers. This is because fractional values of X_1 and X_2 are not meaningful in this problem. It follows that B represents the best solution to the hospital design problem. In other words, allocate the space and funds for 133 inpatient beds and 267 outpatient beds. The total cost of this arrangement is:

$$\$133 \times 7,000 + 267 \times 4,000 = \$1,999,000$$

It requires $133 \div 6 + 267 \div 15 = 39.97 \approx 40$ residents; and the inpatient/outpatient ratio is $133/267 = .498$.

Table 14-1 *Values of the Objective Function*

CORNER	X_1	X_2	$Z = 2X_1 + X_2$
O	0	0	$2 \times \;\;\;0 + \;\;\;0 = \;\;\;0$
A	87	348	$2 \times \;\;87 + 348 = 522$
B	133	267	$2 \times 133 + 267 = 533$
C	200	100	$2 \times 200 + 100 = 500$

Binding Constraints, Slacks, and Surpluses

The solution, $X_1 = 133$ inpatient beds and $X_2 = 267$ outpatient beds, is optimal for the hospital design problem. Before proceeding, let's analyze the implications of following this policy. Note that the constraint due to the budget limitation is:

$$7X_1 + 4X_2 \leq 2,000$$

With $X_1 = 133$ and $X_2 = 267$, the left-hand side of that constraint equals 1,999. This is one unit short of 2,000. This means that the budget could have been one unit (i.e., $1,000) less without affecting the presently optimal solution. Technically, we may express this same finding by saying that the budget constraint is not binding on the optimal solution, since *it has a slack of one unit.*

On the other hand, when $X_1 = 133$ and $X_2 = 267$, the committee must allocate $133 \div 6 + 267 \div 15 \approx 40$ residents. Thus, the number-of-residents constraint is binding on the optimal; one cannot increase either X_1 or X_2 without asking for at least one more resident. In general, slack on a constraint equals the difference:

resource available − resource needed

If slack is zero, the corresponding constraint is binding. If the constraint is not binding, slack would be positive. It equals the amount by which a resource can be reduced without affecting the optimum. (Compare this definition with that of critical tasks and events in the PERT networks of chapter 5.)

You can now check that the ratio ≤ 2 constraint is not a binding constraint, since $X_1 - 2X_2 = -401$ is quite a bit negative. The slack in this case is $0 - (-401) = 401$.

The ratio $\geq .25$ constraint is of a different kind than any of the others. The left-hand side, $4X_1 - X_2$, is required to exceed a certain limit, in this case, 0. In such a case, the difference:

$$\text{left-hand side} - \text{requirement}$$

is known as the *surplus*. If the surplus is zero, the corresponding constraint is binding on the optimal. If it is not, the surplus would be positive.

In the case of hospital design, we found either slacks or surpluses after obtaining the optimal solution. The Simplex technique, to be studied in the next chapter, explicitly introduces slack variables and surplus variables and standardizes the format. More on this topic appears in the next chapter.

Iso-Payoff Lines *(Optional)*

A finite number does not necessarily mean only a few. Thus, if the number of corners becomes extremely large (though finite), the enumeration method might not remain practical. The iso-payoff method might become preferable since only one corner needs to be evaluated.

The objective function Z is assigned a specific value, say $Z = 100$; and the set of all points (X_1, X_2) that yield $Z = 100$ is plotted. The desired set is a straight line. Since the objective function has a constant value along this line, it is also known as the *iso-payoff line*. By varying the values of Z, many iso-payoff lines can be obtained, and they will be mutually parallel. Two iso-payoff lines for the hospital design are shown in figure 14-10. For example, the line with a payoff of 350 is obtained by solving:

$$2X_1 + X_2 = 350$$

Figure 14-10. *Two Iso-Payoff Lines for the Hospital Design*

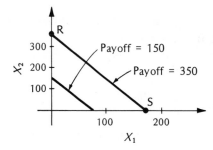

When $X_1 = 0$ on this line, X_2 equals 350; and when $X_2 = 0$, X_1 equals 175. Thus, $(175, 0)$ and $(0, 350)$ both have payoff 350. Similarly, both $(75, 0)$ and $(0, 150)$ yield a payoff of 150.

When one iso-payoff line, say RS, has been plotted, many others can be obtained as follows. Take a pair of rulers. Set one ruler *perpendicular* to RS. Hold it steady. Move the other ruler *parallel* to RS by using the first ruler as a guide. Each position of the moving ruler defines one iso-payoff line.

Notice that the payoff is zero at the origin and it increases steadily as one moves farther away from the origin. The iso-payoff method of finding an optimal solution is based on this observation. Begin by drawing the iso-payoff line $Z = 0$. Then, slide the moving ruler away from the origin.

- If the payoff is undesirable, stop when the moving ruler (i.e., the corresponding iso-payoff line) just touches the solution space.
- If the payoff is desirable, stop when the moving ruler is about to exit the solution space.

In either case, the corresponding corner represents an optimal solution.

Multiple Optima

Occasionally, two neighboring corners will each turn out to be optimal. When this happens, *every point on that boundary represents an optimal solution*. This implies that the boundary of the corresponding constraint is parallel to the objective function, i.e., that boundary is also an iso-payoff line. Algebraically, this situation can be described as follows. Let $P(X_1, X_2)$ and $Q(Y_1, Y_2)$ be the neighboring optima. Choose any fraction r, such that $0 \le r \le 1$. Then, the point $S(S_1, S_2)$ also represents an optimal solution, provided:

$$S_1 = rX_1 + (1 - r)Y_1 \text{ and } S_2 = rX_2 + (1 - r)Y_2$$

Suppose, for instance, that the hospital design committee has reevaluated its utility assessment. It now feels that an inpatient bed is worth 2.5 times an outpatient bed. In that case, the objective function would be:

$$Z = 2.5X_1 + X_2$$

You can check that both $B(133.33, 266.67)$ and $C(200, 100)$ would be optimal so that the entire segment BC has the best payoff. Choose any fraction r between 0 and 1, say $r = .75$. The corresponding point is also optimal and has coordinates (S_1, S_2), where:

$$S_1 = .75 \times 133.33 + .25 \times 200 = 150$$
$$S_2 = .75 \times 266.67 + .25 \times 100 = 225$$

Why bother to report multiple optima? For one, it gives the decision maker a freedom of choice. Also as we have seen earlier (chapter 10), the manager might have multiple objectives of which only one is optimized. Given the choice among a variety of optima, the manager can use it to better satisfy some other, explicit or implicit, objectives.

Example 2: A Minimization Problem

The principal steps required to solve a minimization problem are similar to those outlined for maximization. One difference is simply that the "best" implies least costly, least polluting, least destructive, etc. Obviously, doing nothing (i.e., set $X_1 = X_2 = 0$) could be a potential solution. But, seldom is this a feasible solution. This brings up the other difference between minimization and maximization problems—the origin is usually not in the solution space of minimization problems. The third difference is that the constraints are most often of the requirement type so that the solution space is often unbounded. The dietitian's problem, the paper trim and production scheduling problems in chapter 10 are prototypes of the minimization problem.

Algebraic Formulation We will now introduce a problem directly in its algebraic form. The objective is to:

Minimize:

$$Z = X_1 + 2X_2$$

Subject to:

$$
\begin{aligned}
X_1 + 4X_2 &\geq 40 \\
4X_1 + 3X_2 &\geq 60 \\
X_1 &\leq 30 \\
X_1 - 3X_2 &\leq 0 \\
X_1 \geq 0;\ X_2 &\geq 0
\end{aligned}
$$

Geometric Representation You can verify that boundary $X_1 + 4X_2 = 40$ passes through (40, 0) and (0, 10). Since the requirement is of the $\geq$ type, the corresponding feasible region lies above this line. Similarly, the boundary $4X_1 + 3X_2 = 60$ passes through (0, 20) and (15, 0); the corresponding feasible region lies above that line. The feasible region $X_1 \leq 30$ lies to the left of the boundary $X_1 = 30$. Finally, the line $X_1 - 3X_2 = 0$ passes through (0, 0) and (30, 10); the corresponding feasible region lies above that line. The nonnegativity constraints ensure that the solution space is a portion of the first quadrant. Figure 14-11 represents all these constraints and the resultant solution space (the dotted section). It is unbounded above. In the rest of the directions, it is bounded by the X_2 axis, the line $4X_1 + 3X_2 = 60$, the line $X_1 + 4X_2 = 40$, the line $X_1 - 3X_2 = 0$, and the line $X_1 = 30$. There are four corners A, B, C, and D.

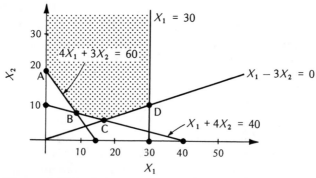

Figure 14-11. *Solution Space of a Minimization Problem*

You should now verify, perhaps by using the cross-multiplication technique, the results displayed in table 14-2. Since the objective is to minimize Z, it follows that the best corner is B. Hence, the optimal solution is:

$$X_1 = 9.23 \text{ and } X_2 = 7.69$$

The same conclusion can be reached by using the concept of iso-payoff lines.

Table 14-2 *Evaluation of the Corners*

POINT	X_1	X_2	$Z = X + 2X_2$
A	0	20	40
B	9.23	7.69	24.61
C	17.14	5.71	28.56
D	30	10	50

The Iso-Payoff Procedure *(Optional)*

Figure 14-12 shows the solution space, the iso-payoff lines, and the guiding edge. Begin by constructing the line $Z = 0$, i.e., $X_1 + 2X_2 = 0$. Obviously, the origin (0, 0) lies on it. You can also verify that (10, −5) lies on this line. The iso-payoff line $Z = 0$ is therefore obtained by joining (0, 0) and (10, −5). Of course, none of the points on this line is feasible. Therefore, create a guiding edge perpendicular to the line $Z = 0$. Using this edge, slide the ruler towards the solution space until it *just* touches the space at point B, which represents the optimal solution. The coordinates of B are found by noting that it lies on two of the boundaries:

AB: $4X_1 + 3X_2 = 60$
BC: $X_1 + 4X_2 = 40$

Multiply the BC equation by 4 and then subtract the AB equation from it. This yields $13X_2 = 100$ or $X_2 = 7.69$. Substituting this from the BC equa-

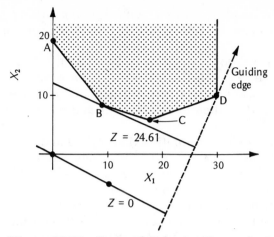

Figure 14-12. *Optimal Solution Using the Iso-Payoff Lines*

tion yields $X_1 = 40 - 4X_2 = 40 - 4 \times 7.69 = 9.23$. Hence, the optimal solution is $X_1 = 9.23$ and $X_2 = 7.69$; the smallest feasible value of Z is $9.23 + 2 \times 7.69 = 24.61$.

INTEGER SOLUTIONS

Thus far, we have ignored the question: what to do if only the integer values of the action variables are meaningful? In this we are not alone. Optimization techniques always begin by ignoring the integer-solution requirement. The problem is formulated and solved in the hope that the resultant optimal values would turn out to be integers. If this does not happen, we have two options: fudge or use a branch-and-bound approach. Each is explored below.

Fudge
Begin by rounding off the optimal (but fractional) values. Check if the rounded solution continues to be feasible. If found to be feasible, compute the corresponding payoff. Accept the rounded solution if its payoff is not too different than the payoff of the fractional valued solution. This is what we did in solving the hospital design problem.

If the above solution is either infeasible or feasible but too far "off the optimum," continue the search in the "neighborhood" of the currently optimal (but fractional) solution. This trial-and-error approach could yield a near-optimal and integer-valued solution in a finite number of steps.

Branch and Bound
To illustrate this approach, we will solve example 2 assuming that X_1 and X_2 must be integers. If this condition were ignored, the optimal solu-

tion would be $X_1 = 9.23$ and $X_2 = 7.69$, with a *minimum payoff* of $Z = 24.61$. Since X_1 and X_2 are fractional, this solution is of course unacceptable.

You can now argue as follows. Insisting on integer-valued solutions is equivalent to adding further constraints. Hence, the solution space would only shrink and consequently, the payoff can only be worse. The minimum payoff, $Z = 24.61$ is, therefore, *a lower bound* to any integer-valued optimum.

Note also that the rounded-off solution (i.e., $X_1 = 9$ and $X_2 = 8$) is feasible and has a payoff of $Z = 9 + 2 \times 8 = 25$. Thus, any acceptable solution should cost less than 25 units. In other words, $Z = 25$ is *an upper bound* to the payoff of any integer-valued solution.

Whether this upper bound is close enough to the lower bound depends on the unit of measurement. Suppose, for instance, that the payoff is measured in millions of dollars. Then, the lower bound would be 24.61 million dollars and the upper bound would be 25 million dollars. The payoff difference then would equal $390,000. Also, one must consider the criterion for being close. For example, if the criterion were:

$$\text{the upper bound} \le 1.01 \times \text{the lower bound}$$

then the rounded-off solution would not be an acceptable solution.

In any case, suppose that the fudged solution is not acceptable. Then, since $X_1 = 9.23$ is unacceptable, the integer-valued solution must have $X_1 \le 9$ (the next smallest integer) or $X_1 \ge 10$ (the next largest integer). Similarly, one should also investigate the possibilities: $X_2 \le 7$ or $X_2 \ge 8$. In other words, the solution could be in one of the four branches as shown in figure 14-13. Each branch leads to one subproblem which can be solved graphically.

The branch-and-bound approach proceeds as follows:

1. If a branch is infeasible, close it. If it is feasible, solve the corresponding problem.

Figure 14-13. *The Branches from the Node with Z = 24.61*

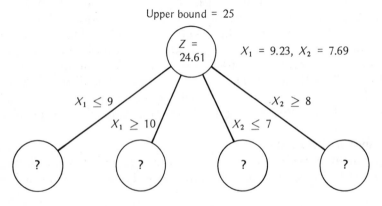

2. If the payoff exceeds the current upper bound, stop searching that branch.
3. If the solution is integer-valued, establish a new upper bound, then close that branch.
4. If none of the above three events happens, establish a new lower bound.
5. A node whose payoff equals the current lower bound is still open for further branching.
6. Continue the search until some stopping criterion is met.

Check the following results by the graphical method:

1. When $X_1 \le 9$; the optimal solution is: $X_1 = 9, X_2 = 8$ with $Z = 25$.
2. When $X_1 \ge 10$; the optimal solution is: $X_1 = 10$, $X_2 = 7.5$ with $Z = 25$.
3. When $X_2 \le 7$; the optimal solution is: $X_1 = 12, X_2 = 7$ with $Z = 26$.
4. When $X_2 \ge 8$; the optimal solution is: $X_1 = 9, X_2 = 8$ with $Z = 25$.

Figure 14-14 displays these findings.

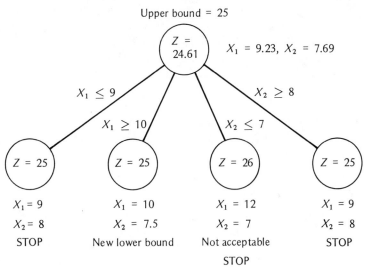

Figure 14-14. *Evaluating the Branches*

You can now argue as follows. When $X_1 \le 9$ or when $X_2 \ge 8$, solution is integer-valued ($X_1 = 9$ and $X_2 = 8$). Since $Z = 25$ is within bounds, this solution is acceptable. Stop searching any further in this branch.

When $X_2 \le 7, Z = 26$ exceeds the current upper bound of 25. Hence, though integer-valued, this solution is not acceptable. Stop searching this branch.

When $X_1 \ge 10$, Z equals 25 which is within bounds. However, the corresponding solution is fractional. Hence, this node is still open for investigation with a *new lower bound of 25*. However, since the new lower bound of 25 equals the upper bound, further search is unnecessary. The solution, $X_1 = 9$ and $X_2 = 8$, is in fact the required integer-valued optimal solution.

SUMMARY AND GENERALIZATIONS

In this chapter, we saw how to obtain optimal solutions of two-variable decision problems. The solution process is rather straightforward: identify all the corners of the resultant solution space and determine the best corner.

This simplicity is a consequence of complete linearity—the objective function is linear and so are the boundaries of every constraint. It follows that so long as the solution space is convex no interior point will ever be optimal. Furthermore, unless the iso-payoff lines are parallel to some boundary, only one corner can be optimal.

Two-variable problems can be solved using graphs since such problems are two-dimensional. An optimization problem with n action variables is a problem in n dimensions. When $n = 3$, it is easy to verify that the iso-payoff triplets lie on a plane; that most of the constraints are bounded by planes; and that the corners lie at the intersection of three or more planes. Any one corner will have three or more neighboring corners. Though theoretically simple, the search process becomes more difficult as the number of corners increases. The number of candidate corners increases rapidly with any increase in n, the number of dimensions. Geometrical procedures become impractical and are replaced by the algebraic ones. Both the Simplex and Dual Simplex algorithms are of this type. These two techniques as well as the Duality Theory will be explored in the next chapter.

SELECTED READINGS

BUDNIK, F. S.; MOJENA, R.; and VOLLMANN, T. E. *Principles of Operations Research for Management.* Homewood, Ill.: Richard D. Irwin, Inc., 1977.

DAELLENBACH, H. G. and BELL, E. J. *User's Guide to Linear Programming.* Englewood Cliffs, NJ: Prentice-Hall, Inc., 1970.

LOOMBA, N. P. and TURBAN, E. *Applied Programming for Management.* New York: Holt, Rinehart and Winston, 1974.

PROBLEM SET 14
TWO-DIMENSIONAL PROBLEMS

1. Explain the following terms: convex set, feasible solution, extreme point or vertex, iso-profit line (*), redundant constraint.

2. Explain, giving an example not discussed in the text, that if an LP problem has two solutions, it has an infinite number of solutions.

3. Why does LP methodology evaluate corner points (extreme solutions) only? Explain.

In problems 4 through 9, find the optimal solution(s) using the graphical method. In each case, assume the nonnegativity constraints: $X_1 \geq 0$ and $X_2 \geq 0$. In each case, identify the slack(s) and/or surplus(es).

4. Maximize:

$$Z = 6X_1 + 5X_2$$

Subject to:

$$\begin{aligned} X_1 &\leq 8 \\ X_2 &\leq 10 \\ 7X_1 + 6X_2 &\leq 84 \\ 3X_1 + 4X_2 &\leq 48 \end{aligned}$$

5. Maximize:

$$Z = 2X_1 + 3X_2$$

Subject to:

$$\begin{aligned} 4X_1 + 5X_2 &\leq 800 \\ 3X_1 + 7X_2 &\leq 700 \\ X_1 + X_2 &\leq 300 \\ X_1 &\geq 50 \end{aligned}$$

6. Minimize:

$$Z = 3X_1 + 4X_2$$

Subject to:

$$\begin{aligned} 2X_1 + 11X_2 &\geq 1{,}000 \\ 5X_1 + X_2 &\geq 400 \\ X_2 &\geq 50 \end{aligned}$$

7. Maximize:

$$Z = 50X_1 + 40X_2$$

Subject to:

$$\begin{aligned} 15X_1 + 11X_2 &\leq 8{,}000 \\ 3X_1 + 2X_2 &\leq 3{,}000 \\ X_1 + X_2 &\leq 900 \\ 20X_1 + 17X_2 &\leq 13{,}000 \\ 5X_1 + 4X_2 &\geq 8{,}200 \end{aligned}$$

8. Minimize:

$$Z = 2X_1 + X_2$$

Subject to:

$$\begin{aligned} X_2 &\geq 3 \\ 2X_1 - X_2 &\geq 0 \\ 3X_1 + 4X_2 &\leq 25 \end{aligned}$$

9. Minimize:

$$Z = X_1 + 2X_2$$

Subject to:

$$\begin{aligned} 7X_1 + 5X_2 &\geq 20 \\ 3X_1 + 2X_2 &\geq 10 \\ X_1 + X_2 &\geq 6 \end{aligned}$$

10. Famous Pizza House makes two kind of pizzas: Best and Super-Deluxe. Each Best pizza yields 50¢ profit and each Super-Deluxe yields 75¢ profit. There are 200 pounds of dough and 600 ounces of topping mix available at present. Each Best pizza needs 1 pound of dough and 4 ounces of topping mix. Each Super-Deluxe pizza needs 1 pound of dough and 8 ounces of topping mix. No more than 100 Super-Deluxe and 125 Best pizzas will be sold today. How many pizzas of which kind should be produced to maximize total profit? Which of the constraints are binding on the optimal?

11. A. B. Tilley Company is in the business of buying soybeans and selling the soybean oil and meal extracted from the beans. The beans are usually sold in bushels, oil in gallons, and meal in tons. However, for the sake of simplicity assume that each product is bought and sold in pounds. This month, the company can buy the beans from Sam Jones and/or Martha Dockett:

- *Sam Jones* can supply 80,000 pounds of beans at 40¢ per pound. Each pound of beans will yield .35 pounds oil and .45 pounds meal; the rest is worthless.
- *Martha Dockett* can supply 100,000 pounds of beans at 45¢ per pound. Each pound of beans will yield .3 pounds of oil and .6 pounds of meal; the rest is worthless.

It costs 10¢ to process a pound of beans from either source. Oil sells for 80¢ per pound and meal for 70¢ per pound. A. B. Tilley cannot sell more than 45,000 pounds of oil, nor can they sell more than 80,000 pounds of meal this month; they also believe in not storing the products. How much should the company buy from either supplier?

12. A midwestern farmer owns 1,000 acres of good farmland. He can plant either corn or soybeans or a combination of both. After accounting for seeds, fertilizers, labor, etc. each acre of corn will yield $100 profit; each acre of soybeans will yield $80. The person-hour requirements are 36 per acre of corn and 40 per acre of soybeans. The farmer can allocate a total of 30,000 person-hours. Also, an acre of corn needs 1/4 ton of fertilizer, an acre of soybeans needs 1/5 ton of fertilizer and the farmer can purchase 200 tons of fertilizer this season. Corn needs 1,000 gallons of water per acre and soybeans need 900 gallons. The county has allotted only 800,000 gallons of water for this farm. How can the farmer maximize his total profit from farming?

13. Nancy Mahoney has just received $100,000 from her dear deceased uncle. She wants to maintain at least $10,000 in cash for a long awaited vacation, home improvements and for other unforeseen expenses. She would like to invest the remainder so as to maximize her annual return on investment. Bonds yield 10 percent with a risk of 1 percent; growth stocks yield 15 percent with a risk of 5 percent. Nancy does not want the average risk to exceed 3.5 percent. How should she divide the investment capital?

14. David Brown, a suburban homeowner, is trying to decide between two fertilizers for his lawn: Instant Green and Roots Multiplier. David's lawn needs at least 200 pounds of nitrogen, 80 pounds of phosphorus, and 100 pounds of potassium to regain its health.

    Instant Green is chemically analyzed as 20-5-20, meaning that a pound of it will release .20 pounds of nitrogen, .05 pounds of phosphorus, and .20 pounds potassium. A 20-pound bag costs $5.

    Roots Multiplier is analyzed as 15-10-10 and costs $7 for a 40-pound bag.

    How many bags of each kind should David purchase? (If necessary, he can store the remains of a bag for use next year.)

15. The Fun-Paints Manufacturing Company produces two types of latex paints: Super Shine and Easy Clean. Currently, they have orders for exactly 200 gallons of Super Shine and 300 gallons of Easy Clean—both in charcoal gray. The company manufactures these paints by blending two premixes; A and B. A gallon of premix A costs $4; that of premix B costs $5. Each gallon of premix A contains 10 ounces of the charcoal gray pigment and 14 ounces of the latex base. Each gallon of premix B contains 5 ounces of the pigment and 20 ounces of the latex base. A gallon of Super Shine must contain at least 6 ounces pigment and 18 ounces base. A gallon of Easy Clean should contain at least 8

ounces pigment and 16 ounces base. How many gallons of premixes A and B must be purchased to exactly fulfill the order at minimal cost?

*16. Obtain X_1, X_2, and X_3 so as to:

Maximize:

$$Z = 3X_1 + X_2 - X_3$$

Subject to:

$$
\begin{aligned}
15X_1 + 11X_2 &\leq 8,000 \\
X_1 + 2X_2 &\leq 900 \\
X_1 + X_2 + X_3 &= 1,500 \\
X_1 + X_3 &\geq 600
\end{aligned}
$$

(Hint: Despite appearances, it is unnecessary to use three decision variables.)

*17. Suppose that the Gordon Morebuck and Company of example 6 in chapter 10 is the only customer of ABC Corporation. Then their aggregate planning problem can be summarized as follows.

Minimize:

$$Z = \$9,600 + 186X_1 + 202X_2 + 219Y_1 + 243Y_2$$

Subject to:

$$
\begin{aligned}
12X_1 \qquad\quad + 15Y_1 \qquad\qquad &\leq 12,000 \\
12X_2 \qquad\quad + 15Y_2 &\leq 10,000 \\
X_1 \qquad + Y_1 \qquad\quad &\leq 800 \\
- X_1 + X_2 - Y_1 + Y_2 &\leq 1,600 \\
X_1 + X_2 \qquad\qquad\quad &= 900 \\
Y_1 + Y_2 &= 600
\end{aligned}
$$

X_1, X_2, Y_1, Y_2 must be integers
$X_1, X_2, Y_1, Y_2 \geq 0$.

Obtain the optimum values of X_1, X_2, Y_1, and Y_2. (Hint: The graphical method is still applicable.)

*18. Obtain X_1, X_2, and X_3 so as to:

Maximize:

$$Z = 5X_1 + 3X_2 + X_3$$

Subject to:

the constraints in problem 16

Then compare the optimal values of X_1, X_2, and X_3 in both problems. Can you explain your findings? Can you generalize your findings to all situations with an equality constraint?

19. To reduce air pollution as well as traffic congestion, a municipality is thinking of banning private automobiles from the downtown area during business hours. The plan includes constructing a number of parking lots around the

downtown area and then providing shuttle service from there. The service will be provided using two types of municipal buses: mini and maxi. Each maxibus costs $45,000 and carries 45 passengers. Each minibus costs $30,000 and carries 20 passengers. A bus will leave a parking lot only when that bus is full. Because of this minibuses will operate on a more frequent schedule than that of the maxibuses. It is anticipated that a maxibus will make 16 trips and a minibus will make 30 trips each day. Consequently, a citizen survey indicates that a minibus will be three times more satisfactory to the riders than a maxibus. To ensure citizen coorporation, the municipality wishes to maximize the rider satisfaction. Each bus needs one driver. The daily usage will be at least 20,000 but no more than 35,000 riders. The municipality has allocated $2,000,000 for purchasing the buses. It can also hire up to 50 drivers. What is the optimal number of buses of each variety and how much will it cost? How will this change if the bus-purchase budget were reduced by $50,000?

20–25. Find the integer-valued optimal solutions of the decision in problems 4 through 9.

15

Simplex, Duality, and Integer Solutions

Many decision problems do not have computationally advantageous structures. In this chapter, the Simplex and Dual Simplex techniques for solving such problems are illustrated. These techniques are based on skillfully solving simultaneous equations. The chapter also discusses how to perform sensitivity analysis, i.e., study the parametric ranges over which the current solution remains optimal. Finally, a branch-and-bound procedure for obtaining integer-valued optimum solutions is shown.

The chapter ends with a review of the topics in the third part, suggesting extensions of this set of techniques.

471

GAME PLAN AND RATIONALE

Many decision problems are not structured in a way that makes computation easy. Nor are the decision variables limited to only two. The Simplex technique is used to solve such problems.

One begins the search for an optimum at the "do-nothing" corner (vertex or extreme point) of the solution space. Nothing happens there since every action variable is zero at this extreme point. The search process begins there only because it is not clear where else to begin. From this point, the Simplex technique locates the most desirable of all the vertices which are "next to" the current vertex. That vertex is analyzed next only if its payoff is better than that of the present one. This process of successively finding better extreme points is repeated until, at some stage, a better vertex cannot be found. At this stage, the search stops since the current solution, by definition, must be optimal.

Algebraic Foundations

Though we have used geometric terminology to briefly describe the search process, it is not practical to use a geometric method to find an optimum when there are more than two action variables. The equivalent algebraic method must be used.

You may recall that in the geometric method, we found the boundaries of the solution space by converting each constraint into an equation. In the algebraic method, each constraint is converted into a suitable equation by *introducing auxiliary variables,* a process called *standardizing the problem format.* In the standard format we end up with n variables which together satisfy m equations, with $n > m$. The role of a corner is played by *a basic solution.* This is obtained by using the following *theorem of simultaneous equations:*

Given a set of m simultaneous equations in n variables, with $n \geq m$, one can always find a solution in which, at most, m variables have nonzero values.

It follows that one can always find a solution by deliberately setting $n - m$ variables to zero. This process yields a basic solution. The variables which are intentionally set to zero are called *nonbasic variables* and the variables whose values are found by then solving the resultant simultaneous equations are known as *basic variables.* The set of all basic variables is known as *the basis.* The act of moving from corner to corner is equivalent to *changing the basis.*

Since we only need to examine the basic solutions to find an optimum, and since there can only be a finite number of such solutions to any decision problem, why not simply make a list of all the basic solutions and then evaluate each one? For a very practical reason. Of the n variables in the decision problem, m will be basic in any one solution. This means that there will be a total of nC_m such solutions. (The symbol, nC_m, denotes total number of ways of choosing m objects out of n.) If, for example, we have a decision problem with 6 action variables and 4 constraints of the $\leq$ type, there will be $6 + 4 = 10$ variables in the standard format of the problem and 4 will be basic at any one time. You can check that even in this small a problem, there are $10C_4 = 210$ basic solutions! Evaluating every basic solution is clearly impractical. It is more practical to conduct a systematic search. This is the rationale for studying the Simplex technique.

Post-Optimality Analysis

Having found an optimal solution, post-optimality or *sensitivity analysis* should be performed. This becomes important because whether or not a specific solution is optimal depends on the actual values of various parameters which jointly define a decision problem. In many real world problems, these parameters are seldom known with the precision assumed by the Simplex technique. The sensitivity analysis consists of identifying the ranges of parametric values within which the current optimal solution remains optimal. The *Dual Theorem* provides an efficient method of recognizing these ranges. It also provides a technique for finding the newer optimal solutions, when necessary. The Dual Theorem also provides a method for solving minimization problems using a maximization format. This will be discussed in more detail in the second part of this chapter.

Optimal solutions obtained by the Simplex technique do not guarantee that the action variables will have integer values. When fractional values are meaningful, one need not proceed further. Occasionally however, only the integer values of some or all action variables are meaningful. Technically, these are known as *integer or mixed* linear optimization problems. One method of solving such problems, the *branch-and-bound approach,* is examined in the last part of this chapter.

Why Bother?

The complex problems involving hundreds of action variables and as many constraints are of course not solved manually. This being the case, why should we study the Simplex technique and the associated theory? For several reasons. Though a computer can solve a problem, you as either a manager or a management scientist are responsible for *interpreting* the computer-generated solution. You are also responsible for *imple-*

menting that solution in real world settings. This, in turn, implies that you must convince your superiors, coworkers, and/or subordinates on the goodness and reasonableness of that solution. Convincing others is easier if you are personally convinced. This means that you must *understand* each step in the solution process. This is best accomplished by completely solving some relatively simple decision problems pretending that you're a computer and thus getting a "feel" for what a computer does in more complex situations.

PRINCIPAL STEPS IN A SIMPLEX TECHNIQUE

There are five major steps in solving a general linear optimization model:

Step 1: Standardize the problem format. The final outcome of this step is the Initial Simplex Tableau. Read the initial basic solution. If the initial basis contains artificial variables, proceed to Step 2; otherwise skip to Step 3.

Step 2: If the objective row contains a penalty, M or $-M$, eliminate the penalty from each column containing an artificial variable. The remaining steps describe an optimization sequence.

Step 3: Check the resultant solution for optimality. If it is found to be optimal, *stop*. Otherwise proceed to Step 4.

Step 4: Decide which of the currently nonbasic variables should become basic. Since the number of variables in the basis must remain constant at each stage in the search process, determine the variable that must leave the basis (i.e., become zero).

Step 5: Change the basis and read the new solution. Return to Step 3 to see if we have arrived.

This short description of steps in the Simplex technique contains several new terms and, thus, you may not have fully understood the search process. In the next few sections we will illustrate these steps in detail by working out one specific problem. We will solve the "community-based organization's problem" which was formulated in example 2 of chapter 10. The corresponding algebraic formulation is reproduced here for ready reference.

The objective of this organization is to maximize its value to the surrounding community. It proposes to do this by employing four types of professionals: X_1 of Type 1, X_2 of Type 2, X_3 of Type 3, and X_4 of Type 4. The objective is to:

Maximize:

$$Z = 6X_1 + 4X_2 + 3X_3 + 3X_4$$

Subject to the constraints:

$$10X_1 + 8X_2 + 5X_3 + 4X_4 \leq 100 \text{ (Budget in \$2000 units)}$$
$$X_1 + X_2 + X_3 + X_4 \leq 20 \text{ (Typists' time in 2-hour units)}$$
$$10X_1 + 8X_2 + 6X_3 + 5X_4 \geq 80 \text{ (Number of clients served)}$$

Nonnegativity requirements:

$$X_j \geq 0 \text{ for } j = 1, 2, 3, \text{ and } 4$$

STANDARDIZE THE PROBLEM FORMAT

The standard Simplex algorithm assumes that the decision maker wants to maximize payoff. It transforms each inequality into a suitable equality, so that the initial solution is always the "do-nothing" solution. To accomplish this, even a managerially meaningful equality constraint is converted into a procedurally more useful equality. In the standard format, the right-hand side constant of each constraint is nonnegative. Also, each action variable in the standard format is nonnegative. Finally, the standard format shows the decision problem in a tabular form known as the *Initial Simplex Tableau*. We will now illustrate how to convert any decision problem into its standard form. Not every one of the following acts are necessary in every problem; each is discussed here for the sake of providing a quick reference.

Introduce the Complementary Variables

The Simplex technique requires that each action variable must be nonnegative. Occasionally, however, both the positive and negative values of some action variable are meaningful. Let X be this type of action variable. For Simplex purposes, it is "split" as follows. Define two new variables, say X^+ and X^-, in the following manner:

$$X^+ = \begin{cases} X \text{ if } X > 0 \\ 0 \text{ if } X \leq 0 \end{cases}$$

It follows that X^+ is a nonnegative action variable which equals X, whenever X is positive. Similarly define the action variable, X^-, as follows:

$$X^- = \begin{cases} -X^- \text{ if } X < 0 \\ 0 \text{ if } X \geq 0 \end{cases}$$

You can check that:

1. Both X^+ and X^- are nonnegative.
2. Only one of these will be positive at one time.
3. The original action variable X always equals the difference:

$$X = X^+ - X^-$$

Rewrite the corresponding objective function using the variables X^+ and X^- instead of X. Also, rewrite each constraint using X^+ and X^- rather than X.

Change Negative Right-Hand Sides

If the right-hand side of a constraint is negative, multiply every term in that constraint by -1 and then change the sense of inequality from $\leq$ to $\geq$, or vice versa. For example, if the constraint reads:

$$4X_1 - 7X_2 + 13X_3 \leq -50$$

it will read:

$$-4X_1 + 7X_2 - 13X_3 \geq 50$$

Change all negative right-hand sides this way.

Introduce Slack and Surplus Variables

To transform an inequality of the $\leq$ type into a useful equality, add a slack variable to the left-hand side of that constraint. A *slack variable* measures the extent to which a resource has been underutilized. For example, the dollars available to hire professionals are a resource. The first constraint in the community organization's decision problem:

$$10X_1 + 8X_2 + 5X_3 + 4X_4 \leq 100$$

shows the limits on this resource. The difference between the left-hand side and 100 represents the extent to which the approved budget will not be used, or the *slack* associated with that constraint. Denote this slack by a new variable, say X_5. Then, rephrase the budget constraint:

$$10X_1 + 8X_2 + 5X_3 + 4X_4 + X_5 = 100$$

Similarly, by introducing another slack variable, say X_6, the constraint on the typists' time can be rephrased:

$$X_1 + X_2 + X_3 + X_4 + X_6 = 20$$

Both X_5 and X_6 represent the corresponding slack, i.e., the extent to which a resource has not been used. When a slack is positive, the corresponding resource is underutilized. When a slack is zero, the associated resource is fully utilized. And, by construction, a slack cannot be negative. For the community organization's problem, we express this condition as:

$$X_5 \geq 0 \text{ and } X_6 \geq 0$$

To transform an inequality of the $\geq$ type into an equation, subtract a *surplus variable* from the left-hand side of such a constraint. For example, the requirement on the number of clients served:

$$10X_1 + 8X_2 + 6X_3 + 5X_4 \geq 80$$

is transformed into an equality by subtracting a surplus variable, say X_7, from the left-hand side. Thus:

$$10X_1 + 8X_2 + 6X_3 + 5X_4 - X_7 = 80$$

A surplus variable, such as X_7, measures the extent to which a requirement has been overfulfilled. It follows that a surplus variable must be either positive or zero; it cannot be negative.

Introduce Artificial Variables (The Big M Method)

Neither slack nor surplus variables represent any action. As such, both are *dummy variables*, introduced solely for standardizing the format. Nonetheless, each such variable has a managerial interpretation. The dummy variables to be described now have no such interpretation. They are known as the artificial variables. Their only purpose is to start search process on an all-dummy basis.

As an illustration, consider again the number-of-clients-served requirement. The all-dummy basis results only if every action variable is zero. If you substitute $X_1 = X_2 = X_3 = X_4 = 0$ in the third constraint, you will run into an impossible situation:

$$-X_7 = 80 \text{ or, equivalently, } X_7 = -80$$

This is impossible because a negative surplus is meaningless. To resolve the difficulty, add an artificial variable, say X_8, to the left-hand side of that constraint. (An alternative technique of resolving this difficulty will be discussed in the section entitled "The Dual Simplex Algorithm and Sensitivity.") With this addition, the constraint now reads:

$$10X_1 + 8X_2 + 6X_3 + 5X_4 - X_7 + X_8 = 80$$

The Simplex technique can thus *begin by setting all the action and surplus variables to zero*. Managerially speaking, this makes sense. When there is no action, there can be no surplus.

An artificial variable is also introduced if a constraint is in fact an equality. Suppose, for example, that the director decided to hire *exactly* 18 professionals in all. This constraint could be represented by:

$$X_1 + X_2 + X_3 + X_4 = 18$$

However, since the standard Simplex technique always begins at the do-nothing corner, we would be faced with an impossible situation:

$$0 = 18$$

As a remedy, we add an artificial variable, say X_9, and then rewrite the equality constraint as:

$$X_1 + X_2 + X_3 + X_4 + X_9 = 18$$

At the do-nothing corner, we have:

$$X_9 = 18$$

Alternatively, in the presence of an equality constraint, eliminate one of the decision variables from the original formulation. For instance, if $X_1 + X_2 + X_3 + X_4 = 18$, then one of these variables, say X_4, can be eliminated by noting that $X_4 = 18 - X_1 - X_2 - X_3$.

The point is that artificial variables help us begin the search on the all-dummy basis. On the other hand, an artificial variable is like a pesticide—the typical farmer cannot survive without it, but it should never be part of his harvest. In fact, if at least one artificial variable remains positive in the optimal basis, this implies that the corresponding decision problem has no feasible solution. Having found the do-nothing solution, therefore, the Simplex technique tries to eliminate each such variable before searching for an optimal solution.

Adjust the Objective Function

There are two steps to standardizing the objective function.

1. If necessary, it is rewritten so that the objective is to maximize payoff.
2. Each action, slack, surplus, or artificial variable is formally introduced in the objective function.

Minimization Objective Note that to minimize Z is equivalent to maximizing its negative, $-Z$. Hence, if the decision maker's objective were:

Minimize:

$$4X_1 + 3X_2 + 7X_3 - 9X_4$$

it could be transformed into a maximization objective by simply changing all the signs and thus stating:

Maximize:

$$Z = -4X_1 - 3X_2 - 7X_3 + 9X_4$$

Introduce the Contribution of Each Variable Note that X_8 is an artificial variable in the community organization's problem. As such, it should never be in the optimal basis. Procedurally, this is accomplished by assigning it a penalty of $-M$ units, M being an extremely large positive number. For this reason, the technique of introducing the artificial variables is known as the Big M Method. Neither a slack nor a surplus variable contributes to the objective function. Formally, the contributions of such variables are set to 0. On the basis of these considerations, the objective function of the community organization becomes:

$$Z = 6X_1 + 4X_2 + 3X_3 + 3X_4 + 0X_5 + 0X_6 + 0X_7 - MX_8$$

THE SIMPLEX TABLEAU

At this stage, all the variables have been defined and the objective has been modified to account for the influence of each variable. Each constraint can also be displayed using every variable. As an illustration, the constraints for the community organization are shown by three equations:

$$10X_1 + 8X_2 + 5X_3 + 4X_4 + 1X_5 + 0X_6 + 0X_7 + 0X_8 = 100$$
$$1X_1 + 1X_2 + 1X_3 + 1X_4 + 0X_5 + 1X_6 + 0X_7 + 0X_8 = 20$$
$$10X_1 + 8X_2 + 6X_3 + 5X_4 + 0X_5 + 0X_6 - 1X_7 + 1X_8 = 80$$

and the nonnegativity conditions:

$$X_j \geq 0, \text{ for } j = 1 \text{ through } 8$$

There are $n = 8$ variables in the standard format and $m = 3$ constraints. A basic solution is found by deliberately setting $n - m = 8 - 3 = 5$ variables to zero. Presumably, we could proceed by displaying and evaluating each basic solution. Since there are $8C_5 = 56$ basic solutions, however, this kind of search is impractical. We will, instead, search rather systematically.

Create the Initial Simplex Tableau

As you can imagine, repeatedly writing the objective function and the constraint equations throughout the search process can be both tedious and error-prone. Besides, the symbols $X_1, X_2, \ldots, X_n$ are unimportant; their coefficients contain all the necessary information. This essential information is separated from the nonessential items by creating a table of coefficients. Such as a table, known as the Initial Simplex Tableau, is shown in table 15-1. It illustrates the tableau for the community organization's problem.

Since it is extremely important to understand this tableau, we will pause to explain each entry. The first line contains the heading of each column. The shorthand, RHS, denotes the "right-hand side" of each equation. For the sake of convenience, the left- and right-hand sides of the objective function are switched. The new right-hand side, Z, is the first entry in the RHS column. The other three entries (100, 20, and 80) are simply copied from the equations defining the constraints. Each row describes one equation. The top row, designated as row 0, describes the

Table 15-1 *The Initial Simplex Tableau*

ROW	X_1	X_2	X_3	X_4	X_5	X_6	X_7	X_8	RHS
0	6	4	3	3	0	0	0	$-M$	Z
1	10	8	5	4	1	0	0	0	100
2	1	1	1	1	0	1	0	0	20
3	10	8	6	5	0	0	-1	1	80

objective function; the next row describes the first constraint; and so on. The entries in each of the eight variable columns are the corresponding coefficients. For example, from table 15-1, you can see that the coefficient of X_1 in the objective row is 6, that of X_2 is 4, . . . , that of X_8 is $-M$. This corresponds to the new form of writing the objective function:

$$6X_1 + 4X_2 + 3X_3 + 3X_4 + 0X_5 + 0X_6 + 0X_7 - MX_8 = Z$$

All other rows are to be interpreted similarly.

Note also, that row 0 is unlike any other row. It is not a constraint. Rows 1 through 3 (m, in general) represent the constraints and these must be solved to obtain a *basis*. The very act of finding the basis provides the current value of the objective function in the RHS of row 0.

An important feature of the Simplex Tableau is that it provides a basic solution without performing any computations. This statement remains true at each stage of the search. Identify a basic variable as follows:

Find a column that contains a 1 in one of the rows and a 0 in every other row. The corresponding variable is a basic variable.

For example, column X_5 of table 15-1 contains a 1 in row 1 and a 0 in every other row. Hence, X_5 is a basic variable. Similarly, X_6 is a basic variable. X_8 would be a basic variable but for the $-M$ in the corresponding objective row. And, since we have found only two (rather than the necessary three) basic variables in table 15-1, it is not yet in the proper form.

Standardize the Artificial Variable Columns

This can be remedied as follows. The search in column X_8 reveals that row 3 contains the only 1 in that column. If we multiply that entry by M and then add it to the $-M$ in row 0, column X_8 becomes proper. *Mathematics believes in fairness.* Thus, to achieve the desired result without violating mathematical laws, we must perform the same operation at each entry in row 0 and row 3.

To each entry in row 0, add M times the corresponding entry in row 3. Symbolically:

New row 0 = Old row 0 + M × row 3

Study this notation carefully since similar operations will be repeated in the future. To illustrate, row 0 contains a 6 in column X_1; and in that same column, row 3 contains a 10. Hence the new entry in column X_1 of row 0 is: $6 + 10M$. Similarly check that the new entry in column X_2 is: $4 + 8M$. Table 15-2 shows the effects in the entire row 0. Note that row 3 is *not* altered in the process.

Table 15-2 *Standardized Initial Simplex Tableau*

ROW	X_1	X_2	X_3	X_4	X_5	X_6	X_7	X_8	RHS
0	$6 + 10M$	$4 + 8M$	$3 + 6M$	$3 + 5M$	0	0	$-M$	0	$Z + 80M$
1	10	8	5	4	1	0	0	0	100
2	1	1	1	1	0	1	0	0	20
3	10	8	6	5	0	0	-1	1	80

Hence, $X_5 = 100$

If there were two or more artificial variables, we would have repeated this process for each such variable. Since the community organization's problem contained only one artificial variable, the problem is now in a completely standard form, because:

1. Each basic variable column, X_5, X_6, and X_8, contains a unique 1 in that column.
2. There are a total of three basic variables.

Read the Initial (All Dummy) Solution

The advantage of using a standard Simplex Tableau is that a solution can be obtained without additional computation. Each nonbasic variable, X_1 through X_4 and X_7 in table 15-2, is automatically set to zero. Finding the values of basic variables is just as simple.

For each basic variable, locate the row that contains the only 1. The corresponding RHS is the value of that basic variable.

For example, column X_5 has its only 1 in row 1 and the RHS of row 1 is 100. Hence, $X_5 = 100$. Similarly, the X_6 column has its only 1 in row 2 and the corresponding RHS equals 20. Hence, $X_6 = 20$. Similarly, $X_8 = 80$. This solution-reading process is illustrated in table 15-2.

The initial solution is, therefore:

$$X_1 = X_2 = X_3 = X_4 = 0, X_5 = 100, X_6 = 20, X_7 = 0, X_8 = 80$$

This is the do-nothing corner of the community organization's solution space since each action variable, X_1 through X_4, is zero. In other words, do not hire any professional of any type; save all the budget ($X_5 = 100$); and leave the secretaries idle ($X_6 = 20$). There will be no surplus of clients served ($X_7 = 0$). The artificial variable equals 80. This solution's "value to the community," obtained by solving $Z + 80M = 0$, is $Z = -80M$. This is much worse than worthless.

Obviously, this initial solution is not optimal. Then why did we bother to find it? For several reasons.

1. The Simplex technique guarantees to find an optimal solution, if one exists, regardless of which solution is used as the first feasible solution. But, the search process must begin somewhere.
2. It is a basic solution. (It has as many positive valued variables, 3, as the number of constraints.)
3. It is feasible, i.e., it satisfies every constraint, and every variable is nonnegative.
4. It is extremely easy to find.

This initial solution corresponds to the "origin" of the graphical method used for solving two action-variable problems. In Simplex terminology, it is the *all dummy* solution, since only the dummy variables are basic.

OBTAINING SUCCESSIVELY BETTER SOLUTIONS

There are three major steps.

1. Test the current solution for optimality.
2. Decide which variable should enter the basis and hence which one should leave the basis.
3. Change the basis and read the new solution. Each is illustrated below by solving the community organization's problem.

Test for Optimality

The coefficients of the variables in the objective row describe the extent to which the objective function can be improved. The coefficients of the basic variables are zero, since their contribution to payoff is already accounted for. If, on the other hand, a currently nonbasic variable has a positive coefficient, this implies that the payoff can be increased by letting that variable become nonzero, i.e., allowing that variable to enter the basis. The optimality test is based on this observation.

> If the objective row contains at least one positive entry, then the current solution is not optimal. Otherwise, it is optimal.

Row 0 of table 15-2 contains four positive entries: $6 + 10M$, $4 + 8M$, $3 + 6M$, and $3 + 5M$. Hence, the corresponding solution is not optimal. A better solution can be obtained by entering *one* of the currently nonbasic variables (X_1, X_2, X_3, or X_4) into the basis. Which one should enter the basis? And, which one of the currently basic variables (X_5, X_6, or X_8) should become zero, i.e., leave the basis?

Determine the Entering and Leaving Variables

There are two parts to this step. *First,* determine which variable should enter the basis. *Then,* determine which variable should leave the basis.

> *Rule for entering a variable.* Examine the coefficients in the objective row. The variable with the largest positive coefficient in row 0 should enter the basis. (If there is more than one qualifying variable, arbitrarily choose one.) The corresponding column is called the pivotal column.

Since $6 + 10M$ is the largest positive coefficient in row 0, the corresponding variable, X_1, should enter the basis. Therefore, *column X_1 of table 15-2 is the current pivotal column.* In the constraint rows, that column contains three positive entries: 10, 1, and 10. These entries are used to determine which variable should leave the basis.

> *Rule for exiting a variable.* Concentrate on the positive entries in the pivotal column. For each such entry, read the corresponding RHS, and compute the ratio:
> $$\text{RHS} \div (\text{positive entry})$$
> The row containing the smallest nonnegative ratio is the pivotal row. (If two or more rows can be pivotal, choose one arbitrarily. Officially, the resultant solution is said to be a *degenerate* solution. But it must be emphasized that this adjective describes a mathematical—rather than a managerial interpretation of the situation.) The basic variable that contains the 1 in this row must leave the basis.

The RHS for row 1 is 100 and the entry in column X_1 of table 15-2 is 10. Hence, in the first row, the ratio equals: $100/10 = 10$. Similar computations yield:

$$\text{Ratio (Row 1)} = 100/10 = 10$$
$$\text{Ratio (Row 2)} = 20/1 = 20$$
$$\text{Ratio (Row 3)} = 80/10 = 8$$

Of the three ratios (10, 20, and 8) the smallest ratio, 8, occurs in row 3. Hence, *row 3 is the pivotal row.*

Of the three basic variables ($X_5, X_6,$ and X_8) the last one, X_8, has a 1 in the pivotal row, row 3. Hence, X_8 must leave the basis. The upshot of these rules is that X_1 should enter and X_8 should leave the basis. How is this accomplished?

Change the Basis

Two operations are necessary to complete this step. First, the pivotal column must contain a 1 in the pivotal row. Next, every other entry in the pivotal column must be zero. The first operation is completed as follows. The entry that lies at the intersection of the pivotal column and row is called the *pivot.* Divide each entry in the pivotal row by the pivot. Symbolically:

$$\text{New Pivotal Row} = \frac{\text{Old Pivotal Row}}{\text{Pivot}}$$

For the problem in table 15-2, the pivotal row is row 3 and the pivotal column is column X_1. The pivot is 10. Hence, the new pivotal row is obtained by the formula:

$$\text{New Row 3} = \frac{\text{Old Row 3}}{10}$$

The results are displayed in the adjoining table 15-3.

Table 15-3 *Restructured Pivotal Row*

ROW 3	X_1	X_2	X_3	X_4	X_5	X_6	X_7	X_8	RHS
Old	10	8	6	5	0	0	-1	1	80
New	1	4/5	3/5	1/2	0	0	$-1/10$	1/10	8

Next, to ensure that every other entry in the pivotal column is zero, proceed as follows. Let A denote the entry in the pivotal column and some nonpivotal row. Then, from every entry in that row, subtract A times the corresponding entry in the newly formed pivotal row. Symbolically:

$$\text{New Row} = \text{Old Row} - A \times \text{New Pivotal Row}$$

Do this for each nonpivotal row.

Let us return again to the problem in table 15-2. Column X_1 is the pivotal column and it contains $(6 + 10M)$ in row 0. In other words $A = 6 + 10M$. Hence, the formula for obtaining the new row 0 is:

$$\text{New Row 0} = \text{Old Row 0} - (6 + 10M) \times \text{New Row 3}$$

That is, from each entry in row 0, subtract $(6 + 10M)$ times the corresponding entry in the new row 3. For example, column X_2 contains $(4 + 8M)$ in the old row 0 and 4/5 in the new row 3. Hence, in the new row 0, it becomes:

$$(4 + 8M) - (6 + 10M) \times 4/5 = -4/5$$

The rest of the entries in the new row 0 are obtained similarly.

Row 1 contains a 10 in the pivotal column. Hence, we obtain the new row 1 by the formula:

$$\text{New Row } 1 = \text{Old Row } 1 - 10 \times \text{New Row } 3$$

Similarly, the old row 2 contains a 1 in the pivotal column. Hence, the appropriate formula is:

$$\begin{aligned}\text{New Row } 2 &= \text{Old Row } 2 - 1 \times \text{New Row } 3 \\ &= \text{Old Row } 2 - \text{New Row } 3\end{aligned}$$

The consequences of applying these formulas to rows 0, 1, and 2 are displayed in table 15-4.

Table 15-4 *The Second Solution*

ROW	X_1	X_2	X_3	X_4	X_5	X_6	X_7	RHS
0	0	−4/5	−3/5	0	0	0	3/5	Z − 48
1	0	0	−1	−1	1	0	1	20
2	0	1/5	2/5	1/2	0	1	1/10	12
3	1	4/5	3/5	1/2	0	0	−1/10	⑧

Reading that $X_1 = 8$

The consequences are summed up as follows. We have established a new basis, i.e., a new set of basic variables: X_1, X_5, X_6. The second basic solution is simply read off table 15-4. For example, the only 1 in column X_1 is in row 3. The RHS in row 3 is 8. Hence, $X_1 = 8$. Similarly, $X_5 = 20$ and $X_6 = 12$. Also, from the RHS of row 0, $Z = 48$. For example, if you employ 8 workers of type 1 and none of any other type, then 20 units of the budget are unused. Also, 12 typing units remain unused, and the value to the community is 48 units.

Whatever happened to column X_8? It was dropped, because the variable X_8 was artificial. It was introduced only to start the solution process at the all-dummy basis. In order to bring in X_1, the artificial variable X_8 was driven out of the basis. Consequently, unlike X_5, X_6, or X_7, it is no more essential to keep column X_8 around. This is usually the fate of artificial variables. When these variables leave the basis, everything about them is forgotten!

Further Tests and Improvements

Is $Z = 48$ the best value of the objective function? According to the optimality test, we should examine the objective row coefficients.

Since X_7 has a positive coefficient (3/5) the current basis is not optimal. One of the currently nonbasic variables must become basic, i.e., must enter the basis. Which one? Again, the coefficients in the objective row provide the answer. Since only X_7 has a positive coefficient, X_7 should enter the basis.

Which variable should leave the basis? Following the rule for exiting a variable, compute the ratio:

RHS ÷ positive entry

for each of the two positive entries: 1 and 1/10 in rows 1 and 2, respectively. The corresponding RHS values are 20 in row 1 and 12 in row 2. Since the ratio $20 \div 1 = 20$ is smaller than the ratio $12 \div 1/10 = 120$, *row 1 is the pivotal row*. The current basic variable X_5 has its 1 in this row. Hence, X_5 must leave the basis.

The computations essential for changing the basis are summed up by the following formulas. First, obtain the new pivotal row:

new Row 1 = old Row 1

This follows because the pivot in this case is already 1. Next, change every other entry in the X_7 column to 0 by using the newly formed pivotal row. The formulas are:

New Row 0 = Old Row 0 − 3/5 × New Row 1
New Row 2 = Old Row 2 − 1/10 × New Row 1
New Row 3 = Old Row 3 + 1/10 × New Row 1

The consequences are displayed in table 15-5. The basic variables are X_1, X_6, and X_7. Their values can be read off as $X_1 = 10$, $X_6 = 10$, and $X_7 = 20$. The objective function Z equals 60. If you employ 10 workers of type 1 and none of any other type, then 10 typing units are unused and 20 more clients than required (i.e., $80 + 20 = 100$ clients in all) can be served. Also, since $X_5 = 0$ (it is no longer basic), the budget will be exhausted. The value of this solution is $Z = 60$. Is this the best possible solution?

Table 15-5 *The Third Solution*

ROW	X_1	X_2	X_3	X_4	X_5	X_6	X_7	RHS
0	0	−4/5	0	3/5	−3/5	0	0	Z−60
1	0	0	−1	−1	1	0	1	20
2	0	1/5	1/2	3/5	−1/10	1	0	10
3	1	4/5	1/2	2/5	1/10	0	0	10

Since the coefficient of X_4 in the objective row is 3/5 (a positive number), further improvements are possible, i.e., the current solution is not optimal. Verify that:

1. X_4 should enter the basis.
2. X_6 should leave the basis.

Also verify the change-of-basis formulas:

New Row 2 = 5/3 Old Row 2
New Row 0 = Old Row 0 − 3/5 × New Row 2
New Row 1 = Old Row 1 + New Row 2
New Row 3 = Old Row 3 − 2/5 × New Row 2

The consequences are shown in table 15-6. Verify that:

1. The variables X_1, X_4, and X_7 form the new basis.
2. Their values are: $X_1 = 10/3$; $X_4 = 50/3$; and $X_7 = 110/3$.
3. The objective function is Z = 70.

Table 15-6 *The Optimal Solution*

ROW	X_1	X_2	X_3	X_4	X_5	X_6	X_7	RHS
0	0	−1	−1/2	0	−1/2	−1	0	Z − 70
1	0	1/3	−1/6	0	5/6	5/3	1	110/3
2	0	1/3	5/6	1	−1/6	5/3	0	50/3
3	1	2/3	1/6	0	1/6	−2/3	0	10/3

Also, since the objective row no longer contains a positive entry, *this solution is optimal.* Now, provide the verbal interpretation of this solution.

Special Cases
Solving the community organization's problem was relatively straightforward. There was only one optimum and the Simplex algorithm led directly to it. Occasionally, there are difficulties.

Cycling When there are ties for entering and/or leaving variables, sometimes the Simplex algorithm might repeat itself. That is, for some $L > 0$ and for some $N > L$, the solution at stage N might be identical to that at stage L. If this happens, break the tie (choose the entering and/or leaving variable) differently than before. Then proceed as usual.

Multiple Optima The basic variables always have zero coefficients in the objective row—their contribution to the objective is fully accounted. Sometimes, one or more of the nonbasic variables might have zeros in the objective row of the optimal tableau. This means that bringing such variables into the basis neither increases nor decreases the value of the objective function. In such cases, *find all other basic optimal solutions.* For example, let $(X_1, X_2, \ldots, X_n)$ and $(Y_1, Y_2, \ldots, Y_n)$ be two such basic optimal solutions. Then, for any fraction r, where $0 < r < 1$, we can always find another optimal but nonbasic solution $(W_1, W_2, \ldots, W_n)$ where $W_j = rX_j + (1 - r) Y_j$. Graphically, the segment connecting these two optima is in fact iso-payoff. When multiple optima exist, you should always present the choice to the decision maker. Other reasons for seeking multiple optima will become clear in the remainder of this chapter.

BEYOND OPTIMALITY

If you were the director of the community organization whose problem we have been discussing, should you accept the optimal solution displayed in table 15-6? After all, you have carefully formulated the decision problem by:

1. Identifying the relevant action variables, $X_j(j = 1$ through 4)
2. Documenting their individual rates of contribution to the objective, i.e., the objective coefficients, C_j
3. Identifying the resource limitations and the output requirements, i.e., the right-hand sides of the constraints, $b_i(i = 1$ through 3)
4. Recording the technological coefficients, a_{ij}.

You have also carefully followed the step-by-step search for the optimum and know that the Simplex technique is an extremely systematic and logical method of obtaining the optimum. Why should you as the director hesitate to accept this carefully derived solution?

The reasons for hesitation stem from the requirement of certainty. Linear optimization models always assume that the input data are perfect. In real world situations, this rarely happens. Hesitating to accept the resultant optimum is, therefore, natural. It is overcome by re-examining the optimal solutions, an activity known as post-optimality analysis, sensitivity analysis, or parametric programming. Each name identifies an aspect of the work. *Post-optimality* indicates that the analysis is conducted after obtaining the optimum solution, a kind of hindsight. *Sensitivity analysis* indicates that we wish to examine the extent to which the current optimum is sensitive to the variations in data. *Parametric programming* focuses our attention on the primary concern— the values of input parameters.

Why might the parameters be inaccurate? Because, most often they are estimates based partly on "concrete" data, partly on out-of-date information, and partly on the estimator's judgment. Furthermore, even if the parametric values were perfectly accurate at the moment of formulating the problem, the passage of time tends to change these values. Thus, a solution which was optimum, say prior to the so-called "oil crisis," is unlikely to be so today. In short, the analysis must continue even after obtaining the optimal solutions.

In such analyses, one can examine the effects of:

1. Additional contraints
2. More action variables
3. New values for the objective coefficients
4. Changes in the technological coefficients
5. New values for the right-hand side constants

Sensitivity analysis, in other words, is valuable for responding to questions of the "what if?" variety.

DUALITY THEORY

The rules for performing a sensitivity analysis are based on the Duality Theory. It is more than just an interesting theory. Interpreting the results of sensitivity analysis is easier with a good grasp of Duality Theory. Also, many primal optimization procedures are direct consequences of the Dual Theorem. (Recall the use of dual variables U_i and V_j in the transportation algorithm in chapter 12.) Finally, it can be used to choose a problem with fewer constraints and thus to save computational expenses.

The Dual Problem

Corresponding to every linear optimization problem of interest to the decision maker, from now on to be designated *the primal problem,* there is another linear optimization problem that uses the same data and shares the same optimum as that of the primal. It is called *the dual problem.* These two problems, the primal and the dual, are two ways of viewing the same data. They are like mirror images—everything in the dual is the reverse of its counterpart in the primal.

As an illustration, consider the primal problem of the community organization. It is reproduced here with a slight modification.

Maximize:

$$Z = 6X_1 + 4X_2 + 3X_3 + 3X_4$$

Subject to:

$$10X_1 + 8X_2 + 5X_3 + 4X_4 \leq 100 \text{ (Budget in \$2,000 units)}$$
$$X_1 + X_2 + X_3 + X_4 \leq 20 \text{ (Typist's time in two-hour units)}$$
$$-10X_1 - 8X_2 - 6X_3 - 5X_4 \leq -80 \text{ (Number of clients served)}$$
$$\text{where } X_j \geq 0, \text{ for } j = 1, 2, 3, \text{ and } 4$$

When the objective is to maximize payoff, all constraints in the standard presentation are of the $\leq$ type. Therefore, every term in the third constraint has been multiplied by -1 so that it is also in the standard form of a $\leq$ inequality. *Always ensure that all the inequalities are of the same type* before proceeding to find the associated dual.

Recognizing the Dual

1. Separate the primal action variables, X_j from their coefficients. As in the Simplex Tableau, this creates a matrix of technological coefficients, a column of right-hand sides and an objective row. See figure 15-1.

	PRIMAL: Read from left to right.					Minimize W	Dual variables
DUAL: Read from top to bottom	10	8	5	4	$\leq$	100	Y_1
	1	1	1	1	$\leq$	20	Y_2
	-10	-8	-6	-5	$\leq$	-80	Y_3
	$\geq$	$\geq$	$\geq$	$\geq$			$=$
Maximize Z	6	4	3	3		Dual objective / Primal objective	W
Primal variables	X_1	X_2	X_3	X_4	$=$	Z	

Figure 15-1. *The Primal/Dual Relationships*

2. For each row of the technological matrix, i.e., for each primal constraint, identify one dual action variable, say Y_i.
3. The right-hand side constants of the primal become the objective row coefficients of the dual. If the primal objective is to maximize payoff (Z), the dual objective would be to minimize payoff, say W.
4. For each primal column, identify the associated constraint as follows. The technological coefficients in a primal column become the coefficients of the dual variables in the corresponding dual constraint. If the primal constraints are of the $\leq$ type, the dual constraints would be of the $\geq$ type. Also, the objective coefficients of the primal variables become the right-hand sides of the dual constraints.
5. If a primal constraint is an inequality, the corresponding dual variable must be nonnegative. If a primal constraint is a strict equality, the corresponding dual variable is unconstrained in sign, i.e., it might be positive, zero, or negative. (For example,

each constraint in the transportation tableau of chapter 12 is an equality; hence U_i and V_j are unconstrained.)

The mathematical relationship between the primal and dual problems can be summarized as follows.

Primal	Dual

Maximize:	Minimize:

$$Z = \sum_{j=1}^{n} C_j X_j \qquad\qquad W = \sum_{i=1}^{m} b_i Y_i$$

Subject to:	Subject to:

$$\sum_{j=1}^{n} a_{ij} X_j \le b_i \qquad\qquad \sum_{i=1}^{m} a_{ij} Y_i \ge C_j$$

for $i = 1, 2, \ldots, m$ $\qquad\qquad$ for $j = 1, 2, \ldots, n$

The Dual of the Community Organization's Problem The primal objective is to maximize its value, Z, to the community. Hence the dual objective is to minimize W. Since the primal problem has three constraints, budget, typist's time, and number of clients served, the dual has three action variables, Y_1, Y_2, and Y_3. The dual objective coefficients are read off the primal right-hand sides. The dual objective is to:

Minimize:
$$W = 100Y_1 + 20Y_2 - 80Y_3$$

Because, the primal problem has four action variables, the dual problem will have four constraints, each of the $\ge$ type. For example, by reading down the first column, you can identify the first dual constraint to be:

$$10Y_1 + Y_2 - 10Y_3 \ge 6$$

Similarly, the other constraints are:

$$8Y_1 + Y_2 - 8Y_3 \ge 4$$
$$5Y_1 + Y_2 - 6Y_3 \ge 3$$
$$4Y_1 + Y_2 - 5Y_3 \ge 3$$

Finally, since every primal constraint is an inequality, every dual variable must be nonnegative.

$Y_i \ge 0$, for $i = 1, 2$, and 3

This completes the identification of the dual problem.

It is now time to solve a mystery—how to obtain the optimal values of dual variables.

Solving the dual.
1. To obtain the optimal values of the dual variables, simply read the coefficients of the corresponding dummy variables in the objective row of the optimal Simplex Tableau. Then change signs.

2. The objective row coefficient of a primal action variable equals the difference:

right-hand side − left-hand side

of the corresponding dual constraint, i.e., that is the value of the associated dummy variable in the dual problem.

An Illustration and Interpretations
The Optimal Simplex Tableau of the community organization's primal problem is reproduced for ready reference as table 15-7. Recall that X_1, X_2, X_3, and X_4 are the action variables and X_5, X_6, and X_7 are the dummy variables in the primal problem. Since the dummy variable X_5 corresponds to primal constraint 1, the corresponding dual variable is Y_1. The corresponding objective row coefficient is $-1/2$. Hence, $Y_1 = 1/2$. Similarly, $Y_2 = 1$ and $Y_3 = 0$. Check that the dual objective function equals 70.

Table 15-7 *The Optimal Simplex Tableau*

ROW	X_1	X_2	X_3	X_4	X_5	X_6	X_7	RHS
0	0	−1	−1/2	0	−1/2	−1	0	Z − 70
1	0	1/3	−1/6	0	5/6	5/3	1	110/3
2	0	1/3	5/6	1	−1/6	5/3	0	50/3
3	1	2/3	1/6	0	1/6	−2/3	0	10/3
					Y_1	Y_2	Y_3	

In fact:

$$W = 100 \times 1/2 + 20 \times 1 - 80 \times 0 = 70$$

The objective row coefficient of X_1 is 0. This means that the first dual constraint: $10Y_1 + Y_2 - 10Y_3 \geq 6$ is satisfied exactly. (Check this.) Similarly, when $Y_1 = 1/2$, $Y_2 = 1$, and $Y_3 = 0$; the left-hand side of the second dual constraint becomes:

$$8 \times 1/2 + 1 - 8 \times 0 = 5$$

The left-hand side exceeds the right-hand side of the second constraint by: $5 - 4 = 1$. This agrees with the X_2 objective coefficient of -1. Similarly, the objective row coefficient of X_3 is $-1/2$ and this means that the left-hand side of the third dual constraint exceeds its right-hand side by $1/2$. Finally, the fourth dual constraint is satisfied exactly since the objective row coefficient of X_4 is 0.

Since the primal objective is to maximize payoff, the dual variables are called the *shadow prices* or *opportunity costs*. In the optimal solution, the ith shadow price, Y_1, measures the per-unit contribution of the ith primal resource to the value of the objective function *as long as* the current basis remains optimal. It is meaningful only as long as changes in the availability of primal resources do not force some current basic variable to leave the basis.

For example, the dual variable Y_1 corresponds to the budget constraint. Currently, 100 units of it are available. Increasing that budget by one unit increases the optimal value Z by $Y_1 = 1/2$ unit. Similarly, increasing the typists' time by 1 unit increases the optimal Z by $Y_2 = 1$ unit. On the other hand, decreasing by 1 the number of clients served does not affect the optimum, since $Y_3 = 0$. This also follows because X_7 is positive, i.e., there is a surplus capacity.

SENSITIVITY ANALYSES

We will now illustrate the responses to a variety of "what if?" questions. In each case, we assume that the primal objective is to maximize payoff. The responses are always obtained by beginning with the currently optimal tableau. It is good to remember throughout the discussion that a solution is managerially meaningful only if it is primal-feasible; and it is optimal only if it is both dual-feasible and primal-feasible.

New Objective Coefficients
The primal feasibility is determined by the primal constraints and not by the objective coefficients. However, the primal objective coefficients might affect the feasibility of the dual problem and hence the optimality. Why might the objective coefficients change? Perhaps due to the passage of time, or perhaps because the initial coefficients were rough estimates only. In any case, there are two possibilities. Each is examined separately.

Changes in the Nonbasic Coefficients Recall that the objective row coefficients of primal action variables in the optimal tableau describe the surplus in the corresponding dual constraints. As long as there is a surplus (i.e., as long as the objective row coefficient is negative) the corresponding dual constraint remains feasible, i.e., the currently optimal basis remains optimal.

For example, in the optimal tableau, the objective row coefficient of X_3 is $-1/2$. Hence, the *initial* coefficient of X_3 can increase by $1/2$, from 3 to 3.5, without affecting optimality. If that coefficient, C_3, exceeds 3.5, the current basis is no longer optimal. Thus, a change of basis operation is necessary when $C_3 > 3.5$.

Suppose $C_3 > 3.5$. It is unnecessary to begin with the initial tableau. If you have followed the arguments thus far, you can see that we only need to begin with the most recent optimal tableau with one change. The objective row coefficient of X_3 would be: $C_3 - 3.5$. Since it is positive, X_3 enters the basis. As before, you can determine the variable that would leave the basis, perform a change of basis operation, and hence obtain the new optimum. The details are left as an exercise.

Changes in the Basic Coefficients Currently, X_1 is a basic variable. Suppose that the objective coefficient of X_1 has since changed from $C_1 = 6$ to $C_1 = 6 + d$, where d is an arbitrary constant, either positive or negative. How does this affect optimality? If we were to perform exactly the same operations as those that yielded table 15-5, the final objective row would be that shown in figure 15-2. That figure also shows the final row 3 for reference purposes.

Row	X_1	X_2	X_3	X_4	X_5	X_6	X_7	RHS
0	d	-1	$-1/2$	0	$-1/2$	-1	0	$Z - 70$
3	1	$2/3$	$1/6$	0	$1/6$	$-2/3$	0	$10/3$

Figure 15-2. *Effect on Final Row 0 of Changing C_1*

Subtract from each entry in row 0, d times the corresponding entry in row 3, so that the objective row coefficient of X_1 is zero. The resultant values of the new objective row coefficients of the nonbasic variables are shown in figure 15-3. (Coefficients of the basic variables would remain unchanged.) As long as *each* of these coefficients remains negative, the current basis remains optimal. If at least one coefficient becomes positive, the corresponding variable will enter the basis. Thus, for example, X_2 remains nonbasic as long as: $-1 - 2/3d < 0$, i.e., as long as $d > -3/2$. By similar computation, you can check that the current basis remains optimal as long as $-1.5 < d < 1.5$. In terms of the original coefficients, this is

Figure 15-3. *Standardizing the Final Objective Row*

X_2	X_3	X_4	X_5	RHS
$-1 - \dfrac{2}{3}d$	$\dfrac{1}{2} - \dfrac{1}{6}d$	$\dfrac{1}{2} - \dfrac{1}{6}d$	$-1 + \dfrac{2}{3}d$	$Z - 70 - \dfrac{10}{3}d$

equivalent to $4.5 < C_1 < 7.5$. That X_1 should leave the basis when C_1 becomes smaller is intuitively obvious. When C_1 exceeds 7.5, X_6 enters the basis, which is not so obvious. Only a systematic search reveals the upper bound for C_1.

New Right-Hand Side Constants
We will now investigate the extent to which a right-hand side constant might change without making the current basis infeasible. As you can imagine, we will proceed by analyzing the corresponding slack and/or surplus variable. There are two possibilities. The dummy variable, slack or surplus, of the associated constraint is either in the optimal basis or it is not. Each possibility must be examined separately.

Dummy Variable Is Basic In that case, the analysis is very simple. The value of the dummy variable equals the amount by which a right-hand side constant can decrease (if the constraint is of the $\leq$ type) or increase (if the constraint is of the $\geq$ type). For example, the third constraint in the community organization's problem is of the $\geq$ variety, and currently b_3 equals 80. The corresponding dummy variable, X_7, is a surplus and it is in the optimal basis with $X_7 = 110/3 = 36\ 2/3$. Hence, b_3 can be as large as $80 + 36\ 2/3 = 116\ 2/3$ without making X_7 negative, i.e., without making that constraint infeasible.

Dummy Variable Is Nonbasic In this case, obtaining the range of values of the right-hand side constant is somewhat more difficult. Consider, for example, the first constraint, viz., budget ≤ 100 units. In this case, $b_1 = 100$. The corresponding dummy variable, X_5, is a slack and is nonbasic, i.e., presently $X_5 = 0$. How much can we change b_1 without making X_5 basic? Suppose $b_1 = 100 + d$, where d is an arbitrary constant. In that case, the first constraint would initially read:

$$10X_1 + 8X_2 + 5X_3 + 4X_4 + X_5 = 100 + d$$

If you now perform *exactly* the same operations that yielded the current optimum, you will find that: *in each row, the coefficient of d equals that of X_5*. In other words, column X_5 also gives the coefficients of d in each row. Column X_5 of table 15-6 and the final RHS values are shown in figure 15-4. You can now argue as follows. In the final basis, the RHS column

Figure 15-4. *Effects on the Final RHS of Changing b_1*

Row	X_5	RHS
0	−1/2	$Z - 70 - d/2$
1	5/6	$100/3 + 5d/6$
2	−1/6	$50/3 - d/6$
3	1/6	$10/3 + d/6$

provides the values of the objective function, as well as those of the basic variables. Each of these must, therefore, be nonnegative. It follows that we must have:

$$Z = 70 + d/2 \geq 0, \text{ so that } d \text{ must be } \geq -140$$
$$100/3 + 5d/6 \geq 0, \text{ so that } d \geq -40$$

You can similarly check that:

$$d \leq 100 \text{ and } d \geq -20$$

Keeping only the most stringent bounds yields the range for d:

$$-20 \leq d \leq 100$$

In other words, if the budget is at least $100 - 20 = 80$ units but no more than $100 + 100 = 200$ units, then the currently basic variables (X_1, X_4, and X_7) will remain basic. The RHS column contains the values of the basic variables and the objective function for each value of d. See figure 15-4.

For example, if the budget becomes 130 units, it would be an increase of $d = 130 - 100 = 30$ units. Similarly, if the budget becomes 88 units, d would be $88 - 100 = -12$. In either case, you can verify the RHS values shown in figure 15-5. As you might expect, when the budget increases, X_1 also increases since the Type 1 professionals are more valuable but also more costly. Converse is true of X_4, so X_4 decreases when the budget increases.

Row	Basic	RHS $d = 30$	RHS $d = -12$
0	—	$Z - 85$	$Z - 64$
1	X_7	175/3	70/3
2	X_4	35/3	56/3
3	X_1	25/3	4/3

Figure 15-5. *Effects of Budget Changes on the Basic Variables*

Changes Beyond Limits The conclusions we have just made and the ease of studying the effects of RHS changes continue to hold as long as the current basis remains feasible. What happens if the change in a right-hand side makes one or more constraints infeasible? We shall respond to this question in the section on the Dual Simplex algorithm.

Adding a New Variable

It is not unusual to want to introduce a new action variable into an existing model. Suppose, for example, that the professionals of type 5 can be employed by the organization; and that each will consume 3 units of budget, need 1 unit of typists' time, and serve 3 clients. Nothing else has changed. It is important to know whether such a variable (product, professional, etc.) will be active in the solution, i.e., will contribute to the objective. It would be good to know what its objective coefficient must be for it to be in the optimal basis. It is possible to determine this without reworking the entire solution process.

Minimum Necessary Contribution As an illustration, let X_8 denote the number of type 5 workers, if any, to be employed and let C_8 denote the relative value of each such worker. Since we have introduced an action variable without increasing the number of primal constraints, the number of dual variables remains at three. On the other hand, there is a new dual constraint:

$$3Y_1 + Y_2 - 3Y_3 \geq C_8$$

If the currently optimal solution, with $X_8 = 0$, is to remain optimal, it must be dual feasible. This means that the optimal values of the dual variables, $Y_1 = 1/2$, $Y_2 = 1$, and $Y_3 = 0$, must satisfy the above constraint. This, then, is the test of whether the Type 5 workers will be hired. Substituting the presently optimal values of Y_1, Y_2, and Y_3 yields the criteria:

$$3 \times 1/2 + 1 - 3 \times 0 \geq C_8, \text{ i.e., } C_8 \leq 5/2$$

In other words, C_8 must exceed 5/2 before X_8 can enter the optimal basis, i.e., before any type 5 workers are hired. This, in itself, is a valuable piece of information.

The Optimal Level Suppose that a type 5 worker is worth 11/4 units on the community organization's test, i.e., $C_8 = 11/4 > 5/2$, so that some Type 5 workers must be hired. How many? As usual, it is unnecessary to begin at the beginning. Since a type 5 worker must score at least 5/2, it follows that the final objective row coefficient of X_8 will be $11/4 - 5/2 = 1/4$. Since X_5, X_6, and X_7 are the dummy variables, their final tableau coefficients, shown in table 15-7, are used to obtain the final technological coefficients in column X_8. The process is summarized in figure 15-6. Since a type 5 worker consumes 3 units of budget, needs 1 unit of typists' time, and serves 3 clients, these *initial* coefficients of X_8 become the multipliers of the final coefficients of the dummy variables.

Figure 15-6. *Obtaining the Coefficients of* X_8

Final coefficients	X_5		X_6	X_7		X_8
Row 1	3 × 5/6	+	1 × 5/3	−3 × 1	=	7/6
Row 2	3 × −1/6	+	1 × 5/3	−3 × 0	=	7/6
Row 3	3 × 1/6	+	1 × −2/3	−3 × 0	=	−1/6
	Number of budget units		Typists' time	Number of clients served		

Computing the optimal value of X_8 now proceeds as usual. Column X_8 in its final form is appended to the Optimal Simplex Tableau of table 15-7. Since the final objective coefficient of X_8 is $1/4 > 0$, X_8 enters the basis and one of the currently basic variables leaves the basis. Compute the new optimum as an exercise in using the Simplex technique.

THE DUAL SIMPLEX ALGORITHM AND SENSITIVITY

Recall that the Simplex algorithm begins with a feasible, though not necessarily optimal basis, and continues to find the better solutions without losing the primal feasibility. At every stage, except the very last one, the solution remains dual-infeasible. The Dual Simplex algorithm is a mirror image of this process. It begins with a dual-feasible basis and continues to establish primal feasibility. At the very last stage, both the dual and primal problems become feasible and hence optimal.

Rationale
Why study the Dual Simplex algorithm?

1. When the primal constraint is of the $\geq$ or $=$ type, this technique finds the optimal basis without introducing the artificial variable (and the consequent penalty, $-M$). It is thus an elegant and computationally advantageous alternative to the "Big M" method discussed earlier. The payoff minimization problems are thus the likely candidates for the use of Dual Simplex.
2. The effects of changes in the right-hand side constants are best investigated using this method since in such cases one or more primal constraints become infeasible.
3. Also, the effects of adding new constraints are best examined using the Dual Simplex technique.

The Dual Simplex algorithm comprises the following sequence of steps:

1. If at least one basic variable is negative, the primal basis is still infeasible.
2. Remove the largest negative variable from the current basis. The corresponding row is the pivotal row.
3. If necessary, multiply the pivotal row by -1 so that the coefficient of the basic variable is a 1. Compute:

$$\text{ratio} = \frac{\text{objective row coefficient}}{\text{pivotal row coefficient}}$$

for each nonzero entry in the pivotal row. The column with the smallest positive ratio is the pivotal column. The corresponding variable enters the basis.

4. Change the basis as in the Simplex technique.
5. Return to step 1.

Additional Constraints

To illustrate the Dual Simplex technique, let us consider the effect of adding more constraints. When new constraints are imposed, apply each one to the currently optimal tableau. If a constraint continues to be feasible, the current basis remains optimal. For example, consider the constraint: $X_1 + X_2 + X_3 + X_4 \geq 20$, i.e., hire at least 20 professionals. It is feasible when $X_1 = 10/3$ and $X = 50/3$. Hence, that solution continues to be optimal. However, if the management wishes to impose the constraint:

$$X_1 \leq 3$$

then a new solution must be found since $X_1 = 10/3$ becomes infeasible.

In that case, introduce a slack variable, X_8, and standardize the constraint to read: $X_1 + X_8 = 3$. Append this to the current Optimal Simplex Tableau of table 15-7 as row 4. Also append column X_8. The result is shown in table 15-8. Note an irregularity. Even though X_1 is a basic variable, column X_1 is no longer in the standard form—row 4 contains a non-zero entry in column X_1. It can be cured easily. Subtract each element of row 3 from every element of row 4. The result is shown as row 4'.

$$\text{Row } 4' = \text{Row } 4 - \text{Row } 3$$

Table 15-8 *Accomodating the Constraint:* $X_1 \leq 3$

ROW	X_1	X_2	X_3	X_4	X_5	X_6	X_7	X_8	RHS
0	0	-1	$-1/2$	0	$-1/2$	-1	0	0	$Z - 70$
1	0	1/3	$-1/6$	0	5/6	5/3	1	0	110/3
2	0	1/3	5/6	1	$-1/6$	5/3	0	0	50/3
3	1	2/3	1/6	0	1/6	$-2/3$	0	0	10/3
4	1	0	0	0	0	0	0	1	3
4	0	$-2/3$	$-1/6$	0	$-1/6$	2/3	0	1	$-1/3$
Ratio		3/2	3		3				

From now on, Rows 0, 1, 2, 3, and 4' constitute the Initial Simplex Tableau. Since the objective row contains no positive entry, the current basis is potentially optimal, i.e., it is dual-feasible. However, since $X_8 = -1/3$, it is not primal-feasible. To restore the primal feasibility without losing dual feasibility, it is best to apply the Dual Simplex algorithm.

Since it is the only negative basic variable, X_8 *should leave the basis*, so that row 4' is the pivotal row. The ratios of objective row coefficients to pivotal row coefficients are shown in table 15-8. Since column X_2 contains the smallest positive ratio, 3/2, that column is the pivotal column and X_2

enters the basis. Using − 2/3 as the pivot, the basis is changed. The appropriate formulas are:

New Row 4 = −3/2 × 4′
New Row 3 = Old Row 3 − 2/3 × New Row 4
New Row 2 = Old Row 2 − 1/3 × New Row 4
New Row 1 = Old Row 1 − 1/3 × New Row 4
New Row 0 = Old Row 0 + New Row 4

The results are shown in table 15-9. The basic variables are: $X_1 = 3$, $X_2 = 1/2$, $X_4 = 33/2$, and $X_7 = 73/2$. None is negative. Hence, this basis is primal-feasible. Dual feasibility has been maintained since none of the objective row entries is positive. In short, table 15-9 displays an optimal solution. Since an additional constraint had to be satisfied, the new optimum, $Z = 139/2 = 69.5$, is smaller than the previous optimum, $Z = 70$. *The difference is the price paid for imposing the additional constraint.*

Table 15-9 *The Optimal Solution When $X_1 \le 3$*

ROW	X_1	X_2	X_3	X_4	X_5	X_6	X_7	X_8	RHS
0	0	0	−1/4	0	−1/4	−2	0	−3/2	Z − 139/2
1	0	0	−1/4	0	3/4	2	1	1/2	73/2
2	0	0	3/4	1	−1/4	2	0	1/2	33/2
3	1	0	0	0	0	0	0	1	3
4	0	1	1/4	0	1/4	−1	0	−3/2	1/2

INTEGER SOLUTIONS

As you have witnessed, both the Simplex and Dual Simplex algorithms provide extremely efficient means of solving the general linear optimization problems. Neither technique, however, guarantees that the optimal values of the action variables will be integers. When the fractional values are meaningful, there is no need to proceed further. In the community organization's problem, for instance, we assumed that part-time professional help was available. Thus, the fractional values were meaningful. Under these circumstances, the Optimal Simplex (or Dual Simplex) Tableau provides all the essential information.

In many optimization problems, however, one or more of the action variables must be integers. For example, suppose that due to the changing employment situation, the part-time help is no longer available, so that we must impose an additional restriction, i.e., that X_1, X_2, X_3, and X_4 must be integers.

Potential Solution Techniques

This innocuous looking condition of requiring integer solutions makes the task of finding optimal solutions considerably harder. Some of the commonly used options are presented here.

Complete Enumeration Since only a finite number of alternatives are meaningful, conceivably one could list all the integer-valued feasible solutions and then compare their objective function values. In one very special case, complete enumeration might be advantageous—when there are only two possible courses of action for each alternative. In that case, one can use the *zero-one algorithm* [see Garfinkel and Nemhauser (1972) for additional details].

Usually, however, such problems are solved by initially ignoring the integer solution requirement. If the resultant optimal values happen to be integers, nothing more need be done. Otherwise, the optimal (or near-optimal) integer-valued solution is obtained through a form of post-optimality analysis.

Fudge Round off the fractional values of the action variables in question. Check that such a solution remains feasible. If feasible, accept that solution if the corresponding payoff does not differ too much from the fractional-valued optimum. If the rounded solution is infeasible or not sufficiently optimal, investigate the solutions obtained by slightly altering the values of the currently fractional variables. This trial-and-error approach could lead to a near optimal solution.

Branch-and-Bound This approach was discussed while solving the traveling salesman problem. It is a special case of the enumeration approach where only a selected set of alternatives is evaluated in detail. Since the objective is to *maximize* some payoff, a feasible solution provides a lower bound, whereas a dual-feasible solution provides an upper bound on the value of the objective function.

Other Methods If there are only two action variables or only two constraints, the graphic approach could be used to find the integer-valued optimal solutions. More generally, Gomory's "cutting plane" algorithm could be employed to obtain the optimal solutions with integer-valued action variables. A host of other methods can be found in research literature, some of which is cited at the end of this chapter.

A Branch-and-Bound Solution of the Community Organization's Problem

As an illustration of the branch-and-bound approach, again consider the dual-feasible solution presented in table 15-7. The maximum payoff is $Z = 70$ units. However, this solution is not acceptable because both X_1 and X_4 are fractional: $X_1 = 10/3$ and $X_4 = 50/3$. Hence $Z = 70$ is an *upper bound* on any acceptably optimal solution.

Rounding off the fractional values gives $X_1 = 3$ and $X_4 = 17$. You can check that this solution is feasible. The corresponding payoff, $Z = 69$, therefore provides the lower bound. This lower bound is so close to the current upper bound that most managers would accept the solution $X_1 = 3$ and $X_4 = 17$ as being sufficiently optimal.

Identifying the Branches To illustrate the branch-and-bound approach, however, let us continue the search for at least one more step. Where should we look? Since $X_1 = 10/3 = 3$ 1/3 is not an integer, one could examine the effect of imposing the condition: $X_1 \leq 3$ (the next smallest integer) or the condition: $X_1 \geq 4$ (the next largest integer). Similarly, the nonacceptability of $X_4 = 50/3 = 16$ 2/3 suggests two more conditions: $X_4 \leq 16$ or $X_4 \geq 17$. In short, as shown in figure 15-7, each of the four "branches" of the node $Z = 70$ must be investigated. In that figure, the optimal values of the action variables are shown alongside the first node. The branches are identified by the corresponding constraints.

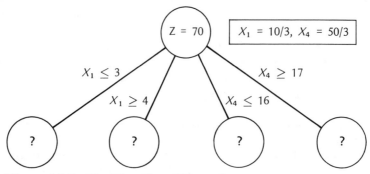

Figure 15-7. *The First Set of Branches*

Solving the Branches We have already evaluated the branch $X_1 \leq 3$. (See table 15-9.) Since the optimal values are $X_1 = 3, X_2 = 1/2, X_3 = 0$, and $X_4 = 33/2$; the corresponding maximal $Z = 139/2 = 69.5$ can only be an upper bound. The other three branches $X_1 \geq 4, X_4 \leq 16$, and $X_4 \geq 17$ are defined by the conditions $X_1 - X_8 = 4$, $X_4 + X_8 = 16$, and $X_4 - X_8 = 17$, respectively. Beginning with the Simplex Tableau of table 15-7, and *augmenting each condition in turn*, the corresponding optimal set can be obtained by an application of the Dual Simplex algorithm. The details are left as an exercise in applying that algorithm. The resulting values of decision variables are shown in figure 15-8.

Evaluating the Nodes It follows that when $X_1 \geq 4$, the acceptable solution yields a payoff $Z = 69$. Further splitting that node is unnecessary. Hence, stop searching along that node. Similarly, when $X_4 \geq 17$, the acceptable solution has the payoff 69. Hence, stop searching in that branch. As a matter of fact, $Z = 69$ *is the lower bound* when $X_1 \geq 4$ or when $X_4 \geq 17$; any additional constraints only reduce the payoff.

Neither $X_1 \leq 3$ nor $X_4 \leq 16$ yields integer solutions. Also, in each

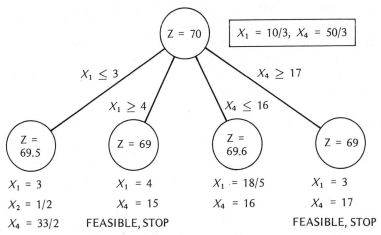

Figure 15-8. *Evaluation of the Branches*

case, the payoff exceeds the lower bound of 69. Thus, both branches are still open. Of these two branches, the one with $X_4 \leq 16$ has the higher payoff, $Z = 69.6$. This, then, is the *new upper bound*. Further search, if you wish to continue, should begin at this node. In that case, you would impose one of the two constraints, $X_1 \leq 3$ or $X_1 \geq 4$, on top of the existing constraint, $X_4 \leq 16$, for creating the new branches out of the node $Z = 69.6$. In case you fail to find an integer solution with $Z \geq 69.5$ (the value of the only other "open" node at this level), further search can be continued out of the node with $Z = 69.5$.

Since the current upper bound of 69.6 is only slightly better than the current lower bound of 69, very few managers would choose to continue the search. We should do likewise.

WHAT A MANAGER SHOULD KNOW

A number of computer programs for solving a variety of optimization problems are available on a number of high-speed computers of today. Also, a number of special-purpose algorithms for solving situation-specific allocation problems have been documented in OR/MS literature. A few are cited at the end of this chapter. However, a manager of tomorrow will be responsible for properly formulating problems and interpreting the computer-generated results. Though it is not possible to present a complete glossary of all possible OR/MS models and/or computer programs, we explored one of the simplest allocation models which turned out to be quite versatile—the general linear optimization model (LP).

In chapter 10, we discussed the techniques for formulating an LP model and presented a wide variety of managerially significant situations which can be approximated by such models. To avoid getting bogged down in computational details, we did not present any solution techniques in that chapter. Specific solution techniques were then examined in chapters 11 through 14 when the models had computationally advantageous structures. In each case, we also discussed the managerially important situations where such models could be applied. We also outlined some of the extensions of such techniques.

The Simplex and Dual Simplex techniques of this chapter have been presented in the same spirit. Enough details of the techniques have been presented so that you, as a manager, can solve such problems in simple situations. At the same time, by working on these simple problems, you will be in a position to interpret the computer-generated solutions of the larger and more complex problems. We have seen how to standardize the problem presentation format (the Initial Simplex Tableau), how to recognize and interpret the dual variables as shadow prices or opportunity costs, how to analyze the effects of additional constraints by an application of the Dual Simplex algorithm, and generally how to perform post-optimality analysis. In particular, we studied how to obtain optimal (or near-optimal) solutions when some or all decision variables must be integer-valued.

The power of the Simplex/Dual Simplex technology lies in its ability to perform this post-optimality analysis. For it is through such analysis that one can evaluate the effects of using less-than-perfect data. As an alternative approach, assume the data to be less than perfect from the very beginning and then formulate a statistical model of the allocation problem. Stancu-Minasian and Wets (1976) present an extensive bibliography of the resultant *Stochastic programming* models developed between 1955 and 1975.

Another natural extension of the LP technology is the formulation and solution of the models wherein the decision maker has multiple and often conflicting objectives. We have already outlined two of the procedures which are gaining wider acceptance—goal programming and multiple objective linear programming. Cochrane and Zeleny (1973) have compiled many articles on this topic. Steuer (1975), and Zionts and Wallenius (1976) have developed the computer programs for solving such models.

Several other algorithms have been cited to help you get started on the way to understand and appreciate the OR/MS work in various aspects of the allocation modeling.

SELECTED READINGS

BALAS, E. "An Additive Algorithm for Solving Linear Programs With Zero-One Variables." *Operations Research* (1965), pp. 517–545.

BALAS, E. *Duality and Pricing in Integer Programming.* Stanford, Calif.: Operations Research House, Stanford University, 1967.

BALINSKY, M. L. "Integer Programming: Methods, Uses, Computation." *Management Science* 12 (1965), pp. 253–313.

BEALE, E. M. L. and SMALL, R. E. "Mixed Integer Programming by a Branch and Bound Technique." IFIP Congress, New York, 1965.

COCHRANE, J. L. and ZELENY, M. eds. *Multiple Criteria Decision Making.* University of South Carolina Press, 1973.

COMER, J. M. "ALLOCATE: A Computer Model for Sales Territory Planning." *Decision Sciences* 5 (1974), pp. 323–338.

DRIEBECK, N. J. "An Algorithm for the Solution of Mixed Integer Programming Problems." *Management Science* 12 (1966), pp. 576–587.

DRIEBECK, N. J. *Applied Linear Programming.* Boston: Addison-Wesley Company, 1969.

GARFINKEL, R. and NEMHAUSER, G. L. *Integer Programming.* New York: John Wiley & Sons, Inc., 1972.

JENSEN, R. W. "Sensitivity Analysis and Integer Linear Programming." *Accounting Review* 43 (1968), pp. 425–446.

KHUMAWALA, B. M. "An Efficient Branch-Bound Algorithm for the Warehouse Location Problem." *Management Science* 18 (1972), pp. B718–B729.

KLINGMAN, D. and RUSSELL, R. "Solving Constrained Transportation Problems." *Operations Research* 23 (1975), pp. 91–106.

LAWLER, E. L. and WOOD, D. E. "Branch-And-Bound Methods: A Survey." *Operations Research* 14 (1966), pp. 699–719.

MITTEN, L. G. "Branch and Bound Methods: General Formulation and Properties." *Operations Research* 18 (1970), pp. 24–34.

RAPPAPORT, A. "Sensitivity Analysis in Decision Making." *Accounting Review* 42 (1967), pp. 441–456.

SALKIN, G. R. and KORNBLUTH, J. S. H. *Linear Programming in Financial Planning.* London: Haymarket Publishing Ltd., 1973.

SAMUELS, J. M. "Opportunity Costing—An Application of Mathematical Programming." *Journal of Accounting Research* 2 (1965), pp. 182–191.

SCHNEIDER, D. P. and KILPATRICK, K. E. "An Optimum Manpower Utilization Model for Health Maintenance Organizations." *Operations Research* 23 (1975), pp. 869–889.

SHARPE, W. F. "A Linear Programming Algorithm for Mutual Fund Selection." *Management Science* 13 (1967), pp. 499–510.

STANCU-MINASIAN, I. M. and WETS, M. J. "A Research Bibliography in Stochastic Programming, 1955–1975." *Operations Research* 24 (1976), pp. 1078–1119.

STEUER, R. E. "ADBASE: A Program for Analyzing Multiple Objective Linear Programming Problems." *Journal of Marketing Research* 12 (1975), pp. 454–455.

TAHA, H. A. *Integer Programming: Theory, Applications and Computers.* New York: Academic Press, Inc., 1975.

WAGNER, H. M. *Principals of Operations Research.* 2d ed. Englewood Cliffs, NJ: Prentice-Hall, Inc., 1975.

ZIONTS, S. and WALLENIUS, J. "An Interactive Programming Method for Solving the Multiple Criteria Problem." *Management Science* 22 (1976), pp. 654–663.

PROBLEM SET 15
OPTIMAL SOLUTIONS AND SECOND THOUGHTS

In each problem the variables are assumed to be nonnegative unless specified otherwise.

1. Below is a Simplex Tableau of a three-variable profit maximization problem. The decision variables are X_1, X_2, and X_3.

ROW	X_1	X_2	X_3	X_4	X_5	X_6	RHS
0	0	0	0	$-5/2$	$-15/4$	0	$Z - 135$
1	0	1	1/4	1/2	$-3/4$	0	3
2	1	0	$-17/8$	$-3/4$	9/8	0	5/2
3	0	0	43/8	$-5/4$	13/8	1	27/2

   a. Identify the basic and the nonbasic variables.

   b. What is the current value of the objective function?

   c. What are the values of the currently basic variables?

   d. Is this an optimal solution? Why or why not?

   e. Which of the constraints are binding? By how much?

   f. Is it possible to obtain another but equally good solution? Why or why not?

2. Construct the Initial Simplex Tableau of the following problem.

   Maximize:

   $$Z = 3X_1 + 2X_2 + 5X_3$$

   Subject to:

   $$5X_1 + 4X_2 + X_3 \le 50$$

   $$X_1 + X_2 + X_3 = 30$$

   Standardize that Initial Simplex Tableau.

3. Given the adjoining Simplex Tableau of a three-variable profit maximization problem,

ROW	X_1	X_2	X_3	X_4	X_5	X_6	RHS
0	3/4	1	0	-2	0	0	$Z - 20$
1	1/4	1/2	1	1/4	0	0	5/2
2	7/4	11/2	0	$-1/4$	1	0	25/2
3	$-1/4$	1/2	0	$-5/4$	0	1	15/2

a. What are the values of the currently basic variables?

b. Is this solution optimal? If yes, skip the rest of this problem. If no, continue.

c. Identify the entering variable, the exiting variable, the pivotal column, the pivotal row, and the pivot.

d. Change the basis.

e. Is the new solution optimal?

4. Given the adjoining tableau, obtain another solution which is equally good.

ROW	X_1	X_2	X_3	X_4	X_5	X_6	RHS
0	0	0	0	-2/5	0	-1/4	Z - 180
1	0	0	1/2	3/5	1	-1/2	5/2
2	0	1	1/4	1/5	0	3/4	3
3	1	0	-1/2	-1/5	0	-1/4	7/4

5. In the following tableau, the decision variables are X_1, X_2, and X_3.

a. Identify the original equality constraint.

b. Identify the surplus variable.

c. Standardize the format.

d. Then identify the entering variable.

ROW	X_1	X_2	X_3	X_4	X_5	X_6	RHS
0	3	2	5	-M	0	-M	Z
1	1	1	1	1	0	0	30
2	-4	5	3	0	-1	1	20

6. Obtain the standardized Initial Simplex Tableau and then identify the entering variable.

Minimize:

$$Z = 8X_1 + 9X_2 + 7X_3$$

Subject to:

X_3 unrestricted in sign
$X_1 + 2X_2 + X_3 \geq 4$
$7X_1 + X_2 - X_3 \geq 6$

7. Using the *graphical* method, obtain the maximum value of $Z = 3X_1 + 2X_2 + 5X_3$; subject to: $5X_1 + 4X_2 + X_3 \leq 50$ and $4X_1 - 5X_2 + 3X_3 \geq 20$. (Hint: Formulate and solve the dual.)

8. Solve the following problem *graphically*.

Minimize:

$$Z = 2X_1 + 4X_2 + 5X_3$$

Subject to:

$$5X_1 + 2X_2 - X_3 \geq 60$$
$$X_1 + X_2 + X_3 = 40$$
$$4X_1 + 3X_2 - 2X_3 \geq 20$$

(Hint: Eliminate an action variable.)

9. A production planning problem and the corresponding optimal tableau are shown below. (X_j = number of units of product j, j = 1, 2, 3)

Maximize:

$$Z = 30X_1 + 20X_2 + 25X_3 \text{ (profit)}$$

Subject to:

$$6X_1 + 5X_2 + 3X_3 \leq 30 \text{ (assembly)}$$
$$4X_1 + 2X_2 + 5X_3 \leq 16 \text{ (packaging)}$$
$$X_1 + 3X_2 + 4X_3 \leq 25 \text{ (inspection)}$$

ROW	X_1	X_2	X_3	X_4	X_5	X_6	RHS
0	0	0	-5/4	-5/2	-15/4	0	Z - 135
1	0	1	-9/4	1/2	-3/4	0	3
2	1	0	19/8	-1/4	5/8	0	5/2
3	0	0	67/8	-5/4	13/8	1	27/2

a. Formulate the dual problem.

b. Obtain the optimal values of the dual variables.

c. Verify that the dual is feasible, i.e., that each dual constraint is satisfied by the optimal values of the dual variables.

d. Give a verbal interpretation of the dual variables.

10. *Graphically* solve the following problem.

Maximize:

$$Z = 40X_1 + 50X_2$$

Subject to:

$$3X_1 + 5X_2 \leq 3,000$$
$$X_1 + X_2 \leq 800$$
$$5X_1 - 3X_2 \geq 0$$

11. Solve problem 10 using the Simplex technique. Create the Simplex Tableau and plot the all-dummy solution as a point in the (X_1, X_2) solution space.

Change the basis and plot the corresponding point. Continue the process till you have plotted the optimal solution. Do you see graphically how the Simplex technique proceeds?

12. Reconsider problem 11. What is the effect on the optimum of adding the constraint:

$$5X_1 + 4X_2 \geq 8,200$$

(Hint: Use the Dual Simplex algorithm, if necessary.)

13. Maximize:

$$Z = 2X_1 + 5X_2 + 8X_3$$

Subject to:

$$X_1 + 2X_2 + 4X_3 \leq 10$$
$$2X_1 + 6X_2 + X_3 \leq 15$$
$$X_1 + 3X_2 + 5X_3 \leq 20$$

14. Maximize:

$$Z = 3X_1 + 2X_2 + 5X_3$$

Subject to:

$$5X_1 + 4X_2 + X_3 \leq 50$$
$$X_1 + X_2 + X_3 = 30$$
$$-4X_1 + 5X_2 + 3X_3 \geq 20$$

(Hint: Introduce and then eliminate the artificial variables.)

15. Minimize:

$$Z = 10X_1 + 11X_2 + 8X_3 \text{ (cost in dollars)}$$

Subject to:

$$X_1 + X_2 + X_3 \geq 2 \text{ (ingredient A)}$$
$$10X_1 + X_2 + 2X_3 \geq 5 \text{ (ingredient B)}$$
$$X_1 + 8X_2 + 3X_3 \geq 8 \text{ (ingredient C)}$$

(Hint: Use the Dual Simplex algorithm.)

16. (Continuation of 15). Formulate the dual problem. Obtain the values of the dual variables. Interpret each variable.

17. Begin with the optimal tableau in table 15-7. Suppose that a consultant to the community organization has determined the relative worth of the Type 1 through 4 professionals to be 6:5:4:3. Does the current solution remain optimal? If not, derive the new optimum.

18. A typical professional of Type 5 scores 2.75 on the community organization's value scale, needs three budget units, one unit of typists' time and can serve three clients. Using this information, derive the new optimum.
(Hint: Augment the final coefficients of X_8 to the Simplex Tableau of table 15-7. Then proceed.)

19. For political reasons, the director of the community organization must hire at least one professional of each type. How does this affect the optimum? If necessary, derive the new optimal solution. What is the "cost" of politics? (Hint: Begin with table 15-6. Augment only the necessary constraints. Then use the Dual Simplex algorithm.)

*20. Reconsider problem 14. Note that the optimal basis would not change if the objective were changed to read:

Maximize:

$$Z = 4X_1 + 3X_2 + 6X_3$$

Why does this happen? Can you generalize your finding?
(Hint: Compare the objective coefficients.)

21. (Continuation of 14.) Suppose that the decision variables must be integer-valued. Obtain a solution whose payoff is within 3 percent of the upper bound.

22. (Continuation of 9). Examine, *in turn*, the effects on optimality of each of the following situations. In each case, derive the new optimum, if necessary.

    a. Profit contribution of product 3 becomes 27 per unit.

    b. Profit contribution of product 1 becomes 28 per unit.

    c. Profit contribution of product 2 becomes 24 per unit.

    d. Only 20 units of assembly time are available.

    e. Packaging time availability has become 20 units.

    f. Only 12 units of inspection time are available.

    g. At least 8 units must be produced.

23. (Continuation of 9). The company in problem 22 is considering the introduction of a new product, say product 4. Each unit of that product would need four units of assembly time, two units of packaging time and three units of inspection time. How large must be its contribution to profit?

24. (Continuation of 23). Suppose that the per unit contribution of product 4 is 18 units. Derive the optimal solution.

PART FOUR

Frontiers of Management Science

16
Appendix

This part consists of a single chapter which reviews the topics discussed in the preceding chapters and presents some suggestions for ensuring successful implementation of OR/MS-derived solutions. The text ends with a discussion of where management science is likely to be in the near future.

16

Frontiers of Management Science

Review of OR/MS Methods
Implementation: A Frontier
Future Possibilities
Selected Readings

A number of commonly used OR/MS techniques for solving managerial problems have been discussed, and many other techniques can also be found by consulting the selected readings at the end of each chapter. Additional sources of information on techniques and their applications are provided in appendix G.

Despite this preponderance of techniques, it must be emphasized that the true test of a management scientist is his/her ability to implement these solutions. This chapter, therefore, discusses some documented suggestions on enhancing the chances of implementing a solution. The chapter ends by discussing the directions in which OR/MS is likely to grow in the near future.

REVIEW OF OR/MS METHODS

In the preceding fifteen chapters, we have studied some of the methods of management science. Chapter 1 suggested that a management scientist should begin by identifying the *object system* and *its environment*. By object system, we mean an organization or its components in which there is a managerial problem that someone wishes to resolve. That someone is the *decision maker*. Some aspects of any decision problem are beyond the control of the object system, but they nonetheless affect the operations of that system. These aspects together constitute the *environment* of that system. *Systems analysis* consists of studying the object system and its environment, the outputs of that system, and the process by which the inputs are transformed into outputs. The success of an operations research project depends on the quality of this systems analysis.

Chapter 1 continues to describe the steps to be followed in a typical operations research project. They are based on a variation of the *scientific method* of inquiry first proposed by René Descartes, a French philosopher, soldier, and mathematician of the seventeenth century.

We have said that *management is decision making*. More often than not, however, all of the parameters that influence a decision are not known with certainty. Thus, a decision maker must be familiar with the techniques of quantifying uncertainty, as reviewed in chapter 2.

The third chapter examined some of the basic concepts in the *decision theory*. These include: *courses of action, states of nature, payoffs, and opportunity costs*. We then discussed how the resultant payoff matrices and decision trees can be used to search for a desirable course of action. Since what is desirable depends on the decision maker's philosophy and the amount of information he/she possesses, we explored a number of commonly used decision criteria. Finally, we discussed a measure of the value of information.

The discussion of decision-making techniques continued in chapter 4, where we saw how one can use *marginal analysis* to make decisions, and *Bayesian analysis* to revise probabilities on the basis of new data. We also explored one more measure of the value of information. Two more concepts, *utility* of money, and *adjusted expectations*, completed the survey of decision theory, and with it, that of the *foundations* of operations research.

Part II applied the concepts developed in Part I to three specific situations: planning and managing a project, determining optimal inventories, and analyzing the properties of waiting lines. In each situation, the formal models often become too complex, too restrictive, or both. In chapters 8 and 9, therefore, we studied the simulation approach of solving such problems.

Part III explored a variety of *linear optimization* (LP) models. We began by exploring the meaning of *linearity* and *certainty*, and the extent to which these assumptions were meaningful in specific situations. Since proper formulation, i.e., algebraic description, of a decision-making situation is a key to its solution, chapter 10 was devoted to the *techniques of formulation*. We then proceeded to examine several specific solution techniques: assignment and traveling salesman techniques in chapter 11; transportation in chapter 12; minimal spanning tree, shortest route, and maximal flow in chapter 13; the graphical method in chapter 14; and Simplex and Dual Simplex techniques in chapter 15. Each chapter examined the managerial applications of the corresponding techniques and their extensions. Chapter 15 also covered Duality Theory and its application to performing sensitivity analysis.

Many other techniques and their applications can be found in the readings at the end of each chapter. A list of additional sources is provided in appendix G.

The computer technology necessary for solving the real life decision problems has also gone through many "generations" of improvement and expansion. The computers are now often accessible in an interactive mode. This means, for instance, that a manager can operate a simulation model to ask a variety of "what if?" questions to a computer.

IMPLEMENTATION: A FRONTIER

Despite the many documented techniques and the almost exclusive attention paid by the present-day management scientists to publish more and varied tools of the trade, it must be emphasized that management science is not synonymous with a collection of techniques. A practicing management scientist must help the manager improve the organization's performance. The real worth of a management scientist lies *not* in the mathematical and technical elegance of solutions alone, but also in the improvements obtained by *applying* those techniques for solving the actual problems. Thus, attention must be focused on the managerial problem and on implementing the appropriate solutions to that problem. *Whatever is not implemented can't be a true solution!* In this final chapter, therefore, we will examine some of the proven ways of accomplishing this.

Why do we stress implementation skills? Because, despite over thirty years of explosive growth of OR/MS as a formal discipline, *implementation continues to be its "weakest suit."* Implementation is the most rewarding aspect of management science and also its most troublesome. Often enough to bother the recognized OR/MS leaders, the solutions proposed by the operations researchers have been ignored by managers or have been abandoned after initial implementation. Why? Because, implementing an operations research solution almost always implies instituting some kind of change within the organization. To successfully initiate change, one must know how to avoid or overcome the potential resistance to change. Those in charge and those affected by the change must be convinced of the need for initiating such changes. It is essential to "sell" or "market" a change. This is an acquirable skill rather than a science. Since there is no unique formula for success in this undertaking, implementation skill constitutes a frontier of management science. We will, therefore, examine some of the useful suggestions as documented by those practicing this art.

Identify the Decision Makers

Based on the reports by practicing management scientists, the first helpful suggestion for enhancing the chances of implementation is: *Begin by identifying the decision maker(s)*. While discussing the conditions necessary for the existence of a decision problem (see chapter 1), we stated that there must be someone who is interested in solving a problem. That someone is the decision maker—the sponsor of an OR/MS project.

Communicate with the decision makers throughout the progress of the OR/MS project—why the problem is what you think it is, where you got the data and how, what assumptions you are making (i.e., what you don't know about the problem, the model, the system, or the environment), what the possible solutions are and how much it will cost to obtain and operate each one. In short, get the decision maker involved—make it *his* problem, *his* model, and *his* solution.

Example: A Grain-Processing Firm in Illinois A firm buys grains (such as, soybeans and potatoes) and sells the processed goods (such as, soybean oil, potato starch, and soybean meal) on the Chicago Exchange. The prices of the grains and the processed goods vary considerably from season to season. The company tries to guard against such fluctuations by selling and buying "futures." This means, for instance, that the company may promise in March to sell so many tank-cars of soybean oil next September at so many dollars per tank-car. If so, the company has sold September futures in March. To meet the above contract, the company may want to ensure receiving an adequate supply of soybeans in August. If so, they have also bought August futures in March.

A managerial problem for this firm is to determine the timings of the buy/sell activities to ensure profitable operations. One decision maker in this case would be the Vice President of Commodity Operations. I also identified two other decision makers: the Manager of Management Systems, who wanted to show that operations research was useful in making the "when to buy and sell" decisions; and the company's Chief Trader, who did not believe in theoreticians telling him what to do. Thus, when I was developing the buy/sell strategies for this firm, I would communicate my findings to these three persons.

Since the Manager of Management Systems was obviously the most sympathetic of my efforts, he became my chief sponsor. I discussed many theoretical issues and technical difficulties with him. The Chief Trader, though skeptical, was also the most knowledgeable about day-to-day buying-and-selling activities. Thus, he became my source of information regarding the Chicago Exchange. To a large extent, the model that I developed for this firm was based on the "psychoanalysis" of the Chief Trader. The Vice President's interest was to use "whatever works." So, in my discussions with him, I concentrated on showing him the monetary advantages of various candidate policies—without stressing the theory, unless he asked for it.

Additional Evidence Why should you worry about identifying a decision maker? Because, if your recommendations are to be put in practice, you must have a corporate sponsor. You must establish rapport with him by close communications during each of the OR phases.

Remember, an operations research project without a sponsor is seldom successful. This is more than just good politics. Though the decision maker may not be a quantitative expert, he knows his organization and its method of working. He got where he is by acquiring this knowledge, and he knows where the "shoe pinches." In this regard, read the articles by Jatinder N. D. Gupta (1977), Lars Lonnstedt (1975), Alan C. Shapiro (1976), Amar J. Singh and Philip R. A. May (1977), and Harvey N. Shycon (1977). Gupta relates his experiences in the U.S. Postal Service, Lonnstedt documents his experiences in Swedish firms, Shapiro relates the problems in a capital-intensive company, Singh and May draw upon their experiences in the health-care field, and Shycon reports on a survey of American firms in 1977 and 1971. In each case, the message is a variation on the theme: *Know and Communicate with Thy Decision Maker* throughout the progress of your OR/MS project.

This becomes even more important when the decision problem you are working on is strategic rather than tactical. See the articles by T. L. Saaty (1972), E. S. Savas (1975); A. H. Rubenstein and D. A. Tansik (1970); R. L. Ackoff (1971); and J. H. Wakelin, Jr. (1971) for potential applications of OR/MS with respect to strategic problems. In such situations, you are developing long-range plans and/or establishing new procedures and guidelines. Well documented and reliable data are seldom on hand. Furthermore, the output is a process rather than a quantity. The intuition of the decision maker is a valuable input for defining the problem, and his creativity is an asset in obtaining and implementing the solution.

How to Identify a Decision Maker? The decision maker has the authority to initiate, modify, and terminate policies governing the organization or the system under study. In some systems, there may be more than one individual performing this function. In any event, one must understand how those who share authority make decisions, because this knowledge determines the format of presenting results and recommendations during and at the completion of the project. Some guidelines are listed below.

The organization of the decision-making group should be determined. Do they make decisions in a body or in a sequence? By majority vote? If not, who has veto power and who has final authority? Is the process a formal or informal one?

Very few cut-and-dried methods are available for identifying the decision makers in an organization. Some questions that may serve as useful guidelines in our search of the decision maker are listed below. A seasoned reader can add to this checklist, which derives from Churchman, et al. (1957).

- Who has the responsibility for making recommendations concerning modification of policies?
- Whose approval is required and how is this approval expressed?
- What constitutes final approval? (A majority vote in group deliberation, approval by a final authority in a sequence of reviews, etc.)
- Does anyone have absolute veto power? If not, how can a recommendation be rejected? Or worse yet, ignored?
- Who has the responsibility for carrying out recommendations once they are approved?
- Who has responsibility for evaluating the actions taken?

If these guidelines reveal the political nature of OR/MS processes, this is intentional. Operations research does involve politics in the best sense of that term.

Further Suggestions

We have already suggested that you must begin by identifying the decision maker. Many other suggestions reported by the practitioners are listed below.

Choose the Right Problem This means, for example, don't begin with statements such as, "This is an integer programming problem," or that "This is a queueing problem." This amounts to identifying a solution before knowing the problem—usually a self-defeating practice.

Bernard H. Rudwick (1969) has cited an interesting case in point. A new forty-story office building was equipped with four elevators. Within a few months of the opening, complaints started pouring in that it took too long to wait for an elevator on the first floor. Looks like a waiting line problem, right? Well, in this case, wrong! In fact, when the problem was attempted as a waiting line problem, each solution turned out to be either unsatisfactory (complaints continued) or expensive ($7,000 to change the existing control device so some elevators could run "express"). Furthermore, it would have cost $50,000 to install another elevator. A *solution* that worked turned out to be the *installation of a television set* in the nearby lobby that riders could watch while waiting for the elevator. Cost = $300 (in 1969); effect = no complaints!

Another case of this type is reported by Robert E. D. Woolsey (1973) who is an expert at unearthing such cases. It seems that the Industrial Engineering group of a steel factory was using a Linear Programming model in blast furnace burdening. They were using a computer for solving the problem. Their objective function had seven action variables. In the notation of chapter 10, they wanted to minimize:

$$Z = C_1X_1 + C_2X_2 + \cdots + C_7X_7$$

This looks like a seven-variable problem, one that would need a computer to solve. But wait. The more Mr. Woolsey listened to the engineers' story, the more equality constraints he found. *Each such constraint reduces the effective number of variables by one.* (We have already seen this phenomenon in chapters 10, 14, and 15.) By the time the engineers had finished their story, only *one* variable was left. The resulting problem could be solved using an ordinary pocket calculator!

This does not mean that they were bad engineers, nor does it mean that their solution was not optimal. It was. However, since they did not concentrate on the problem, their solution technique was more expensive than necessary.

Use the Right Data Note that in order to show that your proposed solution is better, you must know the current state of affairs precisely. If, for example, you are minimizing costs, you must know the cost of the current way of doing things. You should also determine whether your decision maker is concerned with operating costs, capital costs, or a combination of the two. Also, determine whether you are going to measure the costs in today's dollars, dollars one year hence, or what. Then convert all these costs in the same unit. Ask your accountants about the discount rate *they* will use. Make friends with your accountants and your data collectors.

This sounds like common sense, and it is. However, experience shows that it is not always easy to enforce the maxim: *Know Thy Numbers*. I recall working on the development of a simulation model for studying the flows of clients between human service agencies, such as, mental health centers, employment security offices, and public welfare offices. Tremendous difficulties had to be overcome while gathering data because the geographical boundaries of regions as used by the different agencies did not match.

State Your Assumptions If you can prove something, then it must be a fact. What you do not know is an assumption. It is best to make an explicit list of your assumptions before proceeding to construct a model. Make sure that your decision maker fully understands each of these. Write them in his language, if necessary. Only then can the resultant model become the decision maker's model. Failure to do this results either in nonimplementation of your solution or it is abandoned after initial implementation. Jatinder N. D. Gupta (1977) reports how the U. S. Postal Service installed and then abandoned a solution because the corresponding model was based on an implicit (and hence untested) assumption. The unstated assumption also turned out to be untrue, and this led to the solution's demise.

It is good to remember that logically rigorous conclusions can be dangerously incorrect if the relationships and assumptions of the model are incomplete and/or inaccurate. The experience of Robert S. McNamara, former secretary of defense, is a case in point. (See Thomas L. Saaty's article of 1972 for additional details of this issue.) A number of other examples of this phenomenon have been documented by Gene Woolsey, the Editor-in-Chief of *Interfaces*, a bulletin of the Institute of Management Sciences.

To paraphrase an old adage: It isn't what you don't know that hurts you. It's what you know *for sure* that gets you!

Construct a Usable Measure of Effectiveness Most of the models discussed in the preceding chapters measure the effectiveness of a system on an interval scale, meaning that the usual arithmetic operations of addition, subtraction, division, and multiplication are meaningful. However, this need not always be the case, especially when designing solutions (or evaluating the existing ones) for human service agencies. I recall working on a federal project to evaluate the extent of services integration among the human service agencies in an eastern state. Integration was defined as a composite of coordination, joint planning, and joint funding. Each of these components could at best be measured on a preferential (rank order) scale. There was no way to combine these into an interval scale measure of the extent of integration. After an intensive training session on the meaning of numbers, the decision maker in this case was convinced. We then proceeded to create a preferential scale measure of effectiveness. I bring up this story because, applying the OR/MS techniques in the human service arena is the next frontier of management science. And on this frontier, one is constantly faced with the problem of constructing appropriate measures of effectiveness. It was also brought up because the unavailability of data required to run the mathematical models is a serious problem in OR/MS. Though usability of data is determined by the model, the model does not provide data. Thus, when constructing a model, one must *provide mechanisms for securing data*. One must identify the sources, quantity and quality of data, and also establish whether a complete census or sample is to be used. In either case, avoid getting stuck with nonresponse. It gets in the way of deriving definitive conclusions because nonresponse usually implies (an unknown amount of) bias.

Prove with empirical data that the proposed solution will indeed be an improvement over the current state of affairs. This means that:

1. You must know the current state of affairs.
2. You must identify a measure of effectiveness.
3. You must show how to use the readily available data to verify your conclusion.

The same issues as those of the preceding paragraph crop up here. Additionally, you must prove to the satisfaction of your decision maker that the *increase in effectiveness is worth the cost* of obtaining and using your solution.

For example, suppose you invent a scheme for buying and selling commodity futures on the Chicago Exchange and that the anticipated increase in profit is 10 percent *more than* that obtained without such a scheme. Suppose your scheme requires computer time each week to update and run the decision model, and that you must spend a certain number of hours each week revising the data base of this model. Then, the total profit due to your scheme must exceed the expense of performing these activities. If it does, you are earning your keep; if it doesn't, your quantitative sophistication is of no use to the company.

Parenthetically, it should be mentioned that the Chief Trader of the grain-processing firm discussed earlier became a true believer in the utility of management science after he had used my model to make buy/sell decisions for several months. He was convinced that the new model was doing consistently better than their previous guesswork policies.

Use the simplest possible model for solving the problem. Remember the rule: the simpler the model, the simpler it is to explain it to the decision maker as well as to the "line personnel" who must operate it on a regular basis. The less likely it will be misconstrued and the more likely it will continue to be implemented.

This does not mean, of course, that you should abandon a correct model just because it is complex. But if only 5 percent improvement is possible by using a model which is twice as complex, then you should review the situation with your decision maker. Complex models usually need more and higher quality data (which means more costly data) and are likely to be more sensitive to variations in the parametric values (which means it's more costly to operate the model). Since, ultimately, *the decision maker* ends up paying the bill and facing the headaches, he *should be given an option*.

Alan C. Shapiro (1976) reports the same basic finding in somewhat different words. He says that if the model and the manager have different (and possibly conflicting) goals, then the model is likely to be either rejected or misused.

The Final Steps
Let us now assume that you have constructed the decision maker's model of the decision maker's problem. What comes next? *Give the decision maker a choice.* You should *not present* the decision maker with *the solution* of his/her problem. Instead, present the decision maker with a multitude of solutions. Discuss the costs, benefits and difficulties of implementing each candidate solution. Then, let the decision maker make the choice. Two possibilities are outlined.

1. The model may have multiple optima with respect to the stated objective. Table 12-4, for example, shows two basic optimal solutions of the blood-banks-and-hospitals problem. Furthermore, for any fraction, p, between 0 and 1, each solution of the type:

$$p \times \text{Solution A} + (1 - p) \times \text{Solution B}$$

is also optimal for that problem. In such cases, show the various solutions obtained by assigning specific values to p. Then, the decision maker can choose a solution—on the basis of perhaps some as yet unstated criterion.

2. The model has only one optimal solution on the basis of the stated objective, e.g., minimize cost. If so, broaden your perspective and think of the additional criteria which might be important to your decision maker. These might include the cost of operating the solution, convenience in the day-to-day operations, or the extent of noise pollution. Show your decision maker how the value of the primary objective function changes in conjunction with these secondary aspects. Then, let the decision maker pick the best solution. That will be *his* solution to *his* problem.

This is one of the important reasons for performing the sensitivity analysis. For example, reconsider the situation of the Milkland Dairy of chapter 6. Purely on the basis of EOQ analysis, the manager of that dairy should order $Q^* = 645$ gallons of milk each time. Since the total cost is relatively insensitive to moderate departures from Q^*, we had already seen in table 6-1 that ordering as few as 600 or as many as 800 gallons each time would not drastically alter the cost. And ordering either 600 or 800 gallons is *more convenient* than ordering 645 at a time. Let the manager make the final choice.

In other words, *provide the manager with options* so that he can arrive at a workable, if not optimal, decision himself. The manager can then weigh each solution and make a decision based on all factors. Why insist on finding the decision maker's solution? Because, *he is responsible for implementing that solution*. His decision may include an attempt to change political factors, labor contracts, or other imponderables which presently influence him but which are not explicitly stated in the model. If he has participated in the OR/MS process, implementation becomes *his* rather than your responsibility.

In retrospect, this might be an important reason why the grain-processing firm did in fact implement the buy/sell strategies first proposed by me. Though the politics of OR/MS was not a part of my coursework (the OR/MS schools in the 1960's emphasized the techniques), I had always presented the decision makers in that firm with a variety of options. Since they had participated in the selection process, these became their solutions. Perhaps there is some truth in the saying: the meek shall inherit the earth.

There is much empirical evidence behind this suggestion. See, for example, Lars Lonnstedt's report (1975). His data shows that implementation is more likely if:

- The manager (Lonnstedt calls him a user) participates in the process of problem definition.
- The project is initiated by top management rather than by the operations researcher.
- The whole problem, rather than only a portion of it, is considered while constructing the solution.
- The decision maker sees the project to be valuable.

His report also suggests that projects where data is readily available or can be easily collected have better chance of being implemented than when such data are only partially obtainable.

Of course, projects where decision makers participate are usually more costly, but Harvey N. Shycon's survey (1977) shows that such projects are almost always completely successful, i.e., the return on project investment is more than 100 percent per year. In short, the added cost is worth it.

To use Shakun's terminology (1972), what we are advocating may be called *situational normativism*. Jatinder N. D. Gupta (1977) recommends its use for improving the chances of implementation. In fact, Richard F. Barton (1977) suggests building implementation as a goal in the model itself.

Explain the Solution to the Line Workers. Having constructed the decision maker's solution, there is one final step. Prepare an operating procedures manual and explain it, step-by-step, to the persons who must operate the solution. However, avoid getting into mathematical formulas and/or derivations. Remember, you derived the solution. To you, each step is obvious and perhaps, elementary. But, the line workers have to use it. If they don't understand it precisely, they can't use it properly. Result? Loss of effectiveness. This may mean abandonment of your solution after initial implementation (and failure).

Naturally, neither you nor I can anticipate all the difficulties that are likely to arise during implementation. Consequently, you must be "around" to resolve all such difficulties as and when these arise. To quote a Chinese proverb: He who builds a bridge, must be ready to stand under it!

FUTURE POSSIBILITIES

There is now a trend toward analyzing more "ill-structured" problems such as those found in the public sector. Urban development, transportation, pollution control, energy conservation, health, education, and employment security contain the problems of this type. Such problems also exist at top corporate levels. Lack of well-defined quantitative measures is a typical characteristic of the ill-structured problems.

Clearly, the maturing phase will continue for a while. Quantitative measures will be developed for some of the ill-structured problems. Measures such as those describing quality of life will become established. In the human services arena (health, education, welfare, housing), quantitative measures based on the concept of "problem days" are likely to emerge.

As the management students and younger managers of today move up the organization ladder, and as computers continue to become larger, faster, more flexible and more economical, management science will likely play an even larger role in both private and public sectors. In the business world, one may find more truly optimal solutions to the tactical problems such as production and inventory control, scheduling, resource allocation, and replacement and maintenance of equipment. This is because larger and faster computers will enable a management scientist of tomorrow to solve the problem from a corporate rather than departmental standpoint.

Forecasting the developments in the future is, of course, error–prone. However, extrapolating from the present, it seems that the most significant contribution of management sciences is likely to be in attacking the strategic and ill-structured problems, especially in the public sector. The increasing stress on problem solving rather than techniques development will be aided by the increasing use of simulation.

Simulation has already been used to describe and evaluate the operations of human service agencies, urban growth, as well as the effects of population growth on the global economy. Already (as of 1974) Naylor and Schauland have compiled a rather large bibliography on corporate simulation models. But the growth of simulation is likely to be most explosive in the public sector.

We have already seen in chapters 8 and 9 why simulation as a problem-solving approach appeals to most decision makers. Briefly speaking:

- It enables the manager to ask "what if?" questions, often in an in-duces) the problem associated with translation.
- It enables the manager to ask "what if?" questions, often in an interactive mode.
- It forces the management scientist to communicate with the decision maker.
- It does not make restrictive assumptions regarding the decision maker's world.

While discussing the suggestions for improving the chances of implementing the solution, we have already seen that the decision maker's participation is a significant factor. Thus, simulation will perhaps be the most important "technique" for ensuring successful implementation.

The problem solving, rather than techniques, orientation will also mean a need for more, varied and better quality data. This, in turn, would result in better specified management information systems. However, to make the most of it, both the managers and management scientists of tomorrow would end up devoting more time and effort to *specifying* precisely what MIS should do for them.

This, then, is what I see in my crystal ball—time will tell how cloudy or shiny it is!

SELECTED READINGS

ACKOFF, R. L. "Frontiers of Management Science." *The Bulletins of TIMS* 1 (Feb. 1971), pp. 19–24.

AUSTIN, L. M. "Project EOQ: A Success Story in Implementing Academic Research." *Interfaces* 7 (Aug. 1977), pp. 1–14.

BAKER, N. R.; SOUDER, W. E.; SHUMWAY, C. R.; MAHER, P. M.; and RUBENSTEIN, A. H. "A Budget Allocation Model for Large Hierarchical R & D Organizations." *Management Science* 23 (1976), pp. 59–70.

BARTON, R. F. "Models With More Than One Criterion—or Why Not Build Implementation Into The Model?" *Interfaces* 7 (Aug. 1977), pp. 71–75.

BOERE, N. J. "Air Canada Saves With Aircraft Maintenance Scheduling." *Interfaces* 7 (May 1977), pp. 1–13.

CHEN, G. K. C. "What is the Systems Approach?" *Interfaces* 6 (Nov. 1975), pp. 32–37.

CHURCHMAN, C. W.; ACKOFF, R. L.; and ARNOFF, E. L. *Introduction to Operations Research*. New York: John Wiley and Sons, Inc., 1957.

COOK, T. M. and ALPRIN, B. S. "Snow and Ice Removal in an Urban Environment." *Management Science* 23 (1976), pp. 227–234.

DARNELL, D. W. and LOFLIN, C. "National Airline Fuel Management and Allocation Model." *Interfaces* 7 (Feb. 1977), pp. 1–16.

FEENEY, G. J. "The Role of the Professional in Operations Research and Management Science." *Interfaces* 1 (Aug. 1971), pp. 1–4.

FRIES, B. E. "Bibliography of Operations Research in Health-Care Systems." *Operations Research* 24 (1976), pp. 801–814.

GRAYSON, C. J., JR. "Management Science and Business Practice." *Harvard Business Review* 51 (July–Aug. 1973), pp. 41–48.

GUPTA, J. N. D. "Management Science Implementation: Experience of a Practicing O.R. Manager. *Interfaces* 7 (May 1977), pp. 84–90.

HARRISON, E. F. *The Managerial Decision-Making Process*. Boston: Houghton-Mifflin Company, 1975.

HARVEY, A. "Factors Making for Implementation Success and Failure." *Management Science* 16 (1970), pp. B312–B321.

HUYSMAN, J. *The Implementation of Operations Research*. New York: John Wiley and Sons, Inc., 1970.

LONNSTEDT, L. "Factors Related to the Implementation of Operations Research Solutions." *Interfaces* 5 (Feb. 1975), pp. 23–30.

MCDONALD, J. "The Use of Management Science in Making Corporate Policy Decision—Charging for Directory Assistance Service." *Interfaces* 7 (Nov. 1976), pp. 5–18.

MAGEE, J. F. "Progress in Management Sciences." *Interfaces* 3 (Feb. 1973), pp. 35–41.

MARTIN, M. J. C. and PENDSE, S. G. "Transactional Analysis: Another Way of Approaching OR/MS Implementation." *Interfaces* 7 (Feb. 1977), pp. 91–98.

NAYLOR, T. H. and SCHAULAND, H. *Bibliography on Corporate Simulation Models*. Durham, NC: Social Systems, Inc., 1974.

RADNOR, M.; RUBENSTEIN, A. H.; and BEAN, A. S. "Integration and Utilization of Management Sciences Activities in Organizations." *Operational Research Quarterly* 19 (1968), pp. 117–141.

RADNOR, M.; RUBENSTEIN, A. H. and TANSIK, D. A. "Implementation in Operations Research, and R & D in Government and Business Organization." *Operations Research* 18 (1970), pp. 967–991.

RUDWICK, B. H. *Systems Anaylsis for Effective Planning*. New York: John Wiley & Sons, Inc., 1969.

SAVAS, E. S. "New Directions for Urban Analysis." *Interfaces* 6 (Nov. 1975), pp. 1–9.

SAATY, T. L. "The Future of Operations Research in the Government." *Interfaces* 2 (Feb. 1972), pp. 1–9.

SHAPIRO, A. C. "Incentive Systems and the Implementation of Management Science: A Spare Parts Application." *Interfaces* 7 (Nov. 1976), pp. 14–16.

SHAKUN, M. L. "Management Science and Management: Implementing Management Science via Situational Normativism." *Management Science* 18 (1972), pp. B367–B377.

SHYCON, H. M. "Perspectives on MS Applications." *Interfaces* 7 (Aug. 1977), pp. 40–43.

SINGH, A. J. and MAY, P. R. A. "Acceptance of Operations Research/Systems Analysis in the Health Care Field." *Interfaces* (Aug. 1977), pp. 79–84.

WAGNER, H. M. "The ABC's of OR." *Operations Research* 19 (1971), pp. 1259–1281.

WAKELIN, J. H., JR. "Potential Contributions of Mangement Science to the Public Sector." *Interfaces* 1 (Aug. 1971), pp. 13–17.

WEINGARTNER, H. M. "What Lies Ahead in Management Science and Operations Research in Finance in Seventies." *Interfaces* 1 (Aug. 1971), pp. 5–12.

WOOLSEY, R. E. D. "A Candle for Saint Jude, or Four Real World Applications of Integer Programming." *Interfaces* 2 (Feb. 1972), pp. 20–27.

———"The Measures of MS/OR Applications or Let's Hear It for the Bean Counters." *Interfaces* (Feb. 1975), pp. 74–78.

———"Two Digressions on Systems Analysis: Optimum Warehousing & Disappearing Orange Juice." *Interfaces* 7 (Feb. 1977), pp. 17–20.

———"A Novena to St. Jude, or Four Edifying Case Studies in Mathematical Programming." *Interfaces* 4 (Nov. 1973), pp. 32–39.

WYMAN, F. P. and HEFLAND, H. J. "Anaylsis of Revenue Collection Operations in the Washington Metro Rail System." *Interfaces* 7 (May 1977), pp. 28–31.

ZELENY, M. "Managers without Management Science?" *Interfaces* 5 (Aug. 1975), pp. 35–42.

———"Notes, Ideas, and Techniques: New Vistas of Management Science." *Computers and Operations Research* 2, pp. 121–125.

Appendices

APPENDIX A
AREAS UNDER THE NORMAL CURVE

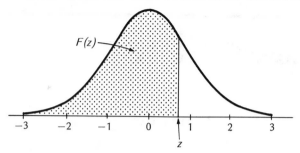

Examples:
1. $F(.37) = .6445$
2. $F(-.5) = 1 - .6917$
         $= .3083$

Table A *Values of F for Positive Values of z*

	.00	.01	.02	.03	.04	.05	.06	.07	.08	.09
.0	.5000	.5040	.5079	.5119	.5158	.5198	.5237	.5277	.5317	.5356
.1	.5396	.5436	.5475	.5515	.5555	.5594	.5634	.5673	.5713	.5752
.2	.5791	.5831	.5870	.5909	.5948	.5987	.6026	.6064	.6103	.6141
.3	.6180	.6218	.6256	.6294	.6332	.6370	.6407	.6445	.6482	.6519
.4	.6556	.6593	.6630	.6666	.6703	.6739	.6775	.6811	.6846	.6882
.5	.6917	.6952	.6987	.7022	.7056	.7091	.7125	.7150	.7193	.7226
.6	.7259	.7293	.7325	.7358	.7391	.7423	.7455	.7487	.7519	.7550
.7	.7581	.7612	.7643	.7674	.7704	.7734	.7764	.7793	.7823	.7852
.8	.7881	.7910	.7938	.7967	.7995	.8022	.8050	.8077	.8104	.8131
.9	.8158	.8184	.8211	.8236	.8262	.8288	.8313	.8338	.8363	.8387
1.0	.8411	.8435	.8459	.8483	.8506	.8529	.8552	.8575	.8597	.8619
1.1	.8641	.8663	.8684	.8705	.8726	.8747	.8768	.8788	.8808	.8828
1.2	.8847	.8867	.8886	.8905	.8924	.8942	.8960	.8978	.8996	.9014
1.3	.9031	.9048	.9065	.9082	.9098	.9114	.9130	.9146	.9162	.9177
1.4	.9192	.9207	.9222	.9237	.9251	.9265	.9279	.9293	.9306	.9320
1.5	.9333	.9346	.9358	.9371	.9383	.9396	.9407	.9419	.9431	.9442
1.6	.9454	.9465	.9476	.9486	.9497	.9507	.9517	.9527	.9537	.9547
1.7	.9556	.9566	.9575	.9584	.9593	.9602	.9610	.9619	.9627	.9635
1.8	.9643	.9651	.9659	.9666	.9673	.9681	.9688	.9695	.9702	.9708
1.9	.9715	.9722	.9728	.9734	.9740	.9746	.9752	.9758	.9763	.9769
2.0	.9774	.9780	.9785	.9790	.9795	.9800	.9805	.9809	.9814	.9818
2.1	.9823	.9827	.9831	.9835	.9839	.9843	.9847	.9851	.9854	.9858
2.2	.9862	.9865	.9868	.9872	.9875	.9878	.9881	.9884	.9887	.9890
2.3	.9893	.9895	.9898	.9901	.9903	.9906	.9908	.9911	.9913	.9915
2.4	.9917	.9919	.9922	.9924	.9926	.9928	.9929	.9931	.9933	.9935
2.5	.9937	.9938	.9940	.9942	.9943	.9945	.9946	.9948	.9949	.9950
2.6	.9952	.9953	.9954	.9955	.9957	.9958	.9959	.9960	.9961	.9962
2.7	.9963	.9964	.9965	.9966	.9967	.9968	.9969	.9970	.9971	.9971
2.8	.9972	.9973	.9974	.9974	.9975	.9976	.9977	.9977	.9978	.9978
2.9	.9979	.9980	.9980	.9981	.9981	.9982	.9982	.9983	.9983	.9984

APPENDIX B
NEGATIVES OF NATURAL LOGARITHMS

	.000	.001	.002	.003	.004	.005	.006	.007	.008	.009
.0		6.908	6.215	5.809	5.521	5.298	5.116	4.962	4.828	4.711
.01	4.605	4.510	4.423	4.343	4.269	4.200	4.135	4.075	4.017	3.963
.02	3.912	3.863	3.817	3.772	3.730	3.689	3.650	3.612	3.576	3.540
.03	3.507	3.474	3.442	3.411	3.381	3.352	3.324	3.297	3.270	3.244
.04	3.219	3.194	3.170	3.147	3.124	3.101	3.079	3.058	3.037	3.016
.05	2.996	2.976	2.957	2.937	2.919	2.900	2.882	2.865	2.847	2.830
.06	2.813	2.797	2.781	2.765	2.749	2.733	2.718	2.703	2.688	2.674
.07	2.659	2.645	2.631	2.617	2.604	2.590	2.577	2.564	2.551	2.538
.08	2.526	2.513	2.501	2.489	2.477	2.465	2.453	2.442	2.430	2.419
.09	2.408	2.397	2.386	2.375	2.364	2.354	2.343	2.333	2.323	2.313
.10	2.303	2.293	2.283	2.273	2.263	2.254	2.244	2.235	2.226	2.216
.11	2.207	2.198	2.189	2.180	2.172	2.163	2.154	2.146	2.137	2.129
.12	2.120	2.112	2.104	2.096	2.087	2.079	2.071	2.064	2.056	2.048
.13	2.040	2.033	2.025	2.017	2.010	2.002	1.995	1.988	1.981	1.973
.14	1.966	1.959	1.952	1.945	1.938	1.931	1.924	1.917	1.911	1.904
.15	1.897	1.890	1.884	1.877	1.871	1.864	1.858	1.852	1.845	1.839
.16	1.833	1.826	1.820	1.814	1.808	1.802	1.796	1.790	1.784	1.778
.17	1.772	1.766	1.760	1.754	1.749	1.743	1.737	1.732	1.726	1.720
.18	1.715	1.709	1.704	1.698	1.693	1.687	1.682	1.677	1.671	1.666
.19	1.661	1.655	1.650	1.645	1.640	1.635	1.630	1.625	1.619	1.614
.20	1.609	1.604	1.599	1.595	1.590	1.585	1.580	1.575	1.570	1.565
.21	1.561	1.556	1.551	1.546	1.542	1.537	1.532	1.528	1.523	1.519
.22	1.514	1.510	1.505	1.501	1.496	1.492	1.487	1.483	1.478	1.474
.23	1.470	1.465	1.461	1.457	1.452	1.448	1.444	1.440	1.435	1.431
.24	1.427	1.423	1.419	1.415	1.411	1.407	1.402	1.398	1.394	1.390
.25	1.386	1.382	1.378	1.374	1.370	1.367	1.363	1.359	1.355	1.351
.26	1.347	1.343	1.339	1.336	1.332	1.328	1.324	1.321	1.317	1.313
.27	1.309	1.306	1.302	1.298	1.295	1.291	1.287	1.284	1.280	1.277
.28	1.273	1.269	1.266	1.262	1.259	1.255	1.252	1.248	1.245	1.241
.29	1.238	1.234	1.231	1.228	1.224	1.221	1.217	1.214	1.211	1.207
.30	1.204	1.201	1.197	1.194	1.191	1.187	1.184	1.181	1.178	1.174
.31	1.171	1.168	1.165	1.162	1.158	1.155	1.152	1.149	1.146	1.143
.32	1.139	1.136	1.133	1.130	1.127	1.124	1.121	1.118	1.115	1.112
.33	1.109	1.106	1.103	1.100	1.097	1.094	1.091	1.088	1.085	1.082
.34	1.079	1.076	1.073	1.070	1.067	1.064	1.061	1.058	1.056	1.053
.35	1.050	1.047	1.044	1.041	1.038	1.036	1.033	1.030	1.027	1.024
.36	1.022	1.019	1.016	1.013	1.011	1.008	1.005	1.002	1.000	0.997
.37	0.994	0.992	0.989	0.986	0.984	0.981	0.978	0.976	0.973	0.970
.38	0.968	0.965	0.962	0.960	0.957	0.955	0.952	0.949	0.947	0.944
.39	0.942	0.939	0.937	0.934	0.931	0.929	0.926	0.924	0.921	0.919
.40	0.916	0.914	0.911	0.909	0.906	0.904	0.901	0.899	0.896	0.894
.41	0.892	0.889	0.887	0.884	0.882	0.879	0.877	0.875	0.872	0.870
.42	0.868	0.865	0.863	0.860	0.858	0.856	0.853	0.851	0.849	0.846
.43	0.844	0.842	0.839	0.837	0.835	0.832	0.830	0.828	0.826	0.823
.44	0.821	0.819	0.816	0.814	0.812	0.810	0.807	0.805	0.803	0.801
.45	0.799	0.796	0.794	0.792	0.790	0.787	0.785	0.783	0.781	0.779
.46	0.777	0.774	0.772	0.770	0.768	0.766	0.764	0.761	0.759	0.757
.47	0.755	0.753	0.751	0.749	0.747	0.744	0.742	0.740	0.738	0.736

Appendix B *Negatives of Natural Logarithms (Continued)*

	.000	.001	.002	.003	.004	.005	.006	.007	.008	.009
.48	0.734	0.732	0.730	0.728	0.726	0.724	0.722	0.720	0.717	0.715
.49	0.713	0.711	0.709	0.707	0.705	0.703	0.701	0.699	0.697	0.695
.50	0.693	0.691	0.689	0.687	0.685	0.683	0.681	0.679	0.677	0.675
.51	0.673	0.671	0.669	0.667	0.666	0.664	0.662	0.660	0.658	0.656
.52	0.654	0.652	0.650	0.648	0.646	0.644	0.642	0.641	0.639	0.637
.53	0.635	0.633	0.631	0.629	0.627	0.626	0.624	0.622	0.620	0.618
.54	0.616	0.614	0.613	0.611	0.609	0.607	0.605	0.603	0.601	0.600
.55	0.598	0.596	0.594	0.592	0.591	0.589	0.587	0.585	0.583	0.582
.56	0.580	0.578	0.576	0.574	0.573	0.571	0.569	0.567	0.566	0.564
.57	0.562	0.560	0.559	0.557	0.555	0.553	0.552	0.550	0.548	0.546
.58	0.545	0.543	0.541	0.540	0.538	0.536	0.534	0.533	0.531	0.529
.59	0.528	0.526	0.524	0.523	0.521	0.519	0.518	0.516	0.514	0.513
.60	0.511	0.509	0.508	0.506	0.504	0.503	0.501	0.499	0.498	0.506
.61	0.494	0.493	0.491	0.489	0.488	0.486	0.485	0.483	0.481	0.480
.62	0.478	0.476	0.475	0.473	0.472	0.470	0.468	0.467	0.465	0.464
.63	0.462	0.460	0.459	0.457	0.456	0.454	0.453	0.451	0.449	0.448
.64	0.446	0.445	0.443	0.442	0.440	0.439	0.437	0.435	0.434	0.432
.65	0.431	0.429	0.428	0.426	0.425	0.423	0.422	0.420	0.419	0.417
.66	0.416	0.414	0.413	0.411	0.409	0.408	0.406	0.405	0.403	0.402
.67	0.400	0.399	0.398	0.396	0.395	0.393	0.392	0.390	0.389	0.387
.68	0.386	0.384	0.383	0.381	0.380	0.378	0.377	0.375	0.374	0.373
.69	0.371	0.370	0.368	0.367	0.365	0.364	0.362	0.361	0.360	0.358
.70	0.357	0.355	0.354	0.352	0.351	0.350	0.348	0.347	0.345	0.344
.71	0.343	0.341	0.340	0.338	0.337	0.335	0.334	0.333	0.331	0.330
.72	0.329	0.327	0.326	0.324	0.323	0.322	0.320	0.319	0.317	0.316
.73	0.315	0.313	0.312	0.311	0.309	0.308	0.307	0.305	0.304	0.302
.74	0.301	0.300	0.298	0.297	0.296	0.294	0.293	0.292	0.290	0.289
.75	0.288	0.286	0.285	0.284	0.282	0.281	0.280	0.278	0.277	0.276
.76	0.274	0.273	0.272	0.271	0.269	0.268	0.267	0.265	0.264	0.263
.77	0.261	0.260	0.259	0.257	0.256	0.255	0.254	0.252	0.251	0.250
.78	0.248	0.247	0.246	0.245	0.243	0.242	0.241	0.240	0.238	0.237
.79	0.236	0.234	0.233	0.232	0.231	0.229	0.228	0.227	0.226	0.224
.80	0.223	0.222	0.221	0.219	0.218	0.217	0.216	0.214	0.213	0.212
.81	0.211	0.209	0.208	0.207	0.206	0.205	0.203	0.202	0.201	0.200
.82	0.198	0.197	0.196	0.195	0.194	0.192	0.191	0.190	0.189	0.188
.83	0.186	0.185	0.184	0.183	0.182	0.180	0.179	0.178	0.177	0.176
.84	0.174	0.173	0.172	0.171	0.170	0.168	0.167	0.166	0.165	0.164
.85	0.163	0.161	0.160	0.159	0.158	0.157	0.155	0.154	0.153	0.152
.86	0.151	0.150	0.149	0.147	0.146	0.145	0.144	0.143	0.142	0.140
.87	0.139	0.138	0.137	0.136	0.135	0.134	0.132	0.131	0.130	0.129
.88	0.128	0.127	0.126	0.124	0.123	0.122	0.121	0.120	0.119	0.118
.89	0.117	0.115	0.114	0.113	0.112	0.111	0.110	0.109	0.108	0.106
.90	0.105	0.104	0.103	0.102	0.101	0.100	0.099	0.098	0.097	0.095
.91	0.094	0.093	0.092	0.091	0.090	0.089	0.088	0.087	0.086	0.084
.92	0.083	0.082	0.081	0.080	0.079	0.078	0.077	0.076	0.075	0.074
.93	0.073	0.072	0.070	0.069	0.068	0.067	0.066	0.065	0.064	0.063
.94	0.062	0.061	0.060	0.059	0.058	0.057	0.056	0.054	0.053	0.052
.95	0.051	0.050	0.049	0.048	0.047	0.046	0.045	0.044	0.043	0.042
.96	0.041	0.040	0.039	0.038	0.037	0.036	0.035	0.034	0.033	0.032
.97	0.030	0.029	0.028	0.027	0.026	0.025	0.024	0.023	0.022	0.021
.98	0.020	0.019	0.018	0.017	0.016	0.015	0.014	0.013	0.012	0.011
.99	0.010	0.009	0.008	0.007	0.006	0.005	0.004	0.003	0.002	0.001

APPENDIX C
BINOMIAL PROBABILITIES

							p					
n	x	0.05	0.1	0.2	0.3	0.4	0.5	0.6	0.7	0.8	0.9	0.95
2	0	0.902	0.810	0.640	0.490	0.360	0.250	0.160	0.090	0.040	0.010	0.002
	1	0.095	0.180	0.320	0.420	0.480	0.500	0.480	0.420	0.320	0.180	0.095
	2	0.002	0.010	0.040	0.090	0.160	0.250	0.360	0.490	0.640	0.810	0.902
3	0	0.857	0.729	0.512	0.343	0.216	0.125	0.064	0.027	0.008	0.001	
	1	0.135	0.243	0.384	0.441	0.432	0.375	0.288	0.189	0.096	0.027	0.007
	2	0.007	0.027	0.096	0.189	0.288	0.375	0.432	0.441	0.384	0.243	0.135
	3		0.001	0.008	0.027	0.064	0.125	0.216	0.343	0.512	0.729	0.857
4	0	0.815	0.656	0.410	0.240	0.130	0.062	0.026	0.008	0.002		
	1	0.171	0.292	0.410	0.412	0.346	0.250	0.154	0.076	0.026	0.004	
	2	0.014	0.049	0.154	0.265	0.346	0.375	0.346	0.265	0.154	0.049	0.014
	3		0.004	0.026	0.076	0.154	0.250	0.346	0.412	0.410	0.292	0.171
	4			0.002	0.008	0.026	0.062	0.130	0.240	0.410	0.656	0.815
5	0	0.774	0.590	0.328	0.168	0.078	0.031	0.010	0.002			
	1	0.204	0.328	0.410	0.360	0.259	0.156	0.077	0.028	0.006		
	2	0.021	0.073	0.205	0.309	0.346	0.312	0.230	0.132	0.051	0.008	0.001
	3	0.001	0.008	0.051	0.132	0.230	0.312	0.346	0.309	0.205	0.073	0.021
	4			0.006	0.028	0.077	0.156	0.259	0.360	0.410	0.328	0.204
	5				0.002	0.010	0.031	0.078	0.168	0.328	0.590	0.774
6	0	0.735	0.531	0.262	0.118	0.047	0.016	0.004	0.001			
	1	0.232	0.354	0.393	0.303	0.187	0.094	0.037	0.010	0.002		
	2	0.031	0.098	0.246	0.324	0.311	0.234	0.138	0.060	0.015	0.001	
	3	0.002	0.015	0.082	0.185	0.276	0.312	0.276	0.185	0.082	0.015	0.002
	4		0.001	0.015	0.060	0.138	0.234	0.311	0.324	0.246	0.098	0.031
	5			0.002	0.010	0.037	0.094	0.187	0.303	0.393	0.354	0.232
	6				0.001	0.004	0.016	0.047	0.118	0.262	0.531	0.735
7	0	0.698	0.478	0.210	0.082	0.028	0.008	0.002				
	1	0.257	0.372	0.367	0.247	0.131	0.055	0.017	0.004			
	2	0.041	0.124	0.275	0.318	0.261	0.164	0.077	0.025	0.004		
	3	0.004	0.023	0.115	0.227	0.290	0.273	0.194	0.097	0.029	0.003	
	4		0.003	0.029	0.097	0.194	0.273	0.290	0.227	0.115	0.023	0.004
	5			0.004	0.025	0.077	0.164	0.261	0.318	0.275	0.124	0.041
	6				0.004	0.017	0.055	0.131	0.247	0.367	0.372	0.257
	7					0.002	0.008	0.028	0.082	0.210	0.478	0.698
8	0	0.663	0.430	0.168	0.058	0.017	0.004	0.001				
	1	0.279	0.383	0.336	0.198	0.090	0.031	0.008	0.001			
	2	0.051	0.149	0.294	0.296	0.209	0.109	0.041	0.010	0.001		
	3	0.005	0.033	0.147	0.254	0.279	0.219	0.124	0.047	0.009		
	4		0.005	0.046	0.136	0.232	0.273	0.232	0.136	0.046	0.005	
	5			0.009	0.047	0.124	0.219	0.279	0.254	0.147	0.033	0.005
	6			0.001	0.010	0.041	0.109	0.209	0.296	0.294	0.149	0.051
	7				0.001	0.008	0.031	0.090	0.198	0.336	0.383	0.279
	8					0.001	0.004	0.017	0.058	0.168	0.430	0.663
9	0	0.630	0.387	0.134	0.040	0.010	0.002					
	1	0.299	0.387	0.302	0.156	0.060	0.018	0.004				
	2	0.063	0.172	0.302	0.267	0.161	0.070	0.021	0.004			
	3	0.008	0.045	0.176	0.267	0.251	0.164	0.074	0.021	0.003		
	4	0.001	0.007	0.066	0.172	0.251	0.246	0.167	0.074	0.017	0.001	
	5		0.001	0.017	0.074	0.167	0.246	0.251	0.172	0.066	0.007	0.001
	6			0.003	0.021	0.074	0.164	0.251	0.267	0.176	0.045	0.008
	7				0.004	0.021	0.070	0.161	0.267	0.302	0.172	0.063
	8					0.004	0.018	0.060	0.156	0.302	0.387	0.299
	9						0.002	0.010	0.040	0.134	0.387	0.630

* All values omitted in this table are 0.0005 or less.

Appendix C *Binomial Probabilities (Continued)*

							p					
n	x	0.05	0.1	0.2	0.3	0.4	0.5	0.6	0.7	0.8	0.9	0.95
10	0	0.599	0.349	0.107	0.028	0.006	0.001					
	1	0.315	0.387	0.268	0.121	0.040	0.010	0.002				
	2	0.075	0.194	0.302	0.233	0.121	0.044	0.011	0.001			
	3	0.010	0.057	0.201	0.267	0.215	0.117	0.042	0.009	0.001		
	4	0.001	0.011	0.088	0.200	0.251	0.205	0.111	0.037	0.006		
	5		0.001	0.026	0.103	0.201	0.246	0.201	0.103	0.026	0.001	
	6			0.006	0.037	0.111	0.205	0.251	0.200	0.088	0.011	0.001
	7			0.001	0.009	0.042	0.117	0.215	0.267	0.201	0.057	0.010
	8				0.001	0.011	0.044	0.121	0.233	0.302	0.194	0.075
	9					0.002	0.010	0.040	0.121	0.268	0.387	0.315
	10						0.001	0.006	0.028	0.107	0.349	0.599
11	0	0.569	0.314	0.086	0.020	0.004						
	1	0.329	0.384	0.236	0.093	0.027	0.005	0.001				
	2	0.087	0.213	0.295	0.200	0.089	0.027	0.005	0.001			
	3	0.014	0.071	0.221	0.257	0.177	0.081	0.023	0.004			
	4	0.001	0.016	0.111	0.220	0.236	0.161	0.070	0.017	0.002		
	5		0.002	0.039	0.132	0.221	0.226	0.147	0.057	0.010		
	6			0.010	0.057	0.147	0.226	0.221	0.132	0.039	0.002	
	7			0.002	0.017	0.070	0.161	0.236	0.220	0.111	0.016	0.001
	8				0.004	0.023	0.081	0.177	0.257	0.221	0.071	0.014
	9				0.001	0.005	0.027	0.089	0.200	0.295	0.213	0.087
	10					0.001	0.005	0.027	0.093	0.236	0.384	0.329
	11							0.004	0.020	0.086	0.314	0.569
12	0	0.540	0.282	0.069	0.014	0.002						
	1	0.341	0.377	0.206	0.071	0.017	0.003					
	2	0.099	0.230	0.283	0.168	0.064	0.016	0.002				
	3	0.017	0.085	0.236	0.240	0.142	0.054	0.012	0.001			
	4	0.002	0.021	0.133	0.231	0.213	0.121	0.042	0.008	0.001		
	5		0.004	0.053	0.158	0.227	0.193	0.101	0.029	0.003		
	6			0.016	0.079	0.177	0.226	0.177	0.079	0.016		
	7			0.003	0.029	0.101	0.193	0.227	0.158	0.053	0.004	
	8			0.001	0.008	0.042	0.121	0.213	0.231	0.133	0.021	0.002
	9				0.001	0.012	0.054	0.142	0.240	0.236	0.085	0.017
	10					0.002	0.016	0.064	0.168	0.283	0.230	0.099
	11						0.003	0.017	0.071	0.206	0.377	0.341
	12							0.002	0.014	0.069	0.282	0.540

Reprinted with permission from J. E. Freund and F. J. Williams, *Elementary Business Statistics: The Modern Approach* (Englewood Cliffs, N. J.: Prentice-Hall, Inc.), 3rd edition, 1977, pp. 518-19.

APPENDIX D
VALUES OF e^{-x}

x	e^{-x}	x	e^{-x}	x	e^{-x}	x	e^{-x}
0.0	1.000	2.5	0.082	5.0	0.0067	7.5	0.00055
0.1	0.905	2.6	0.074	5.1	0.0061	7.6	0.00050
0.2	0.819	2.7	0.067	5.2	0.0055	7.7	0.00045
0.3	0.741	2.8	0.061	5.3	0.0050	7.8	0.00041
0.4	0.670	2.9	0.055	5.4	0.0045	7.9	0.00037
0.5	0.607	3.0	0.050	5.5	0.0041	8.0	0.00034
0.6	0.549	3.1	0.045	5.6	0.0037	8.1	0.00030
0.7	0.497	3.2	0.041	5.7	0.0033	8.2	0.00028
0.8	0.449	3.3	0.037	5.8	0.0030	8.3	0.00025
0.9	0.407	3.4	0.033	5.9	0.0027	8.4	0.00023
1.0	0.368	3.5	0.030	6.0	0.0025	8.5	0.00020
1.1	0.333	3.6	0.027	6.1	0.0022	8.6	0.00018
1.2	0.301	3.7	0.025	6.2	0.0020	8.7	0.00017
1.3	0.273	3.8	0.022	6.3	0.0018	8.8	0.00015
1.4	0.247	3.9	0.020	6.4	0.0017	8.9	0.00014
1.5	0.223	4.0	0.018	6.5	0.0015	9.0	0.00012
1.6	0.202	4.1	0.017	6.6	0.0014	9.1	0.00011
1.7	0.183	4.2	0.015	6.7	0.0012	9.2	0.00010
1.8	0.165	4.3	0.014	6.8	0.0011	9.3	0.00009
1.9	0.150	4.4	0.012	6.9	0.0010	9.4	0.00008
2.0	0.135	4.5	0.011	7.0	0.0009	9.5	0.00008
2.1	0.122	4.6	0.010	7.1	0.0008	9.6	0.00007
2.2	0.111	4.7	0.009	7.2	0.0007	9.7	0.00006
2.3	0.100	4.8	0.008	7.3	0.0007	9.8	0.00006
2.4	0.091	4.9	0.007	7.4	0.0006	9.9	0.00005

Reprinted with permission from J. E. Freund and F. J. Williams, *Elementary Business Statistics: The Modern Approach*, (Englewood Cliffs, N. J.: Prentice-Hall, Inc.), 3rd edition, 1977, p. 536.

APPENDIX E
INTEGER PROGRAMMING ALGORITHM

```
1              DOUBLE PRECISION DABS
2              DOUBLE PRECISION ATAB(8,11), UPBND(12), TPVAL(10), BTHVL(10),
3             1VAL(10), TBSAV(8,11), SAVTAB(9,65), T(11)
4              DOUBLE PRECISION SOLMIN, PCTTOL, TLRNCE, YVECT, ATAB11, AMAX,
5             1RTIO, ALFA, ARTIO, ADELT, ZOPT, ATAB12, X1, AMAX2, AMAX3, ALW,
6             2AUP, RTIO2, DIFF1, DIFF2, DIFF, SVALW, ANDCT4
7              COMMON IROW (8), ITBROW (8)
8              COMMON ICOL (11), ITBCOL (11), IVAR (11)
9              COMMON ISVROW (8, 10)
10             COMMON ISVRCL (10), ICORR (10), ISVN (10)
11             COMMON KSVN (11)
12     C       ARRAY ITEMP USED FOR PACKED FORMAT DATA INPUT ONLY
13             DIMENSION ITEMP (7)
14             X1 = 1.0
15         10 FORMAT (1H0, (7D10.3))
16     C       UNPACKED FORMAT NO. 11
17         11 FORMAT ( 7D10.0     )
18         12 FORMAT ( 1X, 8D13.7)
19         13 FORMAT (1H0,24HPRINT CONTROL PARAMETERS)
20         14 FORMAT (1H0,30HUPPER BOUND ON VARIABLE 1 TO N)
21         15 FORMAT(20I4)
22     C       PACKED FORMAT NO. 16
23         16 FORMAT ( 7(I3,D7.0))
24         17 FORMAT (1H0,18HMATRIX FORMAT CODE)
25         18 FORMAT (4HOI =, I4, 6I10)
26         19 FORMAT (27HOSTRUCTURAL VARIABLES: X(I))
27         20 FORMAT (44HOROWS X COLUMNS AND NO. OF INTEGER VARIABLES//
28            1 I4,2H X, I3, 24X, I6)
29         21 FORMAT (30HOCONSTRAINT TYPES IN ROW ORDER)
30         22 FORMAT (52HOINPUT TABLEAU ECHO, CONSTRAINT VALUE LEFT,  BY ROW.)
31         23 FORMAT (1H0,10D13.3/(1H , 10D13.3))
32         24 FORMAT (1H0,13HITERATION NO.,I6)
33         25 FORMAT ( 1H0,8D13.5/(1H , 8D13.5))
34         26 FORMAT ( 1H , I6, 7I13)
35         27 FORMAT(1H+114X,I5)
36         29 FORMAT (15H0TOLERANCE SET AT E15.7,14H  AT ITERATION,I6)
37         30 FORMAT(21H PROBLEM NOT FEASIBLE)
38         35 FORMAT (21H0OBJECTIVE FUNCTION =, F15.7,14H  AT ITERATION,I6)
39         40 FORMAT (29H0CONTINUOUS SOLUTION COMPLETE)
40         42 FORMAT (38H0FINAL TABLEAU FOR CONTINUOUS SOLUTION)
41         45 FORMAT(40H0CONTINUOUS SOLUTION IS INTEGER SOLUTION,
42         46 FORMAT (1H0,30HNO INTEGER VARIABLES REQUESTED)
43         50 FORMAT (23H0OPTIMALITY ESTABLISHED)
44         55 FORMAT(33H0PROBLEM TOO BIG FOR MACHINE SIZE)
45         60 FORMAT(55H
46         65 FORMAT (30H0END OF PROBLEM, ITERATION NO., I6)
47         70 FORMAT(25H0BRANCH POINT INCREASED TOI4)
48         75 FORMAT (26H0BRANCH POINT DECREASED TOI4)
49         78 FORMAT (24H0INITIAL WORKING TABLEAU)
50             NI = 5
51             NO = 6
52             READ (NI, 15) ISIZE, NMRUNS
53     C       INITIALIZATION
54         68 CONTINUE
55             INDCT7=1
56             KSVN(1)=1
57             INDCTR=1
58             ICNTR=0.
59             IOUT1 = 0
60             I1ROW=1000
61             ADELT = 5.0E-7
62     C***
63     C       READ AND WRITE PROBLEM IDENTIFICATION: PUT 1 IN COL. 1
64             READ(NI,60)
65             WRITE(NO,60)
66     C***
67     C       IOUT2 = INITIAL WORKING TABLEAU
68     C       IOUT3=CONTINUOUS SOLUTION TABLEAU
69             READ (NI, 15) IOUT2, IOUT3, IPACK
70             WRITE(NO,13)
```

Appendix E *Integer Programming Algorithm (Continued)*

```
 71              WRITE(NO,15) IOUT2, IOUT3
 72        C***
 73        C     SOLMIN UPPER BOUND ON OBJ. FUNCTION FOR INTEGER SOLUTION
 74        C     PCTTOL=INPUT TOLERANCE AS FRACTION OF OBJECTIVE FUNCT. FOR CONT. SOL
 75        C     SET EACH ZERO FOR UNKNOWN PROBLEM.
 76              READ ( NI, 11) SOLMIN, PCTTOL
 77        C***
 78        C     INPUT PARAMETERS   M = TOTAL NO. OF ROWS, N = TOTAL NO. OF COLS.
 79        C     NZR1VR = NO. OF INTEGER VARIABLES
 80              READ(NI,15)M,N,NZR1VR
 81              WRITE(NO,20) M, N, NZR1VR
 82         73 DO 72 I=1,N
 83         72 T(I)=0.
 84              NM1=N-1
 85         74 IF(SOLMIN)786,787,786
 86        C***
 87        C     INPUT UPPER BOUND ON OBJECTIVE FUNCTION
 88        786 TLRNCE=SOLMIN
 89              PCTTOL=-1.
 90              GO TO 90
 91        787 ITOL=1
 92              SOLMIN = 1E35
 93              IF(PCTTOL)90,788,90
 94        788 PCTTOL=.1
 95        C***
 96        C     INPUT UPPER BOUNDS ON VARIABLES (ZERO MEANS NO UPPER BOUND)
 97         90 READ (NI,11) (UPBND(I), I = 1, NM1)
 98              WRITE(NO,14)
 99              WRITE(NO,10) (UPBND(I), I = 1,NM1)
100              IROW(1)=0
101        C**      CONSTRAINT TYPES: ( +1, = 0, ' -1 .
102              READ(NI,15)(IROW(I),I=2,M)
103              WRITE (NO, 21)
104              WRITE (NO, 15) (IROW(I), I = 2, M)
105        C**      MATRIX FORMAT: PACKED = 1,  UNPACKED = 0  .
106              WRITE(NO,17)
107              WRITE(NO,15) IPACK
108              IF(IPACK)901,949,901
109        901 DO 92 I=1,M
110              DO 903 J = 1, N
111        903 ATAB(I,J) = 0.0
112        904 READ(NI,16)(ITEMP(K),VAL(K),K=1,7)
113              DO 907 L=1,7
114              IF(ITEMP(L))905,92,905
115        905 K = ITEMP(L)
116        909 ATAB(I,K)=VAL(L)
117        907 CONTINUE
118              GO TO 904
119         92 CONTINUE
120              GO TO 9510
121        C***
122        C     READ MATRIX ELEMENTS
123        949 DO 952 I=1,M
124              READ ( NI, 11) (ATAB(I,J) , J = 1, N)
125        952 CONTINUE
126              IF ( M .LT. 2) GO TO 450
127        C***
128        C     PRINT INPUT TABLEAU FOR ERROR CHECK
129        9510 WRITE(NO,22)
130              DO 80 I = 1, M
131              WRITE (NO, 23) (ATAB(I,J), J = 1, N)
132         80 CONTINUE
133        9520 DO 954 I=2,M
134              IF(IROW(I))953,9521,9521
135        9521 DO 9523 J=2,N
136        9523 ATAB(I,J)=-ATAB(I,J)
137              GO TO 954
138        953 ATAB(I,1)=-ATAB(I,1)
139        954 CONTINUE
140        450 CONTINUE
141        955 DO 98 I=2,N
142              IF(UPBND(I-1))96,96,98
143         96 UPBND (I-1) = 1E3
```

Appendix E *Integer Programming Algorithm (Continued)*

```
144              98 CONTINUE
145        C***
146        C       COMPUTE NO. OF Y VECTORS
147             981 YVECT=UPBND(1)+1.
148                 IF ( NZR1VR .LT. 2) GO TO 322
149                 DO 982 I=2,NZR1VR
150             982 YVECT=YVECT*(UPBND(I)+1.)
151             322 CONTINUE
152        C***
153        C       SET SOLUTION VECTOR OF VARIABLES EQUAL TO ZERO
154        C       AND SAVE ORIGINAL UPPER BOUNDS
155             985 DO 99 I=2,N
156              99 IVAR(I-1)=0
157        C***
158        C       INITIALIZE ROW AND COLUMN IDENTIFIERS,+K=VARIABLE NO. K,
159        C       ZERO = ZERO SLACK, -K = POSITIVE SLACK
160                 IF ( M .LT. 2) GO TO 451
161                 DO 102 I=2,M
162                 IF(IROW(I))100,102,100
163             100 IROW(I)=1-I
164             102 CONTINUE
165             451 CONTINUE
166                 ATAB11=ATAB(1,1)
167                 ICOL(1) = 0
168                 DO 103 J=2,N
169                 IF(ATAB(1,J))1022,1025,1025
170            1022 DO 1023 I=1,M
171                 ATAB(I,1)=ATAB(I,1)+ATAB(I,J)*UPBND(J-1)
172            1023 ATAB(I,J)=-ATAB(I,J)
173                 ICOL(J)=1000+J-1
174                 GO TO 103
175            1025 ICOL(J)=J-1
176             103 CONTINUE
177        C***
178        C       OUTPUT INITIAL TABLEAU
179                 IF(IOUT2)104,254,104
180             104 WRITE(NO,78)
181                 WRITE(NO,26)(ICOL(J),J=1,N)
182                 DO 110 I=1,M
183                 WRITE(NO,25)(ATAB(I,J),J=1,N)
184             110 WRITE(NO,27)IROW(I)
185                 GO TO 254
186        C***
187        C       START DUAL LP
188        C       CHOOSE PIVOT ROW, MAXIMUM POSITIVE VALUE IN CONSTANT COLUMN
189             112 AMAX = 0.0
190                 IF ( M .LT. 2) GO TO 452
191                 DO 120 I=2,M
192                 IF(ATAB(I,1))120,120,115
193             115 IF(ATAB(I,1)-AMAX)120,120,117
194             117 AMAX=ATAB(I,1)
195                 IPVR=I
196             120 CONTINUE
197             452 CONTINUE
198        C***
199        C       IF NO POSITIVE VALUE, LP FINISHED (PRIMAL FEASIBLE)
200                 IF(AMAX)265,265,130
201        C       CHOOSE PIVOT COLUMN, ALGEBRAICALLY MAXIMUM RATIO A(1,J)/A(PIVOTROW
202        C       FOR A (PIVOTROW,J) NEGATIVE. IF NO NEGATIVE A(PIVOTROW,J) PROBLEM
203        C       INFEASIBLE
204             130 AMAX = -1E35
205                 IF(N-2)143,132,132
206             132 IPVC=0
207                 DO 140 J=2,N
208                 IF(ATAB(IPVR,J))133,140,140
209             133 RTIO=ATAB(1,J)/ATAB(IPVR,J)
210                 IF(RTIO-AMAX)140,137,135
211             135 AMAX=RTIO
212             136 IPVC=J
213                 GO TO 140
214             137 IF(ATAB(IPVR,J)-ATAB(IPVR,IPVC))136,140,140
215             140 CONTINUE
216                 IF(IPVC)150,143,150
```

Appendix E *Integer Programming Algorithm (Continued)*

```
217           143 GO TO (145,435,542,610,665),INDCTR
218           145 WRITE(NO,30)
219               GO TO 1001
220       C***
221       C       CARRY OUT PIVOT STEP
222           150 ALFA=ATAB(IPVR,IPVC)
223       C**     UPDATE TABLEAU
224               DO 180 J=1,N
225               IF(ATAB(IPVR,J))152,180,152
226           152 IF(J-IPVC)153,180,153
227           153 ARTIO=ATAB(IPVR,J)/ALFA
228               DO 175 I=1,M
229               IF(ATAB(I,IPVC))157,175,157
230           157 IF(I-IPVR)160,175,160
231           160 ATAB(I,J)=ATAB(I,J)-ARTIO*ATAB(I,IPVC)
232               IF(DABS(ATAB(I,J))-ADELT) 165, 165, 175
233           165 ATAB(I,J) = 0.0
234           175 CONTINUE
235           180 CONTINUE
236               DO 190 J=1,N
237           190 ATAB(IPVR,J)=ATAB(IPVR,J)/ALFA
238       C***
239       C       EXCHANGE ROW AND COLUMN IDENTIFIERS
240               ISV=IROW(IPVR)
241               IROW(IPVR)=ICOL(IPVC)
242               IF(ISV)197,195,197
243       C***
244       C       IF PIVOT ROW WAS ZERO SLACK, SET MODIFIED PIVOT COLUMN ZERO.
245           195 DO 196 I=1,M
246           196 ATAB(I,IPVC)=ATAB(I,N)
247               ICOL(IPVC)=ICOL(N)
248               N=N-1
249               GO TO 200
250           197 DO 198 I=1,M
251           198 ATAB(I,IPVC)=-ATAB(I,IPVC)/ALFA
252               ICOL(IPVC)=ISV
253               ATAB(IPVR,IPVC)=1./ALFA
254       C***
255       C       COUNT PIVOTS
256           200 ICNTR=ICNTR+1
257               IF(IROW(IPVR)+1000)210,205,210
258           205 DO 207 J=1,N
259           207 ATAB(IPVR,J)=ATAB(M,J)
260               IROW(IPVR)=IROW(M)
261               M=M-1
262           210 IF(IOUT1)240,2505,240
263       C***
264       C       OUTPUT CURRENT TABLEAU
265           240 WRITE (NO,24) ICNTR
266               WRITE(NO,26)(ICOL(J),J=1,N)
267               DO 250 K=1,M
268               WRITE(NO,25)(ATAB(K,L),L=1,N)
269           250 WRITE(NO,27)IROW(K)
270          2505 GO TO (254,251,252,253,2535),INDCTR
271       C***
272       C       IF SEEKING INTEGER SOLUTION, TEST OBJECTIVE FUNCTION AGAINST CURRE
273           251 IF(ATAB(1,1)-TLRNCE)254,435,435
274           252 IF(ATAB(1,1)-TLRNCE)254,542,542
275           253 IF(ATAB(1,1)-TLRNCE)254,610,610
276          2535 IF(ATAB(1,1)-TLRNCE)254,665,665
277       C***
278       C       IF CONSTANT COLUMN OF ZERO SLACK ROW IS NEG., REVERSE SIGNS OF ENT
279           254 IF ( M .LT. 2) GO TO 453
280               DO 260 K = 2, M
281               IF(IROW(K))260,255,260
282           255 IF(ATAB(K,1))256,260,260
283           256 DO 258 L=1,N
284           258 ATAB(K,L)=-ATAB(K,L)
285           260 CONTINUE
286           453 CONTINUE
287       C       GO TO NEXT PIVOT STEP
288               GO TO 112
289           265 CONTINUE
```

Appendix E *Integer Programming Algorithm (Continued)*

```
290        C***
291        C      IF ANY BASIS VARIABLE EXCEEDS ITS UPPER BOUND, COMPLEMENT IT, AND
292        C      PIVOT ON CORRESPONDING ROW
293               IF ( M .LT. 2) GO TO 454
294               DO 275 I=2,M
295               IF(IROW(I))275,275,266
296           266 J=IROW(I)
297               IF(J-1000)268,268,267
298           267 J=J-1000
299           268 IF(UPBND(J)+ATAB(I,1))269,275,275
300           269 IF(ADELT+UPBND(J)+ATAB(I,1))270,274,274
301           270 ATAB(I,1)=-ATAB(I,1)-UPBND(J)
302               DO 271 K=2,N
303           271 ATAB(I,K)=-ATAB(I,K)
304               IPVR=I
305               IF(J-IROW(I))272,273,272
306           272 IROW(I)=J
307               GO TO 130
308           273 IROW(I)=IROW(I)+1000
309               GO TO 130
310           274 ATAB(I,1)=-UPBND(J)
311           275 CONTINUE
312           454 CONTINUE
313        C***
314        C      TRUE END OF LINEAR PROGRAMMING
315        C      SET SOLUTION VECTOR VALUES FOR BASIC VARIABLES
316               IF ( M .LT. 2) GO TO 455
317               DO 280 I=2,M
318               IF(IROW(I))280,280,277
319           277 IF(IROW(I)-1000)279,279,278
320           278 J=IROW(I)-1000
321               T(J)=UPBND(J)+ATAB(I,1)
322               GO TO 280
323           279 J=IROW(I)
324               T(J)=-ATAB(I,1)
325           280 CONTINUE
326           455 CONTINUE
327        C***
328        C      SET SOLUTION VECTOR VALUES FOR NON-BASIC VARIABLES IN COMPLEMENTED
329               DO 285 I=2,N
330               IF(ICOL(I))285,285,282
331           282 IF(ICOL(I)-1000)284,284,283
332           283 J=ICOL(I)-1000
333               T(J)=UPBND(J)
334               GO TO 285
335           284 J=ICOL(I)
336               T(J)=0.
337           285 CONTINUE
338               GO TO (286,437,548,615,670),INDCTR
339        C***
340        C      FIRST TIME,WRITE CONTINUOUS SOLUTION TABLEAU
341        C      IF REQUESTED
342           286 WRITE(NO,40)
343               IF(IOUT3)287,291,287
344           287 WRITE(NO,42)
345               WRITE(NO,26)(ICOL(J),J=1,N)
346           288 DO 290 I=1,M
347               WRITE(NO,25)(ATAB(I,J),J=1,N)
348           290 WRITE(NO,27)IROW(I)
349           291 ZOPT =DABS( ATAB(1,1))
350               WRITE (NO, 35) ZOPT, ICNTR
351               WRITE (NO, 19)
352               WRITE (NO,18) (I, I = 1, NM1)
353               WRITE (NO, 10) (I,(I), I = 1, NM1)
354        C***
355        C      COMPUTE ABSOLUTE TOLERANCE
356               ATAB12=ATAB(1,1)
357               ATAB11 =DABS (ATAB11 - ATAB(1,1))
358               IF(PCTTOL)294,293,292
359           292 TLRNCE=PCTTOL*ATAB11+ATAB12
360               GO TO 294
361           293 TLRNCE = 1E35
362           294 CONTINUE
```

Appendix E *Integer Programming Algorithm (Continued)*

```
363        C***
364        C       DETERMINE WHETHER CONTINUOUS SOLUTION IS MIXED INTEGER SOLUTION
365                IF ( M .LT. 2) GO TO 456
366          301 DO 310 I=2,M
367                IF(IROW(I))310,310,302
368          302 IF(IROW(I)-1000)303,303,304
369          303 IF(IROW(I)-NZR1VR)305,305,310
370          304 IF(IROW(I)-1000-NZR1VR)305,305,310
371          305 AJ01 = ATAB(I,1)
372                AJ02 = ADELT
373                AJ03 = X1
374                IF(AMOD(-AJ01,AJ03)-AJ02) 310,310,306
375          306 IF(1.0-AMOD(-AJ01,AJ03)-AJ02) 310,310,295
376          310 CONTINUE
377          456 CONTINUE
378                IF ( NZR1VR) 307, 308, 307
379          307 WRITE (NO,45)
380                GO TO 998
381          308 WRITE (NO,46)
382                GO TO 998
383        C***
384        C DETERMINE WHETHER PROBLEM FITS IN MEMORY , AND IF SO  WHETHER TO SAVE
385        C       ALL INTERMEDIATE TABLEAUS OR ONLY SOME
386          295 IF(N-NZR1VR)297,297,298
387          297 ISVLOC=(N*(N+1))/2
388                GO TO 299
389          298 ISVLOC=(NZR1VR*(2*N-NZR1VR+1))/2
390          299 IF(ISIZE-ISVLOC)3001,3001,300
391          300 I1ROW=0
392                GO TO 315
393         3001 NONBSC=0
394                DO 3006 J=2,N
395                IF(ICOL(J))3006,3006,3002
396         3002 IF(ICOL(J)-1000)3003,3004,3004
397         3003 IF(ICOL(J)-NZR1VR)3005,3005,3006
398         3004 IF(ICOL(J)-1000-NZR1VR)3005,3005,3006
399         3005 NONBSC=NONBSC+1
400         3006 CONTINUE
401                IF(N-NZR1VR)3007,3007,3008
402         3007 ISVLOC=N+((N-NONBSC)*(N-NONBSC+1))/2
403                GO TO 3009
404         3008 ISVLOC=N+((NZR1VR-NONBSC)*(N-NONBSC+N-NZR1VR+1))/2
405         3009 IF(ISIZE-ISVLOC)3010,3010,315
406         3010 WRITE(NO,55)
407                GO TO 998
408          315 CONTINUE
409        C***
410        C       BEGIN INTEGER PROGRAMMING
411          400 I1=1
412          402 AMAX = -X1
413                KSVN(I1+1)=KSVN(I1)
414        C***
415        C       CHOOSE NEXT INTEGER VARIABLE TO BE CONSTRAINE
416        C       TRY NONBASIC VARIABLES FIRST, CHOOSING ONE WITH LARGEST SHAD PRICE
417                DO 4085 I=2,N
418                IF(ICOL(I))4085,4085,405
419          405 IF(ICOL(I)-1000)406,407,407
420          406 IF(ICOL(I)-NZR1VR)408,408,4085
421          407 IF(ICOL(I)-1000-NZR1VR)408,408,4085
422          408 IF(AMAX-ATAB(1,I))4082,4085,4085
423         4082 ISVI=I
424                AMAX=ATAB(1,I)
425         4085 CONTINUE
426        C***
427        C       IF NONE LEFT, TRY BASIC VARIABLES
428                IF ( AMAX + X1) 4087, 420, 4087
429        C***
430        C       VARIABLE CHOSEN
431         4087 IVAR(I1)=ICOL(ISVI)
432                BTMVL(I1)=-1.
433                ISVRCL(I1)=ISVI
434                ICORR(I1)=0
435                VAL (I1) = 0.0
```

Appendix E *Integer Programming Algorithm (Continued)*

```
436        C***
437        C        IF OBJECTIVE FUNCTION VALUE + SHADOW PRICE EXCEEDS TOLERANCE,
438        C        INDICATE UPWARD DIRECTION INFEASIBLE
439                 IF(ATAB(1,1)+ATAB(1,ISVI)-TLRNCE)410,409,409
440          409 TPVAL(I1)=1000.
441                 IF(I1-1)4101,4101,4095
442         4095 ISVN(I1)=0
443                 GO TO 4132
444          410 TPVAL(I1)=1.
445        C***
446                 IF(I1-1)4100,4101,4100
447        C        SAVE ENTIRE TABLEAU OR ONLY COLUMN CORRESPONDING TO CURRENT
448        C        NONBASIC VARIABLE, DEPENDING ON SIZE OF PROB AND 2ND DIM OF SAVTAB
449         4100 IF(I1-I1ROW)4132,4101,4101
450         4101 L=KSVN(I1)
451                 DO 412 J=1,M
452                 ISVROW(J,I1)=IROW(J)
453                 DO 411 K=1,N
454                 I=L+K-1
455                 IF(J-1)4105,4105,411
456         4105 SAVTAB(M+1,I)=ICOL(K)
457          411 SAVTAB(J,I)=ATAB(J,K)
458          412 CONTINUE
459                 ISVN(I1)=N
460                 KSVN(I1+1)=L+N
461         4132 ICOL(ISVI)=ICOL(N)
462                 DO 4135 J=1,M
463         4135 ATAB(J,ISVI)=ATAB(J,N)
464                 N=N-1
465                 GO TO 5000
466        C        CHOOSE NEXT INTEGER VARIABLE TO BE CONSTRAINED FROM
467        C        AMONG BASIC VARIABLES IN CURRENT TABLEAU
468          420 CONTINUE
469                 IF(I1-I1ROW)4204,600,4205
470         4204 I1ROW=I1
471         4205 INDCT7=1
472          421 AMAX = -X1
473                 IF ( M .LT. 2) GO TO 457
474                 DO 425 I2=2,M
475                 IF(IROW(I2))425,425,422
476          422 IF(IROW(I2)-1000)423,424,424
477          423 IF(IROW(I2)-NZR1VR)4241,4241,425
478          424 IF(IROW(I2)-1000-NZR1VR)4241,4241,425
479         4241 AMAX2 = 1.0E35
480                 AMAX3 = -1.0E35
481                 AJO = -ATAB(I2,1) + ADELT
482                 ALW = AINT(AJO)
483                 AUP=ALW+1.
484                 IF(N-1)426,426,4240
485         4240 DO 4246 I3=2,N
486                 IF(ATAB(I2,I3))4244,4246,4242
487         4242 RTIO=ATAB(1,I3)/ATAB(I2,I3)
488                 IF(RTIO-AMAX2)4243,4246,4246
489         4243 AMAX2=RTIO
490                 GO TO 4246
491         4244 RTIO2=ATAB(1,I3)/ATAB(I2,I3)
492                 IF(RTIO2-AMAX3)4246,4246,4245
493         4245 AMAX3=RTIO2
494         4246 CONTINUE
495                 IF ( AMAX3 + 1E34) 430, 430, 4247
496         4247 IF (AMAX2 - 1E34) 4248, 429, 429
497         4248 DIFF1 =DABS (AMAX2 * (ATAB(I2,1) + ALW))
498                 DIFF2 =DABS (AMAX3 * (ATAB(I2,1) + AUP))
499                 DIFF =DABS (DIFF1 - DIFF2)
500                 IF(DIFF-AMAX)425,425,4249
501         4249 AMAX=DIFF
502                 SVALW=ALW
503                 ISVI2=I2
504                 IF(DIFF1-DIFF2)4251,4251,4252
505         4251 ANDCT4=0.
506                 GO TO 425
507         4252 ANDCT4=1.
508          425 CONTINUE
```

Appendix E *Integer Programming Algorithm (Continued)*

```
509          457 CONTINUE
510              ALW=SVALW
511              I2=ISVI2
512              VAL(I1)=ALW+ANDCT4
513              BTMVL(I1)=VAL(I1)-1.
514         4255 TPVAL(I1)=VAL(I1)+1.
515              GO TO 432
516      C***
517      C       IF NO. OF COLS=1 AND RIGHT HAND SIDE=0, DONT GO TO LP
518          426 IF (DABS( ATAB(I2,1) + ALW) - ADELT) 4277 427, 5100
519          427 BTMVL(I1)=-1.
520              TPVAL(I1)=1000.
521              VAL(I1)=ALW
522              IVAR(I1)=IROW(I2)
523              IROW(I2T=0
524              GO TO 5000
525      C***
526      C       CONSTRAINING VARIABLE IN LOWER DIRECTION INFEASIBLE
527          429 BTMVL(I1)=-1.
528              IF (DABS ( ATAB(I2,1) + ALW) - ADELT ) 4295, 4295, 4296
529         4295 ANDCT4=0.
530              VAL(I1)=ALW+ANDCT4
531              GO TO 4255
532         4296 TPVAL(I1)=ALW+2.
533              ANDCT4=1.
534              GO TO 431
535      C***
536      C       CONSTRAINING VARIABLE IN UPPER DIRECTION INFEASIBLE
537          430 TPVAL(I1)=1000.
538              BTMVL(I1)=ALW-1.
539              ANDCT4=0.
540          431 VAL(I1)=ALW+ANDCT4
541      C***
542      C       SAVE ENTIRE TABLEAU
543          432 JSVN=N
544              L=KSVN(I1)
545          438 DO 439 I3=1,M
546              ISVROW(I3,I1)=IROW(I3)
547              DO 439 I4=1,N
548              I6=L+I4+1
549              IF(I3-1)4385,4385,439
550         4385 SAVTAB(M+1,I6)=ICOL(I4)
551          439 SAVTAB(I3,I6)=ATAB(I3,I4)
552              ISVN(I1T=N
553              KSVN(I1+1)=L+N
554              ATAB(I2,1)=ATAB(I2,1)+VAL(I1)
555              ISVRCL(I1)=I2
556              IVAR(I1T=IROW(I2)
557              ICORR(I1)=1
558              IROW(I2)=0
559              IF (DABS ( ATAB(I2,1)) - ADELT) 433, 433T 434
560          433 ATAB (I2,1) = 0.0
561          434 INDCTR=2
562      C***
563      C       RETURN TO CARRY OUT LP
564              IF(IOUT1)240,254,240
565      C       INFINITE RETURN
566          435 IF(ANDCT4)4355,4352,4355
567         4352 BTMVL(I1)=-1.
568              GO TO 5120
569         4355 TPVAL(I1)=1000.
570              GO TO 5120
571      C***
572      C       FINITE RETURN
573          437 GO TO 5000
574      C       TEST FOR ANY INTEGER VARIABLES LEFT TO BE CONSTRAINED
575         5000 IF(I1-NZR1VR)5050,550,550
576      C       INCREMENT POINTER AND RETURN TO CONSTRAIN NEXT INTEGER VARIABLE
577         5050 I1=I1+1
578              IF(IOUT1)5051,402,5051
579         5051 WRITE(NO,70)I1
580              GO TO 402
581      C***
```

Appendix E *Integer Programming Algorithm (Continued)*

```
582        C       DECREMENT POINTER AND CONSTRAIN CURRENT VARIABLE TO
583        C       CURRENT VALUE + OR - 1
584        5100 I1=I1-1
585             IF(IOUT1)5110,5115,5110
586        5110 WRITE(NO,75)I1
587        5115 IF(I1)995,995,5120
588        5120 IF(IVAR(I1)-1000)5151,5151,5152
589        5151 K=IVAR(I1)
590             GO TO 5153
591        5152 K=IVAR(I1)-1000
592        5153 I2=ISVRCL(I1)
593        5155 IF(BTMVL(I1))516,517,517
594         516 IF(TPVAL(I1)-UPBND(K))518,518,5100
595         517 IF(TPVAL(I1)-UPBND(K))530,530,525
596        C***
597        C       TOP END FEASIBLE
598         518 INDCT5=1
599        5181 IF(ICORR(I1))5198,5182,5198
600        5182 IF(I1-I1ROW)5183,5198,5198
601        5183 INDCT8=1
602             IF(I1-1)5185,5198,5185
603        5185 INDCT5=4
604             ISVI1=I1-1
605             I1=1
606             GO TO 5198
607        5190 DO 5194 I3=1,ISVI1
608             I4=ISVRCL(I3)
609             ICOL(I4)=ICOL(N)
610             DO 5193 J=1,M
611             IF(VAL(I3)-1.)5193,5191,5192
612        5191 ATAB(J,I)=ATAB(J,1)+ATAB(J,I4)
613             GO TO 5196
614        5192 ATAB(J,1)=ATAB(J,1)+VAL(I3)*ATAB(J,I4)
615        5196 INDCT8=2
616        5193 ATAB(J,I4)=ATAB(J,N)
617             N=N-1
618        5194 CONTINUE
619        5195 I1=ISVI1+1
620             INDCT5=1
621             GO TO 521
622        C***
623        C       RETRIEVE SAVED TABLEAU
624        5198 N=ISVN(I1)
625           ● L=KSVN(I1)
626             DO 5199 I3=1,M
627             IROW(I3)=ISVROW(I3,I1)
628             DO 5199 I4=1,N
629             I6=L+I4-1
630             IF(I3-1)5197,5197,5199
631        5197 ICOL(I4)=SAVTAB(M+1,I6)
632        5199 ATAB(I3,I4)=SAVTAB(I3,I6)
633        5205 GO TO (521,526,531,5190),INDCT5
634         521 VAL(I1)=TPVAL(I1)
635             TPVAL(I1)=TPVAL(I1)+1.
636             IF(ICORR(I1))541,522,541
637         522 DO 523 I3=1,M
638             ATAB(I3,1)=ATAB(I3,1)+(VAL(I1)*ATAB(I3,I2))
639             IF (DABS ( ATAB(I3,1)) - ADELT) 5225, 5225, 523
640        5225 ATAB(I3,1)=0.
641         523 ATAB(I3,I2)=ATAB(I3,N)
642             ICOL(I2)=ICOL(N)
643             N=N-1
644             IF(ATAB(1,1)-TLRNCE)5235,5100,5100
645        5235 IF(I1-I1ROW)650,5415,5415
646        C***
647        C       BOTTOM END FEASIBLE
648         525 INDCT5=2
649             GO TO 5198
650         526 VAL(I1)=BTMVL(I1)
651             BTMVL(I1)=BTMVL(I1)-1.
652             GO TO 541
653        C***
654        C       BOTH ENDS FEASIBLE
```

Appendix E *Integer Programming Algorithm (Continued)*

```
655        530 INDCT5=3
656            GO TO 5198
657        531 AMAX2 = 1.0E35
658            AMAX3 = -1.0E35
659            DO 536 I3=2,N
660            IF(ATAB(I2,I3))534,536,532
661        532 RTIO=ATAB(1,IN)/ATAB(I2,I3)
662            IF(RTIO-AMAX2)533,536,536
663        533 AMAX2=RTIO
664            GO TO 536
665        534 RTIO2=ATAB(1,I3)/ATAB(I2,I3)
666            IF(RTIO2-AMAX3)536,536,535
667        535 AMAX3=RTIO2
668        536 CONTINUE
669            IF(AMAX2-1.E35)538,537,537
670 C***
671 C       BOTTOM END INFEASIBLE
672        537 BTMVL(I1)=-1.
673            GO TO 521
674        538 IF(AMAX3+1.E35)539,539,540
675 C***
676 C       TOP END INFEASIBLE
677        539 TPVAL(I1)=1000.
678            GO TO 526
679        540 DIFF1 =DABS ( AMAX2 * (ATAB(I2,1) + BTMVL (I1)))
680            DIFF2 =DABS ( AMAX3 * (ATAB(I2,1) + TPVAL (I1)))
681            IF(DIFF1-DIFF2)526,526,521
682        541 ATAB(I2,1)=ATAB(I2,1)+VAL(I1)
683            IROW(I2)=0
684            IF (DABS ( ATAB(I2,1)) - ADELT) 5412, 5412, 5415
685       5412 ATAB(I2,1)=0.
686       5415 INDCTR=3
687            IF(IOUT1)240,2505,240
688 C***
689 C       INFINITE RETURN
690        542 GO TO (544,547,543),INDCT5
691        543 IF(TPVAL(I1)-VAL(I1)-1.)545,544,545
692        544 TPVAL(I1)=1000.
693            GO TO 5120
694        545 IF(VAL(I1)-BTMVL(I1)-1.)546,547,546
695 C***
696        546 CONTINUE
697        547 BTMVL(I1)=-1.
698            GO TO 5120
699 C***
700 C       FINITE RETURN
701        548 GO TO 5000
702 C       FEASIBLE INTEGER SOLUTION OBTAINED
703        550 TLRNCE=ATAB(1,1)
704            SOLMIN=1.
705 C***
706 C       WRITE CURRENT BEST MIXED INTEGER SOLUTION
707            IF ( IOUT3) 552, 553, 552
708        552 ZOPT =DABS( ATAB( 1,1))
709            WRITE (NO, 35) ZOPT, ICNTR
710        553 DO 560 I = 1, NZR1VR
711            IF(IVAR(I))554,560,554
712        554 IF(IVAR(I)-1000)555,555,557
713        555 J=IVAR(I)
714            T(J)=VAL(I)
715            GO TO 560
716        557 J=IVAR(I)-1000
717            T(J)=UPBND(J)-VAL(I)
718        560 CONTINUE
719            WRITE (NO, 19)
720        565 WRITE (NO, 18) (I, I = 1, NM1)
721            WRITE (NO, 10) (T(I), I = 1, NM1)
722            GO TO 5115
723        600 GO TO (605,4205),INDCT7
724        605 INDCTR=4
725            IF(IOUT1)240,254,240
726 C***
727 C       INFINITE RETURN
```

Appendix E *Integer Programming Algorithm (Continued)*

```
728          610 GO TO 5100
729      C***
730      C       FINITE RETURN
731          615 INDCT7=2
732              GO TO 402
733      C***
734      C       IF USING SECOND SOLUTION METHOD, SAVE TABLEAU MODIFIED
735      C       FOR NONZERO VALUE OF NONBASIC VARIABLE IN TBSAV
736          650 DO 655 I=1,M
737              ITBROW(I)=IROW(I)
738              DO 655 J=1,N
739          655 TBSAV(I,J)=ATAB(I,J)
740              DO 660 J=1,N
741          660 ITBCOL(J)=ICOL(J)
742              JSVN=N
743              INDCTR=5
744              IF(IOUT1) 240,254,240
745      C***
746      C       INFINITE RETURN
747          665 GO TO (544,5120),INDCT8
748      C       FINITE RETURN
749      C***
750      C       IF USING SECOND SOLUTION METHOD, RETRIEVE MODIFIED TABLEAU FROM
751      C       TBSAV, AS THIS CORRESPONDS TO SAVED COLUMNS FOR I1 LESS THAN I1ROW
752          670 N=JSVN
753              DO 675 I=1,M
754              IROW(I)=ITBROW(I)
755              DO 675 J=1,N
756          675 ATAB(I,J)=TBSAV(I,J)
757              DO 680 J=1,N
758          680 ICOL(J)=ITBCOL(J)
759              GO TO 5000
760      C***
761      C       OUTPUT FINAL SOLUTION.
762          995 IF(ITOL)996,9976,996
763          996 IF(SOLMIN-1.E35)9976,997,997
764          997 ITOL=ITOL+1
765              TLRNCE=FLOAT(ITOL)*PCTTOL*ATAB11+ATAB12
766              N=ISVN(1)
767              DO 9972 I=1,M
768              IROW(I)=ISVROW(I,1)
769              DO 9972 J=1,N
770         9972 ATAB(I,J)=SAVTAB(I,J)
771              DO 9973 K=1,N
772         9973 ICOL(K)=SAVTAB(M+1,K)
773              GO TO 400
774          998 CONTINUE
775         9976 WRITE (NO, 50)
776         1001 WRITE (NO, 65) ICNTR
777          999 NMRUNS=NMRUNS-1
778              IF(NMRUNS)68,1000,68
779         1000 CALL EXIT
780              END
```

APPENDIX F
SOURCES OF OR/MS INFORMATION

A serious reader of management science needs to know, not only the techniques that have been used in the past, but also their extensions and additional applications. For this reason, additional sources of information regarding OR/MS are listed:

- Accounting Review
- The Bell System Technical Journal
- Decision Sciences
- Geographical Analysis
- Journal of Accounting Research
- Journal of the Association of Computing Machinery
- Journal of Finance
- Journal of Marketing Research
- Management Science
- Naval Logistics Research Quarterly
- Operational Research Quarterly
- Operations Research
- OPSEARCH
- *Proceedings* of the annual conferences sponsored by the Operations Research Society of America, The Institute of Management Sciences, the American Institute of Decision Sciences, and the Operational Research Society of the United Kingdom.
- SIAM Journal of Applied Mathematics

INDEX